# The Pioneers of Psychoanalysis in South America

Shortly before and during World War II many European psychoanalysts found refuge in South America, concentrated in Buenos Aires. Here, together with local professionals, they created a strong, creative and productive psychoanalytic movement that in turn gave birth to theoretical and clinical contributions that transformed psychoanalysis, psychology, medicine and culture in South America. *The Pioneers of Psychoanalysis in South America* is a collection of those pioneers' papers, and introduces the reader to a body of ideas and advancements, many of which have had limited and piecemeal exposure within the psychoanalytic community in the rest of the world until now.

The editors Nydia Lisman–Pieczanski and Alberto Pieczanski present original papers and essays, many of which have never before been published in English; those that have been translated were rarely presented in context. Each one of the chapters is accompanied by a scholarly introduction written by psychoanalysts, many of whom personally knew the pioneers and their oeuvres in depth, tracing the roots of their ideas in the European analytic schools.

*The Pioneers of Psychoanalysis in South America* is divided into six main sections:

- Psychoanalytic process
- Psychoanalytic technique
- Metapsychology
- Psychoanalysis of children
- Culture and society
- Psychosomatic medicine.

Nydia Lisman–Pieczanski and Alberto Pieczanski provide a coherent guide to the seminal ideas and practices of the South American psychoanalysts who have made major theoretical and clinical contributions to the advancement of the psychoanalytic discipline. The chapters present the material in a way that is accessible to psychoanalysts from across the globe and will enable them to incorporate the ideas and practices outlined here into their everyday psychoanalytic work. It will also be of interest to psychoanalytic psychotherapists, academics interested in the history and development of psychoanalytic ideas and psychoanalysis, and advanced students.

**Nydia Lisman-Pieczanski** is a Child and Adult Psychoanalyst. She is the founding chair of the Infant and Young Child Observation Program, Tavistock Method, at the Washington School of Psychiatry. Nydia is a Training and Supervising Analyst at the Buenos Aires Psychoanalytic Association, Member of the British Psychoanalytical Society and a Teaching Analyst at the Washington Center for Psychoanalysis. She is also the Scientific Adviser and Teacher at 'Mind in Mind', Beijing, China.

**Alberto Pieczanski** is a Child and Adult Psychoanalyst. He is a Member of the IPA's (International Psychoanalytic Association) Working Party on the study of the Analyst's Unconscious Theories. He is a Training and Supervising Analyst of the Buenos Aires Psychoanalytic Society (APdeBA), faculty of the Washington Center for Psychoanalysis and faculty member of the Washington School of Psychiatry.

# THE NEW LIBRARY OF PSYCHOANALYSIS
General Editor: Alessandra Lemma

The New Library of Psychoanalysis was launched in 1987 in association with the Institute of Psychoanalysis, London. It took over from the Interna-

a forum for increasing mutual understanding between psychoanalysts and those working in other disciplines such as the social sciences, medicine, philosophy, history, linguistics, literature and the arts. It aims to represent different trends both in British psychoanalysis and in psychoanalysis generally. The New Library of Psychoanalysis is well placed to make available to the English-speaking world psychoanalytic writings from other European countries and to increase the interchange of ideas between British and American psychoanalysts. Through the *Teaching Series*, the New Library of Psychoanalysis now also publishes books that provide comprehensive, yet accessible, overviews of selected subject areas aimed at those studying psychoanalysis and related fields such as the social sciences, philosophy, literature and the arts.

The Institute, together with the British Psychoanalytical Society, runs a low-fee psychoanalytic clinic, organizes lectures and scientific events concerned with psychoanalysis and publishes the *International Journal of Psychoanalysis*. It runs the a training course in psychoanalysis which leads to membership of the International Psychoanalytical Association – the body which preserves internationally agreed standards of training, of professional entry, and of professional ethics and practice for psychoanalysis as initiated and developed by Sigmund Freud. Distinguished members of the Institute have included Michael Balint, Wilfred Bion, Ronald Fairbairn, Anna Freud, Ernest Jones, Melanie Klein, John Rickman and Donald Winnicott.

Previous general editors have included David Tuckett, who played a very active role in the establishment of the New Library. He was followed as general editor by Elizabeth Bott Spillius, who was in turn followed by Susan Budd and then by Dana Birksted-Breen.

Current members of the Advisory Board include Liz Allison, Giovanna di Ceglie, Rosemary Davies and Richard Rusbridger.

Previous Members of the Advisory Board include Christopher Bollas, Ronald Britton, Catalina Bronstein, Donald Campbell, Sara Flanders, Stephen grosz, John Keene, Eglé Laufer, Alessandra Lemma, Juliet Mitchell, Michael Parsons, Rosine Jozef Perelberg, Mary Target and David Taylor.

# TITLES IN THIS SERIES

## THE NEW LIBRARY OF PSYCHOANALYSIS

# Psychoanalysis in South America
## An essential guide

Edited by
Nydia Lisman-Pieczanski
and
Alberto Pieczanski

In collaboration with Karla Loyo for
the Brazilian section

Routledge
Taylor & Francis Group

LONDON AND NEW YORK

First published 2015
by Routledge
27 Church Road, Hove, East Sussex BN3 2FA

and by Routledge
711 Third Avenue, New York, NY 10017

*Routledge is an imprint of the Taylor & Francis Group, an informa business*

© 2015 Nydia Lisman-Pieczanski and Alberto Pieczanski

The right of the Nydia Lisman-Pieczanski and Alberto Pieczanski to be identified as the authors of the editorial material, and of the authors for their individual chapters, has been asserted in accordance with sections 77 and 78 of the Copyright, Designs and Patents Act 1988.

All rights reserved. No part of this book may be reprinted or reproduced or utilised in any form or by any electronic, mechanical, or other means, now known or hereafter invented, including photocopying and recording, or in any information storage or retrieval system, without permission in writing from the publishers.

*Trademark notice:* Product or corporate names may be trademarks or registered trademarks, and are used only for identification and explanation without intent to infringe.

*British Library Cataloguing in Publication Data*
A catalogue record for this book is available from the British Library

*Library of Congress Cataloging-in-Publication Data*
The pioneers of psychoanalysis in South America : an essential guide /
    edited by Nydia Lisman-Pieczanski, Alberto Pieczanski. — First Dual.
        pages cm. — (The new library of psychoanalysis)
    1. Psychoanalysis—South America—History.   2. Psychoanalysts—
South America.   I. Lisman-Pieczanski, Nydia., editor of compilation.
II. Pieczanski, Alberto, editor of compilation.
    BF173.P64196 2014
    150.19'509228—dc23
    2014017581

ISBN: 978-0-415-71372-6 (hbk)
ISBN: 978-0-415-71373-3 (pbk)
ISBN: 978-1-315-75478-9 (ebk)

Typeset in Bembo
by Apex CoVantage, LLC

*For our children Andres, Ana, Juan, Brenden,*
*Eleonore and grandchildren Isabel, Sofia, Alma and Miles.*

The first Argentinian psychoanalysts.
From left to right – Seated: unknown, Roberto Tagliaferro.
Standing: Enrique Pichon-Rivière, Marie Langer,
Arnaldo Raskovsky, Angel Garma, Eduardo Krapf,
Luisa Alvarez de Toledo, Celes Cárcamo, Lucio Rascovsky.
Top row: Arminda Aberastury, Matilde Raskovsky.

# Contents

# Contents

# Contents

## Editors

**Nydia Lisman-Pieczanski**, MD, is a Child and Adult Psychoanalyst trained at the British Psychoanalytical Institute. She is a Training and Supervising Analyst of the Buenos Aires Psychoanalytic Association (IPA) and a member of the Buenos Aires Psychoanalytic Association, the British Psychoanalytical Society, the Washington Psychoanalytic Center for Psychoanalysis, the Washington School of Psychiatry and the Association of Child Psychotherapists, London, UK. She is the founding Chair of the two-year Infant and Young Child Observation Program (Esther Bick model) at the Washington School of Psychiatry. She has written on eating disorders in childhood and adolescence, on unilateral termination in psychoanalysis, on projective mechanisms used as a defense against depressive anxieties, on interpretation and difficulties in psychoanalytic technique and on psychoanalysis with women that were sexually abused in early childhood. She has been a psychoanalytic peer reviewer for the *Journal of the American Psychoanalytic Association*, the *International Journal of Psychoanalysis* and the *New Library of Psychoanalysis*, London, UK.

**Alberto Pieczanski**, MD, is an Adult and Child Analyst trained at the British Psychoanalytic Institute. He is a Training Analyst of the Buenos Aires Psychoanalytic Association. Since his graduation, Dr. Pieczanski has written and presented papers on a number of subjects; his main interest is psychoanalytic technique. Amongst others, he has presented papers on projective identification, analytic treatment of perverse and delinquent patients, and psychoanalytic perspective on films. He was a staff member of the Portman Clinic, which treats perverse and delinquent patients, and the Adolescent

Department of the Tavistock Centre, both in the UK, and did institutional consultations. He has given workshops in the USA, and run study groups on technique from a Kleinian and post-Klenian perspective. He is a member and faculty of the Washington Center for Psychoanalysis and the Washington School of Psychiatry in the District of Columbia USA.

# Contributors

**Samuel Arbiser**, MD, is a Training and Supervising Analyst of the Buenos Aires Psychoanalytic Association, a former member of the Committee of the History of Psychoanalysis (IPA), and faculty of the Institute of Psychoanalysis (APdeBA). He has served on various IPA committees and been a reviewer of the *Argentine Journal of Psychoanalysis* (APA) and the *International Journal of Psychoanalysis*. He has written several scientific papers published in Spanish, English, Italian and Portuguese as well as chapters in psychoanalytic books.

**Ana Bloj**, PhD, is a doctor in Clinical Psychology (PsyD) at the University of Rosario, Argentina; Professor of Educational Psychology U.N.R.; and member of the Department of Children at the Institute Philippe Pinel, Rosario, Argentina. She has published extensively in both papers and books on child psychoanalysis and education.

**Julia Braun**, MD, is a Training and Supervising Analyst of the Argentine Psychoanalytic Association (APA) and the Argentine Society of Psychoanalysis (SAP). She is co-author of the books *Violence d' etat et psychanalyse* (*State violence and psychoanalysis*) and *Argentine, psychoanalysis and political repression*.

**R. Horacio Etchegoyen**, MD, is a Training and Supervising Analyst of the Buenos Aires Psychoanalytic Association and Former Chairman of Psychiatry and Medical Psychology at Universidad Nacional de Cuyo, Argentina. He is also Doctor Honoris Causa (Universidad Nacional de San Luis), Honorary Professor at Universidad de Buenos Aires, a past President of APdeBA, former President of the International Psychoanalytic Association (1993–1997), Honorary Vice President of the IPA (2009), and author of numerous psychoanalytic papers. His book *The fundamentals of psychoanalytic technique* has been published in Spanish and translated into English, Portuguese, Italian and French. A German edition is in preparation.

**Federico Flegenheimer**, MD, is a Training and Supervising Analyst (Adult and Child) of the Argentine Psychoanalytic Association. Since 1979, he has lived in Torino, Italy, where he is a Training and Supervising Analyst of the Italian Psychoanalytic Society and has been twice a member of the Ethics Committee of the Italian Psychoanalytic Society. He is a reviewer for the *International Journal of Psychoanalysis* and is active in several IPA committee positions.

**Dr. Gilda Sabsay de Foks**, full member of the Asociación Psicoanalítica

Chilean Psychoanalytic Association. He has been Vice President and President of the Chilean Psychoanalytic Association and the Deputy Editor for Latin America of the Editorial Board of the *International Journal of Psychoanalysis*. He is a member of the International Association of Relational Psychoanalysis and Psychotherapy (IARPP) and faculty of the Program on Clinical Interventions in Psychotherapy at the School of Psychology of the 'Pontificia Universidad Católica' in Chile. He is co-editor of the book *Cuarenta años de Psicoanálisis en Chile (Forty years of psycho-analysis in Chile)* and the book *Mente y conjuntos infinitos: Aproximaciones a la bi-lógica de matte blanco (Mind and infinite sets: Approximations to Matte Blanco's bilogic)*.

**Sheila Navarro de Lopez**, MD, Adult and Child Analyst and Psychiatrist, did her psychoanalytic training at the Argentine Psychoanalytic Association (APA). She is a Founding Member and Supervising and Training Analyst since 1973 of Buenos Aires Psychoanalytic Association (APdeBA). She worked in Barcelona (Spain) and London (UK) for several years and is a member of the Spanish Psychoanalytic Association and a Guest Member of the British Psychoanalytical Society.

**Karla Loyo**, co-editor for the Brazilian section, is a psychologist currently in psychoanalytic training at the Brazilian Psychoanalytic Society of Rio de Janeiro 2; she holds a Masters in Counseling Psychology from Lesley University, in Massachusetts and completed a Specialization in Brief Psychotherapy at Santa Casa de Misericórdia, Rio de Janeiro.

**Jorge Luis Maldonado**, MD, is a Training and Supervising Analyst (APdeBA), faculty at the Institute of Psychoanalysis, and former Full Professor of Psychopathology, University of El Salvador Buenos Aires, Argentina. A former IPA board member, he has published extensively and is the author of the book *El Narcisismo del Analista (On the analyst's narcissism)*. His paper on positive and negative therapeutic reactions received the FEPAL prize.

**Iñaki Marquez**, MD, PhD in Psychiatry and Neuroscience, is a Forensic Psychiatrist with a Masters in Mental Health, Drug Addiction and AIDS, Public Health and Clinical Management. He is faculty at the University of Deusto and President of OME-AEN, Basque Association of Mental Health and Community Psychiatry. Author or co-author of more than 20 books about mental health and therapeutic intervention in social exclusion (AIDS, substance abuse, immigration, prison) and member of the editorial board of several journals, Alonso is also biographer of Angel Garma's life and work and executor of his papers and unpublished work. He is author of the book *El Bilbaíno Angel Garma (1904–1993), fundador del psicoanálisis argentino (Angel Garma from Bilbao [1904–1993], the Founder of Argentine Psychoanalysis)*.

**Ignacio Maldonado Martinez**, MD, former Member of the Argentine Psychoanalytic Asociation (APA), did advanced training in psycho-neurology in Heidelberg, Germany. He was the Chair of the Psychology Department at the National Autonomous University of Mexico for 17 years and worked in the mental health care of political refugees. He is a founding member of the Latin American Institute of Studies on Families (Systemic Therapy), is particularly interested in domestic violence, and is editor of the magazine *Familias, Una historia siempre nueva (Families, A constantly renewed history)*.

**Roberto Bittencourt Martins**, MD, is the son of Mario and Zaira Martins, pioneers of Brazilian psychoanalysis and founders of the Porto Alegre Psychoanalytic Society. A member and former President of the Brazilian Psychoanalytic Society of Rio de Janeiro, he is author and co-author of psychoanalytic papers published in Brazilian journals of psychoanalysis and books. He is also a fiction writer.

**Maria Angela Gomes Moretzsohn**, Afiliated Member of the Brazilian Psychoanalytic Society. She is coordinator of the Division of Documents and Research of the Psychoanalytic History in the Brazilian Psychoanalytic Society and co-curator of the exhibition 'Freud Conflict and Culture' at the Art Museum of São Paulo, 2000/Modern Art Museum, Rio de Janeiro, 2001.

**Dr. Silvia Neborak**, MD, is a Training and Supervising Analyst at the Buenos Aires Psychoanalytic Association. She worked with Dr. David Liberman (1975–1983) and is co-author of the book *Del cuerpo al símbolo (From body to symbol)*, which she wrote in collaboration with Dr. Liberman and a group of colleagues. She is also co-author of the book *Bion conocido-desconocido (Bion known and unknown)* written in collaboration with

Dr. Elizabeth Bianchedi and Argentine colleagues. Dr. Neborak is Faculty at the Department of Psychoanalytic Technique at APdeBA's Psychoanalytic Institute (currently IUSAM).

**Marialzira Perestrello**, MD, trained as a psychoanalyst at the Argentine Psychoanalytic Association (APA), becoming the first Brazilian female ana-

**Antônio Luiz Serpa Pessanha**, MD, Member and Training Psychoanalyst of the Brazilian Psychoanalytic Society from São Paulo. He is a member of the Brazilian Society of Medicine, and author of the book *Beyond the Couch: A Psychoanalyst Talks about the Everyday*. He is also one of the founders of the Revista Brasileira de Psicanálise.

**Andrés Rascovsky**, MD, is a Training and Supervising Psychoanalyst (APA), President of the Argentine Psychoanalytic Association (APA), member of the International Psychoanalytical Association (IPA), and former Director of APA's scientific publication *Revista de Psicoanálisis*. Former Director of the Racker Center for Research and Development (APA), former Chair of the Scientific Committee (APA), and Professor of Social Psychology, Universidad del Salvador, Rascovsky engages in scholarship at the Research Center on Suicide. He has taught and lectured in Argentina and most South American countries, as well as at the United Nations, and runs for the position of IPA's Secretary.

**Benzion Winograd**, physician, psychiatrist and psychoanalyst. He was a training member of APA (Argentine Psychoanalytic Association) (1976–1996), a professor in the Psychoanalysis Institute APA (1971–1996), a founder and scientific coordinator of SAP (Argentine Society of Psychoanalysis) (1996–2006, 2010–2011), cofounder of ADEP (Epistemology of Psychoanalysis Association) (1979), and a professor and academic board member of the 'Argentinian School of Psychotherapy for graduates'. He was sub-director of the Internet magazine *Aperturas psicoanalíticas* (director: Hugo Bleichmar) (1999–2011).

**José Carlos Zanin**, member of the Psychoanalytic Association Rio 3, Training Analyst, Supervisor, and professor of theoretic courses of this Society's Institute. He received his psychoanalytic training at the Institute of the Brazilian Psychoanalytic Society of Rio de Janeiro and graduated in 1976, where he also became a member and, afterward, a Training Analyst and Supervisor. He attended a study group ministered by Dr. Mário Pacheco de Almeida Prado, and, together with Dr. Pacheco, was the instructor of a course on psychoanalytic technique.

**Dr. Waldemar Zusman** was psychoanalyzed by Dr. Décio Soares de Souza in Brazil, and by Dr. Hans Thorner in London. He was IPA's Vice-President for Latin America and is the author of several scientific papers, published in Brazil and other countries. He was President of the Brazilian Psychoanalytic Society of Rio de Janeiro (SBPRJ) and the founder of the Psychoanalytic Association Rio 3. He is also the author of the book *The Movies Which I Watched with Freud,* and creator of the Forum of Psychoanalysis and Cinema in Rio de Janeiro.

**Samuel Zysman**, MD, Psychiatrist, is a Training Analyst and Supervisor (APdeBA-IUSAM) and a Child and Adolescent Analyst. He is Full Professor of the Theory of Psychoanalytic Technique in APdeBA's Training Institute and Researcher Professor at the IUSAM Research Department. He collaborated with R. Horacio Etchegoyen for many years, both in teaching and in the IPA as member of the Finance Committee and of Etchegoyen's group of advisors. Among his papers are 'Infantile sexual theories and cognitive development', 'Considerations about action in psychoanalysis' and 'Theories as objects'. At present he is working on the genealogy of 'enactment' as part of his collaboration in the IPA's Committee on Conceptual Integration. He is chair of the FEPAL working party on relations between theory and clinical practice that published 'Unconscious theories in the analyst's mind at work'. He has published, in collaboration with R. Horacio Etchegoyen, 'Melanie Klein in Buenos Aires' and 'Psychoanalysis in Latin America: An approach to history and the ideas' (Chapter 1 in *Truth, reality, and psychoanalysis*). In collaboration with R. Horacio Etchegoyen, Tabak de Bianchedi, Ungar and Nemas de Urman, he has published 'Erna and Melanie Klein'.

This overdue anthology must be greatly welcomed.

It has been edited with great competence and moving passion by Nydia Lisman–Pieczanski and Alberto Pieczanski, two Argentinian psychoanalysts who studied first in Buenos Aires during the late sixties, trained in London during the seventies and now are practicing and teaching mainly in Washington, DC, USA.

This is not a collection of papers whose aim is to cover the whole development of psychoanalysis in South America.

There is no doubt that the so-called Argentinian School of Psychoanalysis located in Buenos Aires, and its specificity, due to the creativity of its pioneers and their pupils, has been a very prominent – if not the most prominent – school of psychoanalysis for decades in South America; this collection reflects that reality. Many psychoanalysts coming from Central and South America trained in Buenos Aires and have maintained personal and professional links for years with that school.

Of course, Brazil, Chile, Colombia, Mexico, Peru, Uruguay, and so forth, have developed their own approaches to psychoanalysis, with original results linked to the vicissitudes of their local Psychoanalytic Societies and links with the specific cultural, social and political histories of those countries.

After the period dominated by the work and personalities of Sigmund Freud and particularly of Melanie Klein and her school, whose work during the fifties and sixties of the last century had been studied and accepted with enormous interest much earlier in Argentina than in Europe or in North America, Argentinian psychoanalysts also became very interested in W. Bion and D. Meltzer, and more recently in Lacan, Kohut and others.

That fully explains and justifies the choice made by the Editors to restrict themselves to the generations of the pioneers of South American psychoanalysis and their work.

Furthermore, I think it was not by chance that the first South American President of the IPA was Dr. R. Horacio Etchegoyen, a disciple of Racker who is still practicing in Buenos Aires today.

The Editors have clearly explained to all of us the historical roots and the reasons for the prominence of the Argentinian School of Psychoanalysis.

Its origins and developments confirm that it is impossible to conceive psychoanalysis without taking into account the complex interaction between its internal 'scientific' history and the specificity of the cultural and sociopolitical context in which psychoanalysis has developed in Vienna and also outside Vienna – even before the 'Diaspora' of the Viennese and central European analysts due to the Nazi persecution of the Jews during the late 1930s and the death of Freud in London in 1939 – all factors which enormously contributed to the spreading and the pluralism of modern and contemporary psychoanalysis.

In the case of the Argentinian School of Psychoanalysis, what is so striking is its enormous popularity; for decades it has been a part of the everyday cultural life of the middle class in Buenos Aires, even outside the consulting rooms.

But what matters more is the originality of its contributions. This was due to the creative interaction between the so-called indigenous pioneers, such as E. Pichon-Rivière, A. Raskovsky, C. Carcamo, J. Bleger, and so on, and the group of psychoanalysts who came to Argentina in the late thirties due to the 'Diaspora' I just mentioned, from Berlin, Vienna, Spain and France: A. Garma, M. Langer, H. Racker, M. and W. Baranger and others. Although, even in the case of the so-called indigenous pioneers, many of them belonged to families of immigrants from Europe that 'landed' in Argentina one or two generations earlier.

They seemed to have felt free from the inevitable dogmatisms and strictures that characterized the cradle where psychoanalysis was born. They were not so directly affected by the ferocious controversies between the followers of Freud and Melanie Klein that had threatened the survival of psychoanalysis itself in Great Britain during the 1940s and they courageously counteracted the attempts of North American ego psychology to interfere and control the development of the newly born Argentinian Psychoanalytic Society, as it is well known that North American psychoanalysis mostly rejected M. Klein's work during those years.

The end result of all this is the extremely original contribution those pioneers were able to produce.

This is well documented in this anthology by the work on countertransference of H. Racker, L. Grinberg and H. Etchegoyen and by the pioneering research on the psychoanalytic field and the psychoanalytic process of the two Barangers.

One should not forget the research in the field of child psychoanalysis under the leadership of Arminda Aberastury.

natal and postnatal life of A. Raskovsky and J. Bleger.

The reading of this collection shows that many developments in psychoanalysis have been anticipated by the South American pioneers. Unfortunately their research and hypotheses were ignored by English-speaking colleagues because they wrote in Spanish and were rarely translated.

Many of them have used psychoanalysis to better understand institutional social and political issues as reflected in M. Langer and R. and L. Grinberg's work. We owe to R. and L. Grinberg the first and probably the best psychoanalytic book on migration and exile, which they wrote when they had to leave Argentina during the dictatorship of the seventies.

This book is essential reading for all analysts practicing today that really want to understand the richness and historical roots of so many contemporary developments in psychoanalysis.

We would like to thank the New Library of Psychoanalysis for asking us to edit a book on the pioneers of psychoanalysis in South America, and especially its current editor, Professor Alessandra Lemma, who followed the editing process with much interest and made us always feel that it was worthwhile pursuing this project, and Karla Loyo, who made possible the inclusion in this book of the papers of the Brazilian pioneers.

We want to thank all the colleagues who collaborated with their essays on each one of the pioneers.

Some of the papers were previously published in English and we would like to thank the *International Journal of Psychoanalysis*, *The Psychoanalytic Quarterly* and *Contemporary Psychoanalysis* for granting us permission to republish.

We are grateful to *Revista de Psicoanálisis* (Argentina) and *Revista Brasileira de Psicoanalise* (Brazil) for giving us permission to publish English versions of papers originally written in Portuguese and Spanish.

Full details of the original publications and translations are given at the beginning of each paper.

We would like to also thank Kirsten Buchanan, Routledge's Senior Editorial Assistant, who led us to the 'finishing line' of this complex publishing process, and the Library of the Argentine Psychoanalytic Association, which has an extraordinary collection of psychoanalytic papers from South America and its most helpful librarians.

Ana Pieczanski and Ana de Andrada did a great job translating Spanish and Portuguese papers that required many readings to understand the intended meaning.

Kathy Owen, Thomas Palley and Micheline Klagsburn helped us with thoughtful suggestions for the Introduction.

Heather Frank was efficient and generous with her time and knowledge of the publishing world as well as in reviewing the essays.

We feel especially grateful to our friends and colleagues in Washington, DC, Sharon Alperovitz and Justin Frank, who followed closely our 'journey' and believed that this book was worth the effort, providing us with emotional support in those moments in which it was most needed – when giving up felt a tempting option.

Luis Minuchin was our guide in the complex process of choosing the contributors most suitable to write the essays about each of the pioneers. He was also 'our man in Buenos Aires' that resolved many practical issues that we could not address from Washington.

Andrés Raskovsky generously provided the picture of the pioneers from his family album and gave us permission to publish it.

Finally, our deepest gratitude to the pioneers – some of them our teachers – who taught us to believe in the search for truth and the transformational potential of the psychoanalytic process.

# Early beginnings

Around 1930, Arnaldo Rascovsky, a well-known pediatrician in Buenos Aires, specialized in endocrinology and neurology at Children's Hospital, and Enrique Pichon-Rivière, a psychiatrist at the Central Mental Health Hospital in Buenos Aires, organized several reading groups with papers published by Freud and his collaborators. Although they had diverse back-grounds, they thought that psychoanalysis would enrich them, and they embraced with passion and curiosity the study of the evolving literature. In those days, neither of them had the opportunity to pursue a formal analytic training, but there is no doubt that the two of them created a welcoming setting for the newcomers to this field.

In Latin America, the interest in Freud's works started early in the 20th century. In this book, we would like to acquaint the English-speaking reader with the work of the pioneers of South American psychoanalysis and some of those who have more recently developed further some of their teachers' contributions.

Many of the contributions of South American psychoanalysts are now part of accepted standard analytic theory – as is the case of Heinrich Rack-er's contributions to the theory and clinical use of countertransference – while others, such as Jose Bleger and David Liberman, are less known or almost unknown, primarily due to lack of translation.

Twentieth-century wars created the conditions for an almost seamless continuity between European and South American psychoanalysis. Many of the displaced European professionals moved to South America in search of shelter. As we will describe, the same circumstances prompted the return to their countries of native South American analysts trained in Europe. The arrival of several analysts from Europe created the opportunity to initiate a psychoanalytic movement in Buenos Aires.

In the mid-1930s, the Spaniard Angel Garma trained in Berlin and was analyzed by Freud's analysand, Theodor Reik. He left the Berlin Society as the Nazi regime was increasing its power and moved to Paris, where he met Celes Cárcamo from Buenos Aires. Cárcamo had been trained at the Paris Institute and analyzed by Paul Schiff. During the Spanish Civil War, they both decided to move to Buenos Aires.

They were later joined by Marie Langer (née Glass Hauser), a Polish analyst who had been trained in Vienna and analyzed by Richard Sterba. She migrated first to Montevideo (Uruguay) and shortly after to Buenos Aires. Heinrich Racker, from Poland via Vienna, arrived in Buenos Aires in 1939, finishing his analytic training in Buenos Aires a few years later.

Angel Garma, Celes Cárcamo, Arnaldo Rascovsky, Enrique Pichon-Rivière, Marie Glass Hauser de Langer and Enrique Ferrari-Hardoy founded the Argentine Psychoanalytic Society on the 15th of December 1942. Ferrari-Hardoy migrated to the United States a few years later.

The original working group was organized by Enrique Pichon-Rivière, with Arnaldo Rascovsky and his wife Matilde Wencelblat, Arminda Aberastury and her brother Federico, Teodoro Schlossberg, Luisa Gambier (later called Luisa Alvarez de Toledo), Ferrary-Hardoy, Alberto Tallaferro and Flora Scolni.

The association received the approval of Ernest Jones, then president of the International Psychoanalytic Association (IPA). It was officially accepted as an IPA member at the Zurich Psychoanalytic Conference in 1949. In Santiago (Chile), Ignacio Matte Blanco returned from London after many years of training and joined Allende Navarro, who had been trained in Switzerland. They started training candidates, laying the foundation of a psychoanalytic group that was also accredited by the International Psychoanalytic Association in Zurich in 1949. Between 1949 and 1963, nine Latin American Societies joined the IPA.

Arminda Aberastury and Elizabeth Goode de Garma initiated a strong movement in child and adolescent psychoanalysis, using primarily the theoretical contributions of Melanie Klein.

Upon the first publication in July 1943 of the *Revista de Psicoanálisis* (the scientific publication of the Argentine Psychoanalytic Association), many South American professionals became quite excited about the possibility of acquiring a rigorous training. A significant number moved to Buenos Aires to be trained and then returned to their countries of origin to further create and develop new psychoanalytic institutes. At the same time, the pioneers traveled all over the South American continent as the interest for psychoanalysis was expanding rapidly.

Besides individual analysis, most of the pioneers also worked using a psychoanalytic model for the work with groups, considering the group as a psychological unit but also as the context for the psychological exploration of the group patients.

tion with the British School, particularly the theory of object relations and Melanie Klein.

This created an interesting theoretical and clinical tension between Freud's ideas and the modifications introduced mainly by Klein and her followers regarding the origin and structure of the superego and guilt in the process of cure, particularly with the introduction of the theory of the paranoid–schizoid and depressive positions and the relevance of guilt and reparation in the process of integration of the self, in contrast with Freud's focus on the superego as part of the sado–masochistic configuration.

The concept of guilt was further explored by León Grinberg, describing two kinds of guilt, depressive and paranoid, in his paper "Two kinds of guilt – their relations with normal and pathological aspects of mourning" (1963). This paper has further developed ideas that were present in Klein's model.

All these complex sets of theories and the way they influenced South American psychoanalysis were to a great extent informed by Klein's reelaboration of Freud's theory of the Death instinct, particularly as it appears in *Envy and Gratitude* (1986; Harvard Press, London, England).

The South American pioneers' lines of thinking evolved around a view of the therapeutic process that is nonlinear, multi-structured and nonchronological. Central to this perspective are the ideas about the "psychoanalytic field" of Madeleine and Willy Baranger, Bleger's "psychoanalysis of the psychoanalytic frame", and David Liberman's research on "communication in the therapeutic process". All these contributions were developed with the understanding of the analytic process as a two-person system.

Some of the contributions cross-fertilized the wider psychoanalytic environment very soon after their creation, as in the case of Racker, while others, like the Barangers' idea of "field", are only more recently starting to show their creative potential, as we can see in the extensive use of Madeleine and Willy Baranger's work made by Antonino Ferro in *The bipersonal field* (Routledge, 1999) and Roberto Basile's *The analytic field: A clinical concept* (Karnac, 2009).

Expanding on the relational aspect of the analytic cure, we have the contributions of Heinrich Racker to the subject of countertransference as a fundamental psychoanalytic tool and the added explorations of León Grinberg and David Liberman.

We think that it would be fair to say that the early interest in the dialectic interaction between transference and countertransference is the foundation of the concept of "field".

The early adoption of relational models of the analytic process is a point of view that focuses primarily on the analytic process itself rather than on diagnosis and psychopathology. In other words, it centers on the study of the analytic process and the specific features it acquires when working with different patients. While it is by no means specific to South American psychoanalysis, it is remarkable how strongly this model has predominated since the early days. The analyst, in this approach, works with and from within the experience, exploring the unconscious phantasies, projections, introjections and identifications that these unconscious phantasies promote.

The collection of papers intends to portray a community that emphasized Freud's ideas about freedom and the negative effects on mental health of repression and repressed sexuality at a social and individual level, as in his "Civilization and its discontents" (1930).

Avid readers and thinkers living in what at the time was a significant geographic distance from the European centers had the freedom to expand the field and did not feel the political pressure to show strong allegiance to any particular school.

The choice of papers is our exclusive responsibility. It is our intention to provide a foundation to explore further our rich psychoanalytic tradition. Through our selection we want to show how the diverse theories influenced our pioneers and what core concepts informed each pioneer.

We hope the readers will share our sense of how necessary and relevant many of these papers are today, even though they have been around for decades. Unfortunately, many important papers cannot be included in a volume like this. Since our intention is to encourage and facilitate further exploration, we have added biographical and conceptual essays of each author written by present-day psychoanalysts who are deeply knowledgeable of these pioneers' ideas.

We have divided the content into conceptual segments that are loosely defined, given the fact that one hallmark of South American psychoanalysis has been the attempt to articulate theory, psychopathology and technique in a rational and consistent way.

### Psychoanalytic process

The main section is the one dedicated to psychoanalytic process, an area in which South American pioneers have excelled. As we mentioned above, it has been a specific concern to develop a technique that is solidly articulated with theory.

In this collection, we included Willy and Madeleine Baranger's "The analytic situation as a dynamic field" and "Process and non-process in analytic work" by the Barangers and Jorge Mom. Their theory of the process as a dynamic field became a fundamental tool to understand any clinical

Heinrich Racker is, of course, also present in this collection. His work by now is not restricted by geography. His detailed description of countertransference and its application to our daily clinical work is by now incorporated into all mainstream psychoanalytic schools. His ideas about concordant and complementary countertransference still carry a lot of weight when attempting to explore clinical issues. For anyone interested in a thorough discussion of the merits and limitations of Racker's contributions, we strongly recommend R. Horacio Etchegoyen's book, *The fundamentals of analytic technique*.

By Racker we include the classical "The meanings and uses of countertransference", and for those willing to deepen their understanding of his ideas we recommend "companions" to this paper such as "A contribution to the problem of countertransference" (1948) and the 1956 paper "Counter-resistance and interpretation", that, again, we would have loved to include in this collection but editorial policy issues prevented us from doing so.

Expanding and consolidating these lines of thinking, we have included "The psycho-analytic process", by León Grinberg, Marie Langer, David Liberman, and Genevieve T. de Rodrigué.

From Durval Marcondes, one of Brazil's pioneers, whose work goes as far back as 1927, we have selected his paper "The psychodynamism of the analytic process". In this paper, he revisits Freud's ideas about cure, and he develops his own ideas on identification, countertransference, and the psychoanalytic encounter, paying special attention to interpretation.

In the paper "Lethargy. The ideal Ego and the Dead" that Fidias R. Cesio from Buenos Aires prepared specially for this book, he presents his views about lethargy, one of his lifelong subjects of research. We feel honored by his interest and effort and saddened by his recent death in 2012 at 90 years "young".

Alcyon Baer Bahía from Brazil wrote "Identification and identity". The author revisits ideas formulated in a previous paper on the interaction between the projective and the introjective processes. Presenting clinical material, the author studies two complementary facts that are fundamental for the under-standing of the operative capacities of the ego in the analytical setting. "The interaction of the projective and introjective mechanisms, in constant opera-tion in the ego since its primary development, makes one of the best guides for the comprehension of the therapeutic process in its totality".

Mario Pacheco de Almeida Prado's contribution, "The interference of the destructive impulses in the development of the self notion: States of entanglement", addresses some of the problems that arise in the analytic couple when working with severe pathologies. He focuses particularly on what he calls entanglement states, and his theoretical model is in a line of research with Jose Bleger's and Margaret Mahler's view on symbiosis.

We include in this section a paper by Marie Langer: "Sterility and envy". In it we can see a direct application of Klein's ideas about envy and their clinical manifestations. By the time this paper was published, she had already spent years researching the pathology of infertility in women and published a book on the subject. Here the emphasis is on envy as a useful concept that helped her to expand the understanding of the inner world of the infertile women. Langer is, of course, aware that Freud made envy a cornerstone of his ideas about feminine psychology and addresses in the paper the differences and connections between him and Klein. Klein's *Envy and gratitude* had been published less than three years before this one, and the ideas it contained were not part of the accepted or even generally known analytic concepts. She stud-ies here in some detail dream material and elaborates on the vicissitudes of projective and introjective processes as they appear in the analysis of women. The paper also offers some insight on her technique as she emphasizes the need to work on the transference in the here and now.

"Omnipotence and sublimation" is one of the very few published Adel-heid Koch papers. We believe this is the first translation. She was Klein's contemporary, and they both trained at the Berlin institute. She was the first training analyst in Brazil, once she settled in Sao Pablo; she had been sent by Ernest Jones in 1935 with the intention of organizing the first analytic group in Brazil.

### *Psychoanalytic technique*

This section is in fact a subdivision of the first, and as we mentioned before, a great effort was made in South America to establish a rational connec-tion between technique and the theoretical understanding in the analytic process. The section covers technique and its theory in connection with specific clinical situations. Here we have included a paper that, in our view, belongs to a class of its own: "The analysis of 'associating', 'interpreting' and 'words': Use of this analysis to bring unconscious fantasies into the present and to achieve greater ego integration" by Luisa de Alvarez de Toledo. In it, she articulates multiple layers of theory and, in a style that is sometimes not easy to follow, presents clinical examples and develops important contributions to the theory of technique. It was written at the time in which mainstream psychoanalysts in Buenos Aires were adopting Klein's ideas and an effort was being made to incorporate them in a meaningful way into the

analysis of the syntactic and paralinguistic elements of the patient's speech are a privileged source of data about the underlying unconscious phantasies and that this data should inform the analyst's technique. As he explains in a footnote, the elements that he found most useful to record are "considerations about strength, loudness, rhythm, pitch, length of sounds, length of silences, sighs, whispering, and tremolos. We can also take into account openness, breathiness, articulation, interruptions in the passage of air, and nasalization, as well as the range of deviations from the average for the patient concerned". Clearly, this is the language of a musician. He was an accomplished pianist and played in his father's jazz band.

David Liberman's work is perhaps one of those less known outside Argentina, because of its complexity. We include a second paper of his, "Affective response of the analyst to the patient's communications". Most of his work has not been translated and its understanding requires tutoring by those that worked closely with him, a situation similar to trying to get to know the work of his teacher, Enrique Pichon-Rivière, one of the great thinkers in our field.

Madeleine Baranger's "The mind of the analyst: From listening to interpretation" expands on issues of psychoanalytic process and technique. Baranger also describes some of her and her husband's contributions, such as the analytic field, and tries to define more accurately the ideas on interpretation. Here she uses mostly ideas from Piera Aulagnier and criticizes the Kleinian perspective on transference as well as Strachey's classical paper on the mutative interpretation.

José Bleger had a rich production that includes all psychoanalytic areas, attempting to articulate Marxism and psychoanalysis, social psychology and institutional psychology. Here we include a contribution whose merits are still to be recognized beyond South America: "Psycho-analysis of the psycho-analytic frame". This paper has particular relevance to our contemporary multimodal psychoanalytic field, in which it looks as if a common ground has been lost as far as theory but mainly regarding technique. In this paper, Bleger studies the frame as the institution within which psychoanalysis takes place. In his view it is, ideally, only visible when it is about to break or it has collapsed. Bleger studies the meaning of the frame in the analytic situation in general and regarding particular clinical experiences. This paper is in the same area of concern as many of the Barangers' and Liberman's and shares their conceptual framework.

R. Horacio Etchegoyen's contribution to this volume is in our view quintessential Etchegoyen: "The relevance of the 'here and now' transference interpretation for the reconstruction of early psychic development". Here Etchegoyen shows his thorough knowledge and understanding of the analytic process and literature; he also leaves no doubt as to what his position is regarding such a core subject. It is a combination of scholarship, teachership (an infrequently used word that perfectly describes Etchegoyen's role amongst psychoanalysts) and clarity, rarely found in analytic papers. This paper, unlike Madeleine Baranger's, follows and expands on Strachey's ideas about the mutative interpretation, which Etchegoyen uses as a "presupposed theory", one whose basic validity he does not question, at least at the time when this paper was written in 1983.

The final paper in this section is "On a specific aspect of countertransference due to the patient's projective identification", León Grinberg's expansion of Racker's research on countertransference, particularly the connection between countertransference and projective identification, using Bion's ideas about projective identification as communication comparable to the process that mother and baby use to establish the earliest links.

### *Metapsychology*

There are plenty of contributions to this field. One of the most original is by Enrique Pichon-Rivière, a teacher with many ideas that he rarely put in writing but explored in seminars and workshops.

His paper "Neurosis and psychosis: A theory of illness" is a radical theoretical review of psychopathology from the perspective of a totality in dialectic evolution. Abnormality, in this context, is a failed resolution of a conflict whose understanding must include the study of the antinomies *mind-body*, *individual-society*, and *organism-environment*. It is a model that attempts to understand all aspects of illness: the exploration of how one becomes ill, as well as the cure as a process of regaining health, factoring in the individual, group and society. He attempted to redefine psychoanalysis as a social psychology, trying to re-conceptualize its theories of illness and cure. The theoretical model articulates Freud, Klein – especially her contributions about the positions – and Fairbairn's relational model. Pichon-Rivière's clinical departure is his work with psychotics as well as neurotics and everything in between. This paper also touches on the misconception that psychoanalysis postulates that mental illness, whether psychosis or neurosis, is a psychological entity, something that Freud never said. This misconception is based on the lack of understanding of the body–mind unity sustained by most psychoanalytic thinkers.

Two important contributions that refined and expanded Klein's ideas on

to depressive positions and vice versa. She describes in this paper a pre-depressive position. She says that when tormented by depressive guilt and the inability to work through the depressive position, instead of regressing to the paranoid–schizoid position some patients defend themselves from depressive anxieties through splitting and projective identification in order to deal with guilt. She says: "Thus, instead of feeling guilty because of the aggressions and harm done in fantasy to themselves and their objects, they feel anxious and desperate in facing an object whose only aim is to force them to feel guilty, not deserving of anything good and compulsorily obliged to divide their possessions with them". It is not totally clear that the paper successfully describes a mode different from the paranoid–schizoid position. Nevertheless, we found it an interesting contribution to and exploration of Klein's ideas. The paper is connected with the one by León Grinberg that precedes it, and Bicudo is also interesting as part of a cluster of analysts that thought that the two Kleinian positions do not account for all the object relations modalities observed in clinical work. Bleger was particularly concerned about the un-differentiated phases of the human psyche, and Frances Tustin refers to an autistic mode and phase. We can also see this subject emerge in the work of Bion and Meltzer.

León Grinberg, in "Two kinds of guilt – Their relations with normal and pathological aspects of mourning", explores guilt as an experience that can lead to illness or to health in the process of mourning, depending on the way the patient connects to or denies it. The importance of this paper is twofold. It expands on Klein, but it is also part of the controversy on the role of guilt in neurosis. The first generation of pioneers adopted the model in which guilt is the cause of neurosis persecution and depression. Grinberg, following Klein, sustains that guilt denied is at the core of mental illness, a controversy that is still present amongst psychoanalysts.

Angel Garma, one of the more generous and prolific pioneers of South American psychoanalysis in Buenos Aires, wrote in 1946 the controversial and original paper "The traumatic situation in the genesis of dreams". In that paper, he develops the idea that dreams are hallucinations that mask traumatic experiences. In traumatic neurosis, due to the weakening of the psychic unconscious defense system, the individual is left and exposed to traumatic fantasies. The defense system that is still operating can transform traumatic situations into pleasant wish fulfillment dreams in its manifest content. Well before the Kleinian ideas established themselves to create the possibility of working with psychotic patients, Garma was treating psychotic patients in the early 1930s.

Some of his ideas about psychotic experiences are the ones developed in "The genesis of reality testing a general theory of hallucinations" (not included in this collection); he also departs from Freud's ideas about the psychotic structure, particularly regarding the superego's role in dismantling the ego functions.

Ignacio Matte-Blanco was a Chilean psychoanalytic thinker who created a powerful complement to established metapsychological ideas. His psychoanalytic roots are strictly Freudian in combination with Klein and logical analysis. His research had triggered the interest of analysts as well as researchers in many areas, including theology, philosophy, logic and mathematics. It is striking that his work is barely known and rarely mentioned in analytic papers, and there are very few analysts who have studied his research seriously, in spite of the fact that just a cursory search of the *International Journal of Psycho-Analysis* shows 17 papers since 1940. His work attempts to establish the difference between the logical structures of the primary and secondary processes as well as elaborate a most original thinking about emotionality that has close connections with Bion's ideas. We chose for this collection his seminal paper, "Expression in symbolic logic of the characteristics of the system Us or the logic of the system Us", his first comprehensive presentation of his work in progress.

Jorge Mom is represented in this section by one of his papers on phobia: "Some considerations regarding the concept of distance in phobias", one of his most interesting contributions.

### Psychoanalysis of children

Child analysis was always relevant for psychoanalysts in South America. The understanding was that working with children and primitive anxieties would enhance adult analysts' skills. We believe that this has been true for most psychoanalytic movements around the world a few decades later. In South America, child psychoanalysis developed primarily along Kleinian lines.

Arminda Aberastury was the driving force in conjunction with Elisabeth Goode de Garma. In this area and from her extensive production, we chose "Dentition, walking and speech in relation to the depressive position". In this paper, she describes how by the time of dentition and weaning there is an increase of bodily self-exploration, masturbation and play activity with corresponding unconscious Oedipal phantasies. We believe that her observation adds important weight to Klein's work. She writes in the paper: "Although oral, anal, and genital tendencies operate from the moment of birth, the oral phase is organized and built up because it is the one that

Emilio Rodrigué, one of the most creative and prolific Latin American analysts, was one of the chosen to contribute to *New directions in psychoanalysis* (1957, Basic Books), a collection of 11 of the essays published by the *International Journal of Psycho-Analysis* in 1952 to celebrate Mrs. Klein's 70th birthday. In keeping with the aim of this book to make new sources accessible to readers in English, we did not include his seminal paper "The analysis of a three year old mute schizophrenic", already widely available in English. We did, however, include a unique contribution, "Ludic interpretation: An attitude towards play", that we don't think has been previously translated and is in the book *El contexto del proceso psicoanalitico (The context of the psychoanalytic process)*, published in 1966 with his wife Genevieve.

Décio Soares de Souza, from Porto Alegre, describes in his paper, "Annihilation and reconstruction of object-relationship in a schizophrenic girl", how the analysis goes through phases of "reliving" in the transference the early losses and the particular psychic pain that psychotic patients have to confront in their attempts to move to the depressive position. He describes in this paper the analysis of a 2 year, 10 months old, girl. In it, de Souza attempts to establish a connection between the inability to mourn and schizophrenic deterioration. Herbert Rosenfeld and W. Bion substantially inform the writer's theoretical and clinical model.

### Culture and society

The importance of social, political and cultural subjects as part of the dyad *individual-environment* has been present in South Americans' psychoanalytic thinking from the early days. Psychoanalysis has had a significant impact in popular culture, leaving its mark all across the entire social structure.

Amongst the pioneers' contributions, the work of Arnaldo and Matilde Rascovsky deserves a special mention.

The place of children in our western culture was a subject particularly dear to them. The paper we chose, "The prohibition of incest, filicide and the sociocultural process" is part of a series. The core idea of this paper as expressed concisely by them is that "the assumption that guilt and the original crime stem from parricide calls for serious reconsideration. On the other hand, parricide as the ultimate evolution of object destruction must be regarded as a consequence of filicidal behavior and its principal roots must be attributed to the infant's identification with the parents' aggression". Matilde and Arnaldo Rascovsky have extensively researched how unconscious and conscious filicide phantasies express themselves in myths, culture, education, politics etc.

Fetal psychism, another of Arnaldo's important areas of clinical and theoretical research in the 50s, has found echoes in modern research, as conducted for example by Alessandra Piontelly in her book *From fetus to child: An observational and psychoanalytic study* (1992, Routledge, London), in the use of ultrasound cross-fertilized with psychoanalytic theory and practice plus Ester Bick's Infant Observation methods.

### Psychosomatic medicine

Psychoanalysis has, in a way, always been a holistic approach to the human condition. The study of hysterical phenomena has put psychoanalysis on this path from its inception. The origin of psychosomatic medicine is usually associated with the work of the Hungarian-German analyst Franz Alexander. In South America, a number of papers were published describing the treatment of different conditions like asthma, gastric ulcer, immunological conditions, skin conditions, obesity etc.

Danilo Perestrello, from Brazil, was interested in psychosomatic medicine well before he became an analyst. "Headache and primal scene" was his contribution to the 1953 International Psychoanalytic Congress. At the time, he was the driving force that fueled psychosomatic medicine studies in Brazil. In this paper, he presents interesting and detailed material that helps to follow his understanding of the unconscious phantasies and their correlation with migraine and headaches. His model tries to identify the level of regressed infantile sexuality, along the lines of Freud's 1905 paper "Three essays on the theory of sexuality", and how the vicissitudes of the defenses correlates with the presence or absence of the symptom, as well as an increased interest in the exploration of sadism. The richness of the clinical vignettes also allows us to look at the material using more contemporary analytic models that, in our view, complement and enrich his conclusions.

All the papers in this collection have been at the core of our analytic identity. We learnt them before we initiated our long journey through the English-speaking world, and revisited them many times since. They organized our minds through more than 40 years of work as clinicians and teachers, and for that we feel grateful and privileged.

12

# Part I

# (1920– )

## *Jorge Luis Maldonado*

Madeleine Baranger and her husband, Willy Baranger, both originally from France, settled in Buenos Aires immediately after the Second World War and did their psychoanalytic training with the group of analysts who originally founded the Argentine Psychoanalytic Society. In the mid-1950s, they moved to Montevideo, where they stayed for 10 years and founded the Psychoanalytic Association of Uruguay. They later returned to Buenos Aires, where they continued to teach and train different generations of Argentine psychoanalysts.

The most significant work by Madeleine and Willy Baranger focuses on the problems that emerge from the psychoanalytic field. Both studied the vicissitudes of the psychoanalytic process when this is blocked by the convergence of obstacles that derive from the analyst and the patient, configuring a state of stagnation in the psychoanalytic process. This state of impasse was termed the "bastion" by the authors and is a concept that has similarities with the description that, many decades later, was given to what was termed "enactment". However, the concept of "bastion" confers greater depth and understanding to what occurs in the analytical field in that it refers to the shared, unconscious phantasy which is configured by both analyst and analysand. A typical example of this takes place as a result of the distribution of alternating or fixed roles that are adopted by patient and analyst during states of sadomasochistic transference-countertransference. A summary of Madeleine's ideas about the psychoanalytic process is contained in her paper that explores the workings of the analyst's mind during the process of listening and interpreting (M. Baranger, 1993). An article that predates this paper and that clearly describes the theory of the "dynamic psychoanalytic field" was written together with W. Baranger and J. Mom (M. Baranger et al., 1983).

One of the most significant contributions of Madeleine Baranger was her research into the clinical picture of "bad faith". This disturbance of identity, characterized by the lack of authenticity of the subject both in relation to themselves and to others, imprints an artificial character on object relationships that prevents the subject from having any real contact with their internal objects. The author positions this clinical picture within the pathological organization of the character, and by doing so removes the negative connotation of "value judgment" which the term "bad faith" has in everyday language. She also draws a distinction between J. P. Sartre's phenomenological description of bad faith and her own definition, which is broader in scope and includes the unconscious determinants of this clinical picture. This takes into account the distortions of the fundamental rule of free association as the principal way of understanding this character trait. She differentiates the common transgressions of this rule, which do not respond to a characterological problem, from the intentions of the patient with this clinical picture whose aim is to devalue the fundamental basis of the analytical process. The patient's aim is not only concerned with avoiding the observance of the fundamental rule but is also related to its distortion in response to a desire to radically pervert the course of the analytical process, to reduce the analyst to a state of impotence and to strip the analytical material of all its value. The clinical picture of bad faith falls within disturbances in identity, and relates to the problem of lack of authenticity, which bad faith imprints on the subject, to the vicissitudes of introjection. Baranger states that the identity derives from introjections that are integrated within the structure of the ego, configuring character traits. However, in the case of bad faith, these introjections give the ego masks or personas rather than character traits. This also highlights a characteristic of the internal state of the ego, which consists in a multiplicity of identifications that are current, contradictory and not fixed, so that the analysand becomes and is seen as having many different characters, without knowing which the real one is. She also points out that the subject does not want to relinquish incompatible aspects of these multiple personalities. An interesting characteristic of this condition is that the patient's lack of authenticity is apparent to the observer, but the subject is unaware that he or she is acting out different characters. It is thus possible to appreciate that the problem of lack of authenticity is not only limited to the question of deceit but is also connected to the multiplicity of identifications that determine the analysand, coupled with the subject's lack of awareness of this pathology. This form of defense mechanism enables the subject to retain their omnipotence, and its essential function is to provide a means of avoiding anxiety.

# References

work. *International Journal of Psycho-Analysis, 64*: 1–15.

Baranger, M., Baranger, W., Mom, J. (1988). The infantile psychic trauma from us to Freud: Pure trauma, retroactivity and reconstruction. *International Journal of Psycho-Analysis, 69*: 113–28.

# 2

# INTRODUCTION TO THE LIFE
# AND WORK OF WILLY BARANGER
# (1922–1994)

*Alberto Pieczanski*

Willy Baranger was born in Algeria. After moving to France in his child-hood, he pursued his education, obtaining a PhD in philosophy at the end of World War II. He then started a short-lived teaching career in France, lasting one year, and the Barangers (because Willy was already married to Madeleine) migrated to Argentina, where he taught philosophy.

Willy started analysis with Enrique Pichon-Rivière, one of the pioneers of psychoanalysis in Argentina, and from then on he and Madeleine developed together – to the point that nowadays they constitute, in the mind of those that know their work, "the Barangers" – a conceptual unit. The fertility and originality of their contributions and their joint teaching and publications makes it difficult to establish a proper separation of their individual contributions.

Soon after their arrival in the late 1940s, they started their training at the then-recently founded Argentine Psychoanalytic Association. However, settling down did not seem to be the Barangers' destiny, at least for the time being.

At the time, a group of Uruguayan professionals interested in analysis were traveling regularly to Buenos Aires to train at the Argentine Psychoanalytic Association (APA) and were in analysis in Montevideo with the Uruguayan pioneer Valentín Perez Pastorini. Juan Perón was the Argentine president, relationships with Uruguay were tense, and, eventually, traveling regularly to Argentina from Uruguay was prohibited, leaving the training of professionals from Uruguay interrupted until 1955.

The death of Dr. Pastorini in 1948, compounded by the political tension between Uruguay and Argentina, "orphaned" the Uruguayan group, which started a search for analysts that would be willing to settle in Montevideo. Hanna Segal was seriously considering moving to Uruguay, but she finally decided not to leave England.

Close to the end of Peron's presidency in December 1954, following a

Willy died in 1994.

Possibly, the Barangers' main contribution was the idea of the analytic field, a co-creation of the analyst and the patient, a "third" that operates as an unconscious phantasy (as conceived by Klein) and informs the development of the analytic process. This co-created third is a concept that has its roots in the research by Pichon-Rivière, Heinrich Racker, Luisa Alvarez de Toledo, Jorge Mom, León Grinberg and David Liberman – all of them strongly influenced by Klein – but it goes beyond the strict psychoanalytic origins and includes social psychology, philosophy and literature. Merleau-Ponty is a constant presence in the Barangers' production.

The disruption of the creative field in clinical work was conceptualized in their ideas about the "bastion", a co-created unconscious resistance to the analytic process. Willy Baranger made important research on the psychoanalytic concept of Object and explored it throughout his life, starting with Freud, incorporating the ideas of Klein and finally finding in Lacan the route to a psychoanalysis that goes beyond a one-person or two-person psychology. During his fertile production, he asked questions about Freud's economic theory, Freud's and Klein's Oedipus models, and the absence of the Father in Klein, amongst others.

He was deeply immersed in the epistemological dialogue within psychoanalysis, of extraordinary relevance to today's psychoanalysis. In his paper "Métodos de objetivación en la investigación psicoanalítica" ("Methods of objectivation in psychoanalytic research"), Willy Baranger (1959) invites us to renounce quantitative mechanistic methods and develop our own principles and validation methods as well as truth criteria, and he indicates that those parameters should be primarily rooted in clinical practice.

Finally, I would like to mention a line of research that I would call "foundational" in the analytic chest of tools. I am referring to his idea that Ideology is a core conscious and unconscious organizer of the ego and, as such, should be the object of analysis. Willy introduces his paper "The Ego and the function of Ideology" (1958) with the following paragraph: "As the purpose of psycho-analysis is not to cure isolated symptoms of neurosis, but to modify the life of people entirely, the problems of ideology acquire increasing importance in the process of analysis. Since the ego of a civilized human being is expressed by means of certain ideological attitudes, the patient's ideology becomes 'analytic material', even before we know the exact meaning of this 'material'. It belongs – partly, at any rate – to the ego. It plays a part in psychic balance. We cannot ignore its function or its relationship with the ego" (p. 191).

His extensive list of publications includes four books: *Problemas del campo psicoanalitico*, with Madeleine Baranger (1969), *Posición y objeto en la obra de Melanie Klein* (1971), *Aportaciones al concepto de objeto en psicoanálisis* (1980), and *Artesanias psicoanaliticas* (1994), which has not, unfortunately, been published in English.

Willy Baranger had an intense institutional activity, as well. I have mentioned already his role in establishing the Uruguay Psychoanalytic Society. He actively participated in national and international psychoanalytic congresses, chaired COPAL (Coordinating Committee of Latin American Psychoanalytic Organizations), and had an active role in the creation of the Peruvian Psychoanalytic Society.

# References

Baranger, W. (1958) "The Ego and the function of ideology" *International Journal of Psycho-Analysis* 39: 191–195.
Baranger, W. (1959) "Métodos de objetivación en la investigación psicoanalítica" *Revista Uruguaya de Psicoanálisis* 3(1): 26–41.

# 3

## Madeleine Baranger and Willy Baranger[2]

*This paper was published in 2008 by the* International Journal of Psycho-Analysis, *89: 795–826.*

This paper discusses the consequences of the importance that recent[3] papers assign to the countertransference. When the latter acquires a theoretical and technical value equal to that of the transference, the analytic situation is configured as a dynamic bi-personal field, and the phenomena occurring in it need to be formulated in bi-personal terms. First, the field of the analytic situation is described, in its spatial, temporal and functional structure, and its triangular character (the present–absent third party in the bi-personal field) is underlined. Then, the ambiguity of this field is emphasised, with special weight given to its bodily aspect (the bodily experiences of the analyst and the patient being particularly revealing of the unconscious situation in the field). The different dynamic structures or lines of orientation of the field are examined: the analytic contract, the configuration of the manifest material, the unconscious configuration – the unconscious bi-personal phantasy manifesting itself in an interpretable point of urgency – that produces the structure of the field and its modifications. The authors describe the characteristics of this unconscious couple phantasy: its mobility and lack of definition, the importance of the phenomena of projective and introjective identification in its structuring. The authors go on to study the functioning of this field, which oscillates between mobilisation and stagnation, integration and splitting. Special reference is made to the concept of the split-off unconscious 'bastion' as an extremely important technical problem. The analyst's work is described as allowing oneself to be partially involved in the transference–countertransference micro-neurosis or micro-psychosis, and interpretation as a means of simultaneous recovery of parts of the analyst and the patient involved in the field. Finally, the authors describe the bi-personal aspect of the act of insight that we experience in the analytic process.

There is nothing new in admitting the error of one-sidedness in early descriptions of the analytic situation as a situation of objective observation of a patient in a state of more or less pronounced regression by an analyst-eye[4] that restricts itself to recording, understanding and sometimes interpreting what is happening in the patient.

Direct observation and progressively deeper studies of the countertransference, the unconscious means of communication that develops in the analytic situation with particular ease and intensity, the latent meanings of verbal communication: all these factors imply a very different and much broader concept of the analytic situation, in which the analyst intervenes – in spite of the necessary 'neutrality' and 'passivity' – as a fully participant member.

Therefore, the analytic situation should be formulated not only as a situation of one person who is confronted by an indefinite and neutral personage – in effect, of a person confronted by his or her own self – but as a situation between two persons who remain unavoidably connected and complementary as long as the situation obtains, and involved in a single dynamic process. In this situation, neither member of the couple can be understood without the other. No more than this is implied when it is recommended, and rightly so, that the countertransference be utilised as a technical instrument (Heimann, 1961).

The concept of 'field', as used in particular in Gestalt Psychology and in the works of Maurice Merleau-Ponty,[5] seems to be applicable to the situation created between patient and analyst – at least on the descriptive level – without this implying an attempt to translate analytic terminology into any other.

We think that the need to introduce the field concept into the description of the analytic situation arises from the structural characteristics of this situation. The analytic situation has its spatial and temporal structure; is oriented by specific dynamics and lines of force; and has its own laws of evolution, its general objective and momentary aims. This field is our immediate and specific object of observation. Since observation by the analyst is both observation of the patient and a correlative self-observation, it can only be defined as observation of this field.

# I. Description of the field of the analytic situation

What we notice most immediately about the analytic field is its spatial structure. Two persons meet in the same room, and are generally located in constant places and complementary positions within it. One is lying on the couch and the other is seated, also in a relaxed position, in an armchair next to and slightly behind the other person; any modification of this spatial structure, empirically adopted as being the most favourable, leads to substantial modifications of the analytic relationship itself.

An analysis does not develop in the same way if the armchair is placed a

in the transference–countertransference relation, it undergoes important experiential modifications. Although both are in the same place as in all the previous sessions, the patient may ask the analyst why he or she has changed the position of the armchair, and moved it further away. At other times, patients may experience the distance between themselves and the analyst as being annihilated. The space of the analytic relation may also contract until it includes only the analyst and the patient, with denial of the existence of the natural boundaries of the room and the furniture it contains, or may extend itself to include whatever objects (pictures, books, etc.) are in the room, or may even extend itself beyond the boundaries of the room: the other patient in the waiting room who is listening, the noises from the house or the street, may take on important meaning and form a momentary space that is quite different from the common analytic space.

Any modification of the experienced spatial field naturally means a global modification of the analytic relationship. Many recent studies (Mom, 1956, 1960) of the spatial configurations in agora- and claustrophobia and in phobias in general show the importance of variations in the distances and structure of the spatial field in the analytic situation.

In the temporal dimension we also observe the existence of a common field that is structured in a certain way and the temporary modifications of this structure. The field is constituted by the prior agreement concerning the duration and frequency of the sessions, as well as the interruptions (vacations, etc.) that may break up the uniformity of the field. But the analyst and patient who start to work together also know that, except for an unforeseeable event, they are going to do this for a period of several years. Their work is entered into within a temporal field whose boundaries have been established along general lines.

This does not prevent innumerable modifications from altering this field. The phenomenon of sessions that are experienced as short or long in the transference or the countertransference is quite well known (Spira, 1959).

The procedures used by patients to bring about a halt in the evolution of the temporal field are extremely varied and respond to multiple situations of anxiety (anxiety towards growth, change, the unknown, etc.). Some patients, at certain moments or periods, experience the analytic temporal field as indefinite and come consciously to consider analysis as life-long or even eternal, which sometimes corresponds to a phantasy of unending oral gratification or possession of the idealised object. The future 'cure' or the 'termination' of the analysis is no longer attractive, and still less so when reaching this future means facing intense situations of anxiety.

Other patients, on the contrary, try to force the pace of the temporal field. They try to be analysed in a great hurry, and they always feel that the procedure is too slow. While the former were trying to stop time in order to avoid the next anguishing moment, the latter are 'off like a shot' in response to anxiety and they speed up the changes in order not to find themselves at peace in any situation.

Naturally, these alterations of the analytic temporal field depend on the character structure of the participants and on their particular way of handling objects and anxiety, the temporal field reflecting the global analytic field.

The analytic field is also structured according to a basic functional configuration contained in the initial commitment and agreement. This commitment explicitly distributes the roles between the two participants in the situation: one agrees to communicate to the other, as far as possible, all his or her thoughts; to co-operate with the other's work and to pay for this work. The other agrees to try to understand the former, provides help in resolving conflicts through interpretation and promises confidentiality and abstention from any intervention in the other's 'real' life.

In this way, a functional field is configured in which the two persons expect from each other very determinate behaviour and the maintenance of the basic commitment, whatever the content of momentary modifications may be. Because of the structure of the situation itself, the patient accepts a number of implicit rules in the relation with the analyst – and interpretation will remind the patient of this when he or she fails to observe them; for example, patients accept a considerable limitation of actions in relation to the analyst. They may want to kill him and fantasise the analyst's destruction, but they cannot shoot the analyst down, nor can they move into the analyst's house, even if they think that 'I would be better off here than anywhere else', etc.

The consequences of the structuring of this functional field are extremely important: they place the patient in a position that permits and even encourages regression, and the analyst in a very different one, where the temporary regression of the analyst's ego must be much more limited and partial, leaving the observing aspect of the ego intact and preserving the terms of the contract if the patient tries to bypass them and thus adulterate the analytic situation. The most generalised non-fulfilment of the contract relates to the fundamental rule and, from Freud onwards, everyone has recognised the technical need to analyse and overcome it as an access route to conflicts, and has noted that the particular form of the neurosis in each patient is expressed in the patient's particular way of avoiding the fundamental rule.

or even break into the room in the form of a hallucination.

Neither can we say that these two persons are no more than two, since the general rule is that they are divided experientially into 'parts', each of them and the third persons representing aspects or agencies of the two basic persons. Depending on the moment, the analyst may represent the patient's superego or repressed impulses or repudiated parts of the patient's ego. And naturally the same occurs – though on a smaller scale – with the patient for the analyst.

This situation is the inevitable consequence of the splitting prevalent in the patient's regressive and neurotic situation and of the different type of splitting (Klein, 1955, 1958) involved in the analyst's partial regression. The bi-personal therapeutic situation, therefore, with the basic organisation of the field, disappears under the cover of tri- and multi-personal situations, of multiple splittings in perpetual motion. However, it does not disappear entirely, but only in situations of intense regression when the basic commitment is completely lost and the analytic situation disintegrates, with the consequent danger of interruption of the analytic process. In ordinary situations, the bi-personal therapeutic structuring remains as a background, present but not perceived, on which the constantly changing tri- and multi-personal structures are made and unmade.

Experience shows a clear pre-eminence, within these structures that stand out against the background of the therapeutic situation, of the tri-personal or triangular structure (Pichon-Rivière, 1956–58). The analytic couple is a trio, one of whose members is physically absent and experientially present. Freud expressed the same when he described the Oedipus complex as the nuclear complex of the neuroses. It could be said that all the other structurings are only modifications of this triangular structure, whether in the progressive direction, by distribution of the conflict among secondary characters and by their inclusion, which transforms the tri-personal structure into a multi-personal structure, or in the regressive direction, by elimination or loss of the third party, thus reducing the

25

tri-personal structure to a bi-personal one, but in this case experienced as a relation with a partial object (an example of this situation is the idyllic or marvellous experience of certain patients when they experience the analyst as an inexhaustible, idealised breast, though, of course, in this case the third is still present in a certain virtual way: the patient, anguished by the conflicts in the triangular situation, regressively eliminates one of its terms, which remains as a threat).

Thus, we consider that the field of the analytic situation is always double or multiple. It is never just one situation but superimposed or mixed situations, different but never clearly delimited. This orients us towards a new aspect, of particular importance to this new field.

## II. The essential ambiguity of the analytic situation

It could be said that every event in the analytic field is experienced in the 'as if' category. Of course, this is not the only situation in which things are experienced in this way. An actor playing the part of Hamlet acts and feels as if he were Hamlet, but he is not, and he does not lose consciousness of his own person. In the same way, in love or friendship, the object is always more for us than what it is 'in reality', carrying with it the weight of our former loves and friendships.

However, here the situation is different: in everyday life, we try to relate to people on the basis of their objective reality and not according to our subjective projections; in the analytic situation we try to eliminate as far as possible any references to our objective personality and leave this as indefinite as possible.

If the patients were to experience the analyst exactly as the analyst is (for example, if the patients were to consider the analyst only as his or her analyst), the transference phenomenon would be suppressed, which is obviously inconceivable, and for the same reason any possibility of analysis would be suppressed.

It is essential for the analytic procedure that each thing or event in the field be at the same time something else. If this essential ambiguity is lost, the analysis also disappears. A good example of this would be the episodes when the field is invaded by a situation of persecution. The patient transfers onto the analyst, sometimes with great intensity, a number of internal persecutory figures whose origin is in the patient's history. Transference fear and resentment reach their zenith; however, the patient continues to come to sessions and goes on hoping to get help from the analyst to resolve the situation. In other words, the patient feels and acts as if it were a real situation of persecution, but keeps the therapeutic relation uncontaminated by it. If this ambiguity is lost, the analyst is experienced like any other persecutor and the patient actually attacks the analyst, calls the police or simply runs away.

At the other extreme, certain patients, because of distrust or anxiety, cling to the objective aspects of the background therapeutic situation and what they have been able to learn or perceive about the analyst's 'objective' reality.

The analysis operates between these two extremes of ambiguity: ambiguity rejected for fear of regression and ambiguity dissolved by an excessively regressive situation. It is not only the analyst and the details of the transference relation that are experienced on the level of ambiguity, but all aspects of the analytic field.

The temporal aspect of the field is nothing like the time experienced in everyday situations. The time of the analysis is simultaneously a present, a past and a future. It is a present as a new situation, a relationship with a person who adopts an attitude essentially different from that of the objects of the patient's history, but is at the same time past, since it is managed in a way which permits the patient the free repetition of all the conflicting situations of his or her history. It is this temporal ambiguity, the mixture of present, past and future, that permits patients not only to become aware of their history but also to modify it retroactively. This history is a gross weight, with its series of traumatisms and damaging situations that have been given once and for all, until re-experiencing them in the state of temporal ambiguity permits the patients to take them on again with new meaning. The patients know they had a difficult birth, suffered hunger when a tiny baby, had a wet nurse, etc. But these traumatic situations can now be experienced not as unchangeable deadweight with an attitude of resignation, if they are taken up again, worked through and reintegrated into a different temporal perspective.

For this reason, the future is also present in temporal ambiguity. Most often, patients come to analysis because they feel they have no future. They were prisoners of their neurosis, with no prospect of at least being released from this imprisonment.

The attempt to have an analysis often indicates a last attempt to re-open the future and re-orient existence. Since past and future take on meaning through their correlation, the attempt to revise the past in temporal ambiguity runs parallel to questioning the future. Under these conditions, the dialectical process of the constitution of the past and the future on the basis of the present can be freed to some extent (Baranger W, 1959).

It is essential that the analysis develop in a different temporality from the temporality of action and perception; for this reason, one of the typical ways to avoid the analytic situation through resistance is the chronological narration during the analysis, either of the individual history at the beginning, or of everything the patient did since the last session. The patient clings to a temporality that is already oriented and determined out of fear of ambiguous temporality, in other words, of the joint experience of a present situation with the analyst and a past relation with archaic objects. The loss of a common temporality means a loss of personal identity for these patients.

We could say that the temporal dialectic of analysis progresses from a fixed and determined temporality to a different type (more mobile, with more of a future and a different content), passing through an especially ambiguous temporality. The temporality of the analytic situation is comparable to time in fairy tales or dreams: 'Once upon a time . . .'

We have already pointed out particular features of the space of the analytic field that highlight an equally ambiguous character.

First, because it is the superimposition of two spaces: we have called one of these the common space, onto which a number of momentary spatial experiences are superimposed, though in this superimposition or mixture no one space completely substitutes for any other. The space of the analytic situation is similar to the space in dreams, where the geometric scandal of ubiquity becomes the rule.

The analytic situation seems to obey – like the thinking of primitive peoples, according to Levy Bruhl – not the logical principles of identity, non-contradiction and causality but the law of 'participation'. This explains why the bodies of the patient and the analyst are immersed in the same ambiguity. The taboo against physical contact between analyst and patient, with 'permitted' contact limited to a handshake in greeting and leaving, finds one of its justifications in this, as does the nearly total absence of physical movement during the sessions. The patient's body is disconnected from the need to act, thereby allowing the appearance of bodily experiences that are split or repressed by the need to adapt actively to everyday life. The patient knows that he can recover his 'real' body at any time and that he will effectively recover it when the session ends and he gets up, says goodbye and goes back to his daily activity; but during the session it seems to be a different, unknown body in relation to the different kind of space and time that is being experienced. Any modification of the field of the analytic situation can be expressed by physical changes in the patient, and in practice such changes are always observed, even by the active splitting of the body by the patient. In these extreme cases, patients try to be as if they had no body, keeping it completely still and abstaining from any bodily awareness or any reference to the body. This attempt at elective paralysis corresponds naturally to powerful latent anxieties about what could happen if the body were brought into play in the analytic situation (castration anxiety, fear of sadistic violation, persecutory phantasies relating to bodily integrity, immobilisation by hypochondriacal persecutors, etc.). In these cases, the 'absence' of the patient's body becomes a powerful obstacle to the mobilisation of the field and consequently needs to be interpreted.

manages to institute a body language that we need to understand if we wish to avoid neglecting a very important dimension of the global situation.

The ambiguity of the body in the analytic situation sometimes becomes quite patent at the moment when the patient abandons his 'body' of the session in order to recover the body of his daily life. Particularly when leaving regressive situations of surrender, the patient needs a few moments to recover his physical capacity. The patient gets up with awkward movements and walks unsteadily, sometimes having a feeling of weakness in the legs or dizziness.

The participation of the body in the analytic situation is by no means limited to the patient. Every analyst participates in the physical ambiguity and responds with his or her own body to the patient's unconscious communication. The analyst also elaborates a body language with which to respond to certain modifications of the field. In reference to the observations of León Grinberg (1956), we could call this phenomenon 'corporeal projective counteridentification'. In these bodily manifestations, the analyst responds to an invasion by the patient, who is placing an aspect of his personal experiences in the analyst. For example, it often happens that an analyst will sneeze in the course of a session without having a cold or being in the process of getting one. In this case, the analyst does not consciously feel cold or abandonment, and neither does the patient. However, this sneeze corresponds to a situation of abandonment experienced by the patient as if the analyst had taken on a physical reaction that the patient should be feeling, but does not feel in a manifest way.

In these cases of countertransferential bodily reactions, the reaction stops when the patient's projective identification has been formulated in an interpretation by the analyst and the patient has taken back the projected parts of the self placed into the analyst. The touchstone of validity of the interpretation is therefore the disappearance of the physical state in the analyst and the appearance in the patient of the manifest feeling of which the physical reaction was the equivalent. (The analyst sneezes – interprets the situation of abandonment to the patient – the latter feels sadness.)

We also observe that the fantasies of physical movement that emerge in the analyst during the session always correspond to experiences the patient has actually gone through. Of course, this applies when the analyst is calm and free of upsetting personal worries.

A candidate that one of us had occasion to observe once felt (in a session) invaded by the unusual fantasy of disemboweling and dismembering the patient (without, of course, having the slightest wish to do so). Surprised, he looked through the patient's verbal material in search of anything that might be related to this fantasy and found nothing which pointed that way. He thought, appropriately, that since he hadn't the least desire to disembowel his patient, the fantasy he had had must be a countertransference response to the patient's unconscious phantasy, and he interpreted the wish to be attacked physically (without, of course, mentioning his own fantasy that had motivated the interpretation). Suddenly, the course of the session changed and an intense masochistic transference situation appeared, in which the patient identified him with Jack the Ripper. The analyst's fantasy of physical movement disappeared immediately.

Examples like these abound and have been mentioned in studies of countertransference. We could also quote cases in which the patient physically expresses an unconscious response to circumstantial states of the analyst, not manifested of course by the analyst. Naturally, this latter situation is more infrequent.

From this we conclude that analysts need to use their own bodily ambiguity as an indicator of the unconscious dimensions of the situation, as well as their own particular experiences made possible by the ambiguous character of the space, time and all the rest of the analytic situation.

## III. Orienting lines[6] of the field: Unconscious phantasy

We have pointed out that the field of the analytic situation has at least two superimposed structures: the basic bi-personal therapeutic structure and the changing structures, tri- or multi-personal in general, that overlay it. We immediately recognise the insufficiency of this description. The ambiguity of the analytic situation can never be reduced to these two structures, and between the generally implicit contractual situation, on the one hand, and the manifest content of the patient's verbal communication to the analyst on the other, unconscious structures with decisive importance intervene. The two extreme structures, as they are experienced at a particular moment, have a meaning or latent content. When the situation is expressed verbally, this is obvious. For example, if the patient complains of a frustrating marital situation (manifest content), he or she may be trying to win the analyst over as an ally for wishes of gratification or to consider the analyst unconsciously as causing this situation or be asking the analyst for direct gratification or many other things (latent content). When it concerns the basic contract, the existence of latent content is not always evident, although it is always present in the form of a phantasy of the analytic process and of the treatment.

formulated, is only the superficial aspect of another contract, unconscious for the patient, which is quite different from what was stipulated. It is well known that the patient can accept the analysis, for example, with the unconscious fantasy of acquiring phallic omnipotence or to take revenge on the person of the analyst for ill-treatment and frustrations received in reality or in phantasy from one or another of the childhood objects. In this case, missing a session can mean, for example, 'I do whatever I want, and you're helpless to stop me', or else, 'I stand you up and deprive you of my presence as they did to me'.

In this way, both the basic contract and the manifest material point to another structure and cannot be understood without it. Also, in all the cases of changes of the basic contract, the manifest material, though it has nothing to do with this alteration openly, points to the same underlying situation.

Therefore, we are not twisting the facts when we affirm the existence of three distinct structures. But are things not even more complicated? If the basic situation and the verbally expressed situation are related to a third unconscious situation, this does not happen accidentally at a certain moment in an analysis. It originates in historical childhood situations in the patient's life and has also been reactivated by some external situation experienced by the patient.

Nothing illustrates all this better than the analysis of a dream. The dream has been stimulated by a current situation and includes day residues. It also expresses a historical situation related to the former and has a manifest content that may or may not include the analyst. It is also told to the analyst with a certain phantasy of what the analyst is going to do with this dream, of what the work entails and of what can be expected from the analyst. All this may be a subject of interpretation, but we are not yet really satisfied and we don't have the impression of having interpreted the dream adequately if our interpretation is not placed at the point where all these situations converge.

This point of convergence of different meanings is the third configuration, the most important one from the point of view of the analytic process, because its very essence is rooted therein. It is simultaneously the point of impact of the interpretation. Here, therefore, we find a mixture of two problems: that of the interpretation as seen from the analyst's position and that of the emergence of this configuration of the field from the patient's position. But both problems, though they do not exactly overlap, do come together. The analyst searches through the multiple latent situations that can be perceived in the material offered, which are also related to the manifest content and the current phantasy of the contract, to find the situation that is effectively interpretable. On the other hand, within the patient's multiple historical, current and transference situations intervening in the configuration of the field, one is more vivid than the others, not by chance but because of the double and mixed sequence of the experiences of the analysis and exterior experiences. This is the most urgent situation and consequently the one that must be interpreted preferentially if the interpretation is to become potentially effective for change in the field. It is called the 'point of urgency' (Pichon-Rivière, ibid.).[7]

However, this concept that we habitually use requires some clarification. It may be the interpretive point of urgency (need for interpretation in the patient and the analyst) at a moment of the session, though this interpretation may be only temporary, or it may be the emergent situation in the life of the patient at the moment in which the analytic session in its totality is placed (the patient comes to session with an unconscious problem that he or she wishes both to conceal and to communicate). Most often, this unconscious problem does not appear immediately to the analyst's comprehension and may remain hidden until the end of the session, emerging with different expressions in later sessions.

Access to the main point of urgency can therefore be subordinated to the comprehension and interpretation of a secondary and preliminary point of urgency, whose resolution it needs in order to appear.

The best example of this situation is the patient's silence at the beginning of the session. In certain cases, if we cannot understand and interpret the initial silence, it extends and deprives us of the material that would allow us to understand the point of urgency of the session. The vicious circle thereby created can even thwart the course of an analysis. It goes without saying that the point of urgency provokes a blockage of the field, expressed by the patient's silence, meaning that the point of urgency is already present in the silence. But sometimes, it is hardly useful to know this if we are unable to understand and formulate the content and immediate function of this silence with precision.

Consequently, we need to differentiate various points of urgency in an analytic session or sometimes in a sequence of sessions. There are preliminary points of urgency that particularly express defensive processes of the patient's ego, and a point of urgency of the session, whose interpretation provokes an appreciable modification of this field.

An example of the latter process would be sessions that give the analyst the impression of 'having worked well'; in our experience, these are sessions in which the patient–analyst dialogue has developed along a progressive line. The patient brings up a situation whose point of urgency is understood

tively to include the foregoing material and interpretations, clarifying them and allowing us to integrate them into a seamless 'gestalt'.

The countertransference impression of good communication with the patient and of 'good work' can hardly deceive an analyst with a bit of experience. We may feel very happy to have understood some important point of the structure or the history of a patient, even when our understanding does not at all correspond to the patient's own understanding (although the patient will probably be able to use it later); but this satisfaction is smaller and differs greatly from what the analyst feels when the patient has responded to our understanding with a corresponding understanding and when, because of this understanding, a modification of the field has been produced that is intelligible to us. The patient's material suddenly becomes richer, memories emerge more freely and emotions are manifested with fewer snags.

This is the process of progressive construction of an interpretation in the bi-personal field.

Naturally, it would be fruitless to attempt to understand this process solely from the patient's point of view. Certain sessions are 'good' or 'bad' not only because of the patient's current resistance or due to our greater or lesser intellectual capacity to fathom the situation; it is based on a deeper process of communication, which the expression 'communication from unconscious to unconscious' names without explaining. Situations of control of candidates' analytic work reveal that a candidate who is perfectly capable of understanding what is happening in a session has in fact been incapable of understanding it until someone in a different position explained it. And what is true for candidates is also true, hopefully to a lesser extent, for experienced analysts.

It is essentially an unconscious phantasy that structures the bi-personal field of the analytic situation. However, we would be mistaken to understand it as an unconscious phantasy pertaining only to the patient. Although it is our daily bread to recognise the field of the analytic situation as a couple field, we admit that the structure of this field depends on the patient, while the analyst tries to act accordingly (preserving the patient's freedom). This aim is absolutely laudable.

But it is bad to assume that analysts have total freedom to adapt to the patient's unconscious fantasy without losing their unity and their function as controller of the basic contract. Analysts cannot be 'mirrors' because mirrors do not interpret. Attitudes are demanded of analysts, which are contradictory in some way or at least quite ambiguous. If the patient's position in the analytic process is ambiguous, the analyst's is equally so.

With these restrictions in mind, we can only conceive of the basic phantasy of the session – the point of urgency – as a phantasy in a couple (in analytic group psychotherapy, the appropriate expression is 'group phantasy'). The basic phantasy of the session is not the mere understanding of the patient's phantasy by the analyst, but something that is constructed in a couple relationship. We have no doubt that the two persons have different roles in this phantasy and that it would be dangerously absurd for the analyst to impose his or her own phantasy on the field, but we have to recognise that a 'good' session means that the patient's basic phantasy coincides with the analyst's in the structuring of the analytic session.

Naturally, this implies a position of much renunciation of omnipotence on the analyst's part – in other words, a greater or lesser limit to the persons we can analyse. It goes without saying that this is not a question of the 'liking' or 'disliking' we may feel the first time we meet a patient, but of much more complicated processes.

It is not enough to recognise the existence of this 'phantasy' in the couple; we still need to try to understand the nature of it better. This will mean a change of approach in relation to most analytic studies, and the same change concerning the concept of unconscious phantasy. Discovering the underlying unconscious phantasy of a dream or a symptom is not the same as understanding the unconscious phantasy of an analytic session. In the former process, it suffices to use an adequate frame of reference and to be free of intellectual impediments. In the latter, it is a question of deep contact with a person and the profoundly different structure that is created between that person and us.

Obviously, we are using the term 'unconscious phantasy' in a very different sense from that which is currently attributed to it, when it is defined in uni-personal terms. In this case, unconscious phantasy is the expression of an instinctual impulse of the subject, with a source, an object and an aim in relation to this object.

In her classic paper on this topic, Susan Isaacs (1948) extended the concept considerably, showing the relation of the psychic structure in all its aspects, and thus tending toward a structural conception of the unconscious fantasy (but nevertheless without completely giving up the conception of it as an expression of instinct) (Baranger W, 1956).

It is obvious that the use – for us, inevitable – of the concept of unconscious phantasy to describe the structure and dynamic of the bi-personal field is based on a structural definition of this concept. This structure cannot in any way be considered to be determined by the patient's (or the analyst's)

For example, the analyst may arrive for the session feeling receptive and free of personal worries (the normal case) and the patient may come in with a calm conscious disposition without any urgent external problems or observable manifestations of anxiety. And yet, once the field is established, an intense depressive situation may emerge, perhaps manifested by a feeling of sadness in the analyst and a situation of intense mourning and weeping in the patient. In this case, we say that the patient unconsciously 'brought' a situation of mourning to the analysis. This is true in a sense, but the patient could have continued, if he or she had not come to session, feeling calm and going through daily activities as long as no other stimulating situation evoked the mourning. The patient is not bringing to analysis a situation of repressed mourning that is awaiting an opportunity to unleash itself (which often happens too), but structures the mourning especially in the analytic situation, in relation to the previous course of the analysis. Such phenomena, which occur regularly, oblige us to consider the unconscious phantasy that is produced in the analytic field as a bi-personal phantasy. In this sense, we define phantasy in analysis as the dynamic structure that at every moment gives meaning to the bi-personal field.

Up to now, we have simply affirmed that a melody is not the sum of the notes or that a group is not the sum of its members; in other words, we are emphasising the existence of a 'gestalt' in the analytic situation and we define this gestalt as our specific field of work. But we would be well advised to search further: how is this gestalt constituted? Why isn't it constituted in the same way in all couples? What processes intervene in its production? Perhaps comparison with other couple gestalts might orient us in this investigation. Also, we have already pointed out some of its specific features (the existence of a basic contract with its two functional centres, the specific spatio-temporal limits, the radical ambiguity, etc.). There is obviously a fundamental difference between the analytic couple and a couple of friends or enemies, a couple of lovers, a married couple, a parent–child couple or a couple of siblings, or a doctor–patient couple, though at times it may resemble any of these. The criterion of the difference is given precisely by this: that it is a couple in which all other imaginable couples are experienced while none of them is put into action.

It is true that no non-analytic couple really has the same degree of rigidity that language attributes to it. A couple of friends may become, either temporarily or permanently, a couple of enemies; a couple of spouses may unconsciously become a parent–child couple, etc.; but in these cases, the transformation of the couple, its change of gestalt or meaning, is often a pathological disturbance of the initial couple (unlike the natural growth of couples: lovers who marry, etc.). This is the case when the marital couple gives up its own gestalt in favour of a parent–child situation between spouses.

In natural couples, apart from transformations stemming from growth, any invasion of the initial gestalt by a different one is pathological, and provokes conflicts that lead to its disintegration or its neurotic structuring. In contrast, the analytic gestalt by its nature needs to be invaded (albeit not entirely) by all the other couple gestalts if it is to stay healthy. While it is pathological for a natural couple to lose its structure and become permeable to foreign structuring, the analytic couple is pathological when it becomes crystallised or similar to a natural couple. For example, an analysis in which the analyst is always the patient's 'kindly father' may have beneficial therapeutic results, but it is actually a radically failed analysis.

Therefore, the difference between these two types of gestalts is that the former tends to definition and crystallisation, while the latter tends to mobility and lack of definition. This orients each type toward different uses of the process of projective identification.

We consider Melanie Klein's discovery (1946, 1955, 1958) of the process of projective identification (grounded in Freud's description [1911] of the mechanism of projection) basic to understanding the gestalt of the marital couple (for example, Liberman [1956] and others) or any other couple. Of course, Freud recognised different nuances in the mechanism of projection: projection of an impulse repudiated by the Ego (for example, projection of wishes of infidelity in jealousy [Freud, 1922]), projection of internal images (for example in paranoia), projection of aspects of the Ego (for example, in narcissistic falling in love [Freud, 1921]). But Melanie Klein generalises these discoveries with her concept of the paranoid-schizoid position and with her discovery of the primitive infantile forms of projection related to persecutory and depressive anxieties and to destructive and reparatory impulses (forcing parts of the Ego into objects in order to capture them, the preservation of internal objects and parts of the Ego, keeping them safe within the object, etc.).

If the process of projective identification has the general extension Melanie Klein assigns to it, we can expect it to have decisive importance in the structuring of all couples. The structure of the couple is constituted by the interplay of projective and introjective identifications with their necessary corollary of counteridentifications.

This process appears quite clearly in symbiotic marital couples where each member takes on the other's Ego functions, which the other gives up, or in couples of enemies, where each is invaded by persecutory objects and

cations, but these have special characteristics. The situation is managed in such a way as to avoid or limit the phenomenon of projective counteridentification. If the analyst allows an invasion by projective counteridentification, perhaps because it is flattering to be the depository of an idealised, omnipotent figure of the patient's, the analyst is not doing his job, and the analysis fails.

If the patient feels invaded by a countertransference phenomenon of the analyst, the patient establishes massive defences, either to preserve this state if it is pleasurable or to block it if it generates anxiety, and the entire process is paralysed. The latter is the case when the patient perceives a real countertransference reaction from the analyst and 'makes the analyst pay for it' endlessly. Obviously, the reaction of counteridentification should remain within the analyst and undergo self-analysis until it is solved, to avoid releasing an exchange of secondary reactions that would mix up the analytic situation with a common couple situation and thus vitiate it entirely.

Similarly, the phenomenon of projective identification must have very special characteristics in the analytic couple. It must be allowed to be massive on one side (the patient's) but kept very limited on the other (the analyst's), whereas in natural couples it is reciprocal. The analytic situation consists in permitting the free play of projective identification in the patient, thus giving the patient an exceptional opportunity to structure the couple phantasy according to need, while the 'partner' offers the least hindrance. The analyst's position is quite different: the analyst has to use this projective identification (otherwise the analyst would not be participating in the couple situation and would be unable to understand the patient), but in small doses and by way of experimental exploration. Personal observation and supervision fully confirm that, when the analyst's use of projective identification passes a certain threshold, interpretative work is paralysed: the analyst becomes too involved in the couple structure and loses the opportunity of modifying it.

The involvement of projective identification in the analytic situation and in any psychological comprehension appears clearly in the common term 'empathy', which implies a centrifugal movement in the observer. But introjective identification also takes place in the analyst. If the analyst is a depository of objects or aspects of the patient's 'self', there must necessarily be a corresponding introjective process in the analyst. As in the aspect of projective identification of the situation, this introjective aspect has to be limited and controlled to avoid feelings in the analyst of being inundated by the situation (as sometimes happens, especially with psychotic patients who try to inject their madness into the analyst). An adequate interpretation, with a consequent re-introjection on the patient's part, generally leads to overcoming the danger. This can be seen quite clearly in the management of the countertransference.

When the analytic situation becomes countertransferentially painful for the analyst, the only way to undo this state is to interpret the patient's projective identification with its particular momentary content, which generally leads to relief in both parties.

Summarising: The bi-personal field of the analytic situation is constantly oriented by three (or more) configurations: the basic contract; the apparent configuration of the manifest material, including the analyst's function in it; and the bi-personal unconscious phantasy, which is the object of interpretation. This structure is constituted by the interplay of the processes of projective and introjective identification and of the counteridentifications that act with their different limits, functions and characteristics in the patient and the analyst.

## IV. The dynamic of the field and the course of the treatment

The conclusions above orient us toward recognition of a particular dynamic of the analytic situation, which is a problem that can only be examined by simultaneously taking up its correlative: the problem of the course of analytic treatment.

Although the bi-personal phantasy depends on processes of identification and counteridentification, it remains to be seen how and why these processes are produced in one way and not another, at a certain moment and not another. The nature of the dynamic processes of the analytic situation is obviously impossible to understand without acknowledging the basic role of the interpretation in them. However, for the present discussion, we shall omit certain basic aspects of this topic and take them up elsewhere.

These processes start to be produced in the first interview between possible analyst and possible analysand, or even earlier. Patient and analyst have a certain previous phantasy of each other even before actually meeting each other. The analysand has generally been sent by a colleague who, to a variable extent, has communicated some information on the patient to the future analyst: the patient has an obsessional neurosis, a difficult marital situation, is a very intelligent person … or some such information. The patient also generally 'knows' something about the future analyst (having heard some aspects of the personal myth of the possible analyst in the milieu): the analyst has

phantasy materialises in the first pre-analytic interview and invades the first session, even if, as often happens, the patient takes the greatest care to avoid showing it. For this reason, no time is needed (as some believe) for the 'establishment' of the transference. The bi-personal situation is virtually created before the first session and 'precipitates' in it, with or without interpretation by the analyst.

Whatever the analyst's technical activity may be, the dynamic of the situation begins with the patient's communication and the analyst's reaction (whether this be interpretation or merely silence). In any case, it is the beginning of a dialogue, silence being understood by the patient as (among other things) a wish to wait in order to understand better on the analyst's part. In any case also the analyst chooses the moment and content of the first interpretation. Who would doubt the extreme importance of this choice? It means not only approaching the patient from a certain viewpoint, but also pointing out to the patient the aspect of the communication that we consider the most important or useful, at least at the present moment.

For this reason, the first interpretations can only aim at the point of current urgency: the patient's phantasy about the analysis and the analyst at the moment of initiation. Any other selection of material by the analyst, for example, interpreting a historical element in the material, may superficially calm the patient's paranoid fears ('there is no current situation, we see what happened with your father'), but leaves these fears intact and encourages future acting-out (running away, etc.).

This reveals the immense importance of the analyst's technique in the dynamic of the bi-personal situation. It is by no means true that the patient's conflicts are manifested and worked through in the same way with different analytic techniques. The technique used is part of a dialogue and partly conditions the responses of the other (Racker, 1960).

The analyst's art consists entirely in selecting the interpretable point of urgency in the material, whether this be provided by the patient in a positive way (verbal or other communication) or negatively (silence, omission, etc.).

The use of a certain type of material or a preference for it, the way of taking notes or treating dreams, historical material, bodily positions and manifestations, silences, etc., eventually form a particular language with the patient. It is well known that the successive dreams of the same patient use similar elements, that have already been interpreted, with the intention of communicating something in particular to the analyst (and sometimes to hide something really active behind conventional meanings) (Baranger W, 1960).

It would be as unfair to fail to recognise or value these phenomena as it would be to underestimate the patient's participation in the structuring of the field. Abundant examples show how patients repeat the same latent material over and over again with different means of expression until they have made the analyst understand it. On this basis, we may still ask how far the dynamic of the field depends on the analyst's intellectual and communicational skills. We shall discuss this problem later.

When Freud indicated the way to proceed technically in the dynamic of the field, he recommended acting 'per via di levare' (Freud, 1905), meaning to attack and progressively to dissolve the patient's resistances corresponding to the defence mechanisms of the patient's Ego and thus succeed in permitting the reappearance of repressed elements and forgotten memories. Thus, he showed us the dialectic between analysis of the defence and analysis of the content that should preside over the dynamic of the situation.

This approach implies, with some justification, a fantasy of analytic work conceived as the work of a geologist discovering superimposed strata of buried material (for example, the famous comparison in *Civilization and its discontents* [Freud, 1930]). But in other texts, he uses quite different metaphors that indicate a much more vivid concept of analytic work. He compares analytic treatment to a game of chess, in which the analyst knows the 'classical' moves to open and finish the game, but does not know the structure of the mid-game or what is essential to the game (Freud, 1913).

This metaphor deserves a look into its meaning. Thanks to Freud, we know much about the structure and genesis of the neuroses. Following an analysis, we can re-construct the historical structuring of the case on the basis of anamnesis and transference material. If the analysis consisted only of lifting successive layers of resistance, allowing successive layers of repressed material to appear, we could learn, for each type of neurosis, how all the important stages of the treatment are interconnected. In this case, the analytic treatment might then resemble the work of a geologist or a historian, but not a chess game. The incompatibility of these two metaphors is obvious: the latter makes analysis much more active, in relation to both the analyst and the patient. The 'chessboard' between them is a shared structure and each of them is acting by virtue of it, one through communications and resistances and the other through interpretations. This chessboard could very well symbolise what we have termed the bi-personal field while the game would be the structure of the treatment as a whole.

It would betray not only Freud's thinking but also the whole development of psychoanalysis if were to overlook the dialectic between content and defence that we observe at any moment of our work, but it would be forcing the facts to consider the patient's psyche as a series of superimposed

superficial to the deepest levels.

Freud himself expresses this tendency in different works. It is clearly seen in the historical–geological metaphor above, but also in other texts, particularly in the theory of the complemental series. Analysis regressively attacks the different points of fixation in the subject's history, which form nodules of repressed impulses and defence mechanisms connected to the memory of the circumstances (traumatic situations) in which the fixation was produced.

One might be tempted to draw from these texts the conclusion that Freud accepted the hypothesis of parallelism between the (chronological) progressive course of structuring of the patient's neurosis and the regressive course of the analysis from the most superficial strata: from the most recent and least defended toward the progressively older, deeper and more heavily defended strata and fixations. However, Freud (1916–17) alerts us to this temptation to simplification when he cautions us in absolutely explicit terms in the "Introductory lectures on psychoanalysis" against the hypothesis of this parallelism.

On this occasion, he uses another metaphor: an invading army has left behind forts manned by troops (points of fixation) fighting off re-conquest by the enemy (analytic work). This army can fight inside its fortresses, but may also, if circumstances seem more favourable, fight in the field at any point on the road taken by the re-conquest. The decisive battle may be fought at a point completely lacking importance in the army's advance, the defence against re-conquest being located there rather than in its citadels where all the forces are available. In passing, Freud notes that the most important transference relation for the analysis may very well not be the repetition of the most historically important situation experienced by the patient.

Meditation on this text could have saved analysts overly seduced by the 'geological' tendency a good number of errors. Among these, we can review one example: that of Wilhelm Reich (1949 [1933]) in the psychoanalytic period of his development. Reich formulates the problem of analyses that 'do not work' and the production of what he calls 'the chaotic situation'. In this situation, the patient produces rich and varied material originating in all the 'layers' of the unconscious, but the course of analysis has been altered and the patient does not react to interpretation. Chaos is also produced in the analyst, who cannot fathom what to interpret in this quantity of material. Reich's solution is that this situation occurs when the interpretation has omitted or not solved a special type of resistance in the patient: characterological resistance. This resistance corresponds to the structuring of a character armour during the patient's evolution, that is not experienced subjectively as pathological, and which regulates the patient's relationship with the world and is manifested in the analysis as the greatest obstacle to therapeutic work.

The technical attitude deduced from these concepts is to handle the development of the analysis in a systematic way, abstaining from interpretations of content until the characterological resistance is broken down through consequential interpretation.

Here, we see the hypothesis of parallelism quite clearly. It is the structuring of the patient's character in superimposed layers of impulses and crystallised defences that must determine the regressive structuring of the treatment, starting with the superficial layers of the shell in order to reach the deep and remote ones.

Of course, we do not deny the validity of the concept of characterological shell or the need to resolve it in the treatment. What does seem inadequate to us is to attribute a systematic development to both the treatment and the interpretation and especially to claim that this development is regressive, paralleling the course of evolution of the structuring of the personality and the neurosis (Baranger M, 1960).

Several factors lead us to this conclusion. First, a fact: the depth and temporal remoteness of the material have nothing to do with its appearance in the treatment. A female patient analysed by one of us, who suffered (among other things) a phobia of deflowering and multiple inhibitions, was able to analyse her genital and oral conflicts for several years, but did not react to attempts to analyse the derivatives of anal conflicts (it is worth mentioning that this situation did not correspond to any particular rejection of this type of material in the analyst). Only after this period of time, very rich anal phantasies were unblocked when the anal zone appeared in the conscious as intensely erogenous. If this were an isolated case, we might consider it a particular failing of the analyst (even though the analyst may have consciously tried to detect whether this was true and had reached a negative conclusion). However, it is the rule. We know from our own experience, supervisions and cases narrated or supervised by others, of very few cases where analytic work has followed an order of intelligible stratification. (The cases studied by Reich were analysed for relatively short periods of time and are presented to show the systematic sequence.)

Also, this contradiction of the hypothesis of parallelism by the facts (which might ultimately be dismissed as a general failing of the interpretive technique used by the analysts that could be remedied by a more systematic technique) coincides with very solid theoretical reasons for rejecting it.

Reich and the other representatives of the same line of thinking start from the structuring of the neurosis as it can be reconstructed following

however valid they may be, and more so from subordinating our technique to these pre-established schemes. Our technical attitude must follow concepts developed out of the concrete experience with which we are dealing; in other words, it must follow the dynamic laws of the bi-personal situation. It is truly paradoxical to derive from the bi-personal situation a theoretical reconstruction of the case in terms that are, by definition, uni-personal, and then try to regulate the bi-personal situation according to this reduced and impoverished scheme.

This methodological error is based on denial of the role of the counter-transference in the selection and interpretation of the point of urgency, in other words, in the very essence of the analytic process.

For this reason we consider that the 'depth' of the material in no way designates a generic, chronological or integrative aspect of it, but is instead a technical aspect. The difficulty of gaining access to it by the analytic process usually does not correspond to the stages of development of human psychosexuality.

These considerations show us what the dynamic of the analytic situation is not (the regressive retracing, by overcoming stages of resistance, of the path taken by the patient's personality in its evolution), but they leave us dissatisfied as to what this dynamic is.

Nevertheless, they have shown us a way to approach the solution. We all consider the analytic situation repetitive. With the encouragement of the fundamental rule, the patient's use of projective identification allows the patient to re-actualise the reaction patterns originating in situations in the past that have not been overcome and are crystallised in the form of stereotyped schemes of experience and behaviour. These reaction patterns partly structure the bi-personal field. The impulses, wishes, phantasies, anxieties and defences involved in the original pathogenic situations are again present in the bi-personal field. But they are presented neither in chronological sequence nor in the same way. If repetition were literal, we would have to abandon all hope of seeing the patient get better. A patient who has

always run away from his father would run away from us shortly after starting the analysis (as occurs when we are unable to overcome the problem).

Analytic repetition is neither literal nor stereotyped; when it is, the analysis is interrupted, either by stagnation (the patient continues to come to sessions, but entirely stops evolving) or by flight. Therefore, what is important
in the dynamic of the treatment is not the emergence of emotions, wishes
and past anxieties, but their emergence in one way and not another. They
need to emerge in a new and vivid context and not paralyse it. Of course,
the non-emergence of emotions or impulses is the most frequent way the
analytic field is paralysed, and must be considered a resistance to be attacked
urgently. But this does not mean that the repetition of old impulses and
wishes is the motor of the analytic dynamic.

In other words, we have to consider this dynamic not in terms of reactivation of instinctive impulses, but in situational terms (without, of course,
leaving aside the impulses). Therefore, what is most important is the mobility
or crystallisation of the field. These are the two poles of the analytic dynamic.

The field moves, and the analyst can intervene in it effectively when
the patient 'takes a risk'. Of course, one always takes a risk to some extent
when beginning a psychoanalysis. One risks time, money, effort, hopes (and
a career in the case of a candidate). But all this may be much less important than another aspect of personal life or phantasy that for the patient is
a personal bastion[8] (and is generally the unconscious refuge of powerful
phantasies of omnipotence).

This bastion varies enormously from one person to another, but is never
absent. It is whatever the patient does not want to put at risk because the
risk of losing it would throw the patient into a state of extreme helplessness,
vulnerability and despair (Baranger M, 1959).

The bastion has been described in the literature, especially in relation to
homosexual or perverse patients in general: they want to risk everything,
except their perverse activity, a source of extremely valuable gratifications.
Thus, a homosexual patient said jokingly: 'I'm not a homosexual; it's just
that I like the guys'; another spoke depreciatively of 'fags' or 'fruits'; both
considered their homosexual experience as something radically different
from their book knowledge of homosexual perversion; their bastion consisted in preserving marvellous experiences with chosen beings whose sex
happened to coincide with theirs.

In other persons, the bastion may be intellectual or moral superiority,
their relation with an idealised object of love, an ideology, a phantasy of
social aristocracy, their money or profession, etc.

The most frequent behaviour of patients in defence of their bastion consists of avoiding any reference to its existence. They may be quite sincere
in regard to a multitude of problems and aspects of their life, but become

evasive, disguised, even lying when the analyst comes close to the bastion. We do not think there are patients without bastions, and we believe that the measure of success of the analysis depends greatly on the degree to which they have been able to accept the analysis of them, meaning to accept losing them and with them the basic phantasies of omnipotence and thus giving up to their persecutors.

with intense emotional reactions, even anxiety, and permits considerable mobilisation of the analytic situation. The immobilisation of the field is always a protective measure aimed at preservation from intrusion by the analyst and the analyst's interpretations into a private sector of the analysand's life.

We will offer as an example a person analysed by one of us. A man, still young, came from a former analysis that had allowed him to overcome some of his difficulties, particularly phobias. At this time, he complained of an inability to feel: to be happy or sad, to love or hate, or to participate fully in the events he experienced. He began his analysis with a well-organised and rationalised narrative of his entire life, beginning with the birth trauma and continuing with a series of traumatic situations in his history that would have been horrifying if he had not presented them as a well-reconstructed clinical case, but someone else's. He went on with the analysis, was able to experience transference and historical situations with a good display of diverse emotions, and with this was able to make various improvements. But in the countertransference he always left the impression of someone not entirely authentic. One day he was confronted in his life (an event that coincided with an approach to his bastion by the analyst) with a situation of professional and social failure provoked partly by himself. He was able to admit the possibility that it was really a failure, in spite of his apparent successes, and even considered whether to give up his profession for another with less responsibility. Immediately, the countertransference feeling of lack of authenticity disappeared.

The working through of the multiple phantasies (of omnipotence, persecution, idealisation, impotence for reparation and love, etc.), located and preserved in the professional bastion, marked a decisive turn in the history of his analysis and allowed him to make authentic progress.

The briefly outlined history of this analysis seems illustrative in several ways: first, naturally, of the importance of the bastion. We are certain that this analysis would have been a relative failure if the patient had not been able to risk losing his profession. But it also teaches us something about the course of the treatment.

In outline: this analysis has developed in line with two different processes: the first roughly follows the chronological dialectic between the transference situation and the traumatic situations of the past (whose chronology was not, of course, followed by the patient in the sequence of his repetitions). Forcing it a bit, we could conceive of it as a fluctuation in the course of the time line. But at a certain point, a totally different process occurs that is not essentially situated on any chronological line: the fall of the bastion. If we hold to a spatial representation of things, the process seems to be produced in a direction perpendicular to the chronological line; in other words, a split off and preserved sector of the patient's life, by virtue of a long preparatory process, is integrated brusquely into the field of the analysis of the subject, and in a correlative way into the total field of experience, first as a catastrophic experience and then as positive enrichment.

This event totally changes the patient's position in relation to his history. The uninterrupted series of historical traumata, centred on the figure of a mother that was cold, neurotic and aggressive for the patient (which she doubtless was), changes its meaning. The mother ceases to be a dead weight ('too bad, she was like that') when she is not experienced as a neurotic person, of course, but with her own suffering and wishes for love (she herself a victim through no fault of her own). The infantile traumata cease to be considered as disturbing events in the history of 'a patient' and are accepted in the context of a personal past with the patient's due participation.

In this dialectic movement of historicity, the past is no longer a permanent dead weight but can be transformed to some extent, according to the future that it contributes to creating.

Whereas technically the poles of the dynamic of the analytic situation are mobilisation and stagnation, on the theoretical level they are integration and splitting. This conclusion seems to agree completely with the importance M. Klein assigns to this defensive process, the first of all. The field of the analytic situation is the opportunity, through repetition in a new context of the original situations that motivated the splitting, to break up this defensive process and to re-integrate the split off sectors of experience into the whole of the patient's life. This is why it is necessary to break down the internal bastions.

## V. Interpretive integration and insight[9]

If the analytic situation is radically new and different from other couple fields, if it permits the breaking down and re-integration of split-off bastions more than any other, it is evidently due to its interpretive character. The analyst's attitude of neutral benevolence – as far as possible – is no different from the cathartic role of a good confidante (the person who listens without taking sides).

It is amazing to find in the abundant literature on the subject (or at least the literature we have been able to find) how little we know about

Freud [1926] defined it) is a dialogue.

Our aim here is not to attempt any solution of this problem, which remains open for investigation, but to summarise some contributions toward this solution from the perspective we have chosen. Of course, we shall leave many questions unanswered.

The bi-personal field on which the interpretation will fall has different configurations as described above and includes among its unconscious configurations the person of the analyst as a more or less constant depositary of parts or aspects of the patient's Ego, Superego, objects and repressed impulses. Beneath the unconscious phantasy that structures the field at any moment and that constitutes the point of urgency of the interpretation, there exists a more stable structure that tends to make a certain configuration crystallise in the field and conditions the emergence of recurrent unconscious phantasies. This configuration is quite complex, since it includes reciprocal manifestations of all the patient's psychic agencies and the location of the Ego, Id, Superego and internal objects at different sites in the field, each with certain functions. In the same sense, the corresponding situation in the analyst has been described (Racker, 1960): the micro-neurosis of counter-transference that complements the global structure of the field on this level. The transference neurosis is the repetition of the structure of the patient's neurosis; for this reason, it tends to create a vicious circle: a mobilisation of the parts of self, objects and defences in a stereotyped repetition of childhood conflicts. The micro-neurosis of countertransference is the analyst's participation in this structure, involving, aside from the analyst's limited processes of projective identification, the unresolved remnants of the analyst's infantile conflicts and neurotic structures, which are manifested as counter-resistances. From this arises the fact that the whole transference–countertransference tends to constitute a purely repetitive granite-like block and completely paralyse the analytic process. It is part of the analyst's function to let himself or herself become involved to some extent in these configurations with each patient.

However, the interpretive process as a whole tends to permit the mobilisation of the transference–countertransference neurosis and thereby the gradual modification of all the patient's aspects involved in it, meaning the patient's whole person. In parallel, the process consists, for the analysts, of freeing aspects of themselves that are involved in the countertransference situation and paralysed in the countertransference neurosis.

Interpretation is the tool they use in this double rescue. The process of working through the interpretation in the analyst has been described as a consequence of 'unconscious to unconscious communication', and this is why Freud recommends the analyst's attitude of 'free-floating attention': it allows the emergence of unconscious elements into consciousness and their ulterior formulation in words. This formulation translates the fact that analyst and analysand are involved in the different conscious and unconscious structuring of the bi-personal field. But the patient is as if immersed in it, while the analyst, though regressing partially, is not submerged in the field and keeps his or her Ego free of invasion, but does stay in contact with it. In this way, the analyst can observe the field with a certain degree of 'porosity' and regulate the penetration by its tensions and lines of force. The analyst's observation is both internal and external (auto- and hetero-observation), since its object is the unity of the field.

Without formulating them, the analyst keeps hold of the different conscious and unconscious structurings of the field, the contract and what it is generating, the manifest material, the unconscious phantasy of the couple, the structure of the transference–countertransference neurosis, and the analyst intervenes by interpreting. The effect of this interpretation is clearly perceptible in every concrete analytic situation. The interpretation may have been imprecise, badly formulated, poorly timed or even completely erroneous. In this case, it generally fails to produce any appreciable reaction (apart from the patient's approval or rejection), and this response is not integrated into the sequence of the material, which continues as before. Or, the interpretation was adequate and reached its goal. In this case, it produces an evident change, described below. Alternatively, if it was partially inadequate, it produces a different type of change, and when it is not modified or complemented by subsequent interpretations it leaves a state of confusion in the field and dissatisfaction in the participants, sometimes also an aggravation of the patient's state.

In the normal case of a well-formulated interpretation, given at the right moment and accepted by the patient, we observe a modification of the field that deserves to be described in greater detail. The patient answers the interpretation by expressing a feeling of greater freedom. Sometimes the patient manifests surprise or joy, as if something had suddenly opened up inside the patient or before the patient's eyes. In any case, the patient's mood, feelings and emotions change. The sequence of the material suddenly changes, becoming more unified and oriented. The patient brings up memories, associations and fantasies that confirm, extend and complement the content of the interpretation. The entire situation becomes more understandable for both analyst and patient. Both feel that they are communicating and working together on a joint endeavour.

to extend this formulation.

What has happened is evidently a structural change in the field. The reciprocal location of the conscious and unconscious structures has been modified and the situation expressed in the manifest material has been related to the current unconscious phantasy or point of urgency, thus acquiring new meaning. When the placement in the analyst of a given part of the patient's 'self' or the internal objects is made conscious, together with the motivation for this projective identification, this split off part of the patient is re-introjected, the analyst coming into view in his or her real function in the basic contract: analyst and patient are working together and have just taken a step in their work.

If it is the type of interpretation that Strachey (1934) called the 'mutative interpretation', the inclusion within it of the infantile prototype of situations that was expressed in the unconscious phantasy of the field allows a further type of modification. The unconscious structure whose splitting has been reduced is no longer only the immediate unconscious phantasy, but an aspect of the more durable and rigid structure of the transference–countertransference neurosis. Of course, the restructuring action of the interpretation on this level is much less massive when we consider a more crystallised level, where the defences are more archaic and ironclad, the splitting more difficult to reduce, the objects more stereotyped. But even on this level, some change in the structure of the field is produced that is important at certain moments of the analysis: a modification of the location of objects and parts of the Ego in this field, and the corresponding modification of the nature of the internal objects. These are moments in the analysis when, after long and patient work on more superficial structures of the field, access is gained, prepared by that previous work, to a basic nucleus of the transference–countertransference neurosis and correlatively, a structural change in the patient.

These considerations induce us to define the function of interpretation as mobilising the field, thus permitting re-activation of the projective and introjective processes whose paralysing effect and distortion have provoked the structuring of the neurosis in the patient's life and the structuring of the transference neurosis.

The therapeutic effect of interpretation is obviously a function of the inclusion of the analyst in the field, and of the analyst's ability to regulate the patient's introjective and projective processes, to the extent that the patient gives the analyst the role of depositary of parts of the self that need to be expelled because they are dangerous or damaged, or to be preserved by putting them in a safe place. This is what Strachey points out when he describes the analyst's function as the patient's auxiliary Superego. However, we must differentiate further. In the basic contract, the analyst is certainly an auxiliary Superego, allowing the Ego verbal expression of all its experiences. But the analyst is also an auxiliary Ego, whose analytic function is to regulate psychic processes that – in any circumstance – could become dangerous or disturbing. The patient's phantasy of regression in the basic contract is: 'I can lose control because someone else is now taking control of the situation and will keep it from becoming dangerous'.

In the unconscious structure of the field, the analyst has much more varied and mobile functions. The analyst is the depositary of all the agencies, parts, aspects and objects of the person in analysis. At times, the analyst is the representative of one or another of the idealised or persecutory objects, of this or that aspect of the Ego or Superego or of a repressed impulse of the Id. In re-structurings of the field produced by the adequate interpretation, the analyst stops being the depositary of the aspect the patient had deposited in the analyst, and this is re-introjected by the patient. However, it is not re-introjected in exactly the same form as it was before, since the reasons for the projective identification and the form it takes are not independent of the object's very nature. For example, the need to project a persecutory object cannot be separated from the specific characteristics of that object: the kind of danger it poses, in relation to what concrete childhood experiences, expressed by what phantasies, etc. However, if this object can be re-introjected in the structural change of the field, it is because these characteristics have been modified. The extent of this modification depends on the depth of the re-structuring considered, meaning the degree of strengthening of the structure of the transference–countertransference neurosis that has been reached.

To illustrate the above, I will describe two sessions of a patient that had taken up his analysis again following a severe and prolonged psychotic crisis. In the first of these sessions, the patient came in as if drunk or drugged and presented extremely confused material. He first said that his girlfriend had broken up with him and then he seemed to repeat the former psychotic episode. As he was leaving the session, a quantity of objects fell out of his pocket onto the floor of the consulting room, while he was trying to light a cigarette (coins, lighter, cigarettes, etc.).

The analyst later received a telephone call from one of the patient's friends, saying that 'he was quite badly off, like before' and that the friend feared a relapse.

In the following session, the analyst, who of course understood the friend's role as a spokesman for the patient, told the patient about the telephone call and interpreted the friend as a depositary of the patient's 'sane'

interesting. In the first, he felt invaded by the patient's confusion as if the patient were scattering loose objects and unconnected experiences in the field (he floods the consulting room with the contents of his pockets). This experience got to the point that he was unable to interpret directly the situation of relapse and the invasion of madness. The patient had managed to create, because of his desperate projective identification, a transference-countertransference psychosis in this session. In the meantime, the patient had re-located in the friend and, through him in the analyst, the healthy part of his ego and his ability to control the madness. When he narrated and interpreted the friend's telephone call in these terms, the analyst (also through his behaviour of not making arrangements with the patient's milieu behind his back) had given him back this healthy part, which he had placed into other people in order to preserve it, and had allowed him to take control of himself again. One of the themes of the second session was precisely this: who would take charge of protecting the patient – the analyst, the family, the patient himself – against a relapse?

This dialectical process between the understanding of the point of urgency, its interpretation and the production of a new structure with a new point of urgency, that is in turn interpretable, with the introjective and projective processes involved in it has been described by E. Pichon-Rivière as a 'spiral process', an idea already sketched out in one of Freud's letters to Fliess (May 1897 in Freud, 1892–99, p. 251) and taken up in an expanded and systematic way by Pichon-Rivière (1956–58).

The interpretation provokes a re-structuring of the bi-personal field through processes that have been described in numerous papers, and we could of course mention many more. This is only to complement a little what Freud formulated in terms of 'making conscious the unconscious'. However, although we know fairly precisely what is occurring in the bi-personal field and consequently inside the patient when we give an adequate interpretation, we understand the specific mode of this action much less clearly.

The difference between the 'before' and the 'after' is much more directly accessible to us than the 'how' and the 'why'.

Various authors have tried to understand this process in terms of 'gestalt' (Schmidl, 1955), which we consider allows us to advance a step closer to the solution. The unconscious phantasy of the bi-personal field is a 'gestalt'. This is a complex configuration, with its distribution of objects into precise functions, its lines of force, its global structure. The manifest material is also a 'gestalt'. The immediate goal of interpretation is to connect these two gestalts and sometimes also to link them with the basic structure of the transference–countertransference neurosis.

The manifest material is presented as an incomplete 'gestalt'; interpretation allows its completion using elements of another gestalt that lies behind it, so that something like a fusion of these two gestalts that clarify each other reciprocally is generated. If we try to complete the gestalt of the manifest content with other elements – as in the case of a logical but badly oriented interpretation or one that is given in inadequate terms – we do not get the same result.

Our problem is therefore reduced to this: how can the interpretation reduce the 'gestalt' of the manifest content to the 'gestalt' of the urgent unconscious phantasy in the session? This leads us to the last problem: how can the interpretation, as words, act upon the different structurings of the bi-personal field? In other words, what is the basis of the interpretive power of the word?

The work of L. Alvarez de Toledo (1954) clarifies part of the problem for us. This author points out that 'speaking', 'associating' and 'interpreting' are not a mere intellectual process but a doing with the patient, a doing whose receptive – and also its active – part is based on extremely remote and important object relations (the infant's first relation with the mother's voice). In the same way, words are not experienced in the analytic situation as means of communication but as objects carrying gratifications and aggressions and, in general, innumerable phantasies.

We consider that these studies (which we cannot summarise here), apart from their unquestionable technical value, explain an aspect of our problem, though not all of it.

Each analyst, by directing attention to this problem, can observe the equation that the patient establishes between the words and unconscious objects of analytic exchange. Sometimes the patient only wants to hear our voice, whatever it is that we may say, and experiences this hearing as gratification – our words like warm milk – at other times, our words fall onto the patient like stones, independent of their content, at other times a few of our words suffice to release a certain structuring of the field. In one [female] patient, it was enough to include in an interpretation the words 'current sexual life' or others with the same meaning to provoke a violent headache, associated with the transference fantasy that the analyst was squeezing the patient's head in an iron circle until he 'made her brains jump out of her ears'.[10]

Thus, the bi-personal field is transformed into a scene of torture where sadomasochistic phantasies flourish. Naturally, the incriminating words were

tion. We understand why the word itself provokes intense emotional reactions, but the question of the interpretive effect of the word as a vehicle of intentional meanings remains open. It is one thing for the patient to take our words as milk or stones, and quite another for the patient to understand their meaning and for this understanding to provoke an important modification in the patient's world.

The specific problem is the relation between the word and the insight that the patient acquires with an adequate interpretation.

Elsewhere, one of us (Baranger M, 1956 p. 43) drew the following conclusion regarding insight: ". . . as soon as the patient recognises the analyst's privileged situation as a transactional object between the person and the external world, an experimental situation is created ('phantasy of the analysis') that converts the analyst into a double projection screen. The analyst belongs both to the internal world (projective identification) and to reality, which permits these two worlds to meet in the analyst without much danger, and offers an easier and less anguishing 'external vision' of this meeting. What is seen as outside in this experimental situation, when re-introjected, becomes an internal 'vision' in the insight".

These concepts are quite close to what we discussed before, but do not cover it exactly. A definition of the analyst in terms of the analyst's privileged 'situation' as a transactional object between the person and the 'external world' or as a 'double projection screen' is quite close to the concept of the bi-personal field. However, it is not entirely equivalent to this concept because it sees the analytic situation as essentially transferential instead of transferential– countertransferential.

Consequently, we now consider that the terms 'transactional object' and 'double projection screen' apply not to the analyst but to the analytic situation as a field.

The process of insight acts first on this field. The adequate interpretation opens up the field and connects its conscious and unconscious structures to some degree. The patient's 'vision' of the field expands and is modified at the same time, provoking a re-structuring, but the two successive structurings are not equivalent; this is not a mere re-distribution of agencies, objects and parts of the self in the field. The second structuring is much more differentiated. Let us suppose the interpretation of a persecutory situation experienced in relation to the analyst. It appears later as 'the person I thought was a persecutor and in reality is my analyst who is working with me'. The persecutory object projected onto the analyst is also differentiated. It is not only experienced as an internal object, re-introjected, but its relation to the self has changed: its hatred is no longer considered as being foreign to the patient, but as a split off aspect, and is no longer experienced as present, but as originating in some concrete situation of the past that has given it its particular form. In turn, this differentiation of the present from the past allows the patient to stop experiencing the persecution as eternal and to differentiate the past and the present from a future free (or relatively free) of persecutory anxiety. In sum, it is a general differentiating process that allows the patient's ego to examine anew and work through the aspects of the field involved in the interpretation. This is why we can continue to use the term insight, since the general result of the process is the patient's increased awareness of his or her inner world.

In all this, we see that the word is equipped with three essential functions: it carries object relations and very primitive emotions, connects split off and isolated structurings in the field and differentiates the parts and aspects of the field thus reunified. Thus, the word again acquires the characteristics discovered by M. Klein (1930) in the process of symbol formation: the equivalence of symbol and symbolised, on the one hand, and differentiation between the two on the other. The absence or insufficiency of either of these two aspects constitutes a very great difficulty in the technique of interpretation.

In certain patients, in particular, those with very rigid obsessional structures, the first process seems to be missing. The isolation of the word from the psychic contents it designates becomes so intense that it creates a very great obstacle for the 'entry' of the interpretations. The patient accepts them as 'mere words' and plays with them as if they were an external object unrelated to the inner world. Until this process of intellectualisation has been overcome – re-establishing the relation between symbol and symbolised – interpretations, however theoretically exact they may be, have no practical value. This particular case is only the hypertrophy of a universal process in the creation of words and abstract language. This is why it is so important in all kinds of patients to avoid the intrinsic danger of intellectualisation of the interpretations and of the whole analytic process. For this reason, as we have long been aware, interpretations have to be given in concrete rather than abstract terms, and this is also why the element of surprise they provoke is important.

The problem of the specific action of the word has possibly been formulated backwards: it is not a question of trying to know how words reach the unconscious contents of the analytic situation but why and how words have lost their original power to reach deeply into internal life, a power that they retain in certain circumstances (poetry, song, incantations, a leader's discourse, etc.). The role of interpretation is to overcome the weakening of

the interpretation is experienced in absolutely concrete terms (the patient understands the interpretation of a phantasy of killing the analyst as if the patient were effectively going to kill the analyst, logically expecting a whole sequence of retaliatory reactions). In these cases, the interpretation unleashes emotional manifestations of unsuspected intensity, and will hardly become a factor of working through until this difficulty has been overcome.

These two inverse obstacles to the action of the word in the analytic situation can clarify its two specific functions. The word opens up the communications in the field, uniting its isolated or split off regions. But it also serves to locate, determine and differentiate its multiple aspects. It is both communication and control, and the function of the interpretation can be lost if one of these aspects is exaggerated at the expense of the other.

This can perhaps throw some light on the conditions in which certain words — the interpretation — permit the advent of insight. It is generated when the words of the interpretation possess their characteristic as a medium of communication that is both concrete (in relation to primitive phantasies of object exchange) and abstract (translating the prevalent situation in the field into intelligible terms). A modification of the field then takes place, but not just any modification corresponds to this specific process: one of the parts of the patient that is split off and isolated or deposited in some sector of the field is re-integrated into the patient's self and recognised as the patient's own. It is not simply a change of location of an object that was outside and is now inside. This mere change of location often occurs without leading to the process of insight, particularly when this re-introjection is produced in a brutal and massive way. In this case, the Ego feels violently invaded by a foreign, dangerous body, produces very intense anxiety and needs to change its defensive system in order to confront an enemy that has become internal, if it is a persecutory object. The external persecution has become a demonic possession or the hypochondriacal insertion of the persecutor inside some organ.

All to the contrary, the re-introjection that conditions insight takes place mainly in the Ego, in a measured and a particularly differentiated way. This differentiation is applied first to what belongs to the external object and what the subject has projected into it. The external object thus changes its structure and looks much more like its real characteristics, while the self recovers from the object aspects that were lost because of the projective identification. But this is not all: in this re-introjection, the Ego also differentiates between its own aspects that had been attributed to the object and the internal objects (different from the Ego) that contributed to the structuring of the external object. This is a double process: the Ego recovers what belongs to it as its own and also assimilates something more from its internal objects. This object metabolism provokes an extension of the Ego, which is felt as greater scope and freedom of movement; this state of elation and happiness is quite different from any corresponding hypomania, since it responds to the Ego's increased real potential and improved contact with reality, rather than to denial and omnipotence.

The temporal dimension in this process of insight is much better differentiated: the past and present aspects of the objects are differentiated, which permits their better metabolisation, the assimilation of those aspects of them that are compatible with the Ego and the abandonment of the rest.

Of course, insight with all the aspects that we have just mentioned is only produced as a correlate of the depressive position as described by M Klein (1958), and the strengthening of the Ego produced by the dynamic of the analytic situation allows a decrease in splitting, idealisation and persecution and the synthesis of contradictory aspects of the objects. By this same process, the Ego resorts far less to projective identification and fears re-introjection much less, thus making it possible for the Ego to improve the exercise of its correlative functions of differentiation and assimilation.

The effect of the process of insight on the analytic situation is characteristic: better differentiation makes the bi-personal field appear momentarily as it is – an experimental field, while the analyst loses the phantasised characteristics and is experienced in terms of his or her essential function: the analyst is the analyst and not the patient's father, mother, omnipotence, etc. By this process, in the course of the analysis, the analyst gradually loses those fantastic aspects and the transference relation becomes more serene, more authentically cordial and better communicated.

These considerations allow us to draw some conclusions regarding the process of insight. In spite of its etymology, it can by no means be considered a state of contemplation. For example, the states often observable in patients in beatific contemplation of the idealised object are even quite the opposite of insight. Perhaps its etymology and remnants of introspectionist psychology also contributed to prevent recognition that analytic insight, as a phenomenon of the bi-personal field, can only be described or understood as a bi-personal phenomenon. Of course, we can observe phenomena of self-discovery outside the analytic situation, and certain individuals have more access than others to their own psychological processes. But these phenomena or psychological characteristics are essentially different from the process that we call insight in our practice.

In the analytic situation, insight begins with the comprehension (giving this word its full meaning as both intellection and experienced participa-

there is no insight. Insight is received as an interpretation and immediately recognised by the patient as the patient's own. It provokes or coincides with a modification of the patient's internal situation: what is understood and differentiated in the field is integrated as a part or aspect of the internal world, integrated into the patient's person, and, correlatively, it makes the analyst appear as the analyst.

In this way, a new type of communication is created between patient and analyst: the feeling, not only of seeing the same, but of doing or constructing something together or sharing a reparatory process. Ultimately, insight is the integration of the transference and countertransference phantasies concerning analytic work.

## Notes

1 Translated by Susan Rogers and John Churcher. Originally published in Spanish as Baranger M and Baranger W (1961–1962), and later reprinted in Baranger M and Baranger W (1969), which is the primary source for the present translation.

2 This paper is an attempt at a synthesis of ideas already put forward by both authors in earlier papers, several of which remain unpublished for reasons of discretion. Its technical basis is apparent in those papers. [Added 1969:] The present text was first published in the *Revista Uruguaya de Psicoanálisis*, Vol. IV, no. 1, in 1961–1962. Some of the concepts expressed here will need to be developed – as some of them are in the following chapter, some will need to be modified, others to be radically revised. As it stands, the text gives a good enough idea of the current thinking of both authors. The 'following chapter' referred to here was originally published as Baranger M and Baranger W (1964).

3 The summary was included in the 1961–1962 version only.

4 The Spanish is *analista-ojo*; the word does not appear to have been used elsewhere.

5   The 1961–1962 version has 'Kurt Lewin' where the 1969 version has 'Maurice Merleau-Ponty'.
6   The Spanish 'lineas de orientación' can mean 'guiding principles' as well as, e.g., the orienting lines on a magnetic compass. The context suggests an allusion to the local orientation of lines of force in a physical field.
7   On the relation between Pichon-Rivière's and Klein's notions of 'point of urgency', see Baranger M (1993).
8   The Spanish *baluarte* refers to a type of fortification, projecting from the main walls of a fortress, which enables the defenders to hinder an attack on the main structure by firing laterally on the attackers. It has sometimes elsewhere been translated as 'bulwark'.
9   In the original the English word 'insight' is used, enclosed in quotation marks, and this format is repeated throughout the text.
10  In Spanish, *seso* ('brain') and *sexo* ('sex') are close in sound and morphology, and associatively connected.

# References

Where an English version is available, this is given first, followed by the Spanish in brackets, if this was cited in the original. References to Freud are to the Standard Edition. References marked with an asterisk have been added by the translators.

Álvarez de Toledo L (1954). The analysis of 'associating', 'interpreting' and 'words': Use of this analysis to bring unconscious fantasies into the present and to achieve greater ego integration. *International Journal of Psycho-Analysis, 11*(3): 269–75 [(1996). El analisis del asociar del interpretar y de las palabras. *Revista de Psicoanálisis, 77*: 291–317].

Baranger M (1956). Fantasia de enfermedad y desarrollo del 'insight' en el analisis de un nino [Phantasy of illness and the development of insight in the analysis of a child]. *Revista Uruguaya de Psicoanálisis, 1*(2): 143–82.

Baranger M (1959). Mala fe, identidad y omnipotencia [Bad faith, identity and omnipotence]. Presented to the Argentine Psychoanalytic Association. Unpublished [(1969). Reprinted in: Baranger M, Baranger W, *Problemas del campo psicoanalítico*. Buenos Aires: Kargieman].

Baranger M (1960). Regresion y temporalidad en el tratamiento analitico. Unpublished.

Baranger M (1993). The mind of the analyst: From listening to interpretation. *International Journal of Psycho-Analysis, 74*: 15–24.

Baranger M, Baranger W (1961–1962). La situacion analitica como campo dinamico [The analytic situation as a dynamic field]. *Revista Uruguaya de Psicoanálisis, 4*(1): 3–54.

Baranger M, Baranger W (1964). El 'insight' en la situacion analitica [Insight in the analytic situation]. *Revista Uruguaya de Psicoanálisis, 6*(1) [(1969). Reprinted in: Baranger M, Baranger W, *Problemas del campo psicoanalítico*. Buenos Aires: Kargieman].

Baranger M, Baranger W (1969). *Problemas del campo psicoanalítico* [Problems of the analytic field]. Buenos Aires: Kargieman.

Baranger W (1956). Notas acerca del concepto de fantasia inconsciente [Notes on the concept of unconscious phantasy]. *Revista de Psicoanálisis, 8*(4) [(1969). Reprinted in: Baranger M, Baranger W, *Problemas del campo psicoanalítico*. Buenos Aires: Kargieman].

Congress, Santiago, Chile [(1969). Reprinted in: Baranger M, Baranger W, *Problemas del campo psicoanalítico*. Buenos Aires: Kargieman].

Freud S (1892–99). Extracts from the Fliess papers. *The complete psychological works of Sigmund Freud, 1.*

Freud S (1905). On psychotherapy. *The complete psychological works of Sigmund Freud, 7*: 257–68.

Freud S (1911). Psycho-analytic notes on an autobiographical account of a case of paranoia (dementia paranoides). *The complete psychological works of Sigmund Freud, 12*: 9–82.

Freud S (1913). On beginning the treatment. *The complete psychological works of Sigmund Freud, 12*: 121–44.

Freud S (1916–17). Introductory lectures on psycho-analysis. *The complete psychological works of Sigmund Freud, 15*: 3–239 and *16*: 243–464.

Freud S (1921). Group psychology and the analysis of the ego. *The complete psychological works of Sigmund Freud, 18*: 65–143.

Freud S (1922). Some neurotic mechanisms in jealousy, paranoia and homosexuality. *The complete psychological works of Sigmund Freud, 18*: 221–32.

Freud S (1926). The question of lay analysis. *The complete psychological works of Sigmund Freud, 20*: 177–258.

Freud S (1930). Civilization and its discontents. *The complete psychological works of Sigmund Freud, 21*: 57–145.

Grinberg L (1956). Sobre algunos problemas de tecnica psicoanalitica determinados por la identificacion y contraidentificacion proyectivas [On some problems of psychoanalytic technique caused by projective identification and counteridentification]. *Revista de Psicoanálisis, 13*(4): 507–11.

Heimann P (1961). On counter-transference. *International Journal of Psycho-Analysis, 31*: 81–84 [(1961–1962). Contratransferencia. *Revista Uruguaya de Psicoanálisis, 4*(1): 1–20].

Isaacs S (1948). The nature and function of phantasy. *International Journal of Psycho-Analysis, 29*: 73–97 [(1950). Naturaleza y funcion de la fantasia. *Revista de Psicoanálisis, 7*(4): 555–609].

Klein M (1930). The importance of symbol-formation in the development of the ego. *International Journal of Psycho-Analysis, 11*: 24–39 [(1956). La importancia de la formacion de simbolos en el desarrollo del yo. *Revista Uruguaya de Psicoanálisis, 1*(1): 7–25].

Klein M. (1946). Notes on some schizoid mechanisms. *International Journal of Psycho-Analysis, 27*: 99–110 [(1948). Notas sobre algunos mecanismos esquizoides. *Revista de Psicoanálisis, 6*(1): 82–113].

Klein M (1955). On identification. In *New directions in psycho-analysis*. London: Tavistock, 309–45.

Klein M (1958). Some theoretical conclusions concerning the emotional life of the infant. In *Envy and gratitude and other works 1946–1963*. London: Hogarth Press [(1958). Algunas conclusiones teoricas relativas a la vida emocional del lactante. *Revista Uruguaya de Psicoanálisis, 2*(3): 319–59].

Liberman D (1956). Identificacion proyectiva y conflicto matrimonial [Projective identification and marital conflict]. *Revista de Psicoanálisis, 8*(4): 1–20.

Mom J (1956). Algunas consideraciones sobre el concepto de distancia en las fobias [Some considerations concerning the concept of distance in the phobias]. *Revista de Psicoanálisis, 13*(4): 430–5.

Mom J (1960). Aspectos teoricos y tecnicos en las fobias y en las modalidades fobicas [Theoretical and technical aspects of phobias and phobic modalities]. *Revista de Psicoanálisis, 17*(2): 190–218.

Pichon-Rivière E (1956–58). Seminarios en la Asociacion Psicoanalitica del Uruguay [Seminars at the Uruguyan Psychoanalytical Association]. Unpublished.

Racker H (1960). *Estudios sobre técnica psicoanalítica*. Buenos Aires: Paidos [(1968). *Transference and countertransference*. London: Hogarth Press and Institute of Psycho-Analysis].

Reich W (1949 [1933]). *Character-analysis*. New York: Orgone Institute Press [(1957). *Psicoanálisis del carácter*. Buenos Aires: Paidos].

Schmidl F (1955). The problem of scientific validation in psycho-analytic interpretation. *International Journal of Psycho-Analysis, 36*: 105–113 [(1959). El problema de la validacion cientifica de la interpretacion psicoanalitica. *Revista Uruguaya de Psicoanálisis, 3*(1): 82–100].

Spira M (1959). Etude sur le temps psychologique [A study of psychological time]. *Revue Française de Psychanalyse (Paris), 8*(1).

Strachey J (1934). The nature of the therapeutic action of psycho-analysis. *International Journal of Psycho-Analysis, 15*: 127–59 [(1948). Naturaleza de la accion terapeutica del psicoanálisis. *Revista de Psicoanálisis, 5*(4): 951–83].

# 4

# (1922–1997)

## *Jorge Luis Maldonado*

Mom is one of the second generations of psychoanalysts who were instrumental in the development of psychoanalysis in Argentina. He was a close disciple of E. Pichon-Rivière. The most original and significant contribution that Mom made to psychoanalysis was his work on the pathology of phobias. He studied the relationship established by the phobic patient both with the phobic object and what he called the "accompanying" object in certain phobias. He considered the phobic object as being actively sought out by the subject as opposed to being avoided, the latter being the traditionally held view. This active search enables the phobic patient to associate anxiety with an object (an anxiety linked to the phobogenic object), protecting them from a potential catastrophic situation arising from the dread of experiencing fragmentation anxiety, which derives from the fear of helplessness. Initially, the subject who constructs a phobia looks for an object that he/she does not have, and that he/she lacks. This object is vital for the structuring of the subject's mental order in that it is the very existence of this object that sets a dividing line, a limit, between the self and a negative image of an internal object. Thus, the subject can avoid the terrifying undifferentiation between the self and the internal object, which is the source of the subject's feeling of falling into madness. By creating a feared object, the subject has an object that can be differentiated from the self and that is a "non-me", allowing the subject to have a separate identity: this is the essential function of the phobia.

The world of the phobic patient is divided into subject, phobogenic object (feared) and the accompanying object (protector). However, these functions are not fixed, given that the phobic object needed by the phobic patient may be transformed into the accompanying object. The subject appears to avoid the relationship with the phobic object. However, in fact, this relationship is actively sought out by the subject, as it protects the subject from the real "avoided relationship". This avoided relationship is characterized by the absence of boundaries, the loss of an object and the loss of manifest anxiety. The loss of this phobogenic object would provoke an anxiety caused by undifferentiation, this being the real anxiety that the phobic patient is permanently trying to avoid. The manifest anxiety is a key factor in the structuring of the phobia and if this is lacking, the subject looks for a new phobogenic object to generate this kind of manifest anxiety in order to prevent undifferentiation between the subject and the object. This differentiation is the real function of the phobia, which is achieved by means of an external object, even if this object is feared, as is the case with the phobogenic object.

The concrete and tangible presence of the object that is his, her or its shape and name make a boundary, eliminate absence and demarcate physical spaces, some of which are permitted and others of which are prohibited. This demarcation precludes the undifferentiated and terrifying emptiness of solitude.

Mom considered that the relationship between the phobic subject and the phobogenic object is a fiction. The subject does not avoid but rather needs and seeks to create a relationship with an object that arouses a feeling of uneasiness in order to sustain the dissociation and differentiation with his or her "other-me". This object must be similar but not the same, different but not too different, from the phobic patient. By being different, the object arouses a certain degree of manifest anxiety. If this is not the case, the phobogenic object does not serve its purpose.

The subject needs to keep the object at an optimum distance: not too far, as the subject could run the risk of losing the object; but also not too close, as this might expose the patient to the threat of not being differentiated from the object. The relationship with the object can only be established with a specific distance that demarcates the minimum and maximum limits of a zone. The object must not transgress these boundaries, otherwise the relationship is not useful for the subject. The phobic patient exercises careful control over the feared objects to avoid the risk of their disappearance and to ensure their continued presence. In addition, the subject ensures that there is no contact, neither between the objects nor with the subject, as this might blur the boundaries. Objects who would appear to be phobogenic may, in fact, be transformed into accompanying objects.

In Mom's view, the phobia of open spaces (where incestuous objects are present) enables the subject to establish a differentiation between the subject and a dangerous space outside where there is something that is frightening, but that is not oneself and, as a consequence, generates "a difference". When this differentiation looks tenuous, this causes anxiety, which functions as "anxiety as a signal" acting as a warning against a catastrophic situation; one

generates the phobia, which avoids the anxiety of fragmentation. As a consequence, the phobia is not what the patient is avoiding; on the contrary, it is precisely what the patient is looking for.

From 1953 onwards, Mom developed a series of concepts – such as the notion of "lack", anxiety as a structuring factor, the problem of emptiness, among others – that, in recent times, were dealt with by authors such as Lacan, Green, Laplanche, and Lutenberg, among others. His descriptions, such as the concept of "distancing" in phobias, are of enormous value in their application to other clinical pictures.

Unfortunately, his work on phobias was not translated into English. Only his paper on the analytical process (Process and no-process in analytic work. *International Journal of Psycho-Analysis* 64 (1983): 1–15), and another on trauma (The infantile trauma from us to Freud: Pure trauma, retroactivity and reconstruction. *International Journal of Psycho-Analysis* 69 (1988): 113–28), written together with Madeleine and Willy Baranger, have been published in English.

References for Mom's work on phobias can be found in: Mom, J. (1980). El objeto en la fobia. In: *Aportaciones al concepto de objeto en psicoanálisis.* Willy Baranger y col. Buenos Aires, Amorrortu Editores, 1980; and in the paper translated for this book: Some considerations regarding the concept of distance in phobias. *Revista de Psicoanálisis, 13*(4) 430–435.

------------------------ 5 ------------------------

# PROCESS AND NON-PROCESS IN ANALYTIC WORK

*Madeleine Baranger, Willy Baranger and Jorge Mom*

*This paper was read at the 33rd International Psychoanalytical Congress, Madrid, July 1983, and the present version was published in 1983 by the* International Journal of Psycho-Analysis, *64: 1–15.*

The 'talking cure', named by Anna O. and discovered by Freud, has been widely expanded and diversified throughout our century. Our objective in the following paper is not to summarize the vast literature on the subject but to underline several points that seem to define the analytic process. We believe that progress in psychoanalysis must arise from the study of clinical experience at its frontiers, at its topmost limits, in its failures. For this reason, we have concentrated our search on the analytic non-process, in the very places where the process stumbles or halts. This has led us to propose the introduction of several terms: 'field', 'bastion', 'second look'. When the process stumbles or halts, the analyst can only question himself about the obstacle, by encircling himself and his analysand, Oedipus and the Sphinx, in a second look, in a total view: this is the field. The obstacle involves the analysand's transference and the analyst's countertransference, and poses rather confusing problems. The arrest of the process introduces us fully to the nature of its movement, its inherent temporality. If the process is to continue, then by what main-spring can we accomplish it? Finally, we can only resort to the word, which may lead to an 'insight'. This in turn enables us to describe this particular dialectic of process and non-process as a task of overcoming the obstacles that determine its success or failure.

## I. Analytic field and bastion

Nothing that can happen in an analytic treatment may be considered independent of the analytic situation, which functions as a relatively permanent background in relation to changing forms (in Gestalt terms). This background is a contract or pact, explicit in various aspects, between analyst and

function itself, e.g., the fixed or variable length of the sessions produces two very different types of analytic process.

In terms of function, we must emphasize that the pact establishes a basic asymmetry: one of the members will be the analyst and the other, the analysand, allowing for no possible interchange of functions.

In terms of structure, we insist that the 'fundamental rule' defines the analytic process. The Lacanian concept of 'subject supposed to know', implicit in the fundamental rule, would seem to be enlightening. The fundamental rule places the analyst not only on an imaginary plane of knowing beforehand who the patient really is and what his fate will be, but also as listener and interpreter, committed to the truth of all the patient will associate with or experience. Most of all, it fully opens the doors to transference.

In an attempt to differentiate the circumstantial phenomenal aspects of the analytic situation and its transphenomenal structure, we have already felt it necessary to include in its description the notion of 'field', expressed in several of Freud's descriptions as battlefield or chessboard.

The structure instituted by the pact is intended to permit certain work tending toward a process: experience proves that, beyond the resistances of whose conquest the constitution of analytic work precisely is, situations of obstruction in the process inevitably arise: the idea of field seems appropriate to these circumstances.

In other words, within the functional structure of the process, difficulties arise that involve each member of the pact differently. When examined, they show that other, contingent structures, which interfere in the functioning of the basic structure, have been created.

Our experience supervising many colleagues (from beginners to the most experienced) has taught us that, at those times, the basic asymmetry of the analytic pact is lost and *another*, far more symmetrical *structuring* predominates in which the unconscious attachment between analyst and analysand becomes an involuntary complicity against the analytic process.

This gave us the idea of applying our experience in supervision to the treatments we ourselves practise when they become obstructed. In fact, we all do so spontaneously whenever an obstacle arises that goes beyond the analysand's habitual resistances. At these times, we used a 'second look' in which we see the analytic situation as a field that involves us insofar as we fail to know ourselves.

Each of us possesses, explicitly or not, a kind of personal countertransferential dictionary (bodily experiences, movement fantasies, appearance of certain images, etc.) that indicates the moments in which one abandons one's attitude of 'suspended attention' and proceeds to the second look, questioning oneself as to what is happening in the analytic situation.

These countertransferential indicators, which provide the second look, lead us to realize that within the field exists an immobilized structure that is slowing down or paralysing the process. We have named this structure the 'bastion'.

This structure never appears directly in the consciousness of either participant, showing up only through indirect effects: it arises, in unconsciousness and in silence, out of a complicity between the two protagonists to protect an attachment that must not be uncovered. This leads to a partial crystallization of the field, to a neo-formation set up around a shared fantasy assembly, which implicates important areas of the personal history of both participants and attributes a stereotyped imaginary role to each.

Sometimes the bastion remains as a static foreign object while the process apparently goes forward. In other situations, it completely invades the field and removes all functional capacity from the process, transforming the entire field into a pathological field. We will mention a few brief examples to illustrate the concept of bastion.

A   *A manifestly perverse patient.* He behaves like a 'good patient', complies with the formal aspects of the pact, manifests no resistances, does not progress. The sessions, over a certain period, seem to be a condensed version of the whole of *'Psychopathia Sexualis'* by Krafft-Ebing (1886). The analyst 'has never seen anyone with so many perversions'. The bastion here is set up between an exhibitionist analysand and a fascinated-horrified analyst, the forced 'voyeur', complacent with regard to the perverse display.

B   *An analysand, veteran of a number of analytic treatments.* Apparently, each session bears the fruit of some 'discovery'; in reality, nothing is happening. The analyst is delighted by the subtlety of the analysand's descriptions of his internal states, enjoying his own Talmudism. Until he realizes that, while they are toying with their disquisitions, the analysand is monthly placing the analyst's fees at interest, speculating with his delay in paying.

The analysis of this bastion reveals a shared fantasy set-up: the analysand's old, surreptitious vengeance on his stingy father and the analyst's guilt-ridden compulsion to set himself up as the cheated father.

C   *Example of a bastion that has invaded the field.* A seriously psychopathic patient. The analyst is terrified, fearing the analysand's physical, homicidal aggression without being able either to suspend or to carry the

This series of examples could be infinite. They show not only the interaction between the analysand's transference and the analyst's countertransference, but also the creation of a field phenomenon that could only be produced between *this* analyst and *this* analysand. We could describe it metaphorically as a 'precipitate'. But we must first understand the nature of transference, countertransference and their relation to projective identification.

## II. A jungle of problems: Transference – countertransference – projective identification

Naturally, Freud's discovery of transference led him to deepen and widen this concept, culminating in a representation of the analytic process that is nearly 'pan-transferentialist' – i.e., as a substitution of the patient's initial, natural neurosis for an artificial neurosis in the transference, and its resolution in this place.

As for countertransference, we know that Freud did not give it by any means the sustained attention he did to transference. Even today, many analytic authors consider countertransference an unessential, rather perturbing phenomenon, an undue residue of the analyst's insufficiently 'cured' neurosis. With Heimann's pioneering paper (1950), and Racker's (1953), nearly contemporary to it, countertransference was seen not only as a universal phenomenon, just as constant as transference, but as an indispensable instrument of analytic work as well.

Melanie Klein's discovery of projective identification (1946) profoundly modifies the theory of transference. Although Klein herself did not seek to do so, the theory of countertransference is also consequently modified. Klein's tendency to overextend the concept of projective identification, to the point that transference finally becomes synonymous with a continually

active projective identification, led her to define the movement of the analytic session as a succession of projective and introjective identifications,
resulting from the analyst's interpretive activity.

It was a great temptation to try to arrive at a unified theory of transference, countertransference and projective identification. It would suffice to allow that the field created by the analytic situation consists of a
transferential-countertransferential field formed on the basis of crossed-
over and reciprocal projective identifications between analyst and analysand. Thus, the asymmetrical function of this field would constantly aim
to undo the symbiotic structurings originating in the projective identifications by means of interpretation. In fact, we realized that such a definition
could only apply, and without great precision, to extremely pathological
states of the field: a field characterized either by an invincible symbiosis
between the two participants, or by the annihilating parasiting of the analyst
by the analysand. The simplification and unification of the theory led not
to greater coherence but to flattening. Today, we consider differentiation of
the phenomena indispensable, *since their correct technical management depends
on this differentiation.*

In any case, we cannot content ourselves with defining transference as the
set of thoughts and experiences of the analysand as related to his analyst, nor
countertransference as what the analyst thinks and feels with respect to his
patient, since such a definition would eliminate not only what is structurally determined by the analytic pact but also, beyond this basic structure, the
transferential or countertransferential categories, which indicate to us the
*priorities and characteristics of interpretive management.*

For example, at a certain moment, shadings in an analysand's transferential expressions indicate to us a nearly obligatory turn through his history:
'I dreamt that I was four years old and you were my dad . . .' etc. and another
expression may set another course.

This is one of the many cases in which theoretical coherence works
*against* coherent practice.

Within the set of phenomena that we could term as transferential in the
widest sense of the term, we must differentiate a series of basic categories.

1   Everything in the analysand that responds to the structural position
    and function of the analyst, which has essentially nothing to do with
    the analysand's projections, and which may sometimes be erroneously
    construed as a process of idealization.
2   The momentary and changing transferences corresponding to succes-
    sive structuring of the field that do not necessarily demand interpreta-
    tion, unless transference becomes resistance.

3    The repetitious and structured, basically unconscious, transference that
     Freud referred to with the concept of 'artificial neurosis' (1916–17,
     p. 444), which is always a privileged objective of the interpretive clari-
     fication. In other words: the specific way the analysand positions his
     analyst in the structure of this Oedipus complex, or projects onto him
     the figures of his primary objects of love, hate, identification.

field. It demands interpretation.

The categories that we habitually use to differentiate the forms of transference (positive transference–erotic transference–negative transference) are
actually descriptive and are based on the affective shadings of love and hate
(the love necessary to the pact whose aim is not directly sexual, directly
erotic love concealing hate in erotic transference, the thousand forms
of hate in negative transference). It will be noted that the categorization
we propose is based not on the phenomenal level but on the structures
involved, using Lacan's (1958) distinction between symbolic and imaginary
transference, Freud's repetitious transference and Klein's transference as the
product of projective identification. The latter differentiation involves two
schemes of reference: the first, Freud's, necessarily implies a reference to the
subject's history, while Klein's does not place it in the foreground, though it
does not reject it. We do not in effect consider these to be two alternative
concepts for the same object, but rather different forms and structures of
transference. The apparent simplification suggested by Klein in her concept
of transference as equivalent to projection-introjection or to projective and
introjective identification leads to the idea of a parallelism between positive and negative transference with a greater urgency to interpret (which
for Klein is equivalent to *dissolving*) the expressions of negative transference
insofar as they reveal pathogenic nuclei. Klein's departure from Freud is
immediately perceptible: for him, transference love as the very condition
for analytic work, implies a clear privilege – i.e., a non-parallelism between
these two forms, implying the idea that they do not function in the same
way and in opposition to each other, but in different ways: not as heads or
tails of the same coin, but as two coins of different values.
    As for countertransference, the problems are different, although discrimi-
nation becomes even more necessary. We must adopt the directive idea that
countertransference *is not* the inverse of transference, not simply because

Freud studied the former in depth and the latter very little, but for structural reasons.

If we consider the axis to be the place from which the analyst speaks as such – instituting and maintaining the setting, interpreting – that is, in Lacanian terms, the symbolic register, and this other place (Lacan apart this time) where the analyst is, with his attention evenly suspended and the door to his unconscious open as an apparatus of resonance, then we establish a principle of asymmetry that would seem to constitute the analytic situation. Countertransference is thus shown to be distinct from transference, not only because it is less intense and more instrumental, but also because it corresponds to a different structural position.

Due to his function, and from the outset, the analyst is committed to truth and abstinence from anything *acted out* with the analysand. In the analytic process there is no formalized, computable operation, but a situation in which the analyst is committed, flesh, bone and unconscious. He is so intrinsically, not contingently, because of the fact that an analyst listens and reacts: this implies that countertransference will be prohibited in its expression and condemned to an internal unfolding in him. The analyst's structural position marks certain limits within which his attention is 'suspended' without falling, and the analyst works with the first look without the field as such appearing. In our view, it would be erroneous to define this structural countertransference in terms of projective identification, since this would eliminate differences among extremely contrasting aspects having opposite consequences to countertransference.

In this process of discrimination, we can isolate various forms of countertransference:

1    That which arises from the structure of the analytic situation itself and from the placement and function of the analyst within the process.
2    Transferences of the analyst on to the patient, which, as long as they do not become stereotyped, are a normal part of the process (e.g., 'I know that this patient is not my daughter and that I must guard against my tendency to treat her as if she were').
3    Projective identifications of the analyst toward the analysand and his reactions to the projective identifications of the latter. These phenomena provoke pathological structuring of the field, require a second look toward it, and demand priority in interpretive management. They may also produce the frequent phenomenon that we habitually term 'countertransferential micro-delusions'.

In the jungle of the complex, sometimes mixed and confused, phenomena of transference and countertransference, certain ideas enable us to mark out paths that may guide us. The first consists of placing the constitutive in opposition to the constituted aspects of the transference and countertransference. This opposition, marked by Lacan when he refers to the 'subject supposed to know', is not at all foreign to habitual psychoanalytic thought, at least in certain aspects. It underlies all the descriptions Freud has left us of the technique he invented; it is implicit in all the papers underscoring the opposition between setting and process; it is the basis for the very

perspective'.

Not all phenomena of transference or countertransference correspond to the same model or to the same mechanisms, nor should they be treated in the same way.

## III. The analytic process and its temporality

Among the multiple metaphors that Freud used to describe the analytic process, some refer directly to history: e.g., the battle history of a territory invaded by an enemy (neurosis) and its reconquest (psychoanalytic treatment); another, the archaeological metaphor of reconstruction by excavation of the superimposed layers of the remains of different cities built and destroyed in the same place in different epochs. Other metaphors have no direct connexion with time or with history: the sculptural metaphor ('via di porre', 'via di levare'), the telephonic metaphor, the surgical metaphor. And between these two series is the chess metaphor. Obviously, no one of these metaphors, by itself, fills the concept that Freud had of the analytic process; the choice of one or several over the rest involves a simplification – that is, a limitation – of the original concept. Nor can we say that Freud changed his mind with respect to this problem, but that each of these metaphors describes a facet of a very complex problem.

In any case, up to and including his last two great technical papers, 'Constructions in psycho-analysis' (1937a) and 'Analysis terminable and interminable' (1937b), the subject's history constitutes an essential dimension of what psychoanalysis must uncover.

This originates in Freud's first discoveries on memory: Freud's tendency to define the unconscious as the repressed, the repression having effect basically on *forgetting traumatic situations*. The main-spring of the analytic process is thus defined as a transferential repetition whose interpretation permits a remembrance of the repressed and its eventual working-through.

What happens after Freud?

The sense of history tends to get lost in two, apparently opposite, ways.

The first is partly based on several Freudian metaphors (the telephonic, the surgical, etc.) and also on the Freudian idea that everything is played out in the transference, that is, in the present; and in Freud's (misunderstood) statement that, in the unconscious, the temporal category does not function. Aside from this Freudian groundwork, this position aims to equalize psychoanalysis and the 'natural' or experimental sciences, in which history has no place. The most radical exponent of this position would be Henry Ezriel (1951), who declares that psychoanalysis is an 'a-historic science', but we can perceive the same tendency in Bion and others.

The second tendency, although it does not flatly reject the subject's individual history, aims to dilute it in developmental psychology. Here, a number of misunderstandings have arisen, either because analysts try to adapt the scheme of the developmental phases of the libido described by Karl Abraham (1924) (thereby making Freud's indications on it rigid) to the experimental observations of developmental psychology, or because they attempt to submit analytic hypotheses to the evidence of experimental observation (e.g., Spitz *vs.* Klein). In both cases, the basic prejudice lies in believing that psychoanalysis is continuous with respect to developmental psychology and that descriptions must necessarily coincide if they are true. This prejudice totally sacrifices the Freudian concept of *'Nachträglichkeit'*, according to which, instead of an event constituting a determining cause for a series of ulterior events, this initial event only takes on its meaning *in virtue of* the ulterior events. If one takes Freud's expression *'Nachträglichkeit'* seriously, the discontinuity of psychoanalysis with respect to any developmental psychology cannot fail to be evident. This of course does not imply any basic criticism of the results of developmental psychology. It does however imply a criticism of the contradictory concept of the 'historic–genetic' approach described by some authors (Rapaport, 1973; Gill, 1956; and others).

Past and present discussions to determine whether the analytic process develops and must develop in the 'here and now' of the transferential situation of the session, or whether it aims at recuperating memories, seem to us to overlook the genuine Freudian dialectics of temporality. If analytic work is possible, it is because the subject and the analyst think that exploration of the past permits opening up the future; it is because the complemental series do not constitute a mechanical determinism; it is because it is possible to escape, by means of interpretation, from the eternal, atemporal present of unconscious fantasies. Progressive and regressive movements take place together and condition each other reciprocally.

We do not consider exploration of the past to be the same as regression, although both phenomena are frequently simultaneous. To explore the past is in many ways to relive it, and this involves primitive ways of feeling and levels of psychic organization. Nearly all authors agree that regression is a necessary dimension of analytic work. For that reason, the regularity and uniform duration of the sessions create a fixed temporal framework that permits regressive phenomena to unfold. We consider that one of the subtlest functions of the analyst is regulating the level on which analytic work may take place without the analysand getting lost in regression. We know it

in which we can safely navigate.

It is for this reason that a correct appreciation of the function of regression in analytic work is so important. The idea exists, in certain analytic tendencies, that regression is *in itself* the essential therapeutic factor. These authors consider that the analytic situation, in state of regression, is bound to call up ever more remote phases of the patient's existence. Theoretically, this attitude means searching for the determinant pathogenic factor farther and farther back in the subject's infancy, encouraging the re-experiencing of these badly experienced past situations. The reappearance of the initial symbiosis with the mother, the birth trauma, the primitive relationship with the father, the paranoid–schizoid and depressive positions of suckling, the outcroppings of 'psychotic nuclei', would be indispensable conditions for true progress. Out of this arises the illusion, so often contradicted by experience, that reaching the pathogenic archaic situations, by means of drugs or by systematically favouring analytic regression, suffices to obtain progress. But this loses sight of the fact that re-living a trauma is useless if not complemented by working-through, if the trauma is not reintegrated into the course of a history, if initial traumatic situations of the subject's life are not differentiated from the historic myth of his origins. The necessary working-through discards the magic eagerness to be able to shorten the analytic process by short circuit.

Freud's (1926) discussion of Otto Rank's ideas of the birth trauma and of the technical conclusions derived by the latter from this theory (the birth trauma as basis of all ulterior pathology, its working-through in treatment permitting rapid 'cures' by economizing on analytic process) expresses in prototypical form all the criticisms we could make to several later attempts in the same direction as Rank's.

The time of the session is a parenthesis that suspends the time of life, an unhurried time, which sometimes seems to close in upon an atemporal present or a circular time, and which sometimes produces repeated or new events. In reality, it is the optimal experience for the direct observation of the genesis of temporality and history. The analytic process in some measure rewrites the subject's history and at the same time changes its meaning. The moment in which we can observe this change, in which the subject simultaneously re-assumes a piece of his history and opens up his future, is the moment of 'insight'.

Analytic work takes place in the here and now and in the past, in the dialectics of the closed and repetitious temporality of neurosis and fate, and the open temporality of 'insight'.

## IV. The main-spring of the analytic process: Interpretation and insight

No one would question it: the specific main-spring of the analytic process is the interpretation. The analyst does many things, apart from interpreting: he maintains or imposes the setting, gently or not; he chooses the point that must be interpreted; he internally tries out hypotheses; etc.

From the beginning, Freud describes the main-spring of the process as a dialectic: interpretation is necessary when the analysand's 'free' association stumbles on an obstacle, expressing the appearance of a resistance in him. The model of these fertile moments of the process would be: resistance-interpretation-remembrance.

As the analytic procedure goes beyond the limits of memory and forgetting, the obstacle takes on new forms and the interpretive solution produces broader effects that we will group under the heading of 'insight'.

Thus, we are faced with two enigmas: what is this strange power of the interpretive word? What is 'insight', its result?

The first enigma clears up somewhat if we differentiate two aspects of this power. The first refers to the word in itself, to the fact of speaking, of interpreting or of associating; the second refers to the word as carrier of meanings, expressing 'what one wishes to say'.

The classic papers of Luisa Alvarez de Toledo (1954, 1962) have taught us that, in addition to its semantic value, the word acquires concrete value, most particularly in analytic work, in terms of fantasied action: shooting arrows, throwing rocks, poisoning, suckling, caressing, etc. This is sufficient to lay aside all comparisons of the analyst's interpretation with a translation, much less with a simultaneous translation. Even if we consider only its semantic value, the analyst's interpretation is somewhat similar to the spells of a sorcerer's apprentice, calling up all kinds of demons besides those that were summoned. Because of the polysemy of words and sentences, it is often difficult to determine, among the forever multiple meanings of what we say, which meaning has been chosen and understood by the analysand.

We all know from experience that, in certain treatments, the analysand systematically understands something different or even the opposite to what we meant to say, and we also know, if we think back over our interpretations, that many times our interpretation has been much more meaningful than what we consciously meant to communicate, and that one of its second meanings is the one that has been truly operative. Thus, someone

Every interpretation, in he who pronounces it and in he who listens to it, is necessarily polysemic. It would be a crass error (not infrequently committed) to think that the *precision* of the interpretation, a precision fundamental to any scientific statement (but an interpretation in the analytic process is *not* a scientific statement: its 'truth' resides in another place), allows us to avoid the confusions implicit in the polysemy of the statements.

Quite to the contrary, we think that the analyst's search for theoretical precision in formulating interpretations is directly opposed to what we ask of the patient: to associate – as far as possible – 'freely'. Therefore, we should distinguish between two moments in the act of interpretation: the moments of searching, similar to what children in the country do to catch crickets (they scratch the ground at the entrance to its hole with a straw; the curious cricket comes out of its cave – just the moment to cage it). In our process, this 'caging' would be the second moment of the interpretation: an aspect of the unconscious comes to light and is captured by new meanings; analyst and analysand then coincide on the meaning of the interpretation. The first moment plays on ambiguity and polysemy; the second momentarily reduces them.

It is evident that the analytic power of the word is indeed strange, since in psychoanalytic literature it is described in two diametrically opposite ways. Some take its aspect as rupture, referring ultimately to Freud's (1905) 'via di levare'. To analyse means, etymologically, to un-bind, to un-tie, to break some 'false tie', to reveal a self-deception, to destroy an illusion or a lie: Dora, the 'beautiful soul', believes she is the innocent victim of her family's dirty tricks, and Freud reveals her as their unconscious accomplice.

Others, Melanie Klein more than any, consider it a unifying and integrating power: reducing splitting, permitting the synthesis of the object, broadening and enriching the ego. Freud himself, beginning with his initial model (resistance-interpretation-remembrance), conceives of the power of the interpretive word as permitting the recovery of a piece of repressed history. The 'levare' of the interpretation allows for a 'porre' from another place (from the analysand's unconscious).

In the movement of the analytic process, rupture and integration go together, the analyst not having to add even a pinch of his own salt. The strange power of the interpretation consists – among other things – of unbinding ourselves from the strange power of certain captivating words of our fate. It is to Lacan's credit to have emphasized this, but this power does not stop here: its reach is greater, just as Lacan himself admitted as from 1963, when he introduced the idea of analytic work that would be possible using words about the 'a' object – i.e., about something inexpressible, something beyond words.

Finally, if we wish to place the limit (in our opinion) on Lacan's contribution, we must draw it at the moment in which we are forced to the 'second look'. We coincide with him in recognizing that analytic work does *not* consist in the unflinching exhaustion of 'imaginary petting' (i.e., regressive experiences between two persons without physical contact) but it is not limited to a disruptive power. The main-spring is in the evocative power of the word in so far as it produces 'insight'.

If we wish to remain loyal to the description of our experience, we cannot avoid our obligation to discriminate two categories of what we call 'insight'.

Naturally, this categorization aims to describe two extreme, ideally distinct, forms of 'insight', when in reality they are more often found as mixed forms. The first corresponds to what Freud described as lifting of repression and conscious emergence of the repressed. In this relatively simple case, the analyst is only involved in the analysand's resistance as a transferential screen and in his capacity or difficulty in understanding and interpreting this precise moment of the process. The same unipersonal approach to 'insight' may be held, although with greater difficulty, in the case of the reduction of splitting.

The second category of 'insight' can only appear when the analyst recurs to the 'look toward the field' – i.e., when the dynamics of the field become obstructed and its functioning paralysed, indicating the presence of a bastion.

In this case, the interpretive process is more complex; it aims first for the analysand to realize that the bastion exists by pointing out its most conspicuous effects: detention of the process, stereotyping of his discourse, the feeling that 'nothing's happening'. From here, one may go on to the stereotyping of the reciprocal roles the analysand attributes to himself and to the analyst and then to the fantasies contributing to the structuring of the bastion, whose roots lie in the subject's personal history. This breaking up of the bastion implies returning to the analysand those aspects that he has placed in the analyst by projective identification, without any need for a 'countertransferential confession'. To do so would eliminate the structural and functional asymmetry of the field, introduce interminable confusions for the analysand, and remove the analyst from his specific function.

The rupture of the bastion means redistributing those aspects of both participants involved in the structuring of this bastion, but this redistribution takes place in a different manner in each of them: conscious and silent recuperation in the analyst's case; conscious and expressed in the analysand's.

as well as the analysand's, in the restitution of movement in the field, in the understanding of the obstacle at the moment it is overcome, in the analyst's spontaneous passage from the second look to the first look, which is appropriate to analytic work functioning with no resistance other than the patient's own.

The bastion's extreme form is found in a pathology of field and of process beyond symbiosis that we could describe as parasitism. It is revealed through its countertransferential aspect: the analyst feels as though he were 'inhabited' by the analysand, a prisoner of worry that goes beyond the sessions (either for fear of a self-destructive or criminal act of the analysand; of the imminence of a psychotic 'outbreak'; or of other, less dramatic, situations). These parasitic situations (equivalent to micro-psychoses in the analytic field) tend to lead either to a violent rupture of the analytic situation or to its re-channelling by reducing splitting and by returning the projective identifications to the analysand.

Not all analytic fields reach these pathological extremes, but they all do tend to create bastions, as the Freudian concept of 'transference neurosis' implies.

Thus, the main-spring of the analytic process appears to be the production of resistances and bastions and their respective interpretive dissolution, generator of 'insight'.

This description owes much to James Strachey's (1934) classic paper, 'The nature of the therapeutic action in psychoanalysis', to his idea, rooted in direct clinical observation, that the main-spring of the process resides in certain moments of 'mutative interpretation' in which the entire situation is knotted – past and present, transference and reality, feeling and comprehension – and unknotted, by means of discriminative interpretation that produces the mutation of insight. Aside from some details with which we cannot agree (the idea, taken from Rado, of the analyst's position as auxiliary superego, among others), what was, to our mind, lacking in Strachey's description was the analyst's effective and affective (not only interpretive) participation in this process, something Michael Balint was acutely aware of and that he expounded in many of his later papers without, however, formulating it in terms of field.

The fertile moments of interpretation and 'insight' punctuate the analytic process, described by Pichon-Rivière (1958) as a 'spiral process', an image that expresses the temporal dialectics of the process. 'Here, now, with me' is often said, to which Pichon-Rivière adds 'Just as there, before, with others' and 'As in the future, elsewhere and in a different way'. It is a spiral, each of whose turnings takes up the last turning from a different perspective, and which has no absolute beginning or given end. The superimposition of the spiral's curves illustrates this mixture of repetition and non-repetition, which may be observed in the characteristic events in a person's fate, this combined movement of deepening into the past and constructing the future, which characterizes the analytic process.

## V. Dialectic of process and non-process

Not all analysts have come to realize that the analytic process is an artefact. Not even Freud's clearest warnings (the military metaphor in which Freud explains that the process of reconquest is not played out in the same places where the battles of invasion were fought; the chess metaphor where he explains that, apart from the openings and the end, the intermediate plays are unpredictable) can prevail against the tendency to think of the analytic process in terms of a 'naturalist' model (gestation of a foetus – growth of a tree). The non-parallelism between the pathogenic and the analytic processes is the inevitable evidence to begin with. If analysts have been able to speak of a 'typical cure', of 'variations of the typical cure', of certain 'phases' of the cure, it is because they have a preconceived idea of the development of a treatment as part of their scheme of reference. This idea functions as a Procrustian bed and determines the effective course of a good number of treatments, except in those cases where the patient refuses to comply with the pre-established phases.

We cannot avoid, neither can we renounce our function as 'directors of the cure': we are an integral part of the process and this process is essentially intersubjective. This is not to say that we can or must use this directive function in an arbitrary fashion. We are victims of an 'uncurable idea', the idea of curing (Pontalis, 1981), but what we must do is avoid mistaking the very nature of our work and accept, without feeling intellectually shocked, the fact of the enormous variety of *positive* analytic processes.

To take an example: we consider that Klein's (1934) description of the 'depressive position' as a concrete moment in an analytic process (the patient, through the interpretation of his persecutory anxiety, approximates his persecuting to his idealized objects, unifies the split-off parts of his 'self', realizes his participation in the conflict, feels sadness and hope, etc.) formulates a structure that is observed time and again in treatments, in moments of change and progress. If we set this discovery up as a general rule, taking the access to the depressive position as if it were a basic standard for the evalua-

experiments on the rearing of monkeys, the analyst who is 'programmed' with a prejudice with regard to the analytic process 'manufactures', if he can, orthopaedic patients more or less similar to 'cured' human beings.

What are we left with? Total uncertainty? Exaggeration aside, we do have indicators that a process or a non-process exists in an analytic treatment, and fortunately we take these indicators into account, *even though they do not fit* into our theoretical scheme of reference. We will not now refer to the most frequently mentioned indicators, such as the disappearance of manifest neurotic symptoms, or the patient's progress in different areas of his life (his access to greater genital pleasure, his acquisition of new sublimatory activities, etc.), not because we undervalue their importance, but because they are more or less distant consequences of the process and not its immediate and essential expression.

The indicators of the existence of the process, and those of the non-process, do not correspond to each other exactly as the positive and the negative, as the front and back of the same drawing. Here too, our eagerness for symmetry could deceive us.

One is surprised sometimes to find that the initial indicator Freud described for the existence of an analytic process – the patient's recovery of forgotten (repressed) memories – has fallen into disuse in many descriptions of the process. Can it be that it is taken for granted? Is it that many forget about memory? Is it that *hic et nunc et mecum* is becoming a prejudice and eliminating temporality? We think that the overcoming of infantile amnesia continues to be a valuable indicator of the existence of a process and that, inversely, the specially prolonged persistence of infantile amnesia marks the end point of the process and often concerns a psychotic episode in childhood from which the subject has recuperated at the cost of the erasure of part of his history and a restriction of his person.

Free access to childhood memories goes hand in hand with the possibility of associating freely – i.e., with the richness of the narrative, the easy access to the different areas of the subject's existence, the variability of languages he uses to express himself, especially his capacity for using dream language to allow himself and to allow us access to his unconscious. Fluency of discourse is not enough to indicate the presence of an analytic process unless it is accompanied by affective circulation within the field. Alternating moments of blockage with moments of affective mobilization, the surge of a wide range of feelings and emotions that concord with the narrative, the transformation of transferential and countertransferential affects, all indicate to us the presence of the process. This indicator is not, however, sufficient by itself as evidence of the existence of the process: affective movement is often only a simple stirring, and affective permeability becomes instability. Pure feeling does not cure, contrary to the beliefs of some nonanalytic psychotherapists, advocates of the psychological jolting techniques in fashion in certain circles. Only the convergence of the two indicators (variation in the narrative and circulation of affect) informs us fully as to the existence of the process. An invaluable compass for approaching affective circulation is Klein's (1948) categorization of the different forms of anxiety (persecutory, depressive, confusional anxiety). The dialectic between the production and resolution of anxiety and the qualitative transformations of the latter stakes out the process.

If our description of the main-spring of the analytic procedure is correct, the appearance and frequency of moments of 'insight' are logically our most valuable indicator. But we must first differentiate between true 'insight' and the pseudo-'insight' that the subject uses to deceive both himself and us with regard to his progress. The series of 'discoveries' is bound, in these cases, to conceal absence of process.

True 'insight' is accompanied by a new opening in temporality, most specially in the future dimension; the process in course begins to have goals, and plans and feelings of hope appear. The circular temporality of the neurosis opens up toward the future.

But one of the most important indicators of the process is the analysand's active work as he co-operates with the analyst: an effort to be sincere as far as absolutely possible, to listen to the analyst and to say 'yes' as well as 'no', to allow himself to regress and progress. This becomes evident to us when the analysand says: 'in the last session we found something interesting', and when we share this sentiment.

Some manifestations of the analytic non-process are more difficult to discover than those of the process: aside from the multiple forms of hindrance, non-process is seen in the appearance of all the positive indicators of process, used to dissimulate its non-existence. Non-process usually disguises itself beneath all the positive indicators of process (co-operation that is actually submission, 'insight' that is pseudo-'insight', circulation of crocodile tears, etc.), with which the analysand intends to 'placate' his analyst in order to avoid greater dangers.

These disguises give themselves away as such through their stereotyping, which converges them with the indicators of non-process. The danger intrinsic to every psychoanalytic treatment is stereotyping (of narrative, of feelings, of the respective roles, of interpretation). When this stereotyping is

with his blinkers, who thinking he is advancing, always returns to the same place. If, as we may think, the noria involves not only the patient, we can imagine (remember?) the analyst going the rounds of his own theories without finding the way to break the circle for himself or for his analysand.

In certain cases, the non-process may be expressed in the form of an apparently well-channelled movement: those treatments that 'run on wheels', where the analysand arrives punctually, associates, listens, approves the interpretation, even gratifies his analyst with quite visible therapeutic results, giving him the impression of a job well done. In the analyst, the alarm signal may be that 'this treatment is going *too* well', together with the feeling that 'nothing's happening here'. Generally, the sign that inspires the second look in the analyst is the treatment's tendency to externalization, and the awakening of intense anxiety in the analysand by the mere idea, sent up as a test balloon by the analyst, that 'analysis is terminable'.

The subjacent situations are of very diverse natures, but common to all is the existence of a 'bastion', in the strict sense. This may be, for example, a concealed 'perverse field' (described by us elsewhere), in which analytic activity itself serves as a screen for the analysand's perverse satisfaction (voyeur, masochist, homosexual, etc.). It may also be an anti-death pact, sustained by the analysand's fantasy that 'as long as I'm in analysis, I won't die' and by the analyst's corresponding fantasy, 'if I terminate it, he will die'.

Just as non-process may be concealed beneath the appearance of process, process may also take place surreptitiously. The surreptitious processes may sometimes be seen in patients having great internal obstacles to their own progress, or who wish to carry out an old revenge against their primary objects, or who fear to provoke the wrath of the Gods or some counterattack from Fate if they show their improvement.

The process is achieved through the successive resolution of the obstacles opposing its movement: these are well known, but not all obey the same mechanisms.

These obstacles may be considered resistances if we adopt the definition of resistance formulated by Freud (1900) in 'The interpretation of dreams':

*whatever interrupts the progress of analytic work is a resistance.*

(p. 517)

We are quite familiar with those resistances that are classic expressions of defences and alterations of the ego. Any more-or-less experienced analyst knows how to categorize them and possesses technical resources to deal with them. They are material for our comprehension and interpretation, an intrinsic element of the process, a dialectic part of it. Their resolution is our daily task.

Far more serious are those resistances that, more than an obstacle – foreseeable and familiar – place analytic work in grave danger, compromise the process, and may come to interrupt it, to detract from it, and finally lead to completely opposite results to those intended. Of course, they are in the same range as the 'classic' resistances; we might say that they begin where the latter end, ranking in order of their gravity all the way to the extreme pole of reversal of the intentionality of the process. Among these phenomena, we can distinguish what is commonly called 'uncontrollable resistance', the 'impasse', and finally, the negative therapeutic reaction. Many analytic texts use these terms as if they were comparable or superimposable. However, we consider that a more precise usage of terminology would be useful in view of the technical implications.

The essential difference between these processes and the classic resistances resides in their intensity and durability. They are not elements of the process that appear and are resolved, giving way to other movements; they are far more stable, lasting obstacles manifestly accompanied by the relative or total incapacity of the analyst to deal with and resolve them. The analyst is much more involved and the gravity of the phenomenon is precisely that the analyst becomes powerless to manage it. We think that what we have called 'bastion' is subjacent to all these phenomena: they can only be understood in terms of field.

One commonly speaks of the pair: resistance-counterresistance. This pair leads to the bastion: a collusion between the patient's and the analyst's resistances, which we consider to be a crystallized formation within the field that stagnates its dynamics. Analyst and analysand go round and round an obstacle without being able to integrate it into the process.

The so-called 'uncontrollable resistance', seen in a unipersonal perspective, is a resistance that tends to become chronic and may finally interrupt the process. If it goes on too long, it arrives at the situation that today is called 'impasse'. The analyst feels technically involved in the 'impasse'. He searches in vain for the technical recourse that would allow him to resolve the situation of stagnation. The 'impasse' is resolved through 'acting out' of the patient, who leaves the treatment, or of the analyst, who tends to introduce technical innovations. However, sometimes the analyst hits upon the recourse that allows him to save himself and his patient, and if the treatment

beginning of an analysis, but after a certain time and in an apparently successful treatment. It is a negative response to effective achievements of the patient, or to interpretations that the analyst considers adequate: the patient begins rapidly to go back along the road he has travelled, arriving finally at a suicidal situation or a suicidal accident. He generally does not interrupt the treatment; rather he clings to it up to the catastrophic end. The 'impasse' may be brought to an end without major catastrophes; the negative therapeutic reaction is by definition catastrophic.

We think that a pathognomonic sign of the negative therapeutic reaction is the parasiting of analyst by patient. The analyst is not only concerned scientifically or technically, or even affectively by the patient, as in the 'impasse', but feels totally invaded by the patient. The 'impasse' is comparable to what is sometimes called neurosis of transference-countertransference. The negative therapeutic reaction may be thought of as the psychosis of transference-countertransference: analyst and analysand come to make up a *'folie à deux'*. Precisely because it is at the extreme end of the range of obstacles in the psychoanalytic process, it appears much more clearly to us as a specific product of the analytic field. By examining this extreme end, we can understand that, to a greater or lesser extent, the analyst is actively involved in all the phenomena that are manifestly serious obstacles to the analytic process. For this reason, we maintain that, subjacent to all these obstacles, lies a bastion.

When Freud defined the analytic procedure as the repetition of the initial neurosis and the resolution of this neurosis on the level of the transference, he pointed out the two poles of repetition in the technique: the first, as inertia or 'entropy' or the second, as a moment of the processes or part of progress. The introduction of the concept of field emphasizes a double position – i.e., in each of the participants in the process – of the repetition-compulsion. The analyst also has his ways of repeating: he may enter into collusion with the analysand, unconsciously captured in the fantasy of the field, he may enter into the stereotyping of the analysand when he transforms the sessions into a ritual, he may attempt to break up the repetition by force: can this be the key to understanding the pathology of certain technical innovations, certain undue 'terminations' of analysis? But perhaps the most deceptive form of repetition in the analyst has to do with his enclosure in his own scheme of reference, especially if it has acquired a certain degree of systematization and rationalization, and has tended to become a routine. The analyst's ideal could be the ferret, which never surfaces where it's being awaited, or the hidden prize of the treasure hunt.

The more rigid the analyst's scheme of reference, the more prone he is to accept the role of 'subject supposed to know' – i.e., the more he becomes an accomplice to the paralysing stereotyping of the process. For this reason, it is recommendable to pass through multiple schemes, harvesting for ourselves from several, though avoiding confusing eclecticisms: clinical practice is more varied than our schemes and does not cheat us of opportunities for invention.

As anti-repetition and anti-stereotyping procedure, analysis must constantly fight against the bastions being created, and try to destroy them as they are built up. Some bastions can appear to us as extremely proteiform, others as barely crystallized, and yet others as hard and paralysing for the analyst. *There is process as long as the bastions are being detected and destroyed.* In this sense, the two aspects of the interpretation (rupture and integration) are clearly complementary.

The bastion is always re-born in renewed forms: it is the most conspicuous clinical sign of the repetition-compulsion – i.e., of the death instinct. When the bastion as such is broken down, this expresses the triumph of the process over our intrinsic thanatic dullness – called in the past 'adhesiveness of the libido' – and this victory, though momentary, is perhaps the essence of the joy given us by our analytic work.

## Summary

The 'talking cure', named by Anna O. and discovered by Freud, has been widely expanded and diversified throughout our century. Our objective in this paper is to underline several points that seem to define the analytic process. We believe that forthcoming progress in psychoanalysis must arise from the study of clinical experience at its frontiers, at its topmost limits, in its failures. For this reason, we have concentrated our search on the analytic non-process, in the very places where the process stumbles or halts. This has led us to propose the introduction of several terms: 'field', 'bastion', 'second look'. When the process stumbles or halts, the analyst must question himself about the obstacle. The obstacle involves the analysand's transference and the analyst's countertransference, and poses rather confusing problems. The arrest of the process introduces us fully into the nature of its movement, its inherent temporality. If the process is to continue, then by what main-spring can we accomplish it? We describe this particular dialectic of processes and non-process as a task of overcoming the obstacles that describe its success or failure.

London: Hogarth [1942], pp. 441–504.

Alvarez de Toledo, L. 1954 El análisis del asociar, del interpretar y de las palabras. *Revista de Psicoanálisis,* 11:267–313.

Alvarez de Toledo, L. 1962 Psicoanalisis de la communicación verbal. *Acta Psiquiat. Argentina,* 8:16–24.

Ezriel, H. 1951 The scientific testing of psychoanalytic findings and theory. *British Journal of Medical Psychology,* 24: 30–34.

Freud, S. 1893–1895 Studies on hysteria. *The complete psychological works of Sigmund Freud,* 2.

Freud, S. 1900 The interpretation of dreams. *The complete psychological works of Sigmund Freud,* 4/5.

Freud, S. 1905 On psychotherapy. *The complete psychological works of Sigmund Freud,* 7.

Freud, S. 1910 Five lectures on psycho-analysis. *The complete psychological works of Sigmund Freud,* 11.

Freud, S. 1916–1917 Introductory lectures on psycho-analysis lecture XXVIII. Transference. *The complete psychological works of Sigmund Freud,* 16.

Freud, S. 1926 Inhibitions, symptoms and anxiety. *The complete psychological works of Sigmund Freud,* 20.

Freud, S. 1937a Constructions in psycho-analysis. *The complete psychological works of Sigmund Freud,* 23.

Freud, S. 1937b Analysis terminable and interminable. *The complete psychological works of Sigmund Freud,* 23.

Gill, M. 1956 *Topography and systems in psychoanalytic theory.* New York: International University Press.

Heimann, P. 1950 On transference. *International Journal of Psycho-Analysis,* 31:81–84.

Klein, M. 1934 A contribution to the psychogenesis of manic-depressive states. In *Contributions to psychoanalysis,* London: Hogarth [1948], pp. 282–310.

Klein, M. 1946 Notes on some schizoid mechanisms. In *Envy and gratitude and other works,* London: Hogarth [1975], pp. 1–24.

Klein, M. 1948 On the theory of anxiety and guilt. In *Developments in psychoanalysis,* London: Hogarth, pp. 271–291.

Krafft-Ebing, R. 1886 *Psychopathia Sexualis.* New York: Bell, 1965.

Lacan, J. 1958 The direction of the treatment and the principles of its power. In *Ecrits,* London: Tavistock [1977], pp. 226–288.

Pichon-Rivière, E. 1958 Referential schema and dialectical process in spiral as basis to a problem of the past. *International Journal of Psycho-Analysis,* 39: 294 (abstract).

Pontalis, J. 1981 *Frontiers in psychoanalysis.* London: Hogarth.

Racker, H. 1953 A contribution to the problem of countertransference. *International Journal of Psycho-Analysis,* 34: 313–324.

Rapaport, D. 1973 *The history of the concept of association of ideas.* New York: International University Press.

Strachey, J. 1934 The nature of the therapeutic action in psychoanalysis. *International Journal of Psycho-Analysis,* 15: 127–159.

# 6

# (1910–1961)

## R. Horacio Etchegoyen

The life of Heinrich Racker (1910–1961), short and rich, consists of a lattice of singular acts of creation and existential events, where moments of joy resound with sorrows and troubles that his spirit was able to overcome with temperance and serenity.

In the early 20th century, Naphtali Meyer Racker and Ella Spiegel and their three children – Miriam (1908), Heinrich (1910) and Ephraim (1913) – lived in a small town in Poland. When World War I broke out, the family sought refuge in Vienna.

As a child, Heinrich proved intelligent and musically gifted. He was appointed music professor in a prestigious Viennese institution at a very young age.

His father's illness ruined the family finances, and Heinrich had to replace him in the family business. Despite his desire to study medicine, he opted for the humanities, which also attracted him and was a shorter career.

In 1935, he obtained a doctorate in philosophy, and one year later he was admitted to the Vienna Institute of Psychoanalysis, where he was analyzed by Jeanne Lampl-de Groot. In 1937, he enrolled as a medical student. One year later, the Anschluss took place.

When Hitler annexed Austria in 1938, Racker left Austria. After passing through Denmark and Uruguay, he arrived in Argentina in 1939 when he was 29.

Racker's beginnings in Buenos Aires were difficult. With poor Spanish and economic difficulties, he had a brief analysis with Angel Garma, and made a living playing piano at parties and teaching music (Cesio, 1985).

Racker did his training analysis with Marie Langer, another refugee from Nazism who had arrived in Argentina in 1942. Racker started seminars at the Argentine Psychoanalytic Association (APA) in 1943. In 1947, when he was 37, he became an associate member of the APA. In 1950, he was full member, and one year later he was appointed Training Analyst.

While attending seminars on holiday in Uruguay, Racker met Noune Tronquoy, whom he married a few months later in April 1944, and they had two children. Racker published his first psychoanalytic paper, "On the jealousy of Othello," in 1945.

Racker's second article, "On a case of impotence, asthma and masochistic behavior," was the one he wrote to become an associate member of APA, and it was published in the *Revista de Psicoanálisis* in 1948. Although it is a production of the Argentine Racker, it is based on an analysis of a young Austrian, 20-year-old Peter, whom Racker analyzed for fifteen months in Vienna until his exile. Shortly after, he published a paper on Wagner, which together with one on Othello is part of Racker's lifelong interest in the exploration of art from a psychoanalytic perspective.

Racker was very young and had little clinical experience when he presented his first paper on countertransference, the issue that would establish him as one of the most original and creative analysts in the history of our discipline. "The countertransference neurosis" was read at APA in 1948 and caused quite a stir. (It became Chapter 5 of *Transference and countertransference*). This paper addresses the role of countertransference in the psychoanalytic process, highlighting the analyst as both interpreter and object. Of special interest is Racker's position regarding resistance. In agreement with Fenichel, Racker's opinion is that insofar as resistance is opposed to the analyst's work, it can not fail to arouse anger, but he studies the process not only as a rational response but also as a paranoid reaction of the analyst to be understood according to the dialectic transference / countertransference. Racker's approach is truly revolutionary.

In 1950, Racker lectured on transference, and in 1951 he delivered another lecture entitled "Notes on countertransference as a technical instrument." After the event, he discovered the work of Paula Heimann and found her ideas consistent with his. That encouraged him to publish the lecture in 1952. Among the examples given in the paper is Peter, and it is clear that already in Vienna, Racker foresaw the importance of countertransference.

It can be concluded, therefore, that starting in the early work on countertransference, Racker emphasizes the dialectical relationship between transference and countertransference, challenges the myth of the healthy psychoanalyst (not neurotic) and points out that countertransference reactions can give the analyst important clues regarding the analytic process. This is the main point of the new theory of countertransference, which appeared in the middle of the 20th century, thanks to Racker and Paula Heimann.

Clearly, both reached the same conclusions without knowing about each

explores carefully the relationship between transference and resistance, starting from free association, and argues that repetition serves both the resistance and the development of the analysis, because the repressed past is something current in the transference.

In the 1950s, Racker published the papers that were to appear in his book that was published in English (1988) with the title *Transference and countertransference*, while he simultaneously produced his writings on psychoanalysis and culture, published in 1957, as well as his ideas on psychopathological stratification, an issue that always interested him.

In May 1953, Racker presented what is likely his most accomplished paper, "The meanings and uses of countertransference" (Study VI), (Chapter 4 of *Transference and countertransference*). In it, he describes different types of countertransference, illustrated with clinical material, and distinguishes a direct countertransference, when the analyst's conflict is with the patient, and indirect countertransference, in which the analyst's conflict is with somebody other than the patient but linked to the process.

Following Helene Deutsch, Racker provides a further classification of countertransference, concordant and complementary, which has had a significant impact. In the concordant countertransference, the analyst is identified with a part of his patient's inner world, while in the complementary countertransference, the analyst takes the place of the patient's internal object. There are two more types of countertransference, occurrences and positions, which give a great richness and depth to the relationship analyst / analyzed.

As if it were a musical counterpoint, in 1957 he published in book format his papers on culture under the title *Psicoanálisis del espíritu*.

In early 1960, Racker could feel justified optimism. He was director of the Institute of Psychoanalysis and had decided to create a psychoanalytic clinic, later called Racker Center. He published his second book, *Estudios sobre tecnica psicoanalitica (Studies on psychoanalytic technique)*, which was very well received and later translated to Portuguese, Italian, English and French.

On August 15, Racker received a letter from Karl Menninger in which he was invited to be Sloan Visiting Professor at the Menninger School of Psychiatry.

To complete the exciting picture, he was invited to participate in the 22nd International Psychoanalytical Congress (Edinburgh, 1961). The Congress' theme, "The curative factors in psychoanalysis," would be the adequate stage to show him at the peak of his psychoanalytic development.

In mid-November, without knowing yet that he was sick, Racker delivered at the APA his paper on ethics and psychoanalysis. It was a day of glory. With a room full of friends, colleagues and disciples, Racker maintained a dialogue with Freud on the subject, advancing the idea that ethics comes from the inner world and not only from society. The conference, which was published posthumously, was the culmination of a noble life and a message of love of science and man.

This rosy situation tragically changed. On November 25, Racker knew he had cancer and his remaining days were numbered.

He wrote a farewell letter, which recalls the happy moments of his life and also the difficulties and sufferings he had to endure. There he says: "I was endowed by nature with the gift of feeling great happiness through music and intensely enjoying philosophical, scientific and literary creations." After thanking Oskar Adler and Olga Novakovic, his teacher in Vienna, Racker says: "In Buenos Aires I could realize my old dream of being a psychoanalyst. So I had the opportunity to devote to scientific research and create something."

He told his patients that he could not treat them any more because he was sick, and decided not to receive visitors. He accepted only the presence of Marie Langer; Santiago Chouhy Aguirre; his wife, Noune; and his sons until the end. Racker died at the height of his creativity in Buenos Aires on January 28, 1961, when he was 50 years old.

The highlights of Racker's life are in his writings, but he was also a great analyst and a true master. As an analyst, he was firm and cautious, serene, and not at all authoritarian; he was reserved, as every analyst should be, and not without humor. He was an eminent analyst, fair and democratic. His theory of countertransference is, after all, an attitude strongly psychoanalytic and democratic.

Racker thinks, as Strachey does, that the analyst's task is to break the vicious circle that chains the analysand to neurotic repetition. It also considers that the mutative interpretation is only possible if the analyst is really a good object in the double sense of "good," as a professional and as a person.

Respectful of his patient who suffers and comes to seek relief and love, he was also respectful of the setting, particularly regarding reserve and asymmetry. Racker always maintains balance without falling into the demagoguery of countertransference confession or authoritarian denial of his mistakes.

In the prologue to the Studies, Racker says he had always been surprised and concerned about the significant gap between the extent of knowledge and the limitations of psychoanalytic practice. He dedicated his life to

Cesio, Fidias R. (1985): "Heinrick Racker." *Revista de Psicoanálisis, 42*: 285–304.

Heimann, Paula (1949): "On Counter-transference." *International Journal of Psycho-Analysis, 31*: 81–84, 1950.

Racker, Heinrich (1953): "Contribucion al problema de la Estratificacion Psicopatologica." *Revista de Psicoanálisis, 14*: 276–391, 1957 [*International Journal of Psycho-Analysis, 38*: 223–239, 1957].

——— (1957): *Psicoanálisis del Espiritu*, Buenos Aires, Nova.

——— (1960): *Estudios sobre Tecnica Psicoanalitica*, Buenos Aires, Paidos.

——— (1988): *Transference and countertransference,* Karnac. London: Karnac Books Ltd.

# 7

# THE MEANINGS AND USES OF COUNTERTRANSFERENCE

*Heinrich Racker*

*This paper was originally read at a meeting of the Argentine Psychoanalytic Association in May 1953. The English version was published in 2007 in* Psychoanalytic Quarterly, *26: 303–357.*

## I

Freud describes transference as both the greatest danger and the best tool for analytic work. He refers to the work of making the repressed past conscious. Besides these two implied meanings of transference, Freud gives it a third meaning: it is in the transference that the analysand may relive the past under better conditions and in this way rectify pathological decisions and destinies. Likewise, three meanings of countertransference may be differentiated. It too may be the greatest danger and at the same time an important tool for understanding, an assistance to the analyst in his function as interpreter. Moreover, it affects the analyst's behavior; it interferes with his action as object of the patient's re-experience in that new fragment of life that is the analytic situation, in which the patient should meet with greater understanding and objectivity than he found in the reality or fantasy of his childhood.

What have present-day writers to say about the problem of counter-transference?[1]

Lorand (16) writes mainly about the dangers of countertransference for analytic work. He also points out the importance of taking countertransference reactions into account, for they may indicate some important subject to be worked through with the patient. He emphasizes the necessity of the analyst being always aware of his countertransference, and discusses specific problems such as the conscious desire to heal, the relief analysis may afford the analyst from his own problems, and narcissism and the interference of personal motives in clinical purposes. He also emphasizes the fact that these problems of countertransference concern not only the candidate but also the experienced analyst.

Winnicott (24) is specifically concerned with 'objective and justified

in his re-experience of childhood.

Heimann (11) deals with countertransference as a tool for understanding the analysand. The 'basic assumption is that the analyst's unconscious understands that of his patient. This rapport on the deep level comes to the surface in the form of feelings that the analyst notices in response to his patient, in his countertransference'. This emotional response of the analyst is frequently closer to the psychological state of the patient than is the analyst's conscious judgment thereof.

Little (15) discusses countertransference as a disturbance to understanding and interpretation and as it influences the analyst's behavior with decisive effect upon the patient's re-experience of his childhood. She stresses the analyst's tendency to repeat the behavior of the patient's parents and to satisfy certain needs of his own, not those of the analysand. Little emphasizes that one must admit one's countertransference to the analysand and interpret it, and must do so not only in regard to 'objective' countertransference reactions (Winnicott) but also to 'subjective' ones.

Annie Reich (21) is chiefly interested in countertransference as a source of disturbances in analysis. She clarifies the concept of countertransference and differentiates two types: 'countertransference in the proper sense' and 'the analyst's using the analysis for acting out purposes'. She investigates the causes of these phenomena, and seeks to understand the conditions that lead to good, excellent, or poor results in analytic activity.

Gitelson (10) distinguishes between the analyst's 'reactions to the patient as a whole' (the analyst's 'transferences') and the analyst's 'reactions to partial aspects of the patient' (the analyst's 'countertransferences'). He is concerned also with the problems of intrusion of countertransference into the analytic situation, and states that, in general, when such intrusion occurs the countertransference should be dealt with by analyst and patient working together, thus agreeing with Little.

Weigert (23) favors analysis of countertransference insofar as it intrudes into the analytic situation, and she advises, in advanced stages of treatment, less reserve in the analyst's behavior and more spontaneous display of countertransference.

In the first of my own two papers on countertransference (17), I discussed countertransference as a danger to analytic work. After analyzing the resistances that still seem to impede investigation of countertransference, I attempted to show without reserve how Oedipal and preoedipal conflicts as well as paranoid, depressive, manic, and other processes persist in the 'countertransference neurosis' and how they interfere with the analyst's understanding, interpretation, and behavior. My remarks applied to 'direct' and 'indirect' countertransference.[2]

In my second paper (18), I described the use of countertransference experiences for understanding psychological problems, especially transference problems, of the analysand. In my principal points, I agreed with Heimann (11) and emphasized the following suggestions. 1. Countertransference reactions of great intensity, even pathological ones, should also serve as tools. 2. Countertransference is the expression of the analyst's identification with the internal objects of the analysand, as well as with his id and ego, and may be used as such. 3. Countertransference reactions have specific characteristics (specific contents, anxieties, and mechanisms) from which we may draw conclusions about the specific character of the psychological happenings in the patient.

The present paper is intended to amplify my remarks on countertransference as a tool for understanding the mental processes of the patient (including especially his transference reactions) – their content, their mechanisms, and their intensities. Awareness of countertransference helps one to understand what should be interpreted and when. This paper will also consider the influence of countertransference upon the analyst's behavior toward the analysand – behavior that affects decisively the position of the analyst as object of the re-experience of childhood, thus affecting the process of cure.

Let us first consider briefly countertransference in the history of psychoanalysis. We meet with a strange fact and a striking contrast. The discovery by Freud (7) of countertransference and its great importance in therapeutic work gave rise to the institution of didactic analysis, which became the basis and center of psychoanalytic training. Yet countertransference received little scientific consideration over the next 40 years. Only during the last few years has the situation changed, rather suddenly, and countertransference become a subject examined frequently and with thoroughness. How is one to explain this initial recognition, this neglect, and this recent change? Is there not reason to question the success of didactic analysis in fulfilling its function if this very problem, the discovery of which led to the creation of didactic analysis, has had so little scientific elaboration?

These questions are clearly important, and those who have personally witnessed a great part of the development of psychoanalysis in the last 40 years have the best right to answer them.[3] I will suggest but one explanation.

The lack of scientific investigation of countertransference must be due to rejection by analysts of their own countertransferences – a rejection that represents unresolved struggles with their own primitive anxiety and guilt. These struggles are closely connected with those infantile ideals that survive because of deficiencies in the didactic analysis of just those transference problems that later affect the analyst's countertransference. These deficien-

ing more fully the fact that we are still children and neurotics even when we are adults and analysts. Only in this way – by better overcoming our rejection of countertransference – can we achieve the same result in candidates.

The insufficient dissolution of these idealizations and underlying anxieties and guilt feelings leads to special difficulties when the child becomes an adult and the analysand an analyst, for the analyst unconsciously requires of himself that he be fully identified with these ideals. I think that it is at least partly for this reason that the Oedipus complex of the child toward its parents, and of the patient toward his analyst, has been so much more fully considered than that of the parents toward their children and of the analyst toward the analysand. For the same basic reason, transference has been dealt with much more than countertransference.

The fact that countertransference conflicts determine the deficiencies in the analysis of transference becomes clear if we recall that transference is the expression of the internal object relations; for understanding of transference will depend on the analyst's capacity to identify himself both with the analysand's impulses and defenses, and with his internal objects, and to be conscious of these identifications. This ability in the analyst will in turn depend upon the degree to which he accepts his countertransference, for his countertransference is likewise based on identification with the patient's id and ego and his internal objects. One might also say that transference is the expression of the patient's relations with the fantasied and real countertransference of the analyst. For just as countertransference is the psychological response to the analysand's real and imaginary transferences, so also is transference the response to the analyst's imaginary and real countertransferences. Analysis of the patient's fantasies about countertransference, which in the widest sense constitute the causes and consequences of the transferences, is an essential part of the analysis of the transferences. Perception of the patient's fantasies regarding countertransference will depend in turn upon the degree to which the analyst himself perceives his countertransference processes – on the continuity and depth of his conscious contact with himself.

To summarize, the repression of countertransference (and other pathological fates that it may meet) necessarily leads to deficiencies in the analysis of transference, which in turn lead to the repression and other mishandling of countertransference as soon as the candidate becomes an analyst. It is a heritage from generation to generation, similar to the heritage of idealizations and denials concerning the imagoes of the parents, which continue working even when the child becomes a father or mother. The child's mythology is prolonged in the mythology of the analytic situation,[4] the analyst himself being partially subject to it and collaborating unconsciously in its maintenance in the candidate.

Before illustrating these statements, let us briefly consider one of those ideals in its specifically psychoanalytic expression: the ideal of the analyst's objectivity. No one, of course, denies the existence of subjective factors in the analyst and of countertransference in itself; but there seems to exist an important difference between what is generally acknowledged in practice and the real state of affairs. The first distortion of truth in 'the myth of the analytic situation' is that analysis is an interaction between a sick person and a healthy one. The truth is that it is an interaction between two personalities, in both of which the ego is under pressure from the id, the superego, and the external world; each personality has its internal and external dependences, anxieties, and pathological defenses; each is also a child with its internal parents; and each of these whole personalities – that of the analysand and that of the analyst – responds to every event of the analytic situation.[5] Besides these similarities between the personalities of analyst and analysand, there also exist differences, and one of these is in 'objectivity'. The analyst's objectivity consists mainly in a certain attitude toward his own subjectivity and countertransference. The neurotic (obsessive) ideal of objectivity leads to repression and blocking of subjectivity and so to the apparent fulfillment of the myth of the 'analyst without anxiety or anger'. The other neurotic extreme is that of 'drowning' in the countertransference. True objectivity is based upon a form of internal division that enables the analyst to make himself (his own countertransference and subjectivity) the object of his continuous observation and analysis. This position also enables him to be relatively 'objective' toward the analysand.

## II

The term countertransference has been given various meanings. They may be summarized by the statement that for some authors countertransference includes everything that arises in the analyst as psychological response to the analysand, whereas for others not all this should be called countertransference.

Some, for example, prefer to reserve the term for what is infantile in the relationship of the analyst with his analysand, while others make different limitations (Annie Reich [21] and Gitelson [10]). Hence efforts to differentiate from each other certain of the complex phenomena of countertransference lead to confusion or to unproductive discussions of terminology. Freud invented the term countertransference in evident analogy to transference,

in particular have important influence on the relationship of the analysand with the analyst, but we also know that all these present factors are experienced according to the past and the fantasy – according, that is to say, to a transference predisposition. As determinants of the transference neurosis and, in general, of the psychological situation of the analysand toward the analyst, we have both the transference predisposition and the present real and especially analytic experiences, the transference in its diverse expressions being the resultant of these two factors.

Analogously, in the analyst there are the countertransference predisposition and the present real, and especially analytic, experiences; and the countertransference is the resultant. It is precisely this fusion of present and past, the continuous and intimate connection of reality and fantasy, of external and internal, conscious and unconscious, that demands a concept embracing the totality of the analyst's psychological response, and renders it advisable, at the same time, to keep for this totality of response the accustomed term 'countertransference'. Where it is necessary for greater clarity one might speak of 'total countertransference' and then differentiate and separate within it one aspect or another. One of its aspects consists precisely in what is transferred in countertransference; this is the part that originates in an earlier time and that is especially the infantile and primitive part within total countertransference. Another of these aspects – closely connected with the previous one – is what is neurotic in countertransference; its main characteristics are the unreal anxiety and the pathological defenses. Under certain circumstances one may also speak of a countertransference neurosis (15), (17).

To clarify better the concept of countertransference, one might start from the question of what happens, in general terms, in the analyst in his relationship with the patient. The first answer might be: everything happens that can happen in one personality faced with another. But this says so much that it says hardly anything. We take a step forward by bearing in mind that in the analyst there is a tendency that normally predominates in his relationship with the patient: it is the tendency pertaining to his function of being an analyst, that of understanding what is happening in the patient. Together with this tendency there exist toward the patient virtually all the other possible tendencies, fears, and other feelings that one person may have toward another. The intention to understand creates a certain predisposition, a predisposition to identify oneself with the analysand, which is the basis of comprehension. The analyst may achieve this aim by identifying his ego with the patient's ego or, to put it more clearly although with a certain terminological inexactitude, by identifying each part of his personality with the corresponding psychological part in the patient – his id with the patient's id, his ego with the ego, his superego with the superego, accepting these identifications in his consciousness. But this does not always happen, nor is it all that happens. Apart from these identifications, which might be called concordant (or homologous) identifications, there exist also highly important identifications of the analyst's ego with the patient's internal objects, for example, with the superego. Adapting an expression from Helene Deutsch, they might be called complementary identifications.[6] We will consider these two kinds of identification and their destinies later. Here we may add the following notes.

1    The concordant identification is based on introjection and projection, or, in other terms, on the resonance of the exterior in the interior, on recognition of what belongs to another as one's own ('this part of you is I') and on the equation of what is one's own with what belongs to another ('this part of me is you'). The processes inherent in the complementary identifications are the same, but they refer to the patient's objects. The greater the conflicts between the parts of the analyst's personality, the greater are his difficulties in carrying out the concordant identifications in their entirety.

2    The complementary identifications are produced by the fact that the patient treats the analyst as an internal (projected) object, and in consequence the analyst feels treated as such; that is, he identifies himself with this object. The complementary identifications are closely connected with the destiny of the concordant identifications: it seems that to the degree to which the analyst fails in the concordant identifications and rejects them, certain complementary identifications become intensified. It is clear that rejection of a part or tendency in the analyst himself – his aggressiveness, for instance – may lead to a rejection of the patient's aggressiveness (whereby this concordant identification fails) and that such a situation leads to a greater complementary identification with the patient's rejecting object, toward which this aggressive impulse is directed.

3   Current usage applies the term 'countertransference' to the complementary identifications only; that is to say, to those psychological processes in the analyst by which, because he feels treated as and partially identifies himself with an internal object of the patient, the patient becomes an internal (projected) object of the analyst. Usually excluded from the concept countertransference are the concordant identifications – those

the concept of countertransference. One is thus faced with the choice of entering upon a terminological discussion or of accepting the term in this wider sense. I think that for various reasons the wider sense is to be preferred. If one considers that the analyst's concordant identifications (his 'understandings') are a sort of reproduction of his own past processes, especially of his own infancy, and that this reproduction or re-experience is carried out as response to stimuli from the patient, one will be more ready to include the concordant identifications in the concept of countertransference. Moreover, the concordant identifications are closely connected with the complementary ones (and thus with 'countertransference' in the popular sense), and this fact renders advisable a differentiation but not a total separation of the terms. Finally, it should be borne in mind that the disposition to empathy – that is, to concordant identification – springs largely from the sublimated positive countertransference, which likewise relates empathy with countertransference in the wider sense. All this suggests, then, the acceptance of countertransference as the totality of the analyst's psychological response to the patient. If we accept this broad definition of countertransference, the difference between its two aspects mentioned above must still be defined. On the one hand, we have the analyst as subject and the patient as object of knowledge, which in a certain sense annuls the 'object relationship', properly speaking; and there arises in its stead the approximate union or identity between the subject's and the object's parts (experiences, impulses, defenses). The aggregate of the processes pertaining to that union might be designated, where necessary, 'concordant countertransference'. On the other hand, we have an object relationship very like many others, a real 'transference' in which the analyst 'repeats' previous experiences, the patient representing internal objects of the analyst. The aggregate of these experiences, which also exist always and continually, might be termed 'complementary countertransference'.[7]

A brief example may be opportune here. Consider a patient who threatens the analyst with suicide. In such situations there sometimes occurs rejection of the concordant identifications by the analyst and an intensification of his identification with the threatened object. The anxiety that such a threat can cause the analyst may lead to various reactions or defense mechanisms within him – for instance, annoyance with the patient. This – his anxiety and annoyance – would be contents of the 'complementary countertransference'. The perception of his annoyance may, in turn, originate guilt feelings in the analyst and these lead to desires for reparation and to intensification of the 'concordant' identification and 'concordant' countertransference.

Moreover, these two aspects of 'total countertransference' have their analogy in transference. Sublimated positive transference is the main and indispensable motive force for the patient's work; it does not in itself constitute a technical problem. Transference becomes a 'subject', according to Freud's words, mainly when 'it becomes resistance', when, because of resistance, it has become sexual or negative (8), (9). Analogously, sublimated positive countertransference is the main and indispensable motive force in the analyst's work (disposing him to the continued concordant identification), and also countertransference becomes a technical problem or 'subject' mainly when it becomes sexual or negative. And this occurs (to an intense degree) principally as a resistance – in this case, the analyst's – that is to say, as counter-resistance.

This leads to the problem of the dynamics of countertransference. We may already discern that the three factors designated by Freud as determinant in the dynamics of transference (the impulse to repeat infantile clichés of experience, the libidinal need, and resistance) are also decisive for the dynamics of countertransference. I shall return to this later.

## III

Every transference situation provokes a countertransference situation, which arises out of the analyst's identification of himself with the analysand's (internal) objects (this is the 'complementary countertransference'). These countertransference situations may be repressed or emotionally blocked but probably they cannot be avoided; certainly they should not be avoided if full understanding is to be achieved. These countertransference reactions are governed by the laws of the general and individual unconscious. Among these the law of talion is especially important. Thus, for example, every positive transference situation is answered by a positive countertransference; to every negative transference there responds, in one part of the analyst, a negative countertransference. It is of great importance that the analyst be conscious of this law, for awareness of it is fundamental to avoid 'drowning' in the countertransference. If he is not aware of it he will not be able to avoid entering into the vicious circle of the analysand's neurosis, which will hinder or even prevent the work of therapy.

A simplified example: if the patient's neurosis centers round a conflict with his introjected father, he will project the latter upon the analyst and treat

sis. Hence it is of the greatest importance that the analyst develops within himself an ego observer of his countertransference reactions, which are, naturally, continuous. Perception of these countertransference reactions will help him to become conscious of the continuous transference situations of the patient and interpret them rather than be unconsciously ruled by these reactions, as not seldom happens. A well-known example is the 'revengeful silence' of the analyst. If the analyst is unaware of these reactions there is danger that the patient will have to repeat, in his transference experience, the vicious circle brought about by the projection and introjection of 'bad objects' (in reality, neurotic ones) and the consequent pathological anxieties and defenses; but transference interpretations made possible by the analyst's awareness of his countertransference experience make it possible to open important breaches in this vicious circle.

To return to the previous example: if the analyst is conscious of what the projection of the father-imago upon him provokes in his own countertrans-ference, he can more easily make the patient conscious of this projection and the consequent mechanisms. Interpretation of these mechanisms will show the patient that the present reality is not identical with his inner per-ceptions (for, if it were, the analyst would not interpret and otherwise act as an analyst); the patient then introjects a reality better than his inner world. This sort of rectification does not take place when the analyst is under the sway of his unconscious countertransference.

Let us consider some applications of these principles. To return to the question of what the analyst does during the session and what happens within him, one might reply at first thought that the analyst listens. But this is not completely true: he listens most of the time, or wishes to listen, but is not invariably doing so. Ferenczi (6) refers to this fact and expresses the opinion that the analyst's distractibility is of little importance, for the patient at such moments must certainly be in resistance. Ferenczi's remark (which dates from the year 1918) sounds like an echo from the era when the analyst was mainly interested in the repressed impulses, because now that we attempt to analyze resistance, the patient's manifestations of resistance are as significant as any other of his productions. At any rate, Ferenczi here refers to a countertransference response and deduces from it the analysand's psychological situation. He says '. . . we have unconsciously reacted to the emptiness and futility of the associations given at this moment with the withdrawal of the conscious charge'. The situation might be described as one of mutual withdrawal. The analyst's withdrawal is a response to the analysand's withdrawal – which, however, is a response to an imagined or real psychological position of the analyst. If we have withdrawn – if we are not listening but are thinking of something else – we may utilize this event in the service of the analysis like any other information we acquire. And the guilt we may feel over such a withdrawal is just as utilizable analytically as any other countertransference reaction. Ferenczi's next words, 'the danger of the doctor's falling asleep . . . need not be regarded as grave because we awake at the first occurrence of any importance for the treatment', are clearly intended to placate this guilt. But better than to allay the analyst's guilt would be to use it to promote the analysis – and indeed so to use the guilt would be the best way of alleviating it. In fact, we encounter here a cardinal problem of the relation between transference and countertransference, and of the therapeutic process in general. For the analyst's withdrawal is only an example of how the unconscious of one person responds to the unconscious of another. This response seems in part to be governed, insofar as we identify ourselves with the unconscious objects of the analysand, by the law of talion; and, insofar as this law unconsciously influences the analyst, there is danger of a vicious circle of reactions between them, for the analysand also responds 'talionically' in his turn, and so on without end.

Looking more closely, we see that the 'talionic response' or 'identification with the aggressor' (the frustrating patient) is a complex process. Such a psychological process in the analyst usually starts with a feeling of displeasure or of some anxiety as a response to this aggression (frustration) and, because of this feeling, the analyst identifies himself with the 'aggressor'. By the term 'aggressor' we must designate not only the patient but also some internal object of the analyst (especially his own superego or an internal persecutor) now projected upon the patient. This identification with the aggressor, or persecutor, causes a feeling of guilt; probably it always does so, although awareness of the guilt may be repressed. For what happens is, on a small scale, a process of melancholia, just as Freud described it: the object has to some degree abandoned us; we identify ourselves with the lost object;[8] and then we accuse the introjected 'bad' object – in other words, we have guilt feelings. This may be sensed in Ferenczi's remark quoted above, in which mechanisms are at work designed to protect the analyst against these guilt feelings: denial of guilt ('the danger is not grave') and a certain accusation against the analysand for the 'emptiness' and 'futility' of his associations. In this way a vicious circle – a kind of paranoid ping-pong – has entered into the analytic situation.[9] Two situations of frequent occurrence illustrate both the complementary and the concordant identifications and the vicious circle these situations may cause.

and experiences in this way the domination of the superego over the patient's ego. The relation of the ego to the superego is, at bottom, a depressive and paranoid situation; the relation of the superego to the ego is, on the same plane, a manic one insofar as this term may be used to designate the dominating, controlling, and accusing attitude of the superego toward the ego. In this sense we may say, broadly speaking, that to a 'depressive-paranoid' transference in the analysand there corresponds – as regards the complementary identification – a 'manic' countertransference in the analyst. This, in turn, may entail various fears and guilt feelings, to which I shall refer later.[10]

2   When the patient, in defense against this situation, identifies himself with the superego, he may place the analyst in the situation of the dependent and incriminated ego. The analyst will not only identify himself with this position of the patient; he will also experience the situation with the content the patient gives it: he will feel subjugated and accused, and may react to some degree with anxiety and guilt. To a 'manic' transference situation (of the type called 'mania for reproaching') there corresponds, then – as regards the complementary identification – a 'depressive-paranoid' countertransference situation.

The analyst will normally experience these situations with only a part of his being, leaving another part free to take note of them in a way suitable for the treatment. Perception of such a countertransference situation by the analyst and his understanding of it as a psychological response to a certain transference situation will enable him the better to grasp the transference at the precise moment when it is active. It is precisely these situations and the analyst's behavior regarding them, and in particular his interpretations of them, that are of decisive importance for the process of therapy, for they are the moments when the vicious circle within which the neurotic habitually moves – by projecting his inner world outside and reintrojecting this same world – is or is not interrupted. Moreover, at these decisive points the vicious circle may be re-enforced by the analyst, if he is unaware of having entered it.

A brief example: an analysand repeats with the analyst his 'neurosis of failure', closing himself up to every interpretation or repressing it at once, reproaching the analyst for the uselessness of the analysis, foreseeing nothing better in the future, continually declaring his complete indifference to everything. The analyst interprets the patient's position toward him, and its origins, in its various aspects. He shows the patient his defense against the danger of becoming too dependent, of being abandoned, or being tricked, or of suffering counteraggression by the analyst, if he abandons his armor and indifference toward the analyst. He interprets to the patient his projection of bad internal objects and his subsequent sado-masochistic behavior in the transference; his need of punishment; his triumph and 'masochistic revenge' against the transferred parents; his defense against the 'depressive position' by means of schizoid, paranoid, and manic defenses (Melanie Klein); and he interprets the patient's rejection of a link that in the unconscious has a homosexual significance. But it may happen that all these interpretations, in spite of being directed to the central resistance and connected with the transference situation, suffer the same fate for the same reasons: they fall into the 'whirl in a void' (Leerlauf) of the 'neurosis of failure'. Now the decisive moments arrive. The analyst, subdued by the patient's resistance, may begin to feel anxious over the possibility of failure and feel angry with the patient. When this occurs in the analyst, the patient feels it coming, for his own 'aggressiveness' and other reactions have provoked it; consequently he fears the analyst's anger. If the analyst, threatened by failure, or, to put it more precisely, threatened by his own superego or by his own archaic objects, which have found an 'agent provocateur' in the patient, acts under the influence of these internal objects and of his paranoid and depressive anxieties, the patient again finds himself confronting a reality like that of his real or fantasied childhood experiences and like that of his inner world; and so the vicious circle continues and may even be re-enforced. But if the analyst grasps the importance of this situation, if, through his own anxiety or anger, he comprehends what is happening in the analysand, and if he overcomes, thanks to the new insight, his negative feelings and interprets what has happened in the analysand, being now in this new positive countertransference situation, then he may have made a breach – be it large or small – in the vicious circle.[11]

# IV

We have considered thus far the relation of transference and countertransference in the analytic process. Now let us look more closely into the phenomena of countertransference. Countertransference experiences may be divided into two classes. One might be designated 'countertransference thoughts'; the other 'countertransference positions'. The example just cited may serve as illustration of this latter class; the essence of this example lies in the fact that the analyst feels anxiety and is angry with the analysand – that is to say, he is in a certain countertransference 'position'. As an example of

returning, the fantasy occurs to him that the analysand will take back the money and say that the analyst took it away with him. On his return he finds the thousand pesos where he had left it. When the account has been settled, the analysand lies down and tells the analyst that when he was left alone he had fantasies of keeping the money, of kissing the note goodbye, and so on. The analyst's fantasy was based upon what he already knew of the patient, who in previous sessions had expressed a strong disinclination to pay his fees. The identity of the analyst's fantasy and the patient's fantasy of keeping the money may be explained as springing from a connection between the two unconsciouses, a connection that might be regarded as a 'psychological symbiosis' between the two personalities. To the analysand's wish to take money from him (already expressed on previous occasions), the analyst reacts by identifying himself both with this desire and with the object toward which the desire is directed; hence arises his fantasy of being robbed. For these identifications to come about there must evidently exist a potential identity. One may presume that every possible psychological con- stellation in the patient also exists in the analyst, and the constellation that corresponds to the patient's is brought into play in the analyst. A symbiosis results, and now in the analyst spontaneously occur thoughts corresponding to the psychological constellation in the patient.

In fantasies of the type just described and in the example of the analyst angry with his patient, we are dealing with identifications with the id, with the ego, and with the objects of the analysand; in both cases, then, it is a matter of countertransference reactions. However, there is an important difference between one situation and the other, and this difference does not seem to lie only in the emotional intensity. Before elucidating this dif- ference, I should like to emphasize that the countertransference reaction that appears in the last example (the fantasy about the thousand pesos) should also be used as a means to further the analysis. It is, moreover, a typical example of those 'spontaneous thoughts' to which Freud and others refer in advising the analyst to keep his attention 'floating' and in stressing the importance of these thoughts for understanding the patient. The countertransference reactions exemplified by the story of the thousand pesos are characterized by the fact that they threaten no danger to the analyst's objective attitude of observer. Here the danger is rather that the analyst will not pay sufficient attention to these thoughts or will fail to use them for understanding and interpretation. The patient's corresponding ideas are not always conscious, nor are they always communicated as they were in the example cited. But from his own countertransference 'thoughts' and feelings the analyst may guess what is repressed or rejected. It is important to recall once more our usage of the term 'countertransference', for many writers, perhaps the majority, mean by it not these thoughts of the analyst but rather that other class of reactions, the 'countertransference positions'. This is one reason why it is useful to differentiate these two kinds of reaction.

The outstanding difference between the two lies in the degree to which the ego is involved in the experience. In one case the reactions are experienced as thoughts, free associations, or fantasies, with no great emotional intensity and frequently as if they were somewhat foreign to the ego. In the other case, the analyst's ego is involved in the countertransference experience, and the experience is felt by him with greater intensity and as true reality, and there is danger of his 'drowning' in this experience. In the former example of the analyst who gets angry because of the analysand's resistances, the analysand is felt as really bad by one part of the analyst ('countertransference position'), although the latter does not express his anger. Now these two kinds of countertransference reaction differ, I believe, because they have different origins. The reaction experienced by the analyst as thought or fantasy arises from the existence of an analogous situation in the analysand – that is, from his readiness in perceiving and communicating his inner situation (as happens in the case of the thousand pesos) – whereas the reaction experienced with great intensity, even as reality, by the analyst arises from acting out by the analysand (as in the case of the 'neurosis of failure'). Undoubtedly there is also in the analyst himself a factor that helps to determine this difference. The analyst has, it seems, two ways of responding. He may respond to some situations by perceiving his reactions, while to others he responds by acting out (alloplastically or autoplastically). Which type of response occurs in the analyst depends partly on his own neurosis, on his inclination to anxiety, on his defense mechanisms, and especially on his tendencies to repeat (act out) instead of making conscious. Here we encounter a factor that determines the dynamics of countertransference. It is the one Freud emphasized as determining the special intensity of transference in analysis, and it is also responsible for the special intensity of countertransference.

Let us consider for a moment the dynamics of countertransference. The great intensity of certain countertransference reactions is to be explained by the existence in the analyst of pathological defenses against the increase of archaic anxieties and unresolved inner conflicts. Transference, I believe, becomes intense not only because it serves as a resistance to remembering, as Freud says, but also because it serves as a defense against a danger

becomes anxious and inwardly angry over the intense masochism of the analysand within the analytic situation. Such masochism frequently rouses old paranoid and depressive anxieties and guilt feelings in the analyst, who, faced with the aggression directed by the patient against his own ego, and faced with the effects of this aggression, finds himself in his unconscious confronted anew with his early crimes. It is often just these childhood conflicts of the analyst, with their aggression, that led him into this profession in which he tries to repair the objects of the aggression and to overcome or deny his guilt. Because of the patient's strong masochism, this defense, which consists of the analyst's therapeutic action, fails and the analyst is threatened with the return of the catastrophe, the encounter with the destroyed object. In this way the intensity of the 'negative countertransference' (the anger with the patient) usually increases because of the failure of the countertransference defense (the therapeutic action) and the analyst's subsequent increase of anxiety over a catastrophe in the countertransference experience (the destruction of the object).

This example also illustrates another aspect of the dynamics of countertransference. In a previous paper (20), I showed that the 'abolition of rejection'[12] in analysis determines the dynamics of transference and, in particular, the intensity of the transference of the 'rejecting' internal objects (in the first place, of the superego). The 'abolition of rejection' begins with the communication of 'spontaneous' thoughts. The analyst, however, makes no such communication to the analysand, and here we have an important difference between his situation and that of the analysand and between the dynamics of transference and those of countertransference. However, this difference is not so great as might be at first supposed, for two reasons: first, because it is not necessary that the free associations be expressed for projections and transferences to take place, and second, because the analyst communicates certain associations of a personal nature even when he does not seem to do so. These communications begin, one might say, with the plate on the front door that says Psychoanalyst or Doctor. What motive (in terms of the unconscious) would the analyst have for wanting to cure if it were not he that made the patient ill? In this way the patient is already, simply by being a patient, the creditor, the accuser, the 'superego' of the analyst; and the analyst is his debtor.

# V

The examples that follow illustrate the various kinds, meanings, and uses of countertransference reaction. First are described situations in which the countertransference is of too little intensity to drag the analyst's ego along with it; next, some situations in which the intense countertransference reaction intensely involves the ego; and finally, some examples in which the repression of countertransference prevents comprehension of the analysand's situation at the critical moment.

1. A woman patient asks the analyst whether it is true that another analyst named N has become separated from his wife and married again. In the associations that follow she refers repeatedly to N's first wife. The idea occurs to the analyst that the patient would also like to know who N's second wife is and that she probably wonders whether the second wife was a patient of N. The analyst further supposes that his patient (considering her present transference situation) is wondering whether her own analyst might not also separate from his wife and marry her. In accordance with this suspicion but taking care not to suggest anything, the analyst asks whether she is thinking anything about N's second wife. The analysand answers, laughing, 'Yes, I was wondering whether she was not one of his patients'. Analysis of the analyst's psychological situation showed that his 'spontaneous thought' was possible because his identification with the patient in his Oedipal desires was not blocked by repression, and also because he himself countertransferred his own positive Oedipal impulses, accepted by his conscious, upon the patient.

This example shows how, in the analyst's 'spontaneous thoughts' – which enable him to attain a deeper understanding – there intervenes not only the sublimated positive countertransference that permits his identification with the id and the ego of the patient but also the (apparently absent) 'complementary countertransference' – that is, his identification with the internal objects that the patient transfers and the acceptance in his conscious of his own infantile object relations with the patient.

2. In the following example the 'spontaneous thoughts', which are manifestly dependent upon the countertransference situation, constitute the guide to understanding.

A woman candidate associates about a scientific meeting at the Psychoanalytic Institute, the first she had attended. While she is associating, it occurs to the analyst that he, unlike most of the other didactic analysts, did not participate in the discussion. He feels somewhat vexed, he thinks that the analysand must have noticed this, and he perceives in himself some fear that she consequently regards him as inferior. He realizes that he would prefer that she not think this and not mention the occurrence; for this very reason, he points out to the analysand that she is rejecting thoughts

example shows the importance of observation of countertransference as a technical tool; it also shows a relation between a transference resistance and a countertransference resistance.

3. On shaking hands at the beginning of the session the analyst, noticing that the patient is depressed, experiences a slight sense of guilt. The analyst at once thinks of the last session, in which he frustrated the patient. He knows where the depression comes from, even before the patient's associations lead him to the same conclusion. Observation of the countertransference ideas, before and after the sessions, may also be an important guide for the analyst in understanding the patient's analytic situation. For instance, if a feeling of annoyance before entering the consulting room is a countertransference response to the patient's aggressive or domineering behavior, the annoyance may enable the analyst to understand beforehand the patient's anxiety which, at the most superficial layer, is fear of the analyst's anger provoked by the patient's behavior. Another instance occurs in the analyst who, before entering his consulting room, perceives a feeling of guilt over being late; he realizes that he often keeps this analysand waiting and that it is the analysand's pronounced masochistic submission that especially prompts him to this frustrating behavior. In other words, the analyst responds to the strong repression of aggression in the patient by doing what he pleases and abusing the patient's neurosis. But this very temptation that the analyst feels and yields to in his behavior, and the fleeting guilt feelings he experiences for this reason, can serve as a guide for him to comprehend the analysand's transference situation.

4. The following example from analytic literature likewise shows how the countertransference situation makes it possible to understand the patient's analytic situation in a way decisive for the whole subsequent course of the treatment. It is interesting to remark that the author seems unaware that the fortunate understanding is due to an unconscious grasp of the countertransference situation. I refer to the 'case with manifest inferiority feelings' published by Wilhelm Reich (22). After showing how, for a long period,

no interpretation achieved any success or any modification of the patient's analytic situation, Reich writes: 'I then interpreted to him his inferiority feelings toward me; at first this was unsuccessful but after I had persistently shown him his conduct for several days, he presented some communications referring to his tremendous envy not of me but of other men, to whom he also felt inferior. And then there emerged in me, like a lightning flash, the idea that his repeated complaints could mean only this: "The analysis has no effect upon me – it is no good, the analyst is inferior and impotent and can achieve nothing with me". The complaints were to be understood partly as triumph and partly as reproaches to the analyst'. If we inquire into the origin of this 'lightning idea' of Reich, the reply must be, theoretically, that it arose from identification with those impulses in the analysand or from identification with one of his internal objects. The description of the event, however, leaves little room for doubt that the latter, the 'complementary countertransference', was the source of Reich's intuition – that this lightning understanding arose from his own feeling of impotence, defeat, and guilt over the failure of treatment.

5. Now a case in which repression of the countertransference prevented the analyst from understanding the transference situation, while his later becoming conscious of the countertransference was precisely what brought this understanding.

For several days a patient had suffered from intense anxiety and stomachache. The analyst does not understand the situation until she asks the patient when it first began. He answers that it goes back to a moment when he bitterly criticized her for certain behavior, and adds that he has noticed that she has been rather depressed of late. What the patient says hits the nail on the head. The analyst has in truth felt somewhat depressed because of this aggression in the patient. But she has repressed her aggression against the patient that underlay her depression and has repressed awareness that the patient would also think, consciously or unconsciously, of the effect of his criticism. The patient was conscious of this and therefore connected his own anxieties and symptoms with the analyst's depression. In other words, the analyst scotomatized the connection between the patient's anxiety and pain and the aggression (criticism) perpetrated against her. This scotomatization of the transference situation was due to repression of the countertransference, for the aggression that the patient suspected in the analyst, and to which he responded with anxiety and gastric pains (self-aggression in anticipation) existed not only in his fantasy but also in the analyst's actual countertransference feelings.

The danger of the countertransference being repressed is naturally the greater the more these countertransference reactions are rejected by the ego ideal or the superego. To take, for instance, the case of a patient with an almost complete lack of 'respect' for the analyst, it may happen that the analyst's narcissism is wounded and he reacts inwardly with some degree of annoyance. If he represses this annoyance because it ill accords with the demands of his ego ideal, he deprives himself of an important guide in understanding the patient's transference; for the patient seeks to deny the distance between his internal (idealized) objects and his ego by means

and erotomanic fantasies in the analysand as well as to the situations underlying these. Repression of such countertransference reactions may prevent access to the appropriate technique. What is advisable, for instance, when the patient exhibits this sort of hypomanic behavior is not merely analytic 'tolerance' (which may be intensified by guilt feeling over the countertransference reactions), but, as the first step, making the patient conscious of the countertransference reactions of his own internal objects, such as the superego. For just as the analyst reacted with annoyance to the almost total 'lack of respect' in the patient, so also do the patient's internal objects; for in the patient's behavior there is aggressiveness against these internal objects that the patient once experienced as superior and as rejecting. In more general terms, I should say that patients with certain hypomanic defenses tend to regard their conduct as 'natural' and 'spontaneous' and the analyst as 'tolerant' and 'understanding', repressing at the same time the rejecting and intolerant objects latently projected upon the analyst. If the analyst does not repress his deeper reactions to the analysand's associations and behavior, they will afford him an excellent guide for showing the patient these same repressed objects of his and the relationship in which he stands toward them.

6. In analysis we must take into account the total countertransference as well as the total transference. I refer, in particular, to the importance of paying attention not only to what has existed and is repeated but also to what has never existed (or has existed only as a hope) – that is to say, to the new and specifically analytic factors in the situations of analysand and analyst. Outstanding among these are the real new characteristics of this object (of analyst or of analysand), the patient–doctor situation (the intention to be cured or to cure, to be restored or to restore), and the situation created by psychoanalytic thought and feeling (as, for instance, the situation created by the fundamental rule, that original permission and invitation, the basic expression of a specific atmosphere of tolerance and freedom).

Let us illustrate briefly what is meant by 'total transference'. During a psychoanalytic session, the associations of a man, under treatment by a woman analyst, concern his relations with women. He tells of the frustrations and rejection he has endured, and his inability to form relationships with women of culture. There appear sadistic and debasing tendencies toward women. It is clear that the patient is transferring his frustrating and rejecting imagoes upon the analyst, and from these has arisen his mistrust of her. The patient is actually expressing both his fear of being rejected by the analyst on account of his sadism (deeper: his fear of destroying her and of her retaliation) and, at bottom, his fear of being frustrated by her — a situation that in the distant past gave rise to this sadism. Such an interpretation would be a faithful reflection of the transference situation properly speaking. But in the total analytic situation there is something more. Evidently the patient needs and is seeking something through the session as such. What is it? What is this specific present factor, what is this prospective aspect, so to speak, of the transference situation? The answer is virtually contained in the interpretation given above: the analysand seeks to connect himself with an object emotionally and libidinally, the previous sessions having awakened his feelings and somewhat disrupted his armor; indirectly, he is asking the analyst whether he may indeed place his trust in her, whether he may surrender himself without running the risk of suffering what he has suffered before. The first interpretation refers to the transference only as a repetition of what has once existed; the latter, more complete interpretation refers to what has existed and also to what has never existed and is hoped for anew from the analytic experience.

Now let us study an example that refers to both the total transference and total countertransference situations. The illustration is once again drawn from Wilhelm Reich (22). The analysis has long centered around the analysand's smile, the sole analyzable expression, according to Reich, that remained after cessation of all the communications and actions with which the analysand had begun treatment. Among these actions at the start had been some that Reich interpreted as provocations (for instance, a gesture aimed at the analyst's head). It is plain that Reich was guided in this interpretation by what he had felt in countertransference. But what Reich perceived in this way was only a part of what had happened within him; for apart from the fright and annoyance (which, even if only to a slight degree, he must have felt), there was a reaction of his ego to these feelings, a wish to control and dominate them, imposed by his 'analytic conscience'. For Reich had given the analysand to understand that there is a great deal of freedom and tolerance in the analytic situation and it was this spirit of tolerance that made Reich respond to these 'provocations' with nothing but an interpretation. What the analysand aimed at doing was to test whether such tolerance really existed in the analyst. Reich himself later gave him this interpretation, and this interpretation had a far more positive effect than the first. Consideration of the total countertransference situation (the feeling of being provoked, and the 'analytic conscience' which determined the fate of this feeling) might have been from the first a guide in apprehending the total transference situation, which consisted in aggressiveness, in the original

sified vibration of archaic objects of his own. I wish now to present another example that shows how the analyst, not being conscious of such counter-transference responses, may make the patient feel exposed once again to an archaic object (the vicious circle) and how, in spite of his having some understanding of what is happening in the patient, the analyst is prevented from giving an adequate interpretation.

During her first analytic session, a woman patient talks about how hot it is and other matters that, to the analyst (a woman candidate), seem insignifi-cant. She says to the patient that very likely the patient dares not talk about herself. Although the analysand was indeed talking about herself (even when saying how hot it was), the interpretation was, in essence, correct, for it was directed to the central conflict of the moment. But it was badly formulated, and this was so partly because of the countertransference situation. For the analyst's 'you dare not' was a criticism, and it sprang from the analyst's feel-ing of being frustrated in a desire; this desire must have been that the patient overcome her resistance. If the analyst had not felt this irritation or if she had been conscious of the neurotic nature of her internal reaction of anxi-ety and annoyance, she would have sought to understand why the patient 'dared not' and would have told her. In that case the lack of courage that the analyst pointed out to the patient would have proved to be a natural response within a dangerous object relationship.

Pursuing the analyst's line of thought and leaving aside other possible interpretations, we may suppose that she would then have said to the analy-sand that something in the analytic situation (in the relationship between patient and analyst) had caused her fear and made her thoughts turn aside from what meant much to her to what meant little. This interpretation would have differed from the one she gave the patient in two points: first, the interpretation given did not express the object relationship that led to the 'not daring' and, second, it coincided in its formulation with superego judgments, which should be avoided as far as possible.[13] Superego judg-ment was not avoided in this case because the analyst was identified in countertransference with the analysand's superego without being conscious of the identification; had she been conscious of it, she would have interpreted, for example, the feared aggression from the superego (projected upon the analyst) and would not have carried it out by means of the interpretation. It appears that the 'interpretation of tendencies' without considering the total object relationship is to be traced, among other causes, to repression by the analyst of one aspect of his countertransference, his identification with the analysand's internal objects.

Later in the same session, the patient, feeling that she is being criticized, censures herself for her habit of speaking rather incoherently. She says her mother often remarks upon it, and then she criticizes her mother for not listening, as a rule, to what she says. The analyst understands that these statements relate to the analytic situation and asks her: 'Why do you think I'm not listening to you?' The patient replies that she is sure the analyst is listening to her.

What has happened? The patient's mistrust clashes with the analyst's desire for the patient's confidence; therefore the analyst does not analyze the situation. She cannot say to the patient, 'No, I will listen to you, trust me', but she suggests it with her question. Once again interference by the uncontrolled countertransference (the desire that the patient should have no resistance) converts good understanding into a deficient interpretation. Such happenings are important, especially if they occur often. And they are likely to do so, for such interpretations spring from a certain state of the analyst and this state is partly unconscious. What makes these happenings so important is the fact that the analysand's unconscious is fully aware of the analyst's unconscious desires. Therefore the patient once again faces an object that, as in this case, wishes to force or lure the patient into rejecting his mistrust and that unconsciously seeks to satisfy its own desires or allay its own anxieties rather than to understand and satisfy the therapeutic need of the patient.

All this we infer from the reactions of the patient, who submits to the analyst's suggestion, telling the analyst that she trusts her and so denying an aspect of her internal reality. She submits to the previous criticism of her cowardice and then, apparently, 'overcomes' the resistance, while in reality everything is going on unchanged. It cannot be otherwise, for the analysand is aware of the analyst's neurotic wish and her transference is determined by that awareness. To a certain degree, the analysand finds herself once again, in the actual analytic situation, confronting her internal or external infantile reality and to this same degree will repeat her old defenses and will have no valid reason for really overcoming her resistances, however much the analyst may try to convince her of her tolerance and understanding. This she will achieve only by offering better interpretations in which her neurosis does not so greatly interfere.

8. The following more detailed example demonstrates: (a) the talion law in the relationship of analyst and analysand; (b) how awareness of the countertransference reaction indicates what is happening in the transference and what at the moment is of the greatest significance; (c) what interpretation is most suitable to make a breach in the vicious circle; and (d) how the later associations show that this end has been achieved, even if only in part – for

saying that he feels completely disconnected from the analyst. He speaks with difficulty, as if he were overcoming a great resistance, and always in an unchanging tone of voice that seems in no way to reflect his instincts and feelings. Yet the countertransference response to the content of his associations (or, rather, of his narrative, for he exercises a rigid control over his ideas) does change from time to time. At a certain point the analyst feels a slight irritation. This is when the patient, a physician, tells him how, in conversation with another physician, he sharply criticized analysts for their passivity (they give little and cure little), for their high fees, and for their tendency to dominate their patients. The patient's statements and his behavior meant several things. It was clear, in the first place, that these accusations, though couched in general terms and with reference to other analysts, were directed against his own analyst; the patient had become the analyst's superego. This situation in the patient represents a defense against his own accusing superego, projected upon the analyst. It is a form of identification with the internal persecutors that leads to inversion of the feared situation. It is, in other words, a transitory 'mania for reproaching' as defense against a paranoid-depressive situation in which the superego persecutes the patient with reproaches and threatens him with abandonment. Together with this identification with the superego, there occurs projection of a part of the 'bad ego', and of the id, upon the analyst. The passivity (the mere receptiveness, the inability to make reparation), the selfish exploitation, and the domination he ascribes to the analyst are 'bad tendencies' of his own for which he fears reproach and abandonment by the analyst. At a lower stratum, this 'bad ego' consists of 'bad objects' with which the patient had identified himself as a defense against their persecution.

We already see that it would be premature to interpret this deeper situation; the patient will first have to face his 'bad ego': he will have to pass in transference through the paranoid-depressive situation in which he feels threatened by the superego-analyst. But even so we are still unsure of the interpretation to be given, for what the patient said and did has even at the surface still further meanings. The criticism he made to the other physician about analysts has the significance of rebellion, vengeance, and provocation; and, perhaps, of seeking for punishment as well as of finding out how much freedom the analyst allows, and simultaneously of subjugating and controlling this dangerous object, the analyst.

The analyst's countertransference reaction made clear to the analyst which of all these interpretations was most strongly indicated, for the countertransference reaction was the living response to the transference situation at that moment. The analyst felt (in accordance with the law of talion) a little anxious and angry at the aggression he suffered from the patient, and we may suppose that the patient in his unconscious or conscious fantasy sensed this annoyance in the internal object toward which his protesting behavior was directed, and that he reacted to this annoyance with anxiety. The 'disconnection' he spoke of in his first utterance must have been in relation to this anxiety, since it was because of this 'disconnection' that the analysand perceived no danger and felt no anxiety. By the patient's projection of that internal object the analyst is to the patient a tyrant who demands complete submission and forbids any protest. The transgression of this prohibition (the patient's protest expressed to his friend, the physician) must seem to the analyst – in the patient's fantasy – to be unfaithfulness, and must be responded to by the analyst with anger and emotional abandonment; we deduce this from the countertransference experience. In order to reconcile the analyst and to win him back, the patient accepts his anger or punishment and suffers from stomach-ache; – this he tells in his associations but without connecting the two experiences. His depression today is to be explained by this guilt feeling and, secondarily, by the object loss resulting from his increased 'disconnection'.

The analyst explains, in his interpretation, the meaning of the 'disconnection'. In reply the patient says that the previous day he recalled his conversation with that physician and that it did indeed cause him anxiety. After a brief pause he adds: 'and just now the thought came to me, well . . . and what am I to do with that?' The analyst perceived that these words once again slightly annoyed him. We can understand why. The patient's first reaction to the interpretation (he reacted by recalling his anxiety over his protest) had brought the analyst nearer to satisfying his desire to remove the patient's detachment. The patient's recollection of his anxiety had been at least one forward step, for he thus admitted a connection that he usually denied or repressed. But his next words frustrated the analyst once again, for they signified: 'that is of no use to me, nothing has changed'. Once again the countertransference reaction pointed out to the analyst the occurrence of a critical moment in the transference, and that here was the opportunity to interpret. At this moment also, in the patient's unconscious fantasy, must have occurred a reaction of anger from the internal object – just as actually happened in the analyst – to which the interpretation must be aimed. The patient's anxiety must have arisen from just this fantasy. His anxiety – and with it his detachment – could be diminished only by replacing that fantasized anger by an understanding of the patient's need to defend himself through that denial ('well . . . what am I to do with that?'). In reality the analyst, besides feeling annoyed, had understood that

of the analyst's tyranny – his dominating, exploiting, sadistic character – this dependence had to be prevented.

The analyst by awareness of his countertransference understood the patient's anxiety and interpreted it to him. The following associations showed that this interpretation had also been accurate.

The patient said shortly afterward that his depression had passed off, and this admission was a sign of progress because the patient was admitting that there was something good about the analyst. The next associations, moreover, permitted a more profound analysis of his transference neurosis, for the patient now revealed a deeper stratum. His underlying dependence became clear. Hitherto the interpretation had been confined to the guilt feelings and anxiety that accompanied his defenses (rebellion, denial, and others) against this very dependence. The associations referred to the fact that a mutual friend of the patient and of the analyst had a few days before told him that the analyst was going away on holiday that night and that this session would therefore be his last. In this way the patient admits the emotional importance the analyst possesses for him, a thing he always used to deny. We understand now also that his protest against analysts had been determined beforehand by the imminent danger of being forsaken by his analyst. When, just before the end of the session, the analyst explains that the information the friend gave him is false, the patient expresses anger with his friend and recalls how the friend has been trying lately to make him jealous of the analyst. Thus does the patient admit his jealousy of the analyst, although he displaces his anger onto the friend who roused his anxiety.

What has happened? And how is it to be explained?

The analyst's expected journey represented, in the unconscious of the patient, abandonment by internal objects necessary to him. This danger was countered by an identification with the aggressor; the threat of aggression (abandonment by the analyst) was countered by aggression (the patient's protest against analysts). His own aggression caused the patient to fear counteraggression or abandonment by the analyst. This anxiety remained unconscious but the analyst was able to deduce it from the counteraggression he perceived in his countertransference. If he had not interpreted the patient's transference situation, or if in his interpretation he had included any criticism of the patient's insistent and continuous rejection of the analyst or of his obstinate denial of any with the analyst, the patient would have remained in the vicious circle between his basic fear of abandonment and his defensive identification with the persecutor (with the object that abandons); he would have continued in the vicious circle of his neurosis. But the interpretation, which showed him the analyst's understanding of his conduct and of the underlying anxiety, changed (at least for that moment) the image of the analyst as persecutor. Hence the patient could give up his defensive identification with this image and could admit his dependence (the underlying stratum), his need for the analyst, and his jealousy.

And now once again in this new situation countertransference will show the content and origin of the anxiety that swiftly drives the analysand back to repetition of the defense mechanism he had just abandoned (which may be identification with the persecutor, emotional blocking, or something else). And once again interpretation of this new danger is the only means of breaking the vicious circle. If we consider the nature of the relationship that existed for months before the emotional surrender that occurred in this session, if we consider the paranoid situation that existed in the transference and countertransference (expressed in the patient by his intense characterological resistances and in the analyst by his annoyance) – if we consider all this background to the session just described, we understand that the analyst enjoys, in the patient's surrender, a manic triumph, to be followed of course by depressive and paranoid anxieties, compassion toward the patient, desires for reparation, and other sequelae. It is just these guilt feelings caused in the analyst by his manic feelings that may lead to his failure adequately to interpret the situation. The danger the patient fears is that he will become a helpless victim of the object's (the analyst's) sadism – of that same sadism the analyst senses in his 'manic' satisfaction over dominating and defeating the bad object with which the patient was defensively identified. The perception of this 'manic' countertransference reaction indicates what the present transference situation is and what should be interpreted.

If there were nothing else in the analyst's psychological situation but this manic reaction, the patient would have no alternative but must make use of the same old defense mechanisms that essentially constitute his neurosis. In more general terms, we should have to admit that the negative therapeutic reaction is an adequate transference reaction in the patient to an imagined or real negative countertransference in the analyst.[14] But even where such a negative countertransference really exists, it is a part only of the analyst's psychological response. For the law of talion is not the sole determinant of the responses of the unconscious; and, moreover, the conscious also plays a part in the analyst's psychological responses. As to the unconscious, there is of course a tendency to repair, which may even create a disposition to 'return good for evil'. This tendency to repair is in reality a wish to remedy, albeit upon a displaced object, whatever evil one may have thought or done. And as to the conscious, there is, first, the fact that the analyst's own

his psychological response. The knowledge, for instance, that behind the negative transference and the resistances lies simply thwarted love, helps the analyst to respond with love to this possibility of loving, to this nucleus in the patient however deeply it be buried beneath hate and fear.

9. The analyst should avoid, as far as possible, making interpretations in terms that coincide with those of the moral superego.[15] This danger is increased by the unconscious identification of the analyst with the patient's internal objects and, in particular, with his superego. In the example just cited, the patient, in conversation with his friend, criticized the conduct of analysts. In so doing he assumed the role of superego toward an internal object that he projected upon the analyst. The analyst identified himself with this projected object and reacted with unconscious anxiety and with annoyance to the accusation. He inwardly reproached the patient for his conduct and there was danger that something of this reproach (in which the analyst in his turn identified himself with the conduct of the patient as superego) might filter into his interpretation, which would then perpetuate the patient's neurotic vicious circle. But the problem is wider than this. Certain psychoanalytic terminology is likely to re-enforce the patient's confusion of the analyst with the superego. For instance, 'narcissism', 'passivity', and 'bribery of the superego' are terms we should not use literally or in paraphrase in treatment without careful reflection, just because they increase the danger that the patient will confuse the imago of the analyst with that of his superego. For greater clarity, two situations may be differentiated theoretically. In one, only the patient experiences these or like terms as criticism, because of his conflict between ego and superego, and the analyst is free of this critical feeling. In the other, the analyst also regards certain character traits with moral intolerance; he feels censorious, as if he were indeed a superego. Something of this attitude probably always exists, for the analyst identifies himself with the objects that the patient 'mistreats' (by his 'narcissism', or 'passivity', or 'bribery of the superego'). But even if the analyst had totally solved his own struggles against these

119

same tendencies and hence remained free from countertransference conflict with the corresponding tendencies in the patient, it would be preferable to point out to the patient the several conflicts between his tendencies and his superego, and not run the risk of making it more difficult for the patient to differentiate between the judgment of his own superego and the analyst's comprehension of these same tendencies through the use of a terminology that precisely lends itself to confusing these two positions.

One might object that this confusion between the analyst and the superego neither can nor should be avoided, since it represents an essential part of the analysis of transference (of the externalization of internal situations) and since one cannot attain clarity except through confusion. That is true; this confusion cannot and should not be avoided, but we must remember that the confusion will also have to be resolved and that this will be all the more difficult the more the analyst is really identified in his experience with the analysand's superego and the more these identifications have influenced negatively his interpretations and conduct.

# VI

In the examples presented we saw how to certain transference situations there correspond to certain countertransference situations, and vice versa. To what transference situation does the analyst usually react with a particular countertransference? Study of this question would enable one, in practice, to deduce the transference situations from the countertransference reactions. Next we might ask, to what imago or conduct of the object – to what imagined or real countertransference situation – does the patient respond with a particular transference? Many aspects of these problems have been amply studied by psychoanalysis, but the specific problem of the relation of transference and countertransference in analysis has received little attention.

The subject is so broad that we can discuss only a few situations and those incompletely, restricting ourselves to certain aspects. We must choose for discussion only the most important countertransference situations, those that most disturb the analyst's task and that clarify important points in the double neurosis, la névrose à deux, that arises in the analytic situation – a neurosis usually of very different intensity in the two participants.

1. What is the significance of countertransference anxiety?

Countertransference anxiety may be described in general and simplified terms as being of depressive or paranoid character.[16] In depressive anxiety the inherent danger consists in having destroyed the analysand or made him ill. This anxiety may arise to a greater degree when the analyst faces the danger that the patient may commit suicide, and to a lesser degree when there is deterioration or danger of deterioration in the patient's state of health. But the patient's simple failure to improve and his suffering and depression may also provoke depressive anxieties in the analyst. These anxieties usually increase the desire to heal the patient.

In referring to paranoid anxieties it is important to differentiate between 'direct' and 'indirect' countertransference (17). In direct countertransference

part determined by his professional performance. The feared aggression may take several forms, such as criticism, reproach, hatred, mockery, contempt, or bodily assault. In the unconscious it may be the danger of being killed or castrated or otherwise menaced in an archaic way.

The transference situations of the patient to which the depressive anxieties of the analyst are a response are, above all, those in which the patient, through an increase in frustration[17] (or danger of frustration) and in the aggression that it evokes, turns the aggression against himself. We are dealing, on one plane, with situations in which the patient defends himself against a paranoid fear of retaliation by anticipating this danger, by carrying out himself and against himself part of the aggression feared from the object transferred onto the analyst, and threatening to carry it out still further. In this psychological sense it is really the analyst who attacks and destroys the patient; and the analyst's depressive anxiety corresponds to this psychological reality. In other words, the countertransference depressive anxiety arises, above all, as a response to the patient's 'masochistic defense' – which at the same time represents a revenge ('masochistic revenge') – and as a response to the danger of its continuing. On another plane, this turning of the aggression against himself is carried out by the patient because of his own depressive anxieties; he turns it against himself in order to protect himself against re-experiencing the destruction of the objects and to protect these from his own aggression.

The paranoid anxiety in 'direct' countertransference is a reaction to the danger arising from various aggressive attitudes of the patient himself. The analysis of these attitudes shows that they are themselves defenses against, or reactions to, certain aggressive imagoes; and these reactions and defenses are governed by the law of talion or else, analogously to this, by identification with the persecutor. The reproach, contempt, abandonment, bodily assault – all these attitudes of menace or aggression in the patient that give rise to countertransference paranoid anxieties – are responses to (or anticipations of) equivalent attitudes of the transferred object.

The paranoid anxieties in 'indirect' countertransference are of a more complex nature since the danger for the analyst originates in a third party. The patient's transference situations that provoke the aggression of this 'third party' against the analyst may be of various sorts. In most cases, we are dealing with transference situations (masochistic or aggressive) similar to those that provoke the 'direct' countertransference anxieties previously described.

The common denominator of all the various attitudes of patients that provoke anxiety in the analyst is to be found, I believe, in the mechanism of 'identification with the persecutor'; the experience of being liberated from the persecutor and of triumphing over him, implied in this identification, suggests our designating this mechanism as a manic one. This mechanism may also exist where the manifest picture in the patient is quite the opposite, namely in certain depressive states; for the manic conduct may be directed either toward a projected object or toward an introjected object, it may be carried out alloplastically or autoplastically. The 'identification with the persecutor' may even exist in suicide, inasmuch as this is a 'mockery' of the fantasized or real persecutors, by anticipating the intentions of the persecutors and by one doing to oneself what they wanted to do; this 'mockery' is the manic aspect of suicide. The 'identification with the persecutor' in the patient is, then, a defense against an object felt as sadistic that tends to make the patient the victim of a manic feast; and this defense is carried out either through the introjection of the persecutor in the ego, turning the analyst into the object of the 'manic tendencies', or through the introjection of the persecutor in the superego, taking the ego as the object of its manic trend. Let us illustrate.

An analysand decides to take a pleasure trip to Europe. He experiences this as a victory over the analyst both because he will free himself from the analyst for two months and because he can afford this trip whereas the analyst cannot. He then begins to be anxious lest the analyst seek revenge for the patient's triumph. The patient anticipates this aggression by becoming unwell, developing fever and the first symptoms of influenza. The analyst feels slight anxiety because of this illness and fears, recalling certain previous experiences, a deterioration in the state of health of the patient, who still however continues to come to the sessions. Up to this point, the situation in the transference and countertransference is as follows. The patient is in a manic relation to the analyst, and he has anxieties of preponderantly paranoid type. The analyst senses some irritation over the abandonment and some envy of the patient's great wealth (feelings ascribed by the patient in his paranoid anxieties to the analyst); but at the same time the analyst feels satisfaction at the analysand's real progress which finds expression in the very fact that the trip is possible and that the patient has decided to make it. The analyst perceives a wish in part of his personality to bind the patient to himself and use the patient for his own needs. In having this wish he resembles the patient's mother, and he is aware that he is in reality identified with the domineering and vindictive object with which the patient identifies him. Hence the patient's illness seems, to the analyst's unconscious, a result of the analyst's own wish, and the analyst therefore experiences depressive (and paranoid) anxieties.

ence in his decision to take a trip) and then by using a masochistic defense to escape vengeance.

In brief, the analyst's depressive (and paranoid) anxiety is his emotional response to the patient's illness; and the patient's illness is itself a masochistic defense against the object's vindictive persecution. This masochistic defense also contains a manic mechanism in that it derides, controls, and dominates the analyst's aggression. In the stratum underlying this we find the patient in a paranoid situation in face of the vindictive persecution by the analyst – a fantasy that coincides with the analyst's secret irritation. Beneath this paranoid situation, and causing it, is an inverse situation: the patient is enjoying a manic triumph (his liberation from the analyst by going on a trip), but the analyst is in a paranoid situation (he is in danger of being defeated and abandoned). And, finally, beneath this we find a situation in which the patient is subjected to an object imago that wants to make of him the victim of its aggressive tendencies, but this time not in order to take revenge for intentions or attitudes in the patient, but merely to satisfy its own sadism – an imago that originates directly from the original sufferings of the subject.

In this way, the analyst was able to deduce from each of his countertransference sensations a certain transference situation; the analyst's fear of deterioration in the patient's health enabled him to perceive the patient's need to satisfy the avenger and to control and restrain him, partially inverting (through the illness) the roles of victimizer and victim, thus alleviating his guilt feeling and causing the analyst to feel some of the guilt. The analyst's irritation over the patient's trip enabled him to see the patient's need to free himself from a dominating and sadistic object, to see the patient's guilt feelings caused by these tendencies, and also to see his fear of the analyst's revenge. By his feeling of triumph the analyst was able to detect the anxiety and depression caused in the patient by his dependence upon this frustrating, yet indispensable, object. And each of these transference situations indicated to the analyst the patient's object imagoes – the fantasied or real countertransference situations that determined the transference situations.

2. What is the meaning of countertransference aggression?

In the preceding pages, we have seen that the analyst may experience, besides countertransference anxiety, annoyance, rejection, desire for vengeance, hatred, and other emotions. What are the origin and meaning of these emotions?

Countertransference aggression usually arises in the face of frustration (or danger of frustration) of desires that may superficially be differentiated into 'direct' and 'indirect'. Both direct and indirect desires are principally wishes to get libido or affection. The patient is the chief object of direct desires in the analyst, who wishes to be accepted and loved by him. The object of the indirect desires of the analyst may be, for example, other analysts from whom he wishes to get recognition or admiration through his successful work with his patients, using the latter as means to this end (17). This aim to get love has, in general terms, two origins: an instinctual origin (the primitive need of union with the object) and an origin of a defensive nature (the need of neutralizing, overcoming, or denying the rejections and other dangers originating from the internal objects, in particular from the superego). The frustrations may be differentiated, descriptively, into those of active type and those of passive type. Among the active frustrations is direct aggression by the patient, his mockery, deceit, and active rejection. To the analyst, active frustration means exposure to a predominantly 'bad' object; the patient may become, for example, the analyst's superego, which says to him 'you are bad'. Examples of frustration of passive type are passive rejection, withdrawal, partial abandonment, and other defenses against the dependence on the analyst. These signify frustrations of the analyst's need of union with the object.

In summary, we may say that countertransference aggression usually arises when there is frustration of the analyst's desires that spring from Eros, both those arising from his 'original' instinctive and affective drives and those arising from his need of neutralizing or annulling his own Thanatos (or the action of his internal 'bad objects') directed against the ego or against the external world. Owing partly to the analyst's own neurosis (and also to certain characteristics of analysis itself) these desires of Eros sometimes acquire the unconscious aim of bringing the patient to a state of dependence. Hence countertransference aggression may be provoked by the rejection of this dependence by the patient who rejects any with the analyst and refuses to surrender to him, showing this refusal by silence, denial, secretiveness, repression, blocking, or mockery.

Next we must establish what it is that induces the patient to behave in this way, to frustrate the analyst, to withdraw from him, to attack him. If we know this we shall know what we have to interpret when countertransference aggression arises in us, being able to deduce from the countertransference the transference situation and its cause. This cause is a fantasied countertransference situation or, more precisely, some actual or feared bad conduct from the projected object. Experience shows that, in somewhat general terms, this bad or threatening conduct of the object is usually an equivalent of the conduct of the patient (to which the analyst has reacted internally with aggression). We also understand why this is so: the patient's conduct springs from that most primitive of reactions, the talion reaction, or

tion that is less direct. To exemplify: a woman patient, upon learning that the analyst is going on holiday, remains silent a long while; she withdraws, through her silence, as a talion response to the analyst's withdrawal. Deeper analysis shows that the analyst's holiday is, to the patient, equivalent to the primal scene; and this is equivalent to destruction of her as a woman, and her immediate response must be a similar attack against the analyst. This aggressive (castrating) impulse is rejected and the result, her silence, is a compromise between her hostility and its rejection; it is a transformed identification with the persecutor.

To sum up: (a) The countertransference reactions of aggression (or of its equivalent) occur in response to transference situations in which the patient frustrates certain desires of the analyst. These frustrations are equivalent to abandonment or aggression, which the patient carries out or with which he threatens the analyst, and they place the analyst, at first, in a depressive or paranoid situation. The patient's defense is in one aspect equivalent to a manic situation, for he is freeing himself from a persecutor.[18] (b) This transference situation is the defense against certain object imagoes. There may be an object that persecutes the subject sadistically, vindictively, or morally, or an object that the patient defends from his own destructiveness by an attack against his own ego (19); in these, the patient attacks – as Freud and Abraham have shown in the analysis of melancholia and suicide – at the same time the internal object and the external object (the analyst). (c) The analyst who is placed by the alloplastic or autoplastic attacks of the patient in a paranoid or depressive situation sometimes defends himself against these attacks by using the same identification with the aggressor or persecutor as the patient used. Then the analyst virtually becomes the persecutor, and to this the patient (insofar as he presupposes such a reaction from his internal and projected object) responds with anxiety. This anxiety and its origin is nearest to consciousness, and is therefore the first thing to interpret.

3. Countertransference guilt feelings are an important source of countertransference anxiety; the analyst fears his 'moral conscience'. Thus, for

125

instance, a serious deterioration in the condition of the patient may cause the analyst to suffer reproach by his own superego, and also cause him to fear punishment. When such guilt feelings occur, the superego of the analyst is usually projected upon the patient or upon a third person, the analyst being the guilty ego. The accuser is the one who is attacked, the victim of the analyst. The analyst is the accused; he is charged with being the victimizer. It is therefore the analyst who must suffer anxiety over his object, and dependence upon it.

As in other countertransference situations, the analyst's guilt feeling may have either real causes or fantasied causes, or a mixture of the two. A real cause exists in the analyst who has neurotic negative feelings that exercise some influence over his behavior, leading him, for example, to interpret with aggressiveness or to behave in a submissive, seductive, or unnecessarily frustrating way. But guilt feelings may also arise in the analyst over, for instance, intense submissiveness in the patient even though the analyst had not driven the patient into such conduct by his procedure. Or he may feel guilty when the analysand becomes depressed or ill, although his therapeutic procedure was right and proper according to his own conscience. In such cases, the countertransference guilt feelings are evoked not by what procedure he has actually used but by his awareness of what he might have done in view of his latent disposition. In other words, the analyst identifies himself in fantasy with a bad internal object of the patient and he feels guilty for what he has provoked in this role – illness, depression, masochism, suffering, failure. The imago of the patient then becomes fused with the analyst's internal objects, which the analyst had, in the past, wanted (and perhaps managed) to frustrate, make suffer, dominate, or destroy. Now he wishes to repair them. When this reparation fails, he reacts as if he had hurt them. The true cause of the guilt feelings is the neurotic, predominantly sadomasochistic tendencies that may reappear in countertransference; the analyst therefore quite rightly entertains certain doubts and uncertainties about his ability to control them completely and to keep them entirely removed from his procedure.

The transference situation to which the analyst is likely to react with guilt feelings is then, in the first place, a masochistic trend in the patient, which may be either of a 'defensive' (secondary) or of a 'basic' (primary) nature. If it is defensive we know it to be a rejection of sadism by means of its 'turning against the ego'; the principal object imago that imposes this masochistic defense is a retaliatory imago. If it is basic ('primary masochism') the object imago is 'simply' sadistic, a reflex of the pains ('frustrations') originally suffered by the patient. The analyst's guilt feelings refer to his own sadistic tendencies. He may feel as if he himself had provoked the patient's masochism. The patient is subjugated by a 'bad' object so that it seems as if the analyst had satisfied his aggressiveness; now the analyst is

exposed in his turn to the accusations of his superego. In short, the superficial situation is that the patient is now the superego, and the analyst the
ego who must suffer the accusation; the analyst is in a depressive–paranoid
situation, whereas the patient is, from one point of view, in a 'manic' situation (showing, for example, 'mania for reproaching'). But on a deeper plane
the situation is the reverse: the analyst is in a 'manic' situation (acting as a

influence the analyst's work and because the analysis of the transference situations that provoke such countertransference situations may represent the
central problem of treatment, clarification of which may be indispensable if
the analyst is to exert any therapeutic influence upon the patient.

Let us consider briefly only two of these situations. One is the countertransference boredom or somnolence already mentioned, which of
course assumes great importance only when it occurs often. Boredom and
somnolence are usually unconscious talion responses in the analyst to a
withdrawal or affective abandonment by the patient. This withdrawal has
diverse origins and natures; but it has specific characteristics, for not every
kind of withdrawal by the patient produces boredom in the analyst. One of
these characteristics seems to be that the patient withdraws without going
away, he takes his emotional departure from the analyst while yet remaining with him; there is as a rule no danger of the patient's taking flight.
This partial withdrawal or abandonment expresses itself superficially in
intellectualization (emotional blocking), in increased control, sometimes
in monotony in the way of speaking, or in similar devices. The analyst
has at these times the sensation of being excluded and of being impotent to guide the course of the sessions. It seems that the analysand tries
in this way to avoid a latent and dreaded dependence upon the analyst.
This dependence is, at the surface, his dependence upon his moral superego, and at a deeper level it is dependence upon other internal objects,
which are in part persecutors and in part persecuted. These objects must
not be projected upon the analyst; the latent and internal relations with
them must not be made present and externalized. This danger is avoided
through various mechanisms, ranging from 'conscious' control and selection of the patient's communications to depersonalization, and from emotional blocking[19] to total repression of any transference relation; it is this
rejection of such dangers and the avoidance and mastery of anxiety by
means of these mechanisms that lead to the withdrawal to which the analyst may react with boredom or somnolence.

127

Countertransference anxiety and guilt feelings also frequently cause a tendency to countertransference submissiveness, which is important from two points of view: both for its possible influence upon the analyst's understanding, behavior, and technique, and for what it may teach us about the patient's transference situation. This tendency to submissiveness will lead the analyst to avoid frustrating the patient and will even cause the analyst to pamper him. The analyst's tendency to avoid frustration and tension will express itself in a search for rapid pacification of the transference situations, by prompt 'reduction' of the transference to infantile situations, for example, or by rapid reconstruction of the 'good', 'real' imago of the analyst.[20] The analyst who feels subjugated by the patient feels angry, and the patient, intuitively perceiving this anger, is afraid of his revenge. The transference situation that leads the patient to dominate and subjugate the analyst by a hidden or manifest threat seems analogous to the transference situation that leads the analyst to feel anxious and guilty. The various ways in which the analyst reacts to his anxieties – in one case with an attitude of submission, in another case with inner recrimination – is also related to the transference attitude of the patient. My observations seem to indicate that the greater the disposition to real aggressive action in the analysand, the more the analyst tends to submission.

# VII

Before closing, let us consider briefly two doubtful points. How much confidence should we place in countertransference as a guide to understanding the patient? And how useful or how harmful is it to communicate to the patient a countertransference reaction? As to the first question, I think it certainly a mistake to find in countertransference reactions an oracle, with blind faith to expect of them the pure truth about the psychological situations of the analysand. It is plain that our unconscious is a very personal 'receiver' and 'transmitter' and we must reckon with frequent distortions of objective reality. But it is also true that our unconscious is nevertheless 'the best we have of its kind'. His own analysis and some analytic experience enables the analyst, as a rule, to be conscious of this personal factor and know his 'personal equation'. According to my experience, the danger of exaggerated faith in the messages of one's own unconscious is, even when they refer to very 'personal' reactions, less than the danger of repressing them and denying them any objective value.

I have sometimes begun a supervisory hour by asking the candidate how he has felt toward the patient that week or what he has experienced during the sessions, and the candidate has answered, for instance, that he was bored, or that he felt anxious because he had the impression that the patient wanted to abandon the analysis. On other occasions, I have myself noticed annoyance or anxiety in the candidate relative to the patient. These countertransference responses have at times indicated to me in advance the central problem of the treatment at whatever stage it had reached; and this supposition has usually been verified by detailed analysis of the material

ance whenever his analysands were much occupied with their childhood. The candidate had the idea that only analysis of transference could further the treatment. In reality he also had a wish that the analysands concern themselves with him. But the candidate was able by analyzing this situation quickly to revive his interest in the childhood situations of the analysands, and he could also see that his annoyance, in spite of its neurotic character, had pointed out to him the rejection of certain transference situations in some analysands.

Whatever the analyst experiences emotionally, his reactions always bear some relation to processes in the patient. Even the most neurotic countertransference ideas arise only in response to certain patients and to certain situations of these patients, and they can, in consequence, indicate something about the patients and their situations. To cite one last example: a candidate, at the beginning of a session (and before the analysand, a woman, had spoken), had the idea that she was about to draw a revolver and shoot at him; he felt an impulse to sit in his chair in a defensive position. He readily recognized the paranoid character of this idea, for the patient was far from likely to behave in such a way. Yet it was soon clear that his reaction was in a certain sense appropriate; the analysand spontaneously remarked that she intended to give him 'a kick in the penis'. On other occasions when the candidate had the same idea, this patient was fantasying that she was the victim of persecution; in this case also the analyst's reaction was, in a way, appropriate, for the patient's fantasy of being persecuted was the consequence and the cause of the patient's sadistic impulses toward the transferred object.

On the other hand, one must critically examine the deductions one makes from perception of one's own countertransference. For example, the fact that the analyst feels angry does not simply mean (as is sometimes said) that the patient wishes to make him angry. It may mean rather that the patient has a transference feeling of guilt. What has been said above concerning countertransference aggression is relevant here.

129

The second question – whether the analyst should or should not 'communicate' or 'interpret' aspects of his countertransference to the analysand – cannot be considered fully here.[21] Much depends, of course, upon what, when, how, to whom, for what purpose, and in what conditions the analyst speaks about his countertransference. It is probable that the purposes sought by communicating the countertransference might often (but not always) be better attained by other means. The principal other means is analysis of the patient's fantasies about the analyst's countertransference (and of the related transferences) sufficient to show the patient the truth (the reality of the countertransferences of his inner and outer objects); and with this must also be analyzed the doubts, negations, and other defenses against the truth, intuitively perceived, until they have been overcome. But there are also situations in which communication of the countertransference is of value for the subsequent course of the treatment. Without doubt, this aspect of the use of countertransference is of great interest; we need an extensive and detailed study of the inherent problems of communication of countertransference. Much more experience and study of countertransference needs to be recorded.

## Notes

1   I confine myself in what follows to papers published since 1946. I have referred to a previous bibliography in another paper (17).

2   This differentiation accords in essentials with Annie Reich's two types of countertransference. I would add, however, that also when the analyst uses the analysis for his own acting out (what I have termed 'indirect' countertransference), the analysand represents an object to the analyst (a 'subtransferred' object), not merely a 'tool'.

3   Michael Balint (2) considers a similar problem, the scarcity of papers on the system of psychoanalytic training. Investigation of this problem leads him to several interesting remarks on the relationship between didactic analysts and candidates. (See footnote 5.)

4   Little (15) speaks, for instance, of the 'myth of the impersonal analyst'.

5   It is important to be aware of this 'equality' because there is otherwise great danger that certain remnants of the 'patriarchal order' will contaminate the analytic situation. The dearth of scientific study of countertransference is an expression of a 'social inequality' in the analyst-analysand society and points to the need for 'social reform'; this can come about only through a greater awareness of countertransference. For as long as we repress, for instance, our wish to dominate the analysand neurotically (and we do wish this in one part of our personality), we cannot free him from his neurotic dependence, and as long as we repress our neurotic dependence upon him (and we do in part depend on him), we cannot free him from the need of dominating us neurotically. Michael

Balint (2) compares the atmosphere of psychoanalytic training with the initiation ceremonies of primitives and emphasizes the existence of superego 'intropressure' (Ferenczi) which no candidate can easily withstand.

6   Helene Deutsch (4) speaks of the 'complementary position' when she refers to the analyst's identifications with the object imagoes.

7   In view of the close connection between these two aspects of countertransfer-

ness and futility of the associations express the empty, futile, dead part of the analysand; they characterize a depressive situation in which the analysand is alone and abandoned by his objects, just as has happened in the analytic situation.

10   Cesio (3) demonstrates in a case report the principal countertransference reactions that arose in the course of the psychoanalytic treatment, pointing out especially the analyst's partial identifications with objects of the patient's superego.

11   See Chap. V, example 8.

12   By 'abolition of rejection' I mean adherence by the analysand to the fundamental rule that all his thoughts are to be expressed without selection or rejection.

13   If the interpretations coincide with the analysand's superego judgments, the analyst is confused with the superego, sometimes with good reason. Superego judgments must be shown to the analysand but, as far as possible, one should refrain from uttering them.

14   Cf. Little (15, p. 34).

15   Something similar, although not connected with countertransference, is emphasized by Fairbairn (5).

16   See Klein (12), (13). The terms 'depressive', 'paranoid', and 'manic' are here used simply as descriptive terms. Thus, for example, 'paranoid anxieties' involve all the fantasies of being persecuted, independently of the libidinal phase or of the 'position' described by Klein. The following considerations are closely connected with my observations upon psychopathological stratification (19).

17   By the term 'frustration' I always refer to the subjective experience and not to the objective facts. This inner experience is determined by a complementary series at one end of which is primary and secondary masochism and at the other end the actual frustrating happenings.

18   This 'mania' may be of 'superego type', as for instance 'mania for reproaching' (identification with the persecuting moral superego) which also occurs in many depressive and masochistic states. It may also be of a 'pre-superego type' (belonging to planes underlying that of moral guilt) as occurs, for instance, in certain erotomanias, for erotic mockery is identification with the object that castrates by frustrating genitally (19).

19  This emotional blocking and, in particular, the blocking of aggression seems to be the cause of the 'absence of danger' for the analyst (the fact that the analysand does not run away or otherwise jeopardize the analysis), which seems to be one of the conditions for occurrence of countertransference boredom.

20  Wilhelm Reich (22) stressed the frequent tendency in analysts to avoid negative transference. The countertransference situation just described is one of the situations underlying that tendency.

21  Alice Balint (1), Winnicott (24), and others favor communicating to the patient (and further analyzing) certain countertransference situations. Heimann (11) is among those that oppose doing so. Libermann (14) describes how, in the treatment of a psychotic woman, communication of the countertransference played a very important part. The analyst freely associated upon unconscious manifestations of countertransference that the patient pointed out to him.

# References

Balint, Alice. Handhabung der bertragung auf Grund der Ferenczischen Versuche. *Internationale Zeitschrift für Psychoanalyse* XXII 1936 pp. 47–58.

Balint, Michael. On the Psychoanalytic Training System *International Journal of Psycho-Analysis* XXIX 1948 pp. 163–173.

Cesio, F. Psicoanálisis de una melancolía con ataques histero epilépticos *Revista de Psicoanálisis* IX 1952 pp. 389–412.

Deutsch, Helene. Okkulte Vorgnge whrend der Psychoanalyse Imago, XII 1926 pp. 418–433.

Fairbairn, W. R. D. The Repression and the Return of Bad Objects *British Journal of Medical Psychology* XIX 1943, pp. 327–341.

Ferenczi, Sandor. Missbrauch der Assoziationsfreiheit In: Bausteine zur Psychoanalyse II Vienna: *Internationale Psychoanalytischer Verlag, Wien.* 1927 p. 41.

Freud, S. The Future Prospects of Psychoanalytic Therapy 1910 *Coll. Papers II.*

Freud, S. Further Recommendations in the Technique of Psychoanalysis. On Beginning the Treatment 1913 *Coll. Papers II.*

Freud, S. The Dynamics of the Transference 1912 *Coll. Papers II.*

Gitelson, Maxwell. The Emotional Position of the Analyst in the Psychoanalytic Situation *International Journal of Psycho-Analysis* XXXIII 1952.

Heimann, Paula. On Countertransference *International Journal of Psycho-Analysis* XXXI 1950.

Klein, Melanie. A Contribution to the Psychoanalysis of Manic-Depressive States *International Journal of Psycho-Analysis* XVI 1935.

Klein, Melanie. On the Criteria for the Termination of a Psychoanalysis *International Journal of Psycho-Analysis* XXXI 1950.

Libermann, D. Fragmento del anlisis de una psicosis paranoide *Revista de Psicoanálisis* IX 1952.

Little, Margaret. Countertransference and the Patient's Response to It. *International Journal of Psycho-Analysis* XXXII 1951.

Lorand, Sandor *Technique of Psychoanalytic Therapy* New York: International Universities Press, Inc., 1946.

Racker, Heinrich Contribution to the Problem of Countertransference 1948, *International Journal of Psycho-Analysis* XXXIV 1953 pp. 313–324.

T 1 11 · · 1 1 (T1 · · 1 1 C · · 1

XXIII 1954.

Reich, Annie. On Countertransference *International Journal of Psycho-Analysis* XXXII 1951.

Reich, Wilhelm. *Character Analysis* 1933 New York: Orgone Institute Press, 1945.

Weigert, Edith. Contribution to the Problem of Terminating Psychoanalyses *The Psychoanalytic Quarterly* XXI 1952.

Winnicott, D. W. Hate in the Countertransference *International Journal of Psycho-Analysis* XXX 1949.

# 8

# INTRODUCTION TO THE LIFE AND WORK OF LEÓN GRINBERG (1921–2007)

## R. Horacio Etchegoyen

León Grinberg was born in Buenos Aires on February 23, 1921, and studied medicine in Buenos Aires. He already showed his vocation for psychoanalysis, as did his companion David Liberman. They were great friends and both came to stand out in their field.

Shortly after his qualification in medicine, Grinberg entered the Asociación Psicoanalítica Argentina (APA), becoming an associate member in 1952, at the age of 31. His career was meteoric, and in four years he became professor of the Psychoanalysis Institute and training analyst.

Grinberg belongs to a second generation of APA analysts, along with Resnik, Rodrigué, Arminda Aberastury and many others. He underwent analysis with Arnaldo Rascovsky and continued with Marie Langer to the completion of his studies, becoming, later, her collaborator and friend.

With Langer and Rodrigué, he wrote two books on group psychotherapy. The first, *Psicoterapia del grupo: Su enfoque psicoanalítico* (*Group psychotherapy: A psychoanalytic approach*), was published in 1957. Pleasant and rigorous, it was the first of its genre written in Spanish and of great influence in Latin America and Spain to date.

In 1959 he published *El grupo psicológico: En la terapéutica, enseñanza e investigación* (*The psychological group: In therapy, teaching and research*), divided into three sections in collaboration with more than 20 specialists.

Without a doubt, the stimulating dynamics of the group were an incentive leading Grinberg during those years to study the regressive mechanisms of mental functioning, which at times the group expresses with diaphanous clarity. An outstanding text of these years is "Aspectos mágicos en la transferencia y la contratransferencia" ("Magic aspects in transference and countertransference") that was presented at APA (Argentine Psychoanalytic Association) in 1956 and published two years later. In this paper, Grinberg introduces the concept of projective counteridentification, to which he will refer in many other works.

loved object, while others, with equal ardor, searched to free patients from guilt that condemned them in the dialectics of a sadistic superego and a submissive ego. Grinberg gets round this polemics in perceiving that there are two types of guilt (and not only one): persecutory and depressive guilt, which he relates lucidly to two types of mourning.

The difference between persecutory and depressive guilt is a contribution of great scope. In an audacious move, Grinberg proposes that mourning implies not only loss of the object but also parts of the self in it deposited. This opens to a wider vision of what is lost in the mourning process. A work of lasting influence, its second edition introduces a few important changes.

In 1971, León wrote, in collaboration with his wife Rebeca, *Identidad y cambio* (*Identity and change*), published in Buenos Aires. Its very title poses a great problem going back to Parmenides and Heraclitus. How is it possible at once to be and to change? The Grinbergs approach this issue by defining three relations: spatial, temporal and social. Identity is defined as the capacity to feel one's self in the succession of changes proposed by life. Change implies accepting the unknown, the unpredictable, and mental illness can then be defined as an attempt (desperate) to maintain unity in face of change, so that all continues the same.

This book discriminates carefully between ego and self, parting with Freud, Klein, Bion, Hartmann, Erickson, and others. The Grinbergs start out with Hartmann's ideas on the self (as person) and the ego (as instance) and develop them, using as their basis Edith Jacobson, Wisdom and Erickson. The second part of the book studies identity disorders, focusing on depersonalization and migration, making way for the Grinbergs' next work on migration and exile, full of beauty and nostalgia, published in Madrid in 1984.

*Identidad y cambio* is, in my view, the natural development of the idea of the mourning over the lost parts of the self, and it leads to another book of Grinberg's, *Teoría de la identificación* (*Theory on identification*, 1976b) published in 1976. A brief, penetrating text, it unfolds the development of the concept of identification, beginning with Freud and his disciples, and through to the Kleinian School. It studies in depth the concept of projective identification (Melanie Klein, 1946) followed by the contributions of her disciples Bion, Rosenfeld, Meltzer and Grinberg himself, with special reference to his own concept of projective counteridentification.

Since Grinberg created in 1956 the concept of projective counteridentification, he emphasized its role in communication as well as its essentially passive quality. The strength of projective identification can make the analyst function as the projected object. However, in his last papers Grinberg positions himself "beyond" projective counteridentification, with a wider "three dimensional" perspective, always emphasizing communication.

During his last years in Buenos Aires, he prepared a remarkable book in three volumes entitled *Prácticas psicoanalíticas comprobadas en las neurosis, en las psicosis y en niños y adolescentes* (*Psychoanalytic practice in neurosis and psychosis with children and adolescents*), published by Paidós in 1977. He managed again to gather a distinguished group of scholars in a common intellectual enterprise. Shortly after the preparation of this book, the Grinbergs went into exile in 1976. In Madrid, they joined the Madrid Psychoanalytic Association, where they continued their work as clinicians, teachers and researchers.

In 1987 Grinberg was designated Professor at the historical Ateneo of Madrid. He organized an Introduction to Psychoanalytic Theory, a series of conferences, which show once again his capacity gather psychoanalysts to work together.

At the XXX International Congress of Psychoanalysis (1983), Grinberg presented with Juan Francisco Rodríguez "The influence of Cervantes on the future creator of psychoanalysis", a wonderful text, captivating the audience with its elegance and erudition. The essay shows conclusively the influence of Cervantes on young Freud, who had read *Quixote* and the *Novelas ejemplares* and was enthralled by "El coloquio de los perros".

If Grinberg's scientific trajectory was brilliant, no less so was his performance in the grand politics of psychoanalysis. He was president of APA for three terms (1961, 1962 and 1963) and the first Latin American psychoanalyst to enter the Executive Council of the International Psychoanalytical Association (IPA), as Associate Secretary (1963–1965) and later as Vice President for two periods. He was also Chair of the San Francisco Congress (1995), honorary member of APdeBA (2003) and honorary member of the Asociación Psicoanalítica de Madrid (2003).

His influence as teacher is notable. He is the model of the *porteño* (Buenos Aires inhabitants) psychoanalyst, who follows the path of Freud and Melanie Klein, but includes European, American and Latin American analysts.

A year before his exile, he published a very interesting book on psychoanalytic supervision and, still in Buenos Aires, presented *Psicoanálisis:*

*Aspectos teóricos y clínicos* (*Psychoanalysis, theory and technique*, 1976a, 1981), which compiles a series of works ranging from 1955 to 1976 and ends a cycle of his production.

At the start of the 1960s, Grinberg began seriously examining the work of Bion. His research culminated in *Introducción a las ideas de Bion* (*Introduction to the work of Bion*, J. Aronson, 1977), which he wrote with two of

The story of Grinberg has many peak moments; however, perhaps the topmost was as speaker at the Copenhagen Congress (1967), in which he discussed with Anna Freud the concept of acting out.

The Grinbergs remained in Madrid for 20 years, during which León showed his gift as a master of psychoanalysis. In September 1995, the Grinbergs decided to leave Madrid for Barcelona. Immediately he restarted his teachings with a large group of students until the sad moment of his stroke.

Promolibro published in 1996 two books that summarize his work during his years in Europe: *El psicoanálisis es cosa de dos* (*Psychoanalysis is for two*) and *Psicoanálisis aplicado (Applied psychoanalysis)*.

Grinberg was an outstanding clinician and teacher, committed to psychoanalysis and with an unusual gift, enabling him to bring colleagues together to work in a collaborative way and creative way.

# References

Grinberg, León (1958). Aspectos mágicos en la transferencia y la contratransferencia. Identificación y contraidentificación proyectiva. *Revista de Psicoanálisis*, 15: 347–368.

———— (1963). *Culpa y depresión. Estudio psicoanalítico*. Buenos Aires: Paidós.

———— (1976a). *Psicoanálisis. Aspectos teóricos y clínicos*. Buenos Aires: Alex editor.

———— (1976b). *Teoría de la identificación*. Buenos Aires: Paidós.

————, editor (1977). *Prácticas psicoanalíticas comparadas en las neurosis. En niños y adolescentes. En la psicosis.* Buenos Aires: Paidós.

———— (1981). *Psicoanálisis. Aspectos teóricos y clínicos*. Barcelona: Paidós.

————, editor (1987–1988). *Introducción a la teoría psicoanalítica*. Madrid: Tecnipublicaciones.

———— & Grinberg, Rebeca (1971). *Identidad y cambio*. Buenos Aires: Kargieman.

———— & Grinberg, Rebeca (1984). *Psicoanálisis de la migración y el exilio*. Madrid: Alianza Ed.

————, Langer, Marie y Rodrigué, Emilio (1957). *Psicoterapia del Grupo. Su enfoque psicoanalítico*. Buenos Aires: Paidós.

———— y Rodríguez, Juan Franco (1989). La influencia de Cervantes sobre el futuro creador del psicoanálisis. En *Introducción a la teoría psicoanalítica*.

————, Sor, Darío y Tabak de Bianchedi, Elizabeth (1972). *Introducción a las ideas de Bion*. Buenos Aires: Nueva Visión. [*Nueva introducción a las ideas de Bion*. Madrid: Tecnipublicaciones, 1991].

Klein, M. (1946). Notes on some schizoid Mechanisms. *International Journal of Psycho-Analysis*, 27: 99–110.

# 9

# (1910–1987)

## Ignacio Maldonado Martinez

I met Marie Langer in Santiago de Chile, during an International Congress of Group Psychoanalytical Psychotherapy in March 1959.

In Córdoba, Argentina, where I graduated as a Doctor in Medicine, we didn't know that since 1942 there had been an Association of Psychoanalysis (Argentine Psychoanalytic Association, APA) member of the International Psychoanalytic Association. Through a German colleague, I knew about APA, and he stated "one of the founders is an Austrian, Marie Langer. During the Nazi period she became an exile in Argentina".

Very soon after that, I started my psychoanalysis with her; it lasted 10 years, followed by a friendship and a shared exile in Mexico until her death in December 1983.

The first years were of an orthodox psychoanalysis, with 4 or even 5 meetings weekly; it was more of a Kleinian-oriented analysis. At the time, her affinities were with Arminda Aberastury, who introduced Klein's ideas in Buenos Aires.

She collaborated with Emilio Rodrigué and León Grinberg in the book *El grupo psicológico* (1959) Buenos Aires: Nova. (*The psychological group*), a classic of psychoanalytic South American literature.

The book contains original papers on groups and group therapy that are primarily informed by the work of S. H. Foulkes, E. J. Anthony, and W. Bion.

In some of Langer's conferences, you could feel her preoccupation with spreading psychoanalysis beyond the affluent population to make it available to low-income populations. She did this while preserving core psychoanalytic concepts, such as the unconscious, children's sexuality, mechanisms of defense, etc. She was always clear about the importance of the founding concept in the psychoanalytical science: the unconscious. Among her many publications of that period, her best known was her book *Maternity and sex*, published in 1951.

She was mainly interested in women and their insertion in society. She was aware and interested in the increased importance of women in the labor market, technological changes, the use of contraceptives and its consequences on sexual freedom, mating, fertility problems, and so on. She questioned Freud's phallocentric theory and the concept of penis envy.

In this regard, Langer proposes several hypotheses, such as that envy could possibly be the result of defenses against early anxiety, as can be found in normal babies and children, but especially when the mother isn't satisfied and in conflict with her place as a woman in society. She thought that Freud's phallocentric theories were not corroborated by her clinical work.

Leaning on Isabel Larguia's and Demoulin's studies, she concerned herself with "women's invisibility": her invisible sex, her invisible work, that invisible woman who was becoming visible. Her research led her to dismiss some of Freud's ideas and she started to approach the feminine psyche from the perspective of dualities, such as man–woman, masculine–feminine, professional woman–mother woman, etc.

And then she dedicated herself to a problem that led Michel Foucault to develop ideas on modern power and its consequences: the fact that we are not always aware of the ways through which values enter our psychic world (what Judith Butler called "the psychic life of power").

In a preface to one of the editions of *Maternity and sex*, Janine Puget, a great friend and once a patient of Langer, concludes: "Marie Langer makes us love the woman; she proposes that we build for her a worthy space, the product of an incessant, daily commitment in every social context she participates and belongs . . . There is in this book a message of courage and enthusiasm. We hope that it will reach its readers".

In 1968, it became clear to the psychoanalytic community that the political events such as May in Paris, October in Mexico, and the evolving resistance towards the dictatorship in Argentina, which attained its highest point in the "Cordobazo" in 1969, might have awakened Marie Langer's old and restless social and political worries.

From then on, she started an intense dialogue with Enrique Pichon-Rivière and Jose Bleger, with whom she had great political affinities. All of them opposed restricting psychoanalysis to the confines of the Argentine Psychoanalytic Association (APA), which, in their view, did not openly attempt to blend psychoanalysis with social sciences.

Pichon-Rivière founded a school in which he combined psychoanalysis and social sciences: Escuela de Psicología Social. Bleger did something similar in the School of Psychology in the University of Buenos Aires, and Marie Langer joined the Argentinian Association of Psychiatry in the Capital District, where she soon became the President.

In contrast with the social and political compromise of the Psychiatric were discussing aspects of the institutional development of psychoanalysis, and the narrow approach to theory and technique accepted in the society. We attempted an articulation between psychoanalysis and social psychiatry, and a preventive approach to mental health, that expanded during our exile in Nicaragua.

At this moment it might be relevant to mention that the work we began in Argentina coincided with a split in the Argentinian Psychoanalytical Association in 1971. It was the first splitting in IPA's history for ideological-political and scientific reasons, and it culminated in the resignation of 150 IPA members. At this point, we founded our own organization with a training center, CDI, Centro de Docencia e Investigación, where we began to train all mental health workers, from nurses to psychiatrists, in the rudiments of theory of psychoanalysis, Marxist theory and social theories.

The intention was also to improve the standards of training for those mental health workers (nurses, social workers, etc.) who served the most disadvantaged segments of society. After 1976, during the military dictatorship, mental health providers became one of the groups that suffered persecution, torture and disappearances, triggering a massive exile.

A balance of that period shows as an important accomplishment the publication of several books and papers on mental health and politics. Two of those, *Cuestionamos 1* and *Cuestionamos 2*, have recently been translated into English in London. *Cuestionamos* was a sort of starting point of the critique of psychoanalysis in Latin America, and, at the same time, of its recuperation for the work on mental health in the area. Marie Langer was one of the main contributors to those publications.

In Nicaragua, we had the first opportunity to apply our ideas about mental health. Marie Langer proposed to revise the Freudian "Reality Principle" concept. She explored how reality was a cultural concept informed by the historical moment and the social class to which both the doctor and the patient belonged. She also identified conflicts linked to gender and strongly criticized the lack of interdisciplinary approach in psychoanalysis. She was very critical of Arnaldo Rascovsky's ideas about the origin of wars and their link with his theory of filicide.

This was a turning point in her professional and personal life; she moved her practice away from her private office to become embedded in institutional life. But all this had a short life in Argentina. In October 1974, Langer had to exile herself in Mexico, and in November my family and I left for Cuba, where I was invited to teach. For Marie Langer, it was her second exile. She had friends in Europe, and an international reputation, but chose to stay in Latin America.

I planned to return to Buenos Aires via Mexico so we could visit with the first exiles, amongst them Langer. While in Mexico, we learned that it would be dangerous to return. We were now part of the exiled community.

We organized in Mexico the reception and care of hundreds of expatriates who arrived mainly from Argentina, but also from Chile, Uruguay, Paraguay and Bolivia. All these countries suffered similar military dictatorships, a consequence of the "Plan Condor" orchestrated by the EEUU. We also participated in denouncing the violence to human rights in Argentina during the military dictatorship.

In Mexico, she taught in the postgraduate psychology faculty at UNAM (National Autonomous University of Mexico), saw patients privately and provided a free psychotherapeutic service to political exiles.

Silvia Berman, an Argentinian psychiatrist, also in exile, had been in contact with the Sandinistas in Nicaragua. After the Sandinistas overthrew the Somoza dictatorship in 1979, the Dean of the Faculty of Medicine at Leon asked Silvia Berman to help organize a mental health service for Nicaragua.

After a major effort trying to introduce the study of psychoanalysis in Cuba, Langer sent the Cuban government a letter in which she expressed her gratitude for their efforts in treating her cancer. She says: "I was happy in Cuba . . . at the end of my life I had Cuba and Nicaragua as a reward, a dream. It was like being verified, performing a destiny. I owe it to you. That's why I'm so grateful. I grew young again or better still, I was atemporal. There, I wasn't old or young, and I received the strength to survive".

Before she died, she was acclaimed unanimously as "Permanent Member of the Trust of Intellectuals" to occupy the chair left by Julio Cortazar, the great Argentinian writer, after his death.

# (1920–1983)

## *Silvia Neborak*

David Liberman was one of the great contributors to the development of psychoanalysis in Argentina. He focused his research on the dialogue in the session. He used as raw data for his research detailed records of his patients' sessions at different moments of the analytic process; these were the foundation for his contribution to psychoanalytic theory.

He made use of communication theory and his work is an outstanding example of multidisciplinary approach to psychoanalytic development. He was particularly interested in the relationship between content and style of interpretation convinced that both relate to development fixation points.

Liberman was born in Buenos Aires in 1920 in a middle class, Jewish family. His was a musical family. His father, Sam Liberman, was a well-known jazz musician. David was a gifted piano player and was very aware of the rhythm of spoken language. He once told me that his Oedipal phantasies were shaped by the way his father handled musical instruments.

He met León Grinberg – another pioneer of South American psychoanalysis – in primary school, and they remained friends for the rest of their lives. They both excelled as researchers in different areas of analytic theory but shared psychoanalytic, scientific and ethical values. They went at the same time to medical school, shared Freudian readings, became psychiatrists and did analytic training at the Argentine Psychoanalytical Association (APA).

David Liberman's mentor during his training in psychiatry was Enrique Pichon-Rivière, who eventually became his training analyst. Liberman's dissertation was on "Psychosomatic Semiology", starting a line of research that culminated with the publication of the book *Del cuerpo al símbolo* (*From the body to the symbol*) that we edited with him and a group of colleagues interested in the same subject. We started to meet as a group interested in Liberman's novel approach to psychopathology, which had been published in his book *Lingüística, interacción y proceso psicoanalítico* (*Linguistics, interaction and psychoanalytic process*) and became primarily focused on a number of patients with psychosomatic symptoms. About them Liberman had already written ". . . premature demands plus a premature fugue to the external world by implementing a special kind of body–mind splitting, prevents them from a gradual development of defense mechanisms". We started to think that ultimately we were witnessing an impairment of symbolic function. However, clinically these patients appeared to be very functional and so well adapted that David, ironically, used to say that they "suffered from sanity" – properness and attention to others' needs – in contrast with their inability to be in touch with their own emotional and physical needs.

We started to conceptualize this inner world configuration as a flight into adulthood (obviously pseudo-adulthood) that originated in an attempt to skip normal developmental stages. This attempt resulted in the creation of "symbolization gaps".

Liberman proposed to study sessions in which these patients, initially so well disposed to uphold the setting, started to have difficulties with some aspects of it and showed evidence of conflict. He thought that in those moments of the analytic process, the real self would emerge, letting the analyst visualize incomplete symbolization, and leading to a lack of the flexibility necessary to enable a satisfactory relationship with internal and external reality.

We paid special attention to their relationship with the time and space of the session and their bodies. We then realized that we were dealing with "another patient". One that, having lost the mask of adaptation to Euclidean space and chronologic time, was disorganized and in panic, but unable to identify these mindsets and name them.

Liberman thought that sharing these ideas with the psychoanalytic community was imperative because the transformational potential of the analytic process depended on the analyst's awareness of the failure of symbolic function hidden behind the adaptation mask. Failure to gain insight about this limitation could turn the analytic process into another source of adaptive demands on the patient.

In other words, there would be a repetition in the transference-countertransference relationship of a semantic distortion in which satisfying the analyst's demands is confused with being appreciated and loved.

If the analyst is not aware of this semantic distortion, he will inadvertently promote more splitting and pseudo-adaptation that can trigger the next organic psychosomatic outburst.

Liberman thought that in the process of acquiring insight, patients can, and perhaps should, move from being "hyper-adapted somatizers" to thinkers and demanding patients, even to an excessive degree, to compensate for all the

expressed in a one-person psychological language, while the actual practice in which those ideas originated took place in a bi-personal field. He tried to create operational theoretical definitions that could be applied to real life bi-personal clinical interactions. A thorough reading of his writings shows that he practically reformulated all the analytic concepts from a clinical, interactive perspective.

In his book, *La comunicación en terapéutica psicoanalítica* (*Communication in analytic therapy*) Liberman reformulates the discrete psychopathological syndromes according to communication models based on Jurgen Ruech's concepts. Liberman establishes links between types of communication and the six erogenous zones and the emotions attached to them. Based on this core thesis, he developed a new version of psychopathology based on communicational styles. He also defines an ideal ego model "the ideally plastic (malleable) ego".

Liberman describes six specific illnesses in which the classic classification based on psychiatry is replaced by definitions much closer to their empirical base – namely, the analytic dialogue.

A schizoid character becomes in this reformulation: the person that observes and does not participate. Further research led him to redefine it as the reflecting style fixated to the oral phase. These patients split their emotions and curiosity; they do not look personally involved in the session. These patients create unknowns and trigger the analyst's curiosity. They will induce interpretations that they will interpret as countertransference confessions of our own curiosity, resulting in an analytic dialogue that leads to endless misunderstandings.

Liberman classifies these types as belonging to the class of semantic distortions because "they dilute (distort) the intention of the interpretation, and by extension they distort the meaning of the totality of the analytic situation". In this situation, the interpretation that has more chances of triggering a semantic mutation and repair the therapeutic meaning of the analytic interaction would be an interpretation formulated in a complementary style, the one he calls dramatic with esthetic impact, that brings together in one message affect, thoughts and action. Dramatic with esthetic impact is in Liberman's theory, the complementary style of the reflective style.

Liberman thinks that every style has its complement that represents that part of the patient's ego that did not develop sufficiently. In this way, we offer the patient those modalities of verbal thinking that he could not yet achieve. Liberman states that "we try with each interpretation to introduce verbal thought 'matrices' that are part of the possible syntactic and semantic combinations of the language code that the patient could not build during his development".

As far as the role of interpretation in the analysis, he categorically states: "Psychoanalytic changes can only be achieved with interpretations". David puts as much emphasis on the analyst's as on the patient's verbal language. The latter only gets in touch with the qualities of his links with the breast, with the primal scene and with the vicissitudes of the Oedipus complex in special and infrequent occasions. In those occasions, the analyst learns about it because the patient can use verbal language to communicate insight within the session with a "colloquial style that has . . . linguistic features with roots in early infancy". We can find in these communications some of the preverbal features plus modes that belong to the patient's unique intimate internal slang.

The importance that he attributes to in-session verbalized insight – privileged marker of the modification of repetition compulsion in the transference – separates Liberman from the concept of cure as reconstruction, and privileges the development of a capacity for thinking oneself as a tool in the journey towards self-analysis.

In his theory, analytic process develops a capacity to think one's lived life and evolves into a recreation of the past.

# References

Liberman, D.: *Del cuerpo al símbolo: sobreadaptación y enfermedad psicosomática Colección PSI.* Buenos Aires: Anaké, 1993.

Liberman, D. *ingüística, interacción comunicativa y proceso psicoanalítico.* Buenos Aires: Ediciones Nueva Visión, 1972

Liberman, D.: *La comunicación en terapéutica psicoanalítica.* Buenos Aires: Eudeba, 1962

Genevieve T. de Rodrigue

*This paper was read at the second Panamerican Congress for Psycho-analysis in Buenos Aires, August 1966. The present English version was published in 1967 by the* International Journal of Psycho-Analysis, *48: 496–503.*

The psycho-analytic process is hard to define for two reasons: first, because of its quality as a basic concept, which is liable to have such wide connotation that everything in the realm of theory, technique or clinical data is, in a way, relevant to it, and, second, because of its very nature, which sets it apart from purely biological processes. The analytic happening has the unavoidable quality of the psychobiological process, but it is also induced, magnified and articulated by the appearance of an agent of psychosocial change – namely, the analyst in the exercise of his professional activity (Rapaport, 1959). The interaction of what is already given in the patient with what the analyst gives back to him provides the structure of the therapeutic relationship in a specific and complex manner.

When we speak of analysis as a process we mean both an event that takes place in treatment and the outcome of that event. The second phase – the outcome – may happen within the session or outside it. When dealing with working through, we shall stress the nature of the changes that evolve both in the patient and in the analyst inside and outside the immediate context of the session.

In the same way as the opening of a session contains implicitly the basic unconscious fantasies that will presently unfold in the hour, we believe that the first sessions of a psycho-analytic treatment may present the essential and specific contents that will characterize the whole analytic process. The interplay of fantasies and mechanisms in those early sessions carries the germ of what will later be deployed in the successive phases. One of us (Langer, 1951) published a detailed study of a first analytic session, mapping the series of conflicts and specific mechanisms that were detectable in the patient's transference fantasy. Many of the budding dynamic conflicts of that session later became basic configurations of the way in which that treatment evolved.

The analytic process includes the progressive development of the fantasies that underlie the different object relationships going on in the transference tie. As Riviere (1952) has said, ". . . the world of unconscious feeling and impulse (which we call "phantasy") is the effective source of all human actions and reactions, modified though they are as translated into actual external behaviour or conscious thought."

Freud deals quite clearly with the analytic process in many passages. For example, among his papers on technique, he says (1913, p. 130):

> But on the whole, once begun, it (the process) goes its own way and does not allow either the direction it takes or the order in which it picks up its points to be prescribed for it.

In the last part of his paper on "Remembering, Repeating and Working-through" (1914, p. 155), he also takes as a guideline the dynamic happening in its temporal frame and says:

> One must allow the patient time to become more conversant with this resistance with which he has now become acquainted, to work through it, to overcome it, by continuing, in defiance of it, the analytic work according to the fundamental rules of analysis.

Several questions help to clarify our subject: not only (a) what is the analytic process? but (b) where does it take place? (c) how and when is it registered? and (d) how does it manifest itself?

a. What is the analytic process? With this query we continue with what we already outlined. The analytic process is a temporal succession of dynamic, structural, and economic cycles in the patient. The span of those cycles depends on the type of phenomena to be observed in them and on the analyst's approach. In these cycles conflicts are reactivated with their ensuing crisis. Progress is always the outcome. The analytic process implies progress, but we conceive progress as a development in which the useful regression on the couch is its main leverage. We cannot here deal properly with the notions of progression and regression; but we bring to mind the fact that although we speak of regression in the service of the ego (Kris, 1952), we do not pay enough attention to its counterpart, namely, progression in the

148

disservice of the ego (Rodrigué, 1967). By this concept we do not only mean those states of the so-called improvement connected with a "flight into health" or hypomanic reactions, etc., but have in mind certain striking achievements in some people that are made in a given area of their lives in such a manner that they, so to speak, "make great strides". The whole self suffers from the burden of these unconsolidated gains. Sometimes they

It is not clear to us yet why this progression in the disservice of the ego occurs, and we think that here lies an area where further knowledge about the issue of ego autonomy may prove to be rewarding.

The cycle of conflict, crisis, and progress evolves not only in the patient; it also happens, in a minor key, in the analyst. The therapist is less committed, for the nature of the therapeutic transaction is centered on the patient. (On the other hand, he has greater responsibility.) The analytic relation is bipersonal and asymmetrical. The treatment is of the patient, for the patient, and to the patient. The associative strip of the patient has always reference to himself and us; the interpretative strip from the early sessions onwards has to do with and is centred on the patient. If things do not go that way the analytic process may eventually come to a stop, its direction be reversed and, at its worst, the analyst may start functioning as a patient in the interaction with the resulting deleterious effect. The patient lacks a receptive object that enables him to bring to light his transference and instead becomes subject to a disconcerting and overwhelming transference.

At this stage, we might raise an issue that may be controversial, namely, our belief in the early appearance of transference neurosis. Our viewpoint is that the bipersonal relationship in the analytic situation structures itself from the outset over mutual unconscious fantasies. We share the viewpoint – held by many analysts – from which transference is taken in its widest sense, and postulate that its origins lie in the earliest object relationships, and that it includes not only the conflicts pertaining to those object relations, but also the related anxieties and unconscious defences. In our clinical experience, the transference fantasy, in all its variegated richness, shows itself from the start.

b. Where does the analytic process take place? We shall be brief on this item. The analytic progress, in time, actually starts when the patient is pondering over his wish to be analysed, it begins to shape up from the first session onwards, it deploys itself during the whole analytic situation and it carries on – as an active factor for progress – once the treatment itself has come to an end. It could be said that the analytic process closes its cycle as a bipersonal relationship when it becomes transformed into a disposition, a capacity and natural need for self-analysis (with an internalized analyst).

In space, the process takes place within the frame of the session and in the intervening breaks. The formal opening of the process is sealed by the introduction of the analytic contract whereby both parties convene to comply.[1]

Thus a pledge is made in which the position of the roles of both participants are explicitly stated. We should like to stress here the institutional nature of this setting. The analytic process with its contract, finality, development and closure, creates an institution. The analyst not only receives the transference from the patient's primary objects but he also receives the "transference" of the object analyst as a social role whose position is defined by a manifold of sociocultural patterns that are prevalent in the milieu in which he practises. This image of the "analyst", which is transferred into the analyst, has been slowly evolving with the years and, with the wider acknowledgement of psycho-analysis, tends to become a social constant.

c. How and when is the analytic process registered? Here one must distinguish two types of notations. First comes the conscious and unconscious notation that occurs in the session as the result of the analyst's free-floating attention and his capacity to take in and metabolize the patient's projections. One basic supply for this notation is given by the analyst's countertransference cues that guide him in the configuration of his interpretation.

Here we should also like to make explicit what we consider to be a significant controversial issue. It has to do with the use and conceptualization of countertransference. We admit, of course, that countertransference reactions may come to be factors that disturb the useful communication between analyst and patient; but we think, mainly following Racker (1960) and Heimann (1950), that once countertransference is detected and understood it becomes the logical and unavoidable counterpart of transference and must be used as an important tool in the investigation of the patient's unconscious and in the formulation of mutative (Strachey, 1934) interpretations. In an interesting paper on the subject Gitelson (1952) comes quite close to our views when he remarks that "a countertransference reaction, if the analyst is 'open' enough to analyze it, can be an integrative experience along the road of interminable analysis," and adds that by means of the analysis of his countertransference the analyst "can reintegrate his position from which he can utilize the interfering factor for the purpose of analyzing the patient's exploitation of it".

Finally, we agree with Heimann (1950) and others that the difference existing between the analyst and the patient in the analytical situation is fundamentally one of "degree of feelings that the analyst experiences and the use he makes of them".

Every interpretation is a notation. But in this section we shall refer to another kind of notation — the technique of verification of the analytic process, the objectivation of how things stand in a treatment. And although the analytic process is centred on the analytic situation, its visualization and objectivation can only be made outside the therapeutic context and outside the immediate temporal happening that is the dialogue. In any session,

The working through of the session outside the session, where the bipersonal relationship is taken up as an object of study, fosters a new approach towards treatment, one in which the session is seen as a quasi-experimental situation (Kris, 1956). Hence, analysis ceases to be a postdictive situation only (Rapaport, 1959) — it becomes (quasi-) predictive as well. It changes from a bipersonal to a tripersonal relationship, because the analyst in the act of studying the session outside the session becomes the third object.

d. How does the analytic process manifest itself? To answer this question we shall rely on two concepts that we consider fundamental for the analytic process to be an ongoing one — working through and insight. Then we shall tackle the kind of phenomena that basically interfere with the process — the malignant acting out and the negative therapeutic reaction.

We shall start with working through. We think that the issue of working through should be studied as an intermediate and resulting process but at the same time as independent of them. Working through implies the progression resulting from the overcoming of defences and from the repetitive model of instinctual discharge. But in working through, regression also is at work, if, following Winnicott (1955), we define regression as a process in recovery stemming from "a highly organized ego defence mechanism".

Winnicott points out the latent capacity for regression that is inherent to a highly organized ego. Kris (1952) was the first to refer to this regression in the service of the ego. We understand that Winnicott coincides with Erikson (1963) in considering a useful regression as a moratorium that enables the marshalling of the potentialities of the self.

Thus we regard working through as a process that taps the latent capacity for regression in an organized and systematic way, inducing a moratorium and furthering the back and forth progressive movement. This leads us to consider the role of pain as an element that is always present in working through and in every acquisition of knowledge.

We use Bertrand Russell's term "knowledge by acquaintance" (Richfield, 1954) to characterize a form of getting in touch with the object of

knowledge that is based on experience and involves feelings. This acquaintance is painful and Freud was the first to consider working through (1914)
as a "painful task for the patient". The nature of the psychic pain inherent
in becoming aware "of how oneself is" constitutes a basic characteristic of
the theory and practice of psycho-analysis and sets this discipline apart from
other forms of psychotherapy. The most thoughtful contribution in this area
comes from the notion of the depressive position of the Kleinian school.

The theory of the depressive position is nowadays a basic concept that does
not require further explanation. Here we should only like to add our contribution: the depressive moment implies an essential change in the immature
ego, resulting not only from the pain and suffering of the realization that the
object has been damaged by what-one-is and what-one-has-been, but also
from the simultaneous parallel understanding of the harm done to oneself.
One of us (Grinberg, 1964), pursuing this line of thought, has stressed how
important it is for the patient to make reparations for those parts of his self
that have been damaged, and that this self-reparation is as important as the
object-reparation. The notion of the depressive position, thus widened, has
a lot in common with what we have to say regarding the painful working
through; and in the same way as there is a labour of mourning, with all its
gamuts of readjustments and reparations, there is a mourning-like type of
labour in working through, as a parallel and conjoined process that includes
all the reactions that lead to substantial changes in the attitudes that the self
takes towards its conflicts. An important facet of the painful labour in working through relates to the capacity for renunciation of the infantile self parts
of the personality. The omnipotence one loses has to be adequately mourned.

Bion (1962) also emphasized the element of pain involved in the acquisition of knowledge. In this connexion he describes a certain kind of person
whose mental activity is aimed at distorting understanding in order to avoid
pain and frustration. They hate to face "truth" and repudiate any form of
knowledge. They lean to "misunderstanding" in lieu of understanding.[3]

The opposite of this disposition hostile to knowledge is the disposition to
establish a commensal relationship between subject and object. This relation,
aimed at mutual profit, has its model in the mother-baby pair, when the
projection the baby makes onto the mother's breast mitigates his basic anxiety and he is able to reintroject a more bearable reality that fosters growth.

The "commensal" relationship can be conceived as a working through
model, with its stress on knowledge gained in the fabric of a bipersonal
relationship – a knowledge that is painful and that, in a different way, does
good to both parties.

We should like to relate now the concepts of working through to the process of learning and knowing that leads to the acquisition of insight. Insight
is a type of knowledge. It often happens that analysts seek and conceive

insight as a sudden revealing experience ("a seeing the light"). This "great expectation" reminds one of a similar attitude that was at the base of the theory of the traumatic aetiology of neurosis: at the time the search was for the dramatic causal trauma. We believe that it is more in keeping with clinical reality to consider insight in a more organic, additive role; a factor that unfolds itself with a certain cyclical continuity within the analytic process.

unnoticed or, a posteriori, tend to be minimized.

In that sense we believe that insight and working through are much more akin as processes than they are usually considered to be. We think that by bringing them closer together we make a contribution to the understanding of the analytic process. The moment of insight is a juncture in the working through. It is a juncture in such a process in so far as it stems from the integrating tendencies of the ego, but it is also the cause of a new further integration, made at a higher level. Kris (1956) has touched on this matter when he speaks of a "circular process".

To return to the mother-baby pair, as a model for the analytic process: we know that the setting in analysis fosters regression because it implies limits, frustrations, distance, and a certain psychosocial deprivation. The setting infantilizes the patient. But there is another facet of the analytic situation that also fosters regression that is generally somewhat neglected. This facet, which is actually the opposite of the former, completes the "baby-like condition" of the patient. Just as the infant suffers moments of frustration and despondency, he also experiences moments in which he is received, contained, surrounded and supported by his mother's arms. To give a name to this situation, we call it a holding attitude or condition, for it brings to mind the physical state of protection. This holding is what the analyst offers during his fifty minutes of devoted receptivity. During that time he is truly at the disposition of the baby-patient, by offering him his capacity for free attention, his comprehension and his ability to contain the patient's anxiety. The basis of this holding is the rectifying interpretation of his anxieties. Insofar as the analyst can bear anxiety without anxiousness, he acts as the good mother that makes possible the reintrojection of what has been projected.

We believe that the useful regression in the progress of the analytic process comes from this second aspect of the analytic situation. The frustration-deprivation factors promote regression only and, without the complement of holding, would only generate a repetitive regression to the basic anxieties. That regression would be detrimental.

The process that analysis sets forward by means of frustration is a regression to the condition of infancy and childhood. The patient is witness to all the horror, despair and alienation that a baby is capable of experiencing in the midst of paranoid anxieties and incipient depressive attempts. Holding implies receiving, recognizing, acknowledging, and explicating that state of affairs. It is here where the interpretation makes contact with the inner reality of the patient, in the above-mentioned commensal relationship. The "interpretative holding", in a setting that induces regression, gives psychoanalysis the seal that sets it apart from some kinds of supporting therapies, for we would define the latter as "sham arms for a sham baby".

The holding condition is obtained by the interpretation of both the positive and the negative aspects of transference. But transference interpretation is the main operative factor in the therapeutic action; it is the agent of change in the analytic process. As has been pointed out, the therapeutic effect of the interpretation derives primarily from the inclusion of the analyst in the field and from the possibility of regulating the introjective and projective processes of the patient in so far as he is placing the analyst in the role of depository of those parts of his self that he wants to get rid of for they are felt to be dangerous or damaged or, conversely, because he wants to preserve them by putting them in a safe place (Baranger, 1961).

This would correspond to what Strachey (1934) called the "auxiliary superego" when speaking of the function of the analyst in the first phase of the mutative interpretation. This function allows the patient to make conscious the relation of an id impulse with the analyst, and then, in the second phase, to be able to discriminate between the fantasied object and the real one.

We would like to take up this second aspect of the mutative interpretation and relate it to the notion of actuality (taking the term from Erikson (1962) but using it in a somewhat different way) for it helps, we think, to clarify and to define the nature of the reality and the kind of tie that mediates between the patient and the analyst in an ongoing treatment. With this term we want to elucidate the ambiguous acting-like connotation that is usually ascribed to the patient's transference behaviour.

By *actuality* we also mean a unified experience that we dissociate when we speak of a (spatial) "here" and a (temporal) "now". The notion of actuality integrates the temporal-spatial fabric and describes more aptly the kind of experience the patient has of the analytic happening. We feel that what goes on in a deployed transference, what we called actuality, has more in common with a dream experience than with everyday reality and it is in that matrix that junctures of insight come about.

We believe that transference actuality occurs when the patient, activated by interpretation, can project into the analyst without basically altering his

character of external object. In those cases, the action of projective identification is not insidious and the analyst is able to perceive, meditate, and hand
back in the form of an interpretation, the knowledge he has acquired about
the kind of psychical process that has taken place.

We wish to insist on the role of transference interpretation as the agent of
change in the analytic process. And here we differ from an approach shared by

patient himself.

We do not doubt that in the terminal period of an analysis and when
the patient is about to complete certain culminating phases of the working
through of his depressive position that a lesser participation on the part of
the analyst may be useful in terms of the resolution of transference. But let
us not generalize.

We do not accept the over-use of interpretation. Neither do we uphold
that a particularly active interpretative line is an indication of good analytic
work. The analyst should interpret every time he has understood the patient's
material and he must focus his interpretations on "the emergency points".
We believe this to happen in every session from the outset of treatment.[4]

Our conception of a "good session" – based on what we already said
concerning holding, the commensal relation and the labour of mourning
in working through – is somewhat different. A good session for us implies a
permanent interpretative commitment whereby the analyst receives, understands, and formulates the anxieties that are inherent in the patient's working through, sharing to a certain extent the suffering that such a process
brings about. The therapist acts by means of the interpretation, on which
the unfolding of the session hinges. Thus we would say that an associative
line that does not end up in an interpretation is an incomplete proposition.
And here "incomplete" is used in a similar manner to when we say that an
interpretation that does not include transference is incomplete.

## Interferences in the Analytic Process

Let us now briefly consider the main disturbances in the analytic process:
acting out and the negative therapeutic reaction.

With reference to acting out, besides the serious acting out, inside or
outside the session, that because of its intensity and frequency threatens the whole analysis, we would like to mention another type of acting

out particularly met with at the start of a treatment, when the prevailing transference modality has been called (Rodrigué, 1967) "primary transference", and which is characterized by the massive projection of the internal object into the analyst-external object. This activity is carried out mainly by means of attitudes, gestures and words (Alvarez de Toledo, 1956) that become instruments of action instead of promoting actuality. It is only with a progressing analysis that verbalization becomes less ridden with those elements of induction.

Serious acting out is a phenomenon that has been classically considered as a clinical concept related to the patient's resistances.[5] We think that in this kind of acting out the patient has been the target of massive projective identifications from his primary objects and, feeling so highly charged with destructive contents, he experiences the need to unburden himself of the unbearable psychic tension he harbours. In the analytic situation the analyst becomes the depository of those projective identifications, the end result being that the therapist himself comes to feel a similar parasitic condition that has been described by one of us as projective counteridentification (Grinberg, 1962).

In those states it could be said that the analyst ceases to function, his countertransference loses its quality of cognitive tool for detecting the patient's psychic reality. The analyst suffers the parasitic influence of the patient's feelings and comes to feel that they are his own and this leads him to act on, by counteridentification, the patient's impulses that he has not been able to work through.

We believe that this attack on the analyst's capacity to think, coupled with the parasitic intrusion in the realm of his emotions, constitutes the most malignant form of acting out – that which seriously endangers progress in the analytic process. But malignant acting out can also be conceived as the patient's incapacity to face the depressive position and the painful labour of the mourning-like working through that we have already mentioned.

All this shapes what we know as the "negative therapeutic reaction" that can be considered as an organized compound of narcissistic defences, reinforced by manic and schizoid defences with pervasive paranoid anxieties. This situation makes the junctures of insight impossible and no working through can be set in motion. The patient burdened with excessive persecutory guilt (Grinberg, 1964) will paradoxically fight against his cure and against any progress in his treatment.

Freud, in "The ego and the id" (1923, 48), relates this subject to the unconscious feelings of guilt and explicitly states that they amount to a disturbance that hampers the analytic process:

> There are certain people who behave in a quite peculiar way during the work of analysis. When one speaks hopefully to them or expresses satisfaction with the progress of treatment, they show

156

signs of discontent and their condition invariably becomes worse. One becomes convinced, not only that such people cannot endure any praise or appreciation, but that they react inversely to the progress of the treatment, . . . they get worse during the treatment instead of getting better. They exhibit what is known as a "negative therapeutic reaction".

gression and useful regression that leads to change, the painful working through in the acquisition of knowledge, the correlation between junctures of insight and the overall deployment of working through, the dialectic importance of the transference-countertransference pair and the role of interpretation as sole agent of change, by means of its holding attributes. We have discussed here only two of the possible blocks in the process – acting out and the negative therapeutic reaction – not having time here to deal with all of them.

We should like to close our paper with a quotation from Strachey that, in our opinion, puts the purpose and essence of the analytic process in a nutshell:

> The final result of psycho-analytic therapy is to enable the neurotic patient's whole mental organization, which is held in check at an infantile stage of development, to continue its progress towards a normal adult state. (159)

## Notes

1 Liberman, Ferschtut, and Sor have dealt with this subject in a paper (1961) where they point out that by keeping to a sound analytic contract it is possible to keep the transference regression in controlled doses by means of interpretation. They emphasize the double link of mutual contrasting interdependency: the mature link based on the arrangement of an exchange of time and money and the link of infantile dependency which is the outcome of transference regression. The analytic contract would be like the good lighthouse that allows the risk of sailing through dangerous waters (regression) for it provides the safeguard of being able to find again the reality that the frame of reference affords.
2 Liberman (1962) has paid particular attention to the systematic study of detailed strips of clinical material that were taken in similar circumstances at different stages of treatment, making a study of the intervening variables and taking the theory of communication as starting point for his discussion on

working through. The progress that results from the working through of an epigenetic crisis brings forward a quantitative and qualitative change in the amount of information available. This favourable outcome follows from the patient's positive experience of having participated in the therapist's channel of communication. The increase of output results from the formation of new symbols with a greater capacity to condense a greater quantity of bits of information, thus allowing for an improvement in future experiences.

In one of his latest books, Bion (1964) postulates the possibility of establishing a system of notations of what takes place in analysis, enabling the user, by a system of operations not unlike those of symbolic logic, to evaluate the course of an analysis or the theories that are applied to it.

3   Nunberg (1933) points out that "affirmation and knowledge constitute sequels of the vital instincts, whereas ignorance and denial represent consequences of the destructive impulses."

4   In the Argentine Psychoanalytic Association we have been interested in finding out which is the interpretative modality of the analysts of our group, considering problems such as whether in our milieu therapists interpret from the beginning of an analysis. Langer, Puget and Teper (1964), as a result of their experience of conducting a seminar on technique for several years, and applying Glover's questionnaire, pooled the analysts' interpretative attitudes and found that, in our group, all the analysts used interpretation as the only explicit tool for therapeutic change from the beginning of treatment.

5   Rosenfeld (1965), following Freud, also describes a "partial acting out", playing a necessary and almost inevitable role in every analysis, and sets it apart from a total acting out as it appears in schizophrenic patients with intense hostility and envy who use this mechanism as a defence against confusional states. Greenacre (1950) has pointed out that patients who act out have suffered from emotional upheavals in the early months of infancy which resulted in an increased orality, narcissism, and a low threshold of tolerance to frustration. They also present alterations in their verbal thinking. Michaels (1959), on the other hand, calls "primary acting out" the severe acting out characterized by a condition of chronicity, malignity, and often somatic repercussion.

# References

Alvarez de Toledo, R. 1956 "El anlisis del 'asociar', del 'interpretar' y de 'las palabras'." *Revista de Psicoanálisis* 13

Baranger, W. and M. 1961 "La situacin analtica como campo dinmico." *Revista Uruguaya de Psicoanálisis* 4

Bion, W. R. 1962 *Learning from Experience* (London: Heinemann).

Bion, W. R. 1964 *Elements of Psychoanalysis* (London: Heinemann).

Erikson, E. H. 1962 "Reality and actuality: an address." *Journal of the American Psychoanalytic Association* 10

Erikson, E. H. 1963 *Childhood and Society*, 2nd edition (New York: Norton).

Freud, S. 1913 "On beginning the treatment." *The complete psychological works of Sigmund Freud* 12

Freud, S. 1914 "Remembering, repeating and working through." *The complete psychological works of Sigmund Freud* 12

Freud, S. 1923 "The Ego and the Id." *The complete psychological works of Sigmund*

Greenacre, P. 1950 "General problems of acting out." *The Psychoanalytic Quarterly* 19

Grinberg, L. 1962 "On a specific aspect of countertransference due to projective identification." *International Journal of Psycho-Analysis* 43

Grinberg, L. 1964 *Culpa y Depresin* (Buenos Aires: Paidos.)

Heimann, P. 1950 "On countertransference." *International Journal of Psycho-Analysis* 31

Heimann, P. 1960 "Countertransference." *British Journal of Medical Psychology* 33

Kris, E. 1952 *Psychoanalytic Explorations in Art.* (New York: Int. Univ. Press.)

Kris, E. 1956 "On some vicissitudes of insight in psycho-analysis." *International Journal of Psycho-Analysis* 37

Langer, M. 1951 "Una sesin psicoanaltica." *Revista de Psicoanálisis* 8

Langer, M., Puget, J. and Teper, E. 1964 "A methodological approach to the teaching of psycho-analysis." *International Journal of Psycho-Analysis* 45

Liberman, D. 1962 *La comunicación en al terapia psicoanaltica* (Buenos Aires: Eudeba.)

Liberman, D., Ferschtut, G. and Sor, D. 1961 "El contrato analtico." *Revista de Psicoanálisis* (special issue).

Michaels, J. 1959 "Character disorder and acting upon impulses." In: *Readings in Psychoanalytic Psychology* ed. Levitt. (New York: Appleton-Century.)

Nunberg, H. 1933 *Principles of psychoanalysis* (New York: Int. Univ. Press.)

Racker, H. 1960 *Estudios sobre Tcnica psicoanaltica* (Buenos Aires: Paidos.)

Rapaport, D. 1959 The *structure of psychoanalytic theory.* (New York: Int. Univ. Press, 1960.)

Richfield, J. 1954 "An analysis of the concept of insight." *The Psychoanalytic Quarterly* 23

Riviere, J. 1952 *General introduction to developments in psycho-analysis* by Klein et al. (London: Hogarth.)

Rodrigué, G. de 1967 *El contexto del proceso psicoanaltico* (Buenos Aires: Paidos.)

Rosenfeld, H. 1965 "An investigation into the need of neurotic and psychotic patients to act out during analysis." In: *Psychotic states* (London: Hogarth.)

Strachey, J. 1934 "The nature of the therapeutic action of psycho-analysis." *International Journal of Psycho-Analysis* 15

Winnicott, D. W. 1955 "Metapsychological and clinical aspects of regression within the psychoanalytical set-up." In: *Collected papers* (London: Tavistock.)

# INTRODUCTION TO THE LIFE AND WORK OF DURVAL MARCONDES (1899–1981), "FATHER" OF BRAZILIAN PSYCHOANALYSIS

*Antônio Luiz Serpa Pessanha*

Due to his sharp curiosity and his openness to new ideas, Durval Marcondes understood and valued Freud's theories, becoming one of his loyal disciples. With tireless energy, Marcondes introduced psychoanalysis in São Paulo, taking all the complicated steps for the organization of a Psychoanalytic Society. His enthusiastic leadership easily brought him followers, and by the 1920s he had already created the first Brazilian Psychoanalytic Society, the embryo of our current society.

In 1937, the first training analyses were beginning, conducted by Dr. Adelheid Lucy Koch, who was recommended by the International Psycho-Analytical Association. During the 10 years between his first contact with Freud's work and Dr. Koch's arrival, Durval worked intensely to break down the antagonism of the medical establishment.

Restless and alert, Durval lived through the entire development of psychoanalysis and embodied its very history in Brazil. He was loyal to tradition, yet very sensitive and with a thirst for new contributions. The society in São Paulo inherited this spirit from him, becoming acquainted early on with Melanie Klein's work, which was studied and accepted in European countries long afterwards. He disliked dogmatism and preferred the risks of questioning and innovation.

Broadly cultured, he was interested in all themes – ethical, artistic, literary and political – and often contributed to these sectors of human knowledge.

His knowledge had an effect on those who spent time in his company and who attended his seminars and conferences, which enriched and broadened horizons.

He encouraged the development of the next generations with extreme generosity. He always kept a deep belief in the value of psychoanalytic thinking and the vigor of the institutions and associations he founded. In

containing compliments and encouragement.

He wrote around 50 papers, some of them focused on children, parents and schools. He worked in this area with Virgínia Leone Bicudo and Lygia Alcântara do Amaral, part of the founding group of the Brazilian Psycho-analytic Society of São Paulo.

Out of his countless publications, the organizers of this book have high-lighted "The psychodynamism of the analytic process," published in the *Brazilian Review of Psychoanalysis São Paulo, 14*(3): 277–292, 1980. This work was written and presented at a scientific meeting in 1956; however, it was only published in 1980. Here, the author revisits the bases of psychoanalytic thinking, demonstrating his understanding of Freud's doctrine.

# THE PSYCHODYNAMISM OF THE ANALYTIC PROCESS

## *Durval Marcondes*

*Read at the First Latin-American Congress of Mental Health, São Paulo, on July 22, 1954, and published in the 1956* Psychoanalytic Review, *43: 261–271.*

The analytic process has two different yet interrelated aspects: that which takes place in the analysand and that which occurs in the analyst. In studying this process we must remember that, in the words of Freud (17, p. 378), "the work of analysis consists of two quite different portions, that it involves two people, to each of whom a distinct task is assigned." It is necessary, therefore, to take into account these two aspects, not losing sight of the fact, however, that they influence each other mutually and, in order to understand one of them, it is necessary to understand the other. Let us examine first what occurs in the analysand, and later what takes place in the analyst.

The dynamic element of the analytic process, as in each and every psycho-therapeutic process, is the phenomenon of transference. Already in his early works Freud has demonstrated the importance of this phenomenon in psychoanalysis and its role in the fight against resistances. Analytical cure was accordingly conceived to be a process of overcoming resistances by the use of transference.

A more profound knowledge of this process and how it develops within the personality of the patient was, however, only possible because of the stimulus given it by Freud's studies on hypnosis and on the structural division of the psychic apparatus consolidated in his books *Group Psychology and the Analysis of the Ego* and *The Ego and the Id*, which were published in 1921 and 1923, respectively. Thus it was that in the symposium on the theory

of technique and treatment that took place at the International Psycho-
Analytical Congress of Salzburg in 1924, works appeared (1, 22, 23) that
gave rise to new perspectives for the understanding of the cure, by focal-
izing on the modification of the superego and the effect wrought upon it
in the transference.

Of these studies, the work of Radó (22) was particularly valuable in this

in psychotherapy. In hypnotism, explains Radó, the hypnotizer insinuates
himself into the superego of the patient, thanks to the mechanism of introjection, assuming the position of a "parasitic superego", which then affords
him the possibility of altering the symptomatic manifestations. This hyp-
notic superego usurps, in a provisional way, the functions of consciousness
and vanishes on the patient's awakening, leaving, however, a permanent
trace in the superego that facilitates hypnosis at a subsequent time.

The same conception of a "double" of the superego was readopted by
Strachey in the paper he presented to the British Psycho-Analytical Society
in 1933 (24). In psychoanalytic treatment there is, according to Strachey, a
tendency on the part of the patient to receive the analyst into his superego,
as it was established in Radó's work in reference to hypnosis. The "auxiliary
superego", which is what Strachey calls the image of the psychotherapist
infiltrated into the superego of the patient during the psychoanalytic process, does not work only by assuming temporarily the functions of the
superego but ends by altering it definitively. This permanent transformation
of the superego, effected little by little in the transference situation by means
of successive projections and introjections, is that which results in the definite modifications in the patient translated finally into a lasting cure. The
specific and principal factor in this change is the confronting, proportioned
by the interpretations of the transference, of the archaic phantasy object of
the patient with actual reality, represented in the person of the analyst. Such
interpretations lead the patient to detach himself from his infantile fixations
and to develop freely towards a state of normal adulthood.

This conception of the analytic process as being a succession of experiences that permits the juxtaposition of the past with the present, leading the
individual to the substitution of his childish patterns of reaction for others more in accordance with psychic maturity, constitutes the basis of the
ideas of Alexander and of the psychoanalytical school of Chicago. The decisive element in psychoanalysis is, according to Alexander and French (2),
the opportunity it offers, by means of the so-called "corrective emotional

experience", of having the patient resume the line of development that he had abandoned in childhood. According to the same author the secret of the curative quality of the analytic process is in the contrast, focalized in the transference, between the original conflict and the present situation. The individual can now face under far more favorable conditions, and hence can manage in a more favorable way, affective stimuli that were at an earlier time intolerable for him. The remembering of occurrences repressed in the past, to which such value was given in the classic conception of psychoanalysis, becomes relegated to a secondary position signifying more than anything else that the treatment is progressing satisfactorily. It is rather the result than the cause of therapeutic progress (2, pp. 20, 21). As stated by Alexander and his school, the extratherapeutic experiences of the patient have great significance for the cure since the experiences in the transference relationship are only a training for the real battle (2, p. 38).

As one can see, the Chicago school emphasizes the understanding of the psychoanalytic cure as a process of maturity and growth. This is, really, the fundamental aspect of the problem, allowing for a more appropriate point of view. Freud (14), however, had already defined the psychoanalytic cure as being "a kind of re-education" since in fact the cure consists essentially of the use of the relations of transference to favor and guide the affective development of the individual, helping him establish the forms of psychic reaction that are characteristic of adulthood.

Growth, which is the basic principle of the analytic process, is set in motion in the transference situation and in the transference finds the necessary stimulus for its realization. Transference does not constitute a simple return to the past, which the regressive tendencies of the patient favor, but includes also a constant and ever-renewed effort to regain the starting point, in order to conquer this same past and then progress in the sense of psychic maturity. Transference represents simultaneously a repetition of a previous situation and, according to French (10, p. 191), "an experimental attempt to correct the infantile patterns." It is a natural phenomenon, expressing a permanent search for objects that will reproduce the primitive objects of the patient and that, thus integrated in his problems, can contribute, regressively or progressively, to their solution. From this point of view, psychoanalysis is a form of treatment whose ultimate purpose consists in the exploration of the progressive forces of the transference. It is left to the analyst to mobilize and take advantage of these forces in a constructive way.

The weapon with which to do this is primarily interpretation. Although stretching to excess the significance of the term and risking a difference of opinion with most analysts, I feel justified in broadening the meaning of the word "interpretation" in order that it may include all attitudes of the analyst that have as aim and result in the modification of the way the analysand feels and understands his own psychic happenings. This broadening has the advantage of integrating, under the same denomination, the phenomena whose causes and effects have the same foundation and the same psychological nature. Those who do not agree may restrict the word "interpretation" to designate only simple verbal interpretation and use, in reference to the process I have here set forth, other expressions such as, for example,

therapy, consists in the use of interpersonal relationships in the interests of a cure. For this it uses various means of human communication, including, but not solely, verbal expression. When these relations, by the exchange of the sentiments contained in them and in consequence of the special behavior of the psychotherapist, give way to an alteration in the patient in the direction of a more mature handling of his psychic reactions, the process acquires the character of psychoanalysis. This is the dynamic and economic significance of the classic formulas, translated in the expressions "to turn the unconscious conscious"(14), or "where there was id, there should be ego" (15), etc. On the psychoanalytical level, to interpret is to make something be felt in a different way to that in which it is being understood. It is giving another and clearly defined meaning – intellectual or affective, but not necessarily intellectual – to a situation or an attitude, widening the possibilities of its assimilation by the ego. One may say that the analyst is "interpreting" consciously or unconsciously every minute from the moment the treatment begins: that is, he is presenting to the patient attitudes that give him experiences propitious to an actualization and revision of his defense mechanisms.

In order to be effective, interpretation should be opportune. There is an exact moment when the patient is in condition to receive the useful impact of the analyst's intervention in relation to a certain point in the development of the cure. The analyst should intensively sense the "distance" between the receptivity of the patient and the contents of the message to be transmitted.

The obstacles that the patient erects to the therapeutic process are incorporated in the word "resistance". The resistances have their roots above all in the attitudes of the patient in the transference situation. In order that the analytic process can develop, it is necessary: 1) that the patient reproduce in transference the childhood situation in which he became fixated; 2) that he renounce this situation and accept the frustrations necessary to the establishment of an adult pattern of interrelationship. The first of these two conditions corresponds to the aspect of transference that we might call *regressive* and that tends to establish a position of passive dependence in the search for protection in the person of the analyst. The second reflects the *progressive* aspect of transference; that is, the support found in it for new contacts with objects and ultimately for detachment from the person of the analyst. The first is an indispensable step to the second, and this constitutes in truth the spring-board that gives the patient the necessary impetus for the final adaptation to reality. Both contain, however, a dangerous situation for the patient, who mobilizes his resistance forces against them.

We have, then, to consider first of all the resistance to giving oneself up to the analytical process. The patient declines to participate affectively in the treatment, refusing to relive the primary situations of his object relations. This corresponds to the fear of submitting to the control of an all-powerful and frustrating adult incapable of understanding him or of taking into consideration his emotional needs. On the other hand, there is the refusal to dissolve the transference situation, to abandon an equilibrium in object relations in exchange for an unknown, an unknown that seems to him an enigma, at least in that which is related to the maintenance of his affective security.

The overcoming of these two obstacles depends on the mobilization of the affects provoked at every opportune moment by the analyst. According to the need presented, the analyst should use the two contrasting elements that, according to Ferenczi (7), constitute the foundation of the education of children and of the masses – i.e., love and the imposition of renunciation. These are the expression of the two principles that the same author considers should inspire psychoanalytical technique: the principle of frustration and the principle of indulgence. The aim of psychoanalysis is to make the patient feel that submitting to a frustration does not make him the incurable victim of a lack of love. This is the essence of progress in the principle of reality.

The dynamic and economic conditions that preside over the analytic process are not, of course, its only privileges. They are latent dispositions that psychoanalysis thaws out and uses for the purpose of a permanent cure. "What analysis achieves for neurotics," wrote Freud (16, p. 381), "is just what normal people accomplish for themselves without its help." The disposition to cure oneself, manifested in the tendency to maturity and health as opposed to the tendency towards regression and sickness, finds itself in the warp and woof of all conflicts presented by all patients. On the therapeutic level, analysis simply offers the restorative and propelling stimuli that were lacking in the patient's previous life, and which, without knowing it, he was seeking in coming to the analyst.

Having thus seen the facts of the analytic process unfolded in the patient, we shall now go on to examine the corresponding ones in the conduct of the analyst.

In the conduct of the analyst during the treatment, transpire his attitudes in relation to the analysand consciously or unconsciously determined. The conscious attitudes correspond to the application of his scientific knowledge for the purpose of a cure and constitute the intentional part of his conduct. They are the result of his professional study and of his intention to use objectively and rationally all the technical resources that he possesses.

the outset it should be noted that it does not signify only a determined and specific response to each one of the patient's manifestations of transference as the word alone might lead one to believe, but includes any and every aspect of the therapist's emotional behavior independent of this or that particular stimulus. It is not a simple secondary reaction to transference, but a primary phenomenon, as natural and spontaneous as transference itself.

It can be seen, then, from what has gone before, that there must be considered in psychoanalytic treatment a conscious or intellectual aspect and an unconscious or affective aspect of the behavior of the analyst. These two complement each other in their effect and contribute harmoniously in order to accomplish the cure. Such a duality corresponds to that which Fenichel (6) notes in theatrical representation and that which its two opposite schools of scenic art recommend: one of which believes solely in the intuition of the actor and in the possibility of his feeling, through empathy, the emotions corresponding to his part, to find consequently the most correct way of expressing them; the other, disbelieving in improvisation, insists on the necessity of a detailed study of how each minutia of intonation can impress the audience. Always referring back to the theater, Fenichel thinks that the truth lies between these two extremes. In that which applies to psychoanalysis, the correct and necessary thing is to explore both elements – the intellectual and the affective – which together make the therapeutic process possible.

In view of this, counter-transference constitutes a precious weapon for the analyst. The impression of Paula Heimann (18) is justifiable that, although the analytic situation has been examined and described from various points of view, "it has not been sufficiently stressed that it is a relationship between two persons." Taking into account its importance in the analytic process, it is necessary to conclude that little has been written on counter-transference, a fact that has been registered by Fenichel (5, p. 183) and by Margaret Little (20, p. 32). In general and until very recently, analysts have acted in relation to the difficulties of the patients in treatment much as the parents of problem children, who tend to attribute to these children the conditions responsible for the formation of the symptoms. Ferenczi was one of the first to focalize the negligence with which the personal attitude of the analyst as the sterilizing factor of the process of analysis has been considered. He refused to accept certain conformist explanations for the failure of the cure, and encouraged the question of discovering if the cause of this failure, instead of residing in the patient's resistance, would not rather be for the convenience of the analyst (8).

It is true that in 1910 Freud had affirmed the importance of the analyst's autoanalysis for the adequate control of counter-transference (11, p. 289) and soon after established, in 1912, the necessity of didactic analysis (12, p. 329). The latter became an essential condition of analytical preparation. But it is necessary to recognize that, for a long time, its conscious objective was to provide means of escape from the inconveniences of counter-transference rather than to take advantage of it. The preoccupation with the negative aspect of counter-transference obscured the value and the significance of its positive aspect. In fact, counter-transference has been seen almost solely as an undesirable phenomenon to be avoided and fought against, an untimely intrusion that happens disadvantageously in the analytic process with the sole result of disturbing its satisfactory progress. The constructive and advantageous side of counter-transference was therefore ignored, which is perhaps the reason for the relative disregard of its study and of a better understanding of its utility. The omission of counter-transference as the main object of consideration retarded in an appreciable manner the progress of scientific knowledge of the analytical process and of the development of the technical resources of psychoanalysis. After referring to Freud's statement (13, p. 378) that the fear of coming face to face with the transference retarded the development of psychoanalytic therapy for 10 years, Margaret Little (20, p. 33) stresses the fact that the point of view of the majority of the analysts with regard to counter-transference is precisely the same: "that it is a known and recognized phenomenon but that it is unnecessary and even dangerous ever to interpret it."

This rejection of the study of counter-transference and of the true sense of its practical advantages originated in Freud's well-known recommendations (12) on the impassibility of the analyst. In one of them, he compares the analyst to the surgeon, "who puts aside all his own feelings, including that of human sympathy." In another, included in the same work, he affirms that the analyst "should be impenetrable to the patient and, like a mirror, reflect nothing but what is shown to him." These words were often taken in too rigorous and exaggerated a sense, thus creating, in reference to the affective attitude of the analyst, and as Paula Heimann (18) stresses, the ideal of the "detached" psychoanalyst.

However, in consequence of a more precise experience and founded on a better comprehension of the use of counter-transference, the modern trends of theory and technique have been modifying this method of procedure. Ferenczi was one of those who initiated this revision, proclaiming a wider liberty and naturalness in the affective reactions of the analyst. He focalized (7) the difficulties caused by "cool objectivity", and, based on the

Actually, the "mirror" attitude, cultivated in an extreme way as it almost always has been, is nothing more than an instrument of the analyst's counter-resistance and a narcissistic barrier interposed by him for his protection. It is a defense against his anxiety before the patient and shows the fear of counter-identification and of involvement in the patient's neurosis. This attitude corresponds, on an analytic level, to the classic distinction between the healthy (doctor) and the sick (patient). It is a leftover of the old discrimination that saw in neurotics and psychotics beings different from others, possessed of the devil. This attitude really only began to die at the time of Pinel. At this time the truly "humane" relations in the treatment of patients began; however, an isolation cord was maintained under the guise of considering them victims of "degeneration" or as those who have, unlike most people, a lesion or infection in their brains.

The correct attitude of the analyst demands appropriate identification with the patient and with the objects of his past. This attitude has its roots in a counter-transference that is *protective*, in the sense of making the patient feel he is emotionally accepted by the analyst, and *emancipatory*, in the sense of favoring his possibilities for new experiences. In analysis, the patient has to deal with two kinds of objects represented by the person of the analyst: one that offers him comfort and security, giving him thus the possibility of participating in the analytical process with affection; the other that provokes the renunciations that lead to his independence and maturity. A proper counter-transference meets these basic needs of the patient at the opportune moment. By means of the mobility of his counter-transference, the analyst offers himself to the patient as the needed object at every moment of his psychic development.

The role of identification in counter-transference is implicit in the words of Freud when, in the same paper that refers to the mirror attitude (12), he establishes that the analyst "must bend his own unconscious like a receptive organ towards the emerging unconscious of the patient, be as a receiver of the telephone to the disc." Freud compares in this way the analyst's unconscious, in his relation with the analysand, to the receptor that "trans-mutes the electric vibrations induced by the sound-waves back again into sound-waves."

This function of the unconscious of the analyst, whose psychic sensibility permits him to turn into intimate experiences the original contents of the analysand's unconscious, was already the object of a penetrating study by Helene Deutsch in 1926 (4). She explains this capacity by the permanence in the unconscious of the analyst of the residues of his own psychic devel-opment similar to those of the analysand. In the unconscious, they both have the same infantile desires and impulses, whose memory traces, relived in the analytical situation, permit the analyst to experience them intuitively. In some ways, therefore, this intuitive process of the analyst resembles that which occurs in the patient himself and "revives similar infantile urges in both of them: in the case of the analysand by means of transference, and in the case of the analyst, by means of identification." Deutsch observes that this aspect of the unconscious relations of the analyst and the patient is known as "counter-transference" and adds that counter-transference is not limited to an identification of the analyst with certain portions of the infantile ego of the patient but also entails the presence of certain other unconscious attitudes for which the same author uses the expression "complementary attitude". Once the patient tends to direct his unsatisfied desires to the per-son of the analyst – who is thus identified with the original objects of these desires – the analyst is obliged "to identify himself with these images in a manner compatible with the transference phantasies of his patient." Deutsch calls this process "complementary attitude" in order to distinguish it from the simple identification with the infantile ego of the patient and stresses the fact that only the combination of these two categories of identification constitutes the essence of "counter-transference" and that "the utilization and goal-directed mastery of this counter-transference are some of the most important duties of the analyst."

As one can see, the identification of the analyst is with the ego of the analysand and also with his superego or, speaking in a more general way, with his primary infantile objects, and it takes place by means of the re-animation in the analyst of the historic residues of his own unconscious. For this, the analyst brings into play the phantoms that he harbors in his own mind, giving to the term "phantom" the meaning that Wittels (25) gives it in referring to neurotics. They are personalities existing in the unconscious as a result of identifications in the real experiences of the past that can influence the present behavior. According to Wittels, "the psychotherapist has to do a sculpturing of a kind, artistic work which makes his reluctant patients see and understand the phantoms by which they are vexed and which they cannot control because they usually know very little about them" (p. 143). For this, the analyst must mobilize his own phantoms. To the phantoms of the patient should correspond those of the analyst. Applying this terminology to the theater, Fenichel says (6, p. 150) that "the good actor is characterized by the high multiplicity of his phantoms." One can say the same of the good analyst.

In what relates to the participation of the analyst's ego, the identification

cal situation, which enables him on the one hand to establish the necessary relations of identification with the patient and on the other to detach himself appropriately from them.

The capacity offered to the analyst of utilizing his own unconscious psychic material arises, as explained by Fliess (9), from a particular condition of his own ego: assuming the character of a "work-ego", it has broadened its faculty of critical self-observation in virtue of its special relations with the superego. The latter erected as "therapeutic conscience", abstains from restricting the possibilities of the analyst's ego necessary to its role in the treatment.

The ability to execute this task of fusion and separation of the past and the present, living in a contradictory manner phantasy and reality, supposes in the analyst the complete mastery of his psychic activity. Growth – which, in reference to the patient, constitutes the real object of analysis – depends, as Margaret Little (20, p. 35) has noted, on an alternating rhythm of identification and separation. This is afforded by effecting the proper psychic distance to the patient in each instance of the analyst's behavior. The analyst in this way reproduces the conduct of the parents towards the developing child. For the good performance of this function, he should dispose of the necessary and spontaneous psychic elasticity that is the natural attribute of affectionate, mature parents. "The mature parent," says Berman (3, p. 163), "is the prototype of the analyst at work."

To the extent that this is not possible, the hindrances appear that can come from the counter-transference that functions then as counter-resistance. Typical difficulties now arise that emanate from the person of the analyst and constitute what might be called the pathology of the analytical process. The patient does not find the conditions propitious to the putting in motion and to the regular progress of the evolutive phenomenon inherent in the cure. In the position of father or mother that is conferred upon him by the analytical situation, the analyst presents in this case forms of behavior similar to those that are habitually found in parents of children under treatment in child-guidance clinics. Rejection and overprotection are frequent attitudes, dissimulated and justified in analysis by supposed reasons of technique.

The phenomenon of identification that is the basis of counter-transference can offer great danger. A lack of psychic elasticity on the part of the analyst indicating his insufficient maturation may lead sometimes to a *real* identification, which naturally becomes fatal to the progress of the analysis. The identification in this case ceases to have the restrictive qualities mentioned above, and loses its condition of "trial identification", which is what Fliess (9, p. 213) calls the empathetic identification representative of the normal process of counter-transference.

In neurotic counter-transference, there is the unconscious fear on the part of the analyst of regressing by counter-identification to the level of immaturity presented by the analysand and of losing his suggestive influence (the fear of the patient's counter-magic). As a defense action, the analyst often places himself in the attitude that I would call "authoritarian position", taking inspiration from certain words of Marmor (21). Fearing unconsciously that the analysand will usurp his magic power and with the purpose of keeping him under his affective control, the analyst does not give the latter sufficient opportunities for liberating experiences. Thus, imposing himself as a despotic object upon the superego of the patient, he prevents the emancipatory identification that should take place by introjection into the ego and that constitutes the indispensable mechanism of the phenomenon of growth. In these conditions, a feeling of superiority may develop that Marmor compares to the "God complex" described by Jones (19).

Counter-transference becomes counter-resistance to the degree that the infantile features of the unconscious assume a principal and permanent role in the analytical situation. It interferes, then, in the patient's transference and cultivates in him attitudes of resistance. When the treatment does not progress, it is because there is established, in what relates to the analyst and in accord with a critical moment of the analysis, one of the following contradictory conditions: 1) the analyst does not offer the patient the possibility of accepting the regressive transference in order to integrate himself in the analytical process; 2) the analyst does not detach himself from the patient; thus he does not allow the latter the opportunity to develop the progressive aspects of transference and, thus, to set in motion the phenomenon of psychic maturity.

To sum up, the positive and negative qualities of counter-transference may be synthesized in the following way: In normal counter-transference, the analyst is able 1) to identify himself empathetically with the analysand without fear of the regressive counter-identification; 2) to detach himself naturally and to offer himself as the mature and attainable ego-ideal, which permits the analysand to put into effect the necessary progressive identifications. In neurotic counter-transference (counter-resistance), by the rigidity of his mental set-up, the analyst, on the contrary, is incapable of empathetic identification and of the constructive position of renunciation that is his role in analysis.

# Bibliography

3 Berman, L.: Counter-transference and attitudes of the Analyst in the Therapeutic Process. *Psychiatry*, 12: 159–156, 1949.

4 Deutsch, Helene: Occult Process Occurring during Psychoanalysis. In *Psychoanalysis and the Occult*. Devereux, G., Ed. New York: International Universities Press, 1953. Original paper in German: Imago. Bd., 12: 1926.

5 Fenichel, O.: Problems of Psycho-Analytic Technique. Part. III. *The Psychoanalytic Quarterly*, 8: 164–185, 1939.

6 Fenichel, O.: On Acting. *The Psychoanalytic Quarterly*, 15: 139–160, 1946.

7 Ferenczi, S.: The Principle of Relaxation and Neocatharsis. *International Journal of Psycho-Analysis*, 11: 428–443, 1930.

8 Ferenczi, S.: Child-Analysis and Analysis of Adults. *International Journal of Psycho-Analysis*, 12: 468–482, 1931.

9 Fliess, R.: The Metapsychology of the Analyst. *The Psychoanalytic Quarterly*, 11: 211–227, 1942.

10 French, T. M.: A Clinical Study of Learning in the Course of a Psychoanalytic Treatment. *The Psychoanalytic Quarterly*, 5: 148–194, 1936.

11 Freud, S.: The Future Prospects of Psycho-Analytic Therapy. In *Collected Papers, Vol. II*. London: Hogarth Press, 1924.

12 Freud, S.: Recommendations for Physicians on the Psycho-Analytic Method of Treatment. In *Collected Papers, Vol. II*. London: Hogarth Press, 1924.

13 Freud, S.: Further Recommendations in the Technique of Psycho-Analysis. Observations on Transference-Love. In *Collected Papers, Vol. II*. London: Hogarth Press, 1924.

14 Freud, S.: *A General Introduction to Psychoanalysis*. New York: Boni and Liveright, 1920.

15 Freud, S.: *New Introductory Lectures on Psycho-Analysis*. London: Hogarth Press, 1933.

16 Freud, S.: Analysis Terminable and Interminable. *International Journal of Psycho-Analysis*, 18: 373–405, 1937.

17 Freud, S.: Constructions in Analysis. *International Journal of Psycho-Analysis*, 19: 377–387, 1938.

18 Heimann, Paula: On Counter-Transference. *International Journal of Psycho-Analysis*, 31: 81–84, 1950.

19  Jones, E.: Chapter XII. The God Complex. In *Essays in Applied Psycho-Analysis, Vol. II*. London: Hogarth Press, 1951. Originally published in German: *Internationale Zeitschrift fuer Psychoanalyse*. Bd. I, 1913.

20  Little, Margaret: Counter-Transference and the Patient's Response to It. *International Journal of Psycho-Analysis*, 32: 32–40, 1951.

21  Marmor, J.: The Feeling of Superiority: An Occupational Hazard in the Practice of Psychotherapy. *American Journal of Psychiatry*, 110: 370–376, 1953.

22  Radó, S.: The Economic Principle in Psycho-analytic Technique. *International Journal of Psycho-Analysis*, 6: 35–44, 1925.

23  Sachs, H.: Metapsychological Points of View in Technique and Theory. *International Journal of Psycho-Analysis*, 6: 5–12, 1925.

24  Strachey, J.: The Nature of the Therapeutic Action of Psycho-Analysis. *International Journal of Psycho-Analysis*, 15: 127–159, 1934.

25  Wittels, F.: Unconscious Phantoms in Neurotics. *The Psychoanalytic Quarterly*, 8: 141–163, 1939.

---------- 14 ----------

*Gilda Sabsay de Foks*

Fidias R. Cesio was born on March 15, 1922. He died at the age of 90, with his brilliant mind intact, on October 10, 2012. In fact, he published his last book on actual neuroses a year before his death.

From a very young age he was interested in physiology and did research under the direction of the Argentine Nobel Prize winner Bernardo Houssay. Influenced by his brother-in-law, Luis Storni, who was also a prominent psychoanalyst and is now deceased, he began reading the works of Freud. In 1948, he contacted Enrique Pichon-Rivière and began his psychoanalytic training. His training analyst was Marie Langer, and he always said that his teachers and mentors, in addition to Pichon-Rivière, were Angel Garma, Arnaldo Rascovsky and Enrique (Heinrich) Racker. He held several positions at the Argentine Psychoanalytic Association.

He was Director of the Institute of Psychoanalysis, President of the Argentine Psychoanalytic Association (APA) and, in the international arena, was voted Latin American delegate at the House of Delegates at the International Psychoanalytical Association (IPA).

He was extremely committed to teaching candidates. He was among the analysts who had published the most papers in the journal of the APA. He was often present in National and International Psychoanalytic Conferences.

In 1967, having been interested in psychosomatic medicine for years, he, along with some disciples, founded the Centre for Research in Psychosomatic Medicine (CIMP), which had a successful development in research and training. Their conferences were attended by prestigious national and international professionals as well as writers like Jorge Luis Borges. This institution came to an end around 1977.

In September 1996, along with five colleagues, he founded the psycho-analytic journal *La Plaga de Tebas*.

He was not only an author that I had read and known well; he was also my training analyst.

Fidias was a very formal professional when I started my analysis with him, within what we now call orthodoxy. I had sessions four times a week that offered an impeccable psychoanalytic attitude and a very stable setting. Inside the session, in the transference-countertransference process, he appeared with a less formal attitude than at the beginning and the end of the session.

Although one could say he was an "orthodox" analyst, I have memories where he allowed himself heterodoxies that in those days were regarded as heresy.

While in analysis, even before my analytic training, as I started seeing patients, I was asked to read the material I had written about a patient, and I worked on this material during the session.

To my knowledge the only one who many years later handled this line of work was Jacques Lacan.

Another unorthodox way was that the first four candidates analysed by him during their analytic training became, after graduation, a study group that lasted for many years; all of us continued analysis with Dr. Cesio.

Lacan had also developed something similar. Fidias had no objection taking in analysis a husband and wife separately. An unusual and rare situation; it could be said to be "Ferenzci's way". He had the idea of approaching the psychoanalytic encounter as a dream.

Since the time I met him, his interest was the concept of lethargy and the history of psychoanalysis. Lethargy is one of the aspects to which he devoted himself with force and originality. The concept of lethargy had been very important in his clinical work, as well as in his theoretical elaboration. He explores the subject in the following papers: "The Dead", "Lethargy" and "Lethargy, a contribution to the study of negative therapeutic reaction".

Negative therapeutic reaction was a constant interest for Fidias, as seen in part two of "Lethargy, a contribution to the study of negative therapeutic reaction". Another important work is: "Lethargy, a reaction to object loss, a contribution to the study of negative reaction". Another work that needs to be mentioned is "Lethargy, the expression of the repressed and the buried, the professional disease of the psychoanalyst".

His interest in psychosomatic medicine is revealed in his works, which highlight this theme: "Unlocking the secrets of memory (the Dead)", "The actual neurosis, the psychic act of memory" and "Boredom, its discrimination from lethargy".

In the last years of his life, he became extremely interested by actual neurosis and wrote "The actual neurosis, affect, lethargy and anxiety". The subtitle of this paper is "The second fundamental hypothesis: Jealousy and lethargy, Alzheimer, forgetfulness, homosexuality and memory". Amongst his most important papers are "The castration complex and oedipal tragedy. Sexuality in the etiology of the disease, trauma construction" and "Psy-

with the question: what is lethargy? Up to the end of his life, this remained the subject of his research and understanding, even in the actual neuroses. Fidias describes something like a relationship between the Dead, the ideal Ego and Lethargy. What does Fidias understand about this relationship? He reminds us to note that while the lethargy is a symptom of actual neurosis, sleep is a restorative physiological function.

He gives clinical examples that allowed him to link lethargy as a symptom, its relationship with the ideal Ego and finally its relation with the negative therapeutic reaction. The shortness of this introduction does not allow me to present clinical material, but I could say in general terms that it is the discovery of a narcissistic location of the libido. Several authors, such as Bleger and Willy Baranger, worked later on the same issue of the narcissistic location of the libido, trying to understand this approach.

It is clear that Cesio relates and accepts Arnaldo Rascovsky's idea of the existence of the foetal self in relation to the ideal. But Fidias describes it as constituted by the proto-fantasies that inhabit the Id drive. As Fidias says, paraphrasing Freud, it is precipitated in "earlier selves" of the beings who preceded us. That is why he highlights the Dead buried in the unconscious.

He then proceeds to assert that the ideal Ego originates in the Id. The postnatal Ego contains unconscious configurations, which never became conscious and consequently never underwent repression. These Id components exist in the primary process: timeless and spaceless.

They manifest themselves in neurosis without words; it is absence with physical manifestations, such as anxiety, lethargy and other somatic illnesses. In hypochondria reaches the possibility of language.

According to Fidias, reconstruction and interpretation are the technical tools to make conscious these unconscious materials.

Returning to the lethargy and therefore to the Dead: the Dead is a construction that was made of the contents buried in lethargy and other components, such as the vicissitudes of the original trauma, the phallic castration. In its constitution we find the Primary Oedipus complex – a buried tragic instinct – that becomes conscious as a representation of death, as for example in abortions.

In Cesio's latest book, *Actual neurosis*, he provides the clearest description of what he means by lethargy: how it can be related to a psychotic break-down, how it influences life and how it relates to the negative therapeutic reaction, most of these ideas based on Freud's. Fidias says there is no doubt that patients oppose healing as they consider it a tremendous threat, and what prevails in them is their connection with their disease more than the will to heal.

# References

1  Cesio, Fidias R. (2010) *Actual neurosis*. Editorial La Peste, Buenos Aires.
2  Cesio, Fidias R. (1960) El letargo. Una contribución a la reacción terapéutica negativa, *Revista de psicoanálisis,* vol 17, 3, p 10–26.
3  Cesio, Fidias R. (1964) El letargo. Una rección a la pérdida de objeto; con-tribución al estudio de la reacción  terapéutica negativa. *Revista de Psicoanálisis*, vol 21, 1, p 19–27.
4  Cesio, Fidias R. (1991) El letargo. La enfermedad profesional del analista. In: *Psicoanálisis actual y las patologías graves: teoría, clínica y tecnica*. Editorial APA, Buenos Aires, p 68–74.
5  Cesio, Fidias R. (1978) Psicoanálisis de las manifestaciones somáticas. La seg-unda hipótesis del psicoanálisis. In *Revista de psicoanálisis* vol 35, 2, p 207–219.

$$————— 15 —————$$

*Fidias R. Cesio*

*This paper was written in 2011 for this collection in Spanish and translated by Ana Pieczanski.*

## Introduction

In this chapter, I provide a review of the two cases of analysis that motivated me to begin researching lethargy. In the case 'material', associations and corresponding actions regarding the tragic difficulties of pregnancy, abortion and childbirth were dominant.

Reviewing my most significant work, ranging from the 1950s to 2010, I selected 55 cases for publication in the 2010 book *Actual neurosis*.[1] Many of these address 'lethargy'.

Below is a summary of the analysis for two cases: for Palene, my first publication in 1952;[2] and for Yanira, published four years later, when I discovered[3] – or it was revealed to me – the secret of lethargy.[4]

## Palene

A 39-year-old woman was brought in for a consultation regarding a serious melancholic-lethargic[5] reaction, resulting from the death of her only daughter, Dirse, a 12-year-old girl who was run over by a train.

She experienced an extreme symbiosis with Dirse, and suffered from histero–epileptic attacks shortly after giving birth. Palene began suffering

179

from severe vaginal hemorrhages two years prior to Dirse's accident, which worsened to the point where she was about to undergo surgery. Her husband was hospitalized with paranoid schizophrenia since shortly after Dirse's birth.

When I interviewed her the day after the accident, she had been in a lethargic state for 24 hours. At times, she would leave this state and speak like a child, at other times she pulled at her clothes and hit herself. When I returned two days later, she was more connected. When she saw me she asked for her daughter. A month later, she went home and continued her treatment at my office, accompanied by a family member. During the first two or three months of treatment, she would sometimes experience an attack when leaving the office; she would fall to the ground and become cyanotic, her body rigid. After a few minutes, she would shake and hit her head and body. Once at home, she would remain semiconscious and lethargic until the next day. The hitting and the lethargy – 'death' – seemed to reproduce Dirse's accident.

It is worth pointing out that she did not have a bowel movement until a month after the accident. The fecal matter represented the dead daughter. Once she began to mourn she was able to defecate – to project Author.

Palene's parents had a son who died before the patient was born, and when she was a child another brother died. Palene attempted suicide at age 7 by swallowing pills. At 12, the same age Dirse was when she was run over by a train, she became seriously ill with typhoid fever and the doctors declared her terminally ill. Three months later, as a last resource, her mother called a healer who treated Palene through exorcisms and cured her. The 'exorcist' had appeared once again – the analyst – and just as before, Palene improved drastically.

When Palene received an accounting degree at 22 years old, her father, financially ruined, grew ill because of heart problems and died a few months later. She took his place and maintained the household, working as an accountant. She did not have any sexual experience until she married at 28 years old, and this experience was totally frustrating. She got pregnant against her will. She tried to abort with blows to her abdomen while fantasizing about having a dead child in her womb. She also fantasized about committing suicide to kill the fetus. The accident became the fulfillment of the wish she had had since becoming pregnant – to kill the baby.

Dirse was born a year after the marriage. At that time, Palene's husband was diagnosed with schizophrenia and was hospitalized because of manifestations of morbid jealousy and thoughts of persecution. Palene's histero-epileptic attacks also began at this time. She also suffered from severe vaginal hemorrhage attacks that began two years before Dirse's accident and death. When Dirse entered puberty and her symbiosis with Palene threatened to disappear, she had an accident with mild injuries when boarding a train she used to commute to school. The fatal accident took place one month later. Palene's vaginal hemorrhages remarkably disappeared after Dirse's death, a type of 'somatic conversion' of her fantasies of Dirse's death.

Palene's condition improved after a few months of analysis. The attacks she had experienced when leaving the office and lethargic state became less

Her daughter's accident-suicide was the 'realization'[6] of Palene's fantasies of causing death to Dirse as a fetus: the blows to the womb to cause an abortion, the suicidal fantasies to kill her, the idea that she was already dead inside the womb, and after that, keeping her as a 'fetus-abortion' through the symbiosis.

Palene and Dirse had lived in symbiosis, isolated in their home, since the husband's hospitalization. The fatal accident took place when Dirse reached puberty and the symbiosis threatened to disappear.

Palene continued recovering her health and youthful energy throughout the years of analysis. She began working as an accountant again, which she had abandoned after Dirse's birth. Palene's identification with the 'Dead' daughter – lethargy – was followed by her identification with the pubescent and adolescent 'daughter'.

## Discussion

The symbiosis with Dirse, with the repression of all sexual manifestation, had been a 'continuity' of the pregnancy and the denial of Dirse's birth and the subsequent phallic castration. We were very curious about the fact that Palene, faced with the loss of her supposedly very close daughter, narcis-sistically 'loved' and did not present symptoms of melancholy, but rather lethargy, in identification with the 'Dead'. Furthermore, we were surprised that, without experiencing melancholy and mourning corresponding to the magnitude of the loss, she would experience a noticeable improvement and recover abilities she had prior to Dirse's birth that had been inhibited up until that moment, such as sexual enjoyment and cultural and social experiences.

One explanation is that she identified with the ideal Ego – she was the ideal Ego – and that given this extreme narcissistic constitution, the con-ception of Dirse, regarding the ideal Ego, threatened her with the loss of her 'ideal' identity. She could only live by 'fulfilling' her wishes of death for the new being, by denying its existence and preserving in this way her ideal identity. Dirse, the 'fetus', 'sucked' her blood – the vaginal hemorrhaging – and threatened her life. This is why she attempted to kill the fetus and then 'prolong' the pregnancy through the symbiosis.

Palene made an intense narcissistic transference from the beginning of the analysis, placing her ideal Ego on me and freeing her more mature relational Ego, which she was able to develop in order to recover and increase her abilities prior to Dirse's conception. Dirse had never been a 'postnatal' object for Palene. She was only able to objectify the elements of the 'world' and enter sexuality and affective relationships with her peers during the transference.

During her attacks and vaginal hemorrhages, she would reproduce the violence with which she wanted to 'abort' Dirse – free herself from the slavery of her ideal Ego – and with the lethargy she manifested her identification with the abortion, with the 'Dead' 'daughter' – the ideal, fetal Ego – the 'Dead', buried in her unconscious.

The vaginal bleedings had a double meaning: on the one hand they represented Palene as being 'absorbed' by the fetus, Dirse, when she lived off her blood; and on the other hand they were the realization of her fantasy to abort her. The 'bloody accident', Dirse's death, signified the 'realization' of this fantasy. In the symbiosis, Palene conserved the primary idealized Ego features, which she was in danger of losing with Dirse's puberty.

I believe that the pregnancy, with the appearance of the fetus, was the threat of a phallic castration for Palene, as she experienced it as the loss of her ideal Ego, now alienated in the fetus, and as mentioned before, it made her want an abortion during the pregnancy and later on deny the fetus through the symbiosis.

The accident, like Dirse's birth, was an update of the fundamental trauma, the rupture of the symbiosis; the phallic castration was now dramatically represented by Dirse's death. Her blows during the pregnancy, the fantasy of suicide, the idea of 'Dead' fetus, the hystero-epileptic attacks and the vaginal bleedings set the stage for the original trauma, the birth, the Oedipal tragedy that was objectified by Dirse's accident.

Palene's improvement following Dirse's death can be explained by taking into consideration that, on the one hand, it constituted the 'buried Dead'; on the other hand, it gave way to the appearance of Dirse as an object, subdued by the secondary – postnatal – Ego.[7]

We wondered why she did not experience melancholy with the loss of what we could presume to be such a narcissistically charged object as Dirse was. One hypothesis is that Palene did not objectify Dirse, that she was not an object and that her relationship kept the original narcissistic characteristic up until her death.

## Below is Yanira's case, where the lethargy
## predicted the tragedy

I was consulted about a young woman, Yanira, who suffered from a serious depression after she had an abortion. The first interview took place a few days later. She seemed apathetic, distanced. She was a 'bohemian' – an artist,

a depressed mood.

She was close to her mother until her early 20s.

Over the years, she also showed important physical symptoms. During puberty, she suffered from a progressive inflammation of her respiratory system, most noticeable in her upper respiratory tract. When she consulted me, her nasal mucous membrane was seriously damaged and suffered olfactory loss, and nauseating secretions. She also smelled an unbearable odor of decomposing flesh. Her lungs showed bronchiectasis, she also had renal ptosis and constant and low-grade fever.

Yanira had two abortions, at 26 and 32 years old. The consultation took place after the second, which was followed by a deep depression.

Her appearance was paradoxical. At times she seemed attractive, but when she was depressed and did not perform the necessary hygiene to hide the evidence of her illness, she was repulsive due to the smelly secretions and her untidy appearance.

### The analytical process

During the first months of analysis, in between silences, she spoke about her somatic symptoms, especially about her anosmia, telling me that it was substituted by olfactory hallucinations associated with memories of her infancy. Her silences became progressively more prolonged, until she only spoke during the first few minutes of each session. Adopting a fetal position, she complained about feeling an intense coldness that she associated with death and would lead her to a deep lethargy – apparent death. It is common to say that in these cases the patient, or the analyst, remains silent or 'sleeps', euphemisms that deny the lethargic characteristics, the 'death'[8] of these manifestations. In these circumstances, my interpretations seemed useless.[9]

Later on, the cold and the lethargy were substituted by sexual fantasies that led to a fervent desire to conceive a child, and to that end she established a relationship with a partner and got pregnant, against her doctor's advice. From then on, a noticeable change took place in her life. She only worried about the pregnancy and the future child, and spoke about these issues in a way that, at times, seemed delusional. The pregnancy and the future child would appear as the fruit of the analysis. In fact, she 'decided' to sacrifice her life for her child. She fixed up her apartment, returned to her artwork that had been in storage for a long time, abandoned her other activities and almost all of her friends. When she was in her fifth month of pregnancy, her doctor told her that if she wanted to continue seeing him she would have to stay on almost complete bed rest. She decided to interrupt the analysis, with the conviction that continuing implied an abortion. She had been in treatment for four years.

During the seventh month of her pregnancy, on a night when an extremely close friend was visiting, she spoke about what arrangements to make in case of her hypothetical death. When her friend was leaving, she had a severe eclampsia attack followed by a deep lethargy. She had a cesarean section and the baby girl was saved. She woke up a few hours later, but only for a few minutes, soon relapsing into lethargy. This time, the coldness and the lethargy that had paralyzed progress during the analysis were prolonged until her death; she 'gave' her life to her child, 'she was the abortion' and paradoxically 'survived' in the newborn baby.

# Discussion

Her grandfather's suicide, her father's suicide with the culmination of her Oedipal complex, plus the jealousy she experienced a posteriori due to her mother's relationships, were traumas that prevented her from mourning. The loss was resolved by the consubstantiation[10] with the 'dead', evident in her severe somatic conversions – nasal mucosal destruction and bronchiectasis – as well as in her identification with the 'Dead' grandfather and father, and with the abortions. She died at approximately the same age as her father.

Her silences and lethargy set the stage for her Oedipal tragedy. They were manifestations that during the session presented her identification with the father, crazy with jealousy, suicidal, the 'dead', and the analyst in the transference, which also represented the mother who, we presume, led Yanira's father to commit suicide by stimulating his jealousy.

The Oedipal tragedy,[11] with the installation of the castration complex, is a drama about jealousy and death. It was Yanira's tragedy. Her grandfather and father had committed suicide – the suicide is a crime, the filicide-parricide – a tragedy where we infer that jealousy is the protagonist. Yanira's major suffering as a child was due to jealousy of her mother, and later on, with her voluntary abortions: jealousy of the fetus (?) She also 'committed crimes'. In the analysis, her tragedy expressed itself in the lethargy, in the melancholy-lethargy, a type of suicide identified with the abortions.

The 'Dead', represented above all by the grandfather and the father 'who committed suicide' and the abortions, had such a thanatic power within

consubstantiated with it, since continuing with analysis presumably meant another abortion.

This time, in the analysis she 'simulates' before 'the castrating mother' – with the unconscious complicity of the analyst – that with the conception of a baby she is generating a new abortion, while with the suspension of the analysis she entertains death and 'saves her life' – projected onto her child's life. Now she is the 'abortion', the 'Dead'.

When Yanira managed to get pregnant, stimulating the spark of life that was within her, she zealously took care of it. Paradoxically, while expecting an impossible cure from the analysis, it threatened her with the abortion of this vital 'awakening' of her fertility. The obstetrician recommended an abortion, since continuing with the pregnancy put her life in danger. She 'knew' that the only way to save the life within her was by having a child, and continuing within her. The analysis offered to pour her narcissistic libido into her Ego to keep her alive, and take it away from the fetus; when all is said and done: another abortion. Yanira 'chose' to give her life to her child; she poured her libido into her, and ended up exposed to death. The eclampsia appeared when she was close to eight months pregnant and the daughter was viable; when she was dying, her daughter was taken away from her breast. The most dramatic unmixing took place. By entertaining death, she saved what life she had 'incarnated' in her daughter.

Yanira's analysis became the beginning and foundation of a line of research on which I focused up till now. When she accepted the doctor's recommendation to be on complete bed rest to protect the pregnancy, it apparently prevented her from continuing the analysis. I am not sure why I did not suggest we continue the analysis in her home, as I have done in other cases. She seemed so determined to interrupt it that I presumed she would not accept this solution – an evident manifestation of my resistance – although, as I mentioned above, maybe it was the manifestation of an unconscious vital movement, saving her life by passing it on to her daughter.

185

## Conclusions

The difficulties Palene and Yanira had with conception, pregnancy and birth, beyond the prevailing expression of life, set the stage for the castration complex present in the lethargy, where the primary Oedipal complex, the tragic one, is expressed.

In Palene's case, with Dirse's gestation and birth, despite the attacks on the pregnancy that included suicidal thoughts, a type of extension of the pregnancy continued through their symbiosis, until the first menstruation that was a type of abortion, and then the fatal accident took place. Death wishes for her daughter that were previously manifested in the abortions were 'fulfilled'. For Palene to live, Dirse had to die. She tried to kill the fetus from conception, even fantasizing about her own death to achieve it. Palene tried by all means to restrict her daughter's growth, particularly her sexuality, because they endangered her life. The attacks on the fetus to provoke the abortion, that a posteriori to the accident were manifested in the hystero-epileptic attacks and in her vaginal bleedings, which coincided with Dirse's first menstruation, were a death threat of her being, the one who was aborted. The tragedy ended with Dirse's accident, her vaginal bleedings ceased and she began menstruating, developing her sexuality and a 'normal' social space.

Yanira, whose abortions allowed her to conserve her vital narcissistic libido, reached a point when the abortions no longer saved her. So, to continue her life, instead of the abortion she needed to give birth to the child and continue within her, and she became the abortion.

With conception, the new being is created by the previous Egos, from the 'Dead'[12] – the same ones that gave life to the mother, like the ones in the Odyssey, feeding with blood . . .[13] of the mother. This metaphor indicates that the uterus is where the previous egos, buried, come back to life; the "Mortis et vitae locus," how the tombs were named, where new beings were generated from the 'Dead'.

Yanira's 'Dead', represented by the abortions, were giving life to the fetuses she conceived, even more so when she 'knew' that she could only save her life by 'incarnating herself' in the child; she decided to have her and surrendered to death, Yanira was the abortion.

In the analytical work we find something similar within the limits of the transference; metaphorically we give our blood to give life to the 'Dead' 'buried' in our patient's unconscious.

To clarify the role that conception, pregnancy, abortion and birth play on the makeup of the self, we provide a brief summary of our ideas regarding the fetal Ego.

The ideal, fetal Ego is conceived by the proto-fantasies that inhabit it, by the instinct –the 'Dead'. It is the precipitation of the 'previous egos', of the beings that came before us, of the 'Dead' buried in our unconscious. From this point of view, it is 'ideal' because it has of the Id what could not be achieved in the postnatal Ego. It is what was never conscious and therefore never repressed; it is the buried unconscious, without 'present' time or space. It is manifested in the actual neurosis, without words, particularly in 'absence', 'silence' and in corporal manifestations such as lethargy, anguish

in the lethargy and other actual illnesses. It results from difficulties of the original trauma, the Oedipal tragedy. We find the primary Oedipal complex tragic, instinctual. It appears in the conscience through representations of death, where representations of the abortion are paradigmatic.

## Notes

1   *Actual neurosis*, 2010, Ed. La Peste, Buenos Aires.
2   Psychoanalysis of melancholy with hysteroepilectic attacks and lethargy. *Revista de Psicoanálisis*, 1952, 9, 389–412.
3   A case of negative therapeutic reaction *Revista de Psicoanálisis*, XIII, 522–526.
4   While lethargy – apparent death – is a symptom of actual, ominous neurosis, sleep is a physiological repairing function.
5   While we designate melancholic-lethargic to the symptom Palene presented, the symptoms did not correspond to the typical melancholic symptoms; with her attacks and lethargy, they seemed more like a staged production of the tragedy that was being presented long before the accident. Keep in mind that lethargy is a type of 'suicide' similar to what we see in melancholy.
6   The 'realization' is a setting of the stage for the fulfillment of a wish. 'Realization' is addressed further in "Need, desire and achievement-realization". *The plague of Tebas*, Editorial La Peste, Buenos Aires, 2005, N 32.
7   The postnatal Ego, unlike the narcissistic-ideal-Ego, begins developing at birth, characterized by pulmonary breathing and oral feeding – while the fetus breathed and fed from the mother's blood.
8   Later on we will elaborate on the significance of 'death' – of the 'Dead', the cadaver.
9   With my research on actual neurosis and the technique for analyzing it, years later I concluded that the verbal construction of a scene, which provides words to the current manifestation, is indispensable – as is the lethargy – to proceed to the interpretation, such as with a dream or an occurrence.
10  I call this process 'consubstantiation' due to its nature of 'carnal fusion'; it should not be confused with the direct identification prior to all object cathexis that

Freud refers to when he describes the appearance of the postnatal fundamental Ego in "The Ego and the Id". This same mechanism explains the establishment of the actual transference.

11  The paradigm is King Oedipus, the tragedy of Sophocles.

12  In his poem "Al hijo", Borges addresses this idea: "it is not me who is engendered. It is Author. / They are my father, his father and their elders./ .... "

13  In Chapter 11 of the *Odyssey*, Ulysses pours the blood of a sacrificed animal into a well and the souls of Author come back to life when they try the blood −including that of his mother, Tiresias y Jocasta. In the transference, the analyst, like Ulysses, gives life to the objects buried in the unconscious 'with his blood' − like the mother of the fetus − to the 'dead' buried in the unconscious of his patients.

# References

Some of the citations appear in the chapter endnotes.

Abraham, K.: *Selected Papers on Psycho-Analysis. A Particular Form of Neurotic Resistance Against the Psycho-Analytic Method* (1919), The Hogarth Press, London, 1948.

Freud, S.: The Ego and the Id. *Complete Works*, Ed. Biblioteca Nueva, Madrid, 1948.

Gonzalez, A: Observations about the analysis of the acts of associating and interpreting in a case with a negative therapeutic reaction. (Presented at the Argentine Psychoanalytic Association in March 1956).

Horney, K.: The Problem of the Negative Therapeutic Reaction, *The Psychoanalytic Quarterly*, 1936, 5, 29–45.

Langer, M.: *Maternity and sex*, Ed. Nova, Buenos Aires, 1951.

Racker, H.: The meaning of countertransference. (Presented at the Argentine Psychoanalytic Association in May 1953).

Racker, G.: Aspects of psychoanalysis of a "foreigner". Contribution to the study of the negative therapeutic reaction. (Presented at the Argentine Psychoanalytic Association in May 1955).

Rascovsky, A.: *The fetal psychism*, Ed. Paidós. Buenos Aires, 1960.

Reich, W.: *Character Analysis*, New York, Ed. Orgone Institute Press, 1949.

Riviere, J.: Contribution to analysis of the negative therapeutic reaction. *Revista de Psicoanálisis*, 1949, 7, 121–142. (Trans. from the *International Journal of Psycho-Analysis* 1936, 17, 304).

Segal, H.: A Necrophilic Phantasy, *International Journal of Psycho-Analysis*, 1953, 34, 98–101.

# (1911–1974)

## *Roberto Bittencourt Martins*

"Identification and identity", published in 1969, is representative of the work of Alcyon Bahía. In this paper, Bahía, starting from Freud's ideas and based on significant clinical material, attempts to integrate classic psychoanalytical concepts with authors such as Hartmann, Klein, Winnicott and Bion.

"Identification and identity" is part of a collection of works in which Bahía develops contributions made by authors of his time. It is preceded by "Notes on the interactions of projective and introjective mechanisms in the analytical process".

Bahía was born in 1911; his father was a poet and a journalist and his mother was an accomplished pianist. Bahía was brought up and spent his childhood in a culturally sophisticated family environment where he developed his scientific curiosity and creativity, which he would later on apply to psychoanalysis.

He graduated in medicine at the National University (of Rio de Janeiro) in 1936. He trained as a psychiatrist and from the beginning showed interest in psychoanalysis. He joined other colleagues who were already reading psychoanalytic literature, and with a few members of this group, he decided to go to Buenos Aires in search of personal analysis and training at the then-new Argentine Psychoanalytic Association (APA).

He underwent training analysis with Dr. Celes Cárcamo, an Argentine trained at the Paris Institute. Alcyon became a member of APA in 1952 and, back in Rio, was one of the 14 founders of the Brazilian Psychoanalytic Society of Rio de Janeiro in 1959.

He enjoyed mainly teaching at the Institute of Psychoanalysis as well as being a clinician. He is still remembered as a much-respected professor and supervisor as well as a receptive, sharp and motivating analyst.

His intellectual restlessness and his ethical desire to also help lower income patients at the Mental Health Services of the Ministry of Health drove him to introduce group analytic psychotherapy in Brazil in 1951. Based on teachings received from Pichon-Rivière in Buenos Aires and on Bion's experiences from working with groups during World War II, he established and directed a pioneering public service sector in the country. "Psycho-analytic experiences in group therapy" (1954) and "Secrecy and revelation in the therapeutic group" (1961) are some of his works dedicated to this subject.

Bahía wrote numerous texts based on classical books, such as "Content and defense in artistic creation"(1952), based on *The outsider* by Camus, and "Psychoanalytic interpretation of crime" (1956), based on *Crime and punishment* and other works by Dostoyevsky. He worked with Rorschach tests on convicts and developed psychological research based on texts by Freud and Ferenczi. He came to the conclusion that criminal offences are caused primarily by feelings of guilt. Bound to his time, Bahía examined *Reflections on the edge of tragedy* and *The wedding dress* (1944), by Nelson Rodrigues, which was then revolutionizing Brazilian theatre.

As a true pioneer, he investigated through a psychoanalytic lens some cinematographic works, such as *Rashomon* by Kurosawa, together with the dream of a patient; he then wrote "Repression, memory and amnesia" (1956), a work that sided with Eisenstein's concepts of filmmaking and the Freudian conceptualization of screen memories.

In it, Bahía considers mnemonic function to be "a fantastic construction, in which to remember or not remember are not antagonistic but synchronic instruments with the same intentionality – the transformation of the external reality according to the instinctive needs." We would thus all be "in sickness and in health, in creative activity and in delirious, to a greater or lesser extent, authentic manufacturers of memories."

All this productivity was interrupted by a heart condition, causing his unexpected death in 1974 at 62 years of age. This sudden death caused consternation; however, Bahía's life left behind the solace of reading such texts as "Fear of death" (1944), which deals with the subject of the "great death one brings within", the neurotic fear of death in hypochondria, the intensification of that fear in adolescence and, quoting verses by the poet Rainer Maria Rilke, "his inexorable character".

# I

In an earlier work (1) presented to this Society, I tried to demonstrate that the interaction of projective and introjective mechanisms, constantly operating in the ego from early development, constitutes one of the best guides for understanding the therapeutic process in its entirety.

As I indicated at that time, the importance of projective-introjective interaction in structuring the psyche was first unveiled by Freud, in his anthological comparison of psychic activity with an amoeba's action (6). This was subsequently highlighted and carefully researched in its multiple specific connections, becoming the keynote of Melanie Klein's work (16). And finally, Bion gave it a new dimension in his studies about the coexistence of phenomena and non-psychological aspects, as well as psychotic ones, within the same personality (3), as well as admitting "the existence of a mixed state in which the patient is persecuted by feelings of depression and depressed by feelings of persecution", sentiments which are – according to him – "indistinguishable from bodily sensations" (4).

The simple chronological mention of these facts, which goes from Freud to Bion, passing through Melanie Klein, seems to indicate that, despite the restrictions that some psychoanalysts like Winnicott (20) make, the concept of interaction between the projective and introjective processes grows daily in importance, both for theory and technique.

This paper was translated from Portuguese by Ana de Andrada; the original was read on October 17, 1966, to the Brazilian Psychoanalytical Society in Rio de Janeiro and published in the 1969 *Revista Brasileira de Psicoanalise*, Sao Paulo, 3(1/2): 131–155.

In my earlier work, I believe I demonstrated, using clinical examples, that the isolated interpretation, whether of projective or introjective processes, brings a danger of unilateralism and distortion to understanding the ego in operation. This unilateralism and distortion are reflected, particularly, in the loss of the opportunity to observe – and therefore adequately interpret – the extremely precocious phenomena of the primitive ego's guilt projection characteristics, through which it defends itself from recognizing true guilt via paranoid-schizoid mechanisms such as splitting, idealization of the self and the object and negation of external and internal reality.

The events that constitute and result from the interaction of the projective and introjective processes are revisited, in this work, with the same theoretical and technical implications formulated in the previous work. But now, they are seen from a new, more restricted and more specific angle, therefore better characterizing the facts studied. I refer to the dynamic relationship that exists between the individual's incessant effort to acquire an insight into his own identity and his tendency to merge with the object, whether by projecting parts of himself, or by incorporating parts of the object. In other words, whether by projective identification or introjective identification, as Melanie Klein states on this subject, "the extent to which the individual feels his ego to be submerged in the objects with whom it is identified by introjection or projection is of greatest importance for the development of object relations and also determines the strength or weakness of the ego."

In reality, as clinical experience shows, the ego's "submersion" in objects is not produced by a choice of "introjection or projection", but by both processes. Melanie Klein herself recognizes this fact when she states that "the process of reintrojecting a projected part of the self includes internalizing a part of the object into which the projection has taken place" (18).

But the problem of adequately conceiving the relationships between individual identity and the projective-introjective identification processes does not end with the idea of the ego's "degree of submersion" in objects. This conception must be complemented by the clearest differentiation possible between what should be understood by ego and what should be understood by self. Without this, it would not be possible to avoid that "conceptual imprecision" which, according to Hartmann, "tends to become a serious handicap to an understanding among analysts and also to an understanding of psychoanalysis in general" (10).

The necessity for this differentiation is actually not new. It first appeared in Freud's study about "Analysis Terminable and Interminable", where he categorically stated: "With the recognition that the properties of the ego which we meet with in the form of resistances can equally well be determined by heredity as acquired in defensive struggles, the topographical distinction between what is ego and what is id loses much of its value for our investigation." (7)

Notwithstanding, it was undoubtedly after Hartmann's investigations that the distinction between self and ego became clearest.

"To define it negatively," as Hartmann says, "in three respects, as against other ego concepts: 'ego' in analysis, is not synonymous with 'personality'

world should be highlighted. As Hartmann also recalls, following Freud's train of thought: "The ego organizes and controls motility and perception – perception of the outer world but probably also of the self" (12). However, as he points out, to Freud, "the subjective experience of one's own self was a function of the ego, but not the ego" (13).

Thus, in accordance with Freud's and Hartmann's concepts, I think it is valid to consider that the perception of personal identity is a function of the ego, but organized and directed in the sense of recognizing the self. It is in harmony with Hartmann's concepts, on one hand, and the Kleinian concept of the ego's "submersion" in objects, on the other hand, that I propose to study two complementary facts in this paper. These facts seem to me to be fundamental for understanding the operative capacities of the ego and for a more integrated understanding of the therapeutic process dynamic. First, the fact that the insight of one's own self in the therapeutic work becomes clearer and more vivid when the ego is led to understand that it is continuously "playing" with its environment, via an interaction of projections of parts of the self into objects with introjections, into the self, of parts of the object that have been partially disfigured by prior projections; second, the fact that a lack of understanding of the "interplay" of projective identification with intro-jective identification always causes a stronger "submersion" of the ego into objects, and, consequently, the perception of the self's identity fades.

Before beginning the presentation and discussion of the clinical mate-rial I base myself on, I must say that I don't consider the facts at hand as specific to certain types of patients, but rather as universal manifestations in the structure of the psyche, variable only according to the genetic–historical context of each person.

In the same way, it must be stressed that, when describing and discussing the clinical material, I tried to restrict myself to that moment and those aspects of analysis in which the ego, struggling with its identifications, strives to emerge from the chrysalis of these identifications to give the self the experience of perceiving itself.

193

In other words, this brief study seeks to understand an aspect, undeniably important, of the therapeutic process and the development of the primitive ego. However, it does not have any pretension of constructing a metapsychology of either of these processes. It is essential to complement this work with the study of other aspects and situations that transcend the problems here formulated. This work must be understood, along with the previous one about projective-introjective interaction and a third, about "sublimation", which is to follow, as an inseparable part of a triad that aspires to understanding the analytical process as a totality, but not the totality of the analytical process.

# II

The patient (A.R.), 46, came to analysis for the first time affected by a range of symptoms and difficult external circumstances, most of them caused by failures that he had very imprecise notions about, proving, in this respect as in other aspects of his life, to be semi-indifferent and distant. His symptoms are primarily of a phobic nature, with emphasis on agoraphobia, exacerbated when he has to cross squares or avenues in the midst of traffic, and claustrophobia, especially in movie theaters, where he often feels compelled to exit into the waiting room. On these occasions, he tells his companions he is just "going out for a smoke". As strong as these phobias is his feeling of affective blockage; he has not written to his mother, who lives abroad, for over five years, claiming he feels he has nothing to say to her, and when she sends him money – on a regular basis – she does it through his wife, who is thus the only objective link between the patient and his mother.

Within this framework of blockage and negation of internal reality, all the supremely important events related to the liquidation of his firm's assets are inserted and experienced. He considers it to be "essentially a bankruptcy, like all these immoralities of the capitalist system", which he does not have to bind himself to. That is how two other mechanisms enter the composition of his defenses – the rationalization and the idealization of his Marxist ideology and his militancy, as a student, in his homeland's communist party.

A highly educated, intelligent, cultured and sensitive man, the patient is a clearly schizoid personality. Polite without being affected, he is nonetheless somewhat preoccupied with his physical appearance, doing physical activity every day. He has only one sister, who is six years older than him. Having emigrated due to political circumstances resulting from the Second World War – for he was Jewish in a German-occupied country – he was forced, in order to support himself and his family (wife, daughter and mother-in-law), to perform commercial activities beneath his technical qualifications. This further aggravated the educated resentment and the sarcasm that form the essence of his character and his attitude during transference.

By repeating his psychodynamics in transference, it was possible to reconstitute a large part of his childhood environment and his "family drama".

The patient's memories of his father, even the earliest ones, character-

relationship are also saddening. His father had a small business, which would have supported their family life perfectly well had it not been for his mother's narcissistic ambitions to stand out in their social milieu through bizarre philanthropic attitudes that were far beyond the couple's financial possibilities. The father ended up going bankrupt because of his wife's philanthropic excesses; he lived the last 12 years of his life in a completely parasitic manner, gambling and reading newspapers in his hometown's cafes.

Shame, depreciation and sarcasm are the feelings surrounding the memories of this passive and ridiculous father. The patient's own mother mocked her husband at every step, openly or subtly referring to her marriage as a "mistake". She was – and apparently still is – a determined, authoritarian woman with strong convictions, but lacking consideration for others. Thus she forced a sister, whom the patient idealizes as a "kind auntie", to study medicine and exercise the profession against her will in a rural town, citing "the natural difficulties of competition in a big city." As frequently as she mocked her husband, she used to tell her son she had wanted to abort him, using a method that was then very much in vogue in her town: to "prick the uterus" by introducing small electric needles.

Thus, to sum up, in the patient's fantasy, his parents' marriage and conjugal life were "essentially a bankruptcy", "an immorality typical of the capitalist system". That is, it was an internal regime of violence where the mother submits herself, against her will, to the father's "poor penis", and consequently, angry and sarcastic, tries unsuccessfully to destroy the fruit of this relationship. This way, she brutalizes herself, imposing on herself – as can be seen by the imago of the kind auntie representing the mother's "other side" – forced labor, or repairing the children destroyed in her "interior".

In the interpersonal relationship between analyst and analysand, the "liquidation" represented an attempt to make a deal with the analyst, in a double sense: on one hand, appeasing the "persecuting father" so as to destroy him at a second stage; on the other hand, making a deal with the mother in an idealized relationship, in which both together would murder the "capitalist father" and not feel guilt.

After about two years of treatment, the patient interrupted his analysis, much improved in symptoms and conduct, and apparently with strong external motivation. He had satisfactorily resolved the liquidation affairs, and he had founded another company of the same kind, with a partner, in another state. At the time, he said it was "a less ambitious, healthier company, with fewer avid people around it." Consequently, he had to spend weeks on end without coming to analysis, so he decided to interrupt it, but with the intention of starting again as soon as he could. He fulfilled his promise, restarting analysis about 15 months later.

It must be recognized, however, that despite the apparent magnitude of the external motivation, I largely contributed to this interruption when I lost sight of Freud's wise advice in "Analysis Terminable and Interminable": "We must not take the clarity of our own insight as a measure of the conviction which we produce in the patient" (8). Thus, the understanding of the nature of the parents' relationship as "essentially a conjugal bankruptcy", which was so clear to me, was not experienced by the patient with the same clarity. On the numerous occasions that he mentioned a young male employee of the firm who he claimed was stealing "with the complicity of an older lady" who also worked at the firm, and who he suspected to be the young man's lover, the patient reacted with indifference to the interpretations of his "theft" of the spoils of a relationship of failure and falseness between the mother (analysis) and the father.

Therefore, taking the clarity of my own insight as a measure of conviction produced in the patient was largely what I had done in this first period of his analysis. This became quite clear even before the second phase of treatment began, when it came to time-related matters and updating the price of the sessions, and the patient told me he could "only do eight months of analysis", after which he absolutely had to return to the state where he had founded his new company. But it became clearer still when I perceived in him the anxious need to control the introjection of the analyst, who had become a "persecutor" and "dangerous" precisely because he saw dangerous things. The vicissitudes in this situation can be better observed in the following session fragment, taken from the second month of analysis after we restarted.

FIRST ASSOCIATIVE SEQUENCE

- "A winter season . . . I fell during a skating championship . . . there was no reason for it because I skated well . . . my mother said: you always have to fall twice before getting it right . . . in fact I had only fallen once" . . .

A – Your mother in this instant represents an aspect of you competing with me during this eight-month season, which is the term you have imposed on me. This leads me to believe that I have to fall once more – as I already fell in the earlier analysis period – before I get it right.

A – In your internal reality, I am concerned with your current situation in analysis. Because, like your daughter who is "out of college", you think I feel that you are "out of analysis", that is, afraid of entering into the examination of your fantasies. It will have to be left to a third time, a third period when, as you imagine, I am no longer at risk of falling and failing, as you believe happened the first time.

P – "I had a dream (the patient moves, restless): I was with my mother-in-law, you, who took women's forms, and our dog at home . . . who was quiet" (pauses).

"This dog became really neurotic after a trauma she had, when she found herself in the middle of intense traffic . . . she was nearly run over. I had taken her for a walk, suddenly she broke away from me and rushed in between the cars . . . she nearly died . . . Since then, she always trembles when I take her for a walk."

A – You are telling me you want to escape from analysis, like you did a while ago, and at the same time you want to stay close to me, quietly, like the dog. If I take you for a walk in your internal world, you are afraid of getting lost in the traffic of my interpretations, which make you anxious, now, as in the past the traffic of your mother's coitus with your father made you anxious. This must be the double desire you express in your dreams: to be close to me, in my company, but both of us quiet, without talking about your anxieties regarding this internal traffic. I have to wait some time before you can overcome these fears and talk about all this.

## III

Looking at the three sequences of ideas given by the patient in this session fragment in terms of interaction of projective and introjective identifications – and obviously within the transferential dialogue – we immediately come to a finding of undeniable clinical importance. Indeed, in the first sequence, through projective identification in the form of the "sarcastic mother", the patient attacks the object introjected in his ego, which is undoubtedly fragile and "falling", but is already in a differentiation attempt process. More than a superego imago, this fragile introjected object represents a "supplementary ego" imago, a characteristic, according to Paula Heimann (15), of the analyst's function in the therapeutic process. In the second associative sequence, partly by himself and partly as a result of interpretation, the patient refines the use of projective identification, placing in his daughter those parts of his self in charge of temporarily "immobilizing" the perceptive object which is partly dangerous, partly accepted, constituted by the person of the analyst. In the third sequence, there is an accentuation of the immobilizing role that projective identification has to exercise, at this moment in the therapeutic process, on the introjected object and the perceptive ego in a differentiation process. Projection on a dog, that is, an object that does not verbalize, expresses the patient's desire to silence the "ego-analyst" so that he does not talk about his castration, femininity and childhood dependence fantasies.

In all these three sequences, the ego cannot and should not perceive the differentiation that is at every instant being "imposed" by the "threatening analyst". Of course, if the patient comes to the treatment, it is because he at least partly accepts this "threat". But he accepts it in his own way, which is, dosing the danger, the interference and the intervention. In other words, he is regulating the "entrance" of the interpretations in his psyche.

This leads us to the second finding of clinical and theoretical importance that the confrontation of projective and introjective identification allows us to unveil: the attempt to mold the introjected perceptive object through projective identifications is not necessarily a pathological manifestation, because it largely corresponds to a normal event in the ego's development.

Although he expressed it in terms closer to primitive emotional development than to the therapeutic process, Bion (5) perceived this fact with great lucidity when he underlined the importance of acceptance, on behalf of the mother, of the child's projective identifications. He states: "If the mother and child are adjusted to each other, projective identification plays a major role in management; the infant is able through the operation of a rudimentary reality sense to behave in such a way that projective identification, usually an omnipotent fantasy, is a realistic phenomenon". But he also makes it clear that "if the mother cannot tolerate these projections the infant is reduced to continuing projective identification carried out with increasing force and frequency".

Winnicott, in his magnificent study about communication and non-communication, highlights – although from another angle – the same fact, showing that "there is an intermediate stage in healthy development in which the patient's most important experience in relation to the good or potentially satisfying object is the refusal of it" (21). He adds that "there is something we must allow for in our work, the patient's non-communicating as a positive contribution" (22).

The difficulty in this respect, still according to Winnicott, lies in being able to distinguish positive non-communication "from the distress signal associated with a failure of communication" (23).

should always be in identical circumstances.

If we now examine the presented material, always in light of projective-introjective interaction, in Oedipal terms – even easier to study when we consider them jointly with the elements obtained in the first analysis period – we arrive at a clearer and more clinical formulation of the problem of the relationship between identification and identity. Indeed, in the three associative sequences, observed in light of Oedipal fantasies, it can be seen that the self projects parts of itself (into the mother, into the daughter and into the dog, respectively) at the same time that it introjects, using the person of the analyst, aspects of the paternal imago. In the three sequences, this "interplay" clearly shows that "the internal mother" either denigrates the husband (the patient's fall) or keeps him at a distance, in the "entrance" (the daughter's entrance exam) or "neuroticizes" herself as the dog, for fear of sexual "traffic" with the husband.

In any of the three opportunities, the patient's ego is almost completely "submerged" in the objects, with minimal autonomy to preserve. It is precisely this minimal autonomy that explains the patient's non-communication desire, as any person in identical circumstances would feel. As Winnicott shows, "this preservation of personal isolation is part of the search for identity, and for the establishment of a personal technique for communicating which does not lead to violation of the central self" (24).

It is therefore insofar as he can "emerge" from objects that the individual can find his own identity. But paradoxically, it is only possible to succeed in this task with the help of external objects. The course of the patient's analytical process brought these two facts to light, very clearly, as will be seen below.

# IV

Always within the atmosphere of seeking communication with objects and, at the same time, fearing "submerging" in them, and always seeking that "personal technique for communicating which does not lead to violation of the central self", the patient one day brought to the session some material that was very significant in its double aspect; wanting to better visualize his internal world and daring to understand the meaning of his relationships with me and with his father. Here is the material:

FIRST SEQUENCE

P – "That book, which you had on your table, is no longer there . . . *Psychoanalytical States*, I think that was its name . . ."

A – "You are probably trying to express that I am afraid your fantasies will make me psychotic. They are 'psychotic states' and so I removed them from my interior."

(pause)

SECOND SEQUENCE

P – "Remembering F., Lili's boyfriend . . . he is a nice, friendly guy . . . In her typical language (the patient laughs), she says they're going for it, in his car I think . . . Their relationship is making all of us happy at home: my wife, me, my mother-in-law . . . but (the patient lowers his voice, embarrassed) I'm not sure, I think F. has some black in him".

A – In what you are saying, your daughter represents you and the boyfriend represents me. This means that, in your fantasy, we are both going for it, that is, turning each other on with the things we say to one another. Like everyone in your house, the analysis is also entirely affected by this aspect of your relationship with me. The fact that you lowered your voice when you said maybe F. has some black in him indicates that you imagine me to be ashamed of having some black in me, that is, of having an illegitimate sexuality. As you imagined your father was ashamed of being a Jew, and of having a "Jewish penis".

THIRD SEQUENCE

P – "In my hometown there was a café, like a concert-café, with music etc., but it was strange . . . it was that period between the First and Second World Wars . . . there were 'clausus' numbers, you know what

200

I mean, right? . . . a certain number of tables was set aside for each
group: for Hungarian Jews, for Hungarians, for Romanians, and for
Romanian Jews . . . even for a Slavic minority . . . in other words, it
was all organized".

A – You are trying to say you would rather go back to the period
between the two wars, that is, the period between the two analy-

that do not communicate among themselves.

## FOURTH SEQUENCE

P – "I think you're right. Because, although I'm not religious, I was,
at that moment, visualizing the figure of a Jew in a kaftan and with
curls (gestures) right in the middle of Nazi Germany, as a symbol of
courage".

A – This probably means you already visualize, in your internal world,
your father's figure with his masculine attributes reintegrated and
with no fear of the sarcastic and frustrating mother. This probably
occurred because you felt in me, with the previous interpretation,
this father with no fear of the mother's sarcasm and of her attempt
to denigrate his penis and his person.

As usually took place when he felt affected by an interpretation, the
patient remained in silence for the remaining minutes of the session. But
it was undeniable that, in his central self, a process of mutation and of differentiation was underway that operated in three senses: 1) in the sense
of non-communication for a communication necessity; 2) in the sense
of "emersion" of the ego "out of" primitive objects; and 3) – the most
important – in the sense of acquisition of personal identity.

In relation to the first aspect, that is, the change from non-communication
to the attitude of desiring communication, it is particularly visible in the
first two sequences, although it is also evident, differently of course, in the
last two. Indeed, in the first of the two initial sequences, the patient projects into the object his own fear of the "psychotic state", that is, his fear
of avidness for the maternal breast and the father's penis, almost instantly
reintrojecting this object, which has been modified by the previous projection. Thus, the ego becomes totally "submerged" in the object that it has
largely created itself.

But, unlike what happened in the first fragment of material presented, where the patient "retracted" through the communication that his daughter had to wait eight months to enroll, now he responds to the interpretation with a communication necessity that had previously been strongly denied; showing his avidness for the "analyst-father's" penis, although, due to a partial identification with the "sarcastic-mother", he still tries to denigrate it. In any case, the pleasure derived from the relationship with the analyst's whole person, not excluding his penis, predominates.

In contrast with the first aspect of the mutation and differentiation of the patient's self, the second aspect, that is, the "ego's emersion" out of primitive objects, is more present in the third sequence. Paradoxically, this fragile "emersion" takes place under the regressive form of a strong splitting. But it could be called an "organized" splitting, with all of its aspects, its 'clausus' numbers, well defined by the repression which, at that moment, tries to lead the self to a neutral period, "between the two analyses", where the ego can remain "non-perceptive". There was no doubt that the concert-café symbolized the body of the patient's mother, as divided and racist as a part of him was. But there was also no doubt that, at that instant of his session, this added nothing to his understanding of his fantasy and his self. What was important to perceive and communicate was that, momentarily, it was convenient to retract to "submersion" into the object that seemed to assail him, and go back to being "himself", even if this meant fragmentation and isolation.

Finally, when it comes to the third and most important aspect of the process of the self's differentiation — that of perceiving personal identification — I believe the fourth associative sequence makes it most evident. This is for two reasons: first, because that was the first occasion, in all of his analysis, when the patient "visualized" — to use his own expression — an imago of a father endowed with all his masculine attributes and recognized in the fullness of his existential dignity; second, because this "visualization" emerged as a response to an interpretation about the meaning of his retraction into communication and his anti-black, anti-Jewish, anti-father splitting.

It is clear that the three aspects, through which I am trying to express my understanding of the process of differentiation of the patient's self, are — like almost everything in the psyche — simultaneous and interconnected. Therefore, the four associative sequences contain, in varying shades and intensities, "communication — non-communication" phenomena, phenomena of the ego's "emersion" out of objects, and search and perception of the self's identity phenomena. But the emphasis, qualitatively and quantitatively, on a specific aspect at a given moment, is important for understanding the totality of the differentiation process, which leads to the perception of personal identity.

It is obvious that the process of the self's differentiation leading to the perception of personal identity experiences ascension and descent alternatives that are identical to the progression and regression phenomena observed in any analysis. However, in the clinical material of the patient's first months back in analysis – which forms the basis and expression of this work – there were moments in which the perception of the self's identity became very

thoughts he had had while waiting in my living room. His voice did not reveal anxiety, but rather the impatient determination of someone who is in a rush to perform an important task, without wasting time beating around the bush. As he had arrived early, he had been looking at my bookcase, which he said he admired: "the arrangement of the books, the decorative objects, everything basically". And he added: "except the image of that saint that is there . . . it's unpleasant, heavy with all those dresses; it is truly the image of false sainthood".

I began by interpreting that he wanted to signify that he felt me to be happy with myself, satisfied with "my interior", with the analysis I gave him, but that unpleasant image of "false sainthood" was too "heavy" in his interior as in mine; all those clothes probably represented the garments of false convictions, as "heavy" for me, when I spoke, as for him when listening to me.

Before I could finally "reduce" the interpretation terms to his childhood fantasies around his mother, the patient firmly interrupted me, saying: "Yes! Yes! . . . but do you know? . . . for the first time in my analysis, in all these years, I decided to take a book from your bookcase to read while I waited . . . I chose a book by Hartmann, some essays about the Ego . . . I was beginning to read it, when you came and interrupted me".

With these associations in hand, I was able to complete the interpretation, showing him that he had interrupted me precisely because he felt "interrupted", that is, prevented from being himself by the "weight" of the interpretations that he believed had been given him without conviction. I added that, in his fantasy at that time, I was at the same time the affectionate mother, worthy of being loved, and the mother of the false philanthropic attitudes, who had led his father to ruin and impotence. I also showed him that it was inside this mother and through her that he was finding his true individuality. Probably because he felt that this "false-saint mother", like the "failed father", was a "construction" of his fantasy, aspects of himself placed in the father and the mother to escape guilt for the attacks directed at both.

The patient listened to me without interrupting and, after a few minutes of reflective silence, said in a different tone of voice: "Yes . . . that's exactly what I was thinking, while you finished the interpretation . . . it actually makes me feel like crying . . . Indeed . . . I clung to the mother of defenses, the mother of sarcasm, so that I wouldn't feel the tears that were underneath all this". He was visibly moved.

These facts occurred during a weekend session. On the Monday after this session, the patient didn't come. But on Tuesday, he told me he had thought a lot over the weekend and had reached the conclusion that he had been unreasonable in wanting to limit his analysis time. Business was going well, his partner was capable and trustworthy, and he had the advantage of living where the company was located. He could, therefore, do analysis without concerns about time restrictions. At the most, once or twice a month, he would take a weekend to "see how things were going".

There was certainly some shyness and embarrassment in his attitude when he told me about his decision. However, with his natural alternatives and ups and downs in understanding, the analysis continued and has already surpassed the eight-month barrier.

# V

Now that a reasonable degree of understanding of the patient's fantasy in each fragment of material has been reached, I believe it is worth attempting to integrate this understanding into a broader "gestalt". Because seeking to understand the presented material's meaning as if the three fragments had occurred in a single session, composing an interconnected whole, is an investigation method founded on the best scientific tradition of psycho-analysis. In this case, the attempt has an additional reason – it leads to the very nucleus of the problem of the relationship between identification and the self's identity.

Under these conditions, it seems that the analytical understanding of the patient's material, seen as an interconnected whole occurring during a single session, allows us to unveil the operative capacities of the ego itself with great clarity. Especially in relation to its functions of discriminating and organizing reality's data, as Freud described in "Formulations on the Two Principles of Mental Functioning" (9).

With the first approach under these terms, it can be seen that, in the three sessions, the patient "places" into the analyst (whether by projection, or by "post-projection" introjection), depreciated parts of the self, representative of his failures or – which comes to the same thing – representative of an internal object that is being derided by another internal object, that is, the father denigrated by the mother. In the first session, this part that is "placed" into the analyst is represented by the "skating fall", ironically magnified by the mother. In the second session, this part consists of the daughter's boyfriend, who, although he pleases everyone in the house, "has some black in him". In the third session, the depreciated part of the self, placed into the analyst, is represented by

the third session, who throws the mother's "false sainthood", her castrating philanthropy, in her face.

But the combined analysis of the sessions yields the parallel discovery that the self also seeks to be "non object", even when it expresses itself by projecting its most central aspects into objects.

This happens, for example, when the patient talks about his daughter who has to "wait about eight months" to enroll. It happens when he mentions the concert-café with a "Klaus number" of tables, as expressive of his repulsion to the analyst-father's "interpreting penis" as it represents his ego's capacity to discriminate and organize the data of external and internal reality. And, more than in any other context, it happens when he takes Hartmann's book from my bookcase and discovers himself, and then tries to free himself from entrapment "within" the object.

These considerations lead to the core of the problem of the relationships between identification and identity — to the problem of the relationship between the "False" and the "True" Self.

When discussing the distortions experienced by the ego in terms of False Self and True Self, Winnicott (25) emphatically states that the function of the False Self, which is always defensive, is "to hide and protect the True Self, whatever that may be". At first sight, the clinical data he bases himself on seem to lead him to different concepts than those he proposes, and to obscure, rather than clarify, his points of view about the problem of the True and the False Self.

According to his own expressions, the "best example" he can give is "that of a middle-aged woman who had a very successful False Self, but also the feeling that throughout her life, she had never even begun to exist". In the first phase of this research analysis, Winnicott discovered he was dealing with what the patient called her "Caretaker Self". This "Caretaker Self" played, among others, the functions of "having discovered psychoanalysis", "having chosen analysis as a kind of test of the degree of trust in the analyst", but also the function of taking the analyst's place, "resuming caretaking at times when the analyst failed (analyst's illness, analyst's holidays, etc.)".

As this example illustrates there is, in principle, some confusion in Winnicott's conception between the ego's characteristic functions of discriminating reality – such as having found analysis, coming to analysis, etc. – and more understandable phenomena in terms of persecutory anxiety, with its corresponding omnipotent defenses, such as assuming the function of "guard-analyst" when the actual analyst is absent (due to illness, holidays, etc.).

At first glance, therefore, Winnicott's investigations do not seem very concerned with understanding the process through which the individual tries to use his ego's discriminating functions as a tool for acquiring personal identity. They really seem to confuse the ego's organizational capacities with its defense mechanisms against fundamental anxieties.

But this confusion completely vanishes when we compare Winnicott's points of view about the "False Self" – summarized above – with his concepts about the problem of "communication" and "non-communication". From this comparison there emerges the clear perception of the existence of "a core to the personality that corresponds to the true self of the split personality", which "never communicates with the world of perceived objects" (26) (¹).

In this sense, as Hartmann shows us (14), it seems valid to assert that defense mechanisms "do not originate as defences in the sense we use the term once ego as a definable system has evolved . . . They may originate in other areas and may have served different functions, before they are secondarily used for what we specifically call defence in analysis."

My patient's sequence of associations, relative to the "concert-café with the Klaus numbers", seems to originate from one of these primitive areas in which the ego uses splitting, at the same time, as a defense and as the organizational technique of an ego which needs to free itself from "submersion" in the object in order to be able to provide, to the true self, the perception of its own identity.

In the world of so-called "objective facts" there is a situation that faithfully portrays the set of data that composes what I believe to be the essence of the relationship between identification and identity. This is the situation represented by the legal rituals of concession and acquisition of personal identity.

For a detailed appreciation of the significant data and relationships inherent to the above situation, it would certainly be necessary to examine its multiple and different aspects. But a brief indication of some of these aspects is enough to understand the problem.

Thus, if we consider the situation only from the point of view of institutions themselves, it is obvious that the individual's identity is manifested from birth, even if almost entirely through the ego's "submersion" in identification with the parents or guardians. If, on the other hand, we consider the situation from the point of view of the individual himself, adolescence is the prime example of full, even paroxysmal, affirmation of personal individuality.

However, institutions consider neither the child nor the adolescent to be capable of making a legitimate separation of their external objects in terms

there emerges the clear notion of existence of certain moments when the individual's identity is recognized and desired by both institution and individual. These moments – illustrated by concession and acquisition rituals such as the Certificate of Military Service, Driver's License or Marriage Certificate – symbolize "the moment" when the individual starts "existing" as an adult in the eyes of society.

There is no doubt that a person's "existence" as an independent adult always requires knowledge of "which people" and "which objects" that person comes from. It is not necessary here to recall the difficulties, and even the sinister character of the concession and acquisition of the identity of children of "unknown fathers". However, there is not a shadow of a doubt that, both from the point of view of the institution that concedes it as from the point of view of the individual who acquires it, identity takes on a truer character from the moment that, through the rituals of legal age recognition, both institution and individual recognize that the ego must free itself from "submersion" in objects for the self to acquire and assume the perception of its own identity and the responsibilities it involves.

In the social process, as in the psychic process, the individual seems to follow the same differentiation path, moving from "submersion" in objects to a slow, but progressive, acquisition of identity. The fact that he often fails, as shown by the more or less intense defensive formations of the "False Self" system, only proves the intensity of the ego's struggle against its "absorption" by objects.

Thus, there is a final synthesis of Hartmann's and Winnicott's concepts on the one hand, with Melanie Klein's and Bion's on the other, leading to the following conclusions:

> First – Confirming Melanie Klein's clinical findings and concepts, it must be recognized that the primitive ego is indeed "submerged" in objects to such a degree that it becomes identical to a "psychic amoeba" as Freud imagined. That is, it is only capable of

communicating with the external world through "pseudo-pods", or its projection and introjection function.

Second – Since the perception of the self is also "an ego function" – as Freud and Hartmann showed – it can be deduced that the individual's perception of his true identity becomes clearer and more intense the greater the degree of his ego's "emersion" out of the primitive objects with which it has identified projectively and introjectively.

Third – In the analytical situation, identical facts of supreme importance occur, since the therapeutic process contains the inevitability of regressive phenomena. This means that if the analyst engages in dialogue with his analysand as if the self were already differentiated and the ego already "emerged" from objects, he runs the risk of reinforcing the ego's "submersion" in those objects and of transforming the therapeutic dialogue into a narcissistic monologue, by preventing the patient's perception of his own identity.

# Summary

### *Identification and identity*

The author takes again the ideas formulated, in a previous paper, on the interaction between the projective and introjective processes, in order to use them as a tool for the study of the dynamic relationship that exists between the effort made by the individual to get an insight of his own identity and his tendency to be submerged into the objects, with whom he is identified by projection or introjection. With this purpose, the author emphasizes, on the one hand, the concepts of Freud and Hartmann about the subjective experience on one's self as an expression of an ego function, and, on the other hand, he underlines Melanie Klein's views on the extent to which the individual feels his ego to be submerged in the objects, as a measure at the strength or the weakness of the ego.

In accordance with these concepts, and with the support in clinical material, the author studies two complementary facts, which are fundamental for the understanding of *the operative capacities of the ego* in the analytical setting. The first fact is that the *insight of one's self*, in the therapeutic process, becomes more "lived" whenever the ego is led to understand that it is "playing" continuously with the environment, by way of an interaction of projections of parts of the self in the object with introjections, in the self, of parts of the object partially disfigured by previous projections. The second fact is that the lack of comprehension of the "interplay" between projective and introjective identifications always causes a more strong "submersion" of the ego in the object and, therefore, a fading of the perception of one's own identity.

# Note

1   A valuable contribution to understanding this problem can be found in R.D. Laing's studies about "The False-Self System" (see *The Divided Self* – London Pelican Edition, 1965, pp: 94–105, and *The Self and Others* – Tavistock Publications, 1961; Strongly influenced by Sartre's ideas about bad faith (see *L'etre et le neant*), Laing follows, however, Winnicott's thoughts on the

other people say I am". The Divided self Chapter 5.

# References

1   Bahía, A. B.: "Notas sobre a Interaçao dos Mecanismos Projetivos e Introjetivos no Processo Analitico" – Trabalho apresentado a Sociedade Brasileira de Psicanalise do Rio de Janeiro, em 21 de outubro de 1963. [Paper read at the Brazilian Psychoanalytic Society – Rio de Janeiro, in October 21st 1963.]

2   Bion, W. R.: "Attacks on Linking" – in *International Journal of Psycho-Analysis*, XV, 1959, page 308.

3   Bion, W. R.: "Differentiation of the Psychotic from the Psychotic Personalities" – in *International Journal of Psycho-Analysis* XXXVIII, 1957, page 266.

4   Bion, W. R.: *Elements of Psycho-Analysis* – William Heinemann, 1963, page 39.

5   Bion, W. R.: "The Psycho-Analytic Study of Thinking" – in *International Journal of Psycho-Analysis* XL III, 1962, page 306–310.

6   Freud, S.: "The Libido Theory and Narcissism" in *The Complete Psychological Works of Sigmund Freud* Standard Edition, Vol. XVI, pages 412–430; "The Theory of the Instincts" in *The Complete Psychological Works of Sigmund Freud* Standard Edition, Vol. XXIII, pages 148–151.

7   Freud, S.: *The Complete Psychological Works of Sigmund Freud* Standard Edition, Vol. XXIII, page 241.

8   Freud, S.: *The Complete Psychological Works of Sigmund Freud* Standard Edition, Vol. XII, pages 213–226.

9   Freud, S: *The Complete Psychological Works of Sigmund Freud* Standard Edition, Vol. XII, pages 213–226.

10  Hartmann, H.: "Development of the Ego Concept in Freud's Work" in *Essays on Ego Psychology* – International Universities Press, 1964, page 211.

11  Hartmann, H.: *Essays on Ego Psychology* – International University Press, 1964, pages 113–141.

12  Hartmann, H.: *Essays on Ego Psychology* – International University Press, 1964, pages 113–141.

13   Hartmann, H.: *Essays on Ego Psychology* – International University Press, 1964, pages 268–296.

14   Hartmann, H.: *Essays on Ego Psychology* – International University Press, 1964, pages 124.

15   Haimann, P.: "Notes on Sublimation" – International Congress of Psycho-Analysis, Paris, 1957.

16   Klein, M.: "On Identification" in *New Directions*, Basic Books, 1955; "Some Theoretical Conclusions Regarding the Emotional Life on the Infant" in *Developments in Psycho-Analysis*, Hogarth Press, 1952.

17   Klein, M.: "On Identification" in *New Directions*, Basic Books, 1955, page 342.

18   Klein, M.: "On Identification" in *New Directions*, Basic Books, 1955, page 341.

19   Winnicott, D. W.: *The Maturational Processes and the Facilitating Environment* – Hogarth Press, 1965, pages 179–192.

20   Winnicott, D. W.: Op. cit., pages 171–178.

21   Winnicott, D. W.: Op. cit., pages 179–192.

22   Winnicott, D. W.: Op. cit., pages 179–192.

23   Winnicott, D. W.: Op. cit., pages 179–192.

24   Winnicott, D. W.: Op. cit., pages 179–192.

25   Winnicott, D. W.: Op. cit., pages 140–152.

26   Winnicott, D. W.: Op. cit., page 187.

# ALMEIDA PRADO (1917–1991)

## *José Carlos Zanin*

It is fortunate that the data and text of Mário Pacheco is being included in this valuable historical scientific work on the pioneers of psychoanalysis in South America. It is within the context of scientific training that the implementation and development of psychoanalysis in South America, which happened half way through the last century, will find Mário amongst other pioneers.

He was born in 1917 and died in February 1991. His professional training as a psychoanalyst began in 1948, coinciding with the creation of the first two groups of psychoanalysts, and was completed by 1956.

In 1947 Mário Pacheco was in Buenos Aires, where he found other Brazilians who were searching for training in psychoanalysis – Marialzira and Danilo Perestrelo, Walderedo de Oliveira and Alcyon B. Bahía. In his memoirs, Pacheco enthusiastically recalls a meeting with Pichon-Rivière and how these Brazilians were making the most of the advances in psychoanalysis that already existed in Argentina. Back in Brazil, Pacheco was able to start his personal analysis with Dr. Mark Burke from London, who, thanks to negotiations with IPA (International Psychoanalytic Association) and its president Ernest Jones, consented to come to Rio de Janeiro to psychoanalyze those interested in developing a group for analytical education and training in this city similar to the one that already existed in Sao Paulo.

The pioneers who joined together to found psychoanalytical societies began with the search of their own methods of psychoanalytical treatments. Some of the pioneers went to Buenos Aires to find the opportunity of personal analysis and training, while others went to London. It is worth pointing out that within our group, a strong and advantageous assimilation of evolutionary ideas developed from the Kleinian school of thought. We had, amongst others, Thomaz Lira, who was analyzed by Paula Heimann and had supervision with Melanie Klein and from Décio Soares de Souza, who in turn was analyzed in London, having done his training there too, and then returned to Rio de Janeiro, participating in teaching and analysis that helped form an integrated group that would soon become a psychoanalytical society. We have memories of psychoanalysts from London who came to Rio to present their work, such as Paula Heimann in 1958 and Wilfred Bion and Herbert Rosenfeld in the 70s.

Mário Pacheco had his participation marked by his intense collaboration with a scientific group, the Sociedade Brasileira de Psicanálise do Rio de Janeiro (Brazilian Society of Psychoanalysis of Rio de Janeiro). He carried out numerous functions and roles until reaching the presidency of this society in the 1970s. He organized and directed the 6th Brazilian Congress of Psychoanalysis, and during this time he chaired an important Latin American Congress of Psychoanalysis. In 1977, commemorating the 30th anniversary of Mark Burke's[1] arrival in Rio de Janeiro, Mário Pacheco organized the 2nd Symposium of the Brazilian Psychoanalytic Society of Rio de Janeiro (November 11–13, 1977). Considering the importance of Burke's participation as an analyst and teacher of so many that at that time encouraged the development of this society, the organization of the symposium chose "Evolution of the projective concept" as the theme of the symposium. Later on, Mário Pacheco would provide the publication of the symposium's papers in a 1979 book, *Evolution of the projective concept*.

Mário Pacheco's main contributions to clinical psychoanalysis were published papers and seminars as well as supervisions of the psychoanalytical treatment of psychotic patients. Taking advantage of and extending his knowledge in Kleinian theories, as well as in the development of Wilfred Bion's research, Pacheco was able to expand the application of those theories and research on technique to the treatment of those patients. He expanded his experience of dealing with the most primitive processes and mechanisms of the mind to the analysis of less disturbed patients, since any analysis, regardless of pathological severity, requires working through "psychotic cores", such as narcissism, envy, symbiotic fantasies, and "psychotic transference", with their extensive and excessive use of very primitive mechanisms such as projective identification. This experience led him to the formulation of the concept of *entanglement*. This idea of states of entanglement from the beginning of the analysis was an original formulation of Pacheco's, similar to concepts contributed by other authors such as *symbiosis* and *subject-object*.

In his text, we can find:

> In our formulation the baby initiates his/her life in a state of entanglement "mouth-breast nurturing" due to the initial state of indifferentiation and the condition of intrauterine life. As emotional development takes place, a long progressive process of
>
> mechanisms such as projective identification – seeking relief from this distress, strengthening as well his / her life instinct. The states of entanglement forced in this way, primitively and defensively, result in the re-living of states of indifferentiation prior to physical birth. According to Pacheco, these states are present from the beginning of life.

(Pacheco de A. Prado 1978)

The innumerable scientific works written by Mário Pacheco, published or presented for discussion at scientific meetings and congresses, have addressed many issues, with increasing correlation with clinical psychoanalysis. We will randomly list (quote) some:

- Identification and mechanism of projective identification
- Psychoanalytic treatment of psychotics and their transference and countertransference
- Regression, development and the conflicts and resistances in the analytical relationship
- States of confusion and indifferentiation in the pathological processes observed in the analyst–patient relationship; attacks on the thought process.
- Perception; "the projective identification as basic element of perception".
- Regressions as defenses against depression; manic depressive states.
- Distress; conflicts with life and death instincts.

Pacheco also translated into Portuguese Merell P. Middlemore's (1941) book, *The nursing couple*, and many of her papers in three volumes. The first one was titled The *Projective Identification on the Psychoanalytic Process* (1979) He then published, together with other colleagues, a work that developed from a report for the Latin America Congress about narcissism. Many years

213

later, he resumed this work, developing further his original ideas and adding more related articles, and published them as *Narcissism and states of entanglement*. He then published *Psicoanalise de Psicóticos* (1983) (The Psychoanalysis of Psychotics), a very important collaborative text on technical and theoretical psychoanalysis.

## Note

1   Max Burke was an analyst from the British Psychoanalytical Society.

## References

Middlemore, M.P. (1941), *The nursing couple,* Hamilton.
Pacheco de A. Prado, M. (1978), *Revista Brasileira de Psicanalise*, Sao Paulo, Vol 12, pp 335–346.
Pacheco de A. Prado, M. (1979), *The projective identification on the psychoanalytic process*. Rio de Janeiro: Fon-Fon e Seleta.
Pacheco de A. Prado, M. (1983), *Psicoanálise do Psicóticos*. Plurarte, Brasil.

# THE DEVELOPMENT OF THE
# SELF NOTION

## States of entanglement

*Mário Pacheco de Almeida Prado*

*The English version of this paper was translated from Portuguese by Ana de Andrade from a paper published in 1978 by Revista Brasileira de Psicanalise, Sao Paulo, 12(3): 335–346. In this paper, the author describes ideas of his that resemble those of Margaret Mahler and José Bleger and that were developed based on his own psychoanalytical experiences and clinical investigations. He attempts, following a series of earlier works, to formulate in metapsychological terms his ideas about Self disturbances and the states he calls entanglement. Specifically, he aims to demonstrate, with clinical data, the interference of destructive impulses in the emergence and maintenance of Self distortions and the resulting entanglement of the subject with its objects.*

Starting from a different theoretical-clinical line than Margaret Mahler and José Bleger, this paper arrives at some conceptual points that resemble theirs. Independently of both, whom I only researched subsequently, using my clinical observations of psychotics, borderlines and neurotics whom I analyzed, and fundamentally drawing on Melanie Klein's and Bion's contributions to Freud's works, I developed a theoretical conception that does not differ in essence from the aforementioned authors, but that emphasizes some aspects that are unclear in Mahler's works and highly sophisticated in Bleger's. I believe my formulations aim only to contribute to detailed observations of the conduct of babies as well as to interferences and the theoretical–clinical implications that Mahler and her collaborators later developed. Mahler used data, from the direct observation of psychotic and normal children, of indisputable value for proving many of our psycho-analytical theories. However, her view seems to me – if my pretension can be forgiven – very 'macroscopic' in relation to what I believe I bring in a 'microscopic' sense; moreover, I believe my focus allows a better instrumentation of knowledge, facilitating better penetration into the difficult meanderings of our patients' minds.

However, what I would basically like to highlight in this work is the interference of death impulses in the development of the Self, and as a pathological result of this, the establishment of a state of entanglement between the subject and its primary objects in varying degrees of depth and extension. And corresponding to these varying degrees, there results a greater or lesser degree of the subject's Self distortion, as well as a greater or lesser degree of distortion of current objects and external reality.

Over the course of the paper, I will try to show that this is not a meta-psychological innovation, but almost a result of Freud's, Klein's and Bion's concepts – perhaps even a direct derivation of them.

In a 1969 paper, I developed the idea that perception results from projective identification, followed by reintrojection of what penetrated the external object, as a kind of counterweight. In other words, perception contains a prevailing part of what the subject introduced into the object and a counterpart of what was carried from the object into the subject.

I developed the concept that what primarily penetrates the object can be love (life instinct) or hate (death instinct).

In the model I envisaged, a baby is born undifferentiated from the external world, particularly from the breast and the mother, due to a lack of mental resources that allow differentiation to be a psychological fact. During this initial stage of the baby's life, I postulate that he is undifferentiated from and confused with the breast. Along with Klein, I believe the breast to be the primary object and the mouth the primary subject. Also, as Bion postulates, the preconceptions about a good breast have the opportunity of meeting the reality of a breast that gratifies, relieves and reduces tension and anxiety. If some meeting of this nature does not occur, the child will perish, first psychologically and then physically. The degree of gratifying experience, which forms the nucleus of what a good breast will be, or what a good object will be (as it diminishes the degree of anxiety originated by the action of death impulses), is fundamentally important for the baby's future mental development, because the experience of gratification is what allows the tolerable existence, within a child's mind, of an absent object that can eventually be replaced by a symbolic object. If the experience proves incapable of providing a meeting with a good object that can satisfy and reduce anxiety, then this anxiety will grow and become equal to a concrete, bad object present in the mind. In this case, there is a stop in mental evolution, resulting in difficulties to think thoughts and develop symbolization. To deal with this excessive amount of anxiety, there is a reinforcement of

I have called the state of confusion – secondary and defensive.

The initial state of undifferentiation is what Mahler calls autism, Freud calls the auto-erotic or anobjectal state, Bleger calls symbiosis and Kohut the grandiose Self.

The state of confusion is what Mahler refers to as symbiosis, Freud as primary and secondary narcissism, Bleger as ambiguity and Kohut as archaic self object.

This state of confusion generates the entanglement states.

In my conception, this initial entanglement state, or state of undifferentiation and confusion of the subject with his primary objects, never completely disappears from a person's mental life and constitutes what Bion characterized as psychotic personality parts. I also distinguish a persistent state of undifferentiation during the individual's whole life, which in Mahler's language is the autistic part, or psychotic nucleus, which can manifest itself in any stage of life, originating passing or longer-lasting schizophrenic states.

If personality integration is predominantly reached, because it was possible for the depressive position to develop more firmly, these psychotic levels and nuclei remain active only in the primary process. However, if the depressive position is more precariously reached, these entanglement states will always be actively mixing with and invading the mental field, generating anxiety that sometimes corresponds to the Kleinian depressive position (maniacal-depressive states), sometimes to schizoparanoid states (depersonalization or schizophrenic states), and sometimes to part-objects (hypochondriac states).

My clinical experience has shown me that, as projective identification is a basic and fundamental element for the perceptive phenomenon, there is always an inevitable distortion of external reality, which Bion described as transformation. It is worth noting that everyone has a personal and non-transferable perceptive truth, which makes human communication difficult and means that language is always a precarious instrument from the communicative point of view.

I believe that the greatest and most harmful distortions come from human beings' fundamental, destructive death impulses that manifest themselves as voracity, envy and jealousy. The actions of these impulses, within the baby and his mother, generate a disconnection characterized by an elevated degree of anxiety reigning in the baby's internal world and elevated frustration felt by the baby-mother pair. As a consequence of all this, the omnipotent belief in the perception resulting from projective identification intensifies. Due to its massive use, parts of the Self are evacuated into external objects and situations, and their perceptions are lost. What we call parts of the Self, are the impulses. A person loses the ability to recognize these impulses as his own and believes they belong to the external world. As it is the perception and not the impulses which are being lost, these anxiety increases that can not be recognized as originating in the individuals own impulses. The patients mind becomes like the nucleus of an atom, around which his unrecognizable impulses gravitate, constantly invading his mental field but being recognized as belonging to the external object world and, therefore, not able to be integrated.

Thus, an emptying and shattering of the present and threatening Self occurs. The analyst, who becomes – in the psychotic transference relationship – the holder of these parts of the Self that have been expelled by the subject, in the present as in the most remote past, must try to integrate them, for the patient, by interpreting in the transference in the "here and now". In the analytic session this frequently generates an extremely vivid and acute moment of very strong hate emotions; it generates what we call a crisis moment. This moment can be wrongly understood as the patient's worsening, often leading the analyst to comply with defensive demands. However, if the analyst understands the transference model psychotically acted during the session, this helps the patient to attain integration, followed, in that case, by improved insight, memorization and verbalization that cannot have been achieved otherwise. Simultaneously, there is a positive modification of the Self's internal image.

I believe the destructive triad – voracity, envy and jealousy – is responsible for most of the disturbances in the construction of the Self representation, as I fundamentally believe the Self is *always* a fantastic representation that is altered or modified according to the affective dominance within the subject. I am thus lending *the Self notion* not simply a physical mental representation, but a representation that includes the body and the mind, subject to the dominant emotions in the subject's mental field and parts of the objects.

Below, I will attempt, with clinical material, to pinpoint the role of destructive elements in the Self's composition and in the production of a state of entanglement with the primary objects repeated in the transference situation.

I have selected this patient as an example due to the wealth of material he provides regarding every aspect of his psychopathology.

This patient has been many years in analysis with me. He is a psychotic patient capable of a reasonable social conduct.

As a child he had important feeding difficulties. He showed extreme voracity and a passive behavior. During his first six years he became

silence or uttering incomplete or fragmented sentences, waiting for me, the nanny of the moment, to force-feed him the analytic food. The latter only persisted in his mind for the time it took to pass through his mouth and throat. He seemed to hear, and really did hear the sounds; and these seemed to disappear within him. The nanny episode came up once as a result of interpretations given about his passive position during analysis, which suggested the position of a baby wrapped in diapers and cloths like a pharaonic mummy, having no hands, body or mind capable of thinking and knowing.

It seems clear to me that his mother, and her surrogates, strengthened in the patient the construction of a subject–object confusion state and helped maintain this state, which, during analysis, was very evident. My conceptualization of the case was that the patient was in a state of entanglement with his primary objects, produced as a defense against separation anxiety, and also partly caused by a lack of differentiation, which in analysis took the form of a genuine thinking capacity deficit.

The following material illustrates this point.

"I am incapable of remembering anything . . . I can now read almost a thousand words . . . but I don't understand anything. I can't retain anything. I look at figures and I can't reproduce anything. I remember that at school it was the same thing . . . I would look and I couldn't reproduce anything."

I said he was describing himself like a camera, through which figures passed, but were not recorded.

He corrected me, saying: "That's not it; it's much worse . . . I'm like binoculars!"

I understood, I said, that he felt like an instrument that had figures and sounds passing before it, and that when these were gone, the instrument hadn't seen anything, as if his mind lacked an observer on the opposite side of the figures. That is, inside the binoculars there was no mind capable of understanding the meaning of the figures or words.

He agreed it was so. However, I reminded him that if it had been completely or always that way he would not have been able to correct me or come to my office.

Looking doubtful, he added other examples where, in comparison with another person, he could see that he didn't have the same capacity. It was abstraction he was not capable of, or following a more complex explanation. This made him feel very greedy and triggered an endless repetitive activity, such as reading long texts for hours, as quickly as possible, trying in vain to understand them.

This clinical moment represented enormous progress, because it showed that he perceives the other as the other and recognizes differences. This includes being able to bear separation, the existence of time and space, and the attempt to repair himself. Nonetheless, during years of treatment, he behaved in analysis like the binoculars. His verbal expressions were mostly chaotic, only becoming more complete when interpretation managed to reduce anxiety. However, the interpretations generated an unbearable envy state, followed by the attempt to destroy them as quickly as possible, creating that state of entanglement with the nanny, who knew his desires and sought to satisfy him. Often, in response to some interpretation that led him to see me as separate from himself and capable of giving him something he couldn't achieve alone, he would tell me that it was no use saying what I had said, because he would obtain what he wanted just through the hallucinatory daydreaming. He would spend many hours of the day in bed, fantasizing about his desires in a hallucinatory fashion. His life was practically an endless masturbatory state.

Another element that led him to attack the perceptions that provided the notions of Self and of objects was jealousy. In this jealousy situation, there was a massive projective identification of parts of the Self, so that the other – the object of hate feelings – was experienced as if it were attacking him and depriving him of something he liked. Somebody was receiving what he experienced as being rightfully his – a feeling of being robbed of something that he should receive.

When he was at school, and other students answered the teacher's questions, he would start daydreaming that the teacher was praising him for his beauty and power of thought. In these fantasies, he was able to make important discoveries or inventions that gave him exceptional brilliance and the teacher's approval. In analysis, the jealousy awoken in him when he saw that part of him had a certain admiration for me, led him to remove himself emotionally, and stealthily reverse the situation. Now I was admiring him for the incredible things that he was achieving during the session. He was the admired baby, entirely loved by me, and I belonged to him alone.

This illusion could only be maintained through silence. Fragmented allusions expelled by him were the only thing that allowed me to reconstruct for him the jealous destructive attack unleashed against me and against that part of him that had experienced admiration for me during the analysis instant. At other times, silence did not allow a reconstitution like the one I described, and then there ensued a silence accompanied by some despair with motor disquiet, which sometimes allowed me to interpret that when his attack fragmented me, he experienced despair for having destroyed in

of the Self, and a concrete experience of me as a bad internal object. As a defense, he would isolate himself more, with more silence, and more masturbatory fantasies in which I, as the primary object, was filled with loving idealizations.

I will now report a typical example of the envious situation. Once at school, he heard the chemistry teacher speak highly of a book. He found out the book's name and bought it. Having bought it, he realized it was written in a language he couldn't read. This did not please him, because he had to possess the teacher's book, become him and be admired as he perceived the teacher to be. For weeks, he walked around with the book under his arm – copying the teacher – and felt as if he had his qualities – and the teacher himself. He had physically inserted himself into the teacher, depriving him of everything good he possessed. He no longer felt the need to attend class, to experience the humiliation he had felt. It did not matter to him any longer, and the experience of impoverishment did not hurt any more.

When this experience surged in the transference, he behaved with the greatest indifference, arrived late to his sessions or missed them altogether. When this happened he was unable to connect to any transference interpretation. I could also infer from some fragments of material that he let his friends know about being in analysis while unconsciously reversing roles, making me frustrated and envious.

# References

1   Bion, W. R., "Second Thoughts." *Selected Papers on Psycho-Analysis*, Heinemann, London, 1967.

2   Bleger, J. *Simbiosis y Ambigüedad*. Paidós, Buenos Aires, 1967.

3   Freud, S., "Sobre o Narcisismo: Uma Introdução." In Vol. XIV, *Edição Standard Brasileira*, Imago Editora, págs. 89–119, 1974.

4  Jaffe, D. S., "The Mechanism of Projection: Its Dual Role in Object Relations." *International Journal of Psycho-Analysis*, Vol. 49, 1968.

5  Klein, M., "The Writings of Melanie Klein." *Vols. I, II, III, e IV*, The Hogarth Press & The Institute of Psychoanalysis, London, 1975.

6  Kohut, H. *The Analysis of the Self*. Int. Univ. Press, Nova Iorque, 1971.

7  Mahler, M., S., "On the Concepts of Symbiosis and Separation – Individuation." *Vol. I – Infantile Psychoses*, International University Press, New York, 1969.

8  Mahler, M. S., Pine, F., Bergman, A., *The Psychological Birth of the Human Infant*. Heitchinson & Co. Ltd., London, 1975.

9  Mc Devit, J. B., Settlage, C. F., *Separation-Individuation*. International University Press, New York, 1971.

10  Pacheco, M. A. P., "A Identificação Projetiva como Elemento Básico da Percepção." *Revista Brasileira de Psicanálise*, 4: 5–19, 1970.

11  Pacheco, M. A. P., "Identidade no Processo Analítico: Micro-experiências de Identidades Parciais." *Revista Brasileira de Psicanálise*, 8: 571–579, 1974.

12  Pacheco, M. A. P., Cortes De Barros, J., Juca, G. P., Honigsztejn, H., Sauberman, P. R., *Narcisismo – 61 Anos Depois*. Relatório da S.B.P.R.J., Anais do X Cong. Lat. Amer., Buenos Aires.

$$——————20——————$$

*This paper was read before the 20th Congress of the International Psycho-Analytical Association, Paris, July–August, 1957, and published in 1958 by the* International Journal of Psycho-Analysis, *39: 139–143.*

For several years I have been concerned with the investigation of feminine disorders. Having arrived at certain conclusions, I shall summarize some of them in this paper, although what interests me here is to show how the writings of Melanie Klein – first her discovery of female development (9) and early anxieties (8) and, more recently, her study on envy (7) – have contributed to my greater understanding both of the causes and the underlying psychosomatic mechanisms of these disorders.

In collaboration with Dr. Celes Cárcamo I published a paper on sterility (1944) (2) that was followed by a book (1951) (10) on the subject of female procreative disorders. In the chapter on sterility eight cases of sterile or infertile women were presented, whose study had led me to the following conclusions: one common factor in their family constellation was a predominating mother figure while the father was weak, rejecting or absent. Another factor shared by these patients consisted of their having suffered severe oral frustrations, in half of the cases owing to a new pregnancy of the mother. But what especially drew my attention was a particular circumstance found in seven of the cases, which I was to find again in other patients: unusual tragic events had occurred in the infancy of these patients, for instance, the mother's death during delivery, an outbreak of puerperal psychosis in the mother, the death of a younger and rival sibling, all accidents connected with maternity. The infancy of only one out of eight patients was free from serious external traumata; but she was the youngest child, and as we know, the fantasies that are frequent in such cases refer to having magically prevented the mother from having another baby owing to the strength of their jealousy. Hence they all carried within them the representation of a destroyed mother that the facts of external reality seemed to confirm.

Besides, in childhood they all had extremely hostile fantasies against their mother and the lack of a reassuring reality made them feel that their destructive impulses against the fertile mother had been omnipotently fulfilled; hence the loved object was destroyed beyond repair. Thus I arrived at the conclusion that the main factor that inhibits and renders too-dangerous identification with the mother in her creative function is the fear originating in the bad impulses directed against her.

I agree with Helene Deutsch (3) and Thérèse Benedek (1), who consider the basis for development of normal future maternity to be the girl's good identification with her mother; but I wish to stress that it is precisely the fear resulting from hatred of the fertile mother that often prevents this identification. Helene Deutsch says that the pregnant woman identifies her foetus with herself and with her own mother. It then happens that, on account of her hatred and rivalry of the fertile mother, she comes to compare it either with her angry mother, destroyed by her bad feelings, or with her own destructive parts. These fears interfere with her positive wishes of becoming pregnant, wishes based on their eagerness to restore. Hence the child represents the restored mother and the patient's own good parts. This conflict becomes manifest by means of fluctuations between paranoid and depressive reactions towards pregnancy.

These different processes shall be illustrated with necessarily condensed clinical material. I shall first present two dreams from a patient when she was hoping to become pregnant and a third that, reckoning from the rate of the last menstruation, must have occurred a few days after the consciously desired impregnation. While the first dream, behind a paranoid appearance, showed her depressive fears, the second was frankly paranoid. The recovery of her reparative capacity can be seen in the third dream. From the patient's background I may mention that she was the youngest child; as a young girl she had tried twice to commit suicide, first by taking poison and then by trying to drown herself. During her engagement to her present husband she had several abortions.

Let us see the first dream: She had given birth to twin girls. To one of them she does not give the breast, and thus she remains a weak and silent baby; she feeds the other well, and she grows into a fine strong infant. Then she sees herself among friends, fleeing in panic from the city, for a devil is chasing them, the 'fire-daughter'. She knows it is the daughter she looked after so well, and regrets having neglected the other one, the 'water-daughter', who was a better child. Both daughters stand for the dreamer: the 'water-daughter' is the good and frustrated part of her who would not put up a fight but preferred to drown. The other is the one her mother and I in the analytic situation have fed generously, thus feeding her greed and turning her into a powerful and destructive object – i.e., the ungrateful daughter standing for the 'devil' part. Hence, for her to be a mother means being envied and persecuted by the analyst, who now ceases to be the mother and becomes her greedy daughter. But the dream also refers to a

to an insufficiency of menstrual corpus luteum, until her gynaecologist controlled it with drugs. She now felt trapped, for she was once again in a condition to conceive, and reacted this time in a frankly paranoid fashion. She dreamt of 'a person who wanted to make somebody swallow a dose of poison. This person was already known to have murdered someone in that way. When the sinister character is prevented from carrying this out, he tries to poison himself.' With the poison she associates the medicine prescribed by the gynaecologist, thus condensing his figure and that of her mother with my own. She blames me for poisoning her with my interpretations, which will make her bear a child, just as in her childhood she blamed her mother for having driven her to the brink of actual suicide through poisoning. Therefore pregnancy itself is felt as something poisonous. We shall see later why.

The third dream occurred a few days after conception: She is in the cellar of her childhood home. Everything is full of dust and there are dead cockroaches hanging from the ceiling. One falls down. It disgusts but does not horrify her. She calmly starts cleaning the place. The cellar represents her own and her mother's womb, which are in a neglected and disused condition; Author cockroaches the children she killed inside her mother, and inside her own self (the unborn children she aborted). But as she now feels capable of making reparation, her dread of the past diminishes and she is able to clean the cellar, which symbolically amounts to preparing her womb for a new pregnancy.

I should now like to mention the dream of a young married woman who came to me from abroad with a defloration phobia. When she was finally able to start sexual life, she soon became pregnant. She then considered abandoning her treatment and returning to her country. In this situation she communicated the following dream: She is in her hotel busily packing so as to return home. In a great hurry she stuffs things that do not fit well into her bag. She feels nervous, for the maid is outside and she wants to leave the hotel without her noticing, so as not to have to tip her. The bag represents her womb; the things that do not fit well, the foetus and the penis; the feared chambermaid, myself; and the tip that I could claim, her gratitude.

She is anxious to leave me, because she wants to deprive me of herself, as my daughter, and of the child, who is the result of my work. Her envy of me as a mother in possession of children and of father's penis drives her to rob me, to make me sterile, and thus to obtain a triumph over me. But, at the same time, her envy turns me into a persecutor, capable of robbing her penis and child. This accounts for her anxiety and haste.

In order to demonstrate the frequency of this conflict, I present the dream of another patient. Sterile, until then she was about to interrupt her analysis just when she had a delay in her menstruation; it is probable that she unconsciously perceived her pregnancy. 'She is hurrying down a long staircase and sees some women doing exercises in a courtyard. She steals past, behind the gymnastics teacher's back, without being noticed.' The building stands for the maternity hospital; the women doing exercises for women in childbirth; but also for herself who should go on with her analytical exercises. The gymnastics teacher stands for myself. To hurry downstairs means to bear the child quickly and leave me at once, before I am aware of her pregnancy. This was confirmed in as much as after a few days she did indeed stop her analysis, miscarrying a fortnight later. When she had recovered, she came to see me and confessed that she had unconsciously provoked the miscarriage. Now she hoped to become pregnant again, but she had not wanted that child because it would have meant a 'triumph of the analysis'; that is to say, a triumph obtained through my envied analytical and creative power. It was her envy and hatred that made her feel her child something alien, as belonging to me and therefore as a persecutor.

Owing to lack of space I am unable to present more clinical material. But I should like to stress one fact: In my analytical work the subject of envy did not generally occupy a dominant place, but in the analysis of women with fertility troubles I always interpreted it both on an historical and on a transference level, although I seldom discriminated this emotion from jealousy and hatred. Upon reading Melanie Klein's work on the subject of envy, I was then confronted by the following questions:

i. What difference is there between hatred, jealousy, and envy as emotions towards the fertile mother, which I had found to be causal factors of female disorders? Melanie Klein defines jealousy as based upon envy, but involving three persons. In my patients, in view of the family constellation reported by them – with a dominating mother, existing in reality or in her fantasy only – i.e. not only the owner of children but also of the father and his penis – the jealousy of the father or the brother was based on the envy of the mother as possessor of these objects. Besides, the hatred towards the mother seemed to be far more a consequence of their envy than of other factors. They hated her, then, more for the good that was in her than for her badness (the oral frustrations). The appraisal of the mother's richness is greatly magnified by the girl's fantasies as a result of the guilt feelings already experienced for her primitive envy of the mother.

Hence I conclude that of the jealousy, hatred, and envy my patients felt for the mother, we must consider envy as the basic emotion.

of envy, namely, penis-envy. In 'Analysis Terminable and Interminable' (4) he speaks of penis-envy as a 'virgin-rock', as 'based on biological grounds', and ascribes to it an important part of our therapeutic limitations. In other words, he links it with what we actually call a negative therapeutic reaction. Over a long period this concept held a central position in psycho-analytic investigations and discussions. Karen Horney (5) distinguished between primary and secondary penis-envy. Melanie Klein (9) maintained that the girl's penis-envy arises first as a consequence of her oral conflict with her mother and of her oedipal jealousy. Her fear of being destroyed internally – i.e., in her femininity – for her attacks against the inside of her mother's body, her rivalry with her father and her necessity to restore to both the penis she destroyed in her jealousy are the main causes for her urgent desire to possess a penis. So penis-envy was recognized as being mainly of a defensive nature, but afterwards this concept gradually fell into disuse. Now Melanie Klein makes us direct our attention once more upon envy, but this time with reference to the breast.

At this point it seems necessary to summarize the connections existing between both forms of envy. (i) As Melanie Klein found already in 1928 (6), the voracity of the small girl and her envy of the breast makes her envy and desire father's penis too, because she believes that the possession of this organ enables him to receive mother's breast. So penis-envy is in proportion, in intensity, to the girl's voracity and envy of the breast. (ii) Since envy of the breast leads the girl to attack the mother's body and to fear her counter-attack, and since she defends herself against her fear of being destroyed in her femininity by adopting a masculine position that leads her to penis-envy, this envy is in the last instance, the outcome of her envy of the breast. (iii) Moreover, Melanie Klein has shown us that the girl abandons the breast and turns to the penis because she regards it, in her fantasies, as a richer and virtually inexhaustible breast. But as her envy of the breast originates in the fantasy that, instead of giving itself to her, it feeds itself, she then reacts to the penis with envy and jealousy, in the suspicion that the latter also feeds itself and the mother as well. So her breast-envy becomes directly transformed into penis-envy. (iv) Finally, her lack of any creative organ – be it that of the adult breast or of the penis – forms the root of her envy of both.

It is now better understood why Freud allotted to envy a central role in feminine psychology. We believe that it is indeed a very important factor, though not only penis-envy, but rather envy of the creative force localized in the mother's breast, in her inside and in the father's penis.

Let us return to our subject of the sterile or infertile woman, in order to answer our second question. If envy of the mother's creative power and pleasure has been especially intense, owing to constitutional factors, or if an unfavourable reality has made the young girl feel this envy as very harmful, she will be unable to cope with it. Besides, as we only envy what we do not possess ourselves this envy will be reinforced later when she discovers her infertility – i.e., to be really deprived of the biological power of creation. Thus envy will become the centre of her problem. If the analyst's interpretative capacity is felt to be his creative power, as Melanie Klein stresses, it also becomes clear why envy of the analyst should be in the foreground in the analysis of these women. Besides, Melanie Klein considers envy as the central factor of a negative therapeutic reaction. The interpretation becomes dangerous if the patient feels that through the strength of his envy he has destroyed the analyst. To accept his words means then to swallow something bad and, in the cases described above, it means to be impregnated with something dangerous. We see this process in the first patient who dreamt about being poisoned, and in the miscarriage of the last one. Both had destroyed me with their envy, and for both of them to become pregnant owing to my interpretations amounted to their being poisoned by me. One of them fought against this danger by avoiding conception and the other by miscarrying.

Let us now consider one last question: We have referred to pregnancy as a danger in the transference. But in general, what is the risk that the sterile woman has to face on account of her envy and by what psychosomatic mechanisms does she defend herself against it? Melanie Klein states that envy springs from the first exclusive mother-child relationship, and consists in the wish to steal or destroy her power of creation by putting bad parts and bad excrements inside her. I was able to observe with great clarity this envy of the mother's creative power under the guise of envy of the fertile mother, in sterile or infertile women. Since as a child her envy was felt to be very harmful, she actually believes she has destroyed the mother's creative capacity through its power. Later on the wish to be a mother arises in order to repair the harm she has caused. As a result of the excessive use of projective identification she experiences the penis, semen, or foetus as bad excrements, standing for bad parts of the mother that will be forced into her so as to ruin her and destroy the good objects she carries within herself. But penis-envy also may be tangled up with the envy of the mother's creative power, because as an aspect of the oedipal situation the parents are felt as a combined figure (mother in possession of father's penis). But besides oedipal jealousy, penis-envy per se turns the penis and its products into a dangerous organ and substances. And finally, the sterile woman driven by

ing of paranoid and depressive anxieties, together with the concept of envy as the central factor, enables us to grasp the meaning and the psychosomatic mechanisms of many fertility disorders, which I shall summarize in a condensed and incomplete form.

The superficial barrier to which the woman dreading pregnancy may resort is defloration phobia or vaginismus. We often see how the latter sets in when the former has been overcome.

Frigidity is another attempt at defence, although of fantastic character. The frigid woman, by not feeling the sexual act, denies the fact of the persecuting penis's presence in her vagina, and hopes therefore to elude its dangerous consequences.

Other women resort to the expulsion of the semen, thus preventing its passage through the cervical canal. They use the same defence mechanism of ejecting the enemy as is observed in miscarriage.

Spasm of the Fallopian tubes is the most intimate and primitive defence against impregnation. Beneath its hysterical disguise we perceive the autistic attitude of shutting oneself away from a hostile world.

The sterile woman becomes pregnant, driven chiefly by her need of reparation. But while the child grows within her, she feels that her persecutor, who will spell danger to her and her good objects, is growing too (dream of the 'fire-daughter', p. 140). I have been struck by the intense degree of anxiety observed in some women at the beginning of a consciously desired pregnancy. To get rid of the persecuting foetus they will resort to any means within their power, if the anxiety situation becomes unbearable. For instance, I have seen two women who finally managed to have an abortion performed on psychiatric grounds; a third who achieved the same end by incoercible vomiting that endangered her life, and two others who in all likelihood destroyed the embryo through the sheer force of their anxiety. But the most frequent psychosomatic defence against anxiety that increases with the growth of the foetus is the premature expulsion – miscarriage – of the persecutor, often unresponsive to any medication.

## Summary

Based on analytical investigations of feminine psychosomatic disorders, the girl's incapacity of identification with a fertile mother is considered as the central factor in her future problems of infertility. This incapacity is a consequence of her hostile and invidious fantasies towards her fertile mother and has results more serious and difficult to overcome, when an adverse reality – tragic accidents occurring to her mother or to her siblings – make her feel she has destroyed the loved object beyond repair. As an adult she will oscillate between paranoid and depressive reactions towards pregnancy. This is illustrated with clinical material in the transference level.

As Melanie Klein recently focused our attention on breast-envy and analysed its different consequences, the connections between breast-and penis-envy are summarized, and it is shown how the understanding of early anxieties together with the conception of envy enables us to grasp the meaning and the psychosomatic mechanisms of many fertility disorders.

## Note

1 For the Introduction to the life and work of Marie Langer, see Part 1, Chapter 9, of this volume.

## References

1 Benedek, Thérèse, and Rubenstein, Boris 1945 'El Ciclo Sexual de la Mujer' (The Sexual Cycle in Women), *Biblioteca de Psicoanálisis* (Buenos Aires: Nova).
2 Carcámo, Celes, and Langer, Marie 1944 'Psicoanálisis de la Esterilidad Femenina' *Revista de Psicoanálisis* 2.
3 Deutsch, Helene *The Psychology of Women* (New York: Grune and Stratton, 1945).
4 Freud, Sigmund 1937 'Analysis Terminable and Interminable' *Collected Papers* 5.
5 Horney, Karen 1926 'The Flight from Womanhood' *International Journal of Psycho-Analysis* 7.
6 Klein, Melanie 1928 'Early Stages of the Oedipus Conflict' *Contributions to Psycho-Analysis* (London: Hogarth).
7 Klein, Melanie 1955 *Envy and Gratitude* (London: Tavistock Publications).
8 Klein, Melanie 1946 'Some Schizoid Mechanisms' *Developments in Psycho-Analysis* by Melanie Klein, Paula Heimann and Susan Isaacs (London: Hogarth, 1952).
9 Klein, Melanie *The Psycho-Analysis of Children* (London: Hogarth, 1932).
10 Langer, Marie *Maternidad y Sexo* (Buenos Aires: Editorial Nova, 1951).

# (1896–1880)

## *Maria Angela Gomes Moretzsohn*

## From Berlin to Brazil: A psychoanalytic adventure

Adelheid Lucy Schwalbe, a Jewish doctor born in Berlin in 1896, became a candidate and later a member of the Psychoanalytic Society of that city. She did her training analysis with Otto Fenichel and had Salomea Kempner as her supervisor.

She married the lawyer Ernst Heinrich Koch and then developed her clinical practice in a private office. As the threats regarding the Second World War became more intense, and as she already had two daughters, she considered leaving Germany.

During the 15th IPA Conference in Marienbad, Ernest Jones informed Adelheid Koch that a small Brazilian group interested in psychoanalysis was searching for an analyst with a good background to work in São Paulo. She decided to face this challenge; she arrived in Brazil in 1936 with her family without knowing a word of Portuguese. Dr. Koch, as she became known, dedicated her first months to learning the language and adapting her children to the new country.

At that time, Brazil had just abolished slavery and had become a republic. The rural economy was moving towards a very recently begun industrialization process, stimulated by the arrival of the first European immigrants.

Dr. Durval Marcondes, a young doctor who had heard about the work of Freud through the press since 1919, had been the author of the proposal that Jones presented to Dr. Koch. Durval managed to gather around him a small group of doctors, teachers and intellectuals who were trying to study psychoanalysis using the rare texts available then.

Little by little, they realized that in order to become psychoanalysts, the theoretical study would not suffice and the work of another qualified professional would be necessary, but there was none in the country. They needed to bring someone well prepared from abroad, so Durval got in touch with several people in Europe and abroad, reaching Dr. Koch. Thus, she started working with this small group and from the very beginning was a "Jack of all trades". She was a training analyst, supervisor and teacher for everybody. Together with Durval Marcondes, they became directors and organizers of what would be the embryo of the Brazilian Psychoanalysis Association of São Paulo.

With her workload always on the rise, Dr. Koch started searching for another foreign analyst with whom she could share her work.

In 1950, Nils Haak, a Swedish professional, became interested in the job and came to Brazil with his family, but he didn't adapt to the country and stayed for just a few months. However, another psychoanalyst answered her call and arrived in Brazil in 1950: Theon Spanudis, a doctor educated at the Vienna Psychoanalytic Society, analyzed by August Aichhorn and Otto Fleschman. He collaborated actively with the Brazilian group, but moved away from psychoanalysis a few years later to dedicate himself to his activities as an art critic and collector, making an outstanding contribution to the Brazilian culture.

Dr. Koch counted effectively and permanently on the Brazilian candidates; Durval Marcondes, Virgínia Bicudo, Flávio Dias, Darcy de Mendonça Uchoa and Frank Philips finished their education and started sharing the clinical work and the activities of the institution with her. They set up the Brazilian Psychoanalytic Group, recognized by IPA in December 1942. On August 9, 1951, the Brazilian Psychoanalytic Association of São Paulo was ratified as an IPA member during its 17th International Conference in Amsterdam.

By 1950, Adelheid Koch had been naturalized Brazilian, and, as long as she lived, she worked untiringly in the institution she had founded. She and Durval Marcondes formed a partnership, which was only broken up with their deaths: hers in 1980 and Durval's in 1981. Together they fought for psychoanalysis for 43 years.

Adelheid Koch spent a great part of the 44 years she lived in Brazil developing and institutionalizing psychoanalysis. Her theoretical production was small; she published very little. She seems to have centered most of her writings on questions related to teaching psychoanalysis, for she was in charge of the training analysis of the professionals of the society. Even her text "Omnipotence and sublimation", which was published by the *Revista de Psicoanálisis*, Buenos Aires, in 1956, has been difficult to locate. This work is the result of situations observed in her clinical practice, which led her to postulate a certain kind of relation between omnipotence and sublimation,

structive omnipotence. On the other hand, the perception of an object felt as predominantly bad would promote destructive omnipotence and delay the development of the capacity to sublimate. The text also points out the importance of introjecting good objects of both sexes to develop constructive omnipotence.

## Note

1  Both Melanie Klein and Adelheid Koch did their training in psychoanalysis in the same institution, the Berlin Psychoanalytic Society, almost simultaneously; Klein became a member in 1922 and Koch in 1929, but there's no reference of any contact between them. The initial contact of the Brazilian psychoanalysts with the Kleinian ideas was at the beginning of the 1950s, through some of them who had returned from their studies at the British Society, including Décio de Souza, Virgínia Bicudo and Lygia Amaral.

# OMNIPOTENCE AND SUBLIMATION

## Adelheid Lucy Koch

*The English version of this paper is a translation by Ana Pieczanski from the one published in Spanish in the 1956* Revista de Psicoanálisis, *13(4): 456–460.*

Clinical experience indicates that in certain patients strong tendencies towards omnipotence exist simultaneously with a certain capacity for sublimation. The issue we present in this work is: What is the relationship between the two phenomena, omnipotence and sublimation?

In his work on stages in the development of the sense of reality, Ferenczi described the phenomenon of omnipotence as a child's way to control those objects that are vitally important to his survival. But in that paper, Ferenczi had not established a difference between the internal and external object. The work of M. Klein and her disciples more deeply explains the omnipotence phenomenon, attributing greater importance to the objects introjected by the child during the first years of his life.

Paula Heimann says: While in reality the child is completely defenseless and depends on the mother for support, in phantasy he adopts a position of omnipotence regarding his objects: these belong to him, are a part of him, live exclusively for him.

Correlatively with this development of omnipotence, a denial of reality emerges. According to Paula Heimann, the child does not yet recognize the objects, because his capacity for perception develops gradually. However, the child partially denies, for psychological reasons, what he perceives, through omnipotence and magic.

S. Isaacs describes that when the child cannot control his objects he feels a catastrophic loss due to the inability to satisfy his desires and needs in the "here and now."

Focusing on the phenomenon of sublimation reminds us of a section in Freud's paper "The Ego and the Id" where he expresses the idea that maybe the prerequisite for sublimation is always a transformation of the object libido into narcissistic libido; in other words, the sublimation would necessarily be the relinquishment, be it voluntary or forced upon, of the loved object. This resignation stimulates the aggression and the hatred towards the

Based on this formulation by P. Heimann, we could say the following: The feeling of omnipotence can evolve in two opposite directions: Constructive Omnipotence (equal to sublimation) or Destructive Omnipotence.

Our work with patients can shed light on the special factors that determine the development of one or the other type of omnipotence. These factors seem susceptible to being described as follows: if the introjected object during the first years of life is good, or felt as being good, and therefore stimulating to the libido, to the feelings of love and to affection, the child idealizes his internal object (and also the external) and the identification with this good object leads him to feel omnipotent. In reality, this process of introjection and projection is not so simple. The mother cannot always be good, given that it is unavoidable that she will cause frustration to the child; he then reacts with a crisis of hatred and hostility against the mother because of his frustration. According to M. Klein, this conflict between love and hate results in a dangerous situation: the child fears destroying with his hate not only the bad mother, but also the good one. Faced with this, the child tries to defend himself through idealization of the good mother. If this idealization is achieved, at least partially, the child will feel omnipotent in the constructive sense; he will show self-confidence, intimate well-being and will develop capacity for sublimation. The introjection of a good object makes the child self-sufficient, independent and happy, and also capable of later on merging the idealized object with the real object.

If on the contrary, the first introjected object were or appeared to be more frustrating than satisfying, thus increasing his resentment, hate and aggressiveness, the child would feel threatened by his persecutors (internal and external). As a result of his anxiety and feelings of guilt – the child increases the badness of the objects through his own aggression – he would develop a destructive omnipotence to be able to defend himself from these persecutors. In this case, the capacity for a constructive sublimation would be inhibited.

Naturally, we will not find exclusively one of these types of omnipotence in our patients. Pure destructiveness only manifests itself in paranoia and mania; the patient loses touch with reality, where he believes he is omnipotent in the constructive sense, although, in truth, he may not be capable of any constructive or sublimatory activity.

Clinical material from different patients also presented another factor that seems important in the development of constructive omnipotence: the introjection of two good objects from each sex. In Freud's work "An Infantile Memory of Leonardo da Vinci", we find the following phrase "All the hermaphroditic images of the gods could express the idea that only the union of the masculine and feminine can result in divine perfection."

This process of introjection of two good objects, one masculine and one feminine, explains, in my judgment, the fact that certain patients who have suffered depressions, anxiety, etc., would regardless be able to achieve true sublimations in the professional field or in their private lives. Clinical material:

A man, the youngest of many brothers, always heard his mother remember fondly a younger brother who had died at 4 years of age, prior to the birth of my patient. He felt doted on and loved by his nanny and not by his mother. He fantasized with achieving an ideal union with this nanny that was supposed to have existed between his mother and his dead brother. Also, the mother treated him like a girl, until he was of school age; this caused the patient to lose hope of ever being able to return the lost brother to his mother. Therefore, all his love was directed towards the nanny, hoping to achieve with this the ideal bond that existed in his fantasy between the mother and the other child. When he felt forced to act like a male he also lost hope of being loved by the mother as a male, and developed the tendency of becoming a superman. But this ideal was not the result of identification with the father, but with an imaginary husband of the nanny, who was actually single. The patient not only frequented certain social circles that he belonged to, but also circles of a class much lower than his own. But in the two fields he managed to win and be successful. Within him, feminine sublimations were present alongside the masculine sublimations; in his house the subject did exactly what the nanny used to do: cook, fold clothes and clean objects, take care of the children, etc. And he did these things magnificently well. The conflict of ignoring whether he wished to be a man or a woman would cause him intense anxiety. Despite these, he achieved true sublimations, resulting from the introjection of the good object (nanny) and the fantasy of achieving the ideal union between mother and child, hoping, ultimately, to restore Author brother.

Another male patient, also the youngest of several brothers, suffered a terrible shock at 4 years of age: a brother who was 12 years older got sick with tuberculosis and had to spend 12 years in Europe, where he finally passed away. Since the loss of the sick brother, my patient would always see his mother cry, with a sullen appearance, with no interest in those who surrounded her. For this man the phantasy also included the desire to return the brother to the mother. The love made both, the mother and the brother, introjected within him, which trained him to derive his libidinal instincts towards the task of curing those with tuberculosis. He was tireless in his profession, where he managed to become famous worldwide.

A woman, the eldest of two sisters, would ask herself, whiningly, since the

patient suffered from hatred and jealousy towards her younger sister that she could not overcome. She remembered that she had been an obedient, sweet and exemplary girl, while her sister had been a real little devil. During the course of the analysis it became evident, despite her kindness, that she had always felt like she was bad; on the other hand her sister had been the good sister, the one who had gained more affection and love from the father. The sick one identified herself with the paternal grandfather; from then on, the desire emerged to be a male. During puberty she lived true love scenes – kisses, hugs, etc. – with her mother, finding herself lying in her bed. At that time the father abandoned the home and the mother started to live with lovers. The fantasy of the patient was to become the ideal husband for her mother, and at the same time to become the ideal wife and mother. Her sublimations also had bisexual characteristics: on the one hand she was affectionate and comprehensive with her daughters, and on the other hand, assumed a masculine and dominating position when managing the household, especially on financial issues. Her ideal consisted in first conquering the position of the perfect lady in society and then dedicating herself to cultural activities that for her represented masculine interests.

In my opinion, the interesting factor is that none of these patients was happy in their marriage. It seems that the impulse to repair, based on infantile fantasies, gave origin to the constructive omnipotence and to the capacity for certain sublimations; but the denial of reality, which always accompanies the feeling of omnipotence, prevented the establishment of happy heterosexual relationships in real life.

## Summary

Clinical experiences show in some types of patients strong tendencies of omnipotence and at the same time capacity for sublimation. The author tries to explain the relation between omnipotence and sublimation. It seems

237

as if the primary introjected object is felt more good than bad, this helps to build up a strong feeling of self-confidence, a capacity for real sublimation combined with a feeling of omnipotence that might be called "constructive". If on the contrary, the first objects are felt more bad than good, it arouses in the patient a sense of inner omnipotence of destructive character and they may hinder the development of the capacity for sublimation.

The author puts a second hypothesis for discussion: If two primary good objects of both sexes united in love with each other are introjected, the development of constructive omnipotence seems to be furthered. Such object may be Mother and Father or one of the parents felt by the child in intimate relationship with a sibling of the opposite sex. These two hypotheses are illustrated by some clinical case material.

# References

Ferenczi, Sandor: *Entwicklungsstufen des Wirklichkeitssinnes, Bausteine sur Psychoanalyse.* Intern. Psych. Verlag, 1927.
Freud, Sigmund: Triebe und Triebschicksale. *Ges.* Schriften, 5. Band, 1925.
———— Eine Kindheitserinnerung des Leonardo da Vinci. *Ges.* Schriften, 9. Band, 1925.
———— Das Ich und das Es. *Ges.* Schriften, 6. Band, 1925.
Heimann, Paula: A contribution to the problem of sublimation and its relation to processes of internalization, *International Journal of Psychoanalysis*, XXIII, 1942.
Klein, Melanie: *The psychoanalysis of children.* The Hogarth Press Ltd., 1948.
Klein, Melanie, Heimann, Paula, and Isaacs Rivière, Joan: *Developments in psychoanalysis.* The Hogarth Press Ltd., 1952.
Rosenfeld, Eve: *A case of depression.* Unpublished.

Part II

# TOLEDO (1915–1990)

## *Sheila Navarro de Lopez and Federico Flegenheimer*

Luisa Agusta Rebeca Gambier de Alvarez de Toledo, medical doctor and Argentine psychoanalyst, was born the 13th of June 1915 in 9 de Julio (Buenos Aires Province) and died on the 5th of September 1990 in the city of Buenos Aires. Rebe, as she was known by her friends and relatives, had from her youth a passion for medicine, and she moved to Buenos Aires to study. As a medical student, she showed some interest in psychoanalytic thinking, even before the Argentine Psychoanalytical Association (APA) was founded.

However, she was not a Founding Member of the APA, even though she was actively involved with the founding members, and for 25 years she was involved in the institutional life of the APA. She was elected Associate Member in 1946 and reached the presidency of the society in 1956–57. There she was a deeply committed person and very certain of her way of thinking, regardless of her fragile appearance.

She took very active part in the first psychoanalytic mental health institution in Argentina, Hospicio de la Merced, directed by Enrique Pichon-Rivière. She was part of the Adolescent Department. Between 1955 and 1958 she traveled to Montevideo (Uruguay) and trained professionals through seminars and supervisions, working with the analysts who eventually founded the Psychoanalytic Institute and Society (APU).

She always chose privacy above professional status. This was especially the case during the later years of her life, when she gave up the political institutional activity. However, her retirement was only apparent; she continued analyzing analysts from different analytic groups, giving the chance to other colleagues to undertake analysis with a quite impressive, lucid and highly experienced person.

Each one of us who had an intimate analytic relationship with her realized that Rebe was capable of expressing, through her analytic work, a tremendous wisdom that one gets through a long life of experience. She was capable of exploring the unknown with courage.

## Her work

As we know, every author develops one or two fundamental ideas throughout his or her life, and seeks to formulate them in new ways. In the case of Alvarez de Toledo, the notions that pervaded her entire work, including her classical paper about "Words", are the concern with Life and Death; the intimate relationship with the other; and the fears and anxieties aroused by the unknown, both in others and in oneself.

She was a courageous person and used several tools of investigation not always well known at that time. However, she never gave up her belief in the analytical method. For example, at some point in her career, she experimented with hallucinogenic drugs (for instance, LSD) in the treatment of her patients, probably following previous investigations (see Huxley, Sartre, Merleau–Ponty, etc., in their work with mescaline), but always using psychoanalytic interpretations as part of her psychoanalytic investigations.

The "Artificial Regression" or "Experimental Psychosis" was not used to shorten the analytical process (she insisted on that), but rather to find a way to investigate deeper into the unconscious. Unfortunately she had to give this up when the use of LSD was forbidden by the state.

In our country, many of the outstanding authors of that time had important connections with the world of culture, sculpture, painting and music, which impressed a particular stamp on their productions. Alvarez de Toledo was a representative of that time. Her wide interests – she was well versed in Western and Eastern history and music; she was herself a pianist, organist and sculptor – and her sensitivity are present in all of her writings.

From among her publications – "Contribución al significado simbólico del círculo" (Symbolic meaning of the circle, *Revista de Psicoanálisis* 8(4), 1951); "La musica y los intrumentos musicales" (Music and musical instruments, *Revista de Psicoanálisis* 12(2), 1955); "Mecanismos del dormir y el despertar" (Sleeping and awakening mechanisms, *Revista de Psicoanálisis* 8(2), 1951); etc. – we will focus on her paper "The analysis of 'associating', 'interpreting' and 'words'".

From the beginning, she showed in her work a close connection with her patients. She describes in this paper not only the semantic content of the words spoken in the session but the concreteness of the sounds themselves, as an interchange with unequal values. This conception made for an intimate contact in the analytical couple, breaking through cultural and historic differences.

"The analysis of 'associating', 'interpreting' and 'words'" was first published in 1954 in Issue 3 of Volume XI of the APA's *Revista de Psicoanálisis*

lytic Clinic) in Buenos Aires, where she and the director, Enrique Pichon-Rivière, were known for working without a fixed schedule for long hours into the night. It was a time of lively and fruitful intellectual and ideological exchanges with a sense of discovery and excitement across generations working together.

The paper itself was conceived and written when Argentine psychoanalysis was strongly under the influence of the British School and especially of Melanie Klein and her followers, among whom the most frequently quoted authors were Paula Heimann and Susan Isaacs. Obviously Freud remained the main reference, but there were other influences and a number of trends beginning to emerge that eventually crystallized into new ideas.

The differences between these trends perhaps lie in the place to which they assign guilt in the genesis of suffering and of the curative process. While to a member of the Kleinian school, guilt was the engine of integration, reparation and sublimation, for another, led by Angel Garma, guilt was seen mainly as an obstacle to psychic development owing to the equation of masochism and sadistic superego. These two theoretical orientations were manifested in different techniques of handling the negative transference.

A further group of analysts, led by Pichon-Rivière, were greatly influenced by the French dynamic psychiatrists and by the ideology and philosophy of dialectical materialism, so that they approached Klein's ideas from a different viewpoint. The emphasis fell upon object relations, the field of research being widened to embrace a subtle determination of the status of the object in terms of its place in the subject's external as well as internal world; here the main influence was Fairbairn.

This approach gave rise to an important body of literature that laid stress on the idea of the field and the analytic situation, combined with a profound, original and more pertinent vision of the concept of the transference-countertransference (Bleger, Baranger and Racker).

Alvarez de Toledo, in this paper, combines Kleinian theories of early object relations and early unconscious fantasy with the idea of the defining importance of the erotogenic zones in relational models. Sadism, the need for control, and omnipotence are powerful hypotheses that run through the entire paper; drawing on the ideas of Melanie Klein, Susan Isaacs, Ernest Jones and Sandor Ferenczi, the author attempts a reformulation of symbolism substantially based on the theory of projective and introjective identification. Helen Keller and the philosopher Susanne Langer are recruited in support of her original ideas about speaking and language and her distinction between the abstract and the concrete. Meanwhile, Jean Piaget serves as a reference in the elaboration of these ideas. The author defines her position in relation to science and adopts a non-neo-positivist stance.

The paper has two main aspects. The first is made up by the author's core of original ideas and concerns about what happens in the analytical process, with particular reference to the words spoken by each protagonist. The second comprises detailed observations and reflections on clinical phenomena in both the analysand and the analyst.

Luisa Alvarez de Toledo's observation is that the act of speaking in a psychoanalytical session, irrespective of the semantic content of the words spoken, expresses an object relation accompanied by a particular unconscious fantasy or one that is characteristic of a given libidinal configuration. So, she distinguishes two levels of talking (speaking) in the session. One is symbolic and abstract and the other is concrete. She finds that, when the words spoken fail to assume their symbolic and abstract quality, this is because the necessary transformation is blocked by an excess of cathexis. The concrete component of speaking is the fulfillment or "action" of a primal fantasy; a similar idea led Piera Aulagnier, many years later, to postulate the existence of pictographic inscriptions that remain active throughout life and for other authors to investigate the means of expressions of what is beyond words. David Liberman's rigorous study of styles also deals with this aspect of verbal communication.

Technically, this approach entails a drastic change in the study of the analytical couple.

Nine of the nineteen sections into which this long paper is divided deal in detail with the meaning of speaking, associating and interpreting, while the remainder sections are theoretical–clinical appreciations of various topics. The sections that cover the author's main theme may be summarized as follows:

1   The counter transference is the expression of an emotional language that always arises as a response to what she calls the patient's primal (preverbal) fantasies.
2   Talking, seen in isolation from its semantic content, affords almost direct access to the primitive material.

3 Verbal exchanges are regarded as a form of behavior.
4 When the "words" are analyzed in themselves, there arises "the primitive identity of act, image and object."
5 The relationship between the voice and unconscious primal direct fantasies (again) is a direct access.
6 The release of instinctual impulses through interpretation could be well

to the semantic content.

# Reference

Puget, J., and Siquier, M.I. (1996). Associating and interpreting forty years on. *International Journal of Psycho-Analysis* 77: 319–322.

# 24

# THE ANALYSIS OF 'ASSOCIATING', 'INTERPRETING' AND 'WORDS'

## Use of this analysis to bring unconscious fantasies into the present and to achieve greater ego integration

*Luisa de Alvarez de Toledo*

*This paper was first presented at the Argentine Psychoanalytic Association on the 10th of November 1953, accompanied by extensive clinical material. It was published in this form in the 1994 Revista Latinoamericana de Psicoanálisis, 1: 87–108. It was translated into English for the first time in the 1996 International Journal of Psycho-Analysis, 77: 291–317. The author gives an account of the phenomena that occur when the meaning of 'associating', 'interpreting' and 'words' is investigated. Her presentation is modelled on the manner of appearance and understanding of these phenomena. Because interpretation of a new aspect has always preceded its intellectual understanding, frequent repetitions will be observed, and one theme is sometimes adumbrated within another and developed more fully later. For all its drawbacks, such an exposition has the advantage of coming closest to reality. A schematization would be premature and tend to conceal any errors, thus impeding subsequent understanding of the phenomena concerned. The author discusses the phenomena in their order of appearance. Although the order was the same in every case, she does not rule out the possibility that this might be because of her personal approach. The bibliography lists works that stimulated her interest and were particularly useful in the understanding and formulation of her work.*

## Emotional language in the countertransference

The sensations and emotions that may be experienced by the analyst in relation to his patient are numerous and familiar to all. This emotional language may or may not have a rational explanation or be connected with his countertransference neurosis. However, these reactions often lack any

Using countertransference emotions in this way, I too was able to observe and confirm that they were related to the patient's unconscious wishes, sensations and emotions (themselves linked to his unconscious fantasies). I noticed too that when I was able to understand my emotional reactions in these terms and to verbalise them internally, they disappeared; through the contents supplied to me by the patient and his entire behaviour, I then succeeded in finding a form of expression that allowed him to become aware of his unconscious wishes and defences.

However, this approach being slow and unsatisfactory, especially as regards the patient's emotional experience, I was induced to seek and find a more direct way of bringing his instinctual impulses and defences into the present, permitting the simultaneous expression of the emotion, act and image of the operative unconscious fantasy – that is, a form of bringing-into-the-present accompanied by the experiences corresponding to the primal fantasies.

Underlying the conscious behaviour of analysand and analyst alike, the mutual paranoid anxieties and persecutory fears of the two protagonists are synchronised, and the processes of projective and introjective identification in each constitute the background against which the session proceeds and is structured.

At a deep level below that of the conscious relationship, the analytic situation is a confrontation between two strangers, the analyst and the patient, who, in their dealings with each other, as in any human relationship, will repeat the entire development of their own object relations. Although I shall only discuss the patient, this is equally true of the analyst.

Paranoid anxieties, as well as the defences against them, are manifested in the analyst's sensations and emotions, which express and correspond to the unconscious fantasies of the analysand.

This emotional language may or may not be justified in terms of content. Those emotional reactions that are not justified by the content that the patient is expressing or whose justification is insufficient or inappropriate are precisely the ones that are most directly bound up with the unconscious fantasies.

Emotional reactions in the countertransference show that the patient is repeating and recreating in the analytic setting past situations from his life and, on a deeper level, his primal fantasies. The fact of expression in the form of sensations or feelings already betrays their archaic origin to us. It is a way of coming into contact with and acting on the object, who reacts emotionally in accordance with the fantasies prevailing at that time in the patient. Where analysand and analyst cannot understand each other in any other way, a regressive form of communication arises between them, mediated by a primitive language corresponding to a primitive level of expression and interrelationship (animals – fear – attack).

I was able to observe in one case that countertransference sensations of distress connected with painful memories that then emerged were additionally determined by the patient's wish to move me, with a view to weakening and manipulating me, as a response to the fear of being attacked by me; he also wanted to prepare me for incorporation by him in an oral attack.

If instinct is not elaborated into affect and content, or remains separate from these, it acts independently on the unconscious of the analyst, who feels either the impulse (sensation or emotion) directly or the defence against it.

## Bringing fantasies into the present

I had for various reasons already begun to investigate the meaning of the idea of 'free-associating' and of 'interpreting' when a patient who had decided to break off his analysis, at about the date he had set for himself, insisted that I return his words to him. At the same time he felt and expressed surprise at the absurdity of this demand, which had nevertheless impressed itself powerfully on his imagination. When I asked him to associate to this idea, he told me:

I can't see anything. It is all dark. It occurs to me that the words are like things I gave you, which you have put away in a chest. I don't know, I think of penises . . . wombs . . . whatever . . . anything! I'm very angry, that's for sure! I came to analysis as if I were looking for a formula, something magic that would allow me to solve all my problems, and now I can see that everything I told you about myself was for you to give me that formula.

With 'the formula' he associated ideas of potency, the penis, and he remembered how his mother had looked after him when he was ill. He recalled scenes in which his mother had displayed great affection to get him to take his medicine and had given him enemas. He then connected his anger and complaints with his frustration at the failure of his effort to seduce me, whose aim had been to achieve an oral, anal and phallic relationship in which I was to play the active part. Associating had the significance of a sexual relationship, and it also meant that he was giving me valuable things; this he refused to do because he got nothing in return.

This material made a profound impression on me, not so much because of its content or of the meaning which I had already observed, but on account of my countertransference reaction to the demand to have his words back:

(interpretations), my potency and my knowledge; he was going away and leaving me empty.

This episode taught me that analysis of 'speaking', in the form of both 'associating' and 'interpreting', could bring unconscious fantasies into the present, together with the corresponding experiences. In connecting countertransference sensations and emotions with the act signified by associating and interpreting, I understood the concrete significance of 'speaking and words', as distinct from and in addition to their content.

If countertransference sensations and emotions relating to the patient disappeared when verbalized, then, when the process of verbalization was undone by analysis of the act of speaking, the contents stripped of cathexis should recover that cathexis upon the release of the libido contained in the act and isolated from the verbal representation.

Again, part of this libido had remained isolated from the whole and been locked up in words, which, representing concrete objects on a very primitive level, must have contained the libidinal cathexis directed towards those objects. The analysis of the words as such also allowed the fantasies to be brought into the present, since the analysed word is the object of the fantasy.

This word, the object of the fantasy, acts like an intermediate object between the analysand and the analyst, retaining isolated quantities of cathexis that are thereby withdrawn from the analysand–analyst relationship.

In this way I translated 'speaking and associating' into behaviour; 'interpretation', the behaviour of the analyst, now assumed a different meaning from its content, which had to do with the analysand primal fantasies that could thereby be verbalized.

## Associating and interpreting as behaviour

Associations that link the analysand with the analyst are experienced at a deep level as something the former does to or with the latter, whereas interpretation, the analyst's form of expression and behaviour in his relationship with the patient, will be experienced by the patient as what the analyst is doing or wants to do with him, which, furthermore, is what the patient wants the analyst to do.

The patient treats and manipulates his analyst in the same way as he treats and manipulates his internal objects, and he in turn feels treated and manipulated by the analyst in that way.

On a magic level, interpretation as the behaviour of the analyst completes the Gestalt of the unconscious primal fantasy that he is then carrying out.

To the patient the analyst is an unknown, who can be understood and learnt about only on the basis of the known, by a process of comparison, which takes place by interplay of projective and introjective identifications. The analyst thus acquires the qualities of the introjected objects and the capacity to be manipulated by the patient, who will control him in the same way as he controls his internal objects. Good or bad, he will be manipulable; should it be impossible to sustain this magic conviction, the analytic situation could not come into being. ('Better the bad that is known than the good that is not.') Other instances of this situation are difficulties in forging new relationships and the tendency to find resemblances between new and old friendships. By knowing and understanding someone or something, at a deep level we believe that we are controlling him or it. What arouses the most anxiety is the unknown, because it cannot be controlled.

Little by little during the analysis, in the course of the continuous work of projective and introjective identification, the analyst is incorporated as a real figure, and as this process continues, the analyst's interpretations and behaviour come to be seen in terms of their own content and not of what the patient had projected onto the interpretation.

## Speaking and words

Speaking as behaviour, as distinct from its content, satisfies oral, anal, phallic and genital libidinal impulses. The act of speaking, the utterance of words, as a mode of contact,[1] stands for, replaces and achieves the first form of contact with the object, namely sucking. In those first days of life, the unconscious fantasies lack visual representations and are represented by sensor motor images in which the function, the organ and the object of the function are combined.

When 'associating' and 'interpreting' are analysed as such, the primitive identity of act, image and object arises and becomes a reality in the act of speaking and listening to the analyst. The repressed concrete somatic aspect of the symbols becomes conscious and the verbal images take on the corresponding emotion and content.

When oral fantasies have been analysed and interpreted, it is found that speaking also fulfils anal, urethral and genital fantasies. Speaking thus affords access to the fantasies corresponding to these stages of libidinal development.[2]

The analysis of associating and interpreting as distinct from their content shows that the act thereby symbolized is a fait accompli to the analysand's

and these acts fulfil the patient's unconscious fantasies.

Speaking is an act involving and combining all human structural levels, and words are the end-result of the synthesis of affect, act and image, whereby the individual projects himself into the outside world and connects with objects.

When any one of the elements of speaking (affect, act, image) is dissociated, repressed or distorted, what is authentic is the act whereby the instinctual impulses are discharged on a preconscious level, isolated from the corresponding conscious representations, affects and purposes.

In this situation, instead of forming a link with the object, words become the object projected and introjected by the analysand as he superimposes his internal reality on external reality, as if words were an intermediate object, which combines and separates at the same time, containing as it does in repressed and isolated form the libidinal cathexis connecting the subject with the object.

When analysed, speaking as a symbolic activity, words as symbols in general and symbolic expressions in particular become reconnected with the libidinal cathexis corresponding to the activity they perform and the object they symbolise.[3]

Speaking, as behaviour, combines and fulfils oral impulses – sucking, biting, swallowing, chewing – which are satisfied in verbal activity.

The object of this behaviour is the analyst, who is experienced at a deep level as a breast that the patient wishes to incorporate. This aspect of speaking is repressed and desexualized, while the emotion is wholly or partly repressed or displaced. Its primitive origin in searching, incorporation and pleasurable physical contact, which generated it in the first place, is isolated from conscious knowledge; when speaking as such is analysed, the patient's associations betray its archaic origin in the search for contact and incorporation, which is in fact always current and active. Interpretations to that effect destroy the isolation between these acts and the verbal activity that symbolises them, giving rise to a large-scale release of emotion, in the form

251

of vegetative reactions and sensations that cannot readily be verbalised. This act is always directed towards the person of the analyst and its aim is satisfaction for the analysand, but also destruction of the analyst, although the latter is not the aim of the instinctual impulse. After all, the desire to suck to the point of emptying, swallowing, biting, incorporating etc. stems from the wish to obtain satisfaction or gratification from a valued object; only later will it be a form of destruction that, by damaging the object, will transform it into a persecutor that will need to be controlled and dominated.

Almost simultaneously with the oral fantasies, anal and urethral fantasies appear in rapid succession. Expulsion, destruction and annihilation of the object are accomplished in the act of speaking. However, this act does not have primarily a destructive aim, but is a form of obtaining libidinal satisfaction with the object; the latter's annihilation would prevent its fulfilment, as the aim is to obtain pleasure by acting in this way on what is loved, and the consequence, loss of the object, inhibits this form of love, which destroys what it loves. As these aspects are worked through and reality testing – which shows that the analyst survives in spite of these attacks – strips the instinctual impulses channelled into the act of speaking of their dangerous character, the good aspect of speaking appears, and words take on concrete qualities of good milk, good urine and good faeces. They assume the sense of a valued object, a gift and a son. They symbolise the good internalized objects, penises and breasts and the patient himself, in the aspect he deems most valuable to the object.

The patient will, or will not, give his words to the analyst according to the characteristics attributed to them by his fantasy. He will give them as a token of love and as a form of being with him, while on the other hand fearing what the analyst might do with them, since they are himself, and his person will magically suffer the same treatment as his words receive at the hands of the object. At a deeper level, associating freely (like listening freely) stands for profound and pleasurable sucking, and carries the risk of ending up totally emptied and sucked dry; this is manifested in the fear of unreservedly yielding up all one's associations, lest one 'melt' or 'flow into' the analyst and lose one's individuality. For the same reasons, the analysand defends against interpretations and the affect they arouse, because he feels in danger of being dominated and invaded by the analyst's words and by the emotion and affect they generate in him.

The interpretation, the analyst's words, as both act and object, will be an expression of the unconscious fantasies. Interpretations are commonly experienced as destructive anal and oral penetration, as a homosexual act, as being bitten, defecated or urinated upon, destroyed, castrated etc. This gives rise to various forms of behaviour intended to nullify the pernicious action of the analyst's interpretation.

The conflict of ambivalence and depressive anxieties are expressed in the fear of damaging the analyst by the free association of ideas and in the wish to say good things in order to repair by good words the damage previously done. On the other hand, the desire to present only good things and good words also has to do with the wish to preserve an idealised figure who will protect the patient from persecutory fears aroused by bad objects.

or displaced or both at the same time – are linked to the corresponding representations and integrated with the patient's fantasy as a whole and with the various forms in which they used to be manifested in him; this has repercussions on the expression of his whole personality, his defence mechanisms, his symptoms, his dreams, his object relations, his activity and so on.

Act, sensation, image, body and mind regain on the conscious level their ancient and profound unity when the first oral experiences can be integrated with the corresponding sensations, feelings and images.

The various splits, rents and clefts in the ego then disappear, and the interchange of ego libido and object libido becomes freer.

As Fenichel (1941) notes, the ego as a whole is an apparatus for containing direct discharges; the transitions between affects of discharge and of tension are fluid, and we all constantly have a certain affective tension within us. This tension may be crucial to the interest and liveliness of our conscious actions. Analysis of primal fantasies liberates the instincts and allows past and present symbolisations and representations to acquire the corresponding affect and, with it, their true meaning.

## The process of symbolisation in language

As with both associating and interpreting, when speaking is analysed, the process of symbolisation that gave rise to the formation of language is 'undone'; the instinctual impulses are liberated and the primal fantasies and mechanisms of projective and introjective identification with the analyst, with other people and with things are brought into the present[4] The primitive symbolic relationship with objects and with the world is experienced.

Auditory sensations from the outside world or from the internal world of the subject himself are probably particularly well suited for the structuring

253

of primal fantasies and for the satisfaction of frustrated oral wishes. As far as infantile omnipotence is concerned, they have the great advantage of being produced by the subject himself. Later, when the internal and external worlds become differentiated, the voice – because it comes from inside and acts outside, because it is heard both outside and inside, and because it comes from outside when it issues from an object and is listened to inside by the subject – is a redoubt in which the subject's identity with the world and the identity of the external and internal worlds can persist. The voice as articulated sound and the word-as-object are objects that are as it were 'seen' to come in and go out. The ear as sensory apparatus, as an orifice of communication with the outside world, is a gateway constantly open to pleasing or unpleasing stimuli. Everyone is familiar with the emotional reactions – e.g., crying – aroused in babies in the first months of life by noises and voices according to their tone: sympathetic and querulous voices, angry voices, shrill singing, and so on. The terms used to describe vocal qualities must be related to this primitive oral and tactile meaning (touching with the mouth). Voices are described as warm, soft, gentle or harsh. The concrete and material quality of the voice, as a physical object that may act physically on the subject, is expressed by adjectives such as wounding, irritating or ear-splitting, or a voice may be described by an image – as overwhelming or numbing – or, at the other extreme, as caressing, soothing 'like balm', able to heal wounds, and so on.

Voices that attract and fascinate, not only in singing but also in normal speech, as distinct from what they express, and the importance of the voice in the choice of a love object and in instances of sudden falling in love must all have to do with a primitive voice identity between subject and object, between the internal and the external worlds. When the internal and external worlds become separate, when the libidinal objects move to the outside world, the voice transmitted and received makes it possible to preserve the lost primitive identity, to manipulate both external and internal objects, to obtain gratifications and to secure protection from anxiety. The voice of a person – of the mother – is not only the mother but also the mother inside. The meaning of the voice as milk entering the ear can be readily observed, and when the primal experiences are reactivated, this is felt very concretely and intensely and in a physically gratifying manner.

Words spoken are also experienced as food, as good or bad things (words-as-mouthfuls-to-be-swallowed). The identity of food and words and the action of one on the other and on the individual are evident in ordinary situations; for example, during a meal an argument, a piece of bad news, an instance of verbal aggression or a mere reference to unpleasant events is seen in a particularly bad light and causes much more anger because the subject was eating at the time: 'they upset my stomach' or 'he/she always picks mealtimes to blame me for something'. Family rows at table are much more unpleasant than anywhere else; when a person cannot eat and leaves the table because of an argument or offensive remark, this has to do with the deep, primitive identity of voice, words, milk, swallowing and food, as a result of which the food becomes bad, takes on harmful qualities and is either rejected or, if already ingested, upsets the digestion.

According to Jones, Ferenczi, Kubie, Melanie Klein and Susan Isaacs, the process of symbolization by words takes place as follows:

1   Organs and functions are projected on to objects in the external world.
2   This process results in a projective identification between the subject and external reality, in this case mediated by the voice and by words.
3   The process is followed by an identification through displacement or substitution (a mechanism discussed mainly by Jones and Ferenczi).
4   Finally, the object invested with projections and displacements is reintrojected (introjective identification) and its physical representation takes on the significance of a symbol.
5   Subsequently, the concrete bodily components of the total experience of perception and fantasy are partly repressed, partly deprived of their emotion, desexualized, and made independent of bodily connections on the conscious level. They are transformed into images in the sense of mental representations (but not consciously as bodily incorporations) of external objects recognized as such. It will be understood that the objects are outside the mind, but that their images are inside it. Nevertheless, these images affect the mind because they are inside it, and their influence on feelings, behaviour and personality is based upon their associated somatic elements, which are unconscious and repressed; this shows that, in unconscious fantasy, the objects symbolized by the image will be deemed to be inside the body – i.e., incorporated. (This formulation is due to Isaacs, 1952.)

Countertransference sensations and emotions are signals of the patient's wishes, sensations and emotions (fantasies) that stimulate the analyst and, with the reactivation of his primal fantasies, arouse the necessary emotional response in him.

According to Langer (1942), 'as soon as sensations function as signs of conditions in the surrounding world, the animal receiving them is moved to exploit or avoid those conditions' (p. 29); again, 'man, unlike all other animals, uses "signs" not only to indicate things, but also to represent them' (p. 30). The signals–signs are thus transformed into symbols. The symbol then replaces the object when it is not available or has to be placed in the past, referred to or situated in the future.

Man's wishes, sensations, emotions and fantasies are thus represented by signs, which then assume the character of symbols. The sign is the end-result of the stimulus and of the response, or, in other words, of the subject and his action on the object; similarly, symbols will contain these two components

peratures, shapes and feelings; the most frequent of these are synopsias (coloured hearing). A sensation corresponding to a given sense appears associated with one or more others, and arises regularly when the latter are stimulated. For example, a sound produced by the mouth may be associated with a particular colour, a certain sensation of size, or a pleasing or unpleasing sensation. This is particularly relevant to the process of symbolisation.[5]

At first a sound is a completely free object; as Piaget says, for the newborn child, even 'supposing that there are given simultaneously visual sensations . . . acoustic sensations and a tactile-gustatory and kinaesthetic sensibility connected with the sucking reflex', the breast does not exist as something external but there can only exist awareness of attitudes, of emotions, or sensations of hunger and of satisfaction. Neither sight nor hearing yet gives rise to perceptions independent of these general reactions . . . external influences only have meaning in connection with the attitudes they arouse. When the nursling differentiates between the nipple and the rest of the breast, fingers, or other objects, he does not recognise either an object or a sensorial picture but simply rediscovers a sensor motor and particular postural complex (sucking and swallowing combined) among several analogous complexes that constitute his universe and reveal a total lack of differentiation between subject and object. In other words, this elementary recognition consists . . . of 'assimilation' of the whole of the data present in a definite organisation . . . and only gives rise to real discrimination due to its past functioning . . . this . . . constitutes the beginning of knowledge. More precisely, repetition of the reflex leads to . . . assimilation of objects to its activity, but . . . [through the repetition] assimilation becomes recognitory (Piaget, 1952, pp. 36–7).

Sound, voice and words, considered as something belonging to the subject who has undertaken the process of incorporation, do not bear a fixed relationship to the outside world and are used to satisfy oral needs, acquiring in this way their first symbolic meaning.[6]

As and when objects in the outside world appear, this internal object comes to be identified with and to represent them.

By means of this symbolic representation, the internal object replaces them so that external objects can be obtained at will, but, in accordance with the situations of need or satisfaction that present themselves, the auditory representation will include a certain conception and will be subject and object at the same time, in situations relating to sucking, incorporation and expulsion. Behaviour within, in the form of fantasy, repeats the relationship with the environment in a particular way. Even if the voice, as a substitutive object for the breast, is used successfully when the need is not very pressing, the infant, according to his hunger, attributes unpleasurable sensations to an introjected harmful breast. The auditory representation will then assume a malignant aspect.

The voice and articulated sounds are transformed into representations or symbols: the word and the object are the same thing and, through the act of speaking, the object is projected and introjected. In verbal symbolisation, as in all symbolisations, the unified experience of act, feeling and fantasy acquires a representation.

Subsequently, the relations between what is symbolised and the symbol and the process of projection and introjection, are excluded from consciousness. Furthermore, the total experience is broken down into its different aspects of bodily movement, sensations, images and knowledge. The concrete bodily element, associated with the perception as a whole, is largely repressed; the verbal images acquire their character as such in the most limited sense of the term.[7]

## Voice, words and object relations

Oral wishes have two sources, one of which is libidinal and the other destructive; the endogenous cause of anxiety is the latter. The unconscious fantasy is bound up with the sensation, and the fantasies mobilised in the act of speaking – as in that of eating – determine the character of the object that is the analyst, which will then be incorporated with the interpretation. The analyst's interpretation and the analyst himself become part of the analysand's internal world; however, these doubles are not the same as the original objects but are transformed in accordance with the patient's impulses and fantasies.

When the various stages of development are repeated in the analytic situation, the analyst will be experienced initially as a part-object and the interpretation will be totally good or totally bad. Later the fantasy of incorporation will apply to whole objects, although the part-objects are incorporated. The fantasy fulfilled in the act of speaking and interpreting, although relating to part objects, will refer to whole objects, i.e. the analyst, his family life, other patients, his relational life, his activity etc.

When one analysand refused to tell me important but unpleasant things, I found that this was due to his wish and need to express his affection by telling me only pleasant things, good things that would interest me, give me pleasure and compensate me for other things I had to listen to throughout

infected. By not telling me his bad things, he was protecting and preserving me, and at the same time preserving his good things, which he put in to me, while avoiding the externalization of his internal persecutors and hence also the dangerous action that these, located in myself, might exert on him, since I, damaged and infected as I would be, would not be able to work properly in the treatment.

The representation of the analyst as a good or bad transference figure at a given point in the analysis is determined by the quality attributed to the impulses channelled and fulfilled in speaking and by the character of the words spoken, which will be good or bad according to the greater or lesser degree of integration of the instinctual impulses accommodated within the analyst by the analysand in the act of speaking.

The patient fantasies the analyst's relationships with his objects in the same way as he imagined his parents' relationship; it is a matter of Oedipal fantasies taking the same form as his own polymorphous wishes. Phallic and anal functions are performed in the oral relationship of the analysis, and the act of speaking has cruel aims, such as stealing, dirtying and castrating.

In his relationship with the analyst, the analysand also repeats the parental relationship in the primal scene and his reaction to it. Free-associating then has the aim of eliminating the persecutors, and the words take on the character of destructive urine and faeces.

Paranoid anxiety, the dominant anxiety of the first months of life, then arises, and the patient's ego feels threatened. As the paranoid anxieties are worked through, the figure of the analyst, both good and bad, is gradually integrated, and depressive anxieties appear that are connected with fear of the danger threatening the analyst in the words of the analysand. The persecutory anxieties decline, although they still play an important part. The sense of guilt bound up with the damage done by sadistic and cannibalistic wishes is linked to depressive anxiety. The guilt that carries with it the need to repair the object depends on feelings of love and promotes the object relationship.

## Function of speaking and words in the libidinal economy

Verbal activity and words, by substituting for the act and the object they represent, take possession of quantities of libidinal energy, which they keep isolated, facilitating the mobilisation of the remaining quantities, which, being diminished quantitatively, are modified qualitatively, since large cathexes of libidinal energy are felt to be dangerous owing to their intensity. The process of taking possession of cathexes – which is after all required for the maintenance, bringing-into-the-present and representation of symbols – encourages the phenomenon of repression. When speaking is analysed as behaviour directed at the analyst, this damming up of libidinal cathexes is overcome, words regain their former identity with the object, and the latter now becomes the recipient of the behaviour because it is the concrete object of the primal fantasies. The same thing happens to the analyst's words, which, being totally identified with the act and the object projected and then introjected, recover their total meaning in an act with a specific aim, which will be accompanied by the corresponding emotional and somatic reactions (fantasies).

The objects imprisoned in the soma and in the verbal representation are in effect 'dragged along' by the libidinal current, which is consciously re-established, and its passage from analysand to analyst and from analyst to analysand is experienced almost in the flesh.

Good and bad objects, when externalized, are again subjected to reality testing, forfeiting their extreme qualities; the harmful aspects are eliminated or the positive aspects are assimilated in the personality as a whole. The analyst undergoes the same process and the patient identifies with him, collaborating on the same level.

## Technique of interpretation

When speaking and words are interpreted, the act must be interpreted first and not the content. The latter must not be considered initially, and the interpretation must be immediate, which often necessitates interruption of the course of the patient's associations. What is interpreted is not what he says in words, but what he is doing when he speaks and with the words; although the elaboration of the interpretation calls for use of the contents and associations, the interpretation is always made on the basis of what speaking is for the patient at that moment.

Action always precedes thought and, furthermore, expresses it in its true, total significance. Verbalization is only one moment in the progress of a particular behaviour, but in the act of speaking this entire behaviour is repeated symbolically, its cause and its aim being combined.

Before a patient notices a change of attitude towards an object, his behaviour, and hence his speech, is already indicating it. It is as if, at a given moment, thought were located in the part of the body then being used to connect, whether it be the mouth, the limbs, the anus, the genitals or the

diminishes, and the patient, by means of the defence mechanisms, is seen to fulfil the impulses that these were evidently designed to avoid.

At first, what the patient does and says when speaking directly to the analyst is different from the content of what he is reporting, and it is useful to draw attention to this dissociation. After a time, however, I point out to the patient that, by what he is saying or telling, he is fulfilling the oral, anal, urethral or genital act that speaking at that time signified.

Underlying conscious thought there is always an active primal fantasy, which this thought somehow expresses wholly or partially. When speaking is analysed, the cathexes are liberated, and, when integrated with the sensation and with the total behaviour, the content takes on its true meaning.

The isolation of act, sensation, image and object is gradually reduced and the ego's capacity for integration increases.

The difficulty of associating freely, of connecting, has to do with the fear of the act of projecting as such and of what is projected.

To project is to expel, and this is destructive in so far as the bad is projected. The quality of the bad that is projected is determined by the act, since activity has a deep sense of destructiveness in which erotic and aggressive impulses are satisfied; at a deeper level, the erotism that leads to activity is experienced as hostile, because, in the earliest stages, pleasure and the gaining of pleasure had a destructive character for the object.

What is then eliminated – any act, word, intellectual elaboration or sublimation – is felt to be an action and an elimination of the bad existing in the subject, who has attributed it to an internalised object; the latter, when externalised, will become more dangerous and must be reintrojected so that it can be kept more effectively under control. As the 'internal badness' declines, expelling is transformed into giving. The subject then fears that there may be something bad in the good that he gives, so that he still keeps things back lest the object be damaged by the instincts. Another reason for retention is that this badness is projected on to the object, so that the things he gives it are transformed, in passing through it, into bad things and will have to be introjected; in addition, he fears that the good he gives, which is himself, may be damaged by the object in being given. At a deeper level, he keeps back out of fear that, in giving himself, he himself may be left at the mercy of the object, as if he were his own product. Hence the need to retain for fear of being emptied, just as, on emptying the breast, the subject thought he was taking possession of it and not of its contents.

The difficulty of giving results from a misapprehension, from the belief that what is done and said is the subject himself; when the person is transferred on to his act, words, work or production, these stands for himself, becoming the property of the object to whom they were directed. The subject is then afraid of the treatment that might be meted out to him by the object, while, on the other hand, through being incorporated by and introducing himself into the object, he hopes to control it.

It does not exist for what it is, but for what he thinks it is and what he thinks it has and controls of himself, for the conscious idea and image he has about his person. If he gives his words and thoughts, he feels completely dispossessed.

## Defensive attitudes to interpretation

Words as a magic act are used in analysis for attack and defence. They are used for attacking purposes when interpretations are nullified by expressions of denial or rejection, or by hostile or humorous criticisms, which magically destroy the analyst. The defensive aspect takes the form of control of thought concerning associations, with the aim of watching over thought and hence also the analyst's interpretations, which are experienced at a deep level as hostile. In this way, too, the subject avoids the emergence of anything unforeseen, whether of himself or from the analyst in interpretation.

Another form of defence is denial, expressed not manifestly but by the patient seemingly taking no notice of the interpretation and going on with what he was saying before, or else accepting it but continuing to talk about what 'interests' or 'concerns' him or 'because he has an intellectual interest in understanding a particular conflict'. Another form of defence is acceptance or confirmation of an interpretation outside the session, or experiencing the interpretation, which has been accepted on the intellectual level only, outside the session, beyond the reach of the analyst, who is thereby denied, and with him the action of his interpretation. The latter then becomes the property of the patient, who will manipulate it and thereby also magically manipulate his analyst, whom it symbolises.

The need to control leads to situations of rivalry with the analyst: the patient is reluctant to associate so as to prevent the analyst from interpreting, or he gets angry if the latter sees something that he himself did not see or cannot deny, or he tries to speak while constantly associating and interpreting himself in every known form, to stop the analyst interpreting; with the interpretations he uses, he manipulates the analyst's thought. Hence the anxiety and hostility aroused by an unexpected interpretation, which, after all, not only acts by virtue of its content but also demonstrates the failure of

needs, into something good or bad. In the extreme, whether for the purposes of defence or out of the need to bring a given fantasy into the present, the patient takes no notice at all of the content and only perceives and is gratified by the analyst's voice. He seemingly accepts the interpretations, although what he is actually accepting at this time is the voice, which, as such, then has its own content, usually gratifying; however, sometimes it is also frustrating, whatever the analyst is saying, simply because it comes from him; it becomes unpleasant, and the irritating voice is rejected regardless of the meaning of the words spoken.

## Bringing the omnipotence of wishes, thoughts and words into the present

When primal fantasies are brought into the present, the entire omnipotence of wishes, thought and words emerges and becomes conscious, and the patient experiences his profound conviction of his own omnipotence. Although at the same time he understands that this belief is irrational, that is what he feels, and his primal wishes towards the analyst are acts that operate on the latter and that the analyst, by projective identification, then performs on him. Furthermore, again through projective identification, the analyst's interpretation, speaking and words are the act in which the patient's primal fantasies are fulfilled; the patient transfers on to the analyst his own instinctual needs and wishes, in a process of total omnipotent behaviour directed towards himself.

When the patient becomes conscious of this entire process, he gains a greater awareness of illness. He realises that his conception of the outside world, of objects and events is structured on the pattern of his primitive fantasies; and when his internal reality is consciously externalised, the external reality emerges, followed by a reconsideration and revaluation of that reality.

The omnipotence of the wish demands immediate satisfaction, whether real or symbolic. The most intense and immediate, and hence the most gratifying, idea of libidinal satisfaction is fulfilled in the fantasy of sucking, of totally absorbing what the subject loves, of being totally absorbed by, melting into, fusing or connecting with, manipulating and telepathically possessing the object, controlling it and making it perform the acts necessary for the satisfaction of the wish.

The easier the act that symbolically fulfils the wish and the more independent it is of external action, the more powerful and terrible it proves to be on the level of omnipotence; for this reason, extraordinary power is attributed to the voice, to words, to the look, to gestures and to total or partial movements (the hand is experienced as an omnipotent subject and object). When analysands reach this level, they sometimes cover their mouths or eyes, even if they have them closed, or they put on spectacles if they had previously taken them off in the session, or else they turn their faces to the wall, and so on. All these manoeuvres are to be understood in terms of self-protection and of protecting the object from the force of the subject's wishes, and from his omnipotence, which is experienced as destructive because so intense. They likewise ascribe to the analyst the instinctual power and the danger they feel in themselves. The use of gesture, facial expression and body language is intensified and revealed as nothing but magic wish fulfilment, whether the wish be active or passive, whether for surrender to or defence against activity or passivity.

Everything we can do (project and introject) in relation to the world has greater magic significance the less dependent the action concerned is on reality, and the organ that performs the action takes on the overall significance of the function or of various functions (the mouth) and the associated magic powers. In the same way, the excretion or secretion products arising from the function of an apparatus assume a magic power, and the more they can be manipulated at will, the more powerful they will become. The voice, looks, gestures, movements, the expulsion of secretions and excretions, thoughts, words, actions, everything that expresses and fulfils emotions, affects, love, hate or the results of love and hate – that is to say, ultimately, instinct and libidinal energy – all this has magic significance because it is something that the individual feels within him and can project outside himself, causing an effect in reality.

All behaviour is in the last analysis an instinctual fulfilment, an omnipotent sexual fulfilment whereby the object can be destroyed or restored. The individual hopes in this way to restore and normalize the object, curing it of its ills, and giving it pleasure – ultimately sexual pleasure – that will 'balance' it.

The subject magically expects his loving or destructive action towards the object to have a huge diversity of results. Perhaps for this reason, when the object dashes this expectation by falling ill when it ought to have been thriving because something good is being given or done to it, or when it is somehow being destroyed or has been abandoned, the subject feels violently frustrated (as he also does if the object abandons or loses interest in him) owing to the failure of his omnipotence.

This is because the object then seems to have taken possession of the

# Reduction of anxiety; depersonalization and depression

When the analysand experiences the extent to which his paranoid anxieties stem from the projection and externalisation of the internal objects in which his libidinal impulses had been shaped and structured, his anxiety level drops sharply; people and the world are then seen differently, simply because of the feeling that, as one patient put it, 'they are not doing things against me . . . they are not watching and judging me, but they are all as they are; they are giving me . . . it is like rain, like water on my face'. The analysand feels almost concretely that what bothers him in others is something of himself that he sees in them. He then becomes aware of people, his constellation and the events of his life as they really are, and when he compares his present circumstances with how he used to see them, with his old fantasy images, those primal images 'are undone' and 'dissolve'. At the same time, with the outside world and the persecutors stripped of their dangerous character, the idealised objects assume their real dimensions. Dissociated objects are integrated and the patient enters upon a period of depression. One woman patient said: I am depressed, although I do not really know what is happening to me; it is not how it was before, I don't know if it is depression because it is different, I don't feel unhappy or that things are not worthwhile, and I also have no difficulty in doing things as I used to. When I felt that way, I could not do anything and I used to take to my bed all day; now, though, I can do things easily, yes, and they no longer have the heroic aspect they had in the past.

At the same time, and in some cases before the onset of the depression that arises when patients become aware of the internal origin of their persecutors, depersonalization symptoms of variable intensity are observed. One woman patient described this state as follows: 'It is as if I had inside me something dark and sticky, like an obscure force, like a storm'. This would happen mainly at night: she went through a period of insomnia and anxiety, feeling that something terrible had to come out of her. She associated these sensations with the idea of an earthquake, and it later also seemed to her that she 'was dissolving without being able to explain how or why'. I now realised that, whereas the depersonalization had to do with the fear of her instinctual impulses, which she then held back out of fear of destruction, activity – and especially its most valued form, intellectual activity – although not objectively destructive, fulfilled these instinctual impulses, which, by the mere fact of being active, were felt to be destructive.

I believe that the depersonalization and depression are due to the object loss involved in understanding that the analyst and other objects are different from the objects accommodated in them by the subject. In order to symbolise and to know an object, the individual projects something known, which is himself, but by projecting and introjecting himself he nevertheless acquires not only knowledge of the object but also greater knowledge of himself, like someone looking in a mirror that shows his own projected image.

Since these objects are an image of the subject himself – indeed, they are the subject himself – when he loses them he loses his own person, and that is why he becomes depressed and depersonalized. He then feels a stranger to himself; he is a person unknown to himself and he sees himself as a strange object, because the knowledge he had of the object stemmed from the projection of himself on to the object. At a deep level, he and the object were one. If the object becomes different and strange, the subject too becomes different and strange to himself.

The externalised internal objects used constantly to display their own projected image, and in them the subject observed and controlled his own actions. When these images are lost, he does not see what he is doing; he does not know what he is doing and is afraid of what he may do (withdrawal of libido and phobia).

In order to act in relation to real objects, the individual needs to accommodate in them his internal objects, which, whether good or bad, will have a specific known reaction. He will also in effect continue to possess what he externalises in his behaviour, as these externalised internal objects are a part of himself that he controls.

When he understands that the object is different from himself, he withdraws his libido completely because he is afraid of emptying and losing himself, for lack of a receptacle in a form that belongs to him and is at a deep level a part of himself. The subject cannot then distinguish between the analyst and his own family objects, or invest with libido anyone who is not a member of his family, who is not dependent on him or who does not share his interests.

The depersonalized individual looks at himself as someone unknown; he withdraws his libido from himself and is afraid of investing himself with it, because he would then lose himself as an object of his own which he controls and in which he maintains his link with the world.

If he recognizes and integrates himself, if he accepts himself, then his instinctual impulses will inexorably be directed towards real objects, but this arouses the fear of being emptied out, losing his personality, melting and fusing.

fascination with his own person. He can do what he likes with himself; he is subject and object, and is once again with the introjected good breast, which he can manipulate.

At the same time, however, since he cannot avoid the realisation that he is unable to satisfy all his own needs, he suffers the narcissistic loss of himself as an omnipotent object. He then gets depressed, feeling that he is not good for anything because he is not good for everything. He is not good for anything because he is not totally good for himself, which is what interests him most. He does not want to give to anyone what he is unable to give to himself (charity, of course, begins at home). He is not good for anything because in order to satisfy himself he cannot dispense with everyone, and then he does not want to give anything to anyone, as he cannot give himself entirely to himself.

When the individual becomes depersonalized, withdrawing his libido into himself and not mobilising it, separating from real objects, he loses the notion of external time that he had acquired through movement and through projecting himself into space in the search for the object.

In turning himself into his own object, he becomes his own object world, a space and time that he controls totally. The analysand then manipulates the passage of time with his body, thought or words. He mobilises or immobilises it in accordance with his wishes, and superimposes his own internal time on external time. Both analysis of this situation and reality show him that time is passing notwithstanding his defences.

In addition, the impossibility of satisfying himself totally as an object leads him to seek real objects, and he fears the loss in them, and afterwards with them (in a possible object loss), of all his valuable things, his wishes, his libido, which represent himself, his time as an object of his own that he surrenders. He is also afraid of losing himself through the loss of his control over space and time, and of being absorbed by the space-time world of the object, in which he needs to accommodate his lost omnipotence.

# Falling asleep in the session

With the diminution of paranoid anxieties, patients feel a need to sleep, and they do so long and deeply. They may sometimes also fall asleep during the session; if so, this is not merely a matter of flight and defence, but an expression and fulfilment of the wish to abandon themselves to the analyst, who is no longer a persecutor and in whom they have now accommodated their good objects, the gratifying good mother, the good breast which they reintroject by sleeping in this way, thus repeating the situation of infancy.

## *Identification and introjection*

We have, then, a process of bringing-into-the-present of oral fantasies and mechanisms of projective and introjective identification in relation to internalised objects that are exterminated and reincorporated in the course of association and interpretation. When these fantasies and mechanisms are repeated with the analyst as object, I have observed how this process is disturbed by introjection, the basis of primitive identification, owing to its cannibalistic or vampiristic character, which causes patients to fear my loss or destruction or the possibility that I, damaged, robbed and despoiled, might turn into a persecutor. Because of these fears, they avoided any situation in which the identification they had achieved could be expressed, halted their development, or hid it from themselves and from me. Through analysis of this situation, its repetition and reality testing, they came to understand and accept that identification with the valued aspects of objects did not mean that these aspects were lost to the object, just as, in infancy, the mother's milk they had incorporated was the content and not the source. However, just as they were afraid of stripping the object of the good and thereby emptying it out, destroying and killing it, so they also feared that by giving in free association they might be stripped once and for all of their words, good objects and potency, and then be absorbed, swallowed, dominated and subjugated by the analyst.

Identification with the valued aspects of the analyst and of the internalised objects entailed a process of digestion of these objects, with assimilation of the valued aspects and elimination of the bad; this process, experienced on a very concrete level, caused the object to be lost once and for all.

# Speaking and words as defences against
# the unknown

By projecting good and bad objects into the external world, the individual projects himself; he projects his impulses, condensed and controlled within a specific form, and transforms external reality – or rather, conceals it with his internal reality.

In this way the unknown external world is covered by a known internal world, or rather, one the subject believes he knows totally, in so far as he can name and qualify its contents, which he thinks he thus controls.

For this reason and as a defence against the anxiety aroused by the

controls himself in space and time. So he avoids and forestalls the unforeseen and the unknown (both outside and inside himself) and concomitantly the repetition of the same allows him to deny the passage of time that is leading him towards death, towards the unknown.

In seeing himself as an act, behaviour, a moment in his life, the subject denies his capacity for change and attributes to himself an immutability that defends him from his anxiety at the transience of his life and at the unknown from which he springs, which surrounds him and towards which he is proceeding.

We believe that we know ourselves and others to the extent that we know our thoughts and those of others. In knowing these, we believe that we control them, and we therefore believe that we control our own person, others, and the world, in space and time. When omnipotence fails, death wishes appear; however, these are in fact wishes for a known death that is not death, but a return to the mother, and they are due to the fear of life, as the fear of the unknown that leads to the unknown, namely death. Life and death give rise to one and the same thing: anxiety at the unknown inherent in both.

The need to project good or bad objects is a consequence of the fear of the unknown, which causes us to accommodate in the external world, in space and time, known objects as markers to guide and shelter us. For the same reason, we do not identify with the object or assimilate it, because, were this to happen, we should lose it as such and feel helpless. To be dissociated is to be accompanied, controlled, cared for and protected. It is the same as being persecuted, controlled by a persecutor, in regard to our instinctual impulses and what these might do to real objects; and the same as being protected from other people's instinctual impulses, which are to be feared to the extent that one senses the fearsome and unknown strength of one's own instincts.

However, this defence is more apparent than real, and the fear of what might happen to the externalised objects and what these might then do may perhaps indicate that, simultaneously with our manipulation and for all our conviction that the reality we see is external, it is only a representation of internal reality; we are aware of the fantasy character of this reality and the simultaneous existence of an unknown reality, whether in space, in objects or in time, which we cannot control. Hence the need to deny the reality of objects, space and time and to transform our body into our own world of objects, space and time, which we immobilise (conversion, catatonia or motor inhibition) or mobilise (hyper motility, whether chronic or in relation to certain waiting situations), in response to events that draw our attention to the passage of time against our wishes, as a form of control and mastery over the unforeseen, the unknown, in ourselves, objects, space and time.

In the primitive, the child, the psychotic, the neurotic or indeed any individual, the fear of the unknown within and without, of unknown life and of unknown death, is the linking feature common to all the structures that cause the subject to approach reality by means of connecting mechanisms that are at the same time schizoid defence mechanisms. Gods and demons, the good and the bad breast, the good and the bad object, good and bad theories persecute us and love us, and both aspects protect us.

## Fear of the abstract and need for the concrete[8]

The difference between these structures lies in the capacity to manipulate the abstract; this capacity depends on how the abstract is assessed, in terms of what it symbolises, since the abstract is linked to the idea of the libido.

This assessment of the abstract has to do with the quantity of libidinal energy available for mobilisation, with the capacity to mobilise it from inside to outside, and to feel it as a connecting element that is manipulated, as something that is projected but is not disconnected from ourselves, but instead connects us with others, and which we do not need to introject, since it belongs to us and, furthermore, is the medium and vehicle that allows us to obtain what we need and want from others.

The quantity of mobilisable energy depends on the variation in the intensity of the fear of our instincts, which, when these are accommodated in or transformed into an object that we control outside or inside, is constantly tested and thus demonstrates to us their quality and fate. The greater the level of destructiveness, the more fear, the more destruction and the more difficulty will be experienced in externalising it, and the greater the subject's need will be to incorporate and occupy powerful, good or bad objects; the greater, too, will be the withdrawal from external reality, as a form of magically denying it by evading it. This flight is manifested in every individual and gives rise in some way or other to temporary neurotic behaviour and symptoms; it is more stable in neurosis and even more so in psychosis. The drama becomes ever more internal, until, in schizophrenia, the flight is so extensive that the libido not only withdraws from the world, so that the schizophrenic breaks his links with the objects of reality, but is even disconnected from object representations within the subject himself; it then regresses to lower structural levels,

the quality attributed by the individual to his instincts. This quality requires and gives rise to testing and actions. If the quality is felt to be very bad, the greater will be the need for something concrete in which to accommodate the instinctual impulses 'visibly', so that they can be better controlled. The individual will need and seek concrete forms of activity and will as far as possible translate the abstract into concrete elements. With one analysand who had difficulties of sublimation, I found that even something as abstract as music assumed for him a concrete quality, since it was associated with visual images of a specific form of movement, landscapes, or a time. If he had no basis for such a representation, the various sound images would gradually be split up and arrange themselves into a kind of schema of sound.

The idea of the abstract led him by a series of associations to that of the omnipotence of the look, of thought and of wishes. Furthermore, the abstract, which suggested to him the idea of 'messing around', symbolised his libidinal impulses, which he feared and needed to control by accommodating them in something concrete because their intensity was felt to be destructive.

Science's demand for experimental evidence, for real proof, which never ultimately satisfies and must not be extrapolated, is a paradigm of this situation. The difficulty of understanding another's thought; its total or partial rejection by some rationalisation; the idea of influencing or being influenced by a given conception; and, in the analytic situation, the fear (both the analysand's and the analyst's) of the other's thoughts and words, as well as the precautions taken by each, as manifested in the analyst's personal behaviour and in the entire ceremonial and technical requirements of the analysis – all these are determined by the quality attributed to the instincts, which need to be isolated, incarcerated in the body, in internal representations or in external representations (objects, movements or behaviour governed by strict rules that limit, control and constantly test the instincts).

As and when we lose our fear of the dangerousness of our instincts, the need to control them diminishes. The division of the personality into three agencies – the id, the ego and the superego – apart from its scientific value and necessity for psychological understanding, serves and also expresses this need to control the instincts. By dividing them theoretically in this way, we believe that we are magically dividing and controlling them in reality, even though, at the same time, we know and can verify whenever we like that the id impulses forbidden to the ego by the superego are in any case fulfilled. Indeed, because of the seeming postponements, inhibitions and modifications of a destructive impulse, its aim is achieved much more effectively, albeit indirectly. The individual not only fulfils his aggression but also conceals it, sometimes himself appearing as the victim; he thereby practices the aggression and at the same time protects himself from its consequences.

Conversely, the difficulty of symbolisation in the field of analysis, for example, and in metapsychology – as regards not only the typical agencies and their interrelationship but also the conception of the object – arises from the need to see everything as a single good or bad thing, and to deny the different and hence also the unforeseen that cannot be dominated. This already occurs when we say that a given theory or conception is confused or incomprehensible. The feeling that a theory lacks reality because it is not our own, the difficulty of attributing reality to the abstract, has to do with what the abstract symbolises on the instinctual level; and the lack of a concrete form (evidence or experimental material) prevents us from understanding – that is, from accepting – just as we reject and avoid everything we cannot control, by which we are therefore afraid of being controlled. At the deepest level, the rejection of a theoretical conception, whatever its nature, is an expression of the fear of influencing and being influenced by thought, wishes and libidinal impulses, whose invisible action, lacking concrete expression, we cannot control either in ourselves or in others.

Both difficulties – those of integration and of division – are also a way of denying the continuous and incessant work of integration and disintegration we are performing internally, because this is experienced at a deep level as real action on objects and on ourselves. We regard both our own ideas and those of others as if they were the individual himself and not an emanation from him, and in changing or rejecting some aspects and accepting others, we firmly believe that we are modifying the individual himself.

People with firm ideas and well-defined and powerful convictions are valued highly, as if their own belief in their immutability provided us with a safe haven affording the approval or rejection we need to limit the continuous movement of comparison, division, acceptance, elimination and reintegration of our instincts, impulses, affects and thoughts.

When the quality of the instincts becomes such that they are feared less, they no longer need to be isolated, incarcerated in the body, in internal representations or in external representations of these internal images. They can then flow freely, and libido, soma and thought at all levels of behaviour form a unity that is experienced, fulfilled and completed by integration with reality.

The libido, the libidinal impulses, as a boundary concept between the somatic and the psychic, the concrete and the abstract, is a controversial notion. It is denied concrete reality because it cannot be perceived in a con-

aroused by the idea of the existence in ourselves of an unknown, amorphous force that we cannot dominate.

Precisely the psychologist, who knows the force of the abstract, has the most need to deny it in some way or other; he replaces the abstract by the concrete, substituting a form for the impulse, as a way of denying the latter, although he at the same time perceives and expresses it and it is inexorably sustained by the phenomena of life and of death.

Words are a symbol of libidinal energy. 'In the beginning was the Word . . .' and from it all things were born. Words, as immaterial sounds, are symbols of life, of creative energy, of the unknown, which is constantly transformed, which exists in ourselves, which is the essence of life itself, and which we try to imprison – in order not to lose it – in the body, in objects, in space, and in time, and which we can only possess when we identify with its very essence, with its incessant flow, expressed in the constant variation and transformation taking place in ourselves, in others and in all natural phenomena.

Helen Keller manages to symbolise when she distinguishes the container from its contents – water and glass respectively – and she does this when she feels a trickle of water flow through her hand; she then weeps and feels love for the first time; she weeps for the new doll she had been given as a present and had broken in rage because it was not her own. Her story tells us a great deal: what flows – the water – is the affect, love, what gives pleasure and life to things, to the new doll. She surely did love, but, when it became possible for her to symbolise her affect by something movable and formless, namely water, to which she was also able to give form and which she could control, then she could liberate and accept her affect, because she could manipulate it. She was able to weep for what she had done, because she understood that she could have avoided doing it and it was not now necessary to deny it.

Words are symbols of life, and of human life. How were they transformed into thought, from sign to symbol and to verbal symbol? The sound connected with an image was the channel whereby the external world was introduced, as well as touch and sight; later the voice was projected, its sound images carrying the impulses that acted on the world and on objects; man was then able to act in a new way on his surroundings. In this way he acquired a new form of knowledge of reality and behaviour directed towards it, and this new power was experienced as something marvellous that acted as if it were himself. What emanated from him acted like himself.

The concrete significance of words is an ancient heritage. For a time, a name expresses man's knowledge of a given phenomenon, but it then becomes the phenomenon in itself, the investigation and understanding of which is thereby limited.

In analysis, terms such as confusion, homosexuality, castration, aggression, sadism, masochism, cure, and the like, commonly used by analysands, conceal deeper meanings related to primal fantasies, which are thus isolated with their corresponding cathexes from the whole. In many fields of research, including psychology and philosophy, there are calls to reconsider certain notions that have become mere names that replace and limit the original concepts. Man is once again using metaphor as a way of pointing out, by means of the concrete, the abstract character of his thought, which cannot be expressed in fixed terms but only in metaphorical images, where the abstract, combined with the concrete, conveys the experiential quality essential to understanding. We feel and understand as a single experience, one's thought and feeling about which can be expressed in metaphor. In this way the abstract takes on concrete qualities and acquires a form, while, conversely, the concrete takes on the abstract, the wish, the emotion, which is expressed in form. The two components become fused, and their representation within the individual facilitates the union of libido, emotion and affect with the images that will express them. The kinaesthetic image joins together with sensory images from reality and, through their synthesis in thought, instinct and reality are united.

## Increased ego integration

The ego begins in the mouth, in which it performs the first voluntary act connected with the object, with the world, which is sucking; in this act the ego has a single experience (sucking and fantasying). There is no body–mind dichotomy (Scott, 1950).

Various authors (Klein, 1930; Isaacs, 1952; Kubie, 1934) consider that these fantasies should very probably be understood in terms of motor rather than visual images.

According to the vicissitudes of his breast-satisfaction and frustration – the infant deploys primary defence mechanisms; he deals with frustration situations by dividing the object into good and bad, cancelling out and blocking certain aspects, and hallucinating the good breast when necessary.

When the object is dissociated, so too is the ego. The ego, like the object, is divided into two aspects, one of which is denied and its affects blocked, while it hallucinates in itself one of its aspects – good or bad – as required. When the act of speaking is analysed, these first defence mechanisms are

## Integration in space and time

In order for ego integration to take place, the ego must at the same time be integrated with reality; that is, it must be integrated with the object, and the object to be integrated is the one upon which the ego is projected and which it then introjects in sucking. In integrating the object, the subject projects himself, connects with reality and with space, and in this way acquires the notion of his movement or mobility towards the external world; he consequently regains the notion of time through those of movement and of space. In connecting with the external world, the individual projects himself in space and in time, into the future.

In the analytic situation, the analysand repeats his first experiences when speaking is analysed in a current form, and as he relives his projective mechanisms, so too he relives his introjective mechanisms. Through the object, the analyst – who is identical with his primal object – he reconnects with the first introjected objects, relives all his past identifications, and becomes conscious of the different aspects of the various objects, introjections and identifications made throughout his life. By virtue of the increased capacity for knowledge of reality, all these objects, including the analyst, are reconsidered in their good and bad aspects; the analysand assimilates the good and useful aspects of the introjected objects and eliminates what he now regards as disposable. When the analysand reaches this point, he suffers intense anxieties because he feels that, when the various images are united within him and he is united with reality, he will be absorbed, lost 'in the current', and he fears losing his individuality, melting, and fusing with the object and with things. He is afraid of allowing himself to be carried away by the current and of then no longer being master of himself. In other words, he fears that he will suffer the same fate as that of the breast in himself, which was absorbed and became part of his world. Reality testing gradually shows him that the contrary is the case, as the capacity to cathect is increased by the greater availability of unfettered libidinal energy, which the subject is much freer to accommodate in an object and to summon back to himself so that he can project it again when he so wishes. In reconnecting with past objects, the individual connects with his own past, and reconsiders himself as an object. Everything he previously regarded as negative or positive from the point of view of his affects, acts and thoughts is reconsidered, and his past personality, formerly overvalued or undervalued, is integrated with his present one following this process of 'purification'. Eventually the analysand asserts and repeats that he is the same as he was in the past and that he has always been so; at the same time he cannot fail to see the changes he has undergone, so that he acquires the notion of his capacity for change, which is neither as extreme nor as non-existent as he had thought. The new notion – new in the sense of experience – he then acquires is that he has a capacity for development, which, even if not as sudden or magic as he would like, takes place inexorably, deny it as he will. This notion also arouses anxiety, because the analysand realises that his knowledge, whether of reality, of objects or of himself, is relative and that there is something inside himself which he does not know and over which he does not therefore have total control. The idea of the impossibility of change, the feeling that 'it is always the same' and that the same neurotic situations are repeated, as well as the idea of sudden changes, brought about by the subject himself or by the omnipotent action of the analyst, is merely a defence against the anxiety aroused by the unknown in oneself, in the world, in objects and in time, and which, being unknown, cannot be controlled. The subject then fears what may happen in his relations with people, what he may do, what they may do to him, and what may occur in a future situation. This is always a matter of the analysand's fear of the strength of his own instincts; as reality testing gradually shows him the quality of his instincts, he exhibits greater freedom both directly in his interpersonal relations and in sublimations. He then understands the relativity of his action on others and of their action on himself, and in effect becomes aware of his inner rhythm and freedom, as he realises that his fate is not sealed once and for all. He himself, in this sense, acquires the notion of his own relativity in regard to his ability to influence and act on objects; and even if this frustrates and depresses him and arouses his anxiety, since he loses the hope of finding something definitive, stable and immutable that will protect him, he is compensated by the newly won increase in his capacity for symbolisation. When affect is liberated and integrated in the whole personality and in the subject's actions (thought and movement), the sense of the ego is recovered. Actions that fulfil the individual's instinctual impulses, which are no longer felt to be harmful in fact or in purpose, now give satisfaction simply through their performance.

## Reactivation of masturbation

As the analysand loses his fear of the strength of his instincts and as his capacity to connect with others and with himself increases, there appear fantasies of masturbation involving prohibited or idealised objects, which he then translates into action; alternatively, he may tell of them, if he had

connect with reality, achieved through the diminution of the subject's paranoid anxieties and persecutory fears. He no longer fears being punished for his masturbation, damaging the object of his masturbation fantasy, or damaging himself with his masturbation. Ideas of contracting tuberculosis, becoming an imbecile or going mad through masturbation betray his fear of destruction of the object, totally exhausting it and destroying it within. It seems to me that in masturbation, at a deep level, the hand recovers its primitive identity with the object: in his masturbation, the analysand relives in relation to his hand his earliest relations with the breast, which it represented in very concrete form in the infant's thumb sucking.

## The hand as subject–object

Like the voice, the hand readily lends itself to preserving the primitive identity of subject and object (mouth and breast). It connects the subject with the object and belongs to the former, who therefore manipulates and dominates it; for this reason it always retains the connotation of a good, gratifying object, which can be resorted to in the event of frustrations, and from which pleasure can be obtained at will – in other words, it can be manipulated omnipotently. The persistence of a degree of masturbation throughout life is accepted as normal. The hand, as a regressive object of libidinal satisfaction, is evidently like a bridge between the individual and the world – a real object, on which the individual can stop, which he can cross or over which he can return in the vicissitudes of his relations with the world.

## Pathways of projection and introjection

The senses, the hand and motility, or movement, are the pathways whereby introjection and projection take place and the external and internal worlds

276

meet. From this point of view, speaking and words require a process of introjection and projection and a capacity to receive and to give. The word as object, as a verbal image representing the object, is felt to be omnipotent, since it stands in for and replaces the object, making it possible to possess it magically in space and time beyond and above reality. Perhaps for this reason, the word as verbal image, whether sound or graphic, is the heir par excellence of the individual's omnipotence, as it enables him to survive and act in an extension of space and time not accessible to the individual himself. A word or sentence is often the justification of a long, obscure and seemingly sterile life, retaining through time a value and importance not attributed to the person who uttered it.

When speaking is analysed, it is found that the first defence mechanisms, which are at the same time the first mechanisms of connection with objects, persist throughout life and, moreover, that they are an indispensable condition of the capacity to symbolise – that is, to connect with reality and to survive. Whether we deem an individual 'normal', 'neurotic' or 'psychotic' depends on the abstract or concrete form in which these mechanisms operate for him. This quality of abstraction or concreteness depends on the greater or lesser degree of danger he attributes to his instincts and to the omnipotence of his wishes, as determined both by the intensity of the instinct and by the possibility of fulfilling it.

## Inner rhythm

As the individual loses his fear of his instincts and no longer needs to immobilize them inside himself, others and things, and as he himself becomes integrated by connecting with his past and his future, and understanding that the existing aspects of himself that he values somehow were already there in the past, the current situation being a consequence of them, so he acquires the notion and experience of his inner rhythm, of relativity, of the action exerted by external influences; he then gains a sense of his inner freedom. This inner rhythm is ultimately a consequence of his emotions and instincts. He also becomes aware of the relativity of his action on others when he understands that everyone has his own rhythm. He can then identify with objects without fear, as he is not afraid of being dominated or of entering once and for all into their rhythms. He can surrender, because he knows that he can return to himself and that this same movement of seeking the object and returning to himself is a rhythm that belongs to him. Nor is he afraid of abandoning the object, because, just as he can leave it, so he has been able to return to it. When his own rhythm becomes established, the external and the internal, in a primal sense, lose their former strength.

277

This is not a matter of a lack of affect or capacity for connection, but quite the opposite. Now things, objects, circumstances, success or failure cannot as it were make or break his happiness for ever. This is because what is definitive and lasting is his own capacity to connect and disconnect at will, as and when required by his needs, which are ultimately instinctual.

Movement – rhythm – is an emotional phenomenon. Man is polyrhyth-

Speaking synthesises the abstract and the concrete in the words spoken, while the abstract is at the same time liberated from its form through the emotion transmitted to and aroused in the object. The greater the capacity for abstract connection with objects, the greater the capacity for concrete connection will be, as both forms of connection have the same purpose. However, the concrete always needs the abstract in order to express itself and to achieve its aim of connection (affects – emotion – sensation). It is this abstract quality of objects that is perceived by the analyst and experienced by him in the emotional reactions of his countertransference; as he comes to understand these, he can enable the analysand to grasp their full meaning, appropriateness and value in mediating between his instinctual impulses, on the one hand, and objects and reality, on the other, for the purpose of connection, adaptation and satisfaction.

## Notes

1   The notion that speaking is an act is implicit in "Jokes and their relation to the unconscious" (Freud, 1905). Its intention is to fulfil libidinal, erotic and destructive wishes, which replace sexual contact and physical aggression. The psychogenesis of jokes suggests that the child first touches and then looks; later he exhibits himself in order to arouse admiration; and finally he speaks, as a way of achieving sexual contact with the loved object.

2   Because oral, anal and urethral fantasies appear in quick succession, I first thought that there might be a relationship between the time of acquisition of language and the polymorphous stage of libidinal development. However, I now feel that this phenomenon is due to a primitive identity of all body orifices, which might be represented in a very primitive body scheme by a single orifice, through which the primitive individual – resembling a round vesicle with a communicating orifice – receives and expels elements of the outside world respectively into and from his own world, these two worlds being the same at this time. This hypothesis stems from earlier observations on the body scheme, together with a woman patient's description of her experiences under anaesthetic. Before she

lost consciousness, the anaesthetist had removed the mask and looked into her eyes; the patient described how, already unable to move or speak, she had felt as if she were a lake, lying at the bottom of which she could see through the water someone looming over her. She subsequently recalled that, as a child, she had taken a long time to understand the globe because she had seen the earth as round, like a hollow sphere, surrounded by the ocean. The sky was the space inside the sphere, while the sea was the water on its inner surface, which surrounded the continents where people lived, safe from the danger of falling.

3   Symbolic language and symbolic interpretation, for both analysand and analyst, are thoroughly understood only when the symbols recover their cathexes and are experienced intensely. That may be why symbolism and symbolic interpretations have met with so much interest and so much rejection. Their practical use has always been regarded as highly relative, if anything, more as an aid in the analyst's understanding of the patient's conflicts. Because the symbol and the symbolic interpretation lacked the affective component, they did not produce the necessary emotional mobilisation. The absence of the emotional component from the symbolic representations already betrayed the magnitude of the cathexis that had demanded its repression.

4   Every symbol represents the 'ego', the subject's own body and its parts, as well as the objects and organs of the objects projected by the child onto external objects. 'The child attempts in the middle of the first year of life to reach everything he sees in order to bring it to his mouth. This means that objects are invested with oral libido. The instinctual impulse to introduce things to his mind through the eyes, ears and fingers satisfies some of his frustrated oral wishes. Life, perception and intelligence are due to these sources of libido.' [Translator's note: the author attributes this quotation to Klein, 'The importance of symbol-formation in the development of the ego', but it does not appear there.]

5   *La Nature est un temple où de vivants piliers/Laissent parfois sortir de confuses paroles;/L'homme y passe à travers des forêts de symboles/Qui l'observent avec des regards familiers.*

6   'The utterance of conception-laden sounds, at the sight of things that exemplify one or other of the conceptions which those sounds carry, is first a purely expressive reaction; only long habit can fix an association so securely that the word and the object are felt to belong together, so that the one is always a reminder of the other. But when this point is reached, the humanoid creature will undoubtedly utter the sound in sport, and thus move the object into nearer and clearer prominence in his mind . . . ' (Langer, 1942, p. 134).

7   'Silberer's autosymbolic phenomenon coincides with this conception. The functional aspect, which refers to the mode of functioning of the organism and of the brain; the material aspect, which has to do with the content or, in other words, the meaning of the act; and the somatic aspect, which is related to the bodily sensations, coincide and express the process of symbolisation in more elaborate form; the integration of these three elements is in line with

the ideas of Clifford Scott. Such a representation would combine the conditions of the total experience of bodily movement, sensations and images (knowledge)' (Isaacs, 1952). [Translator's note: this passage does not appear in the English paper by Isaacs with the same title, 'The nature and function of phantasy'.]

8  The terms 'abstract' and 'concrete' are used here in their popular senses of

~~beings are incapable of assimilating external rhythms. The boundary between~~ univocal and polyrhythmic beings appears to be highly fluid, but humans surely take pride of place among polyrhythmic beings. This characteristic of human beings lies at the root of both their superiority and their depravity. In primitive mystical thought, the polyrhythmic nature of human beings seems to be conceived as a combination of different (typical) univocal rhythms, the collision between which gives rise to man's equivocal character and spiritual restlessness. For this reason the specific human rhythms are but reflections of univocal rhythms of animals (or of plants) and the predominant typical rhythm betrays its totem because it indicates its mystical ancestry. However, this typical feature, which is always inconsistent with the other rhythms, is seldom manifested clearly on the surface of the human being; it instead remains hidden, except at certain moments when the predominant rhythm of the nature of an individual is disclosed. That is why the primitive's attention is often directed towards rare or transient phenomena, towards the anomalies or insignificant details of daily life, until he succeeds in discovering the typical animal rhythm reflected in the specifics' (Schneider, 1946).

# References

Delacroix (1952). *El Lenguaje. Nuevo Tratado de Psicología*. Buenos Aires: Kapelusz.

Fenichel, O. (1941). The ego and the affects. *Psychoanal. Rev.*, 28: 49–60.

Freud, S. (1905). Jokes and their relation to the unconscious. *The complete psychological works of Sigmund Freud*, 8.

Freud, S. (1912–13). Totem and taboo. *The complete psychological works of Sigmund Freud*, 13.

Heimann, P. (1949). Some notes on the psycho-analytic concept of introjected objects. *British Journal of Medical Psychology*, 22: 8–15.

Heimann, P. (1950). On counter-transference. *International Journal of Psycho-Analysis*, 31: 81–92.

Heimann, P. (1951). The re-evaluation of the Oedipus complex. *International Journal of Psycho-Analysis*, 33: 84–92.

Isaacs, S. (1952). The nature and function of phantasy. In *New Developments in Psycho-Analysis*, ed. M. Klein et al. London: Hogarth Press, pp. 67–121. Trans. as 'Naturaleza y función de la fantasía'. *Revista de Psicoanálisis,* VII, No. 4.

Jones, E. (1925). *Traité Théorique et Pratique de la Psychanalyse*. Paris: Payot.

Keller, H. (1936 [1902]). *The Story of My Life*. Garden City: Doubleday, Doran & Co.

Klein, M. (1930). The importance of symbol-for-mation in the development of the ego. In *Contributions to Psycho-Analysis*. London: Hogarth, 1948.

Klein, M. (1946). Notes on some schizoid mechanisms. In *Envy and Gratitude and Other Works 1946–1963*. New York: The Free Press.

Klein, M. (1950). On the criteria for termination of a psycho-analysis. In *Envy and Gratitude and Other Works 1946–1963*. New York: The Free Press.

Kubie, L. (1934). Body symbolisation and the development of languages. *The Psychoanalytic Quarterly*, 3: 430–444.

Langer, S. (1942). *Philosophy in a New Key*. Cambridge, MA: Harvard Univ. Press, third edition 1967.

Piaget, J. (1952). *The Origins of Intelligence in Children*. New York: Int. Univ. Press.

Reich, W. (1947). *The Function of the Orgasm – Muscular Attitude and Bodily Expressions*. New York: Orgone Institute Press.

Schneider, M. (1946). *El origen musical de los animales: símbolos en la mitología*. Barcelona: Consejo Superior de Investigación.

Scott, C. (1950). Quoted in S. Isaacs (see above).

# 25

# *David Liberman*[1]

*This paper was published in 1974 by* Contemporary Psychoanalysis, *10: 41–55. Its findings and theoretical hypotheses have been extensively published in Spanish in numerous articles, and his book* La comunicación en terapéutica psicoanalítica (Communication in psychoanalytic therapy) *was published in 1962 by EUDEBA in Buenos Aires.*

In this paper I will support the notions: (a) that some features of the verbalizations in analysis allow us to understand unconscious phantasies; (b) that these traits are valuable when we research psychoanalytic dialogue so as to transmit empirical data in scientific communications, and (c) that what I suggest in (a) has further consequences for effecting strategic, technical, and tactical approaches with which to break up Id resistances (compulsion to repeat).

## Introduction

a   The paralinguistic elements[2] of adult verbalization have an earlier root than articulate language; they somehow resemble infantile ways of communicating inasmuch as they constitute a manner of codifying experiences that cannot as yet be put in verbal language. They provide support for the objectivization of the qualities of unconscious phantasies. One of the advantages of this approach lies in the fact that we can effect deductive inferences on empirical bases in the dialogue during the course of the analytic treatment. I shall, as I have written elsewhere (Liberman, 1962), (1966), (1971), introduce here some findings from different currents of contemporary linguistics that I consider to be useful so as to circumscribe the observations. I have found that the paralinguistic elements of verbalization as components of the patient's "speech" in the session provide the empirical bases for our statements about unconscious phantasy.[3]

b   We must distinguish between our actual work with the patient in the session and our study of psychoanalytic dialogue, taking some elements from the sessions and following a pattern of systematization when sessions are over. In this particular case, systematization must be effected by taking a succession of paraverbal structures in the utterances and observing the sequences of changes and the repetitiousness thereof. Psychoanalysis thus considered becomes the study of the patient's unconscious when we work inside the session, plus the study of the variations of elements in the traits of his verbalization when we research psychoanalytic dialogue outside the sessions. In this way the study of the patient's unconscious inside the session and the study of the psychoanalytic dialogue outside the session acquire a similar status and feed back each other. For the study of unconscious phantasies I apply this method of picking out paraverbal features of the patient's utterances, the structure of their sequences, and their repetitions. Other aspects of current linguistics are also useful sometimes. For example, the study of the options of pronominal phrases in the syntactic structure of the patient's speech is the optimal tool for research into the degree of differentiation between the patient's self and that of the analyst, according to the variation of the transference relationship.

c   The core of compulsion to repeat is contained in the unconscious phantasy, and it is detected in the study of the patent's discursive paralinguistic features. The interruption of the compulsion to repeat is possible when the detection of this core allows us to effect new strategic, technical, and tactical approaches. The compulsion to repeat is expressed as a seriated association of unconscious phantasies.

Now when we study psychoanalytic dialogue, we frequently find that the analyst is unconsciously conditioned towards some sort of "adaptation" – iatrogenic interaction – triggered by the patient's unconscious repetition and reinforced by the duration of the treatment. The discovery of this by the study of the analyst's strategic failures leads us to a new approach to the patient, which, if correct, will eventually break this iatrogenic interaction and switch it to therapeutic psychoanalytic interaction.

## The importance of linguistic elements

This subject requires some references to an inclusive set of contexts in which a psychoanalytic treatment is carried out. In a decreasing degree of inclusion these contexts are (1) the analytic situation and (2) the setting, both of which are almost invariable, and (3) the verbal and paraverbal ele-

that may affect the psychoanalytic process from the psychoanalytic situation include any state of public emergency that, because of its intensity and uncommonness, affects *both analysand and analyst* in such a way that they cannot unconsciously maintain relative stability of the analytic setting.

One patient of mine responded to national economic instability threatening the survival of several private enterprises with unconscious phantasies of helplessness; he felt "as a child who is out of home and cannot find his way towards shelter." The patient's status in his business was for him the only container from which he could expect warmth and food. This state of national economic instability was evidently an element that came from the broad context, namely, *the analytic situation*. The event transcended what was developed in the analytic dialogue, and found its way into the qualities of verbal language and thought. Therefore, fortuitous events[4] outside the psychoanalytic setting may influence the psychoanalytic process by reinforcing or minimizing unconscious phantasies rather than otherwise.

The *psychoanalytic setting* is kept constant from a formal point of view – it includes roles, schedules, and functions that the analyst usually stipulates before beginning treatment. But the setting can be more important if viewed from the points of view of both participants. The patient invests is with changing meanings in the different moments of optimal therapeutic alliance when he approaches the discovery of "what it means to be in analysis." From the analyst's point of view, optimal therapeutic alliance brings about the discovery of "who is the person he once took in analysis." The evolution of the psychoanalytic process inside the setting is considered here as a continuous discovery of new meanings and senses by both patient and analyst.

Therefore, the setting of the therapeutic process has a contextual significance that is somewhat more restricted than that of the analytic situation. In addition to the components of the analytic contract, the context of the setting includes a most important element: a peculiar type of dialogue that I have called *asymmetrical* – the patient speaks to the therapist about himself, whatever the content of what he is saying, whereas the therapist responds to the analysand by speaking to him about him. The psychoanalytic process is *of* the patient, must be developed *by* the patient, and is carried out *for* the patient. This is eventually the therapeutic goal.

Since the study of the patient's unconscious inside the session and the study of psychoanalytic dialogue outside the session become similar, the psychoanalytic process consists of the patient's acquisition of more and more information about himself. He, therefore, stops being at the mercy of uncertainty and of unconscious determinism (Freud, 1962), (1963a), (1963b), (1963c).

In the *linguistic context* it is possible to record and detect with some precision advances and retreats appearing in the therapeutic process by means of those changes and constant elements observed in the course of treatment, and by the therapist's conscious or unconscious working through, out of the session, of situations and conflicts he faces when performing his task with the patient.

This can be found in Freud's self-analysis (1964). His patients were included in his own dreams and in his associations about them. Freud persisted, and further developed psychoanalysis in his work outside the sessions; taking himself as a patient or writing notes after his daily routine. This extra-analytic scrutiny permits the detection of constant elements in the *linguistic context* – the most restricted of the three – and enables the therapist to infer about the patient's compulsion to repeat, one of the resistances most antagonistic to the goals of treatment.

There are different clues to repetitive compulsions, which the therapist may detect through this second avenue of research, namely the investigation of the analytic dialogue outside the session. The empirical bases of psychoanalysis are given by speech and verbal mimicry in the course of the changing succession of structures and functions, plus the changes, crises, and new structures found in the patient; as well as what the patient does not say in the sessions, his silences, the therapist's, the choice of forms of interpreting – all of which imply linguistic styles. Other clues are the patient's gestures and postural attitudes, the consequences of acting out, in and out of the session, the choice of clothes, etc.

When we study the compulsion to repeat out of the context of the session, we can observe a seriated succession of unconscious phantasies potentiated by failures in the therapist's approach. Thus, what we call compulsion to repeat appears in these reformulations as *iatrogenic interaction*. The paralinguistic elements of the patient's utterances are the clues to unconscious phantasies, but are most frequently omitted in the therapist's strategic approach. The duration of treatment may condition the therapist to hearing the patient's utterances only in some ways while unconsciously discarding others. When we discover that our work with the patient becomes "too easy," and if we also sense an impoverishment in the patient's repertoire of subject matter, it becomes necessary to find some way of recording with precision the features of this psychoanalytic dialogue. Iatrogenic interaction, revealed by means of paralinguistic elements in the record of a psychoanalytic session, permits us to discover how

choice of one trait in preference to others and the combinations of these traits imply accepting a set of options and discarding others. This is a valuable tool for the analyst to begin to explore the clues to the significations hinted at by these significants. Linguistics has mostly emphasized syntactic rather than phonological combinations. Yet by examining phonological elements it is possible to effect deductive inferences in reference to certain unconscious phantasies predominating at a given moment, if the therapist takes into account, among other things, the features of the patient's utterances, the irregularities in his intonation, and the pauses separating one utterance from the next.

Thus we reveal that the repetitive compulsion is potentiated by the unconscious phantasies positively fed back by failures in the therapeutic communicative interaction. This phenomenon means a reinforced repetition in the patient and a damaging of the analyst's therapeutic instrument in the therapist. Verbal and paraverbal elements lose their characteristics as temporalized and changing structures. Timelessness and rigidity pervade the psychoanalytic process, turning its direction towards iatrogenic interaction.

## The data of the empirical base

When the patient, male, 38, entered analysis, he was undergoing a depressive state. In the course of treatment the therapist and I (the supervisor), realized how our conception of severe melancholic states had to be reconsidered in the light of the psychoanalytic process. Our diagnostic *psychiatric criteria* must be taken as relative and modifiable, depending on how an analysis proceeds, or else, psychiatric knowledge turns into a hindrance. This might have been the case with this patient who, at the beginning of treatment, did not have the least understanding of his unconscious conflicts and was so taken up by his ideas of failure, self-reproach, and suicide, that he might have been considered unanalyzable.

In such cases, the therapist's contribution to the psychoanalytic process is crucial. The therapist either must work outside the session generating fresh hypotheses that promote the most valid technical attitude. This patient was considered by his relatives a successful man who had surprisingly failed in business. With bankrupt self-esteem, he believed that his partners hated him for his failures and were correct in their attitude. This worried his family group, and a psychiatrist was consulted who referred him to a psychoanalyst. When the patient came to analysis what became immediately apparent was that he had been looking for infantile oral gratification by means of his genital relations. Since this search was unfruitful, frustration mounted. To this he opposed the unconscious phantasy of being "a man who can move mountains to achieve his aim." He then tried to follow with the same phantasy (that of being a "mountain-mover") by attempting to secure a partner's affection as a repetition of his unending and unsuccessful quest for receptive, infantile, narcissistic gratifications. He wished for gratifications, and at the same time, denied others the means he used. Indeed, he wanted to be loved and taken care of, but instead, he gave. He did not allow others to give to him. He was thus frustrated, not only because he did not achieve his aim, but also because, as the people surrounding him did not understand what he wanted from them, all he offered was accepted with his not asking anything in return.

In Kleinian terms, he effected a projective identification in which the oral receptive parts of his self were projected into (1) his wife's vagina and (2) the countenance of one of his partners. As a result, his relationships with both wife and partner were strongly pervaded by his infantile oral receptive self; he had to be the omnipotent breast that took care of and fed others as he would have liked to have been taken care of and fed. This distorted relationship was due to the intense ambivalence and resentment underlying any situation in which depending and receiving affected him.

The foregoing abstract has been necessary for an understanding of the two verbal fragments we shall scan. The first is the opening of a session during the first period of his treatment. Each line includes the fragment of verbalization uttered in five seconds. There are, therefore, 45 seconds of verbalization.

1   I . . . had a *bad day today* . . .
2   Everything *went wrong* . . .
3   Again . . . I heard *the little inner voices* . . .
4   telling me . . . I *won't do things well* . . .
5   Yes . . .
6   You . . . are doing *your best but it doesn't work* . . .
7   it doesn't work . . .

8    well . . .
9    I lose control . . . things escape me, time goes by and there is no end to
     it.

This fragment belongs to the first period of treatment, when the patient's
clinical diagnosis was a melancholic depressive state. Since the analysis pro-

and then from low and slow rising to increasingly high and fast. These traits
of ending at high pitch and high speed showed that he was speaking from a
part of the Self that was trapped inside an object. Verbalization under these
conditions was disturbed because while he tried to verbalize, the internal
object worked on his hearing, and attacked his own voice. In terms of
unconscious phantasy, his voice was being bitten, while it was uttered. This
in turn engendered a defense against the attack on his voice. The result
was the appearance of a shrill quality in the increasingly higher and faster
part of utterances (1), (2), (3), (4) and (6). In these fragments, which appear
in italics, the patient produced a rasping voice with "metallic" qualities.
The deviated pitch was a defense against the phantasy of the voice being
"bitten" and "swallowed" by the speaker's auditory monitoring – listening
to himself. The aggressive shrill voice constituted the clue to this type of
defense the patient unconsciously chose against an inner object equated
with a persecuting Superego. When this defense fails, verbal features correspond to the characteristics of a patient who "bites" what he says, in the
moments of melancholic catastrophe – the patient who wishes to speak
but cannot.

As a generalization we may say that when patients cannot fully manage
to carry out this type of defense against an attacking Superego, the last
syllable or words in some statements are literally swallowed; instead of a
complaining, recriminatory, incisive voice, we hear slurred verbal features
in half-uttered statements as the product of an oral sadistic attack from the
ear, which "bites" the voice as it comes out. As a result the patient sounds
aphasic. That is why melancholic patients are frequently unaware of the difference between what they *have* verbalized and what they have *attempted* to
verbalize. They complain they cannot say all they wish to and that things
remain inside them. In some cases they are not even aware of that, since
they equate *verbal thought* with *verbalization*. The effects of this aggressive
internal object appear in the inquisitive, incisive voice (oral-dental sadism) that also turns against the utterer. The effects of this attack of the

persecuting object (devouring breast introjected as a Superego) are felt by the subject as an attack on his own voice. In the last three five-second fragments of the transcription, phonation acquires other types of verbal features, as if it belonged to someone else. This would correspond to the parts of the Self that remain outside of the inner, entrapping object. The patient's hopes for reparation are deposited in these parts of the Self, but as this is so precarious, he loses strength while carrying it out. Thus the tone of his voice diminishes. Fragments (7), (8) and (9) were delivered with a marked decrease in the intensity of voice and at higher speed. This corresponds to the drainage of good internal contents from the Self, with which the patient tried to placate a bad object, in a Superego mode. The last part of fragment (9) shows an acute crisis of resignation in which the patient's voice sped up and disappeared, as an expression of an unconscious phantasy of dying.

In optimal mental functioning, self-monitoring enables the subject to make an adequate amount of demands with a minimum of impatience. The good internal Superego permits the patient to regulate what he wishes to express while expressing it. To be more precise, demand corresponds to oral – cannibalistic fantasy, which is transformed into constructive self-criticism.

I believe that markedly ambivalent patients who suffer crises of impatience need to speak, but while speaking, the acoustic impact makes them bite their words, so that the ear that listens to them transforms them into bitten feces. My position agrees with Abraham's (1949) statement about an oral – cannibalistic attack and the anal expulsion of the object, which is destroyed and later introjected as destroyed. The high speed and the elevation in tone of the patient's voice were an attempt to prevent his ear, into which he had introjected his analyst, from devouring it.

In (7), (8) and (9) we note that the surviving verbalization was preserved in this patient at a great expense of energy and strength. He could counteract the oral cannibalistic impulses that might attack the word by appealing to the non-trapped parts of the Self. And indeed, this is what was taking place in his life. When he began his analysis, he was struggling to survive, although once in a while he would fall flat, as if paralyzed, as can be seen in the last part of our sample, where his voice dwindles.

Words produce an acoustic self-impact, especially in cases in which there is little distance between the patient's own Self and the listener's Self – the analyst's ear. Survival of the utterance commits the two participants in the psychoanalytic interaction. The therapist's silence is equated with the patient's own ear, which is also attacking him. That is why this patient sped up and raised the tone of his voice in fragments (1), (2), (3), (4) and (6); he phantasied the therapist's silence also stood for his own evil ears. The two auditory areas – his own and the therapist's – overlapped and there was no interpersonal breach. By the very fact of lying down without seeing the therapist, a patient in a melancholic state makes an introjection of the therapist's "evil ears," which are in turn equated to an anus laden with oral cannibalistic impulses. His verbal utterances are then closely connected with this pathological introjection.

It is thus possible to have a very clear notion of the "characters" appear-

and languished while involved in a process of desperate reparation that he could not satisfy (7), (8) and (9).

Let us now scan the second fragment taken from analytic data a year later. In this period the patient was trying to integrate his two Selves, which antagonized each other. The struggle between trapped and non–trapped parts of the Self that we saw in the first fragment turned, in the second, into hard labor towards conciliation. This material will show the empirical data that are the clues to the patient's new state of improvement. They are:

a    Hard–won and progressive insights paved the way for a final and complete understanding of two pathological external links with which his previous melancholic state had been positively fed back.
b    These links consisted of the patient's simultaneously having two women: his wife and a mistress whom he called "the girl." He had reproached himself because he delusionally believed he was damaging his wife with his unconcerned coolness. He realized at this stage that it was actually the other way around: his wife did not care for him and thus pushed him towards "the girl."
c    With regard to his relationship with "the girl," he had originally felt loved and needed, as the hero who can "move mountains." He now realized that actually he did not feel loved but bossed and exploited. Whenever he had believed he was a hero, he had simply been making self-depreciatory remarks that flattered her vanity. He was now aware of the fact that he was committed to a sterile and wasteful process of reparation.

In the second fragment we can see certain differences on the phonological level. Although they may sound unimportant, when the form of response is taken into account, these imply a deep structural change that includes the way the unconscious phantasy is instrumented.

I shall also point at some paraverbal components of the following material taken a year after the previous sample. Because of the nature and the quality of this second fragment, I have had to include the linguistic and paralinguistic components in the text.

1  Today (tense voice and no air intake) . . . is one of those days when . . . (increasingly clearer and more intense; the final sound is lengthened and a pause ensues)

2  I arrive here in a completely (ditto)

3  mechanical and automatic way . . . thinking . . . (there is a progressive slowdown with increased tension on the vocal cords)

4  50 thousand different things and . . . (increased slowdown and increased tension on the vocal cords; voice becomes shrill; in the final word he utters a tremolo)

5  and . . . generally when I am about to arrive (here) I am surprised I am arriving and don't remember the way (there is a progressive relaxation with a slight halt before "don't remember the way"; at the end of the emission the patient sighs; there is also a syllabic lengthening in "remember," "the," and "way")

6  . . . and I come into . . . session (progressively faster) and my mind is completely (a background tremolo)

7  blank (sigh) . . . I mean it is as if I had to . . . change already . . . and de . . . devote myself to thinking of the subject here (there is a passage from tension to relaxation while the patient utters this; then he sighs)

8  . . . here . . . I have to be sorry . . . that (lengthened vowel sound in "that") . . . to

9  this (his voice denotes pain through strength, loudness and tension) that has me worried (final syllabic lengthening) . . . and it may be due to this about the last few sessions that I am fenced in (loud, tense, and slow – emphatic – voice, increasing intensity, lengthening of the final sound) . . . the same (unintelligible utterance)

10  state of the subject . . . due to . . . a . . . state of being accustomed to the subject

11  and . . . have . . . no openings (as from the next metaphor he considerably widens the combination of his phonological features as a consequence of having acquired a higher level in his competence and performance, in Chomsky's sense [1965])

12  and . . . I know I . . . see . . . and

13  along what beaten track I'm driving[5]

14  and . . . perhaps . . . that

15  although I don't see it very clearly it may take very long (a noticeable lengthening of the word "long")

16  (in a louder voice) personally I understand that my . . . (faster) that this depends on me (sighs)

Unlike what happened in the first sample, the patient here gets rid of illusory suicidal reparation. He can emerge from the Superego object that deteriorated him, and a creative process shows up in his speech in the shape of a metaphor. He represents in it, and recreates in the code language, the frustrating and suicidal aspects that now appear as "ploughing a field" unable to escape from the limiting fence.[6] Notice that the metaphor was preceded

resentation in the Ego) surrounded by an imaginary and adequate spatial – temporal environment that fits his performance as a creator of his own language. He therefore gets rid of the illusory suicidal reparation in which he was submerged in the previous sample.

I maintain that when comparative samples of two meetings between the melancholic patient and his analyst have changed so much, in reference to a given parameter (the first five-second fragments of the two sessions), the empirical datum is the discovery of a metaphor that contains the patient as a subject surrounded by his conflict. When this patient began his discourse in the second sample, his paraverbal features and choice of statements denoted a certain mastery of Superego functions over himself, precluding his having the feeling of a physical body lying down and occupying some room. Still, as he progressed in the course of these utterances, the part of the Self that was trapped in suicidal phantasies was able to acquire creativity in the process of verbalization during the session. He began to place outside that part of his Self that had previously been trapped inside a Superego object. This released the feeling of having some Ego functions engulfed and mastered by the Superego. Since suffering had diminished, he could now create metaphors to represent precisely that suffering.

Beyond the phonological elements, the syntactic construction in its semantic sense brings the representation of his body containing a mood, all of which is in a moment of time – space ("generally when I am about to arrive (here) I am surprised I am arriving and don't remember the way"). The patient, as a speaker, verbalizes inner changing states because of the acquisition of the ability to conceive of the therapist as a receiver with an aural area different from his. *We may say that an interpersonal network has now been built up in the transference link.* What appeared in the first fragment as loss of control of his own contents now comes up as a metaphor. The patient is not resigned to an object represented by inner voices that incisively tell him he is doing wrong; he finds this is a hurdle he has to clear. The oral-sadistic phantasies belonging to the devouring breast is an inner object turned into an instrument – the plough[7] – in the metaphor he uses, which analogically reproduces the oral – dental function though with potentially reparative characteristics since it belongs to a human activity – agriculture.

This patient can now control his approach to the therapist without confusing his Self with the therapist's. This control facilitates the creation of the notion of space: the bad object inside him and the good object deposited in his therapist are differentiated. In the course of this second sample, he becomes aware of the ways of thinking he must use in order to reach his therapist: he corrects himself and thus achieves a common universe of discourse with his analyst. In this sense we may say that the self-inflicted torture of the previous sample has turned into a self-criticism that permits him to approach his analyst. He already knows that despite the pain, represented by speaking in the session, therapeutic dependence is much more convenient for him than the isolation and omnipotent unconscious phantasies of the first sample, which had led him to a total imbalance between his needs and his possibilities.

I should like to comment on some phonological clues to his changes in the second fragment. At the end of fragment (7) he lengthens the vowel sound in "that" (in the Spanish original *que* with pronounced lengthening of the vowel sound *e*), indicating the notion of hesitantly moving in space. Progressive speed–ups and slow–downs – in fragments (3), (4), (6) and (16) – are equivalent to the kinetic representations of walking towards, and away from, the mother.

The way he begins to speak is a clue to the fact that he was, at the beginning, taken up by a Superego object. His tense, breathless voice was the expression of his own greediness for speaking, which stopped him from inhaling. His breathing rhythm and verbal utterances change with the appearance in the metaphor of phantasies of two-footedness, deambulation, and discovery of space. The sign denotes the existence of self-pity in the face of pain. The coordination between inhalations and exhalations in verbal utterances reproduce, in the unconscious phantasy, the experiences of union and separation, in the shape of spoken phrases and pauses. They indicate getting nearer and farther from the listener, reproducing the situation of the child who dares to walk (speak) and then rests in silence. Silence then becomes "good," whereas in the first segment it was "devouring" and "evil."

The patient started his session demanding much from himself with no allowance for relaxation and breath intake so as to start his utterance differently. When he synchronized verbalization and emotion, he changed his way of regulating utterances, monitoring his voice by means of obsessional mechanisms of adaptive character.

In the second sample, the patient acquired some mastery over separation anxiety. *Separation anxiety is a threshold that every melancholic patient needs to reach, to preserve himself from an ambivalent pathological dependence*, which, while it persists, exposes him to fall into melancholic states.

The paraverbal features of patients who initiate their analyses deep in melancholic states enable the analyst to detect the quality of the predominant unconscious phantasy. If this is understood and adequately handled by the therapist, it becomes a technical tool that will enable the patient to

with "the girl" as a partial object into an adult couple relationship.

## Notes

1 For the Introduction to the life and work of David Liberman see Part 1, Chapter 10, of this volume.

2 By paralinguistic elements of the patient's verbalization, I mean the universe of phenomena that were described by Pittenger, Hockett and Danehy (1960). The elements that I have found most useful are considerations about strength, loudness, rhythm, pitch, length of sounds, length of silences, sighs, whispering and tremolos. We can also take into account openness, breathiness, articulation, interruptions in the passage of air and nasalization, as well as the range of deviations from the average for the patient concerned.

3 The term "unconscious phantasy" is used here following Isaac (1952). She said, "Phantasies are not dependent upon words, although they may under certain conditions be capable of expression in words. The earliest phantasies are experienced in sensations: later, they take the form of plastic images and dramatic representations. Unconscious phantasies exert a continuous influence throughout life, both in normal and neurotic people, the differences lying in the specific character of the dominant phantasies, the desire or anxiety associated with them and their interplay with each other and with external reality" (Bénassy and Diatkine 1964, 176). See also "On the Ontogenesis of Fantasy," Bénassy and Diatkine, which has several points in common with my own view. "If fantasy has a history, if unconscious fantasy is timeless, and if *language* introduces serial order, we see why fantasies should be analyzed one at a time, at what Heimann calls the 'patient's actual point of growth'. It could be suggested that the emotional content, expressed through language and body behaviour, as well as the whole context sometimes enables the analyst to date the phantasy, and that a very ordinary and ungrammatical language, referred in the end to the patient's and the analyst's body images in a free relationship, enables the patient to introduce his own timing into his own analyst's, to 'assume an active role in his cure'" Bénassy and Diatkine 1964, 176).

4 Isaacs (1952) states: "Through external experience, phantasies become elaborated and capable of expression, but they do not depend upon such experience for their existence."

5 This is roughly equivalent to the Spanish metaphor the patient used, which would translate literally as "on what already-ploughed field I am."

6 In the original Spanish metaphor.

7 In the original Spanish.

# References

Abraham, K. 1949 *Selected Papers on Psychoanalysis* London: Hogarth Press, Chapter XXVI.

Bénassy, M. and Diatkine, R. 1964. Symposiun on Fantasy on the ontogenesis of fantasy *International Journal of Psycho-Analysis* 45, Pp. 171–179.

Chomsky, N. 1965 *Aspects of the Theory of Syntax* Cambridge, Mass.: The M.I.T. Press.

Freud, S. 1962 Third lecture *Five Lectures on Psychoanalysis, Standard Edition. Vol. XI*, P. 38.

Freud, S. 1963a Second lecture *Introductory Lectures on Psychoanalysis (Parts I and II), Standard Edition. Vol. XV*, P. 28.

Freud, S. 1963b Third lecture *Introductory Lectures on Psychoanalysis, Standard Edition.* P. 106.

Freud, S. 1963c Fourth lecture *Introductory Lectures on Psychoanalysis, Standard Edition.* P. 106.

Freud, S. 1964 The dissection of the psychical personality *New Introductory Lectures on Psychoanalysis, Standard Edition.* Pp. 70–79.

Isaacs, S. 1952 The nature and function of phantasy *Developments in Psychoanalysis* Eds. M. Klein et al., London: Hogarth Press.

Liberman, D. 1962 *La Communicatión en Terapéutica Psicoanalítica* Buenos Aires: Eudeba.

Liberman, D. 1966 Criteria for interpretation in patients with obsessive traits *International Journal of Psycho-Analysis* 47, Pp. 212–217.

Liberman, D. 1971 *Lingüística, Interacción Communicativa y Proceso Psicoanalítico* Buenos Aires: Galerna.

Pittenger, R., Hockett, C., and Danehy, J. 1960 *The First Five Minutes* Ithaca N.Y.: Paul Martineau.

# COMMUNICATIONS

## David Liberman[1]

*This paper was read as part of a colloquium on 'Affective Response of the Analyst to the Patient's Communications' at the 30th International Psycho-Analytical Congress, Jerusalem, August 1977; it was published in 1978 in the* International Journal of Psycho-Analysis, *59: 335–340.*

The subject we are dealing with includes two elements. One of them, 'the affective response', is apparently only connected with the term 'counter-transference', and for that reason it might be clear to all of us. Eidelberg (1968) says: 'the term is used by some analysts in connection with all the feelings the analyst experiences for his patients, while others prefer to speak of countertransference only when repressed infantile wishes are involved'. In my opinion, the first part of Eidelberg's definition is the correct one, because it gives room for such elements as empathy, sympathy and decoding, which cover the interaction between patient and analyst.

As to the other element, 'the patient's communications', which I consider much more ambiguous, I should like to explain what I understand by it. With reference to the patient's communications, I stated on several occasions that each and every patient has a repertoire of responses that conform to what I call 'styles of communication'. The styles of communication consist in different structures composed of verbal, non-verbal and para-verbal (or suprasegmental) components that engender a qualitative distinction in the way patient and analyst communicate, and which vary throughout the session. The combinations of such components give a particular style to the patient's communications.

The qualitative distinctive features of the patient's communications require from the analyst an ideally optimal affective response. I shall introduce the term *empathy* in order to effect a link between the two elements in our subject. In general terms, empathy is primarily intellectual, and in the case of psychoanalytic empathy it requires assigning a hierarchy to the participation of affects and to a particular type of identification from the analyst towards the patient (Freud, 1921). That is to say, there is a strong link between affects, special identification with the patient and a capacity to use rationality at the service of the interpretation.

What I suggest in this paper is that the analyst's optimal empathy with his patient leads the latter to attain something which is very difficult to get alone, by himself, outside the session. I am referring to his ability to apprehend some states of mind, or moods, during the session. If he manages to do so, we are to understand that our adequate affective response has led us to an optimal empathy with the patient, which in turn enables him to think of how he feels and behaves during the session and give a name to those states of mind.

## Consequences of the optimal empathic affective response

I shall start from a clinical observation, which I consider the basis for an empirical generalization.

An optimal empathic affective response of the analyst to a patient, in whom the analyst discovered interceptions of thought, ultimately led the patient to insight during that very session. How could that be discovered? Such insights (which consisted in references to the very disturbance in the patient's process of thinking: instead of merely being suffered it could now be named by means of phrase structures) were expressed through original phrases never before uttered by the patient, in which it was possible to see some correlation between the primary empathic affective response and the quality of the mood discovered and stated by the patient.

Such new enunciations always include, among other elements, certain references to past or present moods, and are originally created by the patient, reaching a high degree of competence and performance in Chomsky's (1965) sense. These phrases do not contain the style of the analyst's spoken language; they do however contain the whole of the analytic work done by him in reference to this point. In previous papers (Liberman, 1962), (1975), (1976a), (1976b), (Liberman et al., 1969) I held that when the patient managed to give a name to an emotion (which I shall henceforward call 'mood') it constituted a result for our optimal analytic task.

Summing up all these statements, I wish to establish that the analyst's empathic responses are processed by the patient's process of working through, and the end-product will be these newly created psychoanalytical syntactic enunciations.

at the London Congress of Psychoanalysis (1975). The patient suffered a severe schizoid state covered by hysterical techniques, and during a long first phase of the treatment she gave the impression of being an analysand who had a good capacity to undergo her transference conflicts and whose profession gave her only satisfaction. During this long period the analyst felt frustration and anger towards the patient; however, in his moments of empathy he realized that she tried to force him out to preserve her mental coherence rather than accept analytical assistance from him. The analyst already knew this, but the patient had no idea of it. The technique of actively ignoring the analyst might be considered in theoretical terms as a defensive technique against the analyst as an 'envy-genic object'. In time, still another way of counteracting her envy was discovered, which consisted in a projective identification with severely malformed children as well as with children with suicidal attitudes (poisoning, accidents). She felt at ease with them and was actually successful with them: she gratified herself in her analysis speaking about her frequent successes. Her analyst constantly interpreted to her, among other things, (1) that she needed to have self-assurance in her sessions in order not to feel emotionally pervaded by the feelings coming from the cases she treated; (2) that during the sessions she needed to feel that she was both patient and analyst, in order to avoid feeling that the analyst was another person whom she thought she knew but who, deep down, was a stranger to her; (3) that she never made pauses in her discourse lest her analyst should speak to her and lead her to think of and feel all her suffering and pain during her several early migrations (on account of the war); (4) that she considered the analyst might represent the three different foster-parents she had had in early infancy (for the same reason) and whom she never came to know well; (5) that the analyst in his analytic practice with her was felt as her mirror-double when she worked with her own malformed and suicidal patients; and (6) that the analyst as a person meant for her an 'envygenic' object, since she saw him in a cool, calm and collected state of mind, that is, as she herself wanted to be.

A long time passed before she started discerning between herself and her analyst and somehow overcame her need to exclude him due to her fears (paranoid anxieties) of him. This paranoid transference link was motivated by her envy and her fear of losing her fabricated identity and then having none of her own. During this period the analyst noticed that interceptions appeared every time she wanted to utter such phrases as: 'these damaged children knock me down'. This fear, this aggression (active exclusion) and the interceptions appeared whenever the analyst represented, for her, an anaclitic object relation, dependence on which produced simultaneously pleasure and pain. This weak link, however, was constantly threatened by another link, the narcissistic one, in which the analyst was felt to be as the calm, cool and collected self she wanted to be.

The analyst's previous feeling of being excluded was modified: he now felt and thought he had to be very careful not to damage her, since she had massively included him inside her during the sessions. After working on this point for some time, the patient produced the new syntactic structures created by her, which contained some reference to her moods.

Let me give a verbatim transcription.

Something unusual happened to me today. I was dead beat and didn't hear the alarm . . . [showing her bad temper]. Everything seems balled up at the hospital. Wednesday morning my boss gives classes on adoption. Suddenly all the organization was changed and I went to one of those classes and didn't think I had to ask for permission from the administration. I have always been interested in the subject . . . and I always sidestepped it. [This was an identification with the analyst as an object rejected in the first phase of her analytic process and felt now as forming part of herself.]

She then narrated an incident with a colleague on account of her not having asked for permission to leave her ward and attend that class. She angrily added that her colleague was a very mean woman because she did not accept the reorganization and the problems arising from it. [This mean woman was the part of her rigid self which had rejected the analysis during the first part of the treatment.]

When I entered the classroom I saw a bill posted, reading 'Family therapy classes for residents and visitors only' . . . I thought I'd better not get into trouble . . . Although I was somewhat right in getting angry because it is within my area and I should have been asked . . . Then . . . I don't know how to explain this to you . . . [lowering the tone of her voice] I thought I had to think things by myself. True, the hospital was balled up, confused, but I thought 'I have to clear up my position and see what it is that I really want'.

After speaking about some colleagues who, she felt, sometimes controlled her and other times confused her, she added:

299

It's necessary to put up a big fight not to lose the capacity to think . . . I remember a friend who told me my position at the hospital was important because I had been officially appointed. It is a reference to my professional identity . . . I am surprised I should have to take so long to think of something and to know that it is true . . . I feel strange, but it is true . . .

[Later she added:]

balizing my ideas . . . It's just like when I leave the theatre; ideas come to my head only after the others speak. I never before realized this happened . . . But if this is how I work, I don't know what happens in my life . . . Only when I am not carried away by impatience can I have my own ideas.

[Suddenly her mood shifted precisely to one of impatience, and she quickly started saying things like:]

. . . but it is hard to work in the hospital when everybody has a long face, everybody has a temper [raising the tone of her voice and somewhat angrily]. Well, then I do better when I get disconnected, as I did this morning, and I worked . . . [somewhat surprised:] but I didn't get isolated from the rest . . . I knew what was going on . . . I don't clearly know whether to work with that team of brutes or rather work by myself and isolated . . . I don't want to keep speaking about it. Period.

The analyst showed her how this situation was the exact replica of other situations in other contexts and with other people. She tried to hear, and near the end of the session, interrupted and said, as if to please him: 'Yes, I never thought of that [raising the tone of her voice]. Time here is quite long' [mood of impatience].

Some phrases the product of good analytical work done before, but the interpretation was inadequate because the enunciation of different contexts and situations with the same cliché repeated the confusion-laden situation of 'leaving the theatre'. At that moment the analyst reacted with sympathy instead of empathy, which, as we shall see later on, is feeling for the patient instead of feeling with him.

## Empathetic and sympathetic responses

My best experiences in psychoanalytic empathy have been those in which I was simultaneously able to use affective modulations (which let me feel with the patient) and my own rationality at the service of my technical capacity.

Only when this happens do I feel so free as to have the maximal linguistic resources: this enables me to have the highest degree of competence and effect the passage to the linguistic performance – in Chomsky's sense – to select the one ideal uttered syntactic structure in my style of interpreting. My psychoanalytic empathy, which includes affects among other things, enables me to use my affective responses to the patient's communications with the highest degree of adequacy because this includes an identification with the state the patient is in when he receives the interpretation. Once the patient has the feeling that the use of his analyst's language is so adequate, he will fully understand the senses and meanings conveyed by the formulation with the minimum distortion that may arise at that particular moment. Naturally, this can only happen when the patient and myself are 'keeping step'. Otherwise (which is frequently and unfortunately the case, and I do not wish to lay the blame on either of the participants in this 'duet') in the special case of the unconscious affects, empathy is threatened and may be lost, and we can thus feel for the patient instead of feeling with the patient. Therefore, the affective responses of the analyst to his patient's different styles of communication (understood as previously enunciated) constitute a mordant for the psychoanalyst's empathy to accompany the evolution of his patient all along his changes both in a session and in the psychoanalytic process.

These different styles of communication, or qualitative distinctive features, are the result of a combination of different unconscious fantasies that acquire certain forms or styles through which the patient's ego volunteers his clinical material, which leads us to the second item in our subject, 'the patient's communications'.

## Styles in the patient's communications

The patient's attitude towards the whole of the analytical situation, towards what he says and hears, the significance he ascribes to the psychoanalytical process and to the therapist as a person, the verbal and paraverbal components of his discourse – all of them are the clues that may or may not be detected by us, depending on whether we empathize or sympathize with the state the patient is in. I shall consider six clearly distinguishable states which are always combined in a potentially infinite conjunction of styles that provoke different responses in the analyst. These six states are: (1) schizoid state; (2) depressive state; (3) 'psychopathic state' or acting out; (4) obsessive state; (5) phobic state; and (6) hysterical state. I shall describe each of the six states in order to show the wide spectrum of possible affective responses which may facilitate or impede the analyst's empathy or sympathy.

1. In the schizoid state the patient has a searching attitude of clearing all unknowns and taking all the knowledge for himself in an omnipotent attitude. He has a philosophical Weltanschauung of psychoanalysis. When he speaks he seems to be using a secret code: he unexpectedly lapses into long periods of silence. He is the patient who arouses curiosity and confusion in us, and who makes us silently wonder who this strange person is. With

and the self in panic at such a spoil. I think Melanie Klein's (1957) theory of envy must be completed from the point of view of communicational interaction as well, which is important for our present subject. Thus seen, the mere presence of the analyst as 'the other' inevitably produces what we know as 'double bind'. The example would be, 'if you speak you destroy me with your aggressive intrusion; if you do not speak, you starve me'. This is the revengeful meaning the analyst acquires for the patient.

In the other polarity of the schizoid state, the predominant emotion is what I call 'nostalgia', or the emotion the patient feels when he is longing for something far away and long ago. The outcome of both emotions, when the analysand grows in the psychoanalytic process, consists in feeling as one totality in the presence of another. If the reader remembers Winnicott's (1958) article, 'The Capacity to be Alone', he will see what I mean. If we fall into a countertransference attitude of sympathy, we respond to the patient's communications feeling envy or nostalgia, as if we were the patient himself (projective identification).

2. In the depressive state the patient has a lyrical attitude with strong emotional involvement, that is to say, opposite to what was said about the schizoid state. Instead of splitting off emotions, the patient is eaten and corroded by these emotions arising in his interaction with the analyst and these pervade his link with him. The patient's self is devoured and defecated by impatience externalized as a paranoid-schizoid hypercriticism of himself. He is the patient who gasps, 'bah's, gargles, scratches the couch, etc., and whose monotheme may be summarized in this sentence: 'How mean and dirty I am for feeling rotten. I shouldn't have come to session today.'

In the other polarity, when the depressive state is rigidly consolidated in the first steps of the depressive position, the patient shows what I call 'resignation' in the sense of a passive acceptance, unresisting acquiescence, 'a passive resignation to the authority of other men's [the analyst's] opinions' (Webster's Third International Dictionary). This is the patient who even tells us: 'Today you've hit me hard. Go ahead and you will get something good out of me.' The patient has a sort of masochistic Weltanschauung of psycho-analytic therapy. If the analyst falls into countertransference sympathy, his affective response may be irritation and the wish to kick the patient out of the room and slam the door behind him.

3. In the psychopathic state the patient has a sort of epic attitude and he considers himself a fighter against all past and present injustice done unto him. His communications to the therapist might actually be considered as 'dirty tricks', expressions of revengeful affects motivated by his delusional Weltanschauung. In order to develop his psychopathic techniques in the transference link, he needs to split off himself the shame and humiliation he constantly and silently suffers in the analytical situation. The optimal affective response of the analyst to such patients' communications calls for a great gift, which enables the therapist to be empathic with the consciously hidden shame and humiliation that underlie the patient's revengeful behavior and are embedded in the delusional Weltanschauung. When the analyst is sympathetic, he may feel frightened and think: 'I'd better be careful, anything I say may be taken against me.'

4. In the obsessive state we are faced with a patient who needs firmly obsessive traits to control his feelings of self-diminishment and hopelessness which motivate his specific 'reined-in' ambivalence. He has a narrative style by means of which he states that he will 'announce' something he 'may say' – or again may not – at the end of the session, when the analyst has no more time to interpret. The patient needs to preserve both the therapist and himself from the aggression and the submission contained in his ambivalence. Thus we find a patient who tells us stories carefully organized in time, space or analogies, by means of which he expresses what he unconsciously wishes to communicate, while at the same time he annuls, controls or isolates it. This patient provokes boredom, unless the therapist manages to empathize with his patient's self-diminishing affects and hopelessness. Boredom as an affective response to the obsessive patient's communications means a sympathetic identification with the patient, since he himself suffers it and produces it in others (see Liberman, 1966).

5. In the phobic state the patient looks for unknowns just as the schizoid does, but he creates suspense as well. Interaction with the analyst provokes anxiety, and this anxiety becomes an erotized object. Such a patient will interrupt the narrative and, apparently frightened, will ask in a shrill voice: 'What's the matter?' or 'Can you follow?' or 'Are you there?' or 'Haven't you fallen asleep?'. It is not the case of a hallucinated lunatic but of a person who is chronically frightened and who projects the danger situation in the transference on to the analyst, who is in turn felt as indispensable to dispel these fears.

The analyst is the container of two objects, one of them full of libido and the other full of aggression. That is why a patient in the phobic state is terribly ambitious, some kind of counterphobic hero and coward. Due to these two objects deposited inside the analyst, the patient overtly mistrusts, is openly pessimistic and ostensibly optimistic when going through counterphobic periods. Curiosity in reference to the therapist and erotized fear

becomes for us a person who frightens us and keeps us on the tenterhooks, or else, if he establishes counterphobic defenses, we may eventually behave like big boys who get wise and frighten easily scared little children or, again, like promoters of counterphobia, giving these children such interpretations as 'the thing is, you don't dare to . . .'.

6. In the hysterical state, the patient's goal is that of provoking an aesthetic impact. He tries to produce in us an effect of beauty in order to turn us into his rapturous and stupefied audience. As in the depressive state, the patient seeks emotional gratification instead of insight. The patient is overtly exhibitionistic and tries to be wanted by us merely as the subject of our observation, because he has deposited in us an object cathected with libido. He behaves very much like a commercial TV announcer, using all of his resources (verbal, non-verbal and gestural) reinforced with images, in order to sell the product he is advertising to us. The product may be considered countercathexis, in metapsychological terms. As in the phobic state, empathy can only be preserved if the analyst has the capacity to be a non-participant observer who, from time to time, utters an interpretation with cold emotions that may be grasped by the patient with a maximum of objectivity.

If the analyst succumbs to the state of erotized beauty, two things may happen: the analyst either becomes the foolish observer fascinated by what the patient exhibits and blind to what he hides (and what he hides is right in front of his nose), or else he is possessed by that beauty and also starts dramatizing it. I call this a 'symmetrical escalation' of hysterics, in which both participants organize some sort of dramatic soap-opera dialogue. But this hysterical organization is a defense against states of depersonalization and estrangement analogous to those undergone by adolescents during their changes leading to the acquisition of their sexual identity.

Summing up, I may say that the different styles of communication in the patient produce in the analyst different affective responses. If the analyst is massively pervaded by them, he may sympathize but will not psychoanalytically empathize with his patient. When, on the contrary, this affective response is turned into empathy, the analyst will be able to use his linguistic resources with the highest degree of adequacy, since in the interpretative message he takes into account the state of the receiver. The cumulative work of this type of intervention will provoke the patient to produce phrases never before thought of or uttered, consisting of references to central conflicting aspects which, when verbalized and heard by the patient himself, produce changes in his inner organization that can only be obtained through analytic work. In these 'new' phrases there is always some reference to past and present moods. The instrumentation of the analyst's affective responses will cause the moods to be named.

# Note

1   For the Introduction to the life and work of David Liberman, see Part 1, Chapter 10, of this volume.

# References

Chomsky, N. 1965 *Aspects of the Theory of Syntax* Cambridge, Mass.: M.I.T. Press.

Eidelberg, L. 1968 *Encyclopedia of Psychoanalysis* New York: Free Press.

Freud, S. 1921 Group psychology and the analysis of the ego *The complete psychological works of Sigmund Freud,* 18.

Klein, M. 1957 *Envy and Gratitude* London: Tavistock Publications.

Liberman, D. 1962 *Comunicación en Terapéutica Psicoanalítica.* Buenos Aires: Eudeba.

Liberman, D. 1966 Criteria for interpretation in patients with obsessive traits *International Journal of Psycho-Analysis* 47: 212–217.

Liberman, D. 1970 *Lingüística, Interacción Comunicativa y Proceso Psicoanalítico Vol. 1* Buenos Aires: Galerna-Nueva Visón.

Liberman, D. 1975 Changes in the theory and practice of psychoanalysis *International Journal of Psycho-Analysis* 56: 101–107.

Liberman, D. 1976a *Comunicación y Psicoanálisis* Buenos Aires: Alex.

Liberman, D. 1976b *Lenguaje y Técnica Psicoanalítica* Buenos Aires: Kargieman.

Liberman, D., Achaval, J., Espiro, N., Grimaldi, P., Katz, I.B. De, Lumermann, S., Montevechio, B. & Schlossberg, N. 1969 Modos de reparación y desenlaces de procesos terapéuticos psicoanalíticos *Revista de Psicoanálisis* 26: 123–129.

Winnicott, D.W. 1958 The capacity to be alone *International Journal of Psycho-Analysis* 39: 416–420.

*Madeleine Baranger*

*This paper was read at the 38th Congress of the International Psychoanalytical Association in Amsterdam on the 27th of July 1993; it was published the same year by the* International Journal of Psycho-Analysis, 74: 15–24.

## Introduction

There is no such thing as perception without an object, or without another subject. It is only by an effort of abstraction that we can ask ourselves what passes through the mind of the analyst between listening and interpretation. The analyst's internal process which leads him to interpret belongs from the beginning to an intersubjective situation, however structurally asymmetrical it may be.

Similarly, analytic listening is directed in advance towards an eventual interpretation, whose content is not yet known at the time of listening but which gradually takes shape up to the moment when the interpretation has to be formulated to the analysand. The inter-subjectivity of the analytic dialogue, while describing an essential aspect of the processes with which we are concerned (what happens in the analyst), conceals – and sometimes reveals – another intersubjective type of structure, just as the visible–audible is superimposed on the invisible–unheard of. This second structure, sometimes called the 'intersubjective field', underlies as something unsaid or unsayable both the analysand's material as presented and the analyst's formulations; in the latter, it determines both the content of the interpretation and the feeling-conviction that the interpretation must be formulated.

## Context of the interpretation

Unlike the 'wild' interpretations which may be 'played with' in everyday life, a psychoanalytic interpretation does not arise by chance or in isolation. It belongs to – and is part of – a context whose co-ordinates are fixed by the patient's demand, the analyst's expectations and the contract defining the analytic situation.

The patient – and even the 'training' analysand – asks for analysis because he is suffering from a certain malaise and hopes to improve his conditions of life and pleasure. It matters little at this point whether he brings along a conscious conflict – with his wife, with his children's growing up, with his boss or his workmates – or whether he has been 'sent', for instance by his partner or, in psychosomatic cases, his doctor. Either of his own accord on the basis of cultural information or because of what he has been told, he has decided to try out psychoanalysis as a way – sometimes, indeed, a last resort – of solving his conscious and unconscious problems.

We know only too well that this decision may be fairly ambivalent or be based on expectations of magic actions. Yet we cannot rule out the possibility that he has decided to come and ask for something, even if he himself does not know exactly what he is asking for, but he does suppose that the analyst has the knowledge and the instruments to produce beneficial effects in him.

The analyst, for his part, in making his own decision to accept this subject for treatment, will have done so in the conviction that he can alleviate his suffering or malaise, and that specifically psychoanalysis is the appropriate way, or one of the appropriate ways, in which he can help him. No analyst undertakes the psychoanalysis of a patient without this minimum of expectation. This is the ethical dimension of psychoanalysis. It implies in the analyst a much more precise expectation than the patient's: that his words will be the factor that will give rise to the desired effects.

The terms of the contract, which are minimal, are intended to organise and protect the new relationship, from which ultimately positive changes are expected. First of all, the contract lays down the material conditions of this intersubjective relationship – the place, frequency and length of the sessions – which constitute the framework for the analytic work. The regularity or deliberate irregularity of this framework of time and space is the hallmark of two completely different kinds of analysis and crucially determines the structuring of the field and the internal work of the analyst.

The functional conditions determine the roles assigned to analyst and analysand, which are asymmetrical. The patient is bound by the 'fundamental rule' (Freud, 1904) to say everything that occurs to him, but without acting out. It is assumed that his associations will betray signs of, or information about, his unconscious.

The analyst takes responsibility for and directs the process by his silence or

projective identification). The resonance box is an inadequate metaphor; and projective identification and possibly counter-identification also have their shortcomings. Both concepts attempt to circumvent the active participation of the analyst's conscious and unconscious personal history, to the extent that he may understand and formulate something which he has experienced in the events of his life and his fantasy.

## The concept of 'field'

The conscious and unconscious work of the analyst is performed within an intersubjective relationship in which each participant is defined by the other. In speaking of the analytic field, we are referring to the formation of a structure which is a product of the two participants in the relationship but which in turn involves them in a dynamic and possibly creative process.

The psychology of the last part of the 19th century, whose concepts were broadly adopted by Freud, had an objectivising tendency. Freud's 'complementary series' (1910a) were descended directly from this tendency. However, in laying the foundations of analytic technique, he gave up the opposition between an observing eye and an observed object. Freud thus implicitly accepted a new conception of the intersubjective relationship, which was to be made explicit by phenomenological psychology in the concept of the field, particularly in the work of Maurice Merleau-Ponty (1945).

Freud's discovery of the countertransference (1910b) was an advance compared with the objectivising approach. But even if we take account of the countertransference together with the transference, or regard the transference-countertransference as a unity, this is not the same as what we mean by the concept of *field*. Let us start with intersubjectivity as a self-evident basic datum. Freud described one aspect of this intersubjectivity in referring to communication from unconscious to unconscious (1912), which he stated to be bi-directional. The field is a structure different from the sum of its components, just as a melody is different from a sum of its notes.

The advantage of being able to think in terms of a field is that the dynamics of the analytic situation inevitably encounter many stumbling blocks which are not due to the patient's or the analyst's resistance but reveal the existence of a pathology specific to this structure. The work of the analyst in this case, whether or not he uses the field concept, undergoes a change of centre: a second look (Baranger et al., 1983) is directed at one and the same time to the patient and to oneself functioning as an analyst. It is not simply a matter of allowing for the analyst's countertransference experiences but of acknowledging that both the transference manifestations of the patient and the analyst's countertransference spring from one and the same source: a basic unconscious fantasy which, as a creation of the field, is rooted in the unconscious of each of the participants.

The concept of basic unconscious fantasy is derived from the Kleinian concept of unconscious fantasy, but also from the description given by Bion in his work on groups (1952). For instance, in discussing the basic hypothesis of 'struggle and flight' in a group, Bion is in our view referring to an unconscious fantasy which does not exist in any of the participants outside this group situation. This is what we mean by the basic unconscious fantasy in the field of the analytic situation.

The field is thus structured on three levels: (a) the functional framework of the analysis; (b) the analytic dialogue; and (c) the unconscious dynamic structure underlying this dialogue.

Viewed as movement, the field manifests itself as the analytic process.

## The analytic process

As the analysis proceeds, it becomes possible to follow the steps of a process. From this process, both analyst and analysand will emerge changed, although in different ways and to different degrees. The interpretation, the analyst's instrument par excellence, is both part and agent of this process. This is why I contrasted it with 'wild' interpretations, which do not belong to any process. The process takes place within a history, the history of this analytic relationship, which has its ups and downs, moments of progression and phases of stagnation – and sometimes interruptions. In other words, the interpretation is bound up with this or that particular moment of the process; it will not be the same – even if it change only in form and not in object – at the beginning, after a fairly long period of analysis and towards the end.

The interpretation tends to gather together and put into words something that is occurring at a particular moment in the process: the unconscious fantasy underlying and structuring the present situation of the analytic field. This fantasy is a development and combination of – and sometimes a discontinuity in – everything that has occurred and possibly been interpreted since the beginning of the treatment.

I use the word 'discontinuity' to refer to a phenomenon that every analyst will have encountered with his patients, sometimes spectacularly and

moved to a different position in the analyst's nosography. The process seems to have reached a 'point of inflection'. Not every change in the process or in the patient can legitimately be described as a 'point of inflection'. A process without changes would not be a process. We may speak of a 'point of inflection' when there has suddenly been a mobilisation (whether or not in relation to observed interpretation and insight) of the analytic field and a restructuring of the underlying basic fantasy. The point of inflection marks the opening of access to new aspects of the history.

The idea that the history of the analytic process repeats the steps in the patient's history is mistaken. It is, however, true that obstacles in the work of historicisation correspond to decisive moments in the life of the patient, when he was obliged to mutilate his own history at the same time as he mutilated himself. The history of himself that the patient has brought – sometimes very poorly – changes, enriching and building itself in the analysis. Interpretation – whose aim is to reconstruct this history – becomes necessary when the analyst perceives what we call the 'point of urgency'.

## The point of urgency

What takes place in the analyst's mind between listening and interpretation could be described as the search for the point of urgency.

This concept is originally to be found in Klein, who considered that the onset of the feeling of anxiety (in the analysand) called for interpretation. However, anxiety is often not experienced consciously. Klein then speaks of latent anxiety, replaced on the phenomenal level by other verbal or behavioural manifestations (silence, logorrhoea, bodily tension or insistent repetition of material).

We agree with Klein that anxiety is frequently a sign of the proximity of some unconscious material that is about to emerge, and thus guides our encounter with the point of urgency. However, it is hard to conceive of latent anxiety performing the same function, as we do not know where it is. This leads us to a widening of the concept of anxiety that many would consider improper.

Among our own ranks, the term 'point of urgency' was used by Enrique Pichon-Rivière. His idea differs from Klein's in its central focus. He defines the point of urgency as the moment in the session when something is about to emerge from the analysand's unconscious.

Taking Pichon-Rivière as our basis, we consider the point of urgency to be a moment in the functioning of the field when the structure of the dialogue and the underlying structure (the basic unconscious fantasy of the field) can come together and give rise to an insight. The analyst feels and thinks that he can and must interpret (formulate an interpretation to the analysand).

The point of urgency is not generally known at the beginning of the session, although the course of the process itself may have given the analyst a hypothetical idea of what is about to emerge. The current events in the life of the analysand also guide us towards the probable activation of specific fantasy nuclei (e.g., the death of someone close to the analysand, a birth-day, etc.). The analyst's first interventions, which are most often not interpretive, are aimed at probing the possible directions for the search.

The search for the point of urgency may succeed or fail. Freud (1937) taught us that the analysand's verbal acceptance of the interpretation is not enough to validate it, just as its rejection does not mean than it is necessarily false. The true indicators of its correctness are the opening of the field and the dynamicisation of the process.

## Analytic listening

We define the term 'listening' in its widest sense, as the normally preferential attention we direct towards the patient's verbal discourse. But we also 'listen to' his tone of voice – lively or depressed – the rhythm and pace of his delivery, his attitudes, movements and postures on the couch, and his facial expressions, in so far as we can see them from our vantage point.

Freud recommended the adoption of a state of 'evenly suspended attention' (1912). The aim of this recommendation is that the analyst should be open to whatever arises, without prejudices of any kind and without systematically seeking confirmation of any project. An analyst who plans a treatment on the basis of his knowledge or theoretical interests runs the risk of becoming blind and deaf to the patient's manifestations. The attitude of analytic listening is diametrically opposed to the mental posture of the observer or experimenter in the physical and natural sciences. The latter plans his observation and experiment on the basis of his expectations, which depend both on his general knowledge of his discipline and on an idea or invention that he considers may cause his science to progress. He works with preconcepts that organise the same observation, in order to verify or falsify them. The psychoanalyst, on the other hand, must beware of mentally obstructing access to the unforeseen, to 'surprise', which is precisely what

can appropriately be applied to this.

The analyst must steer a course between two contrasting dangers: the forced application of a pre-existing theory, which will ultimately lead to spurious interpretations, and the whole complex of chaotic theories. The analyst's scheme of reference is what guides both the search for the point of urgency and the formulation of the interpretation.

This scheme of reference is the quintessence, condensed and worked out personally by each analyst, of his theoretical allegiances, his knowledge of the analytic literature, his clinical experience – especially his failures – what he has been able to learn about himself in his analysis, and his identifications with his analyst and supervisors – as well as the theoretical fashions which periodically sweep through the psychoanalytic movement.

The degree of coherence and elaboration of these different influences varies considerably from analyst to analyst. Some have a fairly conscious and synthesised scheme of reference – the danger in this case is that it might become rigid and not be open to anything that does not fit in with itself. But even analysts who declare themselves to be exclusively 'clinical' operate with an implicit scheme of reference, even if it lacks this degree of rationalisation or coherence.

Knowledge of the patient and his history acts as a backcloth to the current drama.

Above all, the history of the analytic relationship and of the process is present in the analyst's mind, with the analytic situation in its totality, in its planned and spontaneous (unconscious) dynamism. The process is governed by the analyst's desire (to know? to understand? to help? to discover?) and the memory of the various moments in it.

We consider it extremely worrying that the concept of 'memory of the process' is lacking from the majority of psychoanalytic contributions. It is well known that the analyst's hyperamnesia, often willingly accepted by patients, is nothing but the counterpart of the relative amnesia of the patients, as de Mijolla-Mellor (1990) points out.

## What does the analyst listen to?

What defines analytic listening and distinguishes it from any other kind of psychotherapy is that it attempts to listen to the unconscious. Freud defined the work of analysis as 'making the unconscious conscious'. However, the very content of the concept of the unconscious is not unambiguous in Freud's work: as we all know, the unconscious of 1915, whose correlate is repression (1915), is expanded in the paper on splitting of the ego and the mechanisms of defence (1938), albeit without forfeiting its validity. This opens the way to the recognition of many forms of rendering unconscious besides forgetting.

Different concepts lie behind the same word, 'unconscious', in all the main analytic schools. When Klein refers to the 'deep layers of the unconscious', she means an organised mass of very archaic unconscious fantasies present and active at every moment of life. The result is the idea, which we consider to be erroneous, that they can be reached directly by interpretation.

Lacan, on the other hand, says that 'the unconscious resists any ontology' (1973) – in other words, that the unconscious is not a thing. If we agree with Lacan on this point, accepting that 'making the unconscious conscious' does not mean moving something from one container to another, which would ultimately leave the unconscious half empty, must we suppose that what we are seeking is a new sense? On the level of our listening, does the latent content lie behind the manifest content, or is the latent content a second sense of the manifest content? We are caught between an impossible ontology and the threat of interpretive arbitrariness. But perhaps this antithesis of thing and sense is badly stated and we should formulate the problem in different terms.

The analyst listens to something other than what he is being told. To imagine that he seeks a latent content that exists behind the manifest content would be to reify something dynamic. The unconscious is not behind but is elsewhere. The listening of the analyst consists in decentring the patient's discourse, stripping it down in order to find a new centre, which at this moment is the unconscious.

The three factors involved are: (1) the patient's explicit discourse; (2) the unconscious configuration of the field (unconscious fantasy of the field), which includes the activated aspect of the transference/countertransference; and (3) what corresponds at this point to something unconscious in the analysand, which must be interpreted.

It is by virtue of the mediation of the unconscious configuration of the field that the analysand's unconscious can express itself and the analyst can find an interpretation. We thus avoid the risk of arbitrariness: it is not just any sense that is appropriate, and not just any interpretation that is valid.

313

This is best illustrated by the use of the analysand's account of his dreams: among the many possible and plausible interpretations of the dream, we choose the one that corresponds to the context lived by the patient, on the one hand, and the current moment in the process, on the other. The account of the dream is addressed to us and involves us, even if we do not appear directly or indirectly in any of the images reported.

If the interpretation has been correct – i.e., if there have not been too many barriers on the part of the analyst to understanding the configuration of the field – the interpretation has a chance of gaining access to some part of the analysand's unconscious. It will be access to a single isolated point, experienced by both participants as insight, and will be followed in the analysand by a new process of rendering unconscious, which, however, will leave behind something new to be contributed to the construction being performed by the analytic process. We are therefore not seeking a thing, and we are not listening to a different sense, but are following the trail of something that (or someone who) is unattainable but always present, whose presence has helped to structure and mould the subject's history and continues to do so at every instant of his life.

## Interpretation

Not everything the analyst says is interpretation. An interpretation is sometimes preceded by verbal interventions intended to facilitate the patient's communication and to demonstrate the listening presence of the analyst. Not everything that is understood is communicated as an interpretation. The analyst withholds many things that he understands until he considers it appropriate to communicate them. Spontaneous interpretations that occur to him may and perhaps must be kept back until it is possible to integrate them in a wider understanding of the field.

The interpretation proper is preceded by exploratory and preparatory interventions that are indicative of the progressive processing carried out by the analyst and his patient. These interventions should not be confused with a simultaneous translation of the patient's material. The interpretation arises at the moment when the analyst considers that he has understood the point of urgency and worked out how to make it accessible, at least in part, to the patient's understanding.

Sometimes the patient himself, if working in unison with his analyst, is capable of integrating the elements previously communicated and of arriving at his own interpretive formulation. We agree with Freud in distinguishing between interpretations of this kind and 'constructions', which are intended to present a plausible picture of the subject's history.

An interpretation is what attempts to throw light on and make convincingly understandable a current aspect of the field of the analytic relationship and hence of the unconscious of the patient involved in it. This mention of the field – of the transference-countertransference – implies that an interpretation is always given within the transference – an idea that is often confused with that of formulating any interpretation in transference terms.

This confusion leads to an indeterminate broadening of the concept of transference and blurs the difference between genuinely transferential phenomena, which are the repetition with the person of the analyst of past links and situations (mésalliances), and the patient–analyst link as structurally defined by the contract. If we regard everything as transference, we in fact lose sight of the transference. This forcing of the transference leads ultimately to interpretations that are off-centre with respect to the point of urgency, and may tend to indoctrinate the patient.

Strachey's historic paper on 'The nature of the therapeutic action of psychoanalysis' (1969) describes a certain type of interpretation, including transference and something resembling a construction, but we do not consider that it can be taken as a general model of interpretation. In our view, there are truly 'mutative' interpretations that have no explicit reference to the person of the analyst.

We referred above to 'withheld' interpretations. They are withheld not only pending a wider understanding, but with a view to having the maximum effect at a specific moment in the session and the process. This is the problem of the timing of the interpretation.

A comprehensive interpretation is not normally given at the beginning of a session, as it would then be liable to be unconvincing and to have a blocking effect. Instead, what is appropriate are interpretations of the different kinds of obstacles in the way of the patient's communication and of the opening of the dialogue.

Towards the end of a session we often think of an interpretation that 'we leave for tomorrow' lest its effect be too disorganising and the patient not have enough time to elaborate it in the session. With other patients we are confident enough to open up a new field for their understanding, in the belief that they can continue the work of elaboration by themselves.

However, towards the end of a session we perhaps tend more to give momentarily 'conclusive' interpretations, which take account of the work performed in the session and fix a moment in the process in detail.

315

Everyone agrees that it is inappropriate to give just any interpretation at just any moment in the process. We do, however, believe that it is impossible to predict an order in which interpretations should be given in a particular treatment – for instance, progressing from superficial to deeper interpretations: the patient does not present his material in the form of superimposed layers, but in accordance with the vicissitudes of the regres-

analysand as something of his own. Only the analyst's empathy, acquired and honed by all his prior experience, gives him the sensitivity that enables him to decide whether a given interpretation can or cannot actually be received by the patient. After all, we are not, of course, speaking to the unconscious, or to the subject of the unconscious, but to the patient to the extent that he can be conscious of himself. The unconscious has no ears. It is only through words and the secondary process in the patient that we can bring him closer to his primary processes and his unconscious.

All the processing that leads to the interpretation does not generally take the form of an explicit deliberation in the analyst's mind, but is spontaneous, except when the analyst is in doubt: can I say this or not? The same doubt is a signal of a difficulty in the field or an obstacle in the process, inviting the analyst to take a 'second look' (Baranger et al., 1983) at the field and to undertake some conscious and reasoned reflection about what he should do. This process, which may be called 'metabolisation', usually takes place in silence.

## Different forms of interpretation

The formula 'making the unconscious conscious' might suggest that the process concerned is unequivocal. However, the effect of appropriate interpretations suffices to show us that interpretation may aim at two different targets at least: ones whereby the analyst seeks to reintegrate a split off aspect of the patient, and ones which irrupt into a system of reassuring representations or illusions, giving rise to anxiety. The former combine aspects and experiences of the patient that are not unknown to him in the sense of being repressed and unconscious.

They may, for example, relate a specific childhood experience (described by the patient) to an event in his present-day life. They normally give rise to relief and even to the pleasure of discovery and understanding. The latter, because they open the way to the unconscious, arouse worry and anxiety in the patient and potentially in the analyst, who may then feel like a sorcerer's apprentice. The disruptive intention and the synthesising intention follow each other in the analyst's mind and act dialectically. Without disruption, the analysis would be idyllic and ineffective. Without unification, it would leave the analysand in a psychological quagmire.

A third form of interpretation, which is particularly important in certain types of patients (e.g., psychosomatics), consists in supplying words to describe experiences that never had any. In this type of interpretation, the analyst proceeds *per via di porre*, and not only *per via di levare*, as Freud demanded in referring to neurotics (1904).

## The language of interpretation

An important part of the mental work of the analyst in arriving at the interpretation is the choice of an appropriate formulation in order to be understood by this particular patient at this moment. The first difficulty in the analyst's way is the universal polysemy of language. However, in our view the analyst's art lies in transforming this difficulty into an instrument. The analyst can never be sure that the patient will understand what he interprets in the same sense as the analyst understands it.

We know from experience that the patient often picks up as an interpretation a fragment of what the analyst has said, sometimes even only a word, and apparently nullifies the analyst's interpretive intention. Yet often this 'bad listening' on the part of the patient also induces in the analyst something that corrects his vision and helps to open up the field.

This does not mean that misinterpretations by the patient due to his resistance do not exist. At any rate, the latter show the analyst that his interpretation ought to be centred differently or aim at a different level. For this reason many analysts' aim of seeking the maximum possible precision in the interpretation seems to us to be wrong: this precision may have the consequence of blocking instead of enriching the analytic dialogue.

Nothing could be more precise than an interpretation formulated in such abstract, theoretical terms, with a metapsychological vocabulary. We are all agreed that such interpretations may be exact but are ineffective.

The analyst should instead, as Aulagnier (1986) points out, concern himself with the representability of the interpretation, i.e. make sure that his words can evoke for the patient thing-presentations and concrete affects. Key words with this power of evocation come to be established in every analysis. They differ from patient to patient and their value is determined by the patient's own history or the history of this particular analysis.

317

This common vocabulary of the treatment is not chosen at random but because, in addition to their evocative power for the patient, some words have for the analyst himself an effect of resonance in his own fantasy world and his own history.

The creation of this common language is a phenomenon that occurs in each analysis, but it may become a trap: abuse of, and confinement within,

open. The use of the improper common vocabulary may eventually result in sterile repetition.

However, not all repetition is sterile. One of the problems the analyst faces before enunciating his interpretation is that it has already been given in some form or another to this patient. He may be loath to repeat it in case the patient retains it intellectually in his memory without the desired insight.

Again, insistence on an interpretation sometimes gives rise in the patient to an apparent conviction, insight being replaced by indoctrination. Yet we know from experience that the interpretation is often obliterated in the patient or that he has only been able to accept a part of what was said.

It is in the nature of the unconscious to close up again after it has partially opened. We therefore believe that one should not be afraid of repeating an interpretation, possibly formulated in a different way. Again, by virtue of the progress of the process, interpretations are complemented with fresh nuances and are deepened by the contribution of more concrete material. We know at the beginning of an analysis that the patient will bring us an Oedipus complex. However, it is only at the end that we will have an exact idea of the individual form in which this complex has manifested itself in the patient's life history.

## Conclusion

The analyst's mind functions so that his interpretation can act as an agent of transformation: it starts from a current context situated between two histories, the one brought by the patient and the one that is constructed during the process. The analyst looks for the point in the session that will mark the urgency of interpreting and the possibility of understanding an aspect of the field and of opening up the dynamics of the process. For this purpose he follows the thread of the basic fantasy of the field and tries to overcome obstacles so as to allow a reconstruction within his patient.

# Summary

The analyst demands two somewhat contradictory attitudes of himself: on the one hand, he listens and interprets on the basis of his theoretical knowledge, experiences and scheme of reference and, on the other, he must open himself to the new, the unforeseen and the surprising.

His work, from listening to interpretation, is situated within a context that includes the history of the treatment as well as the history of the analysand, which is in the process of reconstruction. This context determines the moment of the interpretation (which may vary), i.e., the point of urgency of a given session.

This point denotes the moment when something emerges from the unconscious of the analysand and the analyst believes that it must be interpreted. It is something that occurs within the intersubjective field, which embraces both participants and has its own, partly unconscious, dynamics. This configuration or unconscious fantasy of the field constitutes the common source from which both the discourse of one partner and the other's interpretation spring.

The moments of blockage in the dynamics of the field, the obstacles in the analytic process, invite every analyst to take a 'second look' at the field, focusing on the unconscious intersubjective relationship that determines it.

Focused either on the analysand or on the field, the interpretation can perform its two dialectically complementary functions: it may irrupt into the disguises of the patient's unconscious, or it may allow him to synthesise and reconstruct his history and identity.

# Note

1   For the Introduction to the life and work of Madeleine Baranger, see Part 1, Chapter 1 of this volume.

# References

AULAGNIER, P. 1979 *Les destins du plaisir* Paris: Presses Univ. France.

AULAGNIER, P. 1986 *Du langage pictural au langage de l'interprète. Un interprète en quête de sens* Paris: Payot.

BARANGER, M. et al. 1983 Process and no process in analytic work *International Journal of Psycho-Analysis* 64: 1–13

BION, W.R. 1952 Group dynamics: a review *International Journal of Psycho-Analysis* 33: 235–247

FREUD, S. 1904 On psychotherapy *The complete psychological works of Sigmund Freud*, S.E. 7

FREUD, S. 1910a Five lectures on psycho-analysis: 3rd lecture *The complete psychological works of Sigmund Freud*, S.E. 11

FREUD, S. 1910b The future prospects of psycho-analytic therapy *The complete psychological works of Sigmund Freud*, S.E. 11

FREUD, S. 1912 Papers on technique *The complete psychological works of Sigmund Freud*, S.E. 12

FREUD, S. 1915 ... *... logical works of Sigmund Freud*, S.E. ...

KLEIN, M. 1948 On the theory of anxiety and guilt In *Envy and Gratitude and Other Works, 1946–1963* London: Hogarth Press, 1975 pp. 25–42

LACAN, J. 1973 Les quatre concepts fondamentaux de la psychoanalyse *Le Séminaire Livre XI*. Paris: Seuil.

MERLEAU-PONTY, M. 1945 *La phénoménologie de la perception* Paris: N.R.F., Gallimard.

MIJOLLA-MELLOR, S. de 1990 Le travail de pensée dans l'interprétation *Topique* 46: 192–203

STRACHEY, J. 1969 The nature of the therapeutic action of psychoanalysis *International Journal of Psycho-Analysis* 50: 275–291

# INTRODUCTION TO THE LIFE AND WORK OF JOSÉ BLEGER (1922–1972)

*Benzion Winograd*

José Bleger was born in Argentina, in Santa Fe Province, in 1922. He died in Buenos Aires in 1972. Besides being a prominent psychoanalyst (he published six books in 49 years), José Bleger was a thinker with various interests and intellectual and cultural belongings. He was a political activist with outstanding autonomy who was loyal to his convictions. He deemed his Jewish identity as important as his ideological convictions; this is the reason why some (Volnovich, 1992) called him "the red rabbi" of the Psychoanalytic Association.

In his papers, conferences, classes and institutional activity, he attempted to correlate psychoanalysis with other scientific areas, such as general psychology, academic teaching and also with some issues linked to mental health. In this context, it is worth highlighting that he was faculty at the School of Psychology at the University of Buenos Aires since its creation in 1956. He taught three subjects: "Introduction to general psychology", "Psycho-hygiene and institutional psychology" and "Personality". He actively participated in discussions regarding the professional role of psychologists and the difference between the general psychological field and the psychoanalytic field (Bleger, 1996).

As head of the Argentine Psychoanalytic Association's research center (Enrique Racker Center)[1] from 1967 to 1969, he coordinated a study that gathered data on psychoanalytic therapeutic processes, analytical documentation of diagnosis and psychopathologic indicators. He returned to theses subjects several times in his life.

As I mentioned before, Bleger published six books and several articles, essays, and introductions, as well as making contributions in other papers.

Due to the multiplicity of his subjects and interests, his work was cited and studied by other researchers from other disciplines: some people have highlighted his contribution to the study and teaching of psychology in our environment (Dagfal, 2009a)[2]; some have valued his ideological freedom and autonomy (Itzigsohn, 1973)[3]; others his methodological contribution to psychoanalysis (Klimovsky, 1973)[4] and his theoretical-technical aspects

was studied all over Latin America.

I will now try to mention a possible taxonomy of thematic units that, even if it is not organized orderly and sequentially in the life of the author, it may allow some clarification to the readers.

1   *Contribution to psychoanalytic psychopathology.*

Here we can include (Bleger, 1971b) Bleger's considerations regarding the concept of "psychosis", (Bleger, 1967a, 1967) the clinical aspect of his papers on "symbiosis and ambiguity" and also, his conferences and contributions regarding specific psychopathologic problems such as perversions (Bleger, Cvik and Grunfeld, 1973), schizophrenia and autism (Bleger, 1972a).

2   *Contributions to the technical theory and clinical approach.* Here we can mention Bleger's posthumously published papers regarding "diagnosis" (Bleger, 1972b) and "therapeutic objectives" (Bleger, 1972c).

3   *Contribution to the theories of psychic development included also in his assessment of what we call "symbiosis".* To Bleger, the initial moments of emotional development included an early stage called *syncretism* of non-discrimination of the average subject. This stage entailed (from an observer perspective) the need that the environment (the important characters or the primary maternal objects) ensured a symbiosis, considered necessary and productive. The lack of existence of that method, because of object failures or due to its duration, would result in the hindrance of discrimination and autonomous development, leading to psychological illness.

4   *Contribution to the education of psychologists.* We said that Bleger was one of the first psychoanalysts who taught subjects (Bleger, 1963) that, even if they had psychoanalysis as its main referent, were centered on issues related to other psychological fields. As a professor (Dagfal, 2009b), he

achieved a distinguished prestige among the young generations of psychology students who, at that time, could not get psychoanalytic education. (Only MDs were allowed to train as psychoanalysts.)

5    *Contribution to the knowledge of psychological factors when running institutions.* These are issues on which Bleger (1966) focused, attempting to integrate different disciplines. One of those attempts culminated in the 1966 book, *Psycho-hygiene and institutional psychology.*

I will try to be more specific on three topics included in the previous paragraphs, as I consider them relevant to contemporary psychoanalysis:

1    *Contribution regarding diagnosis.* Bleger's contributions regarding diagnosis may be inferred from his articles on psychoanalytic assessment interview (Bleger, 1964) and his 1971 book, *Psychological topics, interview and groups.* On the article on diagnosis (1972b), Bleger insisted on clearly differentiating the psychoanalytic model from the medical psychiatric model, as he believed they answered to very different conceptual bases (and needs). Bleger remarked that the medical model tended to see the illness as a "thing" with properties. He proposed more functional diagnoses based on certain parameters, which contained indicators or indexes. As an alternative to a medical model, he proposed a multi-dimensional model that he called "pathographic organization"; he also identified what he called "structures" that were combinations of pathological entities and "indexes". Using the three variables, he tried to define two clusters of pathological organizations or modes of mental functioning: psychotic and neurotic.

From this brief review, I believe we can highlight the fact that Bleger does not criticize the medical model and its application in the medical context but its unrestricted application on psychoanalytic diagnosis, which has other methodological basics and conceptual structures. We can say that the method proposed by Bleger is notoriously modern. In fact, from my perspective, *diagnosis, as a non-conjectural activity without labels, does not assess essences but performances, determined by the subject's history, his ties with meaningful characters, his conflicts and deficiencies and how these performances are dramatized in the therapeutic-rational field.* In this field, concepts such as degree dependency, ego range versus restriction or stereotypy versus mobility or rigidity, do not refer to essences but to combinations subjected to the variation in the existential course.

2    *Therapeutic objectives.* The paper (Bleger, 1972c) regarding this issue can be considered one of the most original on this subject matter, and

Bleger insists on the fact that mentioning the therapeutic objectives entails, not only different terminologies, but also the possibility of highlighting two different conceptual perspectives. The first one he called "healing" objectives, which include the resolution of symptoms and changes in dominant psychopathology structures of a subject. The second one is the "maieutic"; these objectives imply changes and move-

functioning changes and quality of life.

3  *Context psychoanalysis.* This aspect has been assessed in his paper (Bleger, 1967) "Psychoanalysis of the analytic frame", in which he links the aspect that he calls "frame", including his ideas regarding development and the functioning of some psychic components, with his research on institutional psychology already mentioned.

## Notes

1  The Racker Center output systematized neurosis and psychosis indicators, an issue to which I will return in this chapter.
2  Dagfal, Alejandro (psychologist dedicated to history).
3  Itzigsohn, José (psychiatrist of Marxist orientation), in "Ideological semblance of José Bleger".
4  Klimovsky, Gregorio (epistemologist, specialist in psychoanalysis).
5  Fiorini, Héctor (specialist psychoanalyst in psychotherapy, in "Comments regarding the mentioned article").

## References

BAULEO, Armando (2003). Bleger, una figura de su tiempo. *Revista de Psicoanálisis* (APA) LX(4), Págs. 1135–1137
BERNARDI, Ricardo (2009). ¿Qué meta psicología necesitamos? Vigencia de J. Bleger. *Revista Uruguaya de Psicoanálisis* 108, Págs. 223–248
BLEGER, José (1952). *Teoría y práctica del narcoanálisis*. Ed. El Ateneo, Buenos Aires.
BLEGER, José (1958). *Psicoanálisis y dialéctica materialista*. Ed. Paidos, Bs. As.
BLEGER, José (1963). *Psicología de la conducta*. Ed. Eudeba, Bs. As.
BLEGER, José (1964). *La entrevista psicológica*, Ficha Departamento psicología Univ. de BsAs.
BLEGER, José (1966). *Psicohigiene y psicología institucional*. Ed. Paidos, Bs. As.
BLEGER, José (1967a). *Simbiosis y ambigüedad*. Ed. Paidos, Bs. As.

BLEGER, José (1967b). Psicoanálisis del encuadre psicoanalítico. *Revista Uruguaya de Psicoanálisis* (APA) XXIV(2), Págs. 241–257

BLEGER, José (1969). Teoría y práctica en psicoanálisis. La praxis psicoanalítica. *Revista Uruguaya de Psicoanálisis* XI(03–04). [Montevideo. Republicado (2003). Revista de Psicoanálisis de la Asociación Psicoanalítica Argentina. Tomo LX, N°4, Pag. 1091–1104.]

BLEGER, José (1971a). *Temas de psicología. Entrevistas y grupos.* Ed. Nueva Visión, Bs. As.

BLEGER, José (1971b). El concepto de psicosis. *Revista de Psicoanálisis* (APA) XXVIII(1), Págs. 5–23

BLEGER, José (1972a). Esquizofrenia, autismo y simbiosis. *Revista de Psicoanálisis* (APA) XXX(2), Págs. 367–376

BLEGER, José (1972b). Criterios de diagnóstico. *Revista de Psicoanálisis* (APA) XXX(2), Págs. 305–316

BLEGER, José (1972c). Criterios de curación y objetivos del psicoanálisis. *Revista de Psicoanálisis* (APA) XXX(2), Págs. 317–342

BLEGER, José – CVIK, Natalio – GRUNFELD, Beatriz (1973). Perversiones. *Revista de Psicoanálisis* (APA) XXX(2), Págs. 351–366

DAGFAL, Alejandro (2009a). José Bleger y los inicios de una psicología psico-analítica en la Argentina de los años 60. *Rev. Universitaria de Psicología* (Fac. Psicología UBA) (2), Págs. 139–170

DAGFAL, Alejandro (2009b). *La entrada precoz del psicoanálisis en las carreras de psicología,* en Entre Paris y Buenos Aires, Ed. Paidos, Bs. As., Cap. 7, Págs. 35–416

FIORINI, Héctor (2003). Comentarios sobre el artículo de José Bleger Teoría y práctica en psicoanálisis. La praxis psicoanalítica. *Revista de Psicoanálisis* (APA) LX(4), Págs. 1123–1126

ITZIGSOHN, José (1973). Semblanza ideológica de José Bleger. *Revista de Psicoanálisis* (APA) XXX(2), Págs. 551–555

KLIMOVSKY, Gregorio (1973). Niveles de integración y relación entre teorías científicas. *Revista de Psicoanálisis* (APA) XXX(2), Págs. 489–507

NASIO, Juan David (2003). Conferencia en homenaje a José Bleger. *Revista de Psicoanálisis* (APA) LX(4), Págs. 1135–1137

PICHON-RIVIÈRE, Enrique (1985). *Esquema conceptual referencial y operativo. En Teoría del vínculo.* Ed. Nueva Visión, Bs. As., Págs. 99–107

VOLNOVICH, Juan Carlos (1992). Bleger, la desgarrada soledad de un analista. *Revista Topía. Buenos Aires Diarios clínicos* 5, Págs. 117–126

WINOGRAD, Benzion (2002). Psicoanálisis rioplatense. *Revista Sociedad Argentina de Psicoanálisis* 5, Págs. 9–29

WINOGRAD, Benzion (2008). ¿Hacia una clínica de la singularidad? *Rev. Asociación Arg. de Psicoterapia para graduados,* 2, Págs. 121–134

## José Bleger

*This paper was read at the Second Argentine Psychoanalytic Congress, Buenos Aires, June 1966, and published originally in Spanish in 1967 by the* Revista de Psicoanálisis, *24(2): 241–257. This English version is from the 1967* International Journal of Psycho-Analysis, *48: 511–519.*

Winnicott (1956) defines "setting" as "the summation of all the details of management." I suggest, for reasons that will become clearer further on, that we should apply the term "psycho-analytic situation" to the totality of phenomena included in the therapeutic relationship between the analyst and the patient. This situation comprises phenomena which constitute a *process* that is studied, analysed, and interpreted; but it also includes a *frame*, that is to say, a "non-process", in the sense that it is made up of constants within whose bounds the process takes place.[1]

The analytic situation may be thus studied from the point of view of the methodology it stands for, its frame corresponding to the *constants* of a phenomenon, a method or technique, and the process to the set of *variables*. Methodological considerations will, however, be left out and they have only been mentioned here to make it clear that a process can only be examined when the same constants (frame) are being kept up. Thus, we include within the psycho-analytic frame the role of the analyst, the set of space (atmosphere) and time factors, and part of the technique (including problems concerning the fixing and keeping of times, fees, interruptions, etc.). The frame refers to a strategy rather than to a technique. One part of the frame includes "the psycho-analytic contract" which "is an agreement between two people into which enter two formal elements of mutual exchange: time and money" (Liberman, Ferschtut and Sor, 1961).

I am here concerned with the psycho-analysis of the psycho-analytic frame, and there is a great deal in the literature about the need for keeping it up and about the breaks and distortions caused by the patient in the course of any psycho-analysis (varying in intensity and features from exaggerated obsessive fulfilment to repression, acting out, or psychotic disintegration). My work in the psycho-analysis of psychotic cases has clearly revealed to me the importance of maintaining and protecting the fragments or elements which might have remained and which can sometimes only be achieved by hospitalization. Yet I do not want to consider now the problem of "disruption of" or "attack on" the frame. I want to study what is involved in the maintenance of an *ideally normal frame*. The problem is similar to what physicists call an ideal experiment, that is to say a problem that does not occur fully and precisely in the way it is being described or stated, but which is of great theoretical and practical use. This is perhaps what Rodrigué had in mind when he once referred to the patient whose history nobody has written and nobody will ever be able to write.

The way I have stated the problem seems to imply that such study is impossible, since ideal analysis does not exist, and I agree with this opinion. The fact is that at times permanently, and at other times sporadically, the frame changes from the mere background of a Gestalt into a figure, that is to say, a process. But even in these cases, it is not the same thing as the process of the analytic situation itself because, whenever "flaws" occur in the frame, we still tend to maintain it or restore it with our interpretation; this is quite different from our attitude in the analysis of the process itself. In this sense, I am interested in examining the psycho-analytic meaning of the frame *when it is not a problem*, in the "ideal" analysis (or at the moments or stages when it is ideal). Thus, I am interested in the psycho-analysis of the frame when it is maintained and not when it is broken, when it remains a set of constants and not when it has turned into variables. The problem I want to look into concerns those analyses in which the frame is not a problem – precisely to show that it is a problem – a problem, however, which has not been defined or hitherto recognized.

A relationship that lasts for years, in which a set of norms and attitudes is kept up, is nothing less than a true definition of *institution*. The frame is then an institution within whose bounds certain phenomena take place that we call behaviour. I was led to this study partly by a series of seminars on Institutional Psychology and as a result of my experience in this field (though at present limited). What became evident to me was that each institution is a portion of the individual's personality; and it is of such importance that identity is always, wholly or partially, institutional, in the sense that at least one part of the identity always shapes itself by belonging to a group, institution, ideology, party, etc. Fenichel (1945) wrote: "Unquestionably the individual structures created by institutions help conserve these institutions." But besides this interaction between individuals and institutions, institutions always work in varying degrees as the limits of the body image and as the

exist. (I do not know who it was who said about love and children that we only know they exist when they cry.) But, what is the meaning of the frame when it is maintained, when "it does not cry"? It is, in all instances, the problem of symbiosis, which is "dumb" and only reveals itself when it breaks or is on the verge of rupture. This is what happens, too, with the body image whose study started with pathology that first proved its existence. In the same way as we speak of the "ghost member", we must accept that institutions and the frame *always* make up a "ghost world", that of the most primitive and undifferentiated organization. What is always there is never noticed unless it is missing; we might apply to the frame the term used by Wallon for what he called "ultra-things", that is to say, all that which in experience appears as vague, undefined, without conception or knowledge of itself. What makes up the ego are not only the steady relationships with objects and institutions but the ulterior frustrations and gratifications with them. There is no awareness of what is always present. Awareness of the missing or gratifying object comes later; the first step is the perception of a certain "incompleteness". What exists in the individual's perception is that which experience has taught him might be missing. On the other hand, steady or motionless relationships (the non-absences) are those that organize and preserve the non-ego, and serve as a basis for the building up of the ego according to frustrating and gratifying experiences. The fact that the non-ego is not perceived does not mean it does not exist psychologically for the organization of personality. The knowledge of something is only apparent in the absence of that something, until it is incorporated as an internal object. But what we do not perceive is also present. And precisely because of this, that "ghost world" is also present in the frame even when this has not been broken.

I want to digress again, hoping to provide more elements for the present study. Until recently, we were comfortably working in the field of science, language, logic, etc., without realizing that all of these phenomena or behaviours (I am interested in all of them in so far as they are behaviours, that is to say, human phenomena) take place within a context of assumptions which we ignored or thought nonexistent or invariable; but we know now that communication contains a meta-communication, science a meta-science, theory a meta-theory, language a meta-language, logics a meta-logics, etc., etc. If the "meta-" varies, the contents vary radically,[2] thus, the frame is constant, and is therefore decisive in the phenomena of the process of behaviour. In other words, the frame is a *meta-behaviour*, and the phenomena we are going to distinguish as behaviour depend on it. It is what remains implicit, but on which the explicit depends.

The meta-behaviour works as a "bulwark", as M. and W. Baranger have called it, a phase in which the analysand tries not to risk avoiding the basic rule. In the meta-behaviour, I am interested in analysing the cases in which the basic rule is fulfilled, and I am concerned precisely with examining that fulfilment. I agree with these authors in regarding the analytic relationship as a symbiotic relationship; but in the cases in which the frame is being respected, the problem lies in the fact that the frame itself is the receiver of the symbiosis and that the latter is not present in the analytic process itself. Symbiosis with the mother (immobility of the non-ego) enables the child to develop his ego. The frame has a similar function: it acts as support, as mainstay, but, so far, we have been able to perceive it only when it changes or breaks. The most powerful, endurable, and at the same time least apparent, "bulwark" is, then, the one that lies on the frame.

I want to illustrate the description I have offered of the frame with the example of a patient, Mr. A., with a phobic character and an intense dependence disguised under the form of reactive independence. For a long time he wavered between hesitation, desire and fear of buying a flat in a purchase that was never accomplished. At a certain point, he came to know by mere chance that I had, some time before, bought a flat that was still being built, and this was the starting point of a period of anxiety and acting out.

One day he told me about what he had learnt and I interpreted his reaction: the way he said it contained reproach at my not informing him of my purchase, knowing it was a fundamental problem of his. He tried to ignore or forget the incident by presenting strong resistance every time I insistently related this fact to his acting out, until strong feelings of hatred, envy, frustration, coupled with verbal attacks, began to appear, and were followed by a feeling of detachment and hopelessness. As we advanced further in the analysis of these situations, the "background" of his childhood experience gradually began to emerge from the narration of different recollections. At home, his parents had done nothing without informing or consulting him about it; he knew all the details of the development of the family life. After the emergence of these memories and my interpretation of them against great resistance, he began accusing me of having broken our connection, and he said that he would not be able to trust me. Fantasies of suicide appeared as well as derangement, frequent confusion and hypochondriacal symptoms.[3]

For the patient, something had broken, something which *was so* and *had to be* as it had always been; and he could not conceive of its being otherwise. He was demanding a repetition of what had been lived, of what for him had "always

element of his personality, his "ghost world". The delusional transference (Little) or the psychotic part of his personality was a non-ego that constituted the groundwork of his ego and his identity. It was only with the "unfulfilment" of his "ghost world" that he was able to see that my frame was different from his, that even before the unfulfilment; his "ghost world" already existed. I must emphasize, however, that the maintenance of the frame was what led to the analysis of the psychotic part of his personality. The important question is not how many of these phenomena are due to frustration or the clash with reality (the frame), but how much of this area does not appear and is therefore never likely to be analysed. I am able not to give an answer to this question, but only to delineate the problem. It is similar to what happens with the character feature that must be turned into a symptom in order to be analysed, that is to say, it must stop being ego-syntonic. Should not whatever is done in the analysis of character be done with the frame? The problem is different and more difficult since the frame is not ego-syntonic on the one hand, and on the other hand is the ground-work on which the ego and the identity of the individual are built up; and it is strongly separated off from the analytic process, from the ego that shapes the neurotic transference.

Even if we assume that, in the case mentioned above, this material would have emerged in one way or another because it was there, the problem persists in reference to the psycho-analytic meaning of the frame.

Summing up, one might say that the frame (thus defined as a problem) is the most perfect repetition compulsion[4] and that actually there are two frames, one which is suggested and kept up by the analyst, and consciously accepted by the patient, and the other, that of the "ghost world", on which the patient projects.[5] The latter is the most perfect repetition compulsion since it is the most complete, the least known, and the least noticeable one. Rodrigué and Rodrigué (1966) talk about a "pending transference" and the "difficulty arises because we are speaking about a phenomenon which, if it existed in its pure form, would have to be dumb by definition."

It has always seemed surprising and exciting to me, in the analysis of psychotic cases, to note the coexistence of a total denial of the analyst with exaggerated sensitivity to the infringement of any detail of the "habitual", the frame, and how the patient might become confused or violent, for example, because of a few minutes' difference in starting or finishing the session. Now I understand it better in that what becomes disorganized is his "meta-ego", which to a great extent, is all he has got. I think it is jumping to conclusions to talk all the time about a patient's "attack" on the frame when he does not adhere to it. He brings what he has got and it is not always an "attack" but his own organization, even though disordered.

In psychotic transference, affection is not transferred but "a total situation, the whole of a development" (Lagache); it would be better to say, the whole of a "non-development". For Melanie Klein, transference repeats the primitive object relationships, but I think that what is still most primitive (the non-differentiation) repeats itself in the frame. The ambiguity of the "as if" of the analytic situation studied by W. and M. Baranger (1961–62) does not cover "all the aspects of the analytic field" as they express it, but only the process. The frame does not accept ambiguity, either on the part of the patient or on the part of the analyst's technique. Each frame *is*, and does not admit ambiguity. Similarly, I believe that the phenomenon of participation (Lévy-Bruhl) or of syncretism admitted by these authors for the analytic situation only applies to the frame.

Jaques (1955) says that social institutions are unconsciously used as a defence against psychotic anxiety. I believe them to be the depository of the psychotic part of the personality, i.e. the undifferentiated and non-dissolved portion of the primitive symbiotic links. Psychotic anxieties take place within the institution, and, in the case of the psycho-analytic situation, within what we have described as the process – what "is in motion" against what is not: the frame. Reider (1953) describes different types of transference to the institution instead of the therapist and psycho-analysis as an institution seems to be a means of recovering the lost omnipotence of sharing in the prestige of a great institution. I believe that what is important here is to consider the psycho-analytic situation as an institution in itself, especially the frame.

The development of the ego, in analysis, in the family, or in any institution, depends on the immobility of the non-ego. This denomination of non-ego makes us think about it as something non-existent, but which actually exists to the extent that it is the "meta-ego" on which the very possibility of formation and maintenance of the ego depends. Hence we might say that identity depends upon the manner in which the non-ego is kept up or handled. If the metabehaviour varies, the whole ego undergoes changes in probably equivalent degrees as regards its quantity and its quality. García Reinoso (1956) has said that just as it is true – as Freud had pointed out – that the ego is corporal, so is the non-ego. We might add something else: that the non-ego is a different ego, having different features, and I suggest (Bleger, 1967) calling it a *syncretic ego*. This also implies that there is not only *one* sense of reality and a lack of it: there are different structures of the ego and sense of reality.

The non-ego is the background or the frame of the organized ego; the

parents in hotels in different countries; the only thing she always carried with her was a small picture. The unsatisfactory relationship with her parents and the constant moving had turned this picture into her "frame", what gave her the "non-change" for her identity.

The frame is the most primitive part of the personality, it is the fusion ego-body-world, on whose immobility depend the formation, existence, and differentiation (of the ego, the object, the body image, the body, the mind, etc.). Patients with "acting-in" tendencies or psychotic patients also bring "their own frame", and *the institution of their primitive symbiotic relationship*; yet not only they, but all patients bring it too. Hence we can better recognize the catastrophic situation which to a variable degree is always created by the analyst's breaking the frame, e.g., holidays, changes of time, etc., because in these breakings a "crevice" is opened into which enters a reality that appears catastrophic to the patient; "his" frame, his "ghost world" remains without depository and it becomes evident that his frame is not the psycho-analytic frame, as happened with Mr. A.

I now want to give an example of a "crevice" that the patient maintained till he felt the need to recover his omnipotence, "his" frame.

Mr. Z., the only son of a family who in his childhood was wealthy and socially influential and united, lived in a huge, luxurious mansion with his parents and grandparents, for whom he was the centre of attention. For political reasons, a lot of their possessions were expropriated, and this brought about a great economic decline. The whole family tried hard for a while to live like rich people, concealing their disaster and poverty, but his parents finally moved into a small apartment and accepted a job. (In the meantime his grandparents had died.) When the family faced and accepted the change, he continued living up to appearances. He withdrew from his parents to live on his profession as an architect and he covered up his great insecurity and economic instability so well that everybody thought him rich. He lived and encouraged his fantasy that "nothing had happened", preserving in this way the safe and idealized world of his childhood, his "ghost world". The impression he gave me in the course of treatment was that of a "well-to-do" person, belonging to the social and economic upper class, who, without the showing-off of a "parvenu", maintained an air of security, dignity, and superiority, of being over and beyond the "miseries" and "pettiness" of life, including money.

The frame was well kept, the patient paying regularly and punctually. As the cleavage in his personality was being more deeply analysed, as well as his acting in two worlds, he began to owe me money, to be unpunctual, and to speak – with great difficulty – about his lack of money, a fact which made him feel very "humiliated". The breaking of the frame meant here a certain disruption of his omnipotent organization, the appearance of a "breach" which became the way to get in "against" his omnipotence (the steady and safe world of his childhood). The fulfilment of the frame was the depository of his omnipotent magic world, his childish dependence, his psychotic transference. His most profound fantasy was that analysis would strengthen that omnipotence and would give him back his "ghost world". "To live" in the past was the basic organization of his existence.

The following material comes from a session just after his parents were seriously injured in an accident. During the previous session he paid me part of his debt, and he began the present session by telling me that he had brought me so much money and still owed me so much. He felt the debt "as a breach, as something missing". After a pause, he went on: "Yesterday I had sexual intercourse with my wife and at the beginning I was impotent and that frightened me". (He had been impotent at the beginning of his marriage.) I interpreted that as he was now living a difficult situation because of his parents' accident, he wanted to go back to the security he enjoyed in his childhood, to his parents and grandparents within him, and the relationship with his wife, with me, and with the present reality made him impotent to accomplish that. He had a need to close the breach by paying me the whole of the debt, so that the money might disappear between us, so that I, and everything that made him suffer now, might also disappear. He answered that the day before he had thought that he in fact only needed his wife not to be alone, she was a mere addition in his life. I interpreted that he also wished me to satisfy his reality-needs so that they might disappear and he might thus go back to the security of his childhood, and to his fantasy of reunion with his grandparents, father and mother, just as had happened in his early years.

After a silence, he said that when he heard the word fantasy he found it strange that I should talk of fantasies, and was afraid of going mad. I told him that he wanted me to give him back all the security of his childhood which he tried to preserve within himself so as to cope with the difficult situation and that, on the other hand, he felt that I, and reality with its needs and sufferings, got in through the breach which his debt had created between us. He finished the session by talking about a transvestite; and I interpreted that he felt like a transvestite: at times like a rich and only son, at times like his father, at times like his mother, at times like his grandfather, and in each one of them both *poor and rich*.

Any variation in the frame brings the non-ego to a crisis, "contradicts"

that the recovery of his "ghost world" was linked to the fulfilment of *my* frame precisely to ignore me or destroy me.

The phenomenon of reactivation of symptoms at the end of a psycho-analytic treatment, which has often been described, is due, too, to a mobilization and regression of the ego because of a mobilization of the "meta-ego". The background of the Gestalt becomes a figure.[6] The frame, in this way, may be considered as an "addiction" which, if not systemati-cally analysed, may become a stabilized organization, the foundation of the organization of the personality, and the individual gets an ego "adjusted" and modeled upon the institutions of which he is part. It is the basis, I believe, of what Alvarez de Toledo, Grinberg and Langer (1964) have called the "analytic character", which the existentialists call a "factic" existence, and which we might recognize as a "factic ego".[7]

This "factic ego" is an "ego of belonging"; it is made up and sustained by the admission of the subject to an institution (which may be the therapeu-tic relationship, the psycho-analytical society, a study group, or any other institution); there is no "internalized ego" to give internal stability to the subject.

Let us say, in other words, that his whole personality is made up of "char-acters", that is to say, of roles, or – to put it another way – that his whole personality is a façade. I am now describing the "extreme case" but quanti-tative variation must be taken into account because there is no way to abol-ish completely this "factic ego"; neither do I think this necessary.

The "pact" or the negative therapeutic reaction represents a perfect fixa-tion of the patient's non-ego in the frame and even its non-recognition and acceptance by the psycho-analyst; moreover, we might say that the negative therapeutic reaction is a real perversion of the transference-countertransference relationship. The "therapeutic alliance" is, on the con-trary, an alliance with the healthiest part of the patient (Greenacre, 1959); and this is true of the process but not of the frame. In the latter, the alli-ance is established with the psychotic (or symbiotic) part of the patient's personality (whether with the corresponding part of the psycho–analyst's personality I do not know yet).[8]

Winnicott (1947) says:

> For the neurotic, the couch and warmth and comfort can be symbolical of the mother's love; for the psychotic it would be more true to say that these things are the analyst's physical expression of love. The couch is the analyst's lap or womb, and the warmth is the live warmth of the analyst's body. And so on.

As to the frame, this is always the most regressive, psychotic part of the patient (for every type of patient). The frame is a permanent presence, like the parents for the child. Without them, there is no development of the ego, but to keep the frame beyond necessity, or to avoid any change in the relationship with the frame or with the parents, there may be even a paralysis of development. Rodrigué and Rodrigué, in a book on transference (1966), compare the psycho-analytic process with the process of evolution.

It has been emphasized that the child's ego organizes itself according to the mobility of the medium that creates and provides his needs. The rest of the medium, which does not generate needs, is not distinguished and remains as a background in the structure of personality, and as yet this has not been given proper considerations.

In every analysis, even one with an ideally kept frame, the frame must become an object of analysis. I do not mean that this is not occurring in practice, but I want to stress the meaning or significance of what is being done or remains undone, and its importance. The de-symbiotization of the analyst-patient relationship is only reached with the systematic analysis of the frame at the right moment. And here we are likely to find the strongest resistance because it is not a repressed thing but something split and never differentiated; its analysis disturbs the ego and the most mature identity reached by the patient. In these cases we don't interpret what is repressed; we give rise to the secondary process. It is not interpreted on amnesic gaps but on what never was part of the memory. It is not projective identification either; it is the expression of syncretism or the patient's "participation."

The frame is part of the patient's body image; it *is* the body image in the part that has not been structured and differentiated. It is thus something different from the body image itself; it is the body-space and body setting non-differentiation. That is why the interpretation of gestures and body attitudes frequently becomes persecutory, because we do not "move" the patient's ego, but rather his "meta-ego".

I want to present now another example that also has the peculiarity that I cannot describe the "dumbness" of the frame but only the moment when it reveals itself, when it has stopped being dumb. I have already compared it with the body image, the study of which was started precisely by the consideration of its disturbances. In this case, however, the psycho-analyst's frame itself was vitiated.

A colleague brought to a supervision session the analysis of a patient whose transference neurosis he had been interpreting for several years; but

had suggested this at the beginning of his analysis, and the therapist had accepted it. The analysis of the therapist's countertransference took many months till he finally "dared" to correct this familiar form of address, interpreting to the patient what was happening and what was hidden behind it. To stop using the familiar "tu" to each other as a result of its systematic analysis revealed the narcissistic relationship and the omnipotent control, and how the person and role of the analyst had been suppressed because of this familiarity.

By using this familiar form of address, the patient imposed his own frame, overlapping the analyst's, but really destroying the latter. The analyst was compelled to cope with a task that represented too great an effort in the session with his patient (and in his countertransference), and this led to an intensive change in the analytic process and rupture in the patient's ego, which was surviving under unsafe conditions and with a very limited "spectrum" of interest, with intensive and extensive inhibitions. The change of the form of address through analysis led to the conclusion that this was not an obsessive phobic character but a simple schizophrenia with a phobic-obsessive characterological "façade".

I do not think it would have been efficient enough to modify the familiar form of address from the very beginning since the candidate did not have the technical experience to handle a patient with a strong narcissistic organization. The analyst must not agree to use the familiar form of address himself, though he may accept it on the part of his patient and analyse it at a suitable time (which I cannot place retrospectively). The analyst should accept the frame the patient brings (which is his "meta-ego") because there the non-solved primitive symbiosis is found summed up. But we must state, at the same time, that to accept the patient's "meta-ego" (the frame) does not mean to abandon one's own, by means of which one is able to analyse the process and to transform the frame itself into a process. Any interpretation of the frame (not altered) stirs the psychotic part of the personality. It makes up what I have called a split interpretation. But the analyst-patient relationship outside the strict frame (as in this example), as well as the "extra-analytic" relationships, enable the psychotic transference to be concealed and favour the "development" of the "psycho-analytic character."

Another patient, Mrs. C., maintained her frame until she progressed in her pregnancy. She had never shaken hands since treatment started, but she now stopped greeting me when arriving or leaving. I strongly resisted including in the interpretation that she had stopped greeting me, but I could see in this the mobilization of her symbiotic relationship with her mother, of highly persecutory features, which became active because of her pregnancy. Not to shake hands when arriving or leaving has been maintained, but there still lies an important part of "her frame" which is different from "mine". I believe that the situation is even more complex, because not to shake hands is not a mere detail that is missing to round up the frame. It is evidence that she has another frame, another Gestalt which is not mine (that of the psycho-analytic treatment) and in which her idealized relationship with her mother remained split. The more we deal with the psychotic part of the personality, the more we must take into account that a detail is not just a detail, but an expression of a Gestalt, that is to say, of a special organization or structure.

Summing up, we may say that a patient's frame is his most primitive fusion with the mother's body and that the psycho-analyst's frame must help to re-establish the original symbiosis in order to be able to change it. The disruption of the frame, as well as its ideal or normal maintenance, are technical and theoretical problems, but what basically blocks off any possibility of a profound treatment is the disruption the analyst himself introduces or admits in the frame. *The frame can only be analysed within the frame*, or, in other words, the patient's most primitive dependence and psychological organization can only be analysed within the analyst's frame, which should be neither ambiguous, nor changeable, nor altered.

## Summary

I propose to call the *psycho-analytic situation* the sum total of phenomena involved in the therapeutic relationship between the analyst and the patient. This situation includes phenomena which make up a *process* and which is studied, analysed and interpreted; but it also includes a *frame*, that is to say "a non-process" in the sense that it represents the constants, within whose limits the process occurs. The relationship between them is studied and the frame is explained as the set of constants within whose limits the process takes place (variables). The basic aim is to study, not the breaking of the frame, but its psycho-analytic meaning when "ideally normal" conditions are maintained.

Thus, the frame is studied as an *institution* within whose limits phenomena occur which are called "behaviours". In this sense, the frame is "dumb" but not non-existent. It makes up the non-ego of the patient, according to which the ego shapes itself. This non-ego is the "ghost world" of the patient,

sonality. The frame as an institution is the receiver of the psychotic part of the personality, i.e. of the undifferentiated and non-solved part of the primitive symbiotic links. The psycho-analytic meaning of the frame defined in this way is then examined, as well as the relevance of these considerations for clinical work and technique.

## Notes

1   Here we might compare this terminology with that used by Liberman (1962) and Rodrigué and Rodrigué (1966) respectively.

2   This variation in the "meta-" or variation of the fixed or constant assumptions is the origin of non-Euclidean geometry and Boolean algebra (Lieber, 1960). In psychotherapy, each technique has its assumptions (its frame) and therefore, its own "contents" or processes.

3   As Little (1958) describes it in patients whose transference is delusional, body associations of very early experiences began to appear in my patient. When he felt immobilized, he associated to having been wrapped up as a baby in a band that kept him motionless. The non-ego of the frame includes the body and if the frame breaks, the limits of the ego made up by the non-ego have to be recovered through hypochondriacal symptoms.

4   This repetition compulsion is not only a way of remembering but a way of life on the requirement to live.

5   Wender (1966) has said that there are two patients and two analysts, to which I now add: two frames.

6   It must be this fact which has led some authors (Christoffel, 1952) to the breaking of the frame as a technique (giving up the couch and having the interview face to face), a point of view I do not share.

7   I have dealt more intensively with the "factic ego" and the "syncretic ego", the "corporal ego" and the "internalized ego" elsewhere (Bleger, 1967).

8   I do not believe that this psychotic split transference which is placed on the frame is the consequence of repression of infantile amnesia.

338

# References

ABRAHAM, K. 1919 "A particular form of neurotic resistance against the psycho-analytic method." *Selected Papers* (London: Hogarth, 1927.)

ALVAREZ DE TOLEDO, L. C., GRINBERG, L. and LANGER, M. 1964 "Termination of training analysis." In: *Psychoanalysis in the Americas* ed. Litman. (New York: Int. Univ. Press, 1966.)

BARANGER, W. and BARANGER, M. 1961–2 "La situatión analítica como campo dinámico." *Revista Uruguaya de Psicoanálisis* 4

BARANGER, W. and BARANGER, M. 1964 "El insight en la situación analítica." *Revista Uruguaya de Psicoanálisis* 6

BLEGER, J. 1964 "Simbiosis: estudio de la parte psicótica de la personalidad." *Revista Uruguaya de Psicoanálisis* 6

BLEGER, J. 1966 *Psicohigiene y Psicología institucional* (Buenos Aires: Paidos.)

BLEGER, J. 1967 *Simbiosis y Ambiguedad* (Buenos Aires: Paidos.)

CHRISTOFFEL, H. 1952 "Le problème du transfert." *Revue Française de Psychanalyse* 16

FENICHEL, O. 1945 *The Psychoanalytic Theory of Neurosis* (New York: Norton.)

FREUD, S. 1914 "Remembering, repeating and working-through." *The complete psychological works of Sigmund Freud,* S.E. 12

GARCÍA REINOSO, D. 1956 "Cuerpo y mente." *Revista de Psicoanálisis* 13

GREENACRE, P. 1959 "Certain technical problems in the transference relationship." *Journal of the American Psychoanalytic Association* 7

JAQUES, E. 1951 *The Changing Culture of a Factory* (London: Tavistock.)

JAQUES, E. 1955 "Social systems as a defence against persecutory and depressive anxiety." In: *New Directions in Psycho-Analysis* ed. Klein et al. (London: Tavistock.)

KLEIN, M. 1955 "The psycho-analytic play technique: its history and significance." *New Directions in Psycho-Analysis* ed. Klein et al. (London: Tavistock.)

LAGACHE, D. 1952 "Le problème du transfert." *Revue Française de Psychanalyse* 16 (Spanish: *Revista Uruguaya de Psicoanálisis*, 1956, 1.)

LIBERMAN, D. 1962 *La comunicación en terapeutica psicoanalítica* (Buenos Aires: Eudeba).

LIBERMAN, D., FERSCHTUT, G., SOR, D. 1961 "El contrato analítico." *Revista de Psicoanálisis* 18

LIEBER, L. R. 1960 "The great discovery of modern mathematics." *General Semantics Bull.* 26–27

LITTLE, M. 1958 "On delusional transference." *International Journal of Psycho-Analysis* 39

NUNBERG, H. 1951 "Transference and reality." *International Journal of Psycho-Analysis* 32

REIDER, N. 1953 "A type of transference at institutions." *Bull. Menning Clin.* 17

RODRIGUÉ, E. and RODRIGUÉ, G. T. DE 1966 *El Contexto del Proceso Analítico.* (Buenos Aires: Paidos.)

WENDER, L. 1966 "Reparación patalógica y perversión." Paper read to the Argentine Psycho-Analytic Assoc.

WINNICOTT, D. W. 1945 "Primitive emotional development." *Collected Papers* (London: Tavistock, 1958.)

WINNICOTT, D. W. 1947 "Hate in the countertransference." *Collected Papers* (London: Tavistock, 1958.)

# INTRODUCTION TO THE LIFE AND WORK OF RICARDO HORACIO ETCHEGOYEN (1919– )

## *Samuel Zysman*

R. Horacio Etchegoyen is alive and still active while I'm writing this essay in 2013. For all of those who know him personally, and for a vast majority of colleagues, he has always been an iconic and charismatic figure – especially so for Latin Americans who know him as the first President of the IPA coming from this geographic area. On the other hand, he is also known as the most obstinate and tireless promoter of Latin American authors in the wide world of international psychoanalysis, through the inclusion of their contributions in his own books and papers, many presented in international congresses. This is surely not a minor merit if we remember that for many years and with few exceptions Latin American psychoanalytic original productions were practically unknown in the northern hemisphere, much in the way that Latin America had to wait to be accepted on equal terms with the colleagues of the USA and Europe in the governing bodies of the IPA.

Some 35 years of a close relationship with R.H. Etchegoyen surely are enough to keep in one's mind a huge repertoire of memories from different moments in various settings. Among them I have to mention his historical seminars on the Theory of Psychoanalytic Technique, whose subject matters we (the then-Associate Professors) previously studied with him as the drafts of what would later become his worldwide known *Fundamentals of Psychoanalytic Technique*. Supervisions, study groups, papers published in collaboration, come to mind, as well as the shared books' readings and the frequent meetings over coffee with common friends for that most Argentine habit of discussing local and international politics. Horacio is known for his hospitality and for his being always accessible. A reasonable conclusion of all this seems to be that to get acquainted with one of the most important Latin American contributors and key figure of psychoanalysis may turn the space here available to be a scarce one.

In the "Festschrift" in honor of R. Horacio Etchegoyen (1) presented in Barcelona at the end of his term in office as President of the IPA, the first

abridged approach to the same matter.

I asked Etchegoyen lately which of his own papers he preferred best, and his immediate answer was: the Helsinki paper. "It's the most creative", he added. He was referring to "The relevance of the transferential interpretation in the 'here and now' for the reconstruction of the early psychic development", presented in the 1981 IPA Congress in Helsinki. The core of this paper is the assertion that the early, pre-verbal stages of psychic development can be detected in the transference, understood, and interpreted verbally to a patient. A clinical material is introduced to sustain the assertion and correlate the transferential interpretations with the changes experimented by the patient along the 9 1/2 years of a classical analytic treatment. Interestingly enough, and in a quick spontaneous answer when I asked which his second preferred paper could be, he said: "Primary narcissism or object relations", presented in 1987 in the 11th Brazilian Psychoanalytic Congress in Canela. "I feel identified with these two papers", he added.

What it is possible to perceive here is the existence of an intimate thread connecting some papers with an ongoing theoretical development that tries permanently to ground itself on epistemological validation requisites. In this particular case, the two papers permit us to see the two faces of one coin: on one side, there is a confrontation of the Kleinian theory of (early) object relations with the classical one of primary narcissism; on the other, we are presented with the technical consequences of the theoretical choice.

This evokes at the same time two other equally linked issues. One is Etchegoyen's pioneering example of the application of epistemological validation rules to psychoanalytic theoretical statements. This leads us to mention his extended relationship with Gregorio Klimovsky, who is the author of a chapter on interpretation in the *Fundamentals*. It's worthwhile to underline the fact that the epistemologist and mathematician Klimovsky was a teacher for many of us for years, and that psychoanalysis in Latin America, and especially in the Rio de la Plata, owes him the possibility of this needful approach. Etchegoyen also cultivated another interdisciplinary link (with ethology: remember the panel on sexuality in the Barcelona Congress, with Alex Kacelnik and other Oxford ethologists), which allows to have a glimpse on how a bright and educated mind can find an honorable place for psychoanalysis in a dialogue among equals with other sciences. To resume, the papers mentioned above show the intimate connections between the theories of early psychic development, transference, and countertransference. It would be impossible to work as Etchegoyen did with his Helsinki paper's patient without a strict adherence to the analysis of the transference, understood as the clinical expression of early psychic development that opens the way to interpret it – most times with the help of the analysis of the countertransference. In it, the emotional involvement of the analyst appears to be a testimony of the presence of the earliest dyadic relations of the patient. Of course, this is how Kleinians work and it may be controvertible, but our present task is to show the importance of Etchegoyen's coherence with his own theoretical assumptions, both for therapeutic and ethical reasons.

Let us move on now to another side of the same matter. As it always happens, identifications with aspects of one's training analyst appear to be of utmost importance in our own careers and developments, and Horacio is not an exception. Although he had a short period of personal analysis with Donald Meltzer while staying in London, he recognizes his training analysis with Heinrich Racker in Buenos Aires for several years as the true one. In his own words: "I remember and I'm grateful to Donald because he helped me to work through some of my manic defenses, but my true analysis was with Racker". Etchegoyen remembers Racker as more neutral; "he always interpreted: never did he try actively to influence my personal life" (which Meltzer seems to have done a couple of times). It would really be difficult to imagine that Racker's well-known studies on transference and countertransference had no relation to his technical approach, and that Horacio did not learn from it. Many of his papers deal especially with the transference; among them and perhaps the most significant may be "The forms of transference" (1978). He states there that every possible psychopathologic state has its own expression in the transference. Again there is a link to the papers mentioned before through the correlation between early mental states, psychopathology, and transference.

While the "true" analysis with Racker developed in what we can call "normal" circumstances, the short analysis with Meltzer took place in quite another situation. He actually went to London to study at the Tavistock Clinic for a fixed term of time with a WHO grant, after resigning his post as Psychiatry Professor in the Argentine city of Mendoza and having had to give up also his psychoanalytic practice there. He had to move with his family, wife and young children, and he would not return to Mendoza but to Buenos Aires after one year. It might have been difficult both for the analyst and the patient to preserve the analytic setting, keeping in mind simultaneously the special circumstances of his case. He actually had won the post, but the Mendoza University never officially materialized his appointment. This had to do with his having published what can be considered one of his earliest psychoanalytic papers, including the case

from it, but he did not. In any case, there is here what we can consider an existential knot from which I would like to pick up a couple of its components and draw some possible conclusions.

We can find a guiding principle that puts in continuity the decisions taken by Horacio in Mendoza with the ones taken in London, namely to preserve his right to behave in accordance with his convictions and his values. Talking especially about his experience with Meltzer, I once asked Horacio what in his opinion might be the difference between the London and the Argentine Kleinians, taking into account that when conflict rose in his analysis with Meltzer, the death of Melanie Klein was still recent. His answer was that probably the London Kleinians had to keep a more militant attitude and therefore be less open, because of the fact of the huge impact and the influence of both Freud's and Anna Freud's presence in London, while Kleinians in LA can feel more open and free because there is no need to stay permanently on watch.

His decision to undertake what was to become a permanent seminar on the Theory of Technique that lasted many years led to the publication of the "Fundamentals". The book itself speaks of Horacio's ability to face the challenge and produce a most complete work.

Finally, I will refer shortly to two very important issues. One is his term in office as President of the IPA. People not acquainted with the IPA's political and administrative problems mainly remember that he was the first Latin American to become President. Some remember his putting an end to the secret of the proceedings of the Executive Board. Others remember the putting in order of the IPA's finances. My preferred memory is the one related to the sad history of Werner Kemper and his appointment as training analyst in Rio de Janeiro by Ernest Jones. Kemper had been a member of the Göring Institute in Berlin, under Hitler. The sequel of Kemper's appointment had to do with one of his analysands, Leao Cabernite, who had a candidate in analysis an Army MD involved in torture during the Brazilian dictatorship. Many complex and painful

344

situations could not be resolved during the years and under different IPA Presidents. Horacio had to face the last act of this tragic situation when he took office, and he did it with courage and respect for the victims, and this is my preferred recollection of that period. It was explained more in detail in an IPA publication on Latin American Psychoanalysis (2). If we have to choose something to justify why Horacio is remembered with respect in LA, I think it must be to a great extent the way he dealt with this most unfortunate legacy.

My last and brief commentary is about Elida, his deceased wife and the mother of his two daughters and one son. Elida's illness was a painful and shocking event that took Horacio in the middle of his IPA Presidency. As a witness to all that Horacio did, on one hand to keep working as President, on the other to take care personally of his wife with love and compassion, I can only say that courage in the face of adversity, as well as determination and strength to sustain and follow one's convictions and to preserve ethical values, constitute the matter of what makes the thread that runs along his long and productive life.

## References and further reading

1  *The perverse transference and other matters*, Aronson, New Jersey 1997. Edited by Jorge Olagaray, Jorge Ahumada, Arlene Kramer-Richards and Arnold Richards.

2  *Truth, Reality and Psychoanalysis. Latin American Contributions to Psychoanalysis*. International Psychoanalysis Library. General Editor Emma Piccioli. Editors Sergio Lewkowicz and Silvia Flechner. London, 2005. (1–21).

3  *Las tareas del Psicoanálisis*, Polemos, Buenos Aires, 2000. Edited by Jorge Olagaray, Jorge Ahumada, Arlene Kramer-Richards and Arnold Richards.

4  Jorge H. Stitzman: *Conversaciones con R. Horacio Etchegoyen*. Buenos Aires, Amorrortu, 1998. (51–52).

# 31

# INTERPRETATION FOR THE RECONSTRUCTION OF EARLY PSYCHIC DEVELOPMENT

*R. Horacio Etchegoyen*[1]

*Etchegoyen wrote this paper to be read at the 32nd International Psychoanalytical Congress, Helsinki, in July 1981, and it was published in 1982 by the* International Journal of Psycho-Analysis, *63: 65–75.*

The purpose of the psychoanalytic treatment is to reconstruct the past filling in the gaps of childhood memories, which are the result of repression. This is achieved by overcoming the resistances and solving the transference through the analysis of dreams, parapraxes and screen memories, no less than symptoms and character traits. The theories on human development, infantile sexuality and the Oedipus complex formulated by Freud using this method were strongly supported not only by the results of the treatment but also by the psychoanalysis of children, which can study these same phenomena *in status nascendi*.

In the small child, lacking verbal instruments for communication, the problems to be investigated cannot be reached directly through language, but there remains the possibility to see them reproduced in the transference and to interpret them, waiting for the patient's associations to support or refute us.

For the purposes of this presentation, we shall call *early* development (or conflict) the pre-verbal period when there is no preconscious record of memories and which approximately covers the pre-oedipal stage described by Freud (1931), (1933) and Mack-Brunswick (1940), and we are going to differentiate it from *childhood* development (or conflict) which corresponds to the Oedipus complex discovered by Freud between 3 and 5 years of age.

On the basis of clinical material, I shall put forward the following points:

Early development is integrated to personality and can be reconstructed during the analytical process, since it is expressed in the transference and it is testable through the response of the analysand.

Early conflict appears in the analytical situation, preferably in the form of pre- or para-verbal language (that is, not articulate language but a language of action), and tends to shape the psychotic aspect of the transference as a function of partial objects, dyadic relationships and early Oedipus complex, while the childhood conflict is mostly expressed by verbal representations and screen memories, that is to say, as a transference neurosis.

Sometimes it is possible to observe the early, the childhood and the actual conflict simultaneously linked to the same structure.

The reports supplied by the analysand about this early development must be considered screen memories, beliefs and familiar myths that actually change in the course of the treatment.

The psychoanalytic treatment reveals the historical truth (psychic reality), how the individual processes facts and how facts influenced the individual, not the material truth, which is unattainable in its infinite variety.

There is no incompatibility between interpretation and construction, since the interpretation of the transference implies a comparison, counterpoint-like, of the present and the past as members of a single structure.

The life history of the patient is always his own *theory* about himself and which the psychoanalytic treatment must re-formulate in more definite and flexible terms.

The concept of traumatic situation should be reserved only for the economic, since the dynamic conflict always takes place between subject and environment in a complemental series.

An adequate and rigorous handling of the transference relationship makes it possible to analyze the early conflict without resorting to any type of active therapy or controlled regression, because the purpose of analysis is not to correct the facts of the past but to *reconceptualize* them.

If it is accepted that there exists an early transference fully able to unfold during the treatment and which could be solved by psychoanalytic methods, it becomes possible to use it as a presupposed theory[2] to investigate early development and test the theories that attempt to explain it, but this subject is beyond the scope of my report.

he was seriously ill and detailed his symptoms: inability to think and concentrate, inclination to drink and take psycho-stimulants, sexual difficulties (lack of desire, impotence) and anti-Semitic feelings despite his being a Jew. He also pointed out the blocking of his affects and illustrated it with his indifference at the death of his analyst.

About my diagnosis it is enough to say that he is a borderline patient with a strong pharmacotimic structure and a manifest perversion – *froteur*. in order to reach orgasm he rubs his genitals on the woman, avoiding coitus. He was not conscious of this perversion, which sometimes he grossly rationalized.

He said he did not remember anything about his childhood although he reported, without expressing any emotion, that *when he was two months old he had almost starved to death because his mother's milk had suddenly stopped flowing.*

This event had never been evaluated by Mr. Brown. It was his former analyst who inferred that he had probably suffered hunger as a child. The patient replied, giving the above-mentioned report, and was surprised by the aptness of the analyst, whom he took more seriously from then on although he never stopped looking down on him.

On the other hand, he liked me from the start, although he considered me a beginner. Having learned from the colleague who sent him to me that I had just arrived from London, he was sure he was my first patient if not the only one in my whole career. When interpreting his jealousy for his siblings in the face of this material, I only succeeded in getting a condescending smile; he did not even listen when I told him that he was putting his need in me, as he saw me hungry for patients.

During the first months he remained cool and distant; sometimes he would suddenly go to sleep when I interpreted something which might appear new to him. He would often feel hungry before or after the session, and then unusually clear coprophagic fantasies appeared. He dreamed that *at a small restaurant he was served cat stew. He felt a terrible loathing, but somebody told him to eat it, that he would not have noticed it if the dish had been presented as hare. The stew smelled of cat's excrement.*

This dream was useful to point out his mistrust of the analyst, who gives him cat for hare, and his desire to feed on his own feces in order not to be dependent.

The boastful tone that Abraham (1920) traced back to the idealization of emunctory functions and excreta was the center of his defensive system, many times linked to anal masturbation (Meltzer, 1966).

His persistent aerophagia, which years later would be a significant indicator of his traumatic suckling period, appeared as a cause of hilarity and mockery. He remembered that he used to belch with his former analyst and that when the latter pointed it out, Brown replied that he was paying for his belching. When I interpreted that he was proud of his belching and his money, he remembered that *he started analysis precisely because of his flatus and his meteorism*, as well as for his gastric problems and his difficulty in studying. On account of these symptoms, a psychiatrist, Dr M, recommended analysis to him.

A few months later he dreamed that

*he was in a bar and they brought him a bottle of some soft drink with a dead fly lying on the crown cap. He hesitated between drinking or complaining to the waiter and finally he decided to complain.*

In relation to his dream he remembered another from his former analysis:

*I dreamed that I was in front of Dr M's Clinic and there was a group of people eating human flesh. One of them took a half putrid skull, rubbed the inside with a piece of bread and ate the brains spread on that piece of bread.*

He associated with a time when he was on the point of discontinuing his analysis for financial reasons, and M proposed group therapy. I told him that these dreams partially explained his difficulties of thinking and concentrating; and, after Freud (1917b) and Abraham (1924), I added that to undergo analysis meant for him to feed on the analyst's thoughts in a very concrete way, but being unable to tolerate them, he expelled them as if they were feces, which he ingested again as food. The patient replied that in that very moment his mouth watered at the thought! He added, with strong resistance, that this often happened to him with nauseating smells, including his feces.

As a result of this session he was anguished; he felt like crying and internally asking me for help. He immediately became angry because the treatment did not cure him and once again entertained the thought of discontinuing it. He constantly stated that psychoanalysis is not a human relationship but a cold business transaction.

The coprophagic fantasies and the manic defenses, always linked to his disorder of thought, took a long stretch of his analysis. At the same time throughout this period, his Oedipal jealousies, the rivalry with his father and his homosexual impulses were being analyzed. The wish to suck the

became evident. For example, he dreamed that

*he was pulling at three thick cords which came out of his throat*

and which he associated with tentacles. This dream was interpreted as his desire to hold fast to the analytical breast and suck it; this seems to be confirmed by another dream he had on that same night:

*I dreamed, also, of a little girl who desperately wanted to suck my cigarette.*
*I took it from her mouth and she stretched desperately to suck.*

Here his orality has been projected while he becomes a father who frustrates the wishes of his little-girl-part. The fact that there are voracious and aggressive feelings for the father's penis inside the mother's body is shown by a third dream in which

*he enters a bank (mother's body) and they want him to kill the cashier (father's penis). He refuses to do it and, when he is arrested, he denies any connection with the crime and succeeds in fleeing.*

Some time afterwards, when paying overdue fees, he remembered again the time in which he suffered hunger during lactation, *when he almost starved to death because his mother did not realize his need, in spite of the fact that he cried and cried the whole day long.*

It is worthwhile comparing this version with that given during his interview, because here there is the added fact that he cried and cried the whole day long. This modification shows, in my opinion, that the blocking (repression) of his affects has shifted, which also implies that the reports concerning early psychic development must be considered screen memories (Freud, 1899), in spite of the fact that they are told as actual facts, as true stories reported by parents and other members of the family.

Once the emotional blockage is overcome he now cries and cries the whole day long: my fees are too high, psychoanalysis is just blah–blah–blah, if he cannot pay me it is because of his difficulties, for which I am also responsible. This acute transference conflict culminates with the following dream:

> *I am in your consulting room, you are sitting beside me like a clinical doctor. Grieving, I am telling you that I suffer terribly because I have opened my feelings to others. You seem to be in sympathy with my suffering and you also have a look of intense suffering on your face, perhaps a little too much. Then three persons burst into the room: a deformed man and a woman, I don't remember the third one. They were friends of yours who came to play cards or for group psychotherapy. I had changed my clothes and was looking for my underpants so that they would not see them soiled with shit. I found some underpants which probably belonged to you. You fondled me and touched me to calm my grief.*

He associated the woman in the dream with one he had seen a few days before in my consulting room and was jealous of. More conscious of his needs, he is now vulnerable to sorrow: he wants me to calm him down, but he is afraid to come close and feel jealous and/or homosexually attracted. In order that his dirty things may not be found out, he confuses himself with me through projective identification (Klein, 1946), by donning my underpants.

At times he admits that analysis is his only company and then he wants to destroy me. His overdue payments now have a shade of provocation and rivalry, while at the same time he wants to keep my money in order not to feel lonely. When he says that my money keeps him company, his mouth waters. When he gets a rise in salary, his first thought is that he has to pay me and he feels angry.

When he is about to buy a flat to live by himself, he dreams that

> *I am analyzing him in the street under a triumphal arch: he shouts because we are quite a distance from each other. While he is being analyzed he quickly creeps closer lying on his back all the time.*

This dream, where his approach is seen plastically, was interpreted in terms of the complete Oedipus complex: he is attracted by the mother's genitals (triumphal arch) which are being guarded by the father's rival penis, which also excites him.

The purchase of the flat, his promotion in the company and the improvement of his erotic life make him feel that he is much better, and this causes him anger and fear: he is afraid of destroying me with his improvements

351

and he is afraid of trusting me. I interpret this fear as springing from an initial trust in the breast which later disappointed him, and he replies with a memory that I consider fundamental: *when he was 7 or 8 years old a maid told him that a child had starved to death because the mother would give him water when he cried out of hunger, to keep him quiet without feeding him.*

This memory is undoubtedly a new version of his breast-feeding period

transference resistance: 'You think that you improve because of your analysis and want to trust me; but something makes you think that the analytic food is only water'. I reminded him of his recent wish to consult a G.P. who 'will fix everything with two injections' and his reiterated assertions that analysis is just blah-blah-blah, as well as a fantasy told a few days before: *I'm going to a service station where they inject air under pressure into me through my anus to clean me.*

This material illustrates the main thesis of my paper: early conflict is not torn off from the rest of the personality, and can be reconstructed from subsequent data that basically have the same meaning. The fact that the pre-verbal experience may be assigned a meaning *afterwards* as proposed by Freud (1918), or have a meaning from the start is not decisive: it is enough that one experience acquires a meaning *a posteriori* to justify the assertion that we can reach it and reconstruct it: the material suggests, on good grounds, that the fantasy of Brown's latency period (the child who was fed water) is isomorphic with the experience of his breast-feeding period.

I also believe that interpretation and construction are complementary phases of a single process.[4] If transference implies superimposing past and present, then we cannot think that an interpretation of the here and now can be given without the perspective of the past, nor that history can be restored without dealing with the ever-present transference involvement. In other words, it is not only essential to elucidate what happens in the present to clear away the past but also to use recollections and memories to enlighten the transference. Racker (1958) humorously used to say that there are analysts who envisage transference only as an obstacle to recover the past while others use the past as a mere instrument to analyze the transference (p. 59); but, as I have just pointed out, a twofold approach is necessary. 'Both the patient dwelling on the past and his persistent adherence to the present can function as resistance', says Kris (1956, p. 56). On the other hand, as suggested by Blum (1980), it is necessary to achieve a synergic action between the analysis of resistance and reconstruction

(p. 40) to restore the continuity and coherence of the personality (p. 50). Thus understood, the analysis of transference delimits the past and the present, discriminates between the objective and the subjective. When this is achieved, the past need not be repeated and remains like a reserve of experiences that can be applied to understand the present and forecast the future – not to misunderstand them.

Since the story of the child who was fed water, he was harassed by meteorism, and his swollen belly made him think of an undernourished baby. He gained 10 pounds in a month and his tendency to sleep when receiving an interpretation was intensified. Now envy had an important place; he progressed in order to awaken envy in other people and he limited his progress in order not to awaken it. Through his somnolence he regulates the session to control his envy (and also to express it); at the same time he puts his hunger and his desperation, his undernourished baby, into me.

He now has this dream:

> I dreamed that we were in bed and you examined my belly, sore and full of flatulence. You palpated it and massaged it gently with a circular movement to ease my pain, while saying in a deep voice that I was ill, that it was a "somatization".

He associated with the other dream of my consulting room approximately a year and a half before, and he remarked that I acted as a physician and there was nothing erotic; once when he was a child he had a stomach-ache and his father told him to massage his stomach.

I interpreted that he needed me as a father to ease his pain: he felt that I could take out of his body, with my hand-penis, the bad air put there by the empty breast of his mother – who is I myself when I speak in vain. In reconstructive terms, I suggested that when he was on the verge of starving to death, his father somehow helped him.

Without understanding the essential part of the interpretation, he accepted that there must be a homosexual wish, and dropped off to sleep. I interpreted that he had now made his dream come true: we were sleeping together in bed, and the undernourished baby turns into the pregnant mother. The former interpretation points at the dependence tie; this one, to the erotization.

The following year, when he has already been five years under analysis, most symptoms have remitted: coprophagic fantasies no longer appear, his mouth does not water at nauseating smells and he does not expel his thoughts, that is, he can pay attention and study, although with a certain difficulty; he now leads a regular, even satisfactory, sexual life. On the other hand, the psychoanalytic process is far from easy. Although his Olympian scorn has disappeared, he strongly resists trusting and his demands and rivalry continuously check the analytic setting.

He remembered that at the age of 5 *he used to play with a little girl at the ballerina and the devil.* This game, which coincides with the peak moment of the Oedipus complex, is related to masturbation in the face of the primal scene and fits in with a screen memory of that time: *he thought there were devils and*

devil was also interpreted after Rosenfeld (1971), as two parts of his self: infantile dependent (ballerina) and omnipotent narcissistic (devil).

About the middle of his fifth year in analysis he brought an important dream to assess his co-operation. At that time he was interested in the treatment and wanted to recover.

> *I dreamed I was with Charles working enthusiastically on air filters. We had become independent from the company and were doing very well. We had built the first absolute filter in the country and were about to manufacture a particle counter, which measures filter efficiency.*

He associated that in the dream he felt as if he had ended analysis and was cured; his sexual problem has not been solved; the absolute filter sterilizes air.

I interpreted the dream as a will to recover, with my help (Charles), from the noxious air that causes his meteorism (therapeutic alliance) and at the same time as masturbatory sexual play between siblings, which makes analysis useless (pseudo-alliance). The dream relates to an important progress: from his new position as manager he actively promoted air filtration and soon became a renowned specialist.[5]

At the beginning of his sixth year under treatment he started a relationship with a woman whom he trusted and who sexually attracted him, whom he later married. He lived this decision as a great achievement of his analysis. During a session which he expressed these feelings, meteorism appeared. I interpreted that he saw me as another who was giving birth to him recovered, and he wanted to imitate me. His meteorism abated dramatically, and this awakened contradictory feelings of trust and rivalry. A short time later, in a session in which he fell sleep, he dreamed that

> *he was with an old and bad woman with empty breasts from which only air flowed.*

Parallel to his progress his defensive system became almost impervious: he interpreted himself, he went to sleep when I spoke, he repeated my interpretations aloud thus making them his own, etc.; he often interrupted me and completed on his own what I was going to say. He was now the perfect example of the patient who is difficult to reach (Joseph, 1975).

As his abdominal symptoms increased, he consulted a G.P. who promised to cure him in a week. This gave him great joy because he was going to prove I was wrong; but he did not give the physician the pleasure of curing him. In the previous session I had once more interpreted his meteorism as pregnancy but he had not listened to me. This time he had to acknowledge, however, that his wife had a brief menstrual delay; he thought she was pregnant and was jealous of the child – just as I had interpreted a few days before.[6]

The meteorism as a model of his identification with the pregnant woman now appeared more linked to envy rather than to jealousy. I tell him he wants it to be he the one who is giving birth to the child, but without being fecundated by my interpretations. Astonished he replies that the abdominal tension has decreased and meteorism has disappeared.[7]

Around this time he had a very significant dream. He arrived with meteorism and abdominal troubles, while his wife's amenorrhea persisted.

> I dreamed that my car had broken down and I took it to the service station. They said that the compressor did not work properly and a thorough examination was necessary to see whether it was serious. I was surprised because my car does not have a compressor. I thought it must be something very serious, equivalent to cancer.

This dream expresses the conflict at all levels: early, childhood and actual. Mr. Brown's *actual conflict* is that he believes that he had made his wife pregnant and is going to be a father; this compels him to be more adult and responsible. The *childhood conflict* is related to the Oedipus complex and sibling jealousy. This time he remembered the strong feeling of grief at 5 when his (only) sister was born. Finally, the *early conflict* appears very clearly expressed by the compressor, an introjected breast that insufflates air instead of feeding.

His meteorism as an air pregnancy is represented in two ways: by the compressor and because he thinks that his car does not have one. This two-fold representation also applied to his wife's pregnancy, which is still imaginary because it is not confirmed and because of his ambivalence; at the same time it symbolizes Mr. Brown's pseudocyesis with a compressor (uterus) that does not exist in his male body.

As representation of the analytical process, the dream shows with dramatic precision the current moment: we are investigating something that does not exist, which is only air, words gone with the wind and which, however, is as serious as a cancer. The analytical process had been arrested; it had no depth and had become a perverse sexual activity (*froteur*) despite all my efforts. Lacking any emotional meaning, the interpretations were water

It is important to point out that this impasse repeats the lactation conflict with astonishing clarity, while the Oedipus complex is remembered and revived at another level of communication. Two organizational forms are thus observed: neurotic and psychotic (Bion, 1957). The neurotic conflict contains the triangular situation of a 5-year-old child who is jealous of his sister's birth, the intense anxiety in the face of the primal scene through the screen memory of witches and devils, child masturbation (the devil and the ballerina) and the sexual games with maids and little friends – which he now remembered vividly.

The conflict with the breast is expressed in a different way, by means of a language of action, without any verbal representations or memories; the same holds for the early Oedipus complex (Klein, 1928), (1945). Analysis reaches them, however, even though the meanders of technique are different and the analyst, on the vortex of repetition, finds himself changed into the empty breast that insufflated flatus into his baby-patient. The fact that this is a very painful process for the analyst does not in any way deny the beauty of our method, the reliability of our theories.

For the purposes of this paper, it is important that the early conflict finds various forms of expression that show its coherent unity with life and history: the adult who went to consult for aerophagea is the child in the latency period who is impressed by the story of the baby fed with water and hears the story of his unfortunate breast-feeding period, as well as the suckling who thought he was receiving air (flatus) instead of food, the man with the coprophagic fantasies who takes feces for food and eructation for words, the specialist in air filtration.

The unity of this story is the basis for our thesis that early experiences leave their imprint and are later on expressed reliably in the latent ideas of the family myths and the subject's fantasies, in screen memories and character traits no less than in symptoms and vocation.

My other thesis is that early experiences can be reached by the classical psychoanalytical technique although it is exceedingly difficult to solve them.

Most ego psychologists think that early conflicts cannot be analyzed. Zetzel (1968) asserts that the boundaries between the transference neurosis and the therapeutic alliance – a necessary condition for analyzability – can only be delimited if the dyadic conflicts with the mother and the father have been solved separately. Although I have just said that early relationships are analyzable, from a practical point of view I share the misgivings of the ego psychology, without ceasing to think that in *every* patient there appear early conflict and psychotic mechanisms.

Some authors, on the other hand, consider that early conflicts can be analyzed by changing the technique. If the primitive emotional development is affected, says Winnicott (1955), the psychoanalytic work must be left in abeyance, 'management being the whole thing' (p. 17). Formerly, the Budapest school had supported similar ideas on the basis of Ferenczi's active technique (1919), (1920) and his theory of trauma (1930), (1931), (1932) which inspires Balint's *new beginning* (1937), (1952) to account for primary object love. This is the line taken by A. & D. Anzieu (1977); for them, serious failures in development demand technical changes, because only concrete experiences can alleviate them: inasmuch as it is a specifically symbolic act, interpretation can never reach what has not been symbolized.

These arguments have the definite support of common sense but, however, the history of science shows us that common sense can be misleading. In the case presented here, a highly traumatic experience during the first months of life was incorporated to the personality of the patient, acquiring a symbolic value, to which we gain access through interpretation. The fact is that the 2-month-old suckling child who 'cannot understand our language' is part of a child and of an adult who communicate us with him.

The corollary is that I did not need to give this patient the opportunity to regress. He fully relived his breast-feeding conflict in the classical analytical setting without any type of active therapy or controlled regression. As an analyst I applied my method rigorously and when I erroneously abandoned it, I tried to recover through a silent analysis of my countertransference, without any concessions for my mistakes.[8]

Finally, the theoretical evaluation of the infantile traumatic experiences must be discussed. In the case reported there appears an environmental situation that actually endangered the subject's life; however, if we intend to continue using the transference theory consistently to understand the past, we must realize that things are not simple. In the transferential repetition we find a baby-patient who is continuously operating on the father and the penis, on the mother and the breast, on the primal scene. It will be said, rightly, that he does it to render that catastrophic experience active; but can this exclude a more complex action between the child and its parents? In the same way that he sleeps in the session so as not to receive the interpretation, he could have gone to sleep on the breast, thus partially conditioning the agalactia. This hypothesis is logical and there is nothing in the material to refute it. I am not saying that this will confirm Klein's primal envy (1957), because other equally plausible explanations could be offered, but I do think that the conflict always occurs between the subject and the human environment with which he interacts, as in Freud's complemental

ment (his abandonment by his parents, the substitute care of Corinthian kings, etc.).

In spite of Freud's warnings (1937) historical truth is often confused with material truth. The *material truth* is the objective facts, which have infinite variables and therefore explanations. What is accessible to the psychoanalytical method is *historical truth* (psychic reality), the way in which each one of us processes facts. That is why I find it is better to speak about psychical reality and factual reality as Freud does in 'Totem and taboo' (1913, pp. 159–61) or about reality and fantasy following Isaacs (1948) and Segal (1964). In the 'Project' (1895), Freud speaks accordingly of thought reality and external reality (p. 373).

The report of a patient about his traumatic situations and in general about his history is a personal version, a manifest content which must be interpreted, and actually changes during the course of analysis.

We have seen that when the affective blockage was lifted, Brown modified the version of his trauma during the suckling period. Two years after the compressor dream, when the impasse had given way and analysis was coming to an end, a new change took place. At that time the analysand, more conscious of his greed and ruthlessness, was afraid of tiring me. Upon the return from his holidays he dreamed that

> *he played sexual games with a girl: he kissed her, and the girl's tongue, growing enormous, remained in his mouth when they moved away from each other.*

I interpreted that he eroticized the psychoanalytic link, denying the separation during the holidays, and I added that the girl's tongue was my complacent nipple which allowed him to be attached to the breast all the time, in order to prevent the repetition of his catastrophic weaning. He made a comment about his being worried because of his payment being once more overdue and suddenly remembered that *the trouble in his breast-feeding period was not that his mother lost her milk and that he starved until they started feeding him with the bottle, but just the opposite: it was with the bottle that he suffered hunger because they gave him a lower ration than the one ordered by the doctor.* This new version responded, in my opinion, to a structural change: there is now a good breast that gave food and a bad bottle; and the father (doctor) is a protective figure, as suggested in previous material.[9]

The purpose of analysis is not to correct facts from the past, which is impossible anyway, but to *reconceptualize* them. If this is achieved and the patient improves, the new version is more equitable and serene, less manicheistic and persecutory. The subject accepts himself as an actor, an agent, not only as a passive factor; he appreciates better intentions in other people, not only neglect and bad faith; there is a better distribution of guilt; a more important role is assigned to unavoidable adversities of life.

Each one of us keeps a set of reports, memories and stories which, in the form of familiar and personal myths, are processed into a series of *theories*, with which we face and order reality, as well as our relationship with others and with the world. I use the word 'theory' in a strict sense, a scientific hypothesis which attempts to explain reality and can be refuted by facts, as taught by Popper (1962); and which, to my mind, coincides with the psychoanalytic concept of unconscious fantasy. Neurosis (and in general mental sickness) may be defined from this point of view as an attempt to maintain our theories in spite of the facts that refute them (Bion's link minus K, 1962); and what we call *transference* from a clinical point of view is the attempt to adjust facts to our theories, instead of testing our theories with the facts.

The aim of the psychoanalytical process is to review the patient's theories and render them more rigorous and flexible. This is attained through the interpretation and particularly through mutative interpretation (Strachey, 1934) where the present and the past are joined for a brief period to show us that our theory of considering them identical was wrong.

## Summary

Early psychic development is included in the personality and appears in the transference; the progress of the analytical process shows in turn that the changes achieved by the treatment transform the text of the original conflict. This twofold modification, concurrent and reciprocal, suggests that the reports concerning the early conflict must be considered screen memories, in spite of their being reported as actual facts.

A complete interpretation throws light on the past from the present and on the present from the past: interpretation and construction complement each other; they cannot be defined separately. Transference analysis distinguishes the past from the present, discriminates between the objective and the subjective. When this is attained, the past need not be repeated and remains as a reserve of experiences that are useful to understand the present and predict the future, not to misunderstand them.

Although early development becomes integrated to personality and

psychotic mechanisms. The early conflict can be analyzed and the classical technique can be used on it, although it is more difficult to solve than neurotic cases, which by the way are never pure.

The psychoanalytic method shows the historical truth (psychic reality), not the material truth, which is unattainable in its infinite variety. Each of us keeps a set of memories and beliefs that, processed into a series of *theories*, regulate our relationship with the world. The purpose of analysis is not to correct facts from the past but to *reconceptualize* them. The aim of the analytical process is to review the patient's theories and make them more rigorous and flexible. This is attained through the interpretation, which links the present to the past, in order to show us that our theory of considering them identical was wrong.

# Notes

1  The author is most grateful to Sheila Navarro de Lopez, Gregorio Klimovsky, David Liberman and Benito M. Lopez for their reading of, and commentary on, the manuscript.

2  By presupposed theory I understand an instrument which is applied without questioning its validity at the time, such as the optical theory of the telescope in the case of an astronomer.

3  The technical aspects were discussed in a seminar conducted by Miss Betty Joseph in Buenos Aires in January 1974. Formerly I discussed this case with León Grinberg.

4  Greenacre says: 'Any clarifying interpretation generally includes some reference to reconstruction' (1975, p. 703).

5  I was referring to this point when speaking of his sublimations.

6  This apparent insight many times only meant that he (and not I) said it.

7  To understand the strength of his defensive system it must be taken into account that the fertile interpretation of this moment may later on become blah-blah-blah which fills his abdomen with gases (imaginary pregnancy).

8  My tolerance in overdue payments could be considered a parameter (Eissler, 1953); but it was not something introduced by me, and I analyzed it as any other symptom.

9  Three years after ending analysis, in a follow-up interview, he challenged the memory once more and said that he *went hungry when he was bottle-fed because the dose indicated by the doctor was insufficient.*

# References

ABRAHAM, K. 1920 The narcissistic evaluation of excretory processes in dreams and neurosis. In *Selected Papers* London: Hogarth Press, 1973 pp. 318–322.

ABRAHAM, K. 1924 A short study of the development of the libido, viewed in the light of mental disorders. In *Selected Papers* London: Hogarth Press, 1973 pp. 418–501.

ANZIEU, A. & ANZIEU, D. 1977 La interpretación en primera persona. In *Prácticas Psicoanalíticas Comparadas en las Neurosis* ed. León Grinberg. Buenos Aires: Paidós.

BALINT, M. 1937 Early developmental states of the ego. Primary object love *International Journal of Psycho-Analysis* 30: 265–273 [1949].

BALINT, M. 1952 New beginning and the paranoid and the depressive syndromes *International Journal of Psycho-Analysis* 33: 214–224.

BION, W. R. 1957 Differentiation of the psychotic from the non-psychotic personalities *International Journal of Psycho-Analysis* 38: 266–275.

BION, W. R. 1962 *Learning from Experience* London: W. Heinemann.

BLUM, H. P. 1980 The value of reconstruction in adult psychoanalysis *International Journal of Psycho-Analysis* 61: 39–52.

BRENMAN, E. 1980 The value of reconstuction in adult psychoanalysis *International Journal of Psycho-Analysis* 61: 53–60 [*Psicoanál.* 2: 1167–1183, 1980].

EISSLER, K. R. 1953 The effect of the structure of the ego on psychoanalytic technique *Journal of the American Psychoanalytic Association* 1: 104–143.

ERIKSON, E. 1950 *Childhood and Society* New York: Norton.

FERENCZI, S. 1919 Technical difficulties in the analysis of a case of hysteria. In *The Theory and Technique of Psycho-Analysis* p. 189 London: Hogarth Press, 1926 Buenos Aires: Paidós, 1967 p. 155.

FERENCZI, S. 1920 The further development of an active therapy in psychoanalysis. In *The Theory and Technique of Psycho-Analysis* p. 198 Buenos Aires, p. 162.

FERENCZI, S. 1930 The principle of relaxation and neocatharsis *International Journal of Psycho-Analysis* 11: 428–443.

FERENCZI, S. 1931 Child-analysis in the analysis of adults *International Journal of Psycho-Analysis* 12: 468–482.

FERENCZI, S. 1932 Confusion of tongues between adults and the child. The language of tenderness and of passion. In *Final Contributions to the Problems and*

*Methods of Psycho-Analysis* London: Hogarth Press, 1955 Buenos Aires: Paidós, 1966.

FREUD, S. 1895 Project for a scientific psychology *The complete psychological works of Sigmund Freud*, S.E. 1.

FREUD, S. 1899 Screen memories *The complete psychological works of Sigmund Freud*, S.E. 3.

~~FREUD, S. 1913~~ *~~The~~ ~~Sigmund Freud, S.E. 14.~~*

FREUD, S. 1918 From the history of an infantile neurosis *The complete psychological works of Sigmund Freud*, S.E. 17.

FREUD, S. 1931 Female sexuality *The complete psychological works of Sigmund Freud*, S.E. 21.

FREUD, S. 1933 Femininity. In *The complete psychological works of Sigmund Freud*, S.E. 22.

FREUD, S. 1937 Constructions in analysis *The complete psychological works of Sigmund Freud*, S.E. 23.

GARMA, A. 1950 On the pathogenesis of peptic ulcer *International Journal of Psycho-Analysis* 31: 53–72.

GARMA, A. 1954 Génesis Psicosomática y Tratamiento de las Alceras Gástricas y Duodenales Buenos Aires: Nova.

GREENACRE, P. 1975 On reconstruction *Journal of the American Psychoanalytic Association* 23: 693–671.

ISAACS, S. 1948 The nature and function of phantasy *International Journal of Psycho-Analysis* 29: 73–97.

JOSEPH, B. 1975 The patient who is difficult to reach. In *Tactics and Techniques in Psychoanalytic Therapy Vol. 2* ed. Peter L. Giovacchini. New York: Aronson, pp. 205–216.

KLEIN, M. 1928 Early stages of the Oedipus conflict. In *Love, Guilt and Reparation and Other Works* London: Hogarth Press, 1975 pp. 186–198.

KLEIN, M. 1945 The Oedipus Complex in the light of early anxieties. In *Love, Guilt and Reparation and Other Works* pp. 370–419.

KLEIN, M. 1946 Notes on some schizoid mechanisms. In *Envy and Gratitude and Other Works* London: Hogarth Press, pp. 1–24.

KLEIN, M. 1957 *Envy and Gratitude* London: Hogarth Press, 1975.

KRIS, E. 1956 The recovery of childhood memories in psychoanalysis *Psychoanal. Study Child* 11: 54–88.

MACK-BRUNSWICK, R. 1940 The preoedipal phase of the libido development *The Psychoanalytic Quarterly* 9: 293–319.

MELTZER, D. 1966 The relation of anal masturbation to projective identification *International Journal of Psycho-Analysis* 47: 335–342.

MIRSKY, I. A., KAPLAN, S. & BROH-KAHN, R. H. 1950 Pepsinogen (uropepsin) excretion as an index of the influence of various life situations on gastric secretion *Proceedings of the Association for Research in Nervous and Mental Disease* 29: 638.

MIRSKY, I. A. et al. 1952 Blood plasma pepsinogen I y II *Journal of Laboratory and Clinical Medicine* 40.

MONEY-KYRLE, R. 1971 The aim of psychoanalysis In *Collected Papers* ed. Donald Meltzer. Perthsire: Clunie Press, 1978 pp. 442–449.

POPPER, K. R. 1962 *La Lógica de la Investigación Científica* Madrid: Tecnos, 1967.

RACKER, H. 1958 Sobre técnica clásica y técnicas actuales del psicoanálisis In *Estudios sobre Técnica Psicoanalítica*, 2 Buenos Aires: Paidós, 1960.

ROSENFELD, H. 1971 A clinical approach to the psychoanalytic theory of the life and death instincts: an investigation into the aggressive aspects of narcissism *International Journal of Psycho-Analysis* 52: 169–178.

SEGAL, H. 1964 Symposium on fantasy *International Journal of Psycho-Analysis* 45: 191–194.

STRACHEY, J. 1934 The nature of the therapeutic action of psycho-analysis *International Journal of Psycho-Analysis* 15: 127–159.

WINNICOTT, D. W. 1955 Metapsychological and clinical aspects of regression within the psychoanalytical set-up *International Journal of Psycho-Analysis* 36: 16–26.

ZETZEL, E. R. 1968 The so-called good hysteric *International Journal of Psycho-Analysis* 49: 256–260.

# 32

# TO THE PATIENT'S PROJECTIVE IDENTIFICATION[1]

## *León Grinberg*

*Paper published in 1962 by the* International Journal of Psycho-Analysis, *43: 436–440.*

In previous papers (3), (4) I have dealt with some changes in the analytic technique resulting from the analysands' massive use of projective identification. The excessive use of this mechanism, in certain situations, gives rise to a specific reaction in the analyst, who is unconsciously and passively 'led' to play the sort of role the patient hands over to him. For this particular reaction, I suggested the term 'projective counter-identification'.

I then pointed out that it had to do with a very specific and partial aspect of the countertransference. But I consider it especially important to stress this aspect in order to show the difference existing between the response I have in mind and the countertransference reactions resulting from the analyst's own emotional attitudes, or on his neurotic remnants, reactivated by the patient's conflicts. With a view to making this difference clearer, I should like to describe in a schematic form the two processes that co-exist in the analyst's mind.

In process A the analyst is the active subject of the patient's introjective and projective mechanisms. In this process, and based on Fliess's remarks (2), three important phases can be described: (i) when the analyst selectively introjects the different aspects of the patient's verbal and non-verbal material, together with their corresponding emotional charges; (ii) when the analyst works through and assimilates the identifications resulting from the said identification of the patient's inner world; and (iii) when the analyst (re)projects the results of this assimilation by means of interpretations.

On the other hand, in process B, the analyst is the passive object of the analysand's projections and introjections. In this case, however, two further situations may still develop: (i) that the analyst's emotional response may be due to his own conflicts or anxieties, intensified or reactivated by the patient's conflicting material; and (ii) that the emotional response may be quite independent from the analyst's own emotions and appear mainly as a reaction to the analysand's projections upon him.

The second process presents for us considerable interest, especially in connection with the problem raised in this paper. In one phase, it is the analysand who, in an active though unconscious way, projects his inner conflicts upon the analyst, who acts in this case as a passive recipient of such projections.

This projective-identification process being constant, the analyst's reactions to it will be similar to his reactions towards the material he has already introjected by an active process of selection. On some occasions, however, the analysand's projective identification mechanism may become too active – owing either to an exaggerated intensity of its emotional charges or to the violence with which this same mechanism was imposed on him during childhood.

Melanie Klein's papers (5), (6), especially those dealing with her concept of projective identification, are sufficiently known to require further comments. I consider that her paper 'On Identification' constitutes, at present, the most complete study of the contents and functioning of the projective identification mechanism; according to her description, it implies a combination of the splitting mechanism, the subsequent projection of the split parts onto another person, with the ensuing loss of those parts, and an alteration of the object-perception mechanism. This process is bound up with the processes that take place during the first three or four months of life (paranoid-schizoid position), when splitting is at its maximum height, with a predominance of persecutory anxieties.

It follows, then, that the essential aspect in the functioning of that mechanism is that the subject projects his own conflicts, emotions, or parts into the object. But should we assume that the analyst does not play a part in this process that he does not react to his patient's active projective identification? In my opinion, there is quite often a specific response more or less intense on the part of the analyst; this fact has been confirmed by experience.

Let me first point out that although there is a dual participation in the process I am describing – as always happens in the analytic situation – the main emphasis should be attributed to the extreme violence of the projective identification mechanism of the analysand. I shall show, later on, in some clinical examples, how the particular intensity of this mechanism is usually related to traumatic infantile experiences, during which the patient suffered the effect of violent projective identifications.

Whenever the analyst has to meet such violent projective identifications,

a   By an immediate and equally violent rejection of the material that the patient tries to project into him.
b   By ignoring or denying this rejection through a severe control or some other defensive mechanism; sooner or later, however, the reaction will become manifest in some way or other.
c   By postponing and displacing his reaction, which will then become manifest with another patient.
d   By suffering the effects of such an intensive projective identification, and 'counter-identifying' himself, in turn.

In fact, the response of the analyst will depend on his degree of tolerance.

When this counter-identification takes place, the normal communication between the analysand's and the analyst's unconscious will obviously be interrupted. In this case, the unconscious content rejected by the analysand will be violently projected onto the analyst, who, as the recipient object of such projective identifications, will have to suffer its effects. And he will react as if he had acquired and assimilated the parts projected on to him in a real and concrete way.

In certain cases, the analyst may have the feeling of being no longer his own self and of unavoidably becoming transformed into the object that the patient, unconsciously, wanted him to be (id, ego, or some internal object). For this particular situation, I propose the term 'projective counter-identification', i.e. the analyst's specific response to the violent projective identification from the patient, which is not consciously perceived by the former. In such a case, even if this situation prevails only for a short time (although occasionally it may persist, with the ensuing danger) the analyst will resort to all kinds of rationalizations in order to justify his attitude or his bewilderment.

Some clinical examples will serve as a basis for the above considerations.

i. A woman patient came to her first session fifteen minutes late; she lay down on the couch and then remained still and silent during a few minutes.

After that, she said she felt the same as she used to feel when passing an oral examination (which usually caused her great anxiety). Then she associated the analytic session with her wedding night, when, even though she was feeling extremely frightened, she was told that she looked like a statue.

I told her then that what she felt was that she was having with me the same experience that she had had at her oral examinations and during her wedding night, because she feared I might deflower her, introduce myself into her to look at things and examine them. Here, too, she was behaving like a statue; the rigidity and stillness she showed at the beginning of her session were intended to disguise her anxiety, but also to prevent the actual possibility of being penetrated.

Although I realized that this interpretation of her paranoid anxiety was correct, I had the feeling that there was something wrong in it; still, I could not understand the reason for such a feeling. I guessed that my interpretation had been rather superficial and that the facts I had pointed out to her were too near her consciousness. I had to find out the deeper motives of her exaggerated fear of my going into her.

On the other hand, her initial attitude of stiffness had particularly attracted my attention, and I found myself, not without considerable amazement, having the phantasy of analyzing a corpse. A thought came at once into my mind, which took the form of a popular Spanish saying: 'She is trying to force Author into me' (which meant that she wanted to burden me with the whole responsibility and guilt). This thought showed me my own paranoid reaction, aroused by the feeling that she was trying to project her fears into me, through projective identification. Based on this countertransferential feeling, I told her that with her rigidity and silence she wanted perhaps to mean something else, besides the representation of a statue; that she wanted to express in this way some feeling of her own, related to death.

This interpretation was a real shock to her; she began to cry and told me that when she was six years old her mother, who suffered from cancer, had committed suicide. The patient felt responsible for her mother's death, because she had hanged herself in her presence, and it had been actually on account of her delay in warning the rest of the family that the death could not be prevented, as had been done in former attempts. She remembered having watched all the arrangements her mother made and being greatly impressed by them; then she went out and waited for a long while (perhaps 15 minutes, she said); only then did she run for help, but when her father came it was too late.

I had the feeling that with her corpse-like rigidity the patient was not only trying to show that she carried inside a dead object, but also, at the same time, to get rid of it by projective identification. From that moment on, she wanted me unconsciously to take over the responsibility, to bear

'Author'. As a defense against her violent projective identification, with which she tried to introduce into me a dead object, I reacted with my first interpretation, which in fact inverted the situation: she was the one who was afraid of my piercing her. Later on, I managed to grasp the actual meaning of the whole situation, I had a much clearer understanding of the deepest sources of her paranoid anxieties and gave her a correct and more

it is very likely that the utter violence of the patient's projective identification was the result of her mother's intense projective identification, not only during the traumatic episode of her suicide, but also on other occasions.

ii. A student under psycho-analytic training came to his session after having analyzed a 'difficult' patient. During the session with his own patient, he had had the feeling of 'killing himself', owing to his very active interpretations, without, however, obtaining any satisfactory result. He was depressed by the feeling of failure, and after communicating his experience and mood to his training analyst, he remained silent. While listening to his analyst's interpretations, which momentarily did not modify his state of mind, the student had the impression that the same situation he had been complaining about was being repeated, although with inverted roles: he realized that now it was his analyst who was killing himself to obtain some reaction from him, while he was acting in the same way as his patient had done. When, with some surprise, he communicated his impression to the analyst, the latter showed him that his behavior during the session had 'compelled' (his own word) him to identify himself with the patient. The interpretation was then completed in the sense that the student envied his analyst for having better and 'easier' patients (the student himself). A very intense projective identification had thus taken place, by means of which the student unconsciously wanted his analyst to experience his own difficulties. The student recurred to splitting and projected his hampered and dissatisfied professional part on to the analyst, remaining himself with the part of himself identified with his own patient, 'who makes one work and does not gratify'. The training analyst had in turn 'succumbed', so to speak, to the analysand's projection, and felt unconsciously compelled to counter-identify himself with the introjected part.

When this occurs – and this process is much more frequent than is usually believed – the analysand may have the magical unconscious feeling of having accomplished his own phantasies, by 'placing' his parts on the object, which also may arouse in him, in certain cases, a maniacal feeling of triumph over his analyst.

iii. During a certain period of a patient's analysis, with a positive outcome, I observed a strange and uncommon reaction in myself. Throughout a number of sessions, every time he spoke about the possibility of getting married, I felt invaded by an intense drowsiness, which interfered with my relationship to him and his subject. It was not due to boredom, since this was a new and very important aspect in his life; on the contrary, the patient himself spoke cheerfully and with great enthusiasm of his projects. Neither could it be attributed to a general weariness on my part, since the drowsiness appeared only in connection with this particular patient. What surprised me most was my own reaction, which was indeed so strange to my nature. I remembered, though, that at the beginning of his analysis, drowsiness had been a frequent characteristic of this patient, and I was able then, by reinterpreting previous material, to realize that marriage unconsciously meant for him transforming his wife into a servant and a prostitute, as he felt his father had done with his mother.

His intense guilt, not yet definitely overcome, prevented him from accepting a situation that had for him the profound significance of damaging his mother's image. In this case, however, his resistance was placed on me through the projective identification process and, owing to my counter-identification reaction, I actually experienced his drowsiness, which in turn inhibited my interpretations and the progress of his analysis.

This reaction of mine – which resulted from very personal characteristics of the patient – is, in fact, a solid argument to show that my attitude was, in this particular case, a direct and specific consequence of his projective identification.

I then interpreted the whole situation and made him conscious of his resistance, which I had been able to perceive through my own sensations.

The patient then confessed that at times, during the sessions, he had had the phantasy that I had fallen asleep; instead, however, of considering this as a disturbing fact, he felt that he should respect my sleep, because I had already done too much for him. This showed that he had set up a limit, beyond which he neither wanted nor dared to progress, owing to his unconscious guilt. His reparative attitude of letting me rest and deliver myself from the servitude to which he felt he was submitting me, just as he wished to do with his mother, was also evident. On another level, it also meant that he had pushed into me his own drowsiness to avoid seeing the primal scene, because of his envy and his unconscious phantasies.

iv. The following episode was with a patient who, during a certain period of her analysis presented hypochondriacal material referred to certain bodily sensations, was reported to me by Marie Langer. During a session, after a prolonged silence, the analyst felt, at a given moment, a sudden need to move. On the basis of this sensation, she pointed out that the patient was becoming rigid. The latter, however, answered that on the contrary she felt very relaxed, and then asked the analyst why she had said this. The analyst explained to the patient her countertransferential sensation; then the patient did confess that her right leg had actually become rigid, but that she had not said so before because she considered it as something independent of herself. It was evident that the patient had unconsciously perceived

facts presented by Hanna Segal in her paper 'Depression in the Schizophrenic' (7), which, in my opinion, are closely related with the process I have called 'projective counter-identification'. These facts refer, especially, to the projection of the patient's depressive anxieties into the object (analyst) by means of projective identification, and to the specific response aroused in the analyst as a result of such identification, as it should appear from some expressions used by Segal. Let us examine some phrases extracted from her paper: '. . . Then one day as she was dancing round the room, picking some imaginary things from the carpet and making movements as though she was scattering something round the room, it struck me that she must have been imagining that she was dancing in a meadow, picking flowers and scattering them, and it occurred to me that she was behaving exactly like an actress playing the part of Shakespeare's Ophelia. The likeness to Ophelia was all the more remarkable in that, in some peculiar way, the more gaily and irresponsibly she was behaving, the sadder was the effect, as though her gaiety itself was designed to produce sadness in her audience, just as Ophelia's pseudo-gay dancing and singing is designed to make the audience in the theatre sad.'

'Projective counter-identification' was successfully dealt with by Segal by integrating it in an adequate interpretation of her patient's attitude. She pointed out to her that she (the patient) had put into her (the analyst) all her depression and guilt, thereby transforming her into the sad part of herself and, at the same time, into a persecutor, since she felt that the analyst was trying to push her unwanted sadness back into her.

In some cases, projective counter-identification may become a positive element in the analysis, since it clarifies to the analyst some of the patient's contents and attitudes determined by projective identification, and makes possible certain interpretations, whose emergence could not be otherwise explained.

When I read lately Bion's paper on 'Language and the Schizophrenic' (1) I found my own ideas confirmed in certain interpretations given to a patient; in view of this, I think it may be interesting to transcribe here a paragraph of Bion's paper. 'The patient had been lying on the couch, silent, for some twenty minutes. During this time I had become aware of a growing sense of anxiety and tension which I associated with facts about the patient that were already known to me from work done with him in the six months he had already been with me. As the silence continued I became aware of a fear that the patient was meditating a physical attack upon me, though I could see no outward change in his posture. As the tension grew I felt increasingly sure that this was so. Then, and only then, I said to him, "You have been pushing into my inside your fear that you will murder me." There was no change in the patient's position, but I noticed that he clenched his fists till the skin over the knuckles became white. The silence was unbroken. At the same time, I felt that the tension in the room, presumably in the relationship between him and me, had decreased. I said to him, "When I spoke to you, you took your fear that you would murder me back into yourself; you are now feeling afraid you will make a murderous attack upon me." I followed the same method throughout the session, waiting for impressions to pile up until I felt I was in a position to make my interpretation. *It will be noted that my interpretation depends on the use of Melanie Klein's theory of projective identification, first to illuminate my countertransference, and then to frame the interpretation which I give the patient.'* [My italics.]

I am not quite sure whether, in this last assertion, Bion considers the process in the same way as I have approached it in these pages, and as shown in the examples I have given.

I do not know, on the other hand, to what extent Bion would agree in denominating 'projective counter-identification' his countertransference illuminated by the patient's projective identification, which gave place to his interpretations. In any case, I feel sure that we coincide a great deal in our appreciation of this type of phenomenon.

## Summary

This paper deals with the disturbance in technique arising from the excessive interplay of projective identification and what is termed 'projective counteridentifications'. The latter came about specifically, on some occasions, as the result of an excessive projective identification, which is not consciously perceived by the analyst, who, in consequence, finds himself 'led' into it. The analyst then behaves as if he had really and concretely acquired, by assimilating them, the aspects that were projected on to him. The various considerations are supported by relevant clinical examples.

# Notes

1 For the introduction to the life and work of León Grinberg, see Part 1, Chapter 8, of this volume.
2 Personal communication.

~~FIELDS, R. 1942 'Metapsychology of the Analyst.' The Psychoanalytic~~ *Quarterly* 11

3 GRINBERG, L. 1957 'Perturbaciones en la interpretación por la contraidentificación proyectivas *Revista de Psicoanálisis* 14
4 GRINBERG, L. 1958 'Aspectos mágicos en la transferencia y en la contratransferencia: Identificatión y contraidentificación proyectivas.' *Revista de Psicoanálisis* 15
5 KLEIN, M. 1946 'Notes on Some Schizoid Mechanisms.' *International Journal of Psycho-Analysis* 27
6 KLEIN, M. 1955 'On Identification' In: *New Directions in Psycho-Analysis* (see [1]).
7 SEGAL, H. 1956 'Depression in the Schizophrenic.' *International Journal of Psycho-Analysis* 37: 339–343

# Part III

## METAPSYCHOLOGY

# 33

# INTRODUCTION TO THE LIFE AND WORK OF ENRIQUE PICHON-RIVIÈRE (1907–1977)

*Samuel Arbiser*

At the beginning of the 20th century, Argentina was, in the eyes of the world, one of the most promising countries in terms of prosperity, freedoms, and upward social mobility. Attracted by these promises, huge numbers of Europeans ventured to try their luck in these lands. Among them was the Pichon-Rivière family. They arrived in the country when Enrique was three years old, and they settled in the inhospitable Chaco region, still threatened at that time by the raids of the Guaraní Indians. By the time Enrique was eight, they had moved to the province of Corrientes and eventually ended up in the city of Goya, where his mother founded the Colegio Nacional (Public High School). Sports, poetry and painting were the great passions of his childhood, adolescence and early youth. In his *Conversations* with Vicente Zito Lema (1976), he confesses that his readings of the Count of Lautréamont, Rimbaud and Artaud exerted a constant influence on his thought during this time and for the rest of his life. In 1946, he published 'Lo siniestro en la vida y en la obra del Conde de Lautréamont' (The Sinister in the Life and Work of the Count de Lautréamont). In Buenos Aires, he got involved in the bohemian literary, journalistic and artistic groups that were part of the city's exuberant intellectual life. After he graduated as a medical doctor in 1936, he started to work at the Hospicio de la Merced, where he put into practice his inexhaustible inventiveness, which was very much out of synch with the conservative psychiatric practices of the overly structured institutions of the time. Finally, the Hospicio ended up firing him. However, it is precisely in this context and environment that the seeds of what would be, in 1958, 'the Rosario experience',[1] which gave rise to the 'operational groups' with the corresponding notions of the 'emergent' and the 'mouthpiece', developed. His singular quality as an innovator in the field of psychiatry and his interest in the articulation of individual and group psychology also became apparent during this period. His passage through psychoanalysis in the early 1940s was by no means innocuous either, and

egoyen, among many others, went on to develop further a large part of the pioneering ideas of this enthusiastic creator. However, his relationship with psychoanalysis and the institution that hosted him was not entirely harmonious. In contrast to the majority of the established psychoanalysts of his time – and, why not, of the present time – who stuck to, and still stick to, a well-defined psychoanalytic identity and an uncontaminated conceptual purity, Enrique Pichon-Rivière did not limit himself to those categorical or exclusive boundaries either in general practice or in theory. He did not focus on the difference between psychoanalytic and psychiatric practice, between the 'group' and the 'individual', or on the exclusiveness of the conceptual sources of psychoanalysis. To illustrate these statements, mention may be made of his paper entitled "Empleo de Tofranil en Psicoterapia individual y grupal" (1960) [The Use of Tofranil in Individual and Group Therapy (1960)]. Neither did his conceptual patrimony draw exclusively on psychoanalytic sources; it also drew on the notion of 'praxis', which had its origin in Marxism and Sartrean philosophy, in Kurt Lewin's Field Theory, G. Bateson's Theory of Communication, and George H. Mead's Symbolic Interactionism, among many others. As for his psychoanalytic sources, special mention may be made of a wide range of authors of that time, but his strong adhesion to a psychology of object relations, a school headed at the time by Melanie Klein and Ronald Fairbairn, cannot be obviated. This peculiarity of the Pichonian thinking that I have tried to highlight, nourished by an extremely rich and varied personal experience and an equally rich cultural background, is consistent with an essential integration effort to endow with coherence the apparently heterogeneous element of that thinking. I say 'apparently' because his scientific cosmic vision took as its point of departure a conception that might be qualified as totalizing or Copernican, versus the habitual Ptolemaic cosmic vision, which focused on the individual. The following quote of Bleger (1963, pp. 47–8) should clarify this point: ". . . all human phenomena are, inevitably, also social [ . . . ] because the human being is a social being. Moreover, psychology is always social, and it also makes it possible to study an individual as a unit". To my mind, the Pichonian notion of internal group as configuration of the psyche, as well as of ECRO as the conceptual baggage through which we address every object of inquiry, constitute the decisive and necessary keys that endow the aforementioned integration endeavor with meaning – the former as articulating instrument of the individual and the collective, and the latter as a broad, open and dynamic conceptual disposition to operate in the context of reality.

The Internal Group[2]: It is not possible to find, among the known articles written by the author who is the subject of this paper, any systematic and complete exposition of this essential piece of his thinking, but only fragments scattered in different works. To choose just one among a range of options, I will transcribe but a paragraph of his paper entitled "Freud: punto de partida de la psicología social" (1971) [Freud: Point of Departure of Social Psychology (1971)]: "We may observe, according to the contributions of the school of Melanie Klein, that these are social relations which have been internalized, relations that we call internal links and that reproduce group or ecological relations in the ambit of the ego. Those linking structures, which include the subject, the object, and their mutual interrelationships are shaped on the basis of extremely precocious experiences, for which reason we exclude from our systems the concept of instinct, replacing it with the concept of experience. Likewise, the entire unconscious mental life, that is, the realm of unconscious fantasy, must be considered the interaction among internal objects (internal group) in permanent dialectic interrelation with the objects of the external world". From this concise paragraph, the following aspects may be highlighted: a) a theory of evolutionary development that differs from the classic Freudian and Kleinian theories. It is no longer a question of the psychic apparatus being built through the internalization of representations (Freud, first topic) or through objects (Freud, second topic, and Klein), but through the internalization of links; b) a definition of link as a complex organization that brings into play not only the subject and the object, but also the content of the mutual interrelations that are incorporated as experience in the earlier stages of human life; c) consequently, this group or ecological (spatial) design of the psychic apparatus can account for the permanent interaction between the psyche thus configured and the different human groups included in true reality. The internal group would therefore consist in conceiving subjectivity as a unified repertory (ideally) of links that have been internalized in the course of evolutionary development that would allow for our better or worse performance in our links with reality.

ECRO (acronym in Spanish for Esquema Conceptual, Referencial y Operativo/Referential, Operational and Conceptual Model): Breaking down the acronym, when Pichon-Rivière employs the term Model he is alluding to an articulate body of knowledge; the term Conceptual responds to the fact that this knowledge is expressed in the manner of statements with a certain level of abstraction and generalization characteristic of scientific discourse; the Referential aspect meets the purpose of setting the jurisdictional boundaries of the object of inquiry; and lastly, the notion of Opera-

formation, both of the object of the inquiry and of the subject that conducts the inquiry. As I understand it, the notion of ECRO advocates a permanent critical revision of our knowledge of internal and external reality, warning against the fossilization of a view of the world that leads to dogmatism. It also advocates, in my opinion, overcoming the gulf between learning from books and learning from life experience, from "the street", if I may employ a colloquial term. In ideal conditions, both types of learning should provide reciprocal feedback.

## Notes

1 See "Técnica de los grupos operativos" (Operational Groups Technique), written in collaboration with José Bleger, David Liberman and Edgardo Rolla, "Acta neuropsiquiátrica" (Neuropsychiatric Act) (1960), and "Del Psicoanálisis a la Psicología Social" (From Psychoanalysis to Social Psychology" (1971).
2 I have devoted a large part of my writings of the past 40 years to this subject. For greater insight into this topic, please see Arbiser, Samuel (2001) and (2003).

## Bibliography

Arbiser, Samuel (2001). El grupo interno. *Revista de la Sociedad Argentina de Psicoanálisis* (SAP), (Argentine Psychoanalytic Society), July 2001.
Arbiser, Samuel (2003). Psiquis y Cultura. *Psicoanálisis APdeBA*, Vol. XXV, N° 1, 193.
Bleger, José (1963). Psicología de la conducta. Buenos Aires, EUDEBA.
Leone, María Ernestina (2003). *La vertiente psicosocial en el Psicoanálisis Argentino.* Magister Thesis, University of San Luis. Argentina. Scientific Advisor: Samuel Arbiser.
Pichon-Rivière, Enrique (1971). *Del Psicoanálisis a la Psicología Social. Volume II.* Buenos Aires, Editorial Galerna.
Zito Lema, Vicente (1976). *Conversaciones con Enrique Pichon Rivière.* Buenos Aires, Editorial Timerman.

# 34

# NEUROSIS AND PSYCHOSIS

## A theory of illness

### *Enrique Pichon-Rivière*

*Pichon-Rivière, one of the most brilliant minds amongst the pioneers of psychoa-
nalysis in Argentina and a founding member of the Argentine Psychoanalytic
Association, was very rarely published; as far as we know, this is the only English
version of any of his papers. It is part of a book (pp. 235–246) published by the
Argentine Psychoanalytic Association in 1997:* Psychoanalysis in Argentina,
selected articles 1942–1997. *This paper appeared in various publications, and
we could not establish which one was used for this translation. It is part of the second volume of* Del psicoanálisis a la psicología social (From psychoanalysis
to social psychology) *published by Galerna in 1970 (Buenos Aires).*

The observation and enquiry into phenomenic aspects of mental illness or
deviated behaviour, which are inherent to our psychiatric work, on the basis
of discovering genetic, evolutional and structural elements, allow us to come
to an understanding of human behaviour as a totality that evolves dialectically. This means that the signs of an 'abnormal', 'deviated' or 'ill' form of
behaviour are pointing to an underlying conflictive situation from which
illness emerges as a failed attempt at solving such conflict.

From a totalising approach, we define behaviour as a structure, as a dialectic and significant system which is in permanent interaction, attempting to solve, from this perspective, the mind-body, individual–society,
organism–environment opposite pairs (Lagache). Including this dialectic
perspective leads us to enlarge the definition of behaviour, understanding it
not only as a structure, but also as a 'structuralising' system, i.e. as a multiple
unit or interactive system. The concept of dialectic interaction involves
the notion of mutual transformation, of intrasystemic and intersystemic
inter-relations. By intrasystemic relationship we understand that which

takes place within the realm of the individual's ego, in which internalised objects and links constitute an internal world, an intrasubjective dimension within which these objects interact and give rise to the individual's internal world. This system is not closed, but rather connected to the external world by means of projection and introjection mechanisms. We call this form of relation 'inter-systemic'. It is in this sense that we speak of solv-

we define as an active or passive adjustment to reality respectively. By 'adjustment', we refer to the adequacy or inadequacy, coherence or incoherence of the response to the demands imposed by the environment, to the individual's expedient and inexpedient relationship with reality. This is to say that the criteria of illness and health, normality and abnormality are not absolute, but rather situational and relative.

Having defined behaviour on the basis of genetic structuralism,[1] as "an attempt at a coherent and significant response", we can now state the basic premise of our theory of mental disease: every "inadequate" response, every "deviated form of behaviour" is the end result of a distorted or impoverished interpretation of reality. This is to say that illness involves a disruption of the process of apprehending (active learning) reality, i.e. a failure in the circuit of learning and communication which establish a mutual feedback.

From this point of view, we consider that the person is sane insofar as he apprehends reality from an integral perspective, in successive attempts at totalising his learning and inasmuch as he has a capacity to transform reality, which shall in turn, transform him. The individual is sane when he can maintain dialectic interplay in his environment instead of a passive, rigid and stereotyped relationship with those around him. As mentioned before, mental health consists in learning from reality by confronting it, and by playing an active role in finding an integral solution to conflicts. We can also say that it consists in a capacity for synthesis and integration into a whole of the opposite pairs that arise in the person's relationship with reality.

We have defined the structure as a multiple unit, as a system, which refers us to the enunciation of the principles that rule the constitution of such structure, whether it is normal or pathological. Such principles are the following:

1   The principle of multicausality
2   The principle of multiple phenomena

3   The principle of genetic and functional continuity
4   The principle of structure mobility

We shall add to these three notions that shall allow us to understand the configuration of a structure – namely, role, link and "loudspeaker" or "spokesman".

## 1. Principle of multicausality

In the specific field of deviated behaviour we can say that in the genesis of neuroses and psychoses, we find there is a multiple causality, an aetiological equation composed of various factors which are subsequently and evolutionally linked, which Freud called 'complemental series'. In this dynamic constitutional process, we shall mention the constitutional factor in the first place. Within this factor, stated by Freud, I will distinguish three elements: a) genetic and hereditary elements, i.e. the genotype or the strictly genetic factor and b) the phenotype, i.e. the elements derived from the social context which are in turn expressed in the biological code. We mean that the foetus is under the influence of the social environment even when it is apparently protected in its intrauterine life, since it receives the impact of the environment through the changes that take place within the mother, the foetus' environment.

Through these changes, there are several factors which affect the development of the foetus: the parental relationship the presence or absence of the father, the conflicts of the family group and its economic vicissitudes, as well as circumstances involving personal or social danger. All this causes an amount of anxiety in the mother, which is transferred to the foetus through metabolic, blood and other alterations Thus, the phenotype and genotype associate in intrauterine life to give rise to the constitutional factor.

Once the child is born, the constitutional factor shall interact with the impact of the presence of the child in the family group, the characteristics that the family constellation acquires thanks to the child's presence in the group and the positive and negative links that are established in this triangular situation (father–mother child). These first feelings and experiences hinge upon the constitutional factor, what Freud called the *dispositional factor* since during birth and during the process of development, the child faces the constant demand of adjusting to its environment. Conflicts arise involving his needs and tendencies, on the one hand, and the demands imposed by the environment, on the other hand. Thus, anxiety is roused as a sign of alarm in the face of the danger caused by the conflictive situation. If this situation is worked through – that is, if the conflict is solved in an integral way – the process of learning from reality continues its normal course. But if the person cannot work through his anxiety and, instead, controls or represses it by means of defensive techniques, which due to their rigidity take on the characteristics of stereotyped defences, the conflict is not solved, but avoided instead and therefore remains latent as a dispositional point, causing the processes of learning and communication to become dammed up (what Freud called fixation of the libido).

try to disengage himself from the situation that causes his suffering.

We mean that, due to a real or phantasied loss of a link, or due to the threat of a frustration or suffering, the individual is inhibited and partially stops his process of apprehending reality. Thus, he resorts to mechanisms that are expedient at that moment, though not entirely so, since he does not solve the conflict but avoids it. This constitutes a pattern of reaction that, upon becoming stereotyped, gives rise to a point of fixation. The degree of inadequacy of the archaic mechanism (which was expedient at the moment of development to which the individual returns but no longer so) and the intensity of the stereotype shall provide us with an indication of the individual's degree of deviation from the standard and of the characteristics of his (both active and passive) adjustment to reality. Hence, we can agree with Freud: "Every individual has the kind of neurosis he is able to, not the kind he wants to have".

The neurosis or psychosis is triggered when the dispositional factor combines with the actual conflict. When the dispositional amount is too high, an actual conflict, no matter how low its intensity is, is sufficient to give rise to illness. This is why we speak of the complementarity of the factors involved.

We would like to point out that the concepts of constitution and disposition are of a psycho-biological nature. By this we insist that psychoanalytical theory of neuroses and psychoses does not postulate the psychogenesis of the neuroses and psychoses, as is mistakenly asserted in certain psychiatric literature, since this would involve a partiality of the psychophysical unit. These three types of factors intricately combine to shape neuroses and psychoses. The enunciation of this aetiological equation allows us to overcome a mechanistic conception that established a futile opposition between the exogenous and endogenous factors. Freud sustained that the correlation between the endogenous and the exogenous must be understood as complementary between disposition and fate. From our point of view, we would like to point out that the so-called "classical" psychiatrists, who insist on the endogenous factors, disregard, among other aspects, the amount of deprivation or actual conflict, whose impact on a variable threshold in each person completes the multidimensional nature of neuroses and psychoses.

## 2. The principle of multiple phenomena

This principle is founded on the consideration of three phenomenic dimensions or areas of behavioural expression. Each area is a projective domain, which the individual occupies with his links, thus establishing an interplay between his internal world and the external context.

In such interplay, the body becomes an intermediate and mediating area.

Each one of these areas – mind, body and external world – has its own code of expression.

As the human being is a totalising totality (Sartre), his behaviour shall always involve the three areas of expression in varying degrees. We speak of degrees of engagement of such areas in the sense that the transposing of objects with which the individual establishes links is situationally more significant in the area seen as prevalent. The self (the presentation of the ego) organises projections of objects and links in the three areas by means of phantasies; thus we call these three domains 'projective areas'. As a result of such projections, the individual shall phenomenically express his relationships and links by means of signs that are manifested in his mind, in his body and in the external world. This implies that in this system of signs (behaviour), the emerging of signs in a certain area is a significant "emergent" (i.e. a sign pointing to the entire underlying process) that refers us to the individual's links, his way of perceiving reality and the specific way of adjusting to it, i.e. to the particular way he solves his conflicts. These modes constitute what we shall call the individual's character structure.

Behaviour is significant; it is a system of signs in which signifiers and signified combine to render it comprehensible and apt to be changed therapeutically. The phenomenic aspects of behaviour, expressed in different space and time dimensions are the end result of the individual's relationship, his transposing of objects and links, the contents of such transposing, along with their negative or positive value and the placing of the objects and links in a symbolical perceptive domain we call 'area'. The individual projects objects and links and acts out that which he projects. For this reason, only the dialectic interaction by the individual with the context will allow him to rectify his reading of reality in which the main task is establishing distinctions. The diagnosis of an illness can be determined according to the prevalence of one of these areas within the multiplicity of symptoms; a study of the strata in which the manifestations appear show that the three areas are always involved.

We would like to point out that the mind, however, acts through the self by means of projection and introjection mechanisms, as a strategy by which it places in the different projective domains the good and bad links in a divalent way, aiming at preserving the good links and controlling the bad ones. Due to this transposing of objects and links, these areas acquire a particular significance for the person as regards the positive or negative value of that which has been transposed.

In this context, the ego, the object and the link (the latter is a structure that includes the ego, the object and the dialectic relationship between them) are split and the defensive task consists in keeping them split, since if the good and the bad were integrated into the same object, the person

three areas, mind-body-external World, with all the variables that can arise from this equation.

By way of exemplifying, we can say that the phobic person shall project and act out the good object and transpose the bad object on the external world. Thus the transposing shall behave elusively, i.e. it shall present flights as though there were an external attack and he shall feel, for example, anxiety in closed places (claustrophobia) or in open spaces (agoraphobia), in which he feels at the mercy of the persecutor.

In schizophrenia, the persecuting object (bad link) can be projected onto the third area (external world) and the good one on the first area, the mind, thus giving rise to the paranoid schizophrenia with a withdrawal from external reality so as to avoid the bad object; here deprivation is reinforced as a triggering factor.

## 3. Principle of genetic and functional continuity

With this principle, we postulate the existence of a central pathogenic nucleus of a depressive nature from which all clinical forms derive as attempts at becoming disengaged from such nucleus. These attempts seem to be implemented through defensive techniques, which are characteristic of the schizoparanoid position described by Melanie Klein, which I call pathoplastic or instrumental. This means that we could speak of a single illness with a depressive pathogenic nucleus implemented by means of a central mechanism, the splitting of the ego, of the object and links established by the ego with the objects. From this splitting, the person resorts to other techniques of the schizoparanoid position, namely, projection (placing the internal objects outside the person), introjection (phantasied passage of the external objects and their qualities to the internal world of the person), omnipotent control of both internal and external objects, idealisation, etcetera. The depressive and the schizoparanoid positions alternate and fuse, thus constituting a continuity that underlies the diverse phenomenic aspects that are characteristic of the different clinical pictures.

Let us consider in mental illness a genesis and a sequence that is linked to these depressive situations, situations of loss, deprivation, pain which are experienced as an internal catastrophe with feelings of ambivalence and guilt, in which the person suffers for feeling he both hates and loves the same object, and at the same he is loved and hated by that object. This means that in the relationship with the object there may be pleasant experiences (good links) or frustrating experiences (bad links).

The forerunners of these patterns are two situations that area part of normal infantile development. Birth represents to the child its first experience of loss of the symbiotic relationship with its mother [loss of mother's warmth]; thus the child remains in a state of total dependence and at the mercy of the demands imposed by the external environment.

In that situation, in which the child shall have pleasant experiences derived from the satisfaction of needs and wishes, as well as frustrating experiences, he shall structure his positive and negative links according to the quality of the experience in whose constitution unconscious phantasies already intervene.

In that stage of development, which covers his first six months of life, the subject resorts for the first time to the above mentioned splitting mechanism, aiming at conferring order to the universe to distinguish his emotions and perceptions. On the basis of splitting, the child relates with what he experiences as two objects, one which is good and entirely gratifying, which he loves and is loved by and another which is entirely bad, frustrating, dangerous and persecutory, which he hates and feels hated by. This splitting and relationship between the ego and the objects of opposite values are called divalent and they are characteristic of the schizoparanoid position.

The prevalent anxiety in this situation is the paranoid anxiety or fear of being attacked by the persecutor, which, the greater the amount of hostility the child has become liberated from by projecting on the internal and frustrating object, the greater is the anxiety.

In the course of its physiological process of maturation and the operative or expedient handling of its conflicts, the child's ego achieves a greater integration, thus entering a new stage, which M. Klein called depressive position of development (between his six months and one year of life). There is a process of change that is an integrative organisation of perceptions. The subject recognizes the total object. He does not divide it, or split it, and relates to it as a totality. This happens when the child stops recognizing his mother as a part–object (breast, voice, warmth, smell) and begins to perceive her as a totality. Due to the development of memory and the integrative capacity it establishes four-way links with the object, i.e. it loves and feels loved, it hates and feels hated by the same object, in which he discovers a

385

potential for gratification and frustration. In the same way, he can recognize feelings of love and gratitude coexisting with hostility and aggression. This causes a feeling of ambivalence, which entails the fear of losing the loved object and guilt feelings out of fear that the hostile impulses might damage the object.

Ambivalence paralyses the subject, who holds inhibition as the only

that will allow him to control anxiety. So the subject emerges from inhibition and the conflict of ambivalence via another dissociation, thus paranoid anxiety (fear of being attacked) replaces the guilt feeling (fear of loss).

Neuroses are defensive techniques against the basic anxieties. Such techniques are the most expedient and closer to health, and although they are failed attempts at adjusting, they have developed further away from the depressive pathogenic nucleus. Psychoses are also attempts at handling basic anxieties, yet they are less successful than neuroses, i.e. they present a greater degree of deviation from the parameters of health.

The case with psychopathies is the same, where the prevalent mechanism is delegation. Within the psychopathies, perversions are manifested as complex forms of working through basic anxieties and their general mechanism revolves around the appeasing of the persecutor (bad object).

Crime (also included in this picture) is an attempt to annihilate the source of anxiety projected on the external world. When this source is placed in the subject himself, the result is suicidal behaviour. The failure at working through suffering in the depressive position inevitably brings about the prevalence of defences that imply the blocking of emotions and phantasy activity. These stereotyped defences particularly hinder a certain degree of self-knowledge or insight that is necessary for a positive adjustment to reality. This is to say that the blocking of affect, phantasy and thought that can be seen in the different clinical pictures determines an impoverished connection with reality and a real difficulty to modify it and modify himself in the dialectic interplay, which, in our view, is a criterion of health.

As regards the depressive situation, taken as the main thread of the process of falling ill and the therapeutic process, we consider the existence of five characteristic forms which we call: a) protodepression, arising from the loss experienced by the child upon abandoning his mother's womb; b) the depressive position of development, marked by the mourning or loss (weaning), a conflict of ambivalence in the process of integrating the ego and the object, guilt feelings and an attempt at working through; c) initial or trigger-ing depression. This is the prodromic period of every mental illness and it is roused by a frustration or loss; d) regressional depression, which implies a regression to the previous dispositional points, characteristic of the infantile depressive position and its failed attempt at working-through; e) iatrogenic depression. We call this type of depression that which takes place within the corrective process, when the patient attempts to integrate the different parts of the ego, i.e. when the task consists in passing from the stereotypy of the mechanisms of the schizoparanoid position to a depressive moment in which the subject achieves an integration both in the ego and in the object as well as in the web of links that includes both. This is what we call insight or a capacity for self-knowledge, which will allow him to imagine a life project including death as a concrete situation that will happen to him. This involves facing the existential problems and achieving an active adjustment to reality with a personal style and personal ideology in life. Yet, the process of integra-tion and self-knowledge entail suffering; that is why Rickman says that "there is no cure without tears", yet we must add that this suffering is expedient.

The psychotherapeutic operation or correcting process is ultimately a process of learning from reality, a reparation of the communication network available to the subject. The confrontation that the corrective experience implies when the person can integrate himself in a situation of suffering, thus tolerating the distinction of his basic fears determines a more adequate handling of the ego techniques in the task of preserving the good and controlling the bad. What does this confrontation consist in? In a process in which the subject shall ascribe to the therapist different roles according to his internal models (transference). In this process of attribution his distorted reading of reality shall become manifested. Such roles are not to be acted but rather retranslated (interpreted) into concepts or hypotheses about the unconscious becoming (or events) in the patient. The subject's response shall be taken up in this dialogue as an emergent, as a sign that refers us again to that becoming, which is the thread that allows us to understand and cooperate with him in the transformation of his perception of the World and the ways in which he adjusts to it.

We have here stated four principles that rule, in our understanding, the configuration of every pathological or normal structure. I shall now refer to the last principle enumerated further above.

## 4. Principle of structure motility

This concept requires placing oneself before the patient with a plastic ref-erential scheme that will allow us to understand that the structures are instrumental and situational in every here-and-now of the process of inter-action; that the modes and techniques of handling the basic anxieties, with its placing of objects and links in different areas are apt to be modified according to the processes of interaction in which the subject is engaged. This affirmation has relevant implications as regards the work of diagnosis.

Going back to what we discussed above as regards the multiplicity of

## Summary

In this article, we pose the existence of a single pathogenic nucleus of a depressive nature implemented by means of a central mechanism, which is the splitting of the ego, the objects and the links, complemented with the repertory of defensive techniques of the schizoparanoid position. The fact that all the clinical pictures appear, from this point of view, as attempts at becoming disengaged from the pathogenic nucleus leads us to postulate, theoretically, the data that has emerged from clinical observation: structure motility and the situational nature of such structures. In the same way that we can see such motility by means of a sequential analysis, an analysis of the strata reveals the degree of engagement of each of the areas, i.e. the amount and quality of the disposition the subject shows to have in each of the areas. Thus in the first place, there is an area involved by the multiplicity of symp-toms, which guides the situational and structural diagnosis and at the same time we take into account the degree of engagement (in terms of transpos-ing) of the other two areas, which shall allow us to reach a prognosis.

## Note

1  We share many of the fundamental concepts supported by this school of think-ing, particularly with the statement that "every form of behaviour has the nature of a significant structure" and that "the positive study of every form of human behaviour lies in attempting to make this meaning come to light". We are particularly attracted by the dialectic approach of this perspective, accord-ing to which "the constitutional structures of behaviour are not universal data, but specific facts, born from a past genesis, which undergo transformations and allow future development" (L. Goldman, *Genése et Structure*, Mouton, The Hague, 1965).

# TWO KINDS OF GUILT

Their relations with normal
and pathological aspects of
mourning

*León Grinberg[1]*

*This paper was presented at the 23rd International Psycho-Analytical Congress, Stockholm, July–August 1963; it was published in 1964 in the* International Journal of Psycho-Analysis, *45: 366–371.*

## Origin and nature of the sense of guilt

The importance of guilt in the aetiology of neuroses and psychoses is well known. In my opinion, however, the question of guilt, of its origin, nature, and different ways of participation in the individual's mental development, is still one of the problems in the field of psycho-analytic research that has not yet been fully elucidated.

In some psycho-analytic circles different groups of therapists have developed varying trends of thought which differ mainly – among other things – in the way they handle guilt in their respective techniques. One of these trends centres interpretation around the necessity of liberating the patient from a guilt which, according to them, is of a negative and pathological nature, to which he is bound in a masochistic manner. Other analysts, on the other hand, seem to follow an utterly opposed theoretical-technical criterion in regard to this problem. For them, the core of any neurotic conflict is, in fact, centred on the denial of guilt experienced by the individual on account of aggressive fantasies directed towards the objects. In my opinion this controversy results from the mistake of dealing with two different kinds of guilt under the assumption that they are one and the same.

One of the classic starting-points established by Freud is that guilt, proceeding from tensions between the ego and the superego, appears as a need for punishment. Freud (1913), when studying the Oedipal conflict in primitive societies, shows how out of the sense of guilt sprang the two main

On the other hand, Freud (1916) showed that guilt arises to a much greater degree from unconscious fantasies than from actual deeds. The actual crime is frequently not the real motive for guilt but rather its consequence.

According to Freud's later work (1930) the guilt belongs to the realm of aggressive instincts, aggression being turned towards the ego as a punishing force, acting through the superego.

Klein (1935) also believes that guilt is linked with the emergence of the superego, though she places it at an earlier period, that is, during the stage in which the infant's sadism plays a dominant role. She points out that the first feelings of guilt arise from the child's oral-sadistic desires to devour the mother, especially the breast (Abraham).

## Two kinds of guilt: Persecutory and depressive

Klein (1935) has described the existence of guilt that is under the influence of the 'depressive position', and which presupposes the existence of an ego sufficiently integrated to experience it and utilize it for reparative purposes.

After Klein, probably Winnicott (1958) more than anyone else has stressed that guilt, although unconscious and apparently irrational, involves a certain amount of emotional maturity, hope, and health on the part of the ego.

In my opinion, however, there is still another kind of guilt, which appears at an earlier period with a weak and immature ego. This guilt increases in intensity parallel with the anxieties of the paranoid-schizoid phase, or in case of frustrations or failures during the evolution towards the depressive phase. Although this guilt begins very early in life, it is my belief that it has a far-reaching effect in later development and appears in such symptoms as inhibitions or masochistic behaviour. It was this kind of guilt with its paranoid undertone that Freud had in mind when he spoke of the formation of the superego.

Money-Kyrle (1955) has described, in relation to guilt, the existence of two different kinds of consciousness, which would appear to be combined in different proportions according as the parental image is felt as a good or an evil one. That is, he described a 'qualitative change' in guilt, pointing out its 'at least' two different components. These would be: 'grief and remorse' [which] 'constitute the other element in guilt which we may describe as depressive as distinct from persecutory'. Money-Kyrle has not explained the origin of these two kinds of guilt. He has neither studied them in a systematic way, nor related them to normal and pathological mourning, as I have endeavoured to do in this and in previous (1962) papers.

I have reached conclusions somewhat similar to Money-Kyrle's. I believe in the existence of two distinct kinds of guilt, which I also have named persecutory and depressive. This provides us with a better understanding of the dynamics of guilt, with a broader picture of the contents and nature of the object relationship, and in connection with our problem should increase our understanding of the likelihood of developing normal or pathological mourning. It also appears to me important to study these two kinds of guilt in connection with the experiences of loss of parts of the self, which I shall develop below.

Klein (1957)[2] has referred to guilt that emerges precociously. This might be thought to be in contradiction with her statement that guilt arises during the depressive position as the result of the integration of part objects into whole objects. I think that this contradiction can be accounted for by assuming the existence of two kinds of guilt. This concept is quite clear in her views on this problem, though she does not refer to it explicitly. But I still find it necessary to add that I think that there is a close relationship between persecutory guilt and the death instinct, and between depressive guilt and the life instinct.

I believe that the concept of instinctual duality plays a fundamental role in the origin and nature of the different mechanisms and feelings, determining whether they will be healthy or pathological. Freud (1924)[3] connected the feeling of guilt with the death instinct. When he studied the superego of melancholia (1923), he ascribed to sadism the extraordinary intensity of the feeling of guilt and suggested that the destructive element, 'a pure culture of the death instinct', abides in the superego and turns against the ego. This I believe to be persecutory guilt.

Among the different situations that contribute to the emergence and intensification of this kind of guilt (birth trauma, a bad relationship with the breast and with the mother, predominance of frustrations, etc.) experiences of loss are highly important. In my opinion, every loss implies a certain degree of guilt, due to the feeling of privation (Isaacs, 1929)[4] and impoverishment of the self. Klein (1955) refers specifically to this when she speaks of 'the guilt due to having neglected and abandoned the precious contents of the self'.

It is my view that one of the main affects involved in the experience of persecutory guilt is resentment. Now *resentment* may be felt towards something or some one previously loved, whom the subject considers responsible for a frustration, loss, or aggression. Spitefulness, as a consequence of

oneself. A resentment is also felt towards Author object for having by its death taken with it certain parts of the self. The greater the resentment, the greater in turn will be the guilt and persecution, and in consequence the elaboration of the corresponding mourning will be disturbed.

Hypochondriacal reactions or psychosomatic disorders so frequently found in pathological mourning are often due to persecutory guilt.[5] In such cases the object is not actually experienced as dead, but it is felt unconsciously as malignantly alive, introjected in the sick organ and threatening and punishing the ego. This is also felt, sometimes, as an attack upon the ego's identity, as I shall show later.

On the other hand, as resentment is mitigated, persecutory guilt will consequently lessen, grief and sorrow for the loss will increase, and depression, concern, and responsibility (depressive guilt) will be intensified, all of which will ultimately lead to reparation.

It is frequently observed in psycho-analysis that when the patient is under the influence of persecutory guilt, he tends to act out in a repetitive compulsive manner and will show marked masochistic attitudes, whereas the progressive and systematic appearance of recollections, subjective experiences and emotions show the gradual transformation of persecutory guilt into depressive guilt.

The proportionally increased participation of the life instinct, as occurs during normal development, determines a real transformation of guilt, its persecuting elements being replaced by depressive elements with the characteristics described by Klein as corresponding to depressive guilt.

However, there always remain elements of persecutory guilt which, under traumatic circumstances – and every loss is in fact a trauma – are intensified.[6]

To synthesize: In *persecutory guilt* the main elements are: resentment, despair, fear, pain, self-reproaches, etc. Its extreme manifestation is melancholia (pathological mourning). In *depressive guilt* the dominant elements are sorrow, concern for the object and the self, nostalgia and responsibility.

This is what we ordinarily see in normal mourning, in which we find sub-limatory activities, discrimination, and reparation.

## Mourning for loss of the object and for loss of parts of the self

In dealing with this particular problem I do not intend to describe or explain in detail the well-known factors involved in the process of mourning for the loss of an object, but rather specifically to point out that in every object loss there occurs simultaneously a loss of parts of the self, which leads to its corresponding process of mourning.

I shall refer in the first instance to the famous example given by Freud (1920), i.e. the one-and-a-half-year-old child who used to play with a reel when his mother was away. The child, according to Freud, consoled himself for his mother's absence by controlling in a displaced manner the appearance and disappearance of the mother.

The child discovered that he could make his own image disappear and reappear in a mirror. By thus controlling his own image he felt that he was controlling his mother's disappearance by identification. In this way he attempted to overcome the anxiety and depression caused by her absence. But this also means that the sensation of transient and permanent loss of an object awakens in the individual the feeling of having lost entirely something that was actually his. I believe that in the unconscious fantasy of this child the mother, the reel, and his reflection were different aspects of a unit that the child considered as his own possession. In other words, when an object-loss occurs, the individual 'runs to the mirror' to observe what has happened to his own image.

Throughout this paper I have pointed out that depression plays a fundamental role in the normal evolution of mourning. The feelings of pain and guilt – whether persecutory or depressive – brought about by the loss of parts of the self, if they become overwhelmingly strong, can impair the work of mourning

To begin with, they may represent one of the answers to the question raised by Freud (1914) when he says that: '. . . Why this compromise by which the command of reality is carried out piecemeal *should be so extraordinarily painful* is not at all easy to explain in terms of economics. It is remarkable that *this painful unpleasure is taken as a matter of course by us*' (My italics). In my opinion 'painful' refers actually to the trauma inflicted on the ego.

I believe that if pain appears in any mourning situation owing to object-loss, it is because it reproduces an experience that in the unconscious fantasy meant an attack upon the ego (in particular upon the body ego, which brings back the birth trauma situation) which provokes physical pain and which has been in turn incorporated as psychical pain.[7]

Living means, necessarily, to suffer a series of mournings: the very fact of growing up, of passing from one stage to another, involves the abandonment of certain attitudes and relationships which, although replaced by more progressive ones, impinge upon the ego as experiences of loss, and provoke

Any concern about the ego means, in general, concern about the feeling of identity. To give a fully satisfactory definition of the concept of identity is not an easy task (Erikson, 1956).[9] It is not the aim of this paper to discuss this concept exhaustively. All the same, it should be taken into account in order to reach a better and more adequate understanding of the value attributed by the ego to the feeling of identity. In my opinion, this feeling refers to the notion of an ego that is built up upon the continuity and similarity of the unconscious fantasies connected primarily with bodily sensations, with the anxieties and emotions experienced by the ego since birth, the tendencies and affects in relation to objects of the inner and outer world, to the superego and the corresponding anxieties, to the specific operation, both in quality and in intensity, of the defence mechanisms, and to the particular type of the assimilated identifications resulting from the processes of projection and introjection.

The specific and permanent interaction of all these elements will endow the ego with a certain cohesion. This cohesion, on which identity is based, is maintained within certain limitations, being subjected in certain circumstances to alterations or experiences of loss. Change and loss must occur during the process of development; under normal conditions, however, it will give the ego sufficient time to elaborate the loss and recover from the transient and tolerable identity troubles that may, in most cases, pass unnoticed. In pathological cases, owing to the failure to elaborate these mournings, serious troubles of identity (psychoses) may appear (cf. Grinberg, 1961).

Any attack against the body (somatic illnesses, physical trauma, hypochondriac sensations) is felt unconsciously as an attack against the ego and its identity, with a fully persecutory content. On another level there is, however, a concern of depressive nature about the condition in which the self has been left as a consequence of such attacks.

The anxiety experienced by the menacing loss of certain aspects of the self may assume different forms. In many individuals it may appear in the form of an inhibition from accomplishing various activities. In fact, what they at depth fear is being exposed to a danger and a threat to the integrity of identity of the self. Such persons exhibit in general stiff personalities, developed in order to avoid change. This is in general observed in cases of repetition compulsion, the origin of which would be, among other things, the necessity to maintain at all costs (even neurosis) aspects or modes of the self which the individual cannot or does not want to risk losing. This fear of change may become at times one of the main causes of a negative therapeutic reaction. In consequence, we can easily understand the paradoxical situation of being unable to bear changes that involve progress. This happens because the change means an alteration of the already known ego (identity), and although the alteration might mean a better development and integration, the result will be a new and different ego.

I shall now give a clinical example to show a patient's response when confronted with the problem of depressive ego feelings.

A female patient of mine had to undergo a rather serious operation, a hysterectomy, shortly after the death of an older, close friend who for various reasons embodied for her a maternal image. During the sessions following the operation she brought up a number of associations which distinctly revealed the existence of two kinds of mourning – one for the loss of the object, and the other for the loss of the removed bodily organ. Both losses were linked in her unconscious. She wavered between a massive identification with Author maternal image, reinforced by the death of her friend (she saw herself as a mother who could not bear any more children), and the feeling of being a newly born infant (birth trauma). In the transference I appeared split as a persecutory mother who exposed her to the surgical castration and death, as well as a saving mother who put life into her, helping her to pull through the operation. In one of the sessions she brought the following dream: 'I had a dream without people. I just saw my old flat, the one I have recently sold; it looked larger. It had an extra bedroom and an extra bathroom. Also the garden seemed to be larger with a cottage in it. I wondered whether it was the same flat. I was sorry that I had sold it so cheaply.' Then she mentioned the following associations: a few days before, when going up to her new flat in the lift, as she was carrying several parcels she forgot a suitcase there. She was puzzled to realize that when she could not remember where she had left it she had given up all hope of finding it. This dream was an attempt to elaborate the loss of such an important organ as the uterus. I have already pointed out that on one level she had felt the operation to be the consequence of a destructive attack coming from persecutory guilt, at times driving her to markedly masochistic attitudes. But she also felt persecutory guilt towards her own self for having neglected it and failed to defend it. That is why on another level she felt the operation to be a violence done to herself. These aspects of self-neglect and self-reproach were clearly expressed in her associations when she remarked that she found it strange to consider her suitcase lost, and also in the dream in which she regretted having sold her flat. Simultaneously, depressive feelings had arisen making her feel a deep sorrow for herself and an awakening of the need to work through the mourning for her self as a reparative attempt. These feelings belong to depressive guilt.

attempt to restore her damaged self by new enriching ego-activities. Actually this patient had at the time, in real life, several constructive experiences. The imagery of the dream that included a larger flat and also a larger garden with a cottage corresponded to the restoration of her inner world and body, but also to the world of the damaged object (her dead friend).

I should like to stress the fact that these depressive feelings for the self are much more frequent than it is usually admitted. Their existence can be recognized in the form of slight depressive states, as part of the phenomena of the psychopathology of daily life. I consider that, if we take into account the appearance of such *microdepressions or micromournings* for the self, we shall have a better understanding of the origin of many states of mind which we cannot consider as real depressions, but which are usually perceived as ill-temper, apathy, weariness, boredom, irritability, etc. A certain purpose not fulfilled, a dream forgotten, an aim not accomplished, an appointment missed, a trip, a move, are some of the many factors which provoke daily depressive microreactions, and at the same time fleeting threats to one's identity. According to how the corresponding depressions of the first stages of life were overcome, they will be favourably solved as minor disorders or turn into deep and serious depressions.

Psycho-analysis gives the patient the possibility of recovering the excluded parts of the self as well as the possibility of giving up those aspects which must inevitably be lost in the process of development, and which he has omnipotently tried to hold on to.

When constitutional and acquired conditions are good enough to allow the ego an adequate elaboration of the self's depression and mourning, the ego will exhibit reparative and constructive tendencies towards itself, which will permit it to become stronger and better balanced. This process will be parallel to the possibility of experiencing reparative drives towards objects (which were first felt as representing lost aspects of the self). I believe that in this way we shall be able to understand more fully the simultaneous process of integration that occurs in the sphere of the object as well as in that of the ego. Finally, this process of integration of the ego, due to the successful elaboration of mourning for the self as well as for its objects, will bring about a progressive strengthening of identity.

# Notes

1   For the introduction to the life and work of León Grinberg, see Part 1, Chapter 8, of this volume.

2   She writes: 'It appears that one of the consequences of excessive envy is an early onset of guilt. If premature guilt is experienced by an ego not yet capable of bearing it, guilt is felt as persecution and the object that rouses guilt is turned into a persecutor.' . . . 'The fact that in the earliest stage (i.e. during the paranoid-schizoid position) premature guilt increases persecution and disintegration, brings the consequence that the working through of the depressive position also fails' (p. 194).

3   Freud points out that 'the third, in some respects the most important, form assumed by masochism has only recently been recognized by psycho-analysis as a sense of guilt which is mostly unconscious'. This, in my opinion, makes part of the 'persecutory guilt'. He adds furthermore that 'Thus moral masochism becomes a classical piece of evidence for the existence of fusion of instinct. Its danger lies in the fact that it originates from the death instinct and corresponds to the part of that instinct which has escaped being turned outwards as an instinct of destruction'.

4   Isaacs here intends to determine, particularly, the process leading from deprivation towards guilt and the emergence of the superego and expresses the view that the first elements of guilt belong to the most undifferentiated levels of experience.

5   I would like to comment briefly on Wisdom's ideas concerning the avoidance of guilt in psycho-somatic disorders (Wisdom, 1959). In his paper he says that: 'Clinically, psycho-somatic disorders are sometimes taken to be ways of avoiding guilt. . . .' This clinical finding, however, is susceptible of two different constructions: one is that a psychosomatic disorder is developed *in order to avoid guilt*, the guilt of a purely psychological disorder. The other – implied by the present hypothesis – is that a patient develops a psychosomatic disorder because he is unable to experience guilt. Following the ideas I have developed in the present paper I consider that a patient develops a psychosomatic disorder (for instance after the loss of a loved object) because he is unable to experience depressive guilt, and instead of this he experiences *persecutory guilt* which he perceives unconsciously as a threat and punishment arising from the persecutory object introjected in the sick organ.

6   Jones (1929) says that these feelings (fear, guilt and hate) are in fact stratified, since any of them may act as a defence against either of the two others. He even points out that a secondary guilt might develop in order to be able to

face the two other attitudes. On the basis of this concept we might explain the alternating character of the two types of guilt I have described. It might happen that, the depressive guilt being unbearable, it was replaced in a regressive way by persecutory guilt which would act, in this case, as a defence mechanism

7  Freud (1915) himself admitted this; when referring to the death or danger of death of loved persons he said: '. . . these loved ones are . . . an inner possession,

us to experience ourselves as something endowed with continuity and uniformity, and allowing us to act accordingly.

# References

ERIKSON, E. H. 1956 'The Problem of Ego Identity.' *Journal of the American Psychoanalytic Association* 4

FREUD, S. 1913 'Totem and Taboo.' *The complete psychological works of Sigmund Freud*, S.E. 13

FREUD, S. 1914 'Mourning and Melancholia.' *The complete psychological works of Sigmund Freud*, S.E. 14

FREUD, S. 1915 'Thoughts for the Times on War and Death.' *The complete psychological works of Sigmund Freud*, S.E. 14

FREUD, S. 1916 'Some Character-Types met with in Psycho-Analytic Work.' *The complete psychological works of Sigmund Freud*, S.E. 14

FREUD, S. 1920 'Beyond the Pleasure Principle.' *The complete psychological works of Sigmund Freud*, S.E. 18

FREUD, S. 1923 'The Ego and the Id.' *The complete psychological works of Sigmund Freud*, S.E. 19

FREUD, S. 1924 *The complete psychological works of Sigmund Freud*, vol 19:3–65.

FREUD, S. 1930 'Civilization and its Discontents.' *The complete psychological works of Sigmund Freud*, S.E. 21

GRINBERG, L. 1961 'Feeling of Identity and Mourning for the Self.' Read at the Symposium on Melanie Klein's Work, Argentine Psychoanalytic Association, June 1961

GRINBERG, L. 1962 'Normal and Pathological Aspects of Mourning.' Read at the Fourth Latin-American Psychoanalytic Congress, Rio de Janeiro, July 1962

ISAACS, S. 1929 'Privation and Guilt.' *International Journal of Psycho-Analysis* 10

JONES, E. 1929 'Fear, Guilt and Hate.' In: *Papers on Psycho-Analysis* (London: Baillière.)

KLEIN, M. 1935 'A Contribution to the Psychogenesis of Manic-Depressive States.' In: *Contributions to Psycho-Analysis* (London: Hogarth, 1948.)

KLEIN, M. 1955 'On Identification.' In: *New Directions in Psycho-Analysis* (London: Tavistock.)

KLEIN, M. 1957 *Envy and Gratitude* (London: Tavistock.)

KLEIN, M. 1959 'On Loneliness.' In: *Our Adult World and Other Essays* (London: Heinemann, 1963.)

MONEY-KYRLE, R. E. 1955 'Psycho-Analysis and Ethics.' In: *New Directions in Psycho-Analysis* ed. Klein et al. (London: Tavistock.)

WINNICOTT, D. W. 1958 'Psycho-Analysis and the Sense of Guilt.' In: *Psycho-Analysis and Contemporary Thought* ed. J. D. Sutherland. (London: Hogarth.)

WISDOM, J. O. 1959 'On a Differentiating Mechanism of Psychosomatic Disorder.' *International Journal of Psycho-Analysis* 40

# (1910–2003)

*Antônio Luiz Serpa Pessanha*

I was analyzed by Professor Virgínia Bicudo in the 1960s for seven years. She was firm but gentle in her relationships. Her communications were clear and precise.

Her speech was concise, sometimes reduced to a short phrase or even a word. The common denominator was the search for truth, which to her was the ethics of psychoanalysis. Generosity, solidarity and a sense of justice stood out in her balanced posture. These resources brought me an adequate model, which began to inhabit my mental world, enriching, correcting and reformulating some of my inadequate thoughts, ideas and judgments. This contributed to my growth, my quality of life and also gave me a greater confidence at work.

I believe she understood the very essence of psychoanalysis. I had the privilege of spending time with a brave, audacious and modern woman, who had a vocation and talent for psychoanalytic work. Another striking characteristic of Virgínia was her great consideration for neutrality and impeccable respect for analytic technique.

After the first years of analysis, I had the honor of collaborating with her on initiatives springing from her creativity. Virgínia had returned from her training in London (1955–1960), where she perfected her knowledge of the contributions of Melanie Klein, with whom she maintained friendship ties. This participation allowed me to witness her countless achievements, which contributed to the development of psychoanalysis in São Paulo and in Brazil in general, considering only the period between 1960 and 1970.

I consider this period, which I will describe below, the most fertile one for the growth of psychoanalysis in Brazil.

In May 1966, on the initiative of Virgínia Leone Bicudo, director of the Institute at the time, the first edition of the *Journal of Psychoanalysis* was published. This journal is still today the only publication in Brazil from a psychoanalytic society affiliated with the IPA. It was created with the aim of furthering the research, teaching, investigation, debate and dissemination of psychoanalysis in our analytic world.

The journal was the first vehicle for this explosion of initiatives. Around it, countless activities blossomed:

1   The First Brazilian Psychoanalytic Day was founded by Bicudo and held in May 1967.
2   Another important event occurred during that meeting, where the creation of the Brazilian Psychoanalytic Association (currently the Brazilian Federation of Psychoanalysis – FEBRAPSI), a national entity that aimed to represent and unite the interests of Brazilian psychoanalysts, was decided.
3   The journal's success and good reception encouraged a distinguished Society group to re-launch the Brazilian *Review of Psychoanalysis*, which was founded in 1927 by Durval Marcondes.

It is important to observe how much was produced in this four-year period, thanks to Virgínia's enterprising spirit: the *Journal* was moving towards its ninth issue, the *Review* towards its fourth, the Third Psychoanalytic Day – after the success of the two previous ones – was growing into the First Congress, and the Brazilian Psychoanalytic Association was fully active.

The *Journal* is still being published, FEBRAPSI is more representative and its attributes and functions have been expanded. During all these years, the Society, through its Institute, has been trying to improve the training of new psychoanalysts, including the selection of candidates and the development of new a curriculum.

For 14 uninterrupted years, Virgínia was the Chair of the Institute, marking her direction by constantly encouraging the study of new contributions. Her mind was full of seeds that were planted and grew in the Society's fertile ground.

Another highlight was the visit by Bion (undeniably influential in our training) to São Paulo in 1974, the first of three visits to our country.

But it is useless to narrate the facts of a story without understanding its meaning, or what is still alive and current about it. Meaning is our memory's rescue and our identity's reinforcement. After all, whoever distances himself from his own story loses himself.

Virgínia Bicudo published countless works. The following chapter stands out; it was initially published as "Persecutory guilt and ego restrictions", in the 1964 *International Journal of Psycho-Analysis* (London, 45: 358–363). In this paper, she explores and expands Melanie Klein's ideas.

# PERSECUTORY GUILT AND EGO RESTRICTIONS

## Characterization of a pre-depressive position

*Virgínia Leone Bicudo*

*This paper was read at the 23rd International Psycho-Analytical Congress, Stockholm, July–August 1963, and it was published in 1964 in the* International Journal of Psycho-Analysis, *45: 358–363.*

In a previous paper (1962) I have described the psycho-analytic process in the case of various patients who exhibited changes in their relationship to external and internal objects after a certain degree of better ego integration. After two years of psycho-analytic treatment in which I interpreted mainly the defenses deriving from persecutory anxiety, these patients reached a state of less tension and more efficiency, followed by the disappearance of the symptoms of which they were most aware. This emotional state, however, was not maintained. The patients were again invaded by persecutory anxiety, and there was a recurrence of inefficiency and a return of symptoms. Accompanying the emotional changes in these patients, I verified that the regressions took place under the pressure of a fantasy that their internal and external objects felt good only when they, the patients, found themselves in some way impaired or inefficient. From the analysis it became clear that the symptoms returned because of the fantasy that they were apportioning certain benefits to their objects. For instance, Mrs. X considered that her becoming efficient and so able to take care of her house and children, made her mother feel useless and her analysis unnecessary, whereas when she felt incapacitated, her mother (and the analyst) felt more important and the analysis was indispensable. This form of regression, related to the fantasy that through it certain benefits are apportioned to the objects, I call 'false reparation'. The psychic mechanisms of defense bound to this sort of false reparation imply, in my view, persecutory anxiety related to a more integrated ego suffering from schizoid–paranoid anxiety described by Klein. The patients

be increased in order to avoid depression, a regression from the depressive to the paranoid–schizoid one' (Klein, 1952).

It is the aim of this paper to call attention to the occurrence of another solution intermediate between progressing to the depressive and regressing to the paranoid–schizoid position. The patients I have observed, after a diminution of their paranoid anxieties, though still unable to support depressive anxieties, protected themselves from these anxieties by utilizing anew the mechanisms of splitting and projective identification, now, however, in order to deal with guilt. Thus, instead of feeling guilty because of the attacks and harm done in fantasy to themselves and their objects, they feel anxious and desperate, facing an object whose only aim is to force them to feel guilty, not deserving of anything good, and in a compulsory way obliged to divide their possessions with them, the objects. Subsequent to the projection of their own feelings of guilt into their objects, the patients see themselves persecuted by their objects, whose only aim, in their fantasy, is to put guilt into the patients, which will force them to share benefits with the objects. The projected guilt, of which the patient is not conscious, is what I designate as persecutory guilt.

I am therefore using the term persecutory guilt in a different context from Melanie Klein. The process that Klein described as persecutory guilt is a regression to the schizoid–paranoid position in order to avoid guilt. Klein (1957) refers to guilt as persecution in the following terms: It appears that one of the consequences of excessive envy is an early onset of guilt. If premature guilt is experienced by an ego not yet capable of bearing it, guilt is felt as persecution and the object that arouses guilt is turned into a persecutor. The infant then cannot work through either depressive or persecutory anxiety because they become confused with each other. A few months later, when the depressive position arises, the more integrated and stronger ego has a greater capacity to bear the pain of guilt and to develop corresponding defenses, mainly the tendency to make reparation.

The process I am describing as persecutory guilt refers to the particular situation subsequent to the projection of guilt into the object, and omnipotent negation of guilt in the self. After the projection of guilt, with which the object is then confused and identified, the patient feels persecuted by the object, who is felt to be unjustly and aggressively forcing guilt into him as a way of obliging him to include the object libidinally in his pleasures, benefits, resources, and successes. This is the situation which I am indicating as a position between the depressive and the schizoid-paranoid positions, a division which, perhaps advisedly, Klein considered too schematic.

The specific defenses of the patient in relation to persecutory guilt correspond to the reverse of the persecutory anxiety connected with sadistic oral–anal–urethral fantasies, that is, they acquire a propitiatory feeling in relation to the objects. By projective identification the patient accuses the object of behaving in such a way that the former is obliged to carry guilt that he feels he should not carry but which should belong to the object. According to the patient's fantasies the one who is dependent, incapable, determined, ambitious, greedy, envious is the object, who is at the same time interested in getting rid of any guilt felt, because of its personal defects, pressing these into the patient. Mrs. X is a patient who in a burst of unrestrained anger expressed herself in the following terms:'I am cooperating in the analysis and I feel better, but why is it that I have to work like this and others don't? Why am I obliged to be better to my mother while nothing is demanded of her? Why is it I am obliged to work so hard to accomplish anything when nobody else is? Everybody in the world has problems, but they don't feel they need treatment; they live well and yet don't feel guilty about it. My mother gets everything without any effort on her part and without feeling guilty. I am a good person. I try to be better, but still I have to submit to this treatment. My mother can be selfish without feeling any guilt whatsoever. I hate her for making me suffer such an injustice. I can't stand the unfairness of my mother's being wrong and my being the one who has to be treated. I don't want to even think about it; it is beyond my comprehension and it makes me furious. Everybody else gets what he deserves, but my mother gets everything without deserving it'.

When Mrs. X felt better, because of a diminution in persecutory anxiety, instead of feeling guilty she came to feel unjustly treated by a mother full of faults but feeling blameless. Mrs. X's desperation came from her unsuccessful projective identifications of guilt into her mother, since the latter showed no signs whatsoever of feeling guilty.

In the case of Mrs.Y, anxiety and desperation because of persecutory guilt are even more evident. 'Now that I have succeeded in getting everything I could possibly want, I have no peace of mind. My children are healthy, my husband is good to me, I am rich. I can buy what I want, but I am sad thinking about my mother. She is a widow and is neither independent nor self-sufficient, and for this reason I feel her as a dead weight upon my shoulders.

If I buy something for myself, I must buy the same thing for her, if not I feel guilty. On Saturdays she comes to my house with the face of a sad person to make me feel guilty because I am happy, and will then include her in all the good things I have. Her presence takes away my freedom with my husband. I even deprive myself of the affection of my children because of her. It is not my fault that she is a widow and that she isn't capable of organizing her life

confrontation by, depressive guilt. The regression to a schizoid-paranoid position corresponds to a loss of possessions and enjoyment of certain ego capacities already attained, while progression to a depressive position is anticipated with anxiety coming from a sentiment of guilt, felt as irreparable, irreversible, unchangeable, and beyond the ego's capacity to bear. The propitiation of the object is a compromise the ego makes in an attempt to protect itself from the anxieties that would accompany either a deeper regression or an evolution to the depressive position. Giving up its capacities, the ego tries to benefit and placate its objects, at the same time that it frees itself from the task of dealing with its own feelings of guilt and need for reparation. Klein (1952) described the above situation as follows:

> During the first three or four months of life, a stage at which (according to my present views) depressive anxiety and guilt arise, splitting processes and persecutory anxiety are at their height. Therefore persecutory anxiety very quickly interferes with progress in integration, and experiences of depressive anxiety, guilt, and reparation can only be of a transitory nature. As a result the loved injured object may very swiftly change into a persecutor, and the urge to repair or revive the loved object may turn into the need to pacify and propitiate a persecutor.

By attacking the capacities of the ego or by creating psychosomatic symptoms or developing adverse situations, the patient suffering from persecutory guilt hopes to compensate the external and internal objects for the crime of being able to use his resources, for progress, for health, etc. To the extent to which the patient from fear of retaliation refuses to utilize his own resources, not only for his own benefit but also for that of his objects, he replaces guilt by self-punishment, as propitiation to his objects. Through self-punishment as a propitiation, the patient tries to gratify the internal and external objects as if, by his suffering and giving up his capacities and good feeling, his objects would become content, happy and exalted in their self-esteem. This intrapsychic situation can be seen in the following reactions of X and Y. Patient X: 'I wanted so much to continue feeling independent and capable, but I have returned to feeling afraid to travel, and so I can't leave the city and live where I would like to live. It only remains for me to accept my mother with all her faults and in this way she will be happy.' Patient Y: 'I was feeling so good, but now everything is the same as it was before. I am again inefficient in everything that I have to do in the house. I get short of breath and the work just doesn't get done, or I keep sitting down without knowing where to begin. It is better, really, for mother to come to the house and take care of everything. That way she will feel of some use'.

The emotional equilibrium resulting from this compromise is short-lived. In a short time the patient will again be using projective identification in an attempt to force his objects to feel guilty. The same symptom used as propitiation is then used for the aggressive aim of projecting guilt once more into the object. Therefore we can consider that persecutory guilt and projective identification are connected with libidinal as well as with aggressive feelings. Consequently the patient is bound to feel and complain of his objects as persecutors who aggressively demand love and reparation from him.

In the two cases above cited, personal independence signifies the expression of rejection of the guilty mother, that is, repulsion of self-guilt with which the mother is identified. On the other hand, the symptomatic dependence of these patients corresponds to the protection of their objects in the sense of not leaving them alone to carry the bad parts of the self, related to the projected guilt. By exhibiting symptoms the patient shows his love for his objects, while projecting guilt into the objects the patient manifests his aggressive feelings towards them. These considerations find support in the hypotheses formulated by Freud and cited by Klein (1932) in the following terms: 'When an instinctive tendency is repressed, its libidinal elements are transformed into symptoms and its aggressive components into a feeling of guilt'.

Owing to continuous experience of projections and introjections and to the progressive development of maturity, processes of ego integration go on from the moment of birth. It is in this situation that the child begins to perceive, inside and outside himself, an object which has the same desire for the good and the same repulsion for the bad as he has, and which tries to obtain its ends by using the same means. This is the emotional climate in which persecutory guilt originates, owing to which the child perceives a bad object hoping to get from him something good, so that he is made to feel guilty as if facing an object of which he is in need. The fantasies of a patient suffering from persecutory guilt clearly show their projective aspect; the object (breast mother) is in need and imperfect (poor, dependent, greedy, envious, widow, etc.), and with no feeling of guilt wants to participate in all the advantages of the child, making him feel bad. Originally the child felt anxious, because of his dependence on the object, which he denied, idealizing himself and seeing the object as worthless. Persecutory guilt is the opposite side of this picture: the object is dependent, denies its deficiencies, and wants to blackmail the

object is caused by the subject's aggressive impulses is the essence of guilt (Klein, 1960). I am suggesting that persecutory guilt follows any integration achieved by the ego before depressive guilt is established. Therefore each small integration that occurs during the schizoid-paranoid position gives rise to guilt, which is immediately projected as a bad quality. This persecutor carrying the ego's guilt differs from the greedy and envious persecutors in the sense that the former intends to get everything good from the ego by making it guilty. Consequently, instead of the reparative tendency arising from the sense of guilt, persecutory guilt tends to propitiation. In order to get rid of the sense of guilt the ego gives up its capacities, thus placating a demanding and harmful object. At the same time making the object feel guilt, the ego gets the reassurance that it can continue to receive benefits from its objects. Persecutory guilt, therefore, has the following characteristics: it appears following processes of ego integration in the form of complaints such as: the ego is not responsible for having good things when the others do not; the object wants to force the ego to feel guilty for something he shouldn't; the object forces the patient to show consideration and obliges him to divide his possessions and share his successes; the patient feels resentful at seeing himself treated so unjustly, he is not to be blamed for the defects of others. Such characteristics of persecutory guilt are a consequence of the relationship of the ego to part objects dealt with by means of projective identifications. Persecutory guilt evolves into depressive guilt only when the ego, with more maturity, becomes capable of establishing relations with whole objects.

Rosenfeld (1962) has considered persecutory guilt connected with the development of the superego, referring to the earliest superego linked with persecution and a superego arising later and related to depression. From this point of view, Rosenfeld pointed out two kinds of superego: (a) one more primitive and characterized by an essentially persecutory and punishing figure or a figure excessively demanding, corresponding to the splitting of the object into a persecutor and an idealized figure; (b) another superego more developed, arising in the depressive position, less primitive and more able to forgive and accept. Money-Kyrle (1955) follows this point of view.

According to the point of view I am putting forward in this paper, I distinguish three aspects in the development of the superego: (i) one superego mostly connected with persecution, and therefore not allowing manifestations of envy and greed; (ii) one superego still connected with idealization and specially connected with guilt and tending to propitiation; and (iii) the more developed superego connected with depression and driving towards reparation. Different methods for dealing with these different superegos emerge at each stage. Rosenfeld has pointed out that one of the methods of dealing with the persecuting superego figures 'is to increase aggression in order to get rid of them by killing'. Another way to get rid of the anxiety of persecutory guilt consists in demanding perfection from the object, therefore the object should never arouse envy or hate or guilt.

Persecutory guilt is the new element in the persecutory picture. It is linked with an ego too weak to confront the demands of a perfectionist superego. The method of defense for dealing with the perfectionist superego consists in diminishing its excessive rights by denigrating the object or by some sort of propitiation.

The more intense, however, the anxiety allied with persecuting guilt, the more impeded is the road to better integration. The regressions to a more primitive schizoid-paranoid state or the fixation on propitiation are indications of emotional difficulties caused by the intensity of the persecutory guilt. Masochistically, the patient gives up his own resources in order to placate the persecutor and feel himself free to deal with guilt and integration. On a deeper level, the self-reproaches of the melancholic are not legitimate but are destined to exempt him from a more deeply feared guilt, at the same time that the ego, blackening itself, thinks it is valuing, exalting, and gratifying its objects. Suicide due to persecutory guilt is linked to propitiatory fantasies.

Grinberg (1962) differentiates two types of guilt: persecutory and depressive. I agree with this differentiation, but I disagree with some aspects of his contention; for example, when he establishes a close relationship between persecutory guilt and the death instincts, between depressive guilt and the life instincts. I maintain the position of Freud and Klein, who agree that hate and aggression are the deepest basis and cause of guilt feelings. Both persecutory and depressive guilt refer to 'the fact that the harm done to the loved object is caused by the subject's aggressive impulses'. As to the characteristics that differentiate persecutory guilt from depressive guilt, these arise from the fact that the former evolves while the child is in relationship with only part objects, and is only capable of feeling depressive guilt, real consideration for the object, after having experienced relationship with whole objects. The pain that accompanies the feelings of persecutory guilt corresponds to the fantasy of an absolute loss of parts of the self or parts of the object, perceived as total. In the depressive position, the pain coming from loss is relative, a fact which makes the way to reparation possible. Nevertheless, to the extent to which persecutory anxiety or anxiety due to persecutory guilt exist, depressive guilt is prevented from appearing because

corresponds to a loss. This fantasy is often responsible for the negative therapeutic reaction of patients described by Joan Riviere (1936). Out of fear of loss, not only is progress towards psychic integration anticipated with anxiety but each progressive step achieved is followed by anxiety with a greater or less intensity, depending on the amount of sadism involved. According to Klein (1960) the guilt of the schizophrenic applies to destroying something good in himself and also to weakening his ego by splitting processes. Bion (1959) has shown that attacks made against anything to do with the function of linking one object with another have the consequence of arresting the psychic development. Grinberg (1962) considers that one of the principal causes for the appearance of persecutory guilt is the deficiency in which the ego finds itself as a consequence of the birth trauma. I agree with these points of view, which reinforce the projective aspect of persecutory guilt, which constitutes an attack on the ego (attack on the perception of psychic reality) and an attack on the object, making it responsible for the loss. Persecutory guilt is then a defense of the ego, making growth possible. Alternatively persecutory guilt can arise as a resistance to the reintegration of the perception of its own aggression against any experience of loss.

The resentment of the ego, feeling itself unjustly accused by the object as an ungrateful and selfish person, is the feeling most characteristic of persecutory guilt. The diminution of this resentment, initially from the analysis of persecutory anxiety (when the ego cannot yet tolerate the analysis of the identifying aspect) results in a better ego integration. When patients come to analysis, all their interest is centralized in wanting the analyst to put an end to their anxieties and symptoms. All lessening of schizoid-paranoid anxieties achieved in the treatment is first utilized for a reintegration of ego capacities. I believe that only then, after restitutive 'reparations' of the ego's capacities have taken place, is the ego in a position to utilize its resources for reparation to the object.

In conclusion, I have described an intermediary position (which I call the pre-depressive position) between the schizoid-paranoid and the depressive positions connected with a perfectionist superego and characterized by persecutory guilt, which is linked with the mechanisms of projective identification, propitiation, and denigration of the object.

# Summary

The process that I describe as persecutory guilt refers to a particular situation subsequent to the projection of guilt into the object and negation of guilt in the self. Consequently the patient feels persecuted by the object, who 'unjustly' and aggressively forces guilt into him as a way of obliging him to include the object libidinally in his pleasures, benefits, resources, and successes.

The aim of this paper is to call attention to the occurrence of another intermediary solution between progressing to the depressive position and regressing to the schizoid–paranoid position. The patients I have observed, after a diminution of their paranoid anxieties, although still unable to bear depressive anxieties, protected themselves from these anxieties utilizing anew the mechanisms of splitting and projective identification, now, however, in order to deal with guilt. Thus, instead of feeling guilty because of the aggressions and harm done in fantasy to themselves and their objects, they feel anxious and desperate in facing an object whose only aim is to force them to feel guilty, not deserving of anything good and compulsorily obliged to divide their possessions with them, the objects.

The struggle of the patient involved in persecutory guilt aims at finding a refuge from the two types of hazard: that of a new regression to the primitive schizoid–paranoid position and that of progression to and confrontation of depressive guilt. The regression to the schizoid–paranoid position corresponds to a loss of possessions and enjoyments of certain ego capacities already attained, while progression to a depressive position is anticipated with anxiety from a sentiment of guilt, felt as irreparable, irreversible, unchangeable, and so beyond the ego's capacity to bear. The propitiation of the object is a compromise that the ego makes as an attempt to protect itself from the anxieties that would bring about either a deeper regression or an evolution to the depressive position. Giving up its capacities, the ego aims to benefit and placate its objects, at the same time that it frees itself from the task of dealing with its own feelings of guilt and need for reparation.

Each progressive step achieved is followed by persecutory guilt with more or less intensity depending on the amount of sadism involved. Persecutory guilt appears following processes of ego integration, and evolves into depressive guilt only when the ego, with more maturity, becomes capable of establishing relations with whole objects. However, the more intense the anxiety allied with persecutory guilt is, the more is the road to a better integration impeded. The regression to a more primitive schizoid–paranoid state or to false reparation is indications of emotional difficulties caused by the intensity of the persecutory guilt in operation.

The resentment of the ego, feeling itself unjustly accused by the object as a person unable to be concerned and to feel gratitude, is the sentiment

In conclusion, I have described an intermediary position, which I call the pre-depressive position, connected with a perfectionist superego and characterized by persecutory guilt, which is linked with the mechanisms of projective identification, propitiation, and denigration of the object.

# References

BICUDO, VIRGÍNIA L. 1962 'False Mourning and False Reparation.' Given at the Fourth Latin-American Congress, Rio de Janeiro.

BION, W. 1957 'The Differentiation of the Psychotic from the Non-Psychotic Part of the Personality.' *International Journal of Psycho-Analysis* 38

BION, W. 1959 'Attacks on Linking.' *International Journal of Psycho-Analysis* 40

GRINBERG, L. 1962 'Normal and Pathological Aspects of Grief.' Given at the Fourth Latin-American Congress, Rio de Janeiro.

KLEIN, M. 1932 *The Psycho-Analysis of Children* (London: Hogarth.)

KLEIN, M. 1952 *Developments in Psycho-Analysis* (London: Hogarth.)

KLEIN, M. 1957 *Envy and Gratitude* (London: Tavistock.)

KLEIN, M. 1960 'A Note on Depression in the Schizophrenic.' *International Journal of Psycho-Analysis* 41

KLEIN, M. 1961 *Narrative of a Child Analysis* (London: Hogarth.)

MONEY-KYRLE, R. 1955 'Psycho-Analysis and Ethics.' In: *New Directions in Psycho-Analysis* ed. Klein et al. (London: Tavistock.)

RIVIERE, JOAN 1936 'A Contribution to the Analysis of Negative Therapeutic Reaction.' *International Journal of Psycho-Analysis* 17

ROSENFELD, H. 1962 'The Superego and the Ego-Ideal.' *International Journal of Psycho-Analysis* 43

# INTRODUCTION TO THE LIFE AND WORK OF ANGEL GARMA (1904–1993)

## Iñaki Marquez

Angel Garma was a world-renowned psychoanalyst and an outstanding symbol of an era of extraordinary dynamic and creative developments in Western Culture and psychoanalysis. He is, in my view, one of the founding "fathers" of psychoanalysis in the Spanish-speaking world, and the Founding Father of psychoanalysis in Spain.

Angel Garma was born on June 24, 1904, in Bilbao, Spain, and died in Buenos Aires on January 29, 1993. He did his medical training at the Universidad Complutense in Madrid and always intended to be a psychiatrist. He was taught by distinguished professors, of the caliber of Ramon y Cajal, Ortega y Gasset and Gregorio Marañon.

He counted amongst his friends Federico García Lorca, Salvador Dalí, Luis Buñuel, Severo Ochoa, José María Hinojosa and other future famous artists of the Generation of '27, with whom he shared the intellectual atmosphere of this extraordinary group of artists during the years leading to the Spanish Civil War.

Garma graduated as a psychiatrist in Tübingen, Germany, in 1929. He then initiated psychoanalytic training in Berlin and became a member of the German Psychoanalytic Society. He had analysis with Theodor Reik and participated in the Society's scientific life together with Alexander, Wilhelm Reich, Spitz, Gustav Jung, Erich Fromm, Alfred Adler, etc. He befriended Ana Freud and Lou Andreas-Salomé.

In 1931, he returned to Madrid, where he was the only analyst trained as such and a member of the International Psychoanalytic Association.

The civil war and the end of the Republic put an end to the attempt to establish a psychoanalytic movement in Spain, sending his only representative into exile. He established residence in Bordeaux and later Paris until the political situation in France deteriorated so much that he was forced to emigrate to Buenos Aires, Argentina, in 1938.

For Franco's dictatorship, psychoanalysis was part of the Jewish-Marxist-Masonic conspiracy, the enemy that had to be eliminated. Garma and psychoanalysis were deprived of a "home", means of communication and

When Garma arrived in Buenos Aires, he brought with him a solid training, strong convictions and creativity. Soon, a group of determined professionals joined him to create the foundations of one of the most productive psychoanalytic groups in the world. He was one of the founders of the first psychoanalytic society in South America, the Argentine Psychoanalytic Association, and was appointed as its first President, a position he held on a few other occasions. He also founded the Institute of Psychoanalysis, and taught there for many years.

He became the paradigm of the ideal psychoanalyst that most Latin American analysts tried to follow. He was a clinician with solid theoretical foundation and an excellent and highly valued teacher who instilled in his students the value of independent thinking. He was a Freudian who rejected orthodoxy where his clinical practice led him to disagree with Freud. He questioned some of Freud's ideas about psychosis and dreams.

In 1931 Garma was accepted as a member of the Berlin psychoanalytic Association after presenting the paper "Die Realität und das Es in der Schizophrenie" (Reality and the Id in Schizophrenia). In this essay, Garma questions Freud's idea that in psychosis reality is repressed and the Id dominates psychic life. Garma asserts that in both pathologies the Id impulses are repressed – in psychosis more radically but in a similar way – resulting in a disturbance of the connection with reality.[1] In this respect, neurosis and psychosis can be seen as a continuum and not as radically different structures.

Garma thought that dreams were the result of conflict, like any other symptom. The hallucinatory satisfaction of wishes is just a defense against the traumatic anxiety expressed and contained in the dream experience. Consequently, dreams are masked nightmares. Although he disagreed with Freud regarding the nature and function of dreams, Garma's view makes Freud's dictum that dream analysis is the "royal road to the unconscious" even more compelling.

414

Garma rejected the body/mind dichotomy. He thought that those divisions are arbitrary and only confuse and mislead the understanding of a human being. Symptoms triggered by physical or chemical triggers may not be different from those triggered by psychic conflict. Furthermore, they may reinforce each other. The foundations of Garma's ideas about psychosomatic medicine can be found in Franz Alexander and Georg Groddeck's research on this subject.

In psychosomatic patients, he found narcissistic psychic structures, early libidinal fixations and failure of symbolic function that obliterates the road to insight and working- through.

A common thread in most of Garma's scientific production is related to what already was present in his 1931 paper: the repression of instinctual impulses (Id impulses) demanded by a sadistic Superego and masochistically accepted by a submissive Ego.

Angel Garma published more than 100 papers and 11 books that he himself organized in several groups: dreams and dreams as trauma; psychopathology; psychosomatic medicine (his work on gastric ulcer and migraine merit special mention); psychoanalytic technique, with special emphasis on sadism and masochism; ornamental art and social subjects. His language was to a great extent devoid of unnecessary analytic jargon and simple; he was always trying to make himself understood.

Unfortunately, the fascism and genocide that he tried to avoid in his own country caught up with him in the Argentinian genocidal "Dirty" War during the 1970s when he was already retired. Although analysts were also targets, he managed to preserve an optimistic outlook for humanity and psychoanalysis.

In his old age, he became reluctant to appear in public due to a neurological condition that impaired his mobility. His wife, Elizabeth Goode, and daughters were his caretakers and encouraged him not to isolate himself and to remain an active participant in the lively scientific activities taking place in Buenos Aires. Elizabeth Goode was a prestigious pioneer of child analysis in her own right.

Angel Garma's work was recognized and honored by psychoanalysts, society and governments. He was honorary Vice President of the IPA and Honorary President of the Latin American Psychoanalytic Association (FEPAL). He was decorated by King Juan Carlos I from Spain, honored in Argentina by the Konex Foundation (Humanities section), and the Institute of the Argentine Psychoanalytic Association was named after him.

It is curious that an originally Spanish father of Argentinian and South American psychoanalysis insisted in his last years that his ashes be thrown in Bilbao in the estuary of el Ebro river. After his death, his wife, in February 1994, fulfilled his dream. It was his last trip to his native Bilbao.

## Note

1   Editors' addenda: Id impulses, in this model, are an integral and necessary component of our capacity to understand and connect with reality. Klein took it further when asserting the existence of an epistemophilic drive. Garma's ideas are also linked to Bion's models of psychotic thought disturbances.

# THE TRAUMATIC SITUATION IN THE GENESIS OF DREAMS

## Angel Garma

*This paper was published in 1946 by the* International Journal of Psycho-Analysis, *27: 134–139.*

Dreams are the gratification of unconscious wishes. This psycho-analytic concept does not conflict even with masochistic dreams, nor with dreams that produce anxiety or that represent punishment by the Superego.

Nevertheless, there is a kind of dream that seems to be an exception – the dreams of traumatic neurosis. When somebody has suffered a great psychic shock, which is relatively frequent in wartime, his dreams are a monotonous reproduction of the unpleasant sensations experienced at the moment of the trauma. In these dreams there is no wish gratified by the hallucinations in the reproduction of the traumatic situation.

There is also another exception. Very frequently the presence of forgotten disagreeable experiences can be discerned in dreams; experiences of the subject's childhood which had a traumatic influence on his psychic evolution. If dreams reproduce these infantile traumatic experiences with great frequency, we have another contradiction to the theory of wish gratification. Not altogether, however, since in these dreams the infantile traumatic situation is often modified and turned towards wish fulfillment.

Freud does not believe that the exception proves the rule. The most one can say, according to him, is that an exception does not nullify the rule. Bearing in mind the exceptions we have mentioned, where the supposed function of a dream fails, Freud made a slight modification in the psycho-analytic theory. Instead of saying that a dream is the gratification of wishes, he says that a dream is an attempt to gratify wishes.

In our opinion, the traumatic situation does not only contribute to the dreams of traumatic neurosis and those reproducing certain infantile traumatic situations. It contributes to all dreams. We believe that the existence of a traumatic situation is a very important factor in the genesis of dreams, possibly the most important factor of all. This opinion is a new point of view in the study of dream psychology. We shall attempt to prove our

to the latter authors, 58% of adult dreams are unpleasant. This last observation is not in itself an unsurmountable objection to the psycho-analytic theory since, as we have already said, on being interpreted, unpleasant dreams may represent the gratification of wishes. The existence in the personality of instincts that trouble the Ego, the intervention of masochism and the existence of the Superego might explain the apparent objection.

But somehow this explanation does not quite satisfy us. It seems as if, even making allowance for all the motives we have mentioned, the frequency of the unpleasant character of dreams is not wholly explained. On studying and interpreting our own dreams and those of others, we get the impression that the dream is attracted by what is disagreeable and painful.

At a time in his treatment when masochism was frequently manifest, a patient told me the following phantasy: 'A man secretly breaks into my sister's room and rapes her. I discover him, and after a struggle I overpower him. I knock him down and crush his skull with the heel of my shoes.' Then the patient asked, 'Is this phantasy of a sadistic or masochistic type?' He had no doubt that the analyst would declare it to be sadistic; he liked to think of himself as a sadist whereas his masochism was distasteful to him. My reply was as follows: 'In your phantasy of crushing the other man's skull, your activity was sadistic; but as the source of your thoughts was the phantasy in which you imagined your sister to be raped, and as you identify yourself with her, the phantasy must rather be classed as masochistic. Your sadism is a superficial attempt to conquer the masochism that is the basis of the phantasy'. I believe that what took place in this phantasy also happens in dreams; the more or less intense satisfaction of wishes screens the disagreeable situations which the dreamer is subject to and which constitute the real basis of the dream.

There is another strange phenomenon in connection with the theory of wish fulfillment. This is the frequency with which the instinctual gratification in dreams is lacking in intensity. Dreams tend to be rather cowardly when it comes to getting satisfaction.

An example will help to make clear what we shall call the cowardice of dreams. During his psycho-analytic treatment a patient dreams: 'I kiss Aurea'. In his association he tells us that it concerns a young woman he met in X . . . and with whom he could have become intimate, as he wished, had he been a little more enterprising. The girl, whom he had visited on several occasions, had offered only slight resistance to his attempts to approach her but he had not dared to make any advances. During his treatment the patient blames himself for his conduct on that occasion.

Knowing the associations it is easy to explain the genesis of the dream. In the dream, the patient corrects a past situation that hurt his pride and was therefore disagreeable. So he turns it into a pleasant situation by daring to kiss the girl. But why does the patient only venture to dream of a kiss, when his associations clearly show that he wanted a more intimate contact? Why does he not dream, for instance, that Aurea is his mistress? The patient is just as unenterprising in his dream as he was before in reality.

Let us suppose that the reason for his real shyness with Aurea was the neurotic inhibition produced in him by the young woman who unconsciously represented his mother to him. In this case we can explain the lack of intensity of the instinctual satisfaction by the connection with the Oedipus complex. But why is he not bold enough to create a dream to destroy his inhibitions, making Aurea completely different from his mother, and in this way to have a happy and complete love affair with her?

We find the same thing in any other dream. For instance, one night after masturbating, X. dreamt the following:

'I have given myself a blow and lost a tooth. The teeth next to it are no longer firm and get loose.'

'I show my fiancée some fire. She is nervous but I keep calm.'

The first part of the dream is easily interpreted, by the symbolism of pulling out a tooth, as masturbation. That is, it repeats the patient's real situation before going to sleep. But the masturbation gave rise to intense fear of castration. The dream overcomes this fear in two ways. Firstly by displacement: the loss of one or several teeth is never as dreadful as castration. And secondly, by projecting his anxiety on to his fiancée: In the dream it is his fiancée and not the patient himself who is disquieted by the fire (or sexual excitement). But even so, in this supposedly soothing dream, X. admits both the loss of a tooth and anxiety. Why does he not achieve a greater satisfaction of his wishes by dreaming, for instance, that there is nothing wrong with him and that if there is fire, it does not destroy anything and that nobody feels anxiety? Of course, it can always be said that what prevents complete satisfaction is the intervention of the Superego that wants to punish the Ego on account of the masturbation. But in our opinion the fixation on the disagreeable ideas that originated the dream also contributes.

Any number of examples could be found but we shall limit ourselves to two more. We shall choose a dream, the first to be published with its psycho-analytic interpretation; the dream about 'Irma's injection'.

Otto, a friend of Freud's, one day gives him very unpleasant news about the condition of one of the latter's patients called Irma. Freud believes he detects in his friend's words certain veiled reproaches against his medical

not of psychogenic origin and consequently Freud is not to blame if he has not managed to cure her by psychological treatment.

Freud writes: 'It is as though Otto had said to me, "You do not take your medical duties seriously enough; you are not conscientious; you do not perform what you promise". Thereupon this train of thought placed itself at my service, in order that I might give proof of my extreme conscientiousness, of my intimate concern about the health of my relatives, friends and patients. Curiously enough, there are also some painful memories in this material, which confirm the blame attached to Otto rather than to my own exculpation . . . the wish to be innocent of Irma's illness. . . .' If the root of this dream is the fear of having been somewhat to blame through professional negligence in Irma's treatment, why does the dream not provide complete satisfaction of his wishes? Why doesn't he dream, for instance, that the treatment has been absolutely successful, that Irma is better than ever and that everyone admires him for the good results he has obtained?

The dream gives one the impression that Freud did not feel strong enough to reject the reproaches he believed himself to have sensed in his friend's words. It is as if the dream accumulated excuses without seriously believing any of them. This agrees completely with something Freud wrote about the interpretation of his dream. He writes: 'The whole plea – for this dream is nothing else – recalls vividly the defence offered by a man who was accused by his neighbour of having returned a kettle in a damaged condition. In the first place, he said, he had returned the kettle undamaged; in the second place, it already had holes in it when he borrowed it; and in the third place, he had never borrowed it at all'. Anyone hearing this man's defence would not hesitate to declare him guilty of having damaged the kettle. His words are a completely clear confirmation of what they intend to deny. The defence is bad just because the man is convinced of his guilt and is not strong enough to free himself from this traumatic situation. Freud's defence in the dream of Irma's injection must be similarly interpreted.

The other dream belongs to one of Freud's patients, Dora. The illustrious author has published it under the title 'Fragment of Analysis of a Case of Hysteria'. Freud gives us the complete interpretation of the dream with the mastery of a true genius – an interpretation that everyone interested in dreams should know. But as regards the theme now under discussion, let us remember only that the dream was a reaction to an unhappy love affair with Mr. K., with whom Dora was very much in love. Grieved by her disappointment, Dora has a dream in which she relives a period of her childhood when she suffered from nocturnal enuresis and her father used to lift her out of bed at nights before the accident happened. Therefore in the dream, she escapes from the present disagreeable situation, that is, her unhappy love affair, and seeks refuge in her father's love to prevent anything unpleasant happening. But why does the dream not dare to change the present situation, by denying, for instance, the existence of the unhappy love affair?

In all the dreams given there is a disagreeable psychic situation which gives rise to the dream. In the dream of 'kissing Aurea' the disagreeable situation is the subject's failure in his amorous attempt owing to internal motives; in the dream of showing his fiancée fire there is fear of castration; in the dream of Irma's injection, the fear of not having conducted the patient's treatment properly and in Dora's dream the disappointment about the man she loved. These disagreeable situations are the starting point for the dreams.

A disagreeable situation for the subject that the dream tries to correct is to be found at the root of the dream. This situation may be described as a disagreeable situation, a situation causing anxiety, a situation of psychic conflict, a traumatic situation, or by any analogous term. Recalling a definition of Freud's, we think the most adequate term is traumatic situation. Indeed, Freud gives the name of traumatic experience to one that produces in a short space of time such an intensity of psychic stimuli that the subject cannot ward them off, or elaborate them in the normal, ordinary way.

The study of some dreams leaves little room for doubt that the most appropriate term to use is that of traumatic situation. It is clearly the case, for instance, in the following dreams of a man who was in a deep depression because his wife had deserted him and eloped with her lover to a distant country onboard a ship. The subject felt he was to blame for this traumatic situation on account of the 'ejaculatio precox' with which he was afflicted. His first dream is as follows:

'With my wife again; I ask her if she wants to marry me. She wants to know whether it will last long. A fellow student is present.'

'To marry' means to have genital relations and 'to last long' refers to the 'ejaculatio precox'. As to the fellow student, through several associations he was found to represent the idea of normal genital potency.

Second dream:

'At X . . ., in the garden of my home. My mother is there and also my wife and a neighbour. There are a lot of clothes – women's clothes – washed and hanging up to dry.'

The dream means: 'To wash dirty linen at home' without anything of what had happened leaking out. This is the situation represented by the

explaining what has happened.'

This dream tries to overcome the traumatic situation by a projection onto his brother. The stolen goods represent his wife; the boat, her means of escape, and the crowd, the patient's condition of social fear.

These three dreams, therefore, are three different ways in which the subject tries to solve his conflict. In the first dream he persuades his wife to come back and live with him; in the second he settles the affair in the privacy of his home without the interference of strangers; in the third it is his brother and not himself who has the conflict and who must solve it. And the three different mechanisms are used with the purpose of allaying the psychic anxiety provoked by the traumatic situation to which he is fixated and which gives rise to his dreams.

The following characteristics leave no doubt as to the wife's desertion being a really traumatic situation. The patient who reacts with intense affects which he is unable to master – affects which bring about a psychogenic depression – believes that he is the one who is responsible for her desertion; besides, he feels that he will not be able to come to any arrangement. These are the characteristics that give the situation a traumatic character; the other terms – disagreeable situation, situation causing anxiety or situation of conflict – are less appropriate descriptions for the psychological phenomenon. We shall illustrate this point by a comparison. Let us suppose that a normal man is in love with a woman and that she leaves him and runs away with another man. The normal man will react by thinking that his conduct has been correct and that the woman's flight is due to some motive that has nothing to do with his own conduct. Also he will feel strong enough to win back the woman or dispense with her without feeling too badly about it; and besides he will feel capable of punishing his rival. The woman's flight is also a disagreeable situation for this man or one that causes anxiety or conflict, but it is not traumatic; for he is able to master and elaborate psychically and normally the affects it has produced. On the other hand, for our patient, besides being disagreeable the situation is traumatic because he is unable to master his affects and react like a normal person.

Continuing our train of thought, we believe that a supposedly normal person would not have dreams like those of our patient, just because he is able to dominate his affects.

Although the external situation is not always as clear-cut as in these last dreams, we can apply the term traumatic situation to what is found, after a deep interpretation, to be the essential motive in dreams. And in nightmares, the traumatic situation is apt to appear in the manifest content with hardly any deformation.

To assert the existence of a traumatic situation as the basis of dreams is completely in accordance with other psycho-analytic findings. The patient's fixation to one or several traumatic situations always proves to be at the root of neurotic symptoms, and the analogy existing between dreams and neurotic symptoms is already known to us. On the other hand, to assert the existence of a fixation to a traumatic situation in dreams does not contradict the theory of wish gratification. Rather, it completes this theory, pointing out an essential fact that must be taken into account for the interpretation. Not only does it not invalidate the theory of wish gratification, but, on the contrary, it strengthens it, for the following reason. If we compare the latent content with the manifest content of dreams, except in dreams of traumatic neurosis, it can be seen that the traumatic situation constituting the basis of the latent content is transformed in the manifest content into a pleasant situation. That is to say, that in the elaboration of the dream a clear evolution towards the gratification of the wish has taken place.

The existence of a fundamental traumatic situation explains the reason for the dream's cowardice in the gratification of wishes. Dreams are incapable of venturing very far towards gratification because the subject is psychically fixed to the traumatic situation. Without this fixation the satisfaction of wishes would be much more complete.

The traumatic situation is in our opinion the principal factor in the dream and it is also the cause for thoughts taking a regressive path, leaving the abstract terms of ordinary thinking for concrete hallucinations. As for traumatic neurosis, there is no doubt at all that in these cases the traumatic situation is the origin of dreams. The same thing must be the case in all other dreams. The satisfied wish is not the cause of the hallucinatory regression, i.e. of the dream, but only an attempt at diminishing the psychic displeasure brought about by the fixation on the traumatic situation.[1]

In the interpretation of dreams an attempt should always be made to find the basic traumatic situation (or situations). In doing so it is necessary to bear in mind the patient's psychology and the fact that a wish that would be pleasurable to a normal individual might be traumatic to a neurotic. This is the case in the following dream produced by a man with genital inhibitions.

'I am lying with my fiancée and I am sexually excited. I want to have intercourse with her, but it is then eight o'clock in the morning and the maid comes in to pull up the blinds. This is annoying to me.'

This dream also came from the subject who brought the above-mentioned dream about the loss of a tooth. In the present dream the traumatic situation is brought about by his desire for a more intimate relationship with his

dream; not the psychic liberation or diminishing of tension that he experiences when the maid enters the room, creating an external obstacle in doing so.

In a more normal person, wishes similar to the patient's, which were clearly sexual desires towards the loved one, would not act traumatically and therefore would not constitute the origin of a dream. This had already been observed by Delage, who in 1891, speaking about the dreams of young married couples, stated that 'if they were very much in love they hardly ever dreamt about each other before marriage or on their honeymoons; and if they did happen to dream about love they committed an infidelity with an indifferent or hateful person in them'.

A dream has one or several traumatic situations as its basis. A traumatic situation, in turn, may revive an analogous situation; not a present one but one of the subject's past experiences. This happens, for instance, in Dora's dream, mentioned before. The present traumatic situation is her disappointing love affair with Mr. K., and she revives an analogous one of her childhood caused by her nocturnal enuresis. The wish satisfaction applies to the infantile traumatic situation; for in her dream Dora hallucinates her father at her bedside as he used to be when she was a child and he went to her to prevent her wetting the bed. This dream clearly describes the characteristic of traumatic situations, which is the subject's incapacity to solve it unaided. Dora has to get her father's help in her dream because she thinks she is incapable of handling the situation. The gratification of wishes in the dream consists in her getting her father's help through reviving her infantile love for him.

The interpretation of two dreams will show in a practical way and more clearly than up to now, the importance of present and past traumatic situations in the genesis of dreams. Here is the first: 'I ask my friends whether any of them is going to Berlin because Delia wishes to send something to her husband Juan Garcia. My friends tell me that Garcia is back again in Buenos Aires and point him out to me at a nearby table. I reflect that Garcia is in Buenos Aires and he has not been to see his wife yet'.

We are dealing with the dream of a patient who had been under psycho-analytical treatment for a long time and had considerably improved his psychical condition but without having yet reached normality. The dream is a reaction to a certain aspect of the patient's present life. At that time he had an intimate friendship with a woman that made him feel happy.

The patient's neurosis made him react to this with intense guilt feelings and great fears of a possible rival when he attempted the conquest of any woman. He was afraid this rival would attack and overpower him. So great were these fears that on one occasion, after having had intercourse with a woman he had the feeling that a man was following him in the street and that he entered his house after him and slipped into his room when no one was looking with the purpose of harming him in some way. At the time of the dream, psycho-analysis had diminished the patient's fears of a rival, without, however, destroying them completely. Even during this period of happy sexual relations the patient could not help thinking of a possible rival who was represented in this case by an ex-lover of his mistress. He was afraid this rival would return and take the woman away from him, for he felt incapable of fighting him. This, then, was the fundamental traumatic situation that gave rise to the dream. As for Delia, i.e. Garcia's wife, she was a woman the patient had thought of courting one or two months before; but he had not dared to do so for fear of her husband. Delia was very neurotic and her conduct was hardly normal. At the time of the dream she had a lover, and unaware of the attraction the patient felt towards her, she tried to confide in him. He rejected this, reacting with intense aggressive wishes.

The patient's first thoughts about the dream were that Garcia had not been to visit his wife because he had found out her infidelity and had decided never to see her again.

In his present love relationship, the patient fears the appearance of his rival who would dispute the possession of the woman on the grounds that she was his first. He dare not fight; and here is the present traumatic situation. In order to overcome it, a former analogous situation is revived in the dream; a situation in which the patient was also in love with a woman (Delia) and feared the coming of his rival (in this case the husband). This former analogous situation meant a failure for the patient, for he did not win the woman who fell in love with someone else. However, this failure has an advantage for the patient, because through it he can overcome his fear of the rival by telling himself that he is not Delia's lover and therefore the rival will never make him answer for his conduct as he probably would do with Delia's lover. Besides the dream reassures him, for the husband does not commit any aggression against his wife but limits himself to not going to see her. Applied to the present traumatic situation this means for him that the man with whom his mistress was formerly in love will not go to see her either, nor will he come between them. The patient could not dream that the husband committed an aggression against his wife, even if by doing so he could have satisfied his own aggressive wishes, because it would have made him fear that his present possible rival would also behave aggressively towards him. The former analogous traumatic situation has the added advantage of allowing the patient to worry over the feared rival (represented in the dream

tion of the patient's behaviour when he learnt that Delia had a lover. He avoided going to a party where he knew Delia and her friends would be, and went elsewhere to be alone while he indulged in fantasies in which he satisfied the aggressive wishes provoked by his disappointment. In short: the traumatic situation is the fear of the rival against whom the patient feels incapable of fighting. The wishes gratified in the dream are: (1) the patient is not guilty; (2) the rival does not interfere; (3) the patient worries over his rival motivated by friendship and not by fear; (4) Delia is punished because her husband discovers her infidelity. This dream bears certain resemblance to Dora's, for in it the present traumatic situation also revives a former analogous traumatic situation where the wish is gratified.

The following dream comes from the same patient and springs from the same traumatic situation; but it is differently elaborated. It is more complicated than the preceding dream, and I believe it, therefore, to be of interest, since it helps to show once again, the channels through which psychic connections are made between the different thoughts of a dream. The dream is as follows:

'A friend of your brother's, Vila or Vela, has died in an explosion. I also dreamt about a woman, Margarita.'

The patient's present lady friend seems to be in love with him and is faithful to him; but his neurosis makes him fear that some day she will leave him for someone else. This fear increases if there is any real event that seems to confirm it, which was what happened on the day of the dream when his friend told him that she had spoken to her former fiancé.

The traumatic situation underlying the dream is the belief that his mistress will leave him for another man, and that he will not know how to retain her. This present traumatic situation, just as in the preceding dream, and in Dora's, revives a former analogous situation connected with Margarita, the woman who appears in the manifest content. Margarita was a woman whom the patient had courted with little success. For instance, he remembers among other things that one day when he went out with her and some other friends, Margarita left him alone and went off with an Italian, X. He felt he was not capable of getting her back. Embittered by his failure, the patient reacted with intense aggressive feelings and death wishes towards his rival. This situation is at the same time associated with another. On one occasion the patient was in real great danger from which he managed to escape with great difficulty. In his flight he met an Italian acquaintance named Vila who treated him badly. Some time later the patient heard that Vila had died in tragic circumstances. The situation of escape has in common with the situation of Margarita the fact that in both of them there is 'an Italian who behaves badly towards the patient'; this common fact psychically associates these two situations. In both cases the patient harboured death wishes against the person who treated him badly. A real event, Vila's tragic death, accidentally satisfied these wishes in the second case. That is why 'the death of Vila', that also represents all the other similar experiences for the patient, appears in the manifest content of the dream.

Another kind of analogous thoughts spring from the affective transference. From infantile motives, the patient also regarded the analyst as a more fortunate rival whom he felt incapable of defeating – here again is the traumatic situation – and against whom he felt death wishes of infantile origin, just as he felt against the other rivals in the situations we have described. The analyst's brother, whom the patient knew, was one of the number of persons who, for the patient's psyche, had the characteristics of a more fortunate rival. On one occasion he heard a woman praise his virile appearance, which roused the patient's envy and consequently the infantile reaction of death wishes. This gave rise to the thought of 'the brother's death', which, as we shall presently see, was also psychically connected.

The psycho-analyst's brother had a friend named Vela who worked in a factory with a brother of his. Once there was an explosion in the factory and Vela's brother was killed. This event is related, through the fact of Author brother, to the thought the patient had before, which was, the wish for the death of the psycho-analyst's brother.

In spite of being the patient's unconscious wish, this last-mentioned thought (the death of the analyst's brother) cannot be included in the manifest content of the dream because it is an immoral thought which the endopsychic censorship rejects. A displacement is made and the objectionable thought is substituted in the dream by the more indifferent one of the death of Vela's brother. It also has the added advantage of having actual facts to lean on.

Now, it is not Vela's brother who dies in the dream but Vela himself. This error in the reproduction of the real event in the dream is due to the fact that the original death wishes were not directed against the analyst's brother but against the analyst himself.

Finally, to bind the dream together, all the thoughts are connected through the similarity in sound of the surnames Vila and Vela. The superficial association through similarity of form, screens a connection on a deeper level due to analogous psychic contents.

In short, the basic traumatic situations of the dream are: the patient's fear of his rival whom he feels incapable of defeating and his regarding his

With the interpretation of this dream, we reach the end of our investigation of the traumatic situation in dreams. And now, if we consider our findings, we may make the following statements:

1   Dreams spring from one or more disagreeable situations that the subject is unable to master or elaborate normally, and to which, using Freud's terminology, we have given the name of traumatic situations.
2   In the dream, the subject is psychically fixated to these traumatic situations.
3   Dreams are generally successful attempts to overcome the psychic displeasure brought about by traumatic situations.
4   The attempt to overcome psychic displeasure is effected through wish fulfillment.
5   The hallucinatory aspect of dreams is due to the influence of traumatic situations and not to the influence of the wishes they gratify.

## Note

1   The influence of the traumatic situation on the genesis of the hallucinatory aspect of dreams has been studied by me (see Garma, 1946).

## Reference

GARMA, A. 1946 'The Genesis of Reality Testing. A General Theory of Hallucination' *The Psychoanalytic Quarterly* 15:161

# INTRODUCTION TO THE LIFE AND WORK OF IGNACIO MATTE BLANCO (1908–1995)

## Juan Francisco Jordan-Moore

Ignacio Matte Blanco was born in Santiago on October 3, 1908, and passed away in Rome on January 11, 1995. The younger son of an aristocratic Chilean family, he was educated at the German *Gymnasium* in Santiago and at the University of Chile, from which he graduated physician-surgeon in 1930. He went to London to become a research fellow in physiology at University College in 1933, but before leaving Chile he had begun an analysis with Dr. Fernando Allende Navarro, the country's first psychoanalyst.

Building on the foundation of this first contact with psychoanalysis, while in London qualifying as a neuropsychiatrist at the Maudsley Hospital and Northumberland House, he also trained as a psychoanalyst in the British Psycho-Analytical Society.

He returned to Chile in 1944, gathering around him a group who established a psychoanalytic study group, later to become the founding group of the Chilean Psychoanalytic Association.

His first two books, *Lo Psíquico y la Naturaleza Humana. Hacia un Planteamiento Experimental* (1954) and *Estudios de Psicología Dinámica* (1955) were published while in Chile. The former contains the germ of many of his later ideas, one of the most innovative sets of ideas in the field of contemporary psychoanalytic theory, and can be read today as a programme of research paving the way for *The Unconscious as Infinite Sets. An Essay in Bi-Logic*, which appeared in 1975, and *Thinking, Feeling and Being. Clinical Reflections on the Fundamental Antinomy of Human Beings and the World*, published in 1988.

Matte Blanco's oeuvre seeks to go beyond Freud while using his inspiration as its start, and it relates firstly to his realisation that psychoanalysis has departed from what is fundamentally the most surprising aspect of Freud's discoveries – namely, the enigmatic character of the unconscious. He asks what has become of the timelessness and spacelessness of the unconscious or the simultaneous existence of opposing ideas and feelings. Psychoanalysis,

described. In this way he is drawing attention to the obvious fact that, if these phenomena were simply the result of chaos, no underlying regularity could be attributed to them, because their very description presupposes that there is some kind of order that can be observed and hence described.

This order is conceptualized in *The Unconscious as Infinite Sets* as two logical principles, generalisation and symmetry, allowing thus a parsimonious explanation of the functioning of the unconscious system.

The principle of generalisation is formulated as follows:

> *The system Ucs. treats an individual thing (person, object, concept) as if it were a member or element of a set or class which contains other members; it treats this class as a subclass of a more general class, and this more general class as a subclass or subset of a still more general class, and so on.*

(1975, p. 38)

The first principle, which Matte Blanco was later (1989) to call the *principle of abstraction and generalisation*, falls within the purview of classical logic and describes the conscious mind as a classifier that abstracts from entities the characteristics which allow them to be attributed to a given class or set by way of a functional proposition.

The principle of symmetry is formulated thus:

> *The system Ucs. treats the converse of any relation as identical with the relation. In other words, it treats asymmetrical relations as if they were symmetrical.*

(1975, p. 38)

To understand this principle, it should be explained that two types of relation can be distinguished in logic: asymmetrical and symmetrical relations.

The former are ones in which the converse of the relation differs from the original relation. The converse of the relation 'Peter is John's father' is the relation 'John is Peter's son'; in other words, the relation changes if its terms are reversed. A symmetrical relation is one in which reversal of its terms does not modify the relation. An example is 'John is Peter's cousin', whose converse is 'Peter is John's cousin'. The relation stays the same notwithstanding the reversal.

The principle of symmetry dictates that the unconscious system treats asymmetrical relations as if they were symmetrical. As an elementary example, a simple sequence such as 'A comes before B' contains an asymmetrical relation, since its converse would be 'B comes after A'. However, application of the principle of symmetry changes the situation radically, as the asymmetrical relation 'A comes before B' is treated as if it were symmetrical, so that, if 'A comes before B', then 'B comes before A'. Alternatively, if 'Peter is John's father', then 'John is Peter's father'.

The simultaneous operation of these two principles has far-reaching consequences. The principle of symmetry is an extraordinary departure from the rules of classical or Aristotelian logic. Its application means that there are no asymmetrical relations in certain areas of the unconscious. Without these, the principle of contradiction or any notion of total order cannot be upheld, as there is no possibility of establishing ordered sequences in the unconscious system. These are necessary to construct the notions of time and space. In the same way, there is no longer any possibility of distinguishing between the part and the whole (an asymmetrical relation), as the two become identical.

Within the classes or sets, delimited by functional propositions of increasing generality, the principle of symmetry reigns. According to Matte Blanco, the unconscious system is organised like a collection of infinite sets. Here he uses the mathematician Dedekind's definition of an infinite set. Dedekind discovered that a set can be defined as infinite when a proper part of the set can be placed in a bi-univocal relationship with the set as a whole. Thus, for example, the set of natural numbers can be placed in a bi-univocal relationship with the set of even numbers, a proper part of the set.

When Matte Blanco introduces the concept of infinite sets as a structuring mode of the unconscious, he does so on the basis of a clinical finding, namely, that when we experience an emotion we tend, from the point of view of the cognitive processes which form part of, and shape, the emotional experience, to slip into the use of symmetrical logic in order to think of the object of our emotion. In this way, for instance, the loved or hated object takes on the characteristics of the entire class in which it is included, so that the part becomes equal to the whole. Matte Blanco also points out that the differences between emotions and the unconscious, if they exist, have yet to be described. As we can see, he is thereby emphasising that *the unconscious cannot know individuals but knows only classes.*

This is the basis of one of the most surprising isomorphisms discovered by Matte Blanco: the similarity between the logic of the unconscious, the logic of emotion and the logic of the infinite.

Matte Blanco also formulates an ontological conception, based on the

to experience reality as a single, inseparable totality, while the latter, by contrast, is made up of parts and sequences. These modes of being stand in an irreducible antonymic relation to each other, so that they exist together and can enter into different relations, but never mix in order to constitute another mode being. These modes of being can manifest themselves logically in either a symmetrical or an asymmetrical logic. These logics can in turn enter into different combinations: bi-logic.

According to Matte Blanco, we human beings *are* always bimodal and we often *think* bi-logically. Emotion, itself a bi-logical structure, is what links the dimension of being with that of thinking, and the continuity and overall unity of our antonymic existence is maintained within it.

In *Thinking, Feeling and Being* (1988), Matte Blanco discusses in detail the bi-logic of thinking and the bimodality of being of man in the world. His studies lead him to describe various configurations of the possible relations between symmetrical and asymmetrical logic and of the modes of being, as discovered in his clinical work. Our author's thought thus includes a structural viewpoint, which enables him to define a number of bi-logical and bimodal structures.

Innumerable questions and potential further developments arise when we investigate the astonishing and marvellous world opened up by the work of Ignacio Matte Blanco. Apart from this powerful incentive, its study has induced me, like many others, to take the infinite seriously into account in research on the human experience.

# References

Matte Blanco, I. (1954). *Lo Psíquico y la Naturaleza Humana.* Santiago de Chile: Editorial Universitaria.

Matte Blanco, I. (1955). *Estudios de Psicología Dinámica.* Santiago de Chile: Editorial Universitaria.

Matte Blanco, I. (1975). *The Unconscious as Infinite Sets. An Essay in Bi-logic*. London: Duckworth.

Matte Blanco, I. (1988). *Thinking, Feeling and Being. Clinical Reflections on the Fundamental Antinomy of Human Beings and the World*. London & New York: Routledge.

Matte Blanco, I. (1989). Bi-logical psychoanalytical technique. A proposal. Presented at the 36th Congress of the International Psychoanalytical Association, Rome, August 1989.

# SYSTEM UCS OR THE LOGIC OF THE SYSTEM UCS

*Ignacio Matte Blanco*

*This paper was originally in Spanish. It was read in Spanish at the First Latin-American Psycho-Analytic Congress in Buenos Aires, August 1956. The English version is from 1959, published by the* International Journal of Psycho-Analysis, *40: 1–5.*

## Introduction and formulation of the problem[1]

The discovery of the characteristics of the system Ucs is the most creative and fundamental of Freud's discoveries because it is on these characteristics that his greatest contributions to psychology, especially all those pertaining to dreams, are based. We have indirect evidence that he valued them particularly. In his preface (1, p. xxxii) to the third English edition of *The Interpretation of Dreams* (1931) he mentions that 'it contains, even according to my present-day judgment, the most valuable of all the discoveries it has been my good fortune to make. Insight such as this falls to one's lot but once in a lifetime'.

On the other hand we know from Jones (4, p. 34) that there were in Freud's writings three things of which he thought highly; one was the last chapter of this book, another his essay on 'The Unconscious'. Now both these rest, so to speak, on the foundations given by the characteristics of the system Ucs, and in both the study of these characteristics occupies a prominent place. Finally, in his *New Introductory Lectures* (3, p. 99) he comments: 'It is constantly being borne in upon me that we have made far too little use for our theory of the indubitable fact that the repressed remains unaltered by the passage of time. This seems to offer us the possibility of an approach to some really profound truths. But I myself have made no further progress here'. This reference to one of the characteristics is worded in a manner that leaves no doubt as to his estimate of its importance. It is obvious that what he says about this particular one could be applied to all. Yet recent analytic researches are, on the whole, sadly uninterested in this fundamental topic.

It is worth remarking that the terminology employed on this subject seems to have changed in the course of years. In *The Interpretation of Dreams* (1, pp. 588–609, esp. p. 597) Freud distinguishes between the primary and the secondary process; and in his work on 'The Unconscious' (2, pp. 118–122) he included the first as one of the 'Special Characteristics of the System Ucs', while earlier he seems to have employed the term primary to designate them all.

These characteristics, we know, are:

i    Absence of mutual contradiction between the presentations of the various impulses. 'When two wishes whose aims must appear to us incompatible become simultaneously active, the two impulses do not detract one from the other or cancel each other …' (2, p. 119). A consequence of this is what he has called the absence of negation.

ii   Displacement.

iii  Condensation.

These two constitute the distinctive traits of the primary process.

iv   Absence of time, in short 'no relation to time at all' (2, p. 119) which comprises lack of temporal ordination and lack of alteration by the passage of time. It seems to me highly probable that the second is a necessary consequence of the first.

v    Substitution of psychic for external reality. In psychiatry, especially in relation to schizophrenia, this characteristic is sometimes designated as literal interpretation of metaphor.

These characteristics might be called the laws by which the system Ucs is ruled. Their inspection soon reveals that any process of thought that conforms to them differs widely, for this very reason, from the habitual logic of scientific thought, which in a rather vague and, on occasion, even inexact manner is frequently designated by the name of Aristotelian logic. But it cannot be said that the processes in the system Ucs happen without conforming to any logical law, for in that case we should only witness a chaos; and if there were a chaos there could be nothing predictable, therefore Freud could not have described the characteristics mentioned at all. There must, then, be implicit in these characteristics one or more logical principles different from those by which scientific thought is ruled. Thus the inevitable

## Formation of two principles

Here I must mention that I personally approached this problem when studying schizophrenic thinking, in which I was able to find a conformity to certain principles. When examining the matter more closely I became aware that such principles referred essentially to the characteristics of the system Ucs and that schizophrenic thinking was only a particular application of them.[2]

To enter directly into the matter, the study of schizophrenic thinking shows that it conforms to two definite principles. The first is the representative of conscious normality or, in other words, of a type of thinking identical with scientific thinking: it is not something different from either. The simultaneous operation of both the first and the second principles may frequently be seen in the same mental product. On the other hand, consideration of these principles, especially the second, reveals that they constitute that aspect or part of schizophrenic thinking which corresponds to the thinking of the system Ucs.[3] For this reason we shall describe them in terms of the latter.

I    *The thinking of the system Ucs treats an individual thing (person, object, concept) as if it were a member or element of a class which contains other members; it treats this class as a subclass of a more general class, and this more general class as a subclass of a still more general class, and so on.*

It seems that the notion of class can be understood by reading or hearing this principle, and I shall illustrate with only one example. John is an element of the class of men, Teresa of the class of women. The class of men (males) is a subclass of the class of rational animals, and the class of women is another subclass of the same class. The class of rational animals is a subclass of the class of animals, and this is itself a subclass of living beings.

The second principle is formulated thus:

II  *The system Ucs treats the converse of any relation as identical with the relation. In other words, it treats relations as if they were symmetrical.*

This principle represents the most formidable deviation from the logic on which all the scientific and philosophic thinking of mankind has been based.

To quote an example: If John is the brother of Peter, the converse is that Peter is the brother of John. The relation that exists between them is symmetrical, because the converse is identical with the direct relation. But if John is the father of Peter, the converse is: Peter is the son of John. In this case, the relation and its converse are not identical. This type of relation, which is always different from its converse, is called asymmetrical. What the second principle affirms is that the system Ucs tends to treat any relation as if it were symmetrical. In the example given: if John is the father of Peter, then Peter is the father of John. In Aristotelian logic this is absurd; in the logic of the system Ucs it is the rule, as we shall see in a moment.

A careful examination of the manner in which this principle is formulated will reveal that according to it in the logic of the system Ucs it is permitted, but not obligatory, to treat as symmetrical relations which in scientific logic are not so considered; in other cases (such as the case of time, to be considered in a moment) it can be affirmed that the system Ucs does not know certain asymmetrical relations which in scientific logic are familiar. I have not found a law that permits us to know or to foresee when relations are treated as symmetrical and when they are not. The most I could say here is that the system Ucs resembles a child who is learning to speak and who at times conforms to the laws of grammar an at other times leaves them aside.

## Application of these principles to the characteristics of the system Ucs

It may be affirmed that the characteristics of the system Ucs described by Freud are the expression either of the second principle or of the operation of both together. With regard to the lack of contradiction and condensation, it is possible that there may be, furthermore, another principle implicit in them, though this is not at all clear to me.

Let us consider these characteristics one by one, beginning with the most obvious.

a    *Absence of time.* I have said that the fact that the processes of the system Ucs are not altered by the passage of time seems to me a consequence of the fact that they are not ordered in time: if there is no time there cannot be any alteration by the passage of time. Now the absence of the temporal process is an inevitable consequence of the second principle, because the existence of a succession of moments requires a serial ordi-

Unconscious is fundamental. It may be said briefly that it is at the base of projection, sublimation, transference, the return of the repressed, and the division of objects: all these mechanisms are in a certain manner examples of displacement, and to a very great extent differ among themselves only with regard to the circumstances in which displacement takes place. This is an interesting subject to elaborate, but will be left on one side for the moment.

In displacement we witness the simultaneous action of two different processes, which I shall try to explain with examples. When an individual displaces, he treats the primitive object and the object towards which he displaces as elements of a class that has a certain specific characteristic, a characteristic that is perhaps not striking to his conscious thinking, but is so to his Unconscious. For example, if he feels his chief to be a dangerous father it is because he considers that both have the same characteristic, dangerousness. If we express this in terms of symbolic logic we may say that in his Unconscious he treats both as elements of a class; it may also happen that he treats one as an element of one class and the other as an element of another class, but in this case both classes are always subclasses of a more general class. For example, a mother who feeds belongs, let us say, to the class of women who feed materially; a professor who teaches belongs to the class of men who feed mentally. When on account of a process of displacement an individual feels the professor as another who feeds he is, first of all, treating both classes as a subclass of a more general class, that of those who feed, either materially or mentally. The same thing can be seen in any example of displacement.

This is the first process visible in displacement; it is easy to grasp that it is nothing else but the operation of our principle I. But this principle *alone* would not suffice for the understanding of displacement. There is yet another aspect. When displacing (for instance, from professor to mother) the Unconscious does not treat both only as possessors of something in common, but in fact it treats them as identical. This is very strange, but with the help of the second principle it becomes comprehensible. In order to reach understanding of this we must first consider a consequence of this principle. Let us consider the relation:

$$y \text{ is a part of } x$$

If the converse of this relation is identical with it, that is, if the relation is symmetrical, we may say:

$$x \text{ is a part of } y = y \text{ is a part of } x$$

For instance, 'the arm is part of the body' is identical with 'the body is a part of the arm'. In other words, the part is identical with the whole, from which it follows logically that it is also identical with any other part. Consequently a subclass may be identical with any other subclass of the same class. All these assertions may appear absurd, but according to what we may call *the logic of symmetrical thinking* they are perfectly legitimate.

Careful reflection about these two processes reveals that the application of both together is enough to explain displacement completely. In other words, *displacement is the resultant of the conjoint operation of that aspect of Aristotelian logic that we have described as principle I and of a logical consequence of principle II.*

c    *Substitution of psychic for external reality.* It seems that in a rigorous for-mulation this characteristic has no right to independence, but on the contrary must be considered as a variety, or better as a particular exam-ple, of displacement. This is easily understandable. Let us consider as examples the identity established by the Unconscious between mental cannibalism and real cannibalism, between an aggressive desire and an aggressive accomplishment, between the emotion described as bursting with rage and a real bursting, etc. It is obvious that in every one of these examples the essential process at work can be described as follows: first, the Unconscious treats both as elements of the same class or as elements of different classes which themselves are subclasses of a more general class; then it treats the two as if they were identical. These are precisely the two processes at play in displacement, and this proves our assertion.

d    *Lack of mutual contradiction and condensation.* Although it seems certain that these two characteristics are different, it is no less certain that there is an especially intimate relation between them, because the second is not conceivable without the first. I have not been able to see them with the same simple clarity that I believe I have achieved in consider-ing the previous ones, and I suspect that, in addition to the principles

I have mentioned, we witness here the operation of another logical principle. But let us consider first the relation between our principles and these mechanisms.

The lack of contradiction between two impulses which appear incompatible to Aristotelian logic and their union in one expression, which is

identical; and (*c*) perhaps even treating as identical various different elements that in scientific logic are mutually exclusive. (In other words, the operation of principles I and II.) In condensation we see that a given element may express more than one meaning or represent more than one person. If we keep in mind that according to II each part contains the potentialities of the whole and of any other part (remember the example of the arm), then it is perfectly understandable that an element may have more than one meaning or represent more than one person. All this can be better understood with the help of a graphic representation of principle II. As with any graphic representation, this reproduces with the help of spatial elements the relations that exist in the thing that is represented according to a previously established convention. The representation of principle II, with the help of the concept of a space of more than three dimensions, enables us to see that if a whole is conceived as possessing more than three dimensions and the parts are considered three-dimensional, then it is possible for several parts to occupy the same space. If we here remember that the Unconscious substitutes psychical for external reality, then it becomes comprehensible that two impulses symbolized by two material (i.e. spatial) objects (to take Freud's already quoted words) 'do not detract one from the other or cancel each other'. And that is precisely what happens in the absence of mutual contradiction and in condensation; all this would be incomprehensible in a three-dimensional representation.

I may add that for years I have occupied myself with the graphic representation of mental phenomena in terms of multidimensional space, and in another publication (5, Ch. viii) I have dealt extensively with this subject, but it is only recently that I have succeeded in reaching the more general formulation of the principle of symmetry, and have come to understand that this graphic representation in terms of multidimensional space is only a particular expression of this principle.

Finally, I am not quite sure that the only principle at play in the absence of contradiction and condensation is the principle of symmetry. Recently it has seemed to me possible that the absence of negation, which Freud has formulated in relation to these characteristics, may be a principle of the logic of the system Ucs. But I should not dare to affirm this.

In summary we may conclude that the special characteristics *of the system Ucs described by Freud reveal the operation of a logic peculiar to this system, whose fundamental distinguishing mark is to treat as symmetrical relations that in scientific logic are not so considered.*

# Notes

1  I wish to express my gratitude to Prof. Gerold Stahl, PhD, whose help has permitted me to purify my first formulations from certain logical imperfections, in order thus to arrive at a more rigorous formulation.

2  The matter is, in fact, more complex and is studied in detail in another (as yet unpublished) work.

3  From this it may be seen that I am asserting that the thinking of the system Ucs is in part identical with scientific thinking.

# References

1  FREUD, SIGMUND 'The Interpretation of Dreams.' *The complete psychological works of Sigmund Freud*, S.E. 4–5

2  FREUD, SIGMUND 'The Unconscious.' *The complete psychological works of Sigmund Freud*, S.E. 14

3  FREUD, SIGMUND 'New Introductory Lectures on Psycho-Analysis.' *The complete psychological works of Sigmund Freud*, S.E. 22: 3–182.

4  JONES, ERNEST 1956 'The Inception of "Totem and Taboo"', *International Journal of Psycho-Analysis* 37

5  MATTE-BLANCO, IGNACIO *Lo Psíquico y la Naturaleza Humana* (Santiago: Editorial Universitaria, 1954.)

6  STAHL, GEROLD *Introducción a la Lógica Simbólica.* (Santiago: Editorial Universitaria, 1956.)

7  WHITEHEAD, ALFRED NORTH, and RUSSELL, BERTRAND *Principia Mathematica 2nd Ed. Vol. I* (Cambridge University Press, 1950.)

# DISTANCE IN PHOBIAS

*Jorge Mom*[1]

*This English version was originally published in Spanish in the 1956* Revista de Psicoanálisis, *13(4): 430–435. It was translated by Ana Pieczanski for this book.*

The work of Ronald Fairbairn, Melanie Klein, and Hanna Segal has, to a great extent, clarified the problem of hysteria. In successive papers on Anxiety Hysteria published since 1953, I have stressed the importance of paranoid-schizoid anxieties and mechanisms underlying phobic structure.

I described the splitting of the Ego, of the objects internal and external, of time and space and how I understand, like Fairbairn, the identity between hysterical and schizoid dissociation.

I also stressed the existence of "two kinds of anxiety" that needed to be kept dissociated, lest integration trigger intense paranoid anxieties, and posited that, particularly in agoraphobia, the primary source of anxiety was the fear of loneliness. In my opinion, this anxiety is always present, irrespective of the manifest expression of the phobia; it is 'the fundamental phobia', while the other, the phobia about the outside or open spaces, a defensive organization designed to preserve two spaces, instead of a unified and un-differentiated one: the space of loneliness.

The preservation of these two spaces implies a "distance" between them, a barrier, or, as one of my agoraphobic patients called it: a bastion.

This attempt to create two separate spaces, one "inside" the other "outside", attempts to blur the experience of an un-differentiated Ego, one that can not tell the difference between inside and outside, equated with non-existence. In this mindset, the object is only useful insofar as it can be the recipient of projective identifications, becoming a dissociated part of the patient's self. By creating this separate part of himself, located inside the object, boundaries are attached to the shapeless un-differentiated self, acquiring in this way Shape, a concept that I consider paramount to the understanding of these patients. This is how in a phobic system an Other is created. The idea of Other is born in this case out of projected bits of the phobic self. It is in this way that the concept of an outside is created.

In other words, the subject uses an object to create separate spaces and defend itself from the anxiety of one, un-differentiated thing; limitless, potentially becoming just an empty space, representative of an 'emptied' image.

So, let's look at agoraphobia as an example of Anxiety Hysteria.

When an agoraphobic steps into the outside, he does not walk aimlessly, nor does he go very far. From a psychoanalytic perspective, there are negative qualitative and/or economic issues to address.

An agoraphobic woman that was in the process of starting to get out of the house, when approaching a nearby wide avenue, looked afar and could not see were it ended. She then decided to walk as far as she could see, because she realized she did not feel anxious. No sooner than she thought that, she had a panic attack and ran back home.

For the agoraphobic, the experience of lack of boundaries, defining barriers that "create" separateness, implies lack of differentiation, and the existence of only one space is anxiety provoking and a threat of annihilation; the impossibility of ambivalence is perceived by the patient as a threat of mental and emotional disaster.

In agoraphobia there is fear of the "outside". So the patient does not go "Out". Out from where? Out from "Inside". By definition, this configuration implies the existence of two spaces that allow splitting. Loneliness implies one character, one space, no dissociation. It is then that the anxiety attack takes place.

The lack of access to schizoid defenses makes it impossible to create a Not-Me, (making it impossible to create a separation between good and bad). The space is perceived as too big for such a poor inner world, so his "things" get lost, triggering an experience of emptiness.

We can see in the example that there is a "here" and a "there". A difference in space and emotion is created. "Here" is tranquility, "there" is horror. Instead of a panic, there is an anxiety associated with the idea of being there, but knowing that he is "here". The separating zone protects from the experience of un-differentiation.

I would now like to propose the hypothesis that anxiety, which never abandons the agoraphobic, is the real accompanying object, partly because it is always there, but also because it creates the two necessary spaces that protect the phobic from that other space where the danger resides.

This hypothesis requires understanding why and for what the agoraphobic does go "outside" in spite of the anxiety, and the danger of losing the protective zone.

The example I mentioned before is clear; there were two clearly defined

the house they shared. Eventually the sister started to change her mind and considered not moving. Although manifestly this should have calmed her down (and it did for a while), it was then that the patient started to feel that something was driving her crazy, and decided to go out.

This is a critical moment, the moment of not having anxiety. Now the Other 'disappears'. It is then that she went out so she could again recreate two spaces, and ascribe the danger to one of them. Now the street became again the place were she could decide not to go if she so wished. The no-anxiety moment acts as a signal that triggers the phobic 'solution': to create a new, controllable, source of anxiety, separated from the one linked to the threatening and destructive loneliness and un-differentiation.

We now can understand the patients' need for anxiety so they can keep living and last.

## About the relationship with the internal object

In previous papers on this subject, I emphasized that the phobic's internalized object, idealized and not assimilated, was perceived as "dead or moribund" and that all the phobic's efforts were geared at "feeding" and keeping the object alive. I found that eating issues are the norm in phobias. Many of the manifest symptoms result from these primitive conflicts.

The idealized object is critical for the patient's survival and the system is designed to feed it and keep it alive, preventing aggression through distance and a safe zone.

The ideal object requires special attention also because it can potentially develop in phantasy a destructive voracity that further threatens the phobic. It can also be said that the subject perceives himself as 'food' to satiate the voracity of the object.

Phobics' eating symptoms express the relationship between aggressive and reparatory impulses. Phobics may not eat so they don't "kill" the parasitic object. However, they can also overeat to calm the fear of being destroyed or destroy the needed "parasitic" object.

A pregnant agoraphobic patient had some bleeding that threatened the pregnancy. Her phantasy about the bleeding was that it was the result of not being able to keep the safe distance between her aggression and the parasitic object; the baby was becoming the concretization of her internalized object, one that she also dearly wished.

This patient then started to overeat, neither putting on weight nor affecting the baby. She then phantasized that due to the disappearance of the protective space between her and the object, destructiveness took over and she was eating herself, her inside disappearing and becoming completely occupied by the baby, and in this way she 'explained' why she did not put on weight.

Here, there is a clear anticipation of her phantasy of loneliness caused by the process of becoming "one" with the baby, causing her ruin. *It is this anticipation accompanied by anxiety – albeit less intense than the anxiety of loneliness – that forces the creation of other distances. In other words, a prior anxiety (signal anxiety) creates distances and spatial configurations to prevent the development of loneliness (traumatic anxiety).*

I think that the subject of the two kinds of anxieties is central to the understanding of phobias and as something to keep in mind in our clinical work.

The clinical vignettes show that the "destructive danger" quality of the object does not depend on its location (internal or external), but on the potential to eliminate the established distance between the split-off parts – the good and necessary ones from the bad and destructive.

It is the fantasized disappearance of distance and a safe zone, felt concretely in the body, that triggers the subsequent splitting and creation of external separations that assign good and bad qualities to places. Projective identification is the main mechanism of defense used to establish the system and protect it from integration, the primary source of traumatic anxiety.

## Final considerations

Distance plays a significant role in the transference. The analyst, as part object, can either trigger anxiety by becoming a bad object or by being the depository of the good aspects of the patient. So "distance" and how it is addressed defines the tone of the analytic interaction.

Irrespective of the actual nature of the split-off and projected part of the self, or the type of transference, the ultimate source of fear is integration – the latent possibility of diminished distance – and the perception of loneliness and un–differentiation is what is felt as destructive by the phobic person.

Based on this conceptualization, I would recommend the analyst not to be primarily concerned with signal anxiety, since in this approach it is ultimately a reassuring company.

Paradoxically, since positive transference brings closeness in the trans-

# Note

1   For the introduction to the life and work of Jorge Mom, see Part 1, Chapter 4, of this volume.

# Part IV

# PSYCHOANALYSIS OF CHILDREN

# 43

# INTRODUCTION TO THE LIFE AND WORK OF ARMINDA ABERASTURY PICHON-RIVIÈRE (1910–1972)

*Ana Bloj*

## Childhood is not a paradise

In 1937, in a corridor in Hospicio de las Mercedes[1] in Buenos Aires, Arminda Aberastury wonders about an eight-year-old girl diagnosed with oligophrenia. The girl is running while her mother sees a psychoanalyst, Enrique Pichon-Rivière.[2] Arminda Aberastury, who is married to Pichon-Rivière, goes with him to the hospital every day, and in the waiting area she plays with the girl and wonders about her diagnosis.

This was the first step into what later would make Aberastury the leading pioneer in child psychoanalysis in Argentina and South America. Aberastury became intrigued while playing with this girl and read the first book on child analysis.[3] When she was 17 years old, one of her brother's friends had given her the *Complete Works* of Sigmund Freud. These readings triggered a strong interest in psychoanalysis. She trained and joined the Argentine Psychoanalytic Association in its early days. Very early in her career she started to teach child analysts, rethinking and deepening understanding of key aspects of the Freudian view on childhood.

She helped to eradicate the ideas of a naive childhood and a Rousseaunian upbringing typical of naturalistic discourses still current in those times: "The paradise of childhood, the idealization of the child, the mother and maternity, the devaluation of the father's role in the first stages of development"[4] were the prevailing representations that Aberastury helped to dismiss.

Her most significant conceptual contributions, as well as her particular modes of sustaining a framework and her contributions regarding technique, were guided by the idea of sex drives expressing themselves from birth onwards. She conceives children as having the ability to observe and understand, as being capable of learning about the truths handled by adults and frequently hidden from children such as sexuality and other key events

that went beyond Klein's ideas.

She understood her practice with children as a very private two-person space where she saw the parents very seldom once she finalized with the assessment period. In the early years of her practice, she even expected the child himself to handle the monthly payment to her.

Aberastury valued the child's intelligence. Children, in her view, are consciously or unconsciously aware of their experiences and culture and of the adult world at large. For her, children can take responsibility and are capable of independent thinking; therefore, they are endowed with rights beyond their parents' expectations. From this perspective, it is necessary to work with the same mindset we apply to work with adults. The only difference would be that the unconscious would speak through the expressive means appropriate for childhood: play and drawing. These aspects of Aberastury's framework allowed her to establish a solid transference, strengthened by the high frequency of the sessions, held almost on a daily basis.

According to Maud Mannoni, Aberastury establishes a new field in Argentina: "For the first time, with her, childhood is a subject of analysis, a subject by themselves, and with their own rights to be listened to, in their words and in their own language of games."[5]

Furthermore, Aberastury observed that in their first interview, the child expressed understanding of their disease and a desire to recover, regardless of their age.[6]

Among her main contributions, this introduction will highlight the concept of an early genital phase, chronologically situated between the fourth or sixth month of life and the end of the first year. It is subsequent to the oral stage and previous to the anal stage. This construction, according to the author, would "fill a gap" in a sliding period not developed in Freudian production.[7]

In 1961, she published "El Juego de Construir Casas".[8] It is considered by many as the first original technical contribution to child psychoanalysis in Argentina. It is a projective play instrument for children inspired in the production of the analyst Erik Erikson, an assembly game that invites the child to build a house. This game has significant advantages when compared with projective tests. Insofar as it is a "play test" and not a graphic test, it allows understanding of unconscious phantasy but also provides possibilities for therapeutic intervention.[9]

Aberastury developed in a systematic way the so-called "diagnostic hour of play", a resource used from the first interview as part of the assessment process. Together with other child psychoanalysts from the Argentine Psychoanalytic Association (APA), Aberastury advocated working with children in the second year of life since, in her experience, they were capable of communicating and establishing transference with the analyst.

Aberastury delimits two stages in her psychoanalytic career[10]:

*Stage 1.* A stage that begins in 1937 and finishes in 1959 with the contribution of the early genital phase previous to the anal stage. In this period, she especially acknowledges Elizabeth Garma's collaboration.[11]

By 1945, Arminda Aberastury had already acquired international recognition in Latin America. She was the Chair of Child Analysis not only at APA and Argentina in general, but also in Uruguay, Brazil and all Latin America.

She had an epistolary correspondence with Melanie Klein from 1945 to 1958. In 1951, Aberastury met Jacques Lacan and Françoise Dolto in Paris and delivered a lecture in Dr. Serge Lebovici's Center in Paris. She was also invited to present the fundamentals of the 'House-Building' play test in Dolto's seminar. Two years later, in 1952, Aberastury met with Melanie Klein in London.

*Stage 2.* From 1959 onwards, psychoanalysis with children is widespread in Buenos Aires and other major cities in Argentina, and it becomes mainstream at the Children's Hospital in Buenos Aires in pediatrics and in the area of dentistry.[12] During this time, Susana Lustig de Ferrer became Aberastury's main collaborator.

All through her career she applied psychoanalytic understanding beyond her private office, educating healthcare professionals, teachers and parents in a variety of settings.

She worked in psychoanalytic groups with parents, as well as sometimes just with mothers. She also had groups with pediatricians, analysts and medical students. These were transgenerational groups that created a new way of approaching the treatment of young children.

The day before she turned 62, on November 13, 1972, Arminda Aberastury committed suicide.

## Notes

1   The current psychiatric hospital called José Tiburcio Borda.
2   In that moment, he was the acting Director of Admission Services in Hospicio de las Mercedes (from 1938 to 1947). In the period 1947–1952, he was Chief of Psychiatric Services for the young.
3   We refer to *The Psychoanalysis of Children*, by Melanie Klein.

4   Arminda Aberastury. "Una nueva psicología del niño a la luz de los descubrimientos de Freud". *Revista de Psicoanálisis*. Buenos Aires: Asociación Psicoanalítica Argentina, July–September 1956, Volume XIII, n° 3, p. 222

5   Maud Mannoni. "Arminda Aberastury". *Diarios Clínicos*. Buenos Aires: Lugar Editorial, 1990, p. 65.

6   Arminda Aberastury (2004). *Teoría y técnica del psicoanálisis de niños* [1962]. Bue-

    p. 6‒7.

8   Editors' addendum: That was later published in English as "House Construction Play its Interpretation and Diagnostic Value". (1958). *International Journal of Psycho-Analysis*, 39: 39–49.

9   Arminda Aberastury (1971). *El juego de construir casas: Su interpretación y valor diagnóstico* [1951]. Buenos Aires: Paidos. (3rd ed.) p. 19.

10  Arminda Aberastury (2004). *Teoría y técnica del psicoanálisis de niños* [1962]. Buenos Aires: Paidos, p. 68.

11  If a historical review is carried out, it is possible to consider Betty Garma as a pioneer rather than a collaborator, due to her novel practices and the contributions she made. See: Bloj, Ana. El niño pensado en clave sexual. *Revista Norte de Salud Mental*. Volume VI n° 26 (November 2006). Also available at: http://www.ome-aen.org/norte.htm

12  In Argentina, psychoanalysis begins to spread among all sectors of the population. Means of mass communication grant airtime to broadcast pieces of advice for parents, and hospital and private practices are sustained by psychoanalysts. Eva Giberti was the best example of the diffusion of psychoanalysis on television, radio and print campaigns. She advertised her "school for parents".

# 44

# DENTITION, WALKING AND SPEECH IN RELATION TO THE DEPRESSIVE POSITION

*Arminda Aberastury Pichon-Rivière*

*Paper read before the 20th Congress of the International Psycho-Analytical Association, Paris, July–August, 1957 and published in 1958 in the* International Journal of Psycho-Analysis, *39: 167–171.*

The second half of the first year of life and the beginning of the second year are characterized by multiple learning convergent with achievements that lead to a fundamental change in attitude towards the external world, a change as significant as birth; the child stands up, walks and is weaned.

I believe that standing erect and walking arise from an overwhelming necessity in the child to break away from the mother in order not to destroy her, although these same achievements serve him later in his need to regain her, and that speech, permitting the magic reconstruction of objects, helps him to work out depressive anxieties increased by dentition. For the child the utterance of the first word means a repetition of the loved-hated object, which he reconstructs inside and flings into the external world. In the second place comes the experience that speech puts him in contact with the world and that it is a means of communication.

Weaning is the consequence of a whole process of detachment whose essential and ultimate motor is the intensification of the depressive anxiety (1), intensification due to the advent of teeth, instruments that render possible the concrete realization of destructive phantasies.

This determines in the child: (i) the need of separation from the mother in order to preserve her, partly losing the communication achieved so far; (ii) the need of seeking new forms of connection with her; and (iii) I postulate the existence a genital phase previous to the anal and polymorphous one.

The starting-point of my observations was Melanie Klein's concepts on the first stages of development, especially those referring to the depressive position and the formation of symbols (2). I consider this paper a develop-

cial increase in the depressive anxiety) throws light upon important aspects of development and certain disturbances that appear during the period of dentition (4).

When a tooth appears the child feels that something hard and cutting that comes out of his body penetrates into something softer, breaking and tearing it (breast – solid food). This experience is at the core of the child's anxiety when he begins to eat solid foods, particularly meat.

The child can verify in real life his ability to destroy with his teeth. The bitten teething-ring, the torn piece of paper, the solid food he bites symbolizes parts of himself and of his mother. Thus he confronts the real effects of his destructiveness; his depressive as well as paranoid anxieties increase according to the degree of destructiveness in him.

The development of locomotion and the child's increasing ability to grasp objects strengthen, on the one hand, his depressive anxiety, but at the same time they help him to work them through; together with walking and speech they have the same significance and ends. Melanie Klein has pointed it out already (5), and I see it mainly from the point of view of the beginning of dentition and its consequences.

Although oral, anal and genital tendencies operate from the moment of birth, the oral phase is organized and built up because it is the one that enables the child to overcome the birth trauma and thus survive. When the teeth appear and the oral link with the object must be abandoned, then, in my belief, an attempt is made at recovering that link through the genital organs.

The fantasies of a genital link with the object expressed as penetrating and being penetrated, are supported by oral experiences that serve as patterns: there appears the fantasy of something that penetrates and nourishes, and that of a cavity that can receive that something, creating the equivalence of breast-mouth and penis-vagina. Melanie Klein (6) places the discovery of the vagina in the baby girl in that period and points out the boy's passive feminine phase in the first stages of the Oedipus complex.

The genital organs would thus seem the most suitable for the reconstruction of the mouth-breast relationship. Based on these finds I postulate the existence of a transitory genital phase previous to the anal and polymorphous one.

Why do genital tendencies fail in their organization? Because they are built on the basis of the oral situation, charged at the moment with its maximum danger. Besides, the necessary frustration of the child's genital desires, in that period of his life, increases his destructive tendencies. His fantasies of a dangerous genital union with an object charge the imago of his parents with a particular destructiveness, and that is one of the reasons why the primary scene, in that period of a child's life, is lived with such cruelty.

The increase in the oral and genital anxieties by the above-mentioned process hastens the need of an organization to expel. The structure of the first anal phase is completed and serves in preserving the good link with the mother by a mechanism similar to the one that, in the first relationship with her, fulfils the projection by acting together with the introjection.

To sum up: Having failed in restoring the connection with the object, the genital organization sets in motion all manner of connection with the object: oral, anal, and genital (polymorphous phase) (7). The primary anal phase of expulsion is built up in order to keep the good link, keeping the oral and genital features active.

These points of view support Melanie Klein's discoveries about the early stages in the Oedipus complex (with the onset of the genital tendencies in the second half of the first year) and are understandable in the light of her ideas about object relation. I intend to explain the reason for the upsurge of the genital phase and its failure as an organization.

I maintain that it is the mechanism of expulsion, serving the preservation of the object, which actuates the impulses to move and walk. The child that walks keeps the mother by withdrawing from her to preserve her, and by approaching her when he needs her.

I wish to discuss an experience closely related to the anal phase that appears in the child when he stands up. Whilst he is lying, wrapped up in napkins, faecal matter and urine form a mass together with the napkins constituting a real wrapper. When he stands up he feels that the faecal matter and the urine detach themselves from his body, and this feeling, plus the evident anxiety in the child under these circumstances, is another phenomenon which determines an increase in the anxiety of separation (depressive anxiety) with the repetition of a situation already lived by him when the foetal membranes become detached from him (8).

Locomotion and the acquisition of new symbolizations facilitate the relationship with the mother by allowing the distribution, displacement, and working out of these anxieties.

455

In the period of development we are describing here, it could be said that the child projects himself and his internal objects into the external world, destroying the bad parts of himself and his mother to save her and himself. The more conscious he becomes of the scope of his destructive weapons: teeth, muscles, growing skill in movement, the more he fears to destroy his mother as a total object, and the more he needs to divide this object and to

mother, were the child immobilized. Furthermore, paranoid anxieties lead the child to explore the external world, in order to verify and ratify the dangers by which he feels he is surrounded.

When his need for movement, exploration, and games is frustrated the child feels an increase of aggressive impulses, and this determines an increase in his depressive and paranoid anxieties. In a normal development the child feels the need of displacing these affects and anxieties on the objects that draw each time further away from him, and I believe that the need of separation from the mother, of moving away not to destroy her, impels him to crawl, climb, walk and play. The clinical observation of infants whose mothers did not understand these needs in their children and subjected them to a regimen of immobility and lack of stimulus, shows invariably that these children suffered from neurotic disturbances.

I have studied one of these disturbances in particular: insomnia. We find it in every case where immobility and lack of stimulus characterize the pattern of life. This condemns the child to kill in fantasy his original objects without having been able to scatter or repeat the experiences, fearing consequently the repetition of an attack against himself, motionless and defenceless. I think that walking is not only a way of overcoming the depressive state, permitting the restoring or discovery of new objects, but that it is the motor realization of one of the means of defence characteristic of this phase, the withdrawing from the love object. In the normal development this is followed later by the restitution of the objects by means of words, using the mechanism of reparation to overcome anxiety.

When Freud (9) described the play of an 18-month-old child, he contributed fundamentally to our understanding not only of the mechanism of play but also of those of the acquisition of speech and the overcoming of the depressive position. You will remember that he observed that a child uttered the same sound at the appearance or disappearance of either the mother or the reel of cotton. The same sound accompanied the appearance and disappearance of his own image in the mirror.

When the baby enters the depressive phase (second half of his first year, M. Klein) his lulling is one of the first attempts to defeat the depressive situation, creating sounds that symbolize something that comes out of his body that makes a noise outside him, and behind it are fantasies and memories, as if making a fantasy of a link with an object; a situation that will occur later with words in an ever clearer sense. The genetic continuity and the original identity between sound and words seem evident (10). The word is for the child a re-creation of the object in his internal world, he can keep it or throw it out into the world.

The anxiety that appears in the child when he begins to speak is enormous; it springs from the fact that his expressible world has enriched itself in a manner disproportioned to his capacity for verbal expression; he is not certain of the efficacy of this new instrument of reparation.

The uttering of the first word means the magic reparation of the loved object for the child, which he reconstructs inside himself and throws out into the external world. Secondly comes the experience that the word puts him in contact with the world and that it is a means of communication.

Actually it is a re-creation of a link with this internal object that he internalizes and externalizes in these verbal games. This egocentric language becomes a social one through learning and coming into contact with the external world, and little by little serves him to build up his system of communication.

The fact that the love object appears when called, the experience that the word links him to the object, as well as the emotional reaction of his environment to his speaking achievements, fortify and ratify his belief in the magic quality of the word.

These theoretical conclusions are the result of observations made during the analytical treatment of several children with speech disturbances and that of a schizophrenic adolescent with difficulties in pronunciation and verbal expression.

There is the case of M, a 6-year-old girl suffering from a serious neurosis. When I began her analysis she uttered only three words: mama, papa, and atta (Spanish for 'there it is'), which she used to say at the appearance or reappearance of some object. M was 7 months old when her mother weaned her suddenly owing to a second pregnancy; the sphincter control had been affected brusquely and severely by the child's nurse during the mother's absence at the time of the little sister's birth. The progress in M's speech stopped from the day her mother, fearing that she would wake the baby, hit her for shouting while trying to pronounce her sister's name. I do think that these external events could, in themselves, have produced similar symptoms in other children, but I believe that the interaction of internal and external situations determined them.

It is during dentition, with growing depressive and paranoid anxieties, that exterior facts of actual loss, transitory or definitive, and the experiences of cruelty of the external world, confirm the fears and are able to provoke serious disturbance in the child.

The intensity of her greed, increased by the abrupt weaning and the mother's new pregnancy, impeded her capacity for reparation.

prevent things from entering or leaving.

For M not to speak meant not to give; it meant opposition to her environment and revenge against her mother. Her deep rejection of the external world was expressed by her mutism and by a serious anorexia. By not speaking and not eating she paralyzed both projection (words) and introjection (food). The non-utterance of words was a way of retaining in herself the excrements which she had actually had to give up to the nurse, to render them motionless, because for her they had acquired the significance of explosive and destructive matter. The fact that the mother hit her when M tried to pronounce her sister's name for the first time was felt by her as a prohibition against repairing that which was harmed in fantasy, condemning her thus to live with a destroyed world inside her, a world that she controlled omnipotently by not speaking.

Analysis brought forth in her the ability for reparation; speech was now for M the recovery of a function she had lost in a regressive process. This function linked to speech consisted in the possibility of freely destroying and reconstructing objects. The capacity for canalizing fantasies into new symbolizations and in a fragmentary and successive way delivered her speech from its previous inhibitions. But during this process of re-creation through speech a failure can occur in the process of symbolization, and it is this failure that led M to an inability to speak. This very failure was shown for the first time by Melanie Klein in the case of Dick (11).

In other cases failure does not take the process of the formation of the symbol itself; there then happens the situation described by Hanna Segal (12) characterized by the impossibility of the subjects differentiating between the symbol and the symbolized object. The symbol becomes charged with the anxieties of the original object and cannot any more be used in the speech.

I observed this mechanism during the analysis of an adolescent schizophrenic of 17 years, whom I shall call R, with a gradual inhibition of speech that had begun at the age of 12. The 'voice of a little man' he had in his heart used to tell him: 'You must not say it, you are a pig, you must not say it.' At first this ban referred only to definite syllables that contained the letter R between a consonant and a vowel, such as: GRA-TRA-PRA. Thus he had to choose carefully the words he pronounced or replace swiftly those that the little man forbade him to use. This had become more and more severe: by the time he started on his analysis, he had been unable to speak to his father for two years.

These symbols were for R the symbol of his parents' sexual relation: the consonant and the vowel together. The letter R, which separated the other two, was the first letter of his name and represented him. He was 12 when he saw his parents' sexual relation. He had repressed the cry and all verbal expression of his emotion; speech turned, for him, into a communication of what he had seen and heard and a magic repetition of the primary scene. This speech disturbance had yet another significance for him: he was the eldest of three brothers, the retention of the syllable TRA meant for him keeping the 'trinity' within himself: he, his mother and his father, nullified the birth of his brothers.

Not only was he incapable of expressing what he had seen, but speech was for him the setting in motion of these original objects, with all the dangerous implications. The symbolic significance of the syllable TRA passed on later to all the synonyms of the words that originally contained it. For instance: *Trabajo* (work) – *Labor* (labour).

In this case the difficulty in differentiating the symbol from what was symbolized (primary scene) led R to an inability to speak. In the case of M it was the inability to create the symbol.

# References

1   KLEIN, MELANIE 1950 'Mourning and its Relation to the Manic-Depressive Psychosis' *International Journal of Psycho-Analysis* 31: 415–450.
2   *The Psychoanalysis of Children* (Buenos Aires: Biblioteca de Psicoanálisis, 1948.) *Contributions to Psychoanalysis* (London: Hogarth, 1951) *Other Developments in Psychoanalysis* (London: Hogarth, 1952.) *New Directions in Psychoanalysis* (London: Hogarth, 1956.)
3   HEIMANN, PAULA 'Re-evaluation of the Oedipus Complex' *New Directions in Psycho-Analysis* (London: Hogarth, 1956.)
4   PICHON-RIVIÈRE, A. A. DE 1951 'Trastornos emocionales en el niño vinculados con la denticion' *Revista de Odontologia* 39 No. 8.
5   KLEIN, MELANIE 'On Observing the Behaviour of Young Infants' *Developments in Psycho-Analysis* (London: Hogarth, 1952.)
6   KLEIN, MELANIE *El Psicoanálisis de niños* (Buenos Aires: Biblioteca de Psicoanálisis, 1948.)

7   HEIMANN, PAULA *El Psicoanálisis de niños*. Amongst us, E. Pichon-Rivière has sustained in his courses the hypothesis that, if the child, at birth, has oral, anal, or genital tendencies, it is because in its intra-uterine life the development of the three phases has already taken place, that there is a genital phase at the moment of birth and that this loses its primacy on account of biological necessities of adaptation. He sustains also that the schizophrenic subject returns to a perverse

was very clear (cf. Aspectos psicosomáticos en Dermatología *Revista de Psi-coanálisis* 6 No. 2 1948 pp. 295–329). In the same paper, we have pointed out that the fact of being covered with crusts has a significance similar to that of Angel Garma's finding in his observations on clothing and the foetal membranes (cf. Garma, Angel: 'El origen de los vestidos' *Revista de Psicoanálisis* 7 No. 2 1949 pp. 191–220).

8   FREUD, SIGMUND 'Mas allá del principio del placer' *Vol. 2 Edición castellana.*

9   TOLEDO, ALVAREZ DE, and PICHON- RIVIÈRE, A. A. DE 'La música y los instrumentos musicales' *Revista de Psicoanálisis* 12 No. 2 pp. 185–200.

10  KLEIN, MELANIE 'La importancia de la formación de símbolos en el desarrollo del yo' *Revista Uruguaya de Psicoanálisis* 1, No. 1.

11  KLEIN, M. 'The Importance of Symbol-Formation in the Development of the Ego' *International Journal of Psycho-Analysis* 1, 1:24–39, 1930.

12  SEGAL, HANNA 'Notes on Symbol Formation' *International Journal of Psycho-Analysis* 38: 1957.

# INTRODUCTION TO THE LIFE AND WORK OF EMILIO RODRIGUÉ, AN UNORTHODOX ANALYST (1923–2008)

## *Julia Braun*

Emilio Rodrigué was born in Buenos Aires in 1923 and died in San Salvador de Bahia in 2008, when he was 85 years old. His career may be divided into two phases. The first one, which Rodrigué himself identified as "orthodox," comprises his first 25 years as a psychoanalyst – from the beginning of his training at age 26, to his resignation from the Argentine Psychoanalytic Association (APA) and the IPA in 1971. The second stage, the "unorthodox" one, stretches from his resignation to his death.

Rodrigué liked to say that his analytic vocation had arisen from an interest in Freud's work that had been transmitted to him by his father. A bon vivant Frenchman and an avid reader – "a master of leisure" – his father would spend hours locked up in his study reading the life of the saints and Freud's writings. Rodrigué also enjoyed calling attention to his own transgressing tendencies. He used to say that halfway through medical school he had announced to his family that he would drop out and take up farm work. Since his mother, who seemed to be the addressee of this statement, had listened to it unperturbed, he had continued studying and had become a physician.

Rodrigué went into analysis with Arnaldo Raskovsky, one of the founders of the APA, during his third year of medical school (when he was 20 years old). Fairbairn's work had made a great impression on him, and he started questioning his analyst so insistently that the latter terminated the analysis. Since he could not continue with his training in Buenos Aires,

Rodrigué decided to move to London, where he became a patient of Paula Heimann.

During his stay in England, Rodrigué excelled at his work both in the British Society and in the Tavistock Clinic – so much so that Melanie Klein entrusted her granddaughter to him for analysis, which she herself supervised. Rodrigué described this peculiar situation as his "first transgressing

develop his ideas on autism, play interpretation, and child analysis technique.

Rodrigué went back to Buenos Aires in 1950, when the APA was strongly Kleinian. He was very well received and became very active in the institution. In 1957, he co-founded the Sociedad de Psicoterapia de Grupo (Group Psychotherapy Society) and published *Psicoterapia del grupo, su enfoque psicoanalítico* (*Group Psychotherapy: A Psychoanalytic Approach*) along with León Grinberg and Marie Langer. This was the first of a series of books and essays on group therapy. In 1958, the Group Psychotherapy Society held its first international conference, which was widely attended. Along with Madé and Willy Baranger, Rodrigué also assisted in the creation of a Uruguayan psychoanalytic group.

While writing a paper on symbolism, he came across a text that exerted great influence on him – *Philosophy in a New Key*, by Suzanne Langer – and he decided to make contact with the author. This was not an easy task, because Langer was an isolated, solitary researcher. When she finally answered his letters, she suggested that he apply for a position at an institution near her, the Austen Riggs Clinic, so that they could be in contact. Austen Riggs was a community psychiatric clinic located in Stockbridge, Massachusetts, and run by Erik Erikson and David Rapaport. Rodrigué worked there for four years, taking on medical and teaching responsibilities. Due to his background, he was appointed director of the group therapy program. He would also meet with Suzanne Langer to work with her once a week, and he viewed these meetings as enormously valuable.

This new and greatly appreciated experience gave rise to one of Rodrigué's most important texts – *La biografía de una comunidad terapéutica* (*The Biography of a Therapeutic Community*). Published in 1965 with a prologue by Mauricio Goldenberg, this book is considered the first Spanish-speaking contribution to the development of therapeutic communities. The latter constitute a social approach to psychiatry that radically changes the notion of doctor–patient relationship and of the appropriate therapeutic context to treat mental illness.

In 1966, he published *El contexto del proceso analítico* (*The Context of the Analytic Process*), co-authored with his then-wife Geneviève T. de Rodrigué. The book's dedication reads: "To Marie Langer and Suzanne Langer who are sisters, in a sense". He considered Suzanne his philosophy guru, and Marie his political one.[1] *El contexto del proceso analítico* is a comprehensive theoretical, technical, and clinical study of the analytic process. This book has the peculiarity of having a theoretical framework that uniquely intertwines Kleinian and ego psychology theories, on which the author drew during his sojourns in England and the United States.

Rodrigué's administrative career continued with his appointment as secretary of the APA board of directors in 1965, during David Liberman's presidency. In 1966, he was elected president. His term was traversed by the country's agitated political life. That same year there was a military coup. The dictatorship took control over public universities and physically attacked professors, researchers, and cultural figures, forcing many of them into exile. The APA reflected the political fervor that permeated the country. Its 1967 symposium was titled "Problemática actual de la APA" (Current Problems in the APA). Due to the country's difficult situation, the organization decided not to broadcast the papers presented at the symposium. A limited-circulation booklet was published that included the opening and closing speeches as well as abstracts of the workshops. These workshops were viewed as a space for introspection where the institutional crisis could be discussed. Issues addressed included scientific power, political power, ideology, decentralization of power, authoritarianism, change process, ethics, morality, boundaries, rigidity, dogmatism, participation of candidates in committees, and analyst-candidate relations. The meeting received a positive evaluation. Soon after that, the Psychoanalytic Institute, headed by Diego García Reynoso, decided to give candidates voting representation in its governing body.

In 1969, the *International Journal of Psycho-Analysis* invited Rodrigué to contribute an article to the issue that celebrated the journal's 50th anniversary. The essay was titled "The Fifty Thousand Hour Patient". In 1970, he expanded on it and turned it into a book with the same title, *El paciente de las cincuenta mil horas*, published in Spain in 1977. In the prologue, Rodrigué writes: "I was already president of the APA and had rejected the vice-presidency of the IPA ( … ) I had become part of the leadership ( … ) One might say that the end of my long English colonization was marked by what I had written [the article for the IJPA] ( … ) The article turned out to be my letter of farewell".

Simultaneously with the IPA 26th Congress, "New Developments in Psychoanalysis", held in Rome in 1969, a "counter-congress" was organized where the International Platform movement was created. This movement developed an in-depth Marxist criticism of the psychoanalytic institutional system that challenged, among other features, institutional hierarchies, the lack of social involvement, the training model, and the candidate selection process. The movement consolidated at the 1971 Congress in Vienna, and had already acquired followers in Buenos Aires. Rodrigué adhered to it and resigned from the APA that same year. Other APA members, gathered in

Docencia e Investigación (Center for Teaching and Research). Rodrigué was elected president of the Federation. International Platform members considered that the political violence that was shaking the world challenged psychoanalysis, and pointed to the need for psychoanalysts to integrate the sociopolitical dimension.

Aware of the risk of political persecution, Rodrigué moved to Brazil in 1974. He settled in Bahia, where he led an intense and creative life as a writer and practitioner of an array of techniques. He engaged in psycho-drama, group therapy, bioenergetics, Gestalt, and social laboratories.[2] He created innovative psychotherapeutic approaches and taught them in study groups. In 1995 – at the height of his unorthodox period – he published a biography of Freud in Portuguese in two volumes. The book took him six years to write and was titled *Sigmund Freud. O século da psicanálise* (*Sigmund Freud: The Century of Psychoanalysis*). He explained in an interview that this biography constituted his own way of looking at Freud and had been the greatest adventure of his life. "In analyzing him, he analyzed me". The translation into Spanish was published in 1996, and the French version in 1999.

The author claims in the prologue that "the main reason behind this biography lies in the crossroads between duty and desire. When duty becomes desiring, it creates such intense motivation that it does not seem like sublimation. My willingness to historicize is facilitated by my incorrigible eclecticism – a virtue that looks like vice, or the other way around" (Rodrigué, 1995, p. 11). And he adds a key observation: "This biography is enriched by the contributions of Southern Hemisphere analysts" (ibid., p. 14). In an interview in Paris with *Le nouvel observateur* on the occasion of the appearance of his book in France, Rodrigué made an oft-repeated statement: "I think like a psychoanalyst, write like a psychoanalyst, psychoanalyze like a psychoanalyst, and woo like a psychoanalyst". In another occasion he went as far as to state that he was not "a dissident from psychoanalysis" but "a dissident from institutions". He kept making the same claim even after he opted for a personal path outside the canonic circuit.

Rodrigué was a prolific writer, both within and without the psychoanalytic field. His novel *Heroína* (*Heroine*), published in 1969, became somewhat of a bestseller and was made into a movie. He started a new literary genre that he called "raw biography", and published a tetralogy. The first volume, *El anti yo-yo* (*The Anti-Ego-Ego* or *The Anti-Yo-Yo*),[3] co-authored with his then-wife Martha Berlín, came out in 1977. Then followed *Lección de Ondina* (*Undine's Lesson*), *Ondina Supertramp* (*Undine Supertramp*), and *Gigante por propia naturaleza* (*A Giant by His Own Nature*), and many other fiction books. He left an unfinished autobiography, *El libro de las separaciones* (*The Book of Separations*), which was published in 2000, and also wrote essays for *Topía. Revista de psicoanálisis, sociedad y cultura* (Buenos Aires). His last, posthumous publication was *Mi prontuario* (*My Criminal Record*), printed by Editorial de la Flor in 2011. Rodrigué stood out for his creativity and unorthodoxy and, as one may easily surmise, was the object of the greatest admiration and the harshest criticism.

## Notes

1  M. Langer was a prestigious Viennese analyst who was also a feminist and a Marxist. She came to Buenos Aires fleeing Nazism and was one of the founders of the APA, which she later presided. She joined Argentina's chapter of International Platform and became its undisputed intellectual leader.
2  One of the body psychotherapy techniques in vogue in the 1960s.
3  Translator's note: The title in Spanish is a play on words between the word "*yo*", both "I" and "ego", and the word "*yoyó*", "yo-yo".

## Reference

RODRIGUÉ, E. (1995). *Sigmund Freud: o século da psicanálise (1895–1995)*. São Paulo, Editora Escuta.

*Emilio Rodrigué*

*This paper was published in Spanish in the 1963 Revista de Psicoanálisis, 20(1), and translated for this book by Ana Pieczanski.*

## Introduction

In this chapter I will write about playing, toys and children more than about adults, but much of what is said about the child relates to the adult.

I begin with a clinical experience that revolutionized my position on analysis: the first child I treated analytically. I recall the impact of this encounter and the clear sensation of the vast therapeutic world opening quickly. With this new perspective, theoretical formulations that had only awakened my lukewarm approval become convincing and solid practical realities. The internal object turned into a presence, into something that the child truly carries within. This new world revealed by a sick child in analysis soon led me to conclude that my attitude towards the patient in therapy would have to change.

When I tried to transmit this experience to other colleagues (especially to candidates in supervision) I realized that they had experienced similar situations. But when there was an attempt to translate our findings into a theoretical formulation in a more or less clear and systematic way, our resulting speculations were ambiguous, "impressionistic" and not very useful. For this reason, this theme is the starting point for this chapter.

I will begin with an explanation that I have formulated many times and that is logically unsustainable. It is as follows: Imagine a child in the playroom during his hour of analysis. This hypothetical child is building a house with wooden blocks. Let us suppose that he is four years old, that the house consists of a simple rectangular wall and that the task is difficult. I am first of all interested in the obvious fact that the child has to "build" his house, block by block, and that this takes him a considerable amount of time.

And now the illogical question is asked: What are the differences between the child that builds his house and the adult patient who talks to us about houses? This question refers to the "way"[1] the psychological material is transmitted and not (or secondarily) the content, since we assume that the child and adult are expressing something that has to do with the symbol "house."

We are obviously dealing with a communication issue that addresses the multiple options provided by the different means of expression. This is based on the assumption that the information provided in both cases, the concept of a "house", varies according to the setting in which the psychological material is expressed. One can say that the word and the toy "serve" as a third factor, with the characteristics of a third object in the analytical relationship, one that has a relatively autonomous impact on the bi-personal therapeutic situation."[2]

The way the "third object" functions becomes evident with the house made out of blocks, since the way each block is aligned will depend on the meaning of the message of the "house" that the child builds. One may object to this by saying that the wall made out of blocks acquires its configuration from operating impulses during the building activity. And, in essence, this is the case – but not completely. The geometry of the block and its physical characteristics (gravity, balance, etc.) operate as variables that influence and modify the basic fantasy developed by the child while playing.

The analyst – in this imaginary example – has been observing the child's play. What type of information is likely to be obtained? While the range of possible expressions is very wide, they are informed by a limited number of vectors. Guidelines will be provided to the analyst by the way in which the house has been built: its mass, solidity, permanence. He will know about the architectural structure of the house. These geographical data are useful to differentiate a range of emotions that reveal what the house specifically means to the child. For example, he will sense whether constructive or destructive impulses stand out. Furthermore, if we assume that the "house" represents an animate object (which can be the actual child), the construction can represent the child's external and internal worlds, as well as the barrier that separates these areas and represents the surface of his body. If one also keeps in mind that the house is built on a site that serves as a framework, the relationship between the house and its surroundings provides a rich source of information regarding the child's object relations.[3]

My hypothesis is that this type of information differs qualitatively from the information collected from adult verbal communication. The toy and the play provide more precise knowledge about the structural configurations of the psychological material, and, at the same time, make the perception of other types of psychic occurrences more difficult. Generalizing, I would say that the ludic activity "projects"[4] more clearly the spatial qualities

If my hypothesis is valid and the expressive medium that the patient uses puts a stamp on the psychological contents, it is worth asking up to what point have Melanie Klein's discoveries, made while she was creating analytic techniques for children on the go, been for the most part determined by the geographical and structural qualities[5] of the content that was being discovered. If this is true, it may partially explain the striking difficulty that adult analysts have in accepting Melanie Klein's understanding. Let us consider, for example, the emphasis that Melanie Klein places on the morphology of the internal object and on the rich differentiation of proposed intrapsychic occurrences. Her most prolific contribution has been, in effect, in the structural differentiation of the psychic apparatus and I believe that the conviction that led her to sketch out such a complex map of the internal world comes from her therapeutic contact with children who played out their fantasies.

There is no doubt that certain children have the tremendous ability to vividly transmit their unconscious fantasies. I recall, for example, a child who would put a bar of chocolate in his mouth when his mother left him in the playroom. The child would then peer through the window and observe the mother walking away down the street, making sure, as a ritual, that he swallowed the last piece of chocolate when his mother turned the corner. The fact that this sequence does not require an explanation is testimony to the power of expression through dramatization.

But let us return to our four-year-old hypothetical child. A basic quality exists in his non-verbal method of communication: the variety of ways he can express the same content. The child can draw, paint, build, model, cut out a house. He can draw with ink, chalk or pencil. He can do this with saliva on the blackboard or with his fingers on the steamed window. The range of expressive resources is practically endless and each one imprints specific characteristics on the communication. The contrast with the adult is noticeable. The adult makes a conscious effort to exclusively use the spoken word to express himself. The imitation, the posture and the expression, are generally not independent means of expression: they serve the same purpose as exclamation marks, which are used to emphasize the verbal tone. In the adult we only interpret the pathology of the expression, both when it stops functioning as an auxiliary sublanguage and comes to the forefront in the form of strange mannerisms or when the tone of the expression differs from the verbal expressive tone (for example, the contrast between a festive story and a dull and apathetic imitation). The expression, the posture and the imitation operate as signs or symptoms of an emotional state and can only rarely be articulated as expressive symbols.

One can say that the child is more of a polyglot than the adult. Maybe "polymorph" is a more adequate word, since a correlation exists between the diversity of means of expression that the child has at his reach and the multifaceted character of his instinctive drives. This expressive polymorphism also includes frustration, since the child does not yet dominate the most simple and convincing means of expression: the spoken word.

I have often wondered, in the playroom, as to why a child leaves his usual means of expression to adopt another one. These changes in means of expression are important and tend to indicate a passage into a new transferential configuration. I would like to illustrate this point by bringing up a fragment of a material from a 5-year-old girl in the beginning of her treatment, when the central theme was her basic insecurity. The girl began almost all of her sessions drawing a conventional picture on her board – the typical flag or the red house with a traditional roof – characteristic of the frozen aspect of fantasies that are present during the latency period. This was her only manifestation in the plastic arts. Two details of her activity were noteworthy: my patient always framed her pictures and then insisted that I erase them with my hand as soon as she finished them. The assignment was for her work to disappear. There was no doubt that the girl feared the result of her creation. The conventionality of the design, the emphasis on framing her work and her insistence that it disappear gave testament to the need for maintaining the picture – whatever its content may be – under her control, and also the need for her external world not to disappear or be confused with her own creation. It is important to point out that when her anxieties and feelings of vulnerability decreased, she could achieve a discovery that helped the subsequent change to a new means of expression. The girl discovered that the water in the faucets of my playroom was also for playing and, several sessions later, she got a wet rag to clean the board. It was obvious that the polished surface – black and shiny – of the wet board had also caused an impression on my patient. This discovery increased her confidence in her ability to control, which allowed her to include a new graphical means of expression to her repertoire: lineal drawing with a stick on wet sand.

In the chapter on discovery, I pointed out how the moment of innovation during a session seemed to emerge from a depressive context. One could add to this that moments of creativity often occur when a medium that up until that moment had been used to carry destructive fantasies also begins to function as a means of reparation.

I now intend to address the theme of expressiveness from another angle,

We are interested in highlighting the word "throughout". The verbal communication is lineal and consists of a discrete series of significant sounds. One word follows the other and this rosary of sounds is only blended by the gestures that, as we mentioned before, serve as punctuation marks that emphasize the discourse.

It is important to point out that currently many analysts do not experience this feeling of free fall when addressing what their patient says.[6] Maybe the expression "distracted attention", coined by Ehrenzweig (7) as the appropriate way to observe art is similar to the type of attention maintained in the analyst's office. It is possible that nowadays we "float" less, as the material flows, because it is no longer lineal, and we are simultaneously listening to the patient while listening to our countertransference. But despite these reservations, there is no doubt that "floating" is the perceptive mode that is sought and often achieved with adults in the analyst's office.

Infantile communication is not lineal. Generally, the child is transmitting different messages through different means of expression in the same temporal space. Let us consider a common situation: that of a child talking and playing, and also assigning to us a complementary role that is integrated with the child's activity.

Sometimes, material from the immediate past continues in the present. One case comes to mind, where the child and analyst play a game while they wait for a broken toy, glued together by the boy, to dry on the table.[7]

I am convinced that floating attention is not useful with children. Furthermore, I believe that "floating" takes place when there is no contact or interaction in the playroom. When this happens, the analyst remains, please excuse the expression, floating, which tends to happen when disconnection takes place.

The child analyst unconsciously adopts another state of mind and perceptive disposition that I call ludic attention. Therefore, ludic attention can be defined as a more active state of mind in the analyst. It is a style of perception. This attention "tracks" the child's different areas of expression. This mindset has to project itself into all areas of the child's world to address the polyphony of stimuli received. This ludic attention creates a willingness to play within the analyst. Maybe a causal relationship does not exist and the ludic attention is simply a willingness to play. The way contact is made with the child's material has a ludic quality. We frequently recapture a forgotten fragment of our childhood play when working with the young patient!

This willingness to play is based on identification with the child who is playing. I am often surprised during a child's silent imitating ludic activity, for example when a child beats a drum to direct an orchestra being heard on the radio. I also realized that this activity helped me better understand the material.

The following can be concluded: there is an analogy between the way something is said and the way it is perceived. In this analogy, I understand that there is a structural similarity. The analyst automatically correlates the type of material with the type of reception.

One has to take into consideration the type of attention – floating or ludic – as a part of the interpretation. It is the beginning of the interpretative process and the final product; the words spoken by the patient will be determined by our attitude when gathering the material. For this reason, I suggest that the ludic attention is followed by a mode of intervention that I will similarly name "ludic interpretation". I prefer to provide my initial understanding of this interpretative mode, and then provide clinical examples, and finally define it more rigorously.

The ludic interpretation begins with making direct and sensorial contact with the material used by the child. It goes from non-verbal and plastic arts expression, to verbal communication. Ludic interpretation consists of two parts: In the first one the analyst imitates the child's game, and in the second he transmits what he has understood verbally, but complementarily using the child's non-verbal means of expression. In practice, these two parts of the interpretation are superimposed.

Let us consider the first example of Ana, who is 5 years old and has made a series of "sausages" with play dough. She takes one, models it, giving it a vague human shape, and, with an anxious gesture, stabs a pencil repeatedly into the belly of the figure. She stabs it compulsively and in a seemingly vicious manner. Around this time, the girl had a sharp conflict of aggression with her mother, linked to her fear of a new pregnancy.

My first step, in line with the technique I want to describe, was to take another play dough "sausage" and a pencil, imitating the child's action while saying: "Ana grabbed her mother like this (shows the "sausage") and, because she was angry with her, she took this (the pencil), which is like a knife and stabbed her like this". Up until this moment,

471

as one can tell, my interpretation does not differ too much from the first trial interventions, in this case outside of the transference, where the child analyst begins to elaborate the infantile material. The only difference stems from the auxiliary use of the elements used by the child for dramatization. But this example has an interesting epilogue. While taking the piece of play dough and lifting the pencil, what caught my

it is because my mother is fat". This leads us to take into consideration her fantasies towards her mother's pregnancy, the notion of vulnerability of the pregnant woman, etc.

What does this example show? First of all: making contact with the material allowed the addition of a factor that I consider specific and very pertinent to understanding the girl's aggressive fantasy. She revealed the meaning of the aggressive game. The fear experienced by the girl when noticing that the play dough gave way so easily could only be captured by me repeating the action. But I believe that the perception of "something soft" is more than a mere physical verification of a piece of information. I believe that through imitation of the medium I was able to detect the quality of the girl's experience. The play dough, serving as the third object, was the matrix that facilitated my identification with the girl and with the attacked object. This play activity provides the ideal vehicle for the externalization of the countertransference.[8]

A practical result of this type of intervention is the fact that Ana followed my interpretation closely. In reality, this type of interpretation awakens a much greater attention in the child. In child analysis, receiving our interpretation tends to be a very problematic issue. We oftentimes have to reach the child from beyond the curtain of noise that they purposely build. I believe the child's resistance is partly due (notice that I only say partly) to the analyst, who exits the game during the interpretation and assumes a teaching role as the therapist-who-is-interpreting.

The ludic interpretation also facilitates the elaboration of the infantile material in the temporal dimension. It provides a strategy where sequences from the previous sessions can be included. When I began working with children, I found it hard to bring material from previous sessions into the current session. On the one hand I did not feel the need to do so – which happens frequently with candidates – or, when I did, the child impatiently interrupted my recaps. Currently, I go over the material by dramatizing it in an abbreviated manner.

During the session following the play dough incident, Ana took the wooden eraser and threw it repeatedly at the blackboard. The game consisted of the following: if the eraser hit the board with the soft side (muted sound), the action was good; if it hit with the wooden side, making noise, and the girl would cover her ears with her hands, showing fear. One thing seemed evident in this game: that the contrast between hard and soft, between silent and loud, was a continuation from the previous session of the theme of anguish for her vulnerable mother. For this reason, instead of only referring to this verbally, I took the eraser and the pencil that were close by and briefly repeated "remember how you were scared?" I then linked the past situation to the current situation.

I predict an objection. One can point out that by actively assuming the role of playing, and also copying the action of the child who is playing, I am introducing a foreign element into the transference. This objection is valid, above all, as a warning. It is not advisable for the analyst to "kill the point" for the child, by playing with him or more than him. Even in cases where the ludic interpretation adequately accompanies the child's play, it is important to consider our ludic activity as a possible stimulus that will influence the outcome of play. Ana's session with the eraser illustrates a fact. I did not understand the meaning of the game at first. Afterwards, it was clear that Ana was throwing the eraser on her and my behalf. If throwing the eraser resulted in a muted sound and was therefore benign, she was the one throwing it; in her fantasy, if it was loud I was throwing it. Meaning, Ana had assimilated my dramatic action from the previous day and was counting on it to direct her aggressiveness towards me. It is important to interpret the use that the patient makes of our interpretation.

By respecting, taking into consideration, and getting in touch with the characteristics of the means of expression, one obtains a series of criteria that serve to understand the levels of the unconscious fantasy used by the child. It is a way to "feel" the material; however, once it is "felt" it is important to turn our understanding into words, making the maximum possible use of the verbal instrument.

In Ana's example, my task consisted of mimicking, in a brief and succinct way, the game and therefore the role that the girl took on. In recent years I have ensured my interpretation, whenever possible, is based on the role that the child has assigned to me. Because my activities in this area are greater than usual, some clarification is needed.

There is a common game that exists in child analysis, where the child assigns us with a very explicit role and expects us to perform it. We play, for example, school, doctor or market. Melanie Klein (14) was the first one to use these situations as a starting point for her interpretations.

In this type of game the child, as mentioned earlier, assigns us with a role and wants us to provide the truest possible version. In some cases I assumed that the child had assigned a role, even when this was not explicit.

The first example is simple. A 7-year-old child with enuresis, orders me, at the beginning of the session, to take out certain toys from his drawer. Following the martial tone of his order I stand up quickly and say: "Yes,

In this example the countertransference played, once again, an important role. As a result, my interpretation achieved two functions: firstly, the sharp order irritated me. My overdramatized interpretation served the purpose of ending my own tension; secondly, I made use of my countertransference reception – clear due to the perception of my irritation – to fill the content of the interpretative monologue.

The second case is more complex. It deals with Pepe, a 6-year-old boy with a very pronounced intellectual delay, with a mental age below 4 1/2 years old.

At the beginning of the session he asks me, in a very low voice, what is in the sandbox (Pepe knew the sandbox well, since he had played with it on several occasions). I get up and go to investigate, assuming a sense of mystery suggested by the child's words. I open the top of the sandbox and explain: "Oh, it is Pepe who is stuck inside Emilio's belly." I then say: "Pepe, do you remember what happened yesterday when you did not want to leave?" (I mimic a game that Pepe played during the previous session where he hid under the table and I had to pretend that I could not see or reach him.)

Pepe looks at his belly and says: "No, it is clearly not," and he adds: "Today I finish work at the garage at 8 because the cars do not 'escarrilan'" (a neologism).

*Escarrilan* is a verb invented by Pepe that sometimes means "derailed" and sometimes means the opposite – to stay on the rails – depending on the context. In this case I understood that Pepe was saying that they did not derail.

I once again whisper: "Look, then Emilio must be the one who is in your belly. An Emilio who is big like your daddy and makes Pepe big like a daddy and then the cars do not derail, they go straight and know a lot, like when Pepe wrote his name yesterday".

Pepe: "Hey, Emilio, will you buy me a Borgward?" (a car's brand).

Analyst: (Pepe sometimes introduces cliché phrases that tend to indicate a quick disconnection. In this case I was not sure.) I ask him: "How much?"

Pepe: (In a convincing tone.) "It works well because it is a Borgward, because it does not drown" (a car that "drowns" is one that "derails" badly).

By not answering with the typical answer ("I will sell it for 50 pesos") I believe Pepe has not disconnected and continue with the previous theme: Pepe is a big person who works in a garage and wants to sell me a car. Therefore, I assume the role of someone buying a car. By asking Pepe-salesman if the car can do all sorts of things, I have the opportunity to interpret the seriousness of the child's fears about growing and the anguish that the perception of his intellectual delay caused him.

In psychoanalytical literature, the possible existing differences between verbal and non-verbal expression have been dealt with a little or not at all. It was believed that both carried the same psychological material. The problem with the form was neglected. Historically, I see a good reason for it being this way: in the beginning it was important to highlight the existing similarity between the word and other means of communication. It was this focus that allowed Freud to infer that the hysterical symptom "tells" something, has syntax and an argument. Subsequently, Melanie Klein adopted a similar position when basing her child analysis technique on the basic assumption that the toy serves the same purpose as the elements of the content manifest in dreams and that the structure of the meaning of play undergoes the same transformations as the primary process in the work regarding dreams.

The analogy is very important in the social sciences. First one tries to generalize by analogy, seeking formal similarities in apparently dissimilar phenomena and then, once the affinity of the studied fields is established, specific differences are sought in each one. I think the time has come to pay more attention to these differences.[10]

At the beginning of this chapter I listed some of the existing differences between the word and the toy (for example, that the toy is a more suitable symbol to indicate the spatial and structural properties of an object relation). I would like to go back to this topic and explain dreams.

The adult dreams; his dream production consists of plastic images, similar to the ones the child conjures up in his game. But the adult brings us his dream, talking to us about this past occurrence; the child "dreams" in his game. The child "imposes" on the analyst his historical present. Everything happens in the present, according to this stated characteristic of non-verbal means of communication. I believe that this timelessness of the infantile play was a factor that led Melanie Klein to concentrate her technique on the here and now.

It was the recognition of these formal differences that provided a conceptual framework for the clinical and empirical tendency to revise my technique, assuming the more active "ludic interpretation". This interpretation, or this interpretive rhythm, is based on an attitude closely related to the non-verbal material in search of significant norms. The subsequent inter-pretation begins in this concrete medium and is based on this method so that the transmission is more faithful, convincing and adequate for the child to receive it. This ludic disposition also allows our countertransference to work in a more truthful and fluid manner.

is to operate outside the transference.

This adjustment in the disposition for perceiving the material and in the way an interpretation is formulated does not have anything to do with the changes that some analysts have recently introduced into the analysis of the child, the psychotic individual and the group. Furthermore, the strategy I am proposing is, in my understanding, opposite to the goals of these modi-fied techniques.

As mentioned in another paper (13) the modified techniques used with the child, the psychotic individual and the group are based on an attempt to turn the child into a non-child, a psychotic into a non-psychotic, and doing the same with the group.[11] The therapeutic contact begins by introducing a framework that leads to minimizing and rejecting the main characteris-tics of the subject seeking treatment. So the previous "pedagogic" period, proposed by A. Freud, and the techniques that only serve and stimulate the positive transference of the psychotic individual are based on the assump-tion and arbitrary limitation that these patients, as such, are inaccessible to the therapeutic action. Therefore, the crazy, the infantile, the group are not qualities that one operates with during the analytical process. So, the basic principles of psychoanalysis are altered: it is the content and not the form of the interpretation that is modified, and the totality of the transference display stops being the center of the analytical process. Our attempt, on the other hand, consists in treating the child as such, using play, his primary means of expression, to the fullest extent.

As previously mentioned, the technique tool that I call ludic interpre-tation, is not something particularly new or original. In my opinion it only consists of applying a more systematic and explicit interpretation that emerges intuitively in most child analysts. Marion Milner, whose work has been very influential on mine, shows great attention and respect for the formal qualities of the infantile play in her clinical examples. Her descrip-tion of "War between the villages" in her work on the formation of symbols (18) clearly proves this. At the same time, Erik Erikson, in his work with children, bases his clinical theories (9) on how the child configures his game in time and space. I believe that the same focus is then used by the author in a different context: In the study of dreams (8) and, especially, in the study of the formal qualities of dreams in borderline patients.[12]

But let us leave the playroom to enter the adult consulting room.

## The adult

First, an example.

Rita, a 21-year-old ballerina, comes to her session after my announcement that I am going abroad and will be interrupting her analysis for the near future (3 months). Rita remains silent for a long time until I break it. I point out that she has been silent for longer than usual, and also that it feels as though it would continue indefinitely if I did not intervene. I add that this is her basic way to communicate how she feels about the interruption of the analysis.

Rita says that she does not feel uncomfortable being silent, that she was drawing a blank and did not feel like talking about anything.

Her words coincide with my experience. Then I tell her that she wants to prove to me and to herself that she is capable of receiving the news about my departure with indifference. Her lack of sadness or rage gives her a sense of security. Then – I add – I thought she showed an air of triumph with her indifference.

Rita agrees and says that she did not expect to be so calm. After a pause she adds: "Today, when I left the bank downtown, I saw the "Cabildo" (historical government building where Argentinian Independence was declared) and, all of a sudden became very interested in it, I looked at it affectionately. I am not sure why."

Up until that moment, I had the feeling that I had been in a pretend game. The word "Cabildo" changed my receptive attitude, and became the central point of my attention.

I interpreted that she was telling me about the change she was experiencing due to my departure. She tells me that all of a sudden she feels a renewed interest for things of the past that are solid, familiar. Her reaction is to transfer her affection for me to her parents.

With a smile Rita says: "Maybe so" and remains silent. Meaning, my interpretation does not trigger a comment that clears up or confirms my stream of thought. Also, incidentally, my first interpretation about the "Cabildo" was, in the best of cases, barely adequate and did not deserve a major reward.

In the silence that followed I found myself doing something that is characteristic of the way I work. I began to ask myself: "Where is the "Cabildo" in this session?" and "where is the separation in this session?" What surprised me was that her reaction had not appeared more explicitly when faced with the separation.

I point out that I am not the one who is separating from her, but that she is the one who is separating from me. The "Cabildo" is the symbol of her independence.[13] One way of separating from me – I add – is to not give me

the statue under her hand became the only real thing that existed for her.

In response to my question, Rita confirms that touching the statue was like clinging on to it and that the "Cabildo" had produced a similar sensation of an unscathed object.

The atmosphere of the session changed. I had the feeling of great expectation, of suspense. I know that Rita shared this feeling.

I pointed out this tendency of suspended time. I later added: "I believe that you are waiting for the 'Cabildo' to suddenly appear here." After a pause, I explain: "This morning, in the street, you suddenly found an object to hold on to, something good and stable. This 'suddenly' represented an awakening. You came here apathetic, in silence, empty, as if you were asleep, but with the hope that suddenly you would be able to find something unscathed in me, denying in this way the separation."

Once again my approach does not leave me completely satisfied. I predicted that the element of holding on, of personal contact, had a greater role than what I had assigned to it.

This time I found myself asking: How does Rita dance in this session? How does she move, how does Rita play in this session?

Rita "danced" less than usual. Her body language, gesture and posture did not have her usual expressivity. This expressionless body was striking, especially when she narrated passages with high narrative connotation (for example, when referring to her experience in the museum). This gave me the idea for a third interpretation that I consider more satisfactory: I point out how little she moves during the session and tell her that she has a great desire to touch me, to join me with the purpose of controlling me, turning me into the "Cabildo", into the object that stays. I point out her inhibition to move for fear of her fantasies of seduction.

Rita responds in an uncomfortable manner. She moves in a peculiar way on the couch, with small angular gestures that can be defined as movements-that-do-not-appear-to-be-movements. She points out that: ". . . the mere idea of dancing in front of you, here in your office, makes me feel extremely embarrassed".

I interrupt the session here that then dealt with the dance and the seduction of the dance as techniques to fight depression in general, particularly the depression due to my departure.

What does my technique during this session consist of? Some elements, like the use of key words in her narrative, will not be addressed here. I only want to mention that my technique tried to make the dramatic quality of the material clear. Therefore, Rita's indifference turned from an apathetic silence and words meant to convey she did not feel anything, into a vivid emotional process that included her hands and her body language. All her being seemed to be involved in an emotional relationship with me. During the session it became clear that her body was the means of expression of an unconscious fantasy. What is usually called "the here and now" is basically interplay, where the analyst seeks to transform the narrative into a process. The here and now is a transformational process; it is what we call the analytical process. I repeat: it is a process and not a situation, and in the last chapter we will point out why we call the process this way.

One of the technical rules for the transformation that takes place during this process consists of finding the extra-verbal[14] connotation in the communication with the patient. I believe that this type of transformation is elaborated in the "kitchen" of the interpretation when the analyst asks, for example: "Where is the dance or the "Cabildo" in this material?" Of course, each analyst has his own way of intrapsychically dealing with the patient's material, but working on the transference process, the goal is to provide a significant communication to the total expressiveness of the patient.[15] In a certain sense the session with the adult takes on dramatic attributes that are similar to those seen in the playroom. But this expressive quality is only conjured up through verbal interpretations.[16]

Before continuing it is important to clear up a contradiction, this time of a conceptual nature. I have just pointed out that each therapeutic situation must be considered unique, adapting the technical mediums to the case's requirements. Following this course, three types, three modes of interpretation could be formulated: Ludic, dialectic (in its Socratic meaning) and sociodramatic, which would be functionally valid for the child, the adult and the group. These differentiations sketched out in previous work (19) lead to the separation of the three therapeutic areas and to react with caution when one of the techniques infringes upon a different area. Especially when individual analysis theories infringe on group techniques.

The contradiction I am referring to is the following: my work with children has influenced my work with adults. The example of Rita illustrates the importance to me – and to analysts in general – of the total, verbal and extra-verbal significance of what the patient expresses. This assumes that I apply certain insights to my understanding of adults and a disposition to perceive that derives from my contact with children.

479

This contradiction is, in reality, only apparent. Nobody who defines thera-peutic situations should confine them to closed compartments. The assump-tion that matrices of basic expression exist in each therapeutic area does not mean that there is no interaction between them, especially in the case of the child and the adult, since they are both bipersonal situations. But we need to include another factor. The adult makes an extensive unconscious use of the

noso (10) and D. Liberman (16) (17), particularly to their work on the value of words by Doctor Álvarez de Toledo (3). From the synthesis of this work, the actual word, "to speak" to avoid confusion, acquires a specific and con-crete emotional meaning, beyond its semantic meaning. This is expressed by Doctor Álvarez de Toledo as follows:

"Deep below the conscious level, verbal activities have the value of, oral, anal, phallic and genital concrete actions that the patient carries out on the analyst, or his own words or those of the analyst, words that, on this level, have the value of concrete objects. In this situation, words, instead of being a link with the analyst as an object, pass on to be an object that the analyst expels or incorporates ... and the words are like intermediary objects that link and separate at the same time, by containing isolated and repressed libidinal cathexis that do not reach the analyst" (page 237).

We see that the author reaches the conclusion that language functions like a third object that simultaneously mediates and separates the bipersonal relationship. The discourse, in the analytical process, is dealt with like a toy: The analyst investigates the extra-verbal connotation that the verbal com-munication has.

In light of these concepts, I would like to revise a comparison made by Susanne Langer (15). This author, while referring to "transparency" of the symbols, points out that: "... if the word 'abundance' were replaced by a real, juicy, succulent peach, not many people would be capable of carefully fol-lowing the description of the concept: 'that is enough,' while contemplating this symbol. The more indifferent and sterile the symbol is – concludes the author – the greater its semantic power will be" (page 75).

We agree with Susanne Langer that it is evident that the abstract language needs an adequate symbolic vehicle that does not distract with emotional overtones, that does not fascinate with its mere presence. This series of phonetic sounds that we call words are ideal means to carry meaning. But we notice that words, scrutinized during the analysis, are much less "trans-parent" than what those who study language assumed. And we precisely work with this "opacity." Our work consists of two aspects: the first one is passive, we investigate the extra-verbal connotation carried by the patient's discourse; the second one is active, we attempt through our interpretations to transform the here and now of the patient so that the reasoning acquires a dramatic, concrete and immanent reality of the extra-verbal significance. Inverting the example of S. Langer, we try, precisely, to transform the verbal concept of "that is enough" in the absence of a vivid peach.

In light of what has been said up until now I would like to begin a revised draft on the operating criteria of interpretations. This draft overlaps with what has been provided in the chapter on "Formulation of the interpretations." With respect to the validity of the interpretations, nowadays we continue supporting the concepts displayed by Strachey in 1933 (20). This author takes credit for placing the transference at the center of the analytical process. Strachey pointed out that the transference interpretation is the only one that creates changes in the patient. He coined the definition of "mutative interpretation" to characterize the transformation generated by the transference intervention. For Strachey, the mutation takes place when the patient compares the existing difference between the fantastic and archaic image that has been projected onto the analyst, and the analyst "as he is". It ends up being a process of rectifying the fantasy by reality.

The dynamic of this mutative mechanism actually seems to be valid but insufficient. Nowadays we know more about the process of projection of images. We propose, as we did in previous chapters, that not only the "imagined" object is projected; part of the subject goes along with it. This is not a mere theoretical digression: the result of this double projection of the objects and parts of the self – this great unit of projection, as described in the chapter on transference – constitutes a very complex defense mechanism called projective identification. Therefore, a smaller difference exists between the object and the subject than what we had previously believed. The projective identification produces confusion between the self and the non-self, as an attempt by the patient to increase the area of influence of the self, acquiring through the omnipotent control mechanism "access," so to speak, to other "selves." There is a fact worth mentioning, that Dr. Grinberg was the first one to explain: This extension of the patient's area of influence is not a "mere" fantasy; it is, in a certain sense, a reality. From the experience of effective control that the patient has over us, to parasitize us, and make us behave in an induced manner, Dr. Grinberg has called this projective counter-identification (11)(12).

Strachey's formula could be completed by saying that the patient projects his fantastic and archaic images in such a way that it tends to turn us into them.

I therefore propose the following provisional hypothesis: mutative inter-pretation is where we reverse the process by which the analyst is affected by the patient's projections, making the patient dramatically experience those aspects of his self that are denied and projected onto his surroundings. Our therapeutic objective is not the mere objectification of the contrast between reality and fantasy; it is a dramatized recreation in the here and now.

on "formulation of the interpretation" and "the toy chest and the fantasy chest".

2   Marion Milner (in: El contexto del proceso analítico Emilio Rodrigue y Gene-vieve T. De Rodrigue. Paidós, 1966, Buenos Aires) poses a similar idea for the draw-ing activity, by considering the graphical trace a third independent object. (18).

3   E. Erikson wrote a very interesting paper about spatial configurations in infan-tile games. (9).

4   Using the terminology in its logic sense that the geometry is projective.

5   Metapsychology has never been a strong suit for Kleinian theorists; this is why I believe that the "structural" contribution has been underestimated in the British school formulations.

6   In a recent conference (1965), Bion presented on a tendency that was oppo-site to the characteristics of his current work. It consists of putting your mind totally blank, not passively resting, but *forgetting everything that the patient has said up until that moment*. This way, the patient is a new being in each moment of each session, a perpetual enigma that has to be resolved. For Bion, knowing how to forget is more important than knowing how to retain.

7   This object waiting to dry, incidentally, is an ideal example of a means of expression serving as a "third object" that determines changes in the transfer-ence, as a way for feedback. Whether the toy dried properly or not is a factor that undoubtedly has an effect on the new material produced by the child.

8   The notion that the expressive vehicle contains the basis for the counter-transference was introduced in Chapter V. This showed that the "how" of an interpretation implies the unconscious reception of an aspect that the patient transmits to the analyst as a means of expression.

9   The game of captain had already appeared in previous sessions, so I was not introducing a new element. As a rule I dramatize from situations and roles that have already appeared in the past.

10  Mauricio Abadi, in recent work (1), also seeks a differential classification of the game, considering ludic in its broadest sense.

11  The techniques used in group interpretations, as is known, do not take into account the transference situation of the group as a social organism and attempt to reduce the multiplicity of the group to the homogeneity of the individual.

12  In our profession, Alberto and Vera Campo have pointed out the role an activity has in our work with children (4) (5). More of this can be observed studying the most recent clinical material of Professor Arminda Aberastury (2).

13  When I discussed this material with Dr. Liberman, his response to the material about the "Cabildo" was immediate. He pointed out that the patient was saying that "the people want to know what it is about," meaning, she was questioning, with a revolutionary tone, the reasons for my departure. I agree and Dr. Liberman, with his usual intuition, touches upon one of the more important aspects of the material.

14  I believe that it is advisable to adopt the term *extra-verbal,* as it is used by Dr. Fidias R. Cesio (6), because by saying "non-verbal' we define all the unconscious expressivity with a prefix of denial.

15  This "plastic" expressive quality of the transference phenomenon will be addressed in the last chapter.

16  In my recent supervisions (1965) with Donald Meltzer and Rosenfeld I proved how frequently they use verbal emphasis and imitation of patients' modes of expression to provide a greater impact to their interpretations.

# Bibliography

1  Abadi, M: "Psicoanálisis del jugar" *Revista de Psicoanálisis* T XXI, 4, 1964.

2  Aberastury, A: *Teoría y técnica del psicoanálisis de niños.* Buenos Aires, Paidós 1962.

3  Álvarez de Toledo: "El análisis del asociar, del interpretar y de las palabras" *Revista de Psicoanálisis* T XIII, 4, 1965.

4  Campo, A.: "La interpretación y la acción en el psicoanálisis de niños" *Revista de Psicoanálisis* T XVII 1–2, 1957

5  Campo, Vera: "La introducción del elemento traumático" *Revista de Psicoanálisis* T XV, 1–2, 1958

6  Cesio, F.: "La comunicación extraverbal en psicoanálisis" *Revista de Psicoanálisis* T XX, 2, 1963.

7  Ehrezweig, A.: *Psychoanalysis of artistic vision and learning*, London, Routledge, 1953.

8  Erikson, E.: "Configuraciones en el juego", *Revista de Psicoanálisis* T VI, 2, 1948.

9  Erikson, E.: "The dream specimen of psychoanalysis" *International Journal of Psycho-Analysis* T XXXVI, 3, 1955.

10  García Reinoso, G.R.: "La actuación en la transferencia en el análisis de un fóbico", *Revista de Psicoanálisis* T XVIII, 3, 1961.

11  Grinberg, L.: "Sobre algunos problemas de la técnica psicoanalítica determinados por la identificación y la contra-identificación proyectiva" *Revista de Psicoanálisis* T XIII; 4, 1956.

12  Grinberg, L.: "Perturbaciones en la interpretación por la contra-identificación proyectiva" *Revista de Psicoanálisis* T XIV, 4 1957.

13 Grinberg, L. Langer, M. Rodrigué, E.: *Psicoterapia de grupo*. Buenos Aires Paidós, 1957.

14 Klein, M.: *El psicoanálisis de niños*. Buenos Aires, Hormé, 1964.

15 Langer, F.: *Philosophy in a new key*. U.S.A., Harvard University Press, 1951.

16 Liberman, D.:"Una nota acerca de la aplicación de la teoría de la cominicación a la comprención y explicación de la situación analítica", *Revista de Psicoanálisis* T. XVIII, 4, 1961.

17 Rodrigué, E.: "Tres analogías", *Anales del primer congreso de psicoterapia de grupo*, 1957.

20 Strachey, J.:"The nature of the therapeutic action of psychoanalysis", *International Journal of Psycho-Analysis* T XIV, 2, 1933.

# 47

# INTRODUCTION TO THE LIFE AND WORK OF DÉCIO SOARES DE SOUZA (1907–1970)

*Waldemar Zusman*

Décio Soares de Souza was born on January, 7, 1907, in Porto Alegre, Rio Grande do Sul. He was the son of Octávio Lisboa de Souza – a preeminent person in the local medical profession and full professor in clinical medicine at the Porto Alegre Medical School – and of Zilda Soares de Souza. He got his degree in medicine in 1929 at the Medical School of Rio Grande do Sul, presenting the thesis "Precocious Dementia and Schizophrenia", which was approved with honors (getting a grade 10). He became a full professor in clinical psychiatry, a position he held until 1950. He then transferred to London, in order to specialize in psychoanalysis. At the Institute of Psychoanalysis of the British Psychoanalytic Society, after five years of training, he received the title of Adult and Child Psychoanalyst.

Between his graduation as a medical doctor and the beginning of his analytic training, he took several extension courses at the university and internships at the Saint'Anne and Salpetrière hospitals in Paris; at the Mount Sinai Hospital he took the Advanced Course in Clinical Neurology; at Columbia University, he took courses in Neuroanatomy, Neuropathology and Educational Psychology, as well as in Mental Hygiene; at the Psychoanalytic Institute, in New York, the Metapsychology course; at the School of Social Research, the Psychology of Personality course.

Since the beginning of his professional life, Décio de Souza was interested in psychiatry and neurology, which at that time were studied in related courses. At the year of his graduation (1929), Décio was already an intern at the Assistance to Psychopathic Patients service. In 1930 he was appointed as staff psychiatrist at the Assistance to Psychopathic Patients, where in 1938 he was promoted, by merit, to chief of division. In 1932, he was an assistant to the 15th Ward of Clinical Neurology. On that same year, he became professor at the Psychiatric Clinic of the Porto Alegre Medical School, becoming the clinical head in that same discipline from 1933 to 1937. Between

Society of Neuropsychiatry of Rio Grande do Sul and professor of Elements of Psychiatry at the Professional School of Nursery of the Assistance to Psychopathic Patients of Rio Grande do Sul, since its foundation, in 1939.

The medical calling of Dr. Décio de Souza was probably inspired by the clinical prestige and by the professional respect attained by his father. Décio's interest in psychiatry and later in psychoanalysis is an expression of his deep attachment to humanism. His philosophical interest wandered through the works of Husserl, Max Scheler and Kant, just to name a few. His contact with Freud and Melanie Klein gave a more defined aim to his cultural journey and brought clarity and methodological order to his thinking about the mysteries of the human soul.

On his return from London, after having finished his psychoanalytic training, Dr. Décio de Souza established himself in Rio de Janeiro. It was in that period (1955) that he gave, at the Brazilian Neurology, Psychiatry and Legal-Medicine Society, the conference entitled Developments of Psychoanalysis, according to the English School. He started his private analytic practice and soon joined the Clinic of Childhood Orientation, a department of the Institute of Psychiatry of the University of Brazil. On the 27th of April of 1956, Professor Adauto Botelho named him director of that clinic, with the objective of making more effective the training of child psychoanalysts. Still a member of the British Psychoanalytic Society, he joined the Brazilian Psychoanalytic Society of São Paulo, where he became a training analyst. With the support of the São Paulo Society, together with Danilo Perestrello, Marialzira Perestrello and other colleagues, he founded a Study Group recognized by the International Psychoanalytical Association. That Study Group became the Brazilian Psychoanalytic Society of Rio de Janeiro in 1959.

Professor Décio de Souza died at 63 years of age, on October 30, 1970.

# 48

# SYMPOSIUM ON PSYCHOTIC OBJECT RELATIONSHIPS

## Annihilation and reconstruction of object-relationship in a schizophrenic girl

*Décio Soares de Souza*

*Read at the 21st Congress of the International Psycho-Analytical Association, Copenhagen, July 1959, and published in 1960 by the* International Journal of Psycho-Analysis, *41: 554–558.*

The clinical material on which I wish to base some suggestions about psychotic object–relationship concerns the case of a girl of 2 years and 10 months who, failing to work through a depressive situation, went on developing more and more regressive defences which pushed her into schizophrenia. This is certainly not new since Melanie Klein taught us about the relationship between the paranoid–schizoid and depressive positions. Klein (3) emphasizes that when paranoid feelings are too strong the individual cannot stand the burden of depressive feelings. 'For if persecutory fears and correspondingly schizoid mechanisms are too strong, the ego is not capable of working through the depressive position. This forces the ego to regress to the paranoid–schizoid position and reinforces the earlier persecutory fears and schizoid phenomena. Thus the basis is established for various forms of schizophrenia in later life.'

The case is as follows. L. was 2 years and 4 months old when her sister was born. In the last months of her mother's pregnancy she was prevented from getting on to her mother's lap on the grounds that the mother could not stand her weight. Until then L. had been the only child and the only grand-child.

Breast-feeding was interrupted after only a month for lack of milk. Apparently she accepted the bottle without much trouble. Sphincter control started rather early – around 6 months. When L. was a year and 4

sister, L. received her with the words: 'Now you haven't got the baby inside you any more. The lap is mine.' In the following months her difficulties increased with the newborn child, mother, and father. She became more and more aggressive towards her sister and her parents. At the same time she tried to put herself into her sister's place, asking to be treated like a baby. She showed terrible feelings of persecution, envy, and jealousy, with attempts at destroying the sister, which produced some sort of alliance between her parents to prevent her aggression against the baby sister. She felt lost regarding their emotional support. During the following weeks she sometimes complained of not being able to walk and at other times of not being able to stand up. Epileptoid convulsions followed, mainly in the evenings. She started biting her nurse, who was looking after her baby sister, and her own wrists. Some months later L. completely lost the control of urethral and anal sphincters; she was unable to learn anything else and was no longer able to handle objects. Her speaking capacity gradually deteriorated and finally was reduced to 'Hum, hum'. At the same time she lost the perception of her position in space among other objects to such a degree that she had to be protected to prevent her from banging against them. At the time when she started analysis she was in this regressed state. During these four months L. showed a first attempt to defend herself against the persecutory and depressive feelings connected with the loss of mother's lap – as a symbol of the total situation of loss and probably with the persecutory situation of having been deprived of milk during the first month of her life.

I treated L. according to Klein's technique of play-analysis for seven months. During treatment, she showed progressive improvement of her capacity for perception, bodily functions and verbalization as well as the rehabilitation of the world of objects in her internal and external reality.

Taking her object-relationships as a sample of psychotic processes of schizophrenia going on in this child, I shall now bring detailed material to show some of the meanings of her regression and subsequent progress.

In the first sessions L. showed a complete indifference regarding play. She used to hold the toys for a moment to look at them and then drop them. Her phantasy life was very inhibited. She followed me without any difficulty when I first took her to the playroom. She approached the table on which were some toys, picked up a woman and a horse together with the same hand and dropped them. I showed her that the woman and the horse were standing for mummy and daddy and the connection between her dropping them on the floor and her being pushed down from mother's lap; that she was fancying I might be going to do the same to her. Although, apparently, she was not paying any attention to me or to what I was saying, the next moment brought me the first response to my interpretation: she picked up a cow and touched the cow's udder with her index finger. I pointed out to her that the cow's udder was standing for mummy's breast, and when she was bringing together the cow and two lambs, the lambs were standing for her and her sister trying to get to mother's breast.

The first sessions went on like this, giving us the opportunity to follow her persecutory anxieties underneath her lack of contact with me and with external reality. When L. repeats the attitude of dropping everything she grasps, she is showing that everything is changed into bad faeces inside her exactly as she had phantasied she had been treated by her parents. When I interpreted this to her she gave me two responses: the first was to try to revive mother's figure by taking a 'woman' and rolling it between her hands. The second was not to drop the objects, but for two or three times to 'put them on' the table. I realized that she was showing some concern for the objects.

The positive movement aroused by my interpretation did not last long; L. goes on dropping mother's and father's figures and houses, showing that she had failed in her attempt to change them from bad into good faeces and from hated into loved objects. When I insisted on interpreting to L. that she was feeling persecuted by the cow, the lambs, the horses, and the human figures, and everything she was grasping and dropping in that session, and that they stood for mother, father, sister, me, and other people she had got inside her and who had been changed into bad faeces because of her feelings of envy and jealousy, her response again shows a positive movement in which she tries to revive Author people inside her, but she does not keep the reparative tendencies long. After the reparative rolling of mother's figure comes now a bit of a smile, a particular way of looking at me or some sort of oral communication, consisting in a kind of babbling. I went on interpreting these rudiments of verbal communication as much as the smile and the look as an expression of people inside her who were just coming alive. These first contacts with L. made me realize how deeply she had regressed.

In the next weeks of treatment L. exhibited a large amount of persecutory feelings and phantasies mainly directed against the inside of mother's body and babies. She dramatized these attacks in many sessions through many ways of playing; sometimes she tried to cut her own tummy with scissors – sometimes she grasped a little bag full of marbles and then started dropping the marbles and emptying the bag. Sometimes she put these marbles in

The other way she chose to express her persecutory anxieties about the mother's inside was a kind of play in which she used to get into the drawer full of toys and stay there the whole session, attacking the inside of the drawer with a ruler, her feet, and her urine. Session after session this type of play was repeated in a very obsessive way. Sometimes the play used to start with the ritual of moving up and down, right in the middle of the drawer, the little bag full of marbles. I interpreted this as a phantasy of controlling the way the babies get inside the mother and come out. I connected that with the phantasy of controlling her sister's birth and the coming in and out of my other patients, the play-room standing for my own and mother's insides.

At some other times we could see the attacks directed against her mother's breast. Very expressive in this sense is a bit of material in which, after playing with the bag and the marbles and after her phantasies of trying to get the babies out of mummy had been interpreted, L. approached me and put her right hand into the pocket of my shirt and then with her index finger tried to open my mouth, pressing down my underlip. I interpreted that I was standing for her sister and she was trying to see whether I had got mummy's breast and milk inside my mouth. After that, she picked up a jeep and broke down the windscreen, which was divided in two parts, and tossed it into the drawer. I explained to her that she was attacking mummy's breast, showing envy of that breast and jealousy because it had been given to her sister and became bad. That she was attacking the breast – windscreen – breaking it, destroying it because she was feeling so much deprived by her mother and sister, as much as she was feeling deprived by me when after the session she believed I was going to give my breast to other children. Next day she picked up the broken windscreen and gave it to me, as if asking me to repair it for her.

Another aspect of conflict L. showed in the first weeks of treatment was against father's penis. Once she was inside the drawer she started rubbing a horse against the drawer's edge until the horse's leg was broken. Then she tossed it inside the drawer. At other times she used to dramatize her persecutory feelings connected with father's penis by bringing two pencil-points together and then breaking them both. At the same time as she acted out such attacks on the penis she used to utter a stereotypic 'Psa-psa'. I interpreted that as L.'s jealousy and envy of her parents' intercourse.

After some weeks in which L. attacked mother's inside by getting into the drawer, she did not approach the drawer any more. She started ignoring it, and it was left shut and untouched. One day when she arrived in the playroom just before the time of her session I was there and had opened the drawer. When she saw the open drawer she started shouting 'No, no' and very anxiously made for the drawer and shut it. I had by now interpreted a great deal of her persecutory anxieties and phantasies without much mitigation of the anxieties that were preventing her from approaching the drawer. I noticed that at that time she did not avoid the drawer and did not take flight from it, but she stood against the drawer as if to prevent its contents coming out. On the other hand, she had shown until then very few open feelings of depression and reparation in comparison with the strong feelings of persecution and open aggression described. When I realized that she had left inside the drawer all her good toys which she had attacked and destroyed previously, without showing any open guilt feelings about it, it seemed to me that by avoiding seeing and touching the drawer she was not defending herself so much against persecutory anxieties connected with destroyed objects and their coming up as persecutors, but predominantly against depressive feelings and anxieties connected with guilt for having destroyed them. I believed that the depressive part of herself, when she was not displaying guilt feelings for such destruction, was left inside the drawer with all the toys for whose destruction she felt responsible. Keeping the inside of the drawer as bad and avoiding it meant that she was trying to evade her feelings of responsibility and depressive anxieties connected with the toys' condition. In the transference, the drawer was standing for my body representing the mother and the attacked toys for the mother's breast and father's penis and the baby sister and other babies inside the mother's womb.

## Words and depression

At that time L. was showing a predominantly negative transference towards me, expressed by her saying as soon as I started interpreting: 'No, no'. She was behaving towards me exactly as she had been behaving towards the drawer: trying to keep my mouth shut. We can see here how much the visual perception of the destroyed objects inside the drawer was equated with the words coming out of my mouth when I was interpreting.

491

L. could not bear seeing the attacked objects, the perception of which would bring depressive and guilty feelings, as much as my words about her hatred and aggressive behaviour towards her sister, mother, and father. In the transference situation the words emerging from my mouth and the contents of the drawer were both the same object with her depressive self inside and the picture of destroyed parents, breast, penis, sister. Denying and annihilat-

came up in her play. The same problem was connected with the annihilation of her perception of the objects. On the other hand it seems to me that mother's words telling her about the baby inside mother's body were linked to L.'s envy and jealousy and depressing feelings of loss which, increasing her greed had pushed her back into persecutory anxieties as the depressive ones became unbearable to her.

Working in this field Bion (1) has described a relationship between verbal thought and depression: 'Verbal thought is so interwoven with catastrophe and the painful emotion of depression that the patient, resorting to projective identification, splits it off and pushes it into the analyst ... at the onset of the infantile depressive position, elements of verbal thought increase in intensity and depth. In consequence, the pains of psychic reality are exacerbated by it and the patient who regresses to the paranoid-schizoid position will, as he does so, turn destructively on his embryonic capacity for verbal thought as one of the elements which have led to his pain.'

When the analysis of her persecutory anxieties was progressing L. went on to reveal a greater capacity to feel guilt and depression during the sessions, as for instance on one day when she came to me just as I arrived, pressed her face against my genital region, and started babbling and crying, showing that she was mourning father's penis.

## The return of verbalization as a means of maintaining an object-relationship

In contradistinction to this phase in which L. was defending herself against verbalization (which reproduces what was going on inside her when she lost her capacity to stand depression) she showed later on, in her treatment, another phase in which she was very demanding as far as verbalization was concerned. By this time she had recovered from the sphincter disturbances and convulsions and had improved her personal contacts.

One day she started pointing with her index finger to objects around her and asking for their names, saying: "Tis, 'tis'. She was reproducing the well-known phase of the exploring index finger. I understood that she was asking for words to give names to these objects and to overcome the splitting between visual and verbal processes. On the other hand she was testing me in order to see whether or not I had destroyed the words standing for the objects inside me, as she had done. Very expressive of this situation was a session in which L. started drawing and asked me soon afterwards to draw for her. As I asked her what she was intending me to draw for her, she said: 'L. – mummy – some grown-up people'. I explained to her that she was expecting that Dad D. (me) might be able to bring together L. and everybody else in her family; that these people were split off inside L. as much as L. herself. And I went on enumerating all the people around her and parts of them like mother's breast and father's penis, which she had bitten and made into pieces as she had bitten her nurse and herself.

As I went on drawing, L. pointed with her finger at different parts of the figures, saying: 'the eyes, the mouth, L.'s eyes, mummy's hair', and so on. I believe that she was trying not only to bring together visual perception and verbal expression, but at the same time asking me to give her back 'as a whole', through drawing and verbalization, the people she had destroyed inside her.

Getting back the split-off parts, the words standing for objects, L. was showing that now she could accept depression and rebuild the objects inside and outside. In this case we see a condensation between perception and action, meaning: 'If I don't see I don't feel responsible for it – its condition is not due to my action' (speaking of the object). We see that the denial of the perception of the object is an attempt to deny responsibility for the object's condition.

At the beginning L. had great difficulties in bringing the syllables of words together correctly, but she soon started more and more integrated words, showing that the same was happening to her self. Her emotional attitude made it evident how much she was enjoying these renewed verbal games. Each "Tis, 'tis' had the function of bringing together the visual and verbal perception and integration previously annihilated after the splitting and projective processes connected with persecutory feelings. By trying to link again visual perception and words, L. was reproducing through progression her previous ways of regression. When she tried to make splits between the visual contents, my words and her own ('Don't talk about that'), she was showing that the same had happened when she split off her phantasies about the contents of her mother's womb with the attacked baby inside and its communication, in words, with her internal reality. The destroyed baby ceased to exist because the ways of expression to indicate its existence and its condition, the words, were annihilated. At the moment in which L. began looking for words it was evident that she was overcoming her difficulties in accepting depression. In the clinical material I could see at that time an open expression of depressive and reparative feelings coming to the fore: she started crying, showing concern for the marbles – standing for children – when they were dropped to the floor, kissing them,

standing for her mother, of the baby she believed she had destroyed in her mother's womb and which was now being given back to her alive. This came up many times during the sessions.

More trust in her internal parents' goodness brought her more confidence in her capacity for reparation and in her own capacity to endure guilt. This increased capacity of accepting guilt connected with attacks against the objects inside the drawer – womb – and outside (sister, mother, and father) and the assurance about her reparative capacity connected with her internal good parents, brought back to her the previous capacity for making use of words: rebuilding a world of whole objects both in her internal and external realities. From the point of view of object relationships, this meant a step from partial to whole objects, from persecution to guilt and reparation, and from splitting to integration. The clinical material at this time showed a better identification of L. with her mother and a stronger nursing attitude towards the baby sister. Thus, she would refer to her baby sister as someone who 'is in her cot'. Her mother told me that she was trying to hold her baby sister and to feed her. At the same time, she completely dropped her previous behaviour, with which she was competing with the baby sister. In the playroom, L. followed a more and more independent role, as for instance when she rejected any help during the play in which she was jumping from the couch to the floor, saying: 'No, no, alone, alone'.

This material points to the fact that the annihilation of the perception of the object and the object-relationship (drawer, toys, mother, father, sister, the analyst and the environment) as much as the annihilation of verbal communication and capacity for integration was related to the ego's integration and capacity for feeling responsible for the object's condition and facing the unbearable guilt connected with the depressive position, as Segal (5) has shown.

We see, as Melanie Klein, Rosenfeld, and Bion have shown, that annihilation of the object that goes with the annihilation of parts of the self is a psychotic type of object-relationship. With splitting and projective identification, it shows the psychotic paradox of an ego which, not being well integrated, in the same process of defence attacks some of its own functions in order to prevent something coming into perception that already existed internally. Freud (2) discusses this type of defence in his paper 'Negation', in which he deals with a defence different from the preservation of the ego and the object, characteristic of repression and of a more integrated ego.

# References

1   BION, W. H. 1954 'Notes on the Theory of Schizophrenia'. *International Journal of Psycho-Analysis* 35: 167–171

2   FREUD, S. 1925 'Negation'. *The complete psychological works of Sigmund Freud,* 19: 233–240

3   KLEIN, MELANIE 'Notes on Some Schizoid Mechanisms'. *Developments in Psycho-Analysis* (London: Hogarth, 1952.)

4   ROSENFELD, H. 1947 'Analysis of a Schizophrenic State with Depersonalization'. *International Journal of Psycho-Analysis* 28: 130–139

5   SEGAL, H. 1956 'Depression in the Schizophrenic'. *International Journal of Psycho-Analysis* 37: 339–343

# Part V

# CULTURE AND SOCIETY

# 49

# INTRODUCTION TO THE LIFE AND WORK OF ARNALDO RASCOVSKY (1907–1995) AND MATILDE RASCOVSKY (1910–2006)

*Andrés Rascovsky*

Arnaldo Rascovsky (1907, Córdoba, Argentina–1995, Buenos Aires) was born to a Rumanian Jewish immigrant family. He graduated From the Buenos Aires University Medical School at 21. He specialized in pediatrics and established a private practice and joined the staff of the Children's Hospital in Buenos Aires. He was passionate as a physician and freethinker.

He married young to Matilde Wencenblat, daughter of Jewish immigrants from Austria and France. Early in his hospital practice he noted the incidence of families' emotional conflicts in the origin of children's illness. His curiosity and "natural" leadership disposition was the driving force that gave birth to the first study group of Freud's papers in Buenos Aires. It was an eclectic gathering of medical doctors, philosophers, lawyers, and artists, together with intellectuals and bohemians.

It was this membership that shaped the spirit of psychoanalysis in Latin America and contributed to its creativity and diffusion. Psychoanalysis was, from the beginning, not a psychiatric or even a medical specialty.

When in 1938 Angel Garma arrived in Buenos Aires fleeing Spain's dictatorship of Franco, this allowed Arnaldo Rascovsky, together with Pichon-Rivière, Matilde Wencelblat, Arminda Aberastury, Celes Cárcamo, Marie Langer and Heinrich Racker to achieve recognition in 1942 as an IPA psychoanalytic society: the Argentine Psychoanalytic Association (APA).

In 1943, Arnaldo created *Revista de Psicoanálisis* and was the first editor, starting the publication of classic papers together with original ones. This journal has been in continuous edition for 70 years (probably the only Argentine journal with no interruptions) and in 1946, Arnaldo succeeded Angel Garma as President of APA.

In 1955, invited by the Medical Students' Organization, Arnaldo gave a

Arnaldo and Matilde were both avid readers of classic and contemporary literature, and Matilde became a psychoanalytic pioneer in her own right.

Arnaldo's leadership, passion and seemingly inexhaustible energy crystallized in his role as founding member of a number of professional organizations in areas such as pediatrics, endocrinology, psychoanalysis, psychotherapy and applied psychoanalysis.

His early contributions were in pediatrics, doing clinical research in psychosomatic medicine (pseudo-epilepsy) and Cushing's syndrome. This work led him to the creation in 1947 of the first journal on psychosomatic medicine in Latin America, becoming its first editor. His psychoanalytic research focused on the psychodynamics of manic as well as psychosomatic illnesses. His research on psychopathy and manic manifestations helped him create an original perspective on fixations prior to the oral stage. This original conception on the birth of human psyche and its structure was published in his book *El Psiquismo Fetal* (*The Fetal Psychism*) in the late 1950s.

His theories were also published in English as "Beyond the Oral Stage" (*International Journal of Psycho-Analysis*, 37: 286–289). Narcissistic phenomena and regression were considered linked to the imaginary relation with bi-dimensional inner objects inherited from fetal life.

Melanie Klein's contributions also influenced Rascovsky, although he was primarily a Freudian reader. While deepening his study and research around early stages of life and regression, his interest and commitment to social issues started to occupy a central role in his professional life.

His writings started to reach a wider professional and lay public. He was one of the more effective promoters of psychoanalysis in Latin America, and his vision was the creation of a Latin American psychoanalysis with its own personality and creative profile.

He was instrumental in making Buenos Aires the main psychoanalytic training center in Latin America. Many of the analysts that developed psychoanalytic study groups and societies in South America received their training in Buenos Aires.

500

In recognition of his contribution as an organizer of a Latin American movement when the Latin American Federation of Psychoanalysis was created, Arnaldo Raskovsky was appointed as its Honorary President.

The clinical confluence of pediatrics and psychoanalysis resulted in his research on the parental disturbances leading to murderousness of parents towards their children. His book on filicide (1961) is a milestone on the subject and unique in its contributions to clinical work as well as theoretical and applied psychoanalysis. In it, he explores subjects like the origin of civilization, Abraham's myth, a contribution to the understanding of Oedipus' psychopathic conduct and the birth of monotheism.

Arnaldo, a gifted communicator, stimulated a line of research regarding childhood in different societies, as well as the unconscious murderous impulses that led over the centuries to the exploitation of, ill treatment of, abuse of and sadism towards children. His work lead to significant questioning of the accepted patterns of parental care, had influence in medical and educational curriculums, and became incorporated into popular culture. The Raskovskys were very active and collaborated in mass media contributions. Their books were sold and became best sellers even at street newsstands.

Matilde Raskovsky co-authored important papers with Arnaldo on filicide and on psychosomatic medicine, amongst other subjects. She was a founding member of APA as well as Filium, an international institution dedicated to the protection of childhood against the multiple expressions of filicide in our culture.

Arnaldo's passionate attitude made him the target of many attacks. Matilde played a key role in helping him to overcome these situations. Matilde's dignity, intellectual strength and psychic balance and conviction were central to Arnaldo's psychoanalytic journey. She continued being an active member of the analytic community until she was 96 years old.

# PROCESS

*Arnaldo Rascovsky and Matilde Rascovsky*

*This paper was read at the 27th International Psycho-Analytical Congress, Vienna, July 1971, and published in 1972 by the* International Journal of Psycho-Analysis, *53: 271–276.*

Psychoanalytic investigation has confirmed that incestuous craving is the most constant and universal sexual force in the life of the individual, and the main obstacle in the socialization process is the difficulty in overcoming the Oedipus complex, i.e. the endogamic sexual tie. We wish to stress, however, the importance of incestuous attraction as the most powerful initial sexual tie, which is a vital and indispensable stimulus for the survival of the child and his later sexual development.

When confronted with the fact that the prohibition of incest is present in all sociocultural groups, we wonder what were the irrevocable, persistent procedures by which the most essential of the instinctual drives were deflected.

Side by side with the universal prohibition of incest, there is another generalized institution to be found in every culture: filicide. Primitive myths (Devereux, 1953),(1966); (Rascovsky, 1970a); (Rascovsky & Rascovsky, 1968), initiation rites (Reik, 1931), a study of human sacrifices (Devereux, 1953) and multiple manifestations of the various social systems reveal that slaughter, mutilation and real or symbolic abasement of children, expressed in quite a number of ways, are practices that have been universal since the dawn of culture (Rheingold, 1964).

In psychoanalytic practice, the endopsychic expression of these phenomena can be constantly observed in the interrelations between the superego and the ego (Berliner, 1966) evidenced by disorders such as obsessional neurosis, melancholia and suicide or by the punitive sanctions imposed on the ego, especially in the case of incestuous fantasies. The unshakable concept of taboo stems from this threat coming from the superego, which results from introjected archaic parental attitudes. Hence, the conceptualization of filicide becomes of paramount importance for psychoanalytical theory as it gives new scope to the Oedipus complex and throws light on the internalized repressive and persecutory forces and the structure of guilt.

The assumption that guilt and the original crime stem from parricide calls for serious reconsideration. On the other hand, parricide as the ultimate evolution of object destruction must be regarded as a consequence of filicidal behaviour and its principal roots must be attributed to the infant's identification with the parents' aggression. This approach stresses the decisive significance of the parental attitude in the regulation of innate infantile aggressiveness and how environment leads the infant to organize the parricide fantasy that is set up at a later developmental stage.

The 'typical' event described by Freud as the 'slaying and eating of the father feeling of guilt' must be modified, inasmuch as the primordial victim was the child and the real 'typical' event is 'slaying and eating of the child or segment of the children – guilt-producing intimidation of all the progeny – denial of the real process'. Thus the substitution of the pars pro toto for the slaughter of the child is found again in the circumcision of newborn infants amongst the Jews and at an older age amongst the Moslems or in the identification with the circumcised, sacrificed Jesus experienced by Christians in Communion. We shall only refer briefly to the serious anthropological criticism to the concept of parricide. According to Kroeber (1939):

> A typical event, historically speaking, is a recurrent one. This can hardly be admitted for the father-slaying, eating, guilt sense . . . certain psychic processes tend always to be operative and to find expression in widespread human institutions.

Filicide is definitely a typical event that recurs with every generation and is kept permanently alive through a large number of human institutions. Of all their various forms, none is more significant than war.

When Freud (1928, p. 183) stated:

> Parricide . . . is the principal and primal crime of humanity as well as of the individual. It is in any case the main source of the sense of guilt, though we do not know if it is the only one.

503

he was influenced by the fear of the father, which prompted him to add (1928, p. 184):

> What makes hatred of the father unacceptable is fear of the father; castration is terrible, whether as a punishment or as the price of love. Of the two factors which repress hatred of the father, the first,

> It can also be asserted that when a child reacts to his first great instinctual frustrations with excessively strong aggressiveness and with a correspondingly severe superego, he is following a phylogenetic model and is going beyond the response that would be currently justified; for the father of prehistoric times was undoubtedly terrible, and an extreme amount of aggressiveness may be attributed to him.

When discussing fear of the father, it is necessary to examine closely the aggressiveness present in the archaic interrelationships with the parents so as to elucidate the internalized factors which may result from the parents' failure to absorb, be depositories of and work through the infant's innate, primitive aggressiveness. We are more often than not confronted with the parents' destructive behaviour towards their children, which ranges from rejection or neglect to abandonment, ill-treatment and slaughter (Berliner, 1966); (Devereux, 1953), (1966); (Rascovsky, 1970a). Recent studies on the effects of the parent–child relationship (Ainsworth et al., 1963); (Bowlby, 1951), (1958); (Bowlby et al., 1956); (Burlingham & Freud, 1943) have led to the assertion that parents initially function as an 'auxiliary ego' (Spitz, 1946),(1951) on which the child relies for survival, as he is unable to adjust to reality without it. The lack of parental function (performed by the real parents or by surrogates) at an early stage causes the infant's death in the same manner as any sort of abandonment causes a damage equal to its intensity and duration. This lack can be expressed through active and/ or passive attitudes, namely circumcision, early or repeated abandonment, mental or physical punishment, cruelty, physical or verbal attacks, despotic refusals, indifference to suffering, insults and so on. They can be occasional or permanent, but the child's self will inevitably bear the brunt and reflect the damage inflicted upon it.

Filicide complements the relationship between the prohibition of incest and parricide. It is the fundamental procedure that established the prohibition and its sociocultural consequences as well as child sacrifice – the basis for human sacrifice – which became the predominant cultural pattern overtly or in disguised ways, the most common being education. It also helps in the understanding of the feeling of guilt, since the paranoiac increase resulting from the direct threat imposed by parents heightens persecutory guilt (Grinberg, 1963, p. 81), (1964). The acknowledgement of filicide introduces a new approach to the aggressive microforms that act on the ego to give form to paranoiac organization and contributes to the understanding of the structure of the internal persecutory objects not only as regards fantasy but mainly in connection with the actual parents.

# The prohibition of incest and the sociocultural process

We should like to emphasize that the overcoming of the initial incestuous tie conditions the entire socialization process in man. Lévi-Strauss (1960, pp. 41–2) supports our view. He states:

> Since the sexual instinct is natural, it does not constitute the transition from the natural state to civilization, as this is inconceivable, but it does explain one of the reasons why it is in the area of sexual life, above all others, where the transition between the two orders should and does operate . . . the prohibition of incest can be found at the dawn of culture, in culture, and in a certain sense, as we shall try to demonstrate, is culture itself.

The prohibition against incest brought about two immediate cultural consequences and a third more indirect one. They are:

1   The institution of exogamy and the enlargement of the social group, including the gradual displacement of basic dependence from the parents to the community.
2   The organization and over-development of sublimation, resulting in a shift of prohibited drives toward acceptable social activities, encouraging creative and practical human expression.
3   These shifts and displacement brought about the necessity to transmit the accumulated experience of previous generations. As a consequence, the entire social group participated in the processes of instruction.

This process, which amounts to individual death in the incestuous society and rebirth in the exogamic society, constitutes the latent content underlying Frazer's description (1944, p. 820) of the ritual of 'death and rebirth' found in all cultures.

This evolution, repeated in the development of each individual, can be observed during the psychoanalytic investigation of the vicissitudes that follow attempts to overcome the genital Oedipal complex around the sixth year of life. When a child reaches the climax of his incestuous desires, he is confronted by increased castration anxiety that means the end of the endogamous and enables him to give up the mother as a sexual object and

increase noticeably. Thus the training that was begun by the parents is now turned over to teachers and other substitutes who are representatives of the community.

The prohibition of incest called for an equally strong force capable of curbing the instinctual desire. This traumatic restraint involved first the immolation of a group of children, which began with the killing of the firstborn son. This requirement, which was subsequently institutionalized through religious systems as a sacred demand from the divine powers, appears explicitly in various historical and religious manifestations (Lorenz, 1966) and must be an ancient pattern whose origins could be traced back to the beginning of culture.

## The origins of filicide

Although it is true that the slaughter of children became the principal procedure that set up the prohibition of incest, it was originally a drive that gradually turned into a well-defined social pattern in the form of 'human sacrifices'. The fact that the primal myths of the main cultures begin with the slaughter or abandonment of children is quite revealing.

Lorenz (1966) states of the higher vertebrates:

> I do not believe that the specifically human tendencies to cannibalism, for which there seems to be ample psychoanalytic evidence, have anything to do with the occasional eating of young mammals by their parents. . . . On the whole 'cannibalism' is quite rare among higher vertebrates.

Referring to infanticide and puerperal cannibalism, Blin & Favreau also state: 'In mammals . . . this does constitute a true behavioural disruption and must be considered to be pathological' (1968, p. 282).

Occasional cannibalism among mammals is the result of excessive stress. This response became permanent in human beings exposed to constant stress, creating an adaptation based on regression to the oral-cannibalistic stage. In this regression, the learned erotic capacities that could have served for child preservation and care were lost.

Cannibalism by ingestion of parts of the mother is a normal process in mammals until the offspring are capable of assimilating more differentiated food than maternal milk. In human beings, it coincides with the part–object relationship and is given up when the child is able to integrate the whole love object. Cannibalism is therefore linked to the schizoid-paranoid position. The transition to a whole-object relationship points to considerable erotic progress and makes it possible to gather the parts into a whole. This erotic development inhibits cannibalism and when the subsequent depressive position is attained, the love object is more easily preserved. To account for the recurrence of filicide and its institutionalized perpetuation, it should be remembered that in early times conditions of extreme stress conducive to oral-cannibalistic regression were quite frequent with the attendant paranoid increase. On such occasions the previously learned inhibitions that had prevented child–slaying were lost. Children became the suitable part objects for intensified oral sadism.

In our practices, we have often observed such regression with the arrival of the firstborn. To give an example:

a     The patient's wife was about to deliver her child. In the following session, he reported she had seen her obstetrician who had told her that dilation of the cervix was well advanced. Then he reported two dreams he had had the night before.

   1     We were in the hall of a hospital. My wife and I saw G. coming towards us; the collar and front of his shirt were stained. He seemed to be drunk. I thought that he had just come from a big dinner at J.'s house. I was furious because she never invited me to dinner, but she did invite G. The hall turned into the hospital where my wife is to be admitted.

His associations led him to G. (a friend for whom he had ambivalent feelings). G., with his shirt stained where the baby's bib would be, stood for his future son breast-feeding. He had had dinner with J. (the wife-mother) leaving him out (from the breast). Oral envy appears as anger at not having been invited.

   2     I am going to the movies with my wife. It is a holiday. The theatre is closed, but they are going to show the film. We are with another couple. I am surprised to learn they are going to show

the film, even though the theatre is closed. They give me gallery seats. They seem too far away for me. I would have preferred orchestra seats.

His associations meant he could not have sexual intercourse because his wife was too big and taken up with the foetus. This was the cinema, which was closed on a holiday (the holiday being like intercourse),

b The baby was born two days later and in hospital with the mother. The next morning our patient reported two dreams:

1 I was with P. [a friend with traits related to the baby], G. [who had previously stood for the baby] and V. [the dreamer]. V. said that they should celebrate the birth with a barbecue that could be held in Luna Park. G. clarified that it would not be in the Rotary Club. P. reproached me for not having received my medical degree and for being incapable of studying.

He associated Luna Park with the boxing arena, in opposition to the Rotary Club, an expression of love among men. The barbecue represented the slaughter and eating of his son. The child complained, as an expression of the superego, accusing him of being immature and not ready for fatherhood because of his uncurbed cannibalism.

2 'I see my brother-in-law's mother, who is sick and about to die.' The patient had this dream after having taken care of the baby during the night. It meant envy and the wish for his wife's death as an attempt to take her place in her relationship with the baby.

c The baby and the mother had been back home for two days. The following dream came after he had again taken care of the baby during the night.

I am going towards the kitchen to get the bottle ready. The door of the apartment is open. I try to close it, but someone is pushing it from outside. I believe it is a burglar, and try to keep him from entering: but he succeeds in opening the door, and it falls on top of me. The supposed burglar was my brother.

That afternoon he had embraced his brother when saying goodbye and he had felt upset because his brother had leaned too much on him. He also associated that little children are told that babies are brought from Paris, his brother having just returned from that city. The burglar stood for the intrusion of the baby threatening to displace him and he felt it was useless to fight against this.

This brief report from a patient's feelings, dreams and reactions before the birth of his first child is just a sample of the universal response to the arrival of children.

## Procedures to impose the prohibition of incest

Let us return now to our first question: what were the procedures that brought about the imposition of the prohibition of incest?

Instinctual demands represent a constant pressure that has been permanently and solidly structured since the earliest stages of phylogenetic development. Conversely their restraint, which came much later historically, calls for a continuous antagonistic action that loses efficiency immediately following cessation. Thus repetition of opposition to the drives, imposed from outside and subsequently introjected as a part of the superego, was always necessary in order to support and maintain the prohibition of incest. The archaic prohibition could be imposed only as long as the parents retained physical, mental and moral power. This supremacy gave way in the face of the children's growing strength and the simultaneous decline of the parents; so much so that it proved impossible to keep the prohibition. After repeated individual and collective experiences of sadistic nature, the primitive gerontocracy understood that it was necessary to establish definite and persistent parental supremacy while it was still possible. It had to be done in the early years of life when the child was still weak and dependent. The principle was followed in all early societies. A body of methods and techniques was created that is still maintained in all its force. The procedure consists of the slaughter of a segment of the offspring, such as the firstborn or the chosen, and the mutilation and abasement of the rest of the progeny. An essential part of the process stresses concealment. There is tacit agreement to keep hidden or to deny all knowledge of the procedures. This denial has lasted into the present, whereas the significance is overstressed. Thus the persecutory guilt, which burdens children, carries a melancholic connotation that intensifies submission. Moreover, the sadism and cruelty to children of parents and other social institutions are denied and converted into justified anger of parents or their substitutes, such as the society or its gods, for the supposed or attributed iniquities of the children. The fact is that the aggression of the children was originally instigated or caused by the persecutors. Once again we are compelled to conclude that the stressing of the parricidal accusation is another form of filicidal action. The parents' fantasies and acts of abasement or abuse of the children are thus transformed by the children into self-blame.

This process can be traced in less obvious forms through anthropological observations of surviving primitive cultures; in the analysis of ancient, mythical narratives, such as Oedipus; in the understanding of the significance of archaic and current rites of initiation; and above all through psychoana-

parents is met, there follows a resurrection of the child out of this voracious act, but now genital rivalry with its threat of castration arises. This process is carried out in many ways ranging from actual castration, which has attained a dramatic reality in many cultures even today, to genital inhibition imposed by means of various disciplinary measures. Trade in castrated boys to be sold as eunuchs and the practice of castrating boys to train them as adult soprano singers (castrati) have continued to modern times. The increasing popularity of self-castration is also of some interest here. Among intermediate procedures is circumcision, practised extensively in contemporary cultures. It is to be noted that in the Christian calendar the year does not begin with the birth of Jesus, December 25th, but on the day that he was circumcised, January 1st.

We do not believe that the prohibition of incest was the earliest motivation for the slaughter and abasement of children. It is more likely, as we observe in psychoanalysis, that the first motivation arose out of parents' envy of the child as a rival in competition for the nurturing woman-mother. Perhaps conditions of extreme stress caused a state of deep regression in the parents, which led to such a heightening of the oral envy that the assassination and ingestion of children resulted, as in the myth of Chronos. Subsequently jealousy and genital rivalry prompted slaughter or perhaps, more conservatively, a pars pro toto real or symbolic castration. Probably the prohibition of incest was a further step to save the child once a sufficiently erotic link had been established with him. This total process reached such intensity, continuity and universality that it became a part of the superego and acted as an inhibitory internal regulator of the genital activity. In psychoanalytic practice, this becomes apparent in the castration complex present in all patients and may be regarded as part of the human condition.

In brief, the prohibition of incest and its sociocultural consequences consisted of:

1   The slaughter of a segment of the offspring, maintained by different techniques, the most characteristic of them consisting of the 'permanent sacrificial pyre that war represents' (Rascovsky, 1970b).

2    To intimidate the progeny intensely, even to an atmosphere of horror, to maintain an extreme paranoid condition in the children.

3    Concealment of the whole process and the inversion of the causality, denying filicide by means of parricide, in order to increase infantile-juvenile feeling of guilt and persecutory anxiety.

Filicide arose from schizo-paranoid regression in the parents, with the ensuing institution of a permanent paranoid exacerbation of the sociocultural process that established the prohibition of incest. The process was integrated through the development of manic defences that culminated in the idealization of the persecutors and the omnipotent denial of the whole process.

# References

AINSWORTH, M. et al. 1963 *Privación de los cuidados maternos* Geneva: World Health Organization.

BERLINER, B. 1966 Psychodynamics of the depressive character *Psychoanal. Forum* 1: 244–264

BLIN, P. C. & FAVREAU, J. M. 1968 Infanticidio y canibalismo puerperal: matadoras y comedoras de pequeños In A. Brion & H. Ey (eds.), *Psiquiatría Animal.* Mexico: Siglo XXI.

BOWLBY, J. 1951 *Los cuidados maternos y la salud mental* Geneva: World Health Organization.

BOWLBY, J. 1958 The nature of the child's tie to his mother *International Journal of Psycho-Analysis* 39: 350–373

BOWLBY, J. et al. 1956 The effects of mother–child separation: a follow-up study *British Journal of Medical Psychology* 29: 211–247

BURLINGHAM, D. & FREUD, A. 1943 *Infants without Families* London: Allen & Unwin.

DEVEREUX, G. 1953 Why Oedipus killed Laius *International Journal of Psycho-Analysis* 34: 132–141

DEVEREUX, G. 1966 The cannibalistic impulses of parents *Psychoanal. Forum* 1: 114–130

FRAZER, J. G. 1944 *La rama dorada* Mexico: Fondo de Cultura Económica.

FREUD, S. 1928 Dostoevsky and parricide *The complete psychological works of Sigmund Freud*, S.E. 21: 173–194

FREUD, S. 1930 Civilization and its discontents *The complete psychological works of Sigmund Freud*, S.E. 21: 57–146

GRINBERG, L. 1963 La culpa persecutoria In *Culpa y depresión* Buenos Aires: Paidos.

GRINBERG, L. 1964 Two kinds of guilt: their relations with normal and pathological aspects of mourning *International Journal of Psycho-Analysis* 45: 366–371

KROEBER, A. L. 1920 Totem and taboo: an ethnologic psychoanalysis *American Anthropologist* 22: 48–55

KROEBER, A. L. 1939 Totem and taboo in retrospect *American Journal of Sociology* 45: 446–451

LÉVI-STRAUSS, C. 1960 *Las estructuras elementales del parentesco* Buenos Aires: Paidos.

LORENZ, K. 1966 Discussion of 'The mutual dynamics of war and peace in C.

tion of war in R. Alonso (ed.), *El psicoanálisis frente a la guerra* Buenos Aires.

RASCOVSKY, A. & RASCOVSKY, M. 1967 Sobre el filicidio y su significación en la génesis del acting-out y la conducta psicopática en Edipo *Revista de Psicoanálisis* 24: 717

RASCOVSKY, A. & RASCOVSKY, M. 1968 On the genesis of acting out and psychopathic behaviour in Sophocles' Oedipus. *International Journal of Psycho-Analysis* 49: 390–394

REIK, T. 1931 *Ritual: Psychoanalytic Studies* New York: Norton.

RHEINGOLD, J. C. 1964 *The Fear of Being a Woman: A Theory of Maternal Destructiveness* New York: Grune & Stratton.

SPITZ, R. A. 1946 Anaclitic depression *The Psychoanalytic Study of the Child* 2

SPITZ, R. A. 1951 The psychogenic diseases in infancy: an attempt at their etiologic classification *The Psychoanalytic Study of the Child* 6

# Part VI

## PSYCHOSOMATIC MEDICINE

# INTRODUCTION TO THE LIFE AND WORK OF DANILO PERESTRELLO (1916–1989)

*Marialzira Perestrello*

Danilo Perestrello obtained a degree in Medicine in 1939. After having worked as a doctor, he was a General Psychology Assistant at the Medical Sciences School and a Propaedeutic and Clinical Medical Assistant at the National College of Medicine, following his teacher, Professor W. Berardinelli.

As a doctor, he was interested in his patients' psychological aspects and thus became a psychiatrist, taking two exams: one for the National Service of Mental Illnesses (1944) and one for Free Psychiatry Teaching (1946). His thesis received praise from Adolf Meyer. He was a doctor at the National Sanitary Education Service (at the Ministry of Education and Health), where he wrote several short books, published officially, including *Almas Infantis (Child Souls)*, a set of 10 lectures giving guidance to parents (broadcast by the Ministry), which had over 10 editions.

An enthusiast of Freud's ideas, he sought analytical training in Buenos Aires in 1946, as there were no psychoanalytical institutions in Rio de Janeiro at the time. In 1952, he qualified as an analyst at the Argentine Psychoanalytic Association. A pioneer of psychoanalysis in Rio de Janeiro, in 1959 he became one of the founders of the Brazilian Psychoanalytic Society of Rio de Janeiro. He was a forerunner of psychosomatic medicine in Brazil; after publishing several works in the field, he launched the book *Medicina Psicossomática (Psychosomatic Medicine)* in 1958, which was translated into Spanish in 1963. In 1973, he published the original work *Medicina da Pessoa (Medicine of the Person)* in which, along with soma and psyche, he emphasized the importance of environment (social and family) for the understanding and etiology of illnesses.

With "Headache and Primal Scene", Perestrello, in 1953, was the first Brazilian to present a paper at an international psychoanalytic congress and to be published in the *International Journal of Psycho-Analysis*. Perestrello was elected the first president of the Brazilian Psychosomatic Association, and

published *Trabalhos Escolhidos de Danilo Perestrello* (*Selected Works by Danilo Perestrello*), a selection of his work in medical psychology, psychosomatics and psychoanalysis.

# HEADACHE AND PRIMAL SCENE

## *Danilo Perestrello*

*Paper read at the 18th International Psycho-Analytical Congress, in London, on the 29th of July, 1953 and published in 1954 in the* International Journal of Psycho-Analysis, *35: 219–223.*

Analysis of a group of patients who, in addition to their psychoneurotic disturbances, had been suffering for several years from headaches of both the common and the migraine type, revealed to me that they presented certain characteristics in their psychological structure and that the headaches were related to phantasies of the primal scene and to the specific way in which the ego attempted to elaborate the situation. Furthermore, it was possible for me, up to a certain point, to clarify the relationship between the common headache and migraine.

The limited extent of this paper prevents me from furnishing the ample supporting material and also obliges me to be somewhat schematic in the exposition of my findings.

My experience deals above all with female patients, of whom I shall select three: O. B., with typical migraine, from scintillating scotoma to the final vomiting; E. S., with common headaches; and M. C., with rather atypical migraine, i.e. a case intermediary between the first two patients. The material from these patients as here set forth should not be taken separately, but rather as fragmentary aspects of a whole to be regarded as if it belonged to one single patient.

In their structures all the patients possessed a common foundation in which the depressive position predominated. The basic conflict was the same, both in the cases of headache and in those of migraine. The deep psychological material showed that there is no reason to separate migraine from other kinds of headache. The two possess the same mechanism and content. The only difference lies in the intensity of the process. Whereas in the common headache the sufferings are restricted to the head, in the migraine – owing to the greater intensity of the conflict – the head is not sufficient to express it and the patient resorts to other means of expression and discharge, such as muscular pains, paraesthesia, etc.

In the analyses my first finding was the relationship between the crises

when she began pregenital sexual play with her fiancé. As intimacy between them grew her crises became more frequent and intense, and still more so when she started with coitus. O. B. seemed to have escaped from this rule, for her first crisis made its appearance at only 13 years of age, one day when she was riding in a tram. As a matter of fact, however, her associations with this ride led infallibly to unconscious phantasies of masturbation and coitus, starting from the vibration of the tram.

The psychological material connected with the subjective sensations during the crises was related, in the first layer, with elements of the phallic level, as may be seen in the following dream of E. S.:

> 'I dreamt I had such a bad headache that I went and saw a gynaecologist. I went into the consulting-room, but I didn't see him. On the examining table there was a man lying in the gynaecological position wearing ballet tights.'

The patient associated that the day before she had woken up with such a violent headache that she could neither hear nor see all day. She felt as though her head were swollen. The position the man was in reminded her of one she sometimes assumed on my couch with her knees bent. She remembered a paper on cancer of the penis that she had read in a medical journal: There are cases in which it must be extirpated, in which event the man has to urinate just like a woman, which the patient found very depressing. The ballet tights led her to the dancers who are usually homosexual, with subsequent associations concerning homosexuality.

The interpretation is obvious: the gynaecologist she does not see is myself, and she is the man under examination. In the grip of a severe headache she comes to me to extirpate the penis she possesses in phantasy (her homosexuality). The swollen head, i.e. erection, is the displacement upwards of the penis.

The patient M. C. had a feeling as though an airplane had embedded itself in her head, and O. B. talked of having her head congested through the effort of urinating in a jet as her brother used to do in her infancy.

From what has been said above one might suppose that it was only a question of phallic conversion, but deeper analysis brought to light characteristics belonging to more regressive levels directly related to the symptoms of the attack.

O. B.'s jet of urine not only represented her penis-envy but was also interwoven with her urethral sadism; it was seen in transference that she unconsciously desired to urinate on me with obvious destructive intentions, just as in her childhood, together with her brother, she had tried to direct a jet on a maidservant on whom she wished to take revenge. The above-mentioned journey on which her first crisis broke out was associated by her with horror with a tram that had crushed a little girl's head. The description she gave was that of a veritable butchery, 'as if it were chicken flesh torn to pieces by someone's teeth, as at royal banquets of olden days, flesh eaten with wine and with one's fingers', which of course revealed her intense oral destructive impulses.

On the other hand, E. S. referred to 'haemorrhoids in her head', and on one occasion when the headache disappeared during the analytic session, it was shown, from certain phantasies about enemas she used to have during coitus, that her relief was represented by the intestinal discharge. Shortly before she had said that she could not feel quiet with her head full of such filth.

From what I have presented so far we may sum up the situation of my patients in the following way: Starting from the repressed and undischarged sexual excitement owing to a lack of maturity in their libidinal organizations, and with a very regressive sadistic idea of coitus, the patients presented headaches through the mobilization of phallic, anal, oral, and urethral elements.

Nevertheless, the characteristic element in all this is the meaning of these pregenital elements in relation to the internalized objects.

Thus, the airplane embedded in M. C.'s head arose in a dream:

> '*An airplane in flames crashes on to my house, it sets it on fire and buries itself in the roof, the smoke covers it all and I can't see anything; I escape in my nightdress and outside I think of the lovely things my mother will lose.*'

She associated this with airplanes that frighten one by going into a spin and with the headache, as if she were in a desert and the sun scorching her eyes and forehead. She also associated my matrimonial relations, adding that my wife might have been in the park that sunny day – sunny and cloudy like her head.

The airplane (the father's penis) in flames (excited and in erection) crashes on to the house and causes the loss of the mother's lovely things (loss of her mother). The house, in its turn, is the patient herself who has the airplane embedded in her roof (head). She loses the mother in a destructive coitus. Her eyes and forehead burn (excitement, headache) and everything looks cloudy (the darkness of her parents' room).

It seems clear that M. C. lived the whole of this drama in her head.

Moreover, M. C. practised the sexual act with a very special ritual. She lay on top of her fiancé and he had to describe to her the conquest and posses-

watching the coitus between the parents with whom she identified herself. When she had slept in her parents' room she had been present at their sexual relations and after being moved out she continued being spectator within herself.

As for her paraesthesia it could clearly be seen that it also represented the same thing: she often compared her parents to ants, and used to say that the sensation of crawling ants was as though the creatures were fighting inside her.

O. B.'s ride in the tram was shown by her associations to stand for one of the many journeys she used to make as a girl when accompanying her mother to the doctor. This doctor was her mother's lover and a surgeon of the head; the patient had often been operated on by him in her childhood (deviation of the nasal septum, tonsils, etc.). She often used to sit waiting for hours while her mother was in the consulting-room.

I think it now becomes clear why the vibration of the tram was associated with the movements of masturbation and coitus and why she was horrified at the girl with the crushed head who was none other than herself. One day when she had woken up with muscular pains in her back, a symptom that used to accompany her headaches, she related a dream in which a little girl was crushed between a couple who pressed against her head and back.

O. B. was perhaps the one who felt most vividly the experience of becoming conscious of her infantile phantasies. The doctor and her mother, her father and her mother, myself and my wife, always in copulation in every imaginable position obsessed her with such exceptional intensity that 'she simply couldn't get us out of her head'. At this time it came to light that the jet of urine was plainly directed at the parental couple in copulation. Apropos of the feelings my voice aroused in her she said, 'I thought of the first time I masturbated; my mother was talking over the telephone to A. He was a flirt of hers, as she has now admitted, and her voice was soft. I was excited to hear her and felt like urinating. I left the room and did it on to my hand. I liked the feeling and repeated it afterwards pressing my hand against my genitals'. In a certain period after this she used to masturbate when watching from her window couples caressing in the street.

I will next refer to a perverse mechanism presented by this patient when her analysis was already at an advanced stage. She had had unsatisfying coitus and had woken up in the morning with a headache. She then decided to lie down and make free association of thought in her own home, just as if she were at a session. She thought over her crises and the relation they bore to her sexual life. She thought of her parents, and their coitus at once came powerfully to her imagination. At that moment she had an orgasm and her headache went away.

As for the scintillating scotoma, she associated it with something like lightning that illuminates things fleetingly and then leaves everything in the dark again; she also associated it with something that suddenly struck her. Here we see that the illumination of the parents' room, i.e. the light thrown upon the parents in copulation, struck her like a flash, which is not only due to the traumatic character of her spying upon the primal scene, but also to the projection of her own destructive impulses upon the couple.

E. S. possessed a rather marked hyperacusis, and her first words before lying down at the first interview were to the effect that my consulting-room was indiscreet, for she had been able to overhear something while waiting outside. Evidently, from her very first contact with analysis, this represented for her an encounter with the phantasies of the primal scene. Throughout the analysis the problem of noise seemed inexhaustible and was always connected with the aforementioned basic conflict. One day when she was suffering from a severe headache she related a dream. She is at the hairdresser's. In the next compartment a hairdresser and a female client are in conversation, and she hears something about 25 past 10. Her associations to 25 past 10 are related with the meal-times in her childhood, with her parents at table with everyone sitting around, and with the times of her analytic sessions; the day before she had arrived at 10.25, i.e. five minutes before time; she says she saw my front door ajar and noticed a smell like the inside of a wardrobe. While waiting she heard voices in my consulting-room. She added excitedly, 'I know; you want me to go into details, to say that I should like to have been there in that room with you, doing the dirty things you and your wife must do'. The patient spoke with unaccustomed anger and on arriving next day she declared that at the end of that interview her headache had left her. She added in a questioning tone: 'That means that the headache had some connection with what was discussed in the session. . . .' In this dream we clearly meet with the primal scene with both oral contents (the mealtimes) and anal ones (the dirty things and the wardrobe smell) and their relation with the headache. From this dream on, I could observe that her infantile memories and phantasies centred round her parents' coitus in which they mingled their urine and faeces, as well as sucking and biting at each other.

To sum up: *it was to be seen that the jealousy,* envy, hatred, and anxiety in these patients were basically directed at the parents in coitus whom they had internalized.

As the analysis advanced and the defences broke down, the primal scene

as though one were dealing with a traumatic neurosis in which the reproduction of the original event took place and, as the primal scene was more and more adequately elaborated, the headaches proportionately diminished.

The connection headache–primal-scene was such an intimate one that, broadly speaking, we may say that there was not one session to which the patients had come with a headache where they did not present the primal scene in the latent content of either the dreams or the associations. Moreover, these phantasies were virtually limited to the days on which they had such attacks. It was as if these phantasies were concentrated in the symptom, and only as the analysis progressed and more repressed material came to the surface did this concentration gradually lose strength and become diluted, i.e. seek other means of expression.

The relationship stated was so close that from the dreams or the associations I was able to know whether the patients had a headache without their telling me; and *vice versa,* when they complained of a headache I was able to foretell the content of the previous night's dream.

Of course the auditory and visual functions formed an integral part of the material. At the time when they remembered or reconstructed the primal scene in an intense and vivid form, O. B. was totally blind for some seconds on leaving my consulting-room, and both she and E. S. were rather deaf for almost a week.

Now, it is commonly maintained that the precipitating factor in attacks of headache is the turning of aggression against the self as a consequence of frustrations that are not followed by discharge.

I do not believe that any undischarged frustration whatsoever will have this effect, but consider that a specific frustration is necessary, i.e. a frustration with a specific content – something symbolizing the primal scene.

By way of illustration, let me mention a crisis of headache of O. B.'s apparently precipitated by a trivial and unspecific frustration. She had arranged to meet her daughter at 7.30 to go to the theatre, and the girl was not on time. She was seized with fury, but on her daughter's arrival she controlled herself, reflecting that she ought not to traumatize her. As a result of this she had a crisis. An excellent example, one might say, of an attack owing to the lack of discharge of hostility resulting from frustration. A dream of the patient's, however, sufficed to show that the facts did not happen quite so simply. That night she dreamt that she was on a couch with a doctor. I was present. The man lies on top of her and she does not know what is happening but has a very pleasant sensation. All of a sudden she comes to and finds that the man is no longer there. She then sees her daughter standing at the foot of her bed and is worried by the thought: 'Perhaps I have traumatized her?' I will add the associations: She notices my couch is scented; the scent must be from the patient who usually precedes her; it seems to her to be a smell of rot; Dr. X, her mother's ex-lover, used a great deal of scent; the patient before her has an air of superiority like Dr. X, and I must be a victim of this patient's just as her mother was of Dr. X. At the previous session she had been full of fury because this patient and I had been in the consulting room while she was outside; by her watch it was past 4.30; she heard our voices but could not make out what we were saying; she had left the consulting-room filled with hatred; she does not know why she made no mention of all this at the time.

It seems unnecessary to enter into very lengthy interpretations. It is clear that the frustration of waiting for her daughter is in reality the frustration with me. I (the mother) and the other patient, a representative of Dr. X (the father) were in the consulting-room, while she waited outside. In reality the waiting for the daughter merely represented the manifest content, a kind of displacement of the waiting outside my consulting-room. Besides, she and her daughter were going to the theatre *to see a show*.

I think that in every case if the analysis is carried deep enough one will discover that the factor immediately provocative of the crisis is of the specific nature referred to above.

In psycho-analytical literature, to the best of my knowledge, attention has not been drawn to this close connection: primal-scene–headache. Nevertheless *the very phenomenology of the crisis is in itself expressive, and exactly reproduces the attitude of the child in the room where the parents are in coitus.*

In fact, a person in a strong crisis, with his *head congested and throbbing*, wishes to *lie still*, and avoids any kind of *visual* or *auditory* stimulus whatsoever. Photophobia is almost always present and the slightest notice is disturbing, sometimes even that of the person's own *breathing*.

It is upon the basis of these data, as I have attempted to summarize them in the foregoing pages, that I have outlined a theory of headaches from the psycho-analytic point of view.

The experience of the primal scene in a small child has the effect of a traumatic stimulus upon his mind. The traumatic character is given by the following three situations which are as a rule concomitant: (*a*) the union of the parents *in itself* signifies for the child that he is overlooked and that they are doing things between themselves and not with him; (*b*) the spectacle offered by the couple is, to an onlooker, in itself one of great brutality, simply through the muscular activity displayed, and seems, to the child's tender mind, more like a struggle; (*c*) in view of the fact that at a time when

but it must be stressed that we are here dealing with a *double* object-loss, for he loses both father and mother together. It is easy to imagine the degree of the child's anxiety in such a situation, as a result of which he resorts to the *introjection* of these objects in an endeavour to recover them. Without doubt the introjected objects are 'bad', but the child is left with no other resource since he *needs* them and cannot live without them. Furthermore, by having the parents inside himself he sees them as good outside. Thus we may say that the parents are introjected just because they are bad, for the child prefers to be bad himself rather than see his parents as such, and hence decides to bear the badness of his objects himself.

Here thus takes place the repression of the bad objects, in the concrete case of the parents in copulation with all its destructive character. When, at a later date, some stimulus that, through its likeness to the primal scene (which is repressed), happens to reactivate the latter, this stimulus constitutes a danger of this trauma's being brought to consciousness, thereby bringing to consciousness the degree of badness in the objects. In this way the stimulus in question comes to act as a traumatic agent.

The external stimuli reminding the subject of the primal scene act, then, traumatically and the ego seeks to elaborate the trauma by means of the headache, which here assumes the same function as the dreams in classical cases of traumatic neurosis.

> *The headache, with all its symptomatology, which, as we have seen, reproduces the attitude of the child in his parents' bedroom, may thus be said to represent the repetition of the trauma of the primal scene.*

The function of the introjection of the primal scene is aimed, besides, at the internal control of the same in an omnipotent manner, in which the ego resorts to various mechanisms (isolation, obsessive control, paranoid expulsion, manic denial). In the particular case of the migraine headache, owing to the amount of aggression and the breakdown of the defences against the activation of the internalized objects, the only possibility left to the ego of annulling their action, which has been mobilized by the specific stimuli I have described, is through the destruction of these said internalized objects (the parents in active copulation). The headache attack would represent, in the last analysis, the administration to oneself of this destructiveness in a paroxysmal form.

# Index

Aberastury, Arminda 2, 10, 11, 134, 499; "El juego de construir casas" 450; *see also* Pichon-Rivière, Arminda Aberastury

Abraham, Karl 72, 125, 289, 349, 501

Adler, Alfred 413

Adler, Oskar 90

Alexander, Franz 12, 163, 164, 415

Alvarez de Toledo, Luisa (Luisa Gambier) 7; "The analysis of 'associating', 'interpreting' and 'words': Use of this analysis to bring unconscious fantasies into the present and to achieve greater ego integration" 246–81; analytic character 334; associating and interpreting as behaviour 249–50; bringing fantasies into the present 248–9; bringing the omnipotence of wishes, thoughts, and words into the present 262–4; countertransference 247–8, 249, 255, 278; defensive attitudes to interpretation 261–2; ego integration 273–4; emotional language in countertransference 247–8; falling asleep in the session 267; fear of the abstract and need for the concrete 269–73; function of speaking and words in the libidinal economy 259; hand as subject-object 276; inner rhythm 277–8;

integration in space and time 274–5; interpretation technique 52, 74, 156, 259–61; introduction to life and work 241–5; pathways of projection and introjection 276–7; reactivation of masturbation 276; reduction of anxiety 264–6; speaking and words 250–3; speaking and words as defences against the unknown 267–9; symbolisation in language 253–7; transference 258; voice, words, and object relations 257–8, 480

ambiguity 21, 217, 322, 331; essential to the analytic situation 26–30

analytic character 334, 337

analytic listening 306, 311, 314

Anzieu, A. 357

Anzieu, D. 357

Arbiser, Samuel 375–8

Argentine Psychoanalytic Association (APA) 18, 88, 90, 135, 136, 139, 140, 141, 143, 175, 189, 241, 451, 461, 462, 463, 464, 465n1, 499, 500, 501

Argentine Psychoanalytic Society 2, 15

artificial neurosis 67, 69

Asociación Psicoanalítica Argentina (APA) 134

Asociación Psicoanalítica Madrid 136

auto-erotic 217

527

45958197R00317

Made in the USA
Middletown, DE
18 July 2017